THE INTERNATIONAL LAW
ON FOREIGN INVESTMENT

Second edition

M. SORNARAJAH

Professor of Law
National University of Singapore

CAMBRIDGE
UNIVERSITY PRESS

1004 938 8 53

PUBLISHED BY THE PRESS SYNDICATE OF THE UNIVERSITY OF CAMBRIDGE
The Pitt Building, Trumpington Street, Cambridge, United Kingdom

CAMBRIDGE UNIVERSITY PRESS
The Edinburgh Building, Cambridge, CB2 2RU, UK
40 West 20th Street, New York, NY 10011–4211, USA
477 Williamstown Road, Port Melbourne, VIC 3207, Australia
Ruiz de Alarcón 13, 28014 Madrid, Spain
Dock House, The Waterfront, Cape Town 8001, South Africa

http://www.cambridge.org

First published 1994 (reprinted 1995, 1996)
Second edition first published 2004
Reprinted 2005

Printed in the United Kingdom at the University Press, Cambridge

Typeface Minion 10.75/12.75 pt.   *System* LATEX 2_ε [TB]

A catalogue record for this book is available from the British Library

ISBN 0 521 83713 8 hardback
ISBN 0 521 54556 0 paperback

To
Ramanan

CONTENTS

PREFACE TO THE SECOND EDITION

The international law on foreign investment has witnessed an explosive growth since the last edition. The decade had witnessed a proliferation of bilateral and regional investment treaties, and a dramatic rise in litigation under such treaties. The attempt to fashion a multilateral instrument on investment within the World Trade Organization has given the debate on issues in the area a wider focus. This edition seeks to capture such developments.

In the course of the decade, I have had the good fortune of being involved actively in many facets of the operation of this area of the law. During such activity, I have acquired many friends who work in the area. My association with UNCTAD has brought me in contact with Karl Sauvant, Anna Joubin-Brett, Victoria Aranda and James Chan. It has also given me the opportunity to work with Arghyrios Fatouros, Peter Muchlinksi and Kenneth Vandevelde, the academic leaders of this field. They have added much to my understanding of the law. The many hours of arguments with them, in various parts of the world, have added to the pleasure of studying this area of the law.

The first edition was written while I was a visiting fellow at the Lauterpacht Centre for International Law, University of Cambridge. The successive Directors of the Centre, Professor Sir Eli Lauterpacht and Professor James Crawford, have continued to encourage my efforts in this and other areas of international law.

My many students in Singapore and Dundee have always challenged me so that I was taught by them to know and remember that there are other ways in which the law could be looked at. To my critics, my answer would be that I am constantly made aware of their criticisms in the classroom. I have accommodated those criticisms in the text.

I thank Finola O'Sullivan, Alison Powell and Martin Gleeson for the care taken over the production of my book.

My research student, Lu Haitian, prepared the bibliography.

Thanga was there, as always. Ahila, Ramanan and Vaishnavi happily are now old enough to let their father alone.

PREFACE TO THE FIRST EDITION

This book was written while I was on sabbatical leave from the National University of Singapore. I thank the Vice-Chancellor, the Council and Dean of the Faculty of Law for the generous terms on which I was granted the leave.

I spent the sabbatical year as a Visiting Fellow at the Research Centre for International Law of the University of Cambridge. I thank Eli Lauterpacht, the Director of the Centre, for many acts of kindness in making this year a happy and productive one.

I am grateful to Professor James Crawford, Whewell Professor of International Law at Cambridge, who read and commented on an early draft of this work, to Professor Detlev Vagts, Bemis Professor of International Law at Harvard, who enabled me to spend a month of research at the Harvard Law School and to Robin Pirrie, Fellow of Hughes Hall, Cambridge, who was helpful with his advice. I remain responsible for any errors and omissions.

As always, Thanga has been an unfailing source of strength. Ahila, Ramanan and Vaishnavi have given up time that should have been theirs.

TABLE OF CASES

ABBREVIATIONS

ABAJ	American Bar Association Journal
AC	Appeal Cases
AD	Annual Digest of Public International Law Cases
AJCL	American Journal of Comparative Law
AJIL	American Journal of International Law
All ER	All England Reports
ALR	Australian Law Reports
AMPLA Yearbook	Yearbook of the Australian Mining and Petroleum Association
Ann Fr	Annuaire Française de Droit International
Arb Int	Arbitration International
ASIL Proceedings	American Society of International Law Proceedings
Buffalo LR	Buffalo Law Review
BYIL	British Yearbook of International Law
Calif. LR	California Law Review
CLR	Commonwealth Law Reports
CMLR	Common Market Law Review
Cornell ILJ	Cornell International Law Journal
Cornell LQ	Cornell Law Quarterly
Cornell LR	Cornell Law Review
Dalhousie LJ	Dalhousie Law Journal
Duke LJ	Duke Law Journal
EHRR	European Human Rights Reports
EJIL	European Journal of International Law
F Supp	Federal Supplement
Florida JIL	Florida Journal of International Law
Fordham ILJ	Fordham International Law Journal
Ga JIL	Georgia Journal of International Law
GYIL	German Yearbook of International Law
Hague Recueil	Hague Recueil des Cours
Harvard LR	Harvard Law Review

Harvard ILJ	Harvard International Law Journal
ICJ Rpts	International Court of Justice Reports
ICLQ	International and Comparative Law Quarterly
ICSID Rev	ISCID Review – Foreign Investment Law Journal
IJIL	Indian Journal of International Law
ILM	International Legal Materials
Int Conc	International Conciliation
Int Lawyer	International Lawyer
Int Org	International Organization
Iran–US CTR	Iran–United States Claims Tribunal Reports
JIA	Journal of International Arbitration
JWTL	Journal of World Trade Law
KB	Kings Bench Reports
Ky LJ	Kentucky Law Journal
LQR	Law Quarterly Review
Mich LR	Michigan Law Review
Michigan JIL	Michigan Journal of International Law
Minn LR	Minnesota Law Review
MLR	Modern Law Review
NYUJIL&P	New York University Journal of International Law and Politics
NYULR	New York University Law Review
NYIL	Netherlands Yearbook of International Law
PCIJ	Permanent Court of International Justice
Pol Sci Qty	Political Science Quarterly
SJ	Solicitors Journal
Stanford LR	Stanford Law Review
Texas ILJ	Texas International Law Journal
UNRIAA	United Nations Reports of International Arbitral Awards
Virginia JIL	Virginia Journal of International Law
WLR	Weekly Law Reports
Yale LJ	Yale Law Journal
YBECHR	Yearbook of the European Commission on Human Rights
YBWA	Yearbook of World Affairs
YCA	Yearbook of Commercial Arbitration

1

Introduction

Few areas of international law excite as much controversy as the law relating to foreign investment.[1] Such controversy resulted from the law on the subject being the focus of conflict between several forces released at the conclusion of the Second World War. The cyclical nature of the ebbs and flows of the controversy is evident. The ending of colonialism released forces of nationalism. Once freed from the shackles of the colonialism, the newly independent states agitated not only for the ending of the economic dominance of the former colonial powers within their states but also for a world order which would permit them more scope for the ordering of their own economies and access to world markets. The cold war between the then superpowers made the law a battleground for ideological conflicts. The non-aligned movement, which arose in response to this rivalry, exerted pressure to ensure that each newly independent state had complete control over its economy. One avenue for the exertion of such pressure by the non-aligned movement was the formulation of new doctrines through the use of the numerical strength of its members in the General Assembly of the United Nations. Several resolutions were enacted asserting the doctrine of permanent sovereignty over natural resources and calling for the establishment of a New International Economic Order, the aim of which was to ensure fairness in trade to developing countries as well as control over the process of foreign investment. The oil crisis in the 1970s illustrated both the power as well as the weakness of the states which possessed natural resources. It brought about industry-wide shifts through collective action organised by the oil producing states. The producers of other mineral resources were not able to achieve the same success.

---

[1] Compare Harlan J in *US* v. *Sabbatino*, 374 US 398 (1964), who said, regarding one aspect of the branch of the law: 'There are few if any issues in international law today on which opinion seems to be so divided as the limitation of the state's power to expropriate the alien's property.'

The ability of the developing states to exert their collective influence on shaping the law shifted dramatically towards the end of the twentieth century. Sovereign defalcations associated with the lending of petro-dollars dried up private lending by banks. Aid had already dried up due to recession in the developed states. The rise of free market economics associated with President Reagan of the United States and Prime Minister Thatcher of the United Kingdom gave a vigorous thrust to moves to liberalise foreign investment regimes. The acceptance of an open door policy by China and the success of the small Asian states like Hong Kong and Singapore, which had developed through liberal attitudes to foreign investment, made other developing states choose a similar path. The dissolution of the Soviet Union led to the emergence of new states committed to free market economics. Developing states began to compete with each other for the foreign investment that was virtually the only capital available to fuel their development. Third world cohesion, which drove the ideas behind the New International Economic Order, was on the verge of collapse, though it had by then evolved competing norms challenging the previously existing ones. The vigorous espousal of free market economics by the International Monetary Fund and the World Bank also led to pressures being exerted on developing countries to liberalise their regimes on foreign investment. In the context of this swing in the pendulum, the developing states entered into bilateral treaties containing rules on investment protection and liberalised the laws on foreign investment entry. They also participated in regional treaties like the North American Free Trade Agreement (NAFTA) and sectoral treaties like the Energy Charter Treaty. The World Trade Organization (WTO) came into existence with the avowed objective of liberalising not only international trade but also aspects of investment which affected such trade. The link between international trade and international investment was said to justify the competence of the WTO in this area. The Singapore Ministerial Conference of the WTO decided to study the possibility of an instrument on investment. New factors had entered the area of the international law on foreign investment. Many of the new instruments of the WTO dealt with areas of foreign investment directly.[2]

---

[2] Intellectual property was covered by Trade Related Intellectual Property Measures (TRIPS). The General Agreement on Trade in Services dealt with the services sector and covered the provision of services through a commercial presence in another country, which is foreign investment in the services sector. The Trade Related Investment Measures (TRIMS) dealt

Economic liberalism was generally triumphant at the end of the last millennium. The impact of its triumph was felt on the international law on foreign investment. The incredible proliferation of bilateral investment treaties was evidence of this triumph. The treaties created jurisdiction in arbitral tribunals at the unilateral instance of the foreign investor. This in turn led to the articulation by these tribunals of principles which confirmed and extended notions that favoured movement of foreign investment and their treatment in accordance with external standards. It also restrained governmental interference with such investment significantly by considerably expanding the notion of compensable taking to include regulatory takings.

There appears to be evidence of yet another swing taking place at the beginning of the new millennium. Successive economic crises in Asia and Latin America attributed to the sudden withdrawal of foreign funds have led to the re-evaluation of whether the flow of foreign funds and investments is the panacea for development as originally thought. The Organization of Economic Cooperation and Development (OECD) attempted to draft a Multilateral Agreement on Investment (MAI) thinking that the time was ripe for it, given the willingness of developing countries to liberalise their economies and enter into bilateral economic treaties. But, during the discussions, the members of the OECD, all developed states, found that they could not agree among themselves on the principles of the rules on foreign investment protection. The attempt also spawned a protest coalition of environmentalists and human rights activists who complained that the draft emphasised the protection of investment without adverting to the need to protect the environment and human rights from abuse by multinational corporations. The collective protests against the MAI were a prelude to the protests against globalisation that were to mar the meetings of economic organisations like the WTO, the IMF and the World Bank at Seattle, Prague, Montreal and other capitals of the world. The new phenomenon that has emerged in the area is the role of non-governmental organisations (NGOs) committed to the furtherance of environmental interests and human rights. These NGOs operate within developed states and espouse, to a large extent, what they believe to be the interests of the people of the developing world and the world as a

with performance requirements associated with foreign investment. The Singapore and Doha Ministerial Meetings of the WTO decided to consider an instrument on investment and one on competition which will directly impact foreign investment.

whole. In addition, there are the protest movements against globalisation which also seek to espouse causes that favour developing world interests, ranging from economic development, the writing-off of Third World debt and foreign investment.[3] It has been suggested that, with the increase in the gap between rich and poor within developed states brought about by globalisation, there is a Third World within developed states ready to protest against excessive reliance on free market ideas.[4]

Though assailed by these changes, the developed states have taken positions on foreign investment which have seldom changed despite the swings that take place. As the power of the multinational corporations increases,[5] the developed states will continue to espouse their interests not only because of the enormous power that these corporations achieve through lobbying but also because it is in their interests to do so. The expansion of trade and investment increases the economic power of the developed states. They have traditionally seen the need to ensure the protection of the multinational corporations responsible for such trade and investment as coincidental with their interests.

The multinational corporations themselves must be seen as distinct bases of power capable of asserting their interests through the law. Their individual economic resources far exceed those of sovereign states. Their collective power to manipulate legal outcomes must be conceded. It is a fascinating fact that through the employment of private techniques of dispute resolution, they are able to create principles of law that are generally favourable to them. That they can bring about such outcomes through pressure on their states is obvious.[6] The role of these actors in the international legal system is seldom studied due to the dominance in the field of positivist views which stress that states are the only relevant actors in international relations. The subject calls for an understanding not only of the role of states and multinational corporations but also the role of non-governmental associations. In addition, since much of the exploitation

---

[3] This clash of globalisations is discussed in M. Sornarajah, 'The Clash of Globalisations: Its Impact on the International Law on Foreign Investment' (2003) 10 *Canadian Foreign Policy* 1.

[4] Caroline Thomas, 'Where is the Third World Now' in Caroline Thomas (ed.), *Globalisation and the South* (1997) 1.

[5] It has been pointed out that multinational corporations exist in the developing states as well. But, they are nowhere near as large as US and European multinational corporations and cannot wield the same degree of influence.

[6] Clare Cutler, *Private Power and Global Authority: Transnational Global Law in the Political Economy* (2003).

of natural resources takes place on the land of minorities and tribal and aboriginal groups, the interests of these groups also have to be taken into account in the development of the law. It is an area in which international law is clearly moving away from the old positivist notion that international law is shaped entirely by the activities of states. As much as in one direction, techniques of protection of foreign investment are coming to be explored more fully through the creation of standing in multinational corporations, in the other direction, there is pressure to ensure that the subject reflects the concerns of human rights and environmental interests through the imposition of liability on these corporations. These emphasise, not the protection of the investment of the multinational corporations but their social and corporate responsibility to the host communities in which they operate.

The interplay of various economic, political and historical factors shaped and continues to shape the development of international law on foreign investment. If international law is generated by the eventual resolution of conflicting national, business and social interests, the international law of foreign investment provides an illustration of these processes of intense conflicts and their resolution at work. It is an area in which the interests of the capital-exporting states have clashed with the interests of capital-importing states. The resultant resolution of the conflict, if any resolution is indeed achieved, indicates how international law is made and how open-ended the formulation of its principles are in the face of intense conflicts of view as to the law among states. These conflicts become accentuated when other actors in the field divide behind the states and support the contesting norms that each camp supports.

As a result of such clashes, the field provides for the study of international law as an interdisciplinary subject in which ideas in the sphere of economics, political science and related areas have helped to shape the arguments. Yet, for all its richness, the field has seldom been looked at as a whole, until recently.[7] It is necessary to carve out a niche for the

---

[7] After the first edition of this book, a spate of new books on this and related areas appeared. See Peter Muchlinski, *Multinational Enterprises and the Law* (1995); Robert Pritchard (ed.), *Economic Development, Foreign Investment and the Law* (1996); and Daniel D. Bradlow and Alfred Escher (eds.), *Legal Aspects of Foreign Investment* (1999). For earlier studies, see Ingrid Delupis, *Finance and Protection of Foreign Investment in Developing Countries* (1987); Zuhair Kronfol, *Protection of Foreign Investment* (1972); and Georg Schwarzenberger. *Foreign Investment and International Law* (1969). There are now specialist journals: *Foreign Investment Law Journal,* published by the World Bank, and the *Journal of World Investment* (Geneva). For a French study, see P. Laviec, *Protection et Promotion des Investissements: Etude*

subject within international law so that the manner in which the norms of international law are affected by the seemingly irreconcilable interests that operate in this area could be studied more intensely.[8]

Interest in the area also arises from the fact that the trends in this field cannot be explained on the basis of any existing theory of international law. Most theories of international law are rooted in positivism and are aimed at explaining law as an existing, static phenomenon, unaffected by political and other trends. These theories are incapable of being applied to a situation where the existing principles of law, formulated at a time when they were kept in place by hegemonic control and dominance, are under attack. Other theories are idealistic, seeking to achieve objectives based on morality and conscience. These theories are also inadequate to explain a situation in which different value systems of somewhat equal moral validity are in collision. Where existing rules supported by the established group of nations are subject to attack by relatively new members of the international community,[9] they become feeble and, until they are replaced, a situation of chaos or normlessness will exist. The task of decision-makers and scholars will be to examine the conflicts in the norms in the area and ensure that adjustments are made to bring about some acceptable norms so that the normless state may be ended. This book is a

---

de Droit International Economique (1985). Specific areas of the law on foreign investment have also attracted book-length studies. See e.g. Rudolf Dolzer and Marguerite Stevens, *Bilateral Investment Treaties* (1996); M. Sornarajah, *The Settlement of Foreign Investment Disputes* (2000); and Christoph Schreuer, *Commentary on the ICSID Convention* (2001).

[8] The creation of new subjects within international law must be addressed with caution as the charge is made that these are studied without any foundation in the major discipline of international law. This is a legitimate criticism. Specialisation helps to enhance the law. Also, often in modern times, the law has to be explained to persons who may not have the inclination to study the whole area of international law. The fact is that the areas of international law are burgeoning so rapidly that they cannot be addressed by a generalist with sufficient depth. There is a need for specialist works, well grounded in basic principles of international law. As indicated in the previous footnote, there are studies on more specialised aspects of this area of international law.

[9] The European origins of international law have been extensively commented on. One view is that new nations are born into the world of existing law and are bound by it. See Daniel P. O'Connell, 'Independence and State Succession' in William V. Brian (ed.), *New States in International Law and Diplomacy* (1965). The opposing view is that they may seek revision of existing principles of international law as they are not bound by these rules. This dispute takes an acute form in many areas of international law. For general descriptions of the disputes, see Ram P. Anand, *The Afro-Asian States and International Law* (1978). The attack on Eurocentric international law is more evident in this field as the conflict is between the erstwhile colonial powers which are now the principal exporters of capital and the newly independent nations which are the recipients of such capital.

contribution to this process in an area of abundant normative conflicts. The identification of the conflicts in norms will itself facilitate the process of a future settlement of the conflicts and bring about a clearer set of rules on the international law of foreign investment.

1. The definition of foreign investment

Foreign investment involves the transfer of tangible or intangible assets from one country into another for the purpose of their use in that country to generate wealth under the total or partial control of the owner of the assets.[10] There can be no doubt that the transfer of physical property such as equipment or the physical property that is bought or constructed such as plantations or manufacturing plants constitute foreign direct investment. Such investment is contrasted with portfolio investment. Portfolio investment is normally represented by a movement of money for the purpose of buying shares in a company formed or functioning in another country. It could also include other security instruments through which capital is raised for ventures. The distinguishing element is that, in portfolio investment, there is a divorce between management and control of the company and the share of ownership in it.[11]

1.1. The distinction between portfolio investment and foreign direct investment

In the case of portfolio investment, it is generally accepted that the investor takes upon himself the risks involved in the making of such investments.

---

[10] Compare the definition of foreign investment in the *Encyclopaedia of Public International Law* (vol. 8, p. 246), where foreign investment is defined as 'a transfer of funds or materials from one country (called capital exporting country) to another country (called host country) in return for a direct or indirect participation in the earnings of that enterprise'. The difficulty with this definition is that it is broad enough to include portfolio investment. The IMF, *Balance of Payments Manual* (1980), para. 408, used a narrower definition which excluded portfolio investment. It defined foreign investment as 'investment that is made to acquire a lasting interest in an enterprise operating in an economy other than that of an investor, the investor's purpose being to have an effective choice in the management of the enterprise'. A definition that includes portfolio investment should demonstrate that its inclusion for the purposes of the international law on foreign investment is justified.

[11] Such a distinction is drawn in the texts on economics and is a sound basis for distinguishing direct and portfolio investment in the law as well. Thus, control is stressed in the following definition in E. Graham and Paul Krugman, *Foreign Direct Investment in the United States* (1991) 7: 'Foreign direct investment is formally defined as ownership of assets by foreign residents for purposes of controlling the use of those assets.'

He cannot sue the domestic stock exchange or the public entity which runs it, if he were to suffer loss. Likewise, if he were to suffer loss by buying foreign shares, bonds or other instruments, there would be no basis on which he could seek a remedy. Portfolio investment was not protected by customary international law. Such investment was attended by ordinary commercial risks which the investor ought to have been aware of. But, customary international law protected physical property of the foreign investor and other assets directly invested through principles of diplomatic protection and state responsibility.

One viewpoint maintains that there should be no distinction between portfolio investments and foreign direct investments as to the protection given to either by international law. This view is based on the assumption that there is no distinction between the risks taken by either type of investor, both being voluntarily assumed.[12] But, this view is not accepted generally in international law, where it is clear that foreign direct investment is subject to the protection of customary law. Several reasons are given for this differential treatment. The foreign investor takes out of his home state resources which could otherwise have been used to advance the economy of the home state.[13] The home state is said to be justified in ensuring that these resources are protected.[14] Portfolio investments, on the other hand, can be made on stock exchanges virtually anywhere in the world. Since the host state cannot know to whom linkages are created through the sale of shares on these stock exchanges, there can be no concrete relationship creating a responsibility. This is otherwise in the case of foreign direct investment where the foreigner enters the host state with the express consent of the host state. Nevertheless, the trend of the law in the area may be to create responsibility towards those who hold portfolio investments through treaties. This is a trend associated with the liberalisation of the movement of assets. Opinions are found in some

---

[12] Ian Brownlie, 'Treatment of Aliens: Assumption of Risk and International Law' in W. Flume, H. J. Hain, G. Kegel and K. R. Simmond (eds.), *International Law and Economic Order: Essays in Honour of F. A. Mann* (1997) 309 at 311.

[13] This is not much of a reason as portfolio investment also constitutes resources within the state which could have been used within the state if not committed to a company overseas. But, sums of money that are used in portfolio investments are often small, shares being bought by individuals on stock exchanges.

[14] But, again, the reason breaks down. The home state itself takes a risk in allowing these resources to leave the state. The question is why it should not have to bear the consequences of its own risk if the resources were to be harmed. Obviously, there is no answer to this logical issue, other than a pragmatic one that powerful states have conferred protection on the person and property of its citizens who work or invest abroad.

publications that portfolio investments are now to be included in foreign direct investments. To a large extent, such opinions are influenced by the fact that treaties defining investments include shares in the definition of foreign investment. But, as will be demonstrated, shares in this context mean the shares of a joint venture company in which the foreigner present in the host state has invested, and is not meant to include shares held by a non-resident and purchased entirely outside the host state. There will be continued uncertainty attached to the question whether portfolio investment is protected in the same manner as foreign direct investment in international law. The better view is that portfolio investment is not protected unless specifically included in the definition of foreign investment in the treaty.[15]

1.2. Definition of foreign investment in treaties

The tendency of many treaties in the area of foreign investment, particularly the model treaties drafted by the United States and other capital-exporting states, has been to broaden the scope of the definition of foreign investment.[16] The objective behind this is to ensure that treaty protection could be given to a wide variety of activities associated with foreign direct investment. This objective has to a large extent been facilitated by the attitudes taken by arbitration tribunals and writers in the area. It is important for those who negotiate treaties to understand the purpose behind the making of these extensions.

1.3. The evolution of the meaning of the term 'investment'

It is clear that from early times the meaning of investment in international law was confined to foreign direct investment. The evolution of the international law was towards the idea that the responsibility of the state would arise if it did not treat the alien in accordance with a minimum standard of treatment. This standard of treatment was extended to his physical property. The early discussion of the law on state responsibility for injuries to aliens took place in the context of either physical abuse or

---

[15] There are treaties, like the ASEAN Framework Agreement on Investment, which specifically exclude portfolio investments from the scope of the treaty.

[16] Vandervelde has explained the concerns behind the definition of foreign investment in US bilateral investment treaties. See K. Vandervelde, *United States Investment Treaties* (1992), 261.

the violation of the rights of the alien to physical property held by him in the host state. The genesis of the international law on foreign investment was in the obligation created by the law to protect the alien and his physical property and state responsibility arising from the failure to perform that obligation. In terms of customary international law, the obligation was largely created through the practice of the United States which asserted the existence of such an obligation in its relations with its Latin American neighbours. As foreign investments grew, the law was extended to protect the tangible assets of the foreigner from governmental interference by way of the taking of such property. The early cases dealt with the destruction of property or the taking of land belonging to the foreigner. The concept of taking was also narrow, for only tangible assets could be taken by the state. This original feature of an economic asset in the form of physical property protected by a legal right under the law of the host state has always remained the starting point of the definition of an 'investment' for the purposes of this area of the law.

Progressively, consistent with this essential feature, the term 'investment' was extended to include intangible assets. These initially consisted of contractual rights in pursuance of which the foreign investor took his assets, such as machinery and equipment into the host state. The rights associated with the holding of property such as leases, mortgages and liens came to be included. There are cases that indicate that loans also fell into this category. There was difficulty in the case of shares in companies. In the *Barcelona Traction Case*,[17] the International Court of Justice held that a shareholder's rights in a company that was the vehicle of the foreign investor could not be protected through the diplomatic intervention of the home state of the shareholder. The much criticised view taken by the Court was that only the state in which the company was incorporated could intercede on behalf of the company and that the shareholders of the company had no independent interests that were protected by international law. It indicated a problem as to the protection of the rights of the shareholder which continues to befuddle international law.[18] The situation becomes more difficult where the foreign investor operates his

---

[17] [1970] ICJ Rpts 1.

[18] This is particularly seen in the case law under the International Convention on the Settlement of Investment Disputes. In the ICSID Convention, shareholder rights are to be protected only where the host state gives its consent to treat the corporate vehicle for the investment as a foreign corporation for the purpose of ICSID arbitration. Complex litigation has resulted on the issue of corporate nationality. See further on this, M. Sornarajah, *The Settlement of Foreign Investment Disputes* (2000), 194–207.

investment through a company that is incorporated under the laws of the host state or is a minority shareholder in such a company. The International Convention on the Settlement of Investment Disputes seeks to overcome this through the requirement that the host state specifically agrees to regard the company as a foreign company despite its incorporation as a local company.

In response to the *Barcelona Traction Case*, the issue of shareholder protection was addressed directly in the bilateral investment treaties by including shares in companies within the meaning of the term 'investment'. The shares that are referred to in such treaties are shares in a company that is to serve as a vehicle for the investment that is contemplated and presumably not portfolio investments.[19]

There were further developments which took place in the area since the *Barcelona Traction Case* and the inclusion of shares in corporations established by the foreign investor within the meaning of foreign investment. There are now statements in publications which state that shares are investments that are protected by investment treaties, without having regard to the specific history that led to the inclusion of shares in investment treaties. These statements give the impression that portfolio investments are protected by international investment law the same way foreign direct investments are. This view, which is expansive, does not accord with the context in which the law was developed. Some treaties expressly counter the possibility of such a view being adopted by excluding portfolio investments from the definition of protected investments.

The next phase was the inclusion of intellectual property rights within the meaning of foreign investment. Widespread copying of inventions made in developed states was the reason for the extension of protection to intellectual property rights. Many of these rights were associated with the making of foreign investments. When a new invention was to be manufactured in the developing state or when new technology was to be

---

[19] But, it is evident that, whatever change is made by the treaties, this will not affect the manner of the protection that could be given to companies under the ICSID Convention. This nicely proves the point that the definition of investment in the ICSID Convention remains unaffected by the changes to the meaning of the term 'investment' that are later made through treaties and other means of developing international law. The different approaches to shareholder protection under the ICSID Convention and the BIT show that the meaning of the term 'investment' in the different treaty instruments do not coincide. If this view is correct, then the use of the term 'investment' has a temporal meaning varying from treaty to treaty and depending on the period at which it was drafted.

transferred by a foreign investor to a local partner within a joint venture, it would be necessary to provide for the protection of the intellectual property rights associated with the venture. When such a need for the recognition of intellectual property rights arose, the treaties extended the meaning of foreign investment to include intangible rights associated with intellectual property thus making a leap in the meaning of foreign investment which had hitherto been confined to the physical assets of the foreign investor. Analytically too, the situation was different, for the intellectual property was created by the local law through the recognition of the right by an act of the host state. So, technically, it was property that was created by the host state in the foreigner that was being protected. The types of intellectual property that are to be recognised are often elaborately spelt out in the treaties to include patents and copyright which are rights technically granted to the foreign investor by the host state laws, as well as lesser rights such as know-how. The policy justification for the protection of intellectual property rights through investment treaties is that there will be more technology transferred to developing countries if such intellectual property is protected through investment treaties. When a state interferes with these intellectual property rights it is interfering with property it had itself created in the foreign investor. The treaty internationalised the rights once they had been created and required them to be protected in accordance with the standards of the treaty. The argument that the state can control the property it had created can no longer apply as a result of the operation of the treaty. This process of the internationalisation of the property that was created under the local law is the basis of the protection of intellectual property which is adopted in the field of both foreign investment and international trade. It is clear that, in the area of international trade, the TRIPS instrument (Trade Related Intellectual Property Measures) attached to the World Trade Organization operates on the basis of the same technique. As a result of this internationalisation, any state interference with intellectual property thereafter becomes a breach of treaty which amounts to an expropriation and has to be compensated. Wide interpretations are sometimes given to the concept of taking of property in treaties. As a result, there is a danger that compulsory licensing of patents and parallel imports by the state can amount to takings and involve the state in liability for breach of the treaty standards. This danger arises in areas such as pharmaceuticals. The parallel import of an AIDS drug manufactured cheaply in another state stands in danger of being regarded as a violation of treaty standards as a result of this widening of the meaning and scope of the term 'foreign investment' and of the notion of 'taking'.[20]

The protection of intellectual property under bilateral and multilateral investment treaties, the WTO regime and the earlier regimes will mean that there will be an absence of coordination as to how the law in the area will be developed. The remedies provided and the mechanisms employed are different. The investor may have a unilateral remedy under an investment treaty whereas only a state could invoke the dispute settlement mechanism of the WTO. The substantive law on protection may also be differently stated. No real claims have yet arisen in which the law has been considered.

Once the idea that the concept of foreign investment need not be confined to tangible assets took hold, there were further inclusions of intangible rights in the list of matters which are to be included in the definition of the term foreign investment in the treaty. One such inclusion is the contractual rights which the foreign investor acquires as a result of its relationship with the state and its agencies. It is generally conceded that a breach of a contract which the state has made with a foreign investor does not by itself give rise to an international remedy.[21] There are obvious reasons for this. There may be good reasons for the breach by the state, for example defective performance by the foreign investor. There is also the possibility of settling the claims that arise through domestic litigation. The treaty inclusion of contractual rights in the definition of the term 'foreign investment' would mean that upon the breach of a contract by the state an international obligation arises in the state that caused the breach of contract. As a result a right arises in the foreign investor to seek remedies under the treaty. Again, the contract which is ordinarily subject to the laws of the host state becomes effectively internationalised as a result of this technique being adopted in the treaty. This internationalisation enables the foreign investor to have recourse to the remedies that are provided for him in the event of a violation of his rights under the treaty.[22] So, crucial to the strategy of protection is the definition of foreign investment

---

[20] The argument would be that such a parallel import interferes with the expectations of profits of the patent holder and therefore amounts to a taking. The question as to what amounts to a taking is discussed in Chapter 9 below.

[21] See further Chapter 10 below.

[22] Awards have established that the claims arise not from the breach of the contract but from the consequent breach, if any, of the treaty rights of the foreign investor. The manner of the breach may indicate such breach of treaty rights.

to include the contractual rights of the foreign investor in the definition of foreign investment.

A further extension of foreign investment is to include the administrative rights that the foreign investor acquires in the host state. Why is the extension to include administrative rights so important? In the 1970s, influenced to a large extent by the views of the United Nations Committee on Transnational Corporations that foreign investment could be beneficial to the host economy if the foreign investment is harnessed to the economic development of the host economy, developing states began to enact in legislation that was designed to screen foreign investment having regard to the effects it would have on the domestic economy. Much of the screening was done through administrative machinery that was instituted. Every one of these administrative agencies has undergone various transformations in accordance with the prevailing and changing philosophies relating to foreign investment in that country. Obviously when economic liberalism takes hold, there will be a more permissive approach. The dismantling of these screening procedures and the recognition of a right to entry is one of the aims of treaties based on economic liberalism.[23] But, there will be greater control when there are more restrained attitudes to foreign investment, especially if some crisis, such as a financial crisis, results which is attributed to foreign investment. The tide of economic liberalism did not result in the dismantling of screening legislation in many states.

The functions of these administrative agencies change from time to time. Their basic functions are to take administrative measures both to facilitate as well as to control foreign investment. Such roles are carried out in almost all Asian states to varying degrees. Even where it is not carried out at the stage of entry, there would be various administrative procedures involved such as environmental licences and planning permissions, which the foreign investor has to secure before he can commence on his investment project. These are all administrative rights he acquires at either the entry or the post-entry stages. The treaties now define all these administrative rights as constituting foreign investment. The justification for this is easy to understand. If the government were to withdraw any of these administrative rights, the foreign investor will not be able to operate his foreign investment. His plant and machinery will remain his and, to that extent, there has been no interference with his physical assets

---

[23] The NAFTA recognised a right of entry and establishment. The draft Multilateral Agreement on Investment (MAI) of the OECD also sought to recognise such a right.

but they will be of no use to him for he cannot operate them without having the necessary administrative licences. Hence, from the point of view of the capital-exporting states, it is only logical that there be protection given to these administrative rights which are indispensable to the purpose for which the foreign investor entered the host state. But, the inclusion of these administrative law rights within the definition of investments greatly restricts the right of the state to exercise regulatory control over the foreign investment. It also enhances the possibility of interferences with the licences for regulatory reasons being regarded as taking of property.

So far the discussion has shown that, in defining the foreign investment which is to be given protection, the capital-exporting state adopts the obvious strategy of defining the foreign investment protected by the treaty to include three principal concerns. These are, first, to protect the physical property of the foreign investor; secondly, to extend protection to the intangible rights which are themselves to be regarded as property and to be protected as such; and, thirdly, to include within foreign investment the administrative rights that are necessary for the operation of the investment project. The latter rights are granted by the state, as are intangible rights relating to most intellectual property. Technically, the state which gives can take back what it gives. But, the treaty has the effect of lifting out of the realm of domestic law the right that is given to the foreign investor and subjecting it to treaty protection so that the right cannot be withdrawn without engaging the responsibility of the state.

There has been a tendency in the law to extend the meaning of investment in treaties. A variety of attempts have been made to test out the limits to which the meaning could be extended. Arguments have been made that the costs associated with preparations for the making of the investment should be included in the definition of investment. In *Mihaly v. Sri Lanka*,[24] the strategy of litigation was based on the notion that costs involved in tendering for a project and negotiating it should be considered as investment if the negotiations are unsuccessful for improper reasons after an expectation as to their success has been created. There have also been efforts to argue that the legitimate expectations of the foreign investor constitute rights which can be protected through expansive interpretations of treaty provisions. If new rights are effectively created by treaties for foreign investors, the meaning of investments for the purpose

[24] (2002) 17 ICSID Rev 21.

of those treaties will be correspondingly enlarged. This meaning, however, will not be received into general law. In the *Ceskoslovenska Case* (1997),[25] the ICSID tribunal considered the question whether the failure to repay a loan, which the Slovak government had guaranteed, could be regarded as a foreign investment within the meaning of the ICSID Convention. The tribunal said that there was 'support for a liberal interpretation of the question whether a particular transaction constitutes a foreign investment'. It took the view that the language in the Preamble to the ICSID Convention permits 'an inference that an international transaction which contributes to cooperation designed to promote the economic development of a contracting state may be deemed to be an investment as that term is understood in the Convention'. This purposive view that any activity that is considered to promote economic development should be considered an investment is again too expansive to receive acceptance. A loan may benefit economic development but it lacks the other essential criteria of foreign investment such as the entry of personnel into the state and the direct generation of profits as a result.[26] Such expansive views are the product of the dominance of economic liberalism and must be regarded as passing fashions that do not accord with legal prescriptions. Financial transactions are commercial transactions and are settled through mechanisms provided by domestic law. It was not in the contemplation of states that the treaties on foreign investment should affect such transactions. It is not within the function of tribunals to read into treaties meanings that extend concepts beyond what sovereign states had intended so as to enlarge their own roles. To do so overzealously would invite non-compliance and consequent injury to the system that has been built up.

Another case in which an expansive interpretation was taken was *Fedax NV v. Venezuela*.[27] In this case, there was an assignment of promissory notes. The respondent state, Venezuela, argued that the assignment did not amount to 'a direct foreign investment involving a long term transfer of financial resources-capital flow from one country to another'. The claimant had in fact acquired interest in the promissory notes by way of endorsement of the notes by a separate company with which Venezuela

---

[25] *Ceskoslovenska Obchodni Banka v. Slovak Republic* (1999) 14 ICSID Rev 251.
[26] Loans are traditionally protected through other techniques. Because of the immense bargaining power of the lender, he will be able to secure dispute resolution before the courts of his country and ensure that there is enforcement against the assets of the borrower in his own state. The need for the protection of loans as investment has seldom arisen.
[27] (1998) 37 ILM 1378.

had made a contract. The tribunal dealt with academic views on the subject and held that they all supported 'a broad approach to the interpretation' of the term 'foreign investment' in the ICSID Convention.

Some academic writers have also formulated wide definitions of the term 'foreign investment'. Thus, Schreuer, after stating that the forms that foreign investment has taken have undergone changes, observed that 'the precise legal forms in which these operations are cast are less important than the general economic circumstances under which they are undertaken'.[28] This is again a policy-oriented approach which invites the ICSID tribunal to broaden the meaning of the term 'foreign investment' beyond what the parties may have had in mind. It is clear that an opportunity for making new law by broadening the scope of foreign investment is being created by the *dicta* of the ICSID tribunal and in the academic views. But, these views must be confined, even if correct, to the practice under ICSID and as interpretations that are based on the ICSID Convention. They do not affect the general international law on foreign investment.

Foreign investment attracts the greater attention of international law for the simple reason that it involves the movement of persons and property from one state to another and such movements have the potential for conflict between two states. It involves the securing of competitive advantages over local entrepreneurs both within the market as well as from the state authorities. The resulting integration of the foreign investor into the host economy makes his involvement in the internal economic and political affairs of the host state inevitable.[29] Conflict is inherent in such situations. Disputes that arise between parties to sales and financial transactions are largely settled through domestic courts. The intervention of the machinery of international law may become necessary for the settlement of disputes arising from foreign investment. Because movement of persons is involved, it is possible to link the protection of foreign investment to the already existing norms on the diplomatic protection of aliens. Historically, this area of the law has been built up as a part of the area of the diplomatic protection of citizens abroad and of state responsibility for injuries to aliens.[30] Since the function of diplomatic missions was the

---

[28] Christoph Schreuer, *ICSID Convention: A Commentary* (2002).

[29] R. Gilpin, *The Political Economy of International Relations* (1987), 33.

[30] For early works on the area, see E. M. Borchard, *The Diplomatic Protection of Citizens Abroad* (1915); F. Dunn, *The Protection of Nationals* (1932); A. V. Freeman, *The International Responsibility of States for Denial of Justice* (1938); C. F. Amerasinghe, *State Responsibility for Injuries to Aliens* (1964); and R. B. Lillich (ed.), *International Law of Resonsibility for Injuries to Aliens* (1983).

protection of nationals living in the states to which the missions were assigned. The protection of the property of these nationals also became a concern of such missions.[31] The right of diplomatic missions to intercede on behalf of the property rights of their nationals came to be asserted in the diplomatic practice of capital-exporting states. Since this right of protection of the alien can be extended to the protection of foreign investment, it was a logical step to argue that this right could be utilised to protect the investments made by aliens. The roots of international law on foreign investment lie in the effort to extend diplomatic protection to the assets of the alien. The extension of the right was contested from the time it was attempted on the ground that it leads to unwarranted interference in the domestic affairs of the host state. Foreign investment is an essentially intrusive process which takes place essentially within the territory of a host state. To be able to lift that process out of the domestic sphere and subject it to international norms requires a nice balancing of international interests in the protection of the investment and the interests of the host state in regulating the process having its own benefits in mind. That is essentially what the international law on foreign investment is about. The definition of foreign investment must be rooted in this historical sense and not be extended beyond the meaning attributed to it in state practice and the precise words used in the treaties.

2. The history of the international law on foreign investment

2.1. The colonial period

The history of foreign investment in Europe can be traced to early times. There is no doubt that such investment existed in Asia, the Middle East, Africa and other parts of the world.[32] Early European institutional writings on the treatment of aliens by their host states set the stage for later controversies in the area of foreign investment law. One view was that aliens should be given equal treatment with the nationals. Vitoria suggested that, because trading was an expression of the feeling of community that is inherent in man, the alien trader must be given equality with the

---

[31] Luke T. Lee, *Consular Law and Practice* (1991), 124.

[32] Each of these systems had laws which governed trade and investment between nations. See C. H. Alexandrowicz, 'The Afro-Asian Nations and the Law of Nations' (1968) 123 *Hague Recueil* 117.

national.[33] This view would have justified trade and investment as natural rights. The alternative view required that aliens be treated in accordance with some external standard, which was higher than the national standard.[34] The latter view was motivated by the concern that the standards of treatment provided to nationals in a host state may be low and therefore unacceptable. Both views were premised on the idea that the law should be designed to further the free movement of trade and investments across state boundaries. They were intended to serve the interests of states which had the ability to expand their overseas trade. The espousal of these views, and more famously the freedom of the seas, by Grotius is seen by some historians as enabling the access of European powers into Asia and Africa.[35] In the context of modern times, the question whether history is repeating itself or is not at an end remains a relevant one.

In the eighteenth and nineteenth centuries, investment was largely made in the context of colonial expansion. Such investment did not need protection as the colonial legal systems were integrated with those of the imperial powers and the imperial system gave sufficient protection for the investments which went into the colonies.[36] In this context, the need for an international law on foreign investment was minimal.[37] Within the imperial system, the protection of investments flowing from the imperial

[33] Vitoria, *De Indis*, III, 5. The assumption was that this standard of national treatment was the highest he could expect and that he should not be discriminated against in the host state. The view was stated at the time of Spanish expansion in Latin America. Some writers have noted the duplicity that was inherent in this view. A. Anghie, 'Francisco Vitoria and the Colonial Origins of International Law' (1996) 5 *Social and Legal Studies* 256. Grotius also stated the freedom of trade and investment, but many believe that the sanctimonious efforts to promote such rights as natural rights hid the purpose of promoting Dutch colonial expansion in the Indies.

[34] Vattel was among the first writers to favour an external standard. Vattel, *The Law of Nations* (1758); II, 8, 104.

[35] Martine van Ittersum, 'Profit and Principle: Hugo Grotius, Natural Rights Theories and the Rise of Dutch Power in the East Indies' (PhD thesis, Department of History, Harvard University, Cambridge, MA 2002).

[36] One facet of this protection was to ensure that colonial legal systems were changed in order to accommodate European notions of individual rights of property and freedom of contract. See A. G. Hopkins, 'Property Rights and Empire Building' (1980) 40 *Journal of Economic History* 787, who pointed out that notions of collective ownership of property which were widely prevalent in the colonies were replaced by European notions of individual property.

[37] This explains the reason why the law first grew in the American context, where investment flows from the United States into Latin America had to be secured in a non-colonial context.

state was ensured by the imperial parliament.[38] The power to lobby for such laws would have been enormous as it was the major trading companies which had first established colonial power in the states that were later integrated into the imperial system.[39] Since the imperial system ensured the protection of the flows of capital within the system, there was no need for the growth of a separate system of law for the protection of foreign investments. Where investments were made in areas which remain uncolonised, a blend of diplomacy and force ensured that these states did not interfere with foreign investors too adversely. In states which stood outside the imperial system, enclaves into which the jurisdiction of the state did not extend were established so that trade and investment could be facilitated. The system of 'extraterritoriality' was imposed by treaties resulting from the use of force. In these enclaves, the law that was applied to European traders was the law of their home states.[40]

Power was the final arbiter of foreign investment disputes in this early period. The use of force to settle investment disputes outside the colonial context was a frequent occurrence. The use of overt or covert force in order to coerce the settlement of disputes continued even after the Second World War into the post-colonial period. There were spectacular instances of such uses of force.[41] But, doctrine had to be constructed to justify the use of force.[42] Capital-exporting countries, which operated outside the colonial context, were keen to devise some legal justification for pursuing the claims of their nationals and for the use of force if such use became necessary.

It was in the relations between the United States, still a fledgling power, and its Latin American neighbours that the need for the development of an international law relating to foreign investment played a role during the period prior to the Second World War. These developments have dictated the course of the law for a considerable period of time. In the foreign

---

[38] Thus, Britain relinquished control over the legislatures of the Empire settled by Anglo-Saxons in 1932 with the Statute of Westminster. The Asian and African colonies had to wait till after the end of the Second World War.

[39] The British East India Company and the Dutch East India Company played major roles in the establishment of their states' colonial rule.

[40] The system of extraterritoriality caused as much resentment as colonialism. In Asia, such enclaves existed in China, Thailand and Japan. The practice was also prevalent in the Middle East. See L. T. Lee, *Consular Law and Practice* (1991), 8–9.

[41] The incident involving the *Rosemary* [1953] 1 WLR 246 is an example. The overthrowing of the governments of Mosadegh in Iran and Allende in Chile were the more obvious instances of forcible intervention to assist foreign investment in recent history.

[42] As, some would argue, was the case with the invasion of Iraq in 2003.

investment relations between the United States and the Latin American states, one witnesses the clash between the idea that an alien investor should be confined to the remedies available in local law to the citizen and the idea that he must be accorded the treatment according to an external, international standard. It is an interesting aside to note that the United States in its formative years, as an importer of European capital, had experiences similar to those which developing countries presently have and took stances not dissimilar to those developing countries now take.[43] But, after its emergence as a regional economic power, it insisted that its Latin American neighbours should provide treatment in accordance with international standards to foreign investors. The Latin American states kept the debate vigorous by insisting in a series of conventions and in their own laws and constitutions that the provision of equal treatment to foreign investors satisfied the requirements of international law.[44] In many ways, this tussle between the United States and the Latin American states was to be replayed on a global scale in the post-colonial period. But, the law that was generated in the early period of this confrontation between the United States and the Latin American states had little to do with the taking of alien property to bring about economic reforms. It involved cases of attacks by mobs or political vendetta carried out for profit by juntas in power. The takings of foreign property that were involved in these early disputes are qualitatively different from the takings that resulted from economic reforms in later periods both in Latin America and elsewhere. The uniform application of principles to both types of interference with foreign investment is an unfortunate facet of the law which was introduced by early writers who failed to see the distinction between the two types of interference with foreign investment. The capricious grabbing of property for personal advancement of elite groups is different from the taking of property by a government for the institution of economic reform. But, early writings failed to emphasise this distinction.

---

[43] A. Chayes, T. Ehrlich and A. F. Lowenfeld, *International Legal Process* (1969), 851: 'When the United States was a less developed state, it had experiences with foreign investors not unlike those of today's developing societies.'

[44] The inspiration was provided by the writings of Carlos Calvo, an Argentinian foreign minister and jurist. In his *Le Droit International* (vol. 6, 5th ed., 1885), he had said: 'Aliens who established themselves in a country are certainly entitled to the same rights of protection as nationals, but they cannot claim any greater measure of protection.' This statement, that aliens are entitled to national treatment only, was adopted in the First International Conference of American States (Washington, DC, 1889) and included in the Convention on the Rights and Duties of States adopted at the Seventh International Conference of American States (Montevideo, 1933).

The Russian revolution and the spread of communism in Europe led to the taking of foreign property which was justified on the basis of economic philosophy. This initiated a debate among international lawyers as to the standards that should be satisfied to make such interference with foreign property acceptable in terms of international law. Many of the claims which arose as a result of these nationalisations were eventually settled by lump-sum agreements which reflect a compromise between the two conflicting views as to the appropriateness of the standards that have to be met for valid interference with foreign property. Though important as indicating state practice, the use of lump-sum agreements did not shed any light on the resolution of the question as to the external standard that had to be satisfied for a valid interference with alien property rights.

2.2. The post-colonial period

It was only after the dissolution of empires that the need for a system of protection of foreign investment came to be felt by the erstwhile imperial powers which now became the exporters of capital to the former colonies and elsewhere. It is convenient to divide the post-war developments into three periods in order to trace the developments which took place. The period immediately following the ending of colonialism witnessed hostility and antagonism towards foreign investment generated by nationalist fervour.[45] Such nationalism was itself a result of the anti-colonial movements which spread throughout the colonised parts of the world. There was also a need felt on the part of the newly independent states to recover control over vital sectors of their economies from foreign investors, largely nationals of the former colonial powers. The result was a wave of nationalisations of foreign property. These nationalisations resulted in intense debates as to what the international law on foreign investment protection was, each opposing group of states contending for a different set of norms in the area. In this period of political nationalism, there was more rhetoric generated than law. But, in the course of the conflict, there was also an effort to articulate the conflicting principles through the use of legal terminology. The capital-exporting nations argued for an external international law standard protecting foreign investment, whereas the newly independent nations argued for national control over the

---

[45] Much of it lingered on for some time. See e.g. C. Himavan, *The Foreign Investment Process in Indonesia* (1980), for the antagonism that the prolonged colonial struggle left in Indonesia.

process of foreign investment, including the ending of foreign investment by nationalisation.

These feelings of hostility have now been largely assuaged as the rearrangement of the economies of the newly independent states has been completed. In the natural resources sector, particularly in the oil industry, dramatic changes took place as a result of the collective action by the oil producing nations which ended the dominance of the industry by the major oil companies. These processes were accompanied by the articulation of new principles by the capital-importing states. Though nationalism still remains a threat to foreign investment,[46] it is unlikely that a new wave of nationalism will sweep across a vast area of the globe as it did during the immediate post-war era. Yet, individual states or regions may go through the same phenomenon, and the arguments which were used during the period of nationalism will once more be dusted off and used.[47] If one looks at the controversial areas of international law as involving a process of argument, then the arguments used during one period are likely to be used when conditions similar to those in that earlier period recur. The arguments which were formulated during this period of nationalism to oppose the more established norms of the capital-exporting states will be used again in appropriate circumstances.

One major change in this period was the increasing acceptance that nationalisation in pursuance of economic reform or reorganisation will not be considered unlawful in international law.[48] This change indicates the capacity of movements within international relations to displace

---

[46] On the role of economic nationalism in international society, see J. Mayall, *Nationalism and International Society* (1994), 70–110.

[47] As in the case of Iran, for example, where a once-thwarted nationalism took a more virulent form later, leading to the overthrow of the Shah and the expulsion of US business from the country. In both instances, the nationalisations which resulted gave rise to celebrated disputes. The first resulted in the *Anglo-Iranian Oil Company Case* [1952] ICJ Rpts 93 and the second led to the creation of the Iran–US Claims Tribunal which considered the claims of US citizens who had suffered injury during the uprising.

[48] It is difficult to show that nationalisation in pursuance of economic reform was ever considered unlawful in international law. It is simply the case that in earlier times the law was discussed in the context of takings by states controlled by dictators for the benefit of the ruling coterie and the rule extended to takings in pursuance of economic reforms. However, there are assertions of the legality of takings in pursuance of economic reforms in early literature. See J. Fischer Williams, 'International Law and the Property of Aliens' (1928) 9 BYIL 20, who denied the existence of any rule preventing nationalisation in international law. Also, see A. P. Fachiri, 'Expropriation and International Law' (1925) 6 BYIL 159, in accord. Both writers discussed the issue in the context of takings inspired by economic reforms.

prevailing norms with those which more readily reflect the trends within the international community.

The second period was a period of rationalisation undertaken by the state. Though at the international level, the capital-importing states continued to maintain collective stances, requiring changes to the rules relating to the conduct of international economic relations (including foreign investment), they were also busy adjusting their own legal systems. These adjustments reflected more pragmatic approaches to issues of foreign investment. Thus, there was a divergence between the attitude a state may take at the international level and what it may take at the domestic level. While at the international level, a state may join other states in taking a stance as to the international law position it supports, its domestic position may be different as it may seek to attract foreign investment as a strategy of economic development. It may also sign bilateral investment treaties that are at variance with its international position. This pragmatic position was in response to the need to maintain the idea of sovereign control over foreign investment at the international level while at the same time being able to attract multinational corporations into the state through the creation of an appropriate climate favourable to foreign investments. This explains the variance that exists between the stances that states have taken at different levels of interaction in this field.[49]

Several factors have led to this inconsistency of attitudes at these different levels. At the domestic level, the debates as to the role of the multinational corporations within the host economy of the developing state led to the view that even small states could utilise the resources of multinational corporations to launch into economic development. The success of small states like Singapore and Hong Kong demonstrated this. Ideological predispositions and economic nationalism gave way to more pragmatic attitudes which saw value in the stances that had been made in the past to assert the sovereignty of the state over foreign investment but now sought to use that sovereignty in a more meaningful fashion. This explains the apparent inconsistency in the stances of developing countries. While supporting normative changes at the global level that were protective of sovereign control over foreign investment, they were busy

---

[49] Sometimes the wrong conclusions are made from this variance. It is an error to conclude from the fact that a state had altered its domestic law on foreign investment favourably to such investments or has concluded a large number of bilateral investments that it had given up its stance on sovereign control over foreign investment. Such an error is too often made in the literature on the subject. This point is discussed further in Chapter 3 below.

making bilateral investment treaties strengthening the structure of foreign investment protection and foreign investment codes providing tax and other incentives.[50]

The modern period takes pragmatism in the area further. There have been significant shifts in the international economic scene. Communism has receded and the existence of an ideologically based source of counternorms that were hostile to notions of property on which foreign investment protection is based has lost its force. Developing countries have progressively introduced more open policies on foreign investment. This was not only because the economic philosophy favoured the liberalisation of foreign investment regimes, but also because there was competition for the limited amount of foreign investment that could flow into these states.[51] The old distinction between capital-importing and capital-exporting countries was also becoming diffused. Europe and the United States are now among the largest recipients of foreign investments. The free movement of investments within areas in North America and Europe where liberal regimes of foreign investment flows have now been established through regional treaties will create tension among these states.[52] The inflexible stances that were taken to foreign investment in the past on the basis of ideological predispositions do not have any force. There will, as a result, be a willingness to attempt compromise positions as to what the law is.[53]

One feature of the law is that developed states are undergoing experiences that were in the past confined to developing states. The UK and Canada changed petroleum contracts by legislation on the ground that

[50] S. Krasner, *Sturctural Conflict: Third World Against Global Liberalism* (1985).
[51] Aid had dried up due to recession as well as policies which did not favour the granting of aid. Banks did not provide loans to states after the petro-dollar crisis leading to a greater awareness of risks in sovereign lending. This left foreign investment as the only available means of external finance for economic development.
[52] The European Union is committed to internal flows of investment within its member states. In North America, Chapter 11 of the North American Free Trade Agreement (NAFTA) contains investment protection rules which parallel the US model bilateral investment treaty. Clashes will occur when the treaty rules are seen as eroding the sovereignty of the participating states to an unacceptable degree.
[53] There are two clear instances of such compromise positions in recent times. One is the *Restatement on Foreign Relations of the American Law Institute* which deviates from the previously accepted official position of the State Department of the United States on the issue of compensation for nationalisation. The other is the World Bank's Guidelines on Foreign Investment (1992) which also departs from the traditional norm of full compensation in favour of the formula of appropriate compensation but redefines appropriate compensation to mean usually market value compensation.

these had become disadvantageous to state interests.[54] The United States has legislation controlling the influx of foreign investments which raise national security concerns. Canada has been concerned with decisions under the provisions of NAFTA which seemed to interfere with its power to regulate the environment.[55] The extent of the litigation brought under the investment provisions of NAFTA have subjected the developed states to the same experience of having to defend regulatory policies before foreign tribunals that developing countries had been subjected to. There is considerable opposition to the system within the United States and Canada to this restraint on the regulatory powers of the state. The developed states have become the largest recipients of foreign investments. As a result, they may come to question facets of the law that they themselves had helped to fashion as they increasingly become targets of litigation under regional and other treaties. Evidence of this is beginning to appear. The issue as to whether an interference on environmental grounds amounts to a taking of property which has to be compensated has arisen in many cases concerning Canada, the United States and Mexico.[56] Likewise, the issue as to whether a foreign investor should be given the same treatment as a state corporation in a mixed economy under the national treatment provisions of an investment treaty has arisen in a case involving Canada.[57]

The thrust in the 1990s was made by economic liberalism which required a market-oriented approach to the problems of the world. Aspects of the theory were the liberalisation of capital markets and the assurance of freedom of movement to multinational corporations. The glamorous economic progress made by the East Asian states fuelled notions of economic liberalism and the pressure to open up markets was directly applied. The World Trade Organization (WTO), committed to a philosophy of free trade, came into existence in 1995. It had instruments which affected investments.[58] The OECD embarked on an attempt to draft a Multilateral Agreement on Investment (MAI) which was

---

[54] P. D. Cameron, *Property Rights and Sovereign Rights: The Case of North Sea Oil* (1983).

[55] The *Ethyl Case* was based on the claim that an announcement that the production of a chemical additive manufactured by the US company would be banned caused a depreciation in the price of the shares of that company and hence amounted to a taking. Canada asked for a reconsideration of the takings provision in NAFTA after this case.

[56] Apart from the *Ethyl Case*, other recent cases involving environmental issues are *Metalclad v. Mexico* (2001); *Methanex v. United States* (2003); and *Santa Elena v Costa Rica* (2002). *Methanex* is still being litigated. *Ethyl* was settled through the payment of a sum by Canada.

[57] *United Parcel Services v. CanadaPost* (pending, 2003).

[58] The extent to which they affect investments is surveyed in Chapter 6 below.

discontinued in 1998. But, the endeavour showed that, by the middle of the 1990s, the fervour for economic liberalism had reached a high point. Ideas such as rights of entry and establishment dominated discussion of investment principles and found their way into some treaties.[59] There were also treaties which were made giving prior consent of states to arbitration of any disputes which may arise from foreign investments at the unilateral instance of the foreign investor. The ability of the foreign investor to invoke such arbitral procedures gave rise to an increase in the number of arbitration awards involving foreign investments, thus contributing further precedents to the law.

This was a period that generally saw the triumph of the liberal economic views of foreign investment and the attempt at the transportation of these views into international law. However, the fervour for economic liberalism itself was rolled back somewhat by economic crises precipitated by the onrush of liberalisation that induced flows of funds into developing states but as speedy an outflow when things turned bad. The successive economic crises in Russia, Mexico, Asia and Argentina have led to much rethinking of the prescriptions of economic liberalism. The increasing gap between the rich and the poor on a global scale and the resulting schism in the attitudes to globalisation has also led to reviewing the wisdom of unmitigated capitalism. This rethinking too is reflected in the law. The ability of capital to move around unrestricted has been seen as the cause of much of the woes, and capital controls have been seen as a remedy by some states as well as by economists.[60] Coming at a time when the opposition to the MAI led to its withdrawal, the Asian economic crisis also contributed to a rethinking of the premises on which foreign investment law was based. The attitudes that will be adopted to foreign investment will go through cyclical changes. It could well be that the very favourable climate that existed for foreign investment in the last decade of the twentieth century may give way to a lukewarm attitude in the future, particularly if the promises of liberalisation do not materialise. Globalisation which proved favourable to foreign investment has also released forces of fundamentalism and ethnicity which compete against further liberalisation of the economy. In ensuring that these forces are placated, the state may have to rein in the trend towards further liberalisation.

---

[59] The US bilateral investment treaties recognise such rights but they are entered into subject to broad sectoral exceptions. NAFTA also contains provisions on pre-entry rights.

[60] Malaysia and Argentina had resorted to capital controls in order to deal with their economic crises. George Soros, at whose door the Asian economic crisis was laid by the Malaysian Prime Minister, himself advocated the need for controls.

But, the institutions that were created on the basis of economic liberalism will maintain their vigour for many years to come. Despite the demonstrations against it, the World Trade Organization will remain in place and function as an institution based on ideas of free trade which will attempt increasingly to take in investment issues as well on the basis that investment issues are not severable from issues of international trade. The WTO is already discussing issues relating to investment. Some of its new instruments like TRIPS and GATS which deal with intellectual property and services are in fact areas that would traditionally have fallen within investment. The impact of the law developed by the WTO in these areas will have an effect on the international law of investments. The latter body of law has to concern itself with the developments that take place within the WTO in areas such as intellectual property, services and competition. At the Singapore Ministerial Meeting of the WTO, the issue of an investment code was mooted, but at Doha there was a requirement that the issue of investment should be considered in the light of the development dimension. At the Cancun Ministerial Meeting, which was concluded in September 2003, the larger developing countries opposed consideration of investment unless there was agreement to expand the discussion to include not only protection of investment but also the potential liability of multinational corporations for the harm they may cause to the host state. Another episode during the height of the period of economic liberalism was the effort on the part of the OECD to draft the MAI. Though the MAI failed, there will be fresh efforts to bring about multilateral and regional investment treaties which have the promotion of investments through their protection as their aim. But, the effect of the MAI was to marshal the forces opposed to the impact of economic liberalism and the expression of the principles behind it in the form of binding codes. These groups argued that there was too great a concentration on the protection of foreign investment, thus favouring multinational corporations, without any concern for issues such as the protection of the environment, the development of the poorer states and the protection of human rights.

The forces hostile to liberalisation have already left their mark on the law. They will also gather strength. The movement for corporate responsibility will not be confined to the domestic spheres but will seek to create a global system that recognises the liability of multinational corporations. There is an increasing awareness of the need to develop rules relating to the environmental liability of multinational corporations through international law. There will be greater concern with the impact of the activities of multinational corporations on human rights, economic development and the rights of indigenous communities in the host states. These trends will counterbalance the trends towards the enhancement of the protection of the investment of multinational corporations and their ability to traverse the world freely. New interests have been brought into the existing conflict of interests.

These developments have shifted the focus onto new areas that had hitherto not been the focus of international investment law. The developments in the area of human rights gave an impetus to some of these changes. As domestic courts declared that they would exercise domestic jurisdiction over crimes against humanity, there were a larger number of prosecutions brought against multinational corporations before the courts of the home states of the parent companies for the damage they caused to the environment or human rights in other states. In the United States, the Alien Torts Act, an obscure statute enacted in 1876, gave jurisdiction to the US courts over any wrongs against public international law. The statute was the basis on which many actions against torture committed in various countries of the world were brought in the United States. An offshoot of such litigation were allegations of torture done in the course of the exploitation of natural resources or the construction of large projects by multinational corporations. There have been many instances of such litigation in which jurisdiction was assumed. So far, there have been no instances in which damages have been awarded. There is receptivity to litigation concerning torts committed by multinational corporations outside the jurisdiction in other common law jurisdictions as well.

Disparate forces have been at work within the law in this area. The forces of economic liberalism did have a near complete sway in the last decade of the twentieth century but competing forces had begun to appear as a result of a succession of economic crises. Each of these rival forces will support a different set of norms relating to investment protection. They will also differ on issues such as rights of access, types of treatment of investment and dispute resolution. The impact of the interplay of these forces on the international law on foreign investment is difficult to assess. These forces will always be extant within the international community, with ascendancy of one group of norms at a period and a decline at another. At each stage of this cycle, marks will be left on the law because law is the instrument through which expression is given to the fundamental tenets of each group of ideas. There is no total erasure of the marks left by either set of norms which makes the study of the area challenging. The law that can be stated lacks clarity. To those who see law not as a set of static rules but as an evolving process, this situation should be taken as the normal phenomenon in the law.

3. An outline of the book

The purpose of Chapter 2 is to identify the factors which work to shape the law on foreign investment. The major events in the historical development of the subject are identified at greater length than explained in this chapter. The nature of the multinational corporation and its counterpart, the state corporation, and the legal problems involved in the manner of their organisation are identified. The sources of international law which have been used to fashion the contending principles are described. It is shown that the sources in the construction of the contending sets of principles are weak sources of international law. What is passed off as custom by the different contending groups can hardly satisfy the stringent standards required by international law for graduating state practice into custom. There is an absence of multilateral treaties which have a direct bearing on the subject of foreign investments. Indeed, the recent unsuccessful efforts of the OECD in bringing about such an instrument demonstrate the difficulties inherent in such an attempt. There are many arbitral awards and opinions of jurists supporting one system of rules, and there is a series of General Assembly resolutions supporting the other. It will help in the understanding of the nature of the area to accept that both contending sets of principles are, at present, based on the weakest sources of a weak system of law. There is little to be achieved through the pretence that one set of norms has displaced the other. Both rely on weak sources of the law. Chapter 2 outlines the nature of the sources that have been used to construct the competing structures of the international law on investment.

Chapter 3 contains a study of the nature of the control that legislation in developing countries seeks to exert over foreign investment. The assertion of control over the process of foreign investment has been an aspect of the strategy of the capital-importing countries in seeking to contest the older norms on foreign investment protection. While contesting these norms at the international level, they also enacted legislation which exerts national control over entry, establishment and operation of foreign investments. The aim of such legislation is to attract foreign investment into the state while ensuring that the investment is geared to the economic goals of the state and that the potential harmful effects to such goals are eliminated. There are three levels at which host states make stances. These stances may be at variance with each other but they are explicable on grounds other than inconsistency in attitudes. At the domestic level, states are inclined to enact legislation having their domestic goals in mind and in such a manner as to exploit fully the advantages of foreign investment and diminish the possible harmful effects. At the bilateral level, states make treaties, again often having particular objectives in mind. These objectives may be at variance with the stances they take at the multilateral level. At the multilateral level, developing states may have common objectives which they seek to pursue so that a global change may be effected to international law. The charge of inconsistency merely fails to take into account the fact that the objectives at the three levels are induced by different considerations.

Chapter 4 deals with the controls that a home state of a multinational corporation could exercise over the corporation's activities abroad. Flowing from this control, the issue is addressed as to whether the home state has the duty to control abuses committed by the multinational corporations that affect the host state and its people. The extent to which home state measures could control the misdeeds of multinational corporations has increasingly attracted attention, particularly in stances made by states and other actors in opposing multilateral agreements on investment.

Chapter 5 traces the development of the customary rules advanced by developed states which constrain the power of the host state of foreign investment and create rules which confer protection on foreign investment. This chapter is important as it illustrates the system that had been advanced on the basis of an international minimum standard which creates responsibility in the host state. Such a minimum standard and other standards of treatment act as constraints on the power of the host state. This chapter bridges the two parts of the book, for it demonstrates how the rudimentary system of investment protection was supported. It thus serves as a prelude to the later chapters discussing liability arising from failure to conform to treatment standards and from expropriation.

Chapter 6 contains an analysis of the trends that can be seen in these bilateral investment treaties. The rapid increase in the number of these treaties has been a phenomenon of the modern law. Many claims are made that they constitute customary international law. Such claims are based on superficial analyses. It is evident that, though the outer shell of these treaties is similar, their contents vary markedly. They strike internal balances between notions of protection and notions of sovereignty in different ways. The chapter contains a study of the content of these treaties and an analysis of their impact on the law.

Chapter 7 contains a survey of the efforts made by international institutions to bring about uniform norms in the area. There have been many guidelines and draft codes generated by these organisations. None of them has been successful. The most recent of them has been the draft Multilateral Agreement on Investment (MAI) prepared by the OECD. The inability to bring about a multilateral code indicates the existence of a division of views among the developing states and the developed states. The failure of the MAI illustrates that even developed states may disagree on certain aspects of the law on foreign investment. The protests generated by the MAI indicated the extent to which the international law on foreign investment has become embroiled in the politics of globalisation. Yet, there have been in the recent past successes with regional agreements on investments. They have been able to set up viable dispute settlement processes which give effect to the rules contained in these agreements. Also, the project to bring about a multilateral agreement has been transferred to the World Trade Organization, where it has met with resistance from developing countries. Yet, it has to be recognised that in certain areas such as technology and services, there has been progress made in the context of the WTO and there is a possibility that the impact of the WTO on the international law of investment will be greater in the future. Its present and future impact therefore has to be assessed and this is an additional task this chapter attempts.

The final three chapters deal with issues of liability. Such liability flows from breaches of treaty and other obligations. Chapter 8 deals with the breach of treatment standards. The breach of treatment standards has become an important cause of action in recent times, as a result of NAFTA litigation. Developed countries seldom expropriate property. The opportunity to level charges of violations of treatment standards particularly in the context of the use of regulatory powers, however, remains. The NAFTA litigation against Canada and the United States is a novel phenomenon in that developed states have now become the targets of the law that they themselves helped to create. The use of treatment standards in such litigation opens up new possibilities in the area.

Chapter 9 deals with liability for breach of foreign investment agreements. It examines the internationalisation theory which deems a foreign investment contract to be subject to a transnational system of law and regards breaches of it as actionable wrongs. Chapter 10 deals with the controversial question as to the nature of compensation for the expropriation of foreign property. Inflexible stances have been taken in the past on this issue. There is a general acceptance that compensation must be paid. The ideological position that no compensation needs to be paid has lost support. The quantum of compensation still remains subject to dispute. The Hull standard of full compensation seems to have accumulated support, particularly in bilateral investment treaties, but the alternate standard of appropriate compensation still retains vigour. There has been an effort to transfer the emphasis onto valuation standards but these efforts have not diminished the fact that the issue of the standard of compensation has to be settled first.

The issue of compensation for expropriation is of historical value as most litigation takes place on the basis of treaties which specify the standard of compensation. Yet, the debate exposes the extent of the divisions that existed on this subject and provides an interesting clash in international law between the different groups of states. For that reason and for the reason that there are still cases which are brought on the basis of customary law, the area will continue to be of importance.

The work seeks to identify the major features of an international law on foreign investment. It demonstrates that such a branch of international law is in the process of development and can be isolated for separate study. The fact that many of the areas in it are replete with controversies is not a reason against its separate treatment. The major areas of international law, such as the law on the use of force, are similarly controversial. But, that has not impeded its treatment as a distinct branch of international law. The time is now ripe for the isolation and separate development of this branch of international law. The separate treatment of controversial areas, such as that of foreign investment, will help in the identification of the nature of the disputes and lead to the formulation of acceptable solutions. This book is a contribution to such development of an important area of international law.

2

The shaping factors

All law involves a resolution of conflicting interests. But, unlike other areas of law, international law lacks a centralised authority which could resolve conflicts of interest. Whereas in a domestic system there are decision-making authorities which can resolve such conflicts, in international law the absence of such an authority means that conflicts will be protracted. This situation will exist until some adjustment of the conflict is made in the course of time, either through negotiated settlements resulting in treaties or practices resulting in custom. The adjustment will contain principles which receive a measure of acceptance by the states. All these involve consensual processes. International law embodies a long series of adjustments made in response to conflicts.[1] As the process of adjustment never ends, the law continually remains in a state of flux.

The international law on foreign investment is an example of this process of adjustment. Its lack of clarity in many areas results from the intensity of conflict of divergent interests. Essentially, the conflict relates to the nature of the control that could be exercised over the foreign investment. The host states argue for national control subject to a minimum of external constraints, whereas capital-exporting states argue for greater constraints against national control in the hope of ensuring the protection of foreign investment.[2] Various other actors such as non-governmental organisations with a diversity of interests have come onto the scene, further complicating the existing situation of uncertainty. The elucidation of the nature of the conflict in the different areas of this field of law will help

---

[1] Part of this sentence is taken from Phillip Jessup, *The Use of International Law* (1959), 12. He identified some of the conflicts which have shaped international law. At pp. 17–20, Judge Jessup referred to the conflicts involved in the area of foreign investment, pointing out that there was no 'balanced bargaining power' in this area but that 'Latin American leadership contributed to the balancing Calvo doctrine which has been slowly making its way toward general acceptance'.

[2] The external controls which developed states seek to impose are manifested in the efforts to create multilateral instruments on investments.

in understanding the issues involved. The historical factors which shaped the law were set out briefly in the introductory chapter and the changes that have taken place in the framework within which foreign investments are made were discussed. There is a further elaboration of the legal context in which foreign investment operates in this chapter.

The chapter then goes on to consider the risks to foreign investment. The changes in the international political context in which foreign investment takes place have also increased the risks to foreign investment. In the colonial period, risks to foreign investments were virtually non-existent. But, the ending of colonialism and the consequent emergence of economic nationalism have brought about greater risks to the whole process. The nature of these risks has to be understood, for much of the law in this area is aimed at the reduction of the risks that arise to foreign investment. In the past, it was thought that risks to foreign investment arise only in developing states and socialist states. The experience of the disputes under NAFTA belies this belief.[3] It indicates that governments of both developed and developing countries take measures which are protective of their own economic interests and take refuge in sovereignty-centred arguments in order to justify them.[4]

The success of the legal solutions in countering the risk of government interference will depend on the extent to which this aim of reduction of risks to foreign investment is achieved. After dealing with the nature of the risks, this chapter discusses the major actors in the foreign investment scene and the legal problems which arise in connection with dealing with each of them. Some of the complexities which arise come about because of the structure of the multinational corporations which make the investments. The nature of state corporations in developing countries, with which multinational corporations have often had to co-operate in making investments in developing countries, adds to the problems. Despite the movement towards privatisation, state corporations still exist and play a dominant role in many industrial sectors of different states. The description of the roles these different entities play in the making of investments is necessary for the understanding of the law in the area. A section of this chapter identifies the problems which

---

[3] NAFTA cases, which can involve only the three states, Canada, Mexico and the United States, have increased in numbers in recent times. Many of the cases involve the United States and Canada.

[4] In the case of the United States, see *Methanex* v. *United States*. The pleadings are available at www.naftaclaims.com.

the different legal characteristics of these actors create. The final part of the chapter deals with the sources of the international law of foreign investment.

In effect, the chapter is intended to emphasise the major changes that have taken place in the present political economy of foreign investment. The shift in emphasis in the sources of law is a consequence of these changes, and the clear identification of these changes is a necessary prelude to the study of the subject. The first is the release of the major part of the world from colonialism and the impact this change had on the legal thinking related to the creation of new structures for foreign investment as well as for the protection of such foreign investment. Unlike in the past where power alone was the arbiter, it became necessary to construct legal methods for the protection of such investments. The second is the nature of the actors on the scene. The growth of multinational corporations and the emergence of state corporations have been factors with which the law has had to contend. The third factor is the democratisation of the process of law-making within the international society. The Eurocentric nature of international law has been subject to challenge in the field of international economic relations through an attempt to fashion law by means other than the traditional source of law-making, sometimes with success.[5] The subject also lends itself to the analysis of how neo-liberalism and globalisation have shaped the law, particularly in the period since the writing of the last edition. In this period, there was an evident, though short lived, triumph of neo-liberalism which emphasised the free movement of capital and investments and consequently stricter standards of investment protection and resolution of investment disputes. These immediately came to be reflected in the law, changing the balance in favour of the views held by capital-exporting countries. There was a profusion of bilateral treaties incorporating high standards of investment protection. However, a multilateral instrument on investment is yet to come about. The effort to create competence in the WTO over investment seems also to be mired in controversy. With the increasing disenchantment caused by successive economic crises, there is a restoration of the balance as neo-liberalism comes to be countered by opposing ideas. The aim of this chapter is to survey the nature of these changes as a prelude to the

---

[5] Whether the powerless majority can meaningfully make law without the consent of the powerful is a thorny issue. Some would support the democratic, quantitative principle as the best method of law-making.

exploration of legal norms relating to foreign investment in the succeeding chapters.

1. The historical setting

It is necessary to elaborate on some of the historical information provided in the Introduction so that the evolution of the law may be better understood. Prior to the Second World War, foreign direct investment did not face any risks except in states which were not under colonial rule. But, many of these states which were nominally independent were either protectorates, such as the states of the Middle East, or were subject to some form of dominance so that European investments had sufficient protection.[6] Protection of foreign investment in these areas was based on military power. Power ensured that foreign investment, usually flowing from the metropolitan power into its colonies was adequately protected. Gun-boat diplomacy was sufficient to ensure that both trade and investment were protected.

1.1. State responsibility for injuries to aliens

The system of state responsibility for injuries to aliens and their property was therefore first established in the part of the world where such a colonial relationship did not exist, but power, nevertheless, played a determining role.[7] The genesis of many of the rules of state responsibility is to be found in the relationship between the United States and Latin America. The early rules on diplomatic protection were devised in the context of injuries suffered by US citizens in Latin American states. The struggle again reflected the binary nature of the norms in this area. The United States sought to externalise the norms that governed aliens and their property. It argued for an international minimum standard in accordance with which the foreigner should be treated. It built into the international minimum standard, norms that were favourable to the foreign investor and were, to a

---

[6] Most of these areas were subject to capitulation treaties which imposed a system of extraterritoriality on them. The system insulated the foreigners living and trading in these areas from the application of the local laws and subjected them instead to the laws of their home states. This system prevailed in China and Thailand and in many areas of the Middle East.

[7] E. M. Borchard, *The Diplomatic Protection of Citizens Abroad* (1915); F. S. Dunn, *The Protection of Foreign Nationals* (1932); C. F. Amerasinghe, *State Responsibility for Injuries to Aliens* (1964); and M. Sornarajah, *The Pursuit of Nationalized Property* (1986).

large extent, based on US domestic law standards. The foreign investor was entitled to compensation according to an external standard, which came to be described in the hallowed formula used by Cordell Hull that compensation should be 'prompt, adequate and effective'.[8] The foreign investor was entitled to dispute resolution before an overseas tribunal. The Latin American states countered this stance by focusing on the fact that the foreign investor entered the host state voluntarily, assuming the risks of the investment there. On this basis, they argued that the foreign investor, like any other person in the state including their own citizens, was entitled only to a national standard of treatment provided to both foreigner and citizen alike by the local laws. Enunciated in the form of the Calvo doctrine, this came to be accepted generally by the Latin American states.[9] Later, both stances were to be internationalised.[10] The European states, once they gave up their colonies, had to structure a system of invest-ment protection, and they found the already existing American system a convenient one to adopt.[11] The developing states of Africa and Asia, once independent, espoused the Calvo doctrine. Its universalisation was sought to be accomplished by instruments associated with the New International Economic Order which the developing states sponsored in the General Assembly of the United Nations. At the inter-state level, diplomatic pro-tection and state responsibility became the bases on which investment protection was accomplished. But, there was no guarantee of the success of such a method of protection. For one thing, a state may refuse to espouse a claim because it may consider a foreign investment claim expendable in the pursuit of other foreign policy objectives. There was also no guaran-tee of success in that it was unclear as to what the international law was, in view of the conflict of norms. There was a general reluctance to take issues of foreign investment law to the International Court of Justice. The uncertainty in the law that may be exposed by a ruling by the Court may

---

[8] Cordell Hull, who was Secretary of State during the Mexican expropriations of 1938, stated this to be the standard in a letter to his Mexican counterpart. Ever since, the standard has been espoused by the United States and has been referred to as the Hull doctrine of compensation.

[9] The doctrine is associated with Carlos Calvo, an eminent Latin American jurist and diplo-mat.

[10] See, for example, Article 2(2)(c) of the Charter of Economic Rights and Duties of States.

[11] There is a paucity of state practice regarding investment protection. The state responsibility cases involved European states but the heavy influence of US practice and US writings on the subject in the early twentieth century is evident.

be a reason not to force an authoritative pronouncement. The developed states may prefer to maintain at least the mirage that their set of norms constituted international law.[12]

State responsibility in this area, though feasible, remains a solution of last resort. It is for this reason that the devising of remedies that multinational corporations can themselves resort to has played a more important role. This is an instance in which private power has played the dominant role in shaping international norms for quite some time. The employment of international law by private corporations flies in the face of traditional theory but yet has gone largely unnoticed. No doubt, the more successful techniques of protection have been created through such private power acting in tandem with state power but yet, the ideas that have driven the field were initiated through largely private means. The area of international foreign investment law effectively belies the old notion that only states are the effective arbiters of what international law contains. Private power, in the form of both multinational corporations and, more recently, non-governmental organisations, always has a significant role in the shaping of this area of international law.[13] Positivism provided a convenient cloak to hide this fact by insisting that only states acted in the international sphere.[14] The accommodation of such private power in the theory of international law is a challenge that awaits the international lawyer. It will probably not be taken up because there is little incentive to remove the cloak and reveal the extent to which international law is an instrument of both private and public power. The manner of the evolution of the law through such power can now be stated. It developed largely in the different sectors in which investments were traditionally made. The oil sector played the dominant role.

---

[12] The *ELSI Case*, which was the most recent instance in which such a dispute was heard by the International Court of Justice, was heard by a Chamber. See further M. Sornarajah, *The Settlement of International Disputes* (2000).

[13] There are studies of the role of private actors in international relations. See Leslie Sklair, *The Transnational Capitalist Class* (2001). For the role of non-govenmental organisations, see Robert O'Brien, *Contesting Global Governance* (2000).

[14] It is evident that many of the early doctrines were advocated to enhance the power of the old colonial companies like the Dutch East India Company. The freedom of the high seas attributed to Grotius was, according to historians, not a neutral doctrine, but a doctrine articulated to favour the privateers employed by the Dutch East India Company. The tract on *mare liberum* was originally written by Grotius to justify the sinking of the Portuguese vessel, the *Santa Catarina*, off the coast of Malacca, by Dutch privateers.

1.1.1. The natural resources sector

Foreign investment in natural resources was necessary to ensure the raw materials for production in the Western states. The cycle of trade during the colonial period was to transfer resources from the colonies to the metropolitan states so that they could be converted into manufactured products or used to fuel industries in these states. The early oil companies and companies which operated in the other natural resources sectors used concession agreements to tie up production in large areas of land for considerable periods of time.[15] This picture which formed in the oil industry was reproduced in other mineral industries. The similarity of the pattern around the world was another feature of this process. International business transactions up to modern times take features that are similar, facilitating the formulation of a seemingly uniform law around the world.[16] The concession agreements often effected transfers of sovereign powers over vast tracts of land, to the foreign corporation for long periods of time, for payment of royalty calculated on the quantity of oil produced at a fixed rate.[17] The system was kept in place by an elaborate web of power exerted by the home state and a concerted dominance exerted within the international system itself by the dominant powers.[18]

---

[15] The evolution and the politics of the oil industry are well described in Daniel Yergin, *The Prize* (1992).

[16] This phenomenon becomes the basis for the arguments relating to a *lex mercatoria*. The wide prevalence of the joint venture form in foreign investment is an example in modern times. See M. Sornarajah, *The Law of International Joint Ventures* (1992). The existence of a common form facilitates the formation of what is referred to as *lex mercatoria*, the claim to the existence of a universally valid international business law, again created through entirely private processes. Its bases are to be found in writings of scholars and in arbitral awards rather than in the normal sources of international law such as treaties harmonising the law. The *lex mercatoria* is, in the conception of some writers, the law that applies to foreign investment contracts.

[17] The *Aminoil Arbitration* indicates the classic situation of a petroleum agreement. The concession, which was made in 1948, was to last for sixty years. The royalty was fixed at two shillings and six pence per barrel of oil. These agreements are described in Henry Cattan, *The Law of Oil Concessions in the Middle East and North Africa* (1967); A. Z. El Chiati, 'Protection of Investments in the Context of Petroleum Agreements' (1987) 204 *Hague Recueil* 9; Kamal Hossain, *Law and Policy in Petroleum Development* (1979); and A. S. El Kosheri and T. Riad, 'The Law Governing a New Generation of Petroleum Agreements' (1986) ICSID Rev 259.

[18] Thus, the Iranian revolution in 1952 which affected the oil interests of the major British and American companies was ended through the collective exercise of power by Britain and the United States. The rule of Mossadegh was ended and the rule of the monarchy was restored. In the context of what happened two decades later, when the Shah was overthrown and an Islamic form of government established, it is contestable whether such interventions

Some of these concession agreements have been subjected to legal analysis as they were subjects of international arbitrations. Thus, in *Aminoil* v. *Kuwait*,[19] the concession agreement which was involved was originally entered into between the Sheik of Kuwait, at a time when Kuwait was a protectorate of Britain, and a US oil company. The royalty which was to be paid was two shillings and six pence for every barrel of oil. The arrangement was to last for sixty years. The terms of the contract were not to be changed without the consent of both parties. Events showed that the agreement was not able to withstand the political and economic changes which took place within the industry. The agreement was renegotiated on two occasions. In the 1970s, the price of oil sky-rocketed during the oil crisis. But, the oil company insisted on paying the same sum of two shillings and six pence per barrel that had been originally agreed upon in the concession agreement. The windfall profits were not due to any inherent merit on the part of the company but due to external industry trends. As the company was not willing to part with a larger share of these profits, the state intervened and took over the production of the oil. In these circumstances, it is inevitable that a state would intervene. The case nicely illustrates that power balances within long-term contracts involved in the area of foreign investment could shift as a result of external circumstances and that if the contract proves inflexible, it will provoke a conflict that results in government intervention.

Concession agreements were not confined to the petroleum sector but were utilised in other mineral resources sectors as well.[20] The Ashanti goldfields concession concluded in Ghana provides an example of an agreement to prospect for gold that was to last for one hundred years from the date of the agreement. The ruby mines in Burma were subject to similar concessions.[21] Similar agreements existed throughout the developing world. They were executed in the context of unequal bargaining power, the rulers of the states either not having the power to resist the terms that were imposed on them or not having the expertise or desire to bargain for

---

accomplish a useful purpose. They merely fuel more extreme forms of nationalism. A. W. Ford, *The Anglo Iranian Oil Dispute* (1954); J. Walden, 'International Petroleum Cartel – Private Power and the Public Interest' (1962) *Journal of Public Law* 64.

[19] *Aminoil* v. *Kuwait* (1982) 21 ILM 976. For a discussion of the dispute, see Alan Redfern, 'The Arbitration Between the Government of Kuwait and Aminoil' (1984) 55 BYIL 65.

[20] David Smith and Louis Wells, *Negotiating Third World Mineral Agreements* (1975).

[21] For an interesting account of the scheming and exploitation that accompanied these transactions, see R. V. Turrell, 'Conquest and Concession: The Case of the Burma Ruby Mines' (1988) 22 *Modern Asian Studies* 141.

better terms. The people of the state were seldom beneficiaries of these transactions.

These agreements were obnoxious from the point of democratic notions of sovereignty. Often, they were signed by rulers who did not understand the implications of the contracts they were concluding or they did not care as they, being absolute rulers, could utilise the royalties they received for their own benefit.[22] In some instances, these agreements were facilitated by the fact that alien governments were in control of the states in which they were made. Thus, in Namibia, the South African government, during the period of the mandate, ensured that the concessions that were made favoured the interests of their own multinational corporations. The validity of such contractual arrangements made through coercion or with unrepresentative governments is doubtful in modern international law.[23]

The structure of the mineral industries had to undergo change with the independence of the states in which they were made.[24] In the petroleum sector and, to a lesser extent, in the other mineral resources sectors, there was rapid change brought about by collective action initiated by cartels of producer countries. There were dramatic shifts particularly in the petroleum sector where state oil corporations were created and vested with ownership of the oil resources of the state. The old oil concessions were cancelled. Thereafter, the concession agreement ceased to be the norm within the oil industry and was replaced by the production sharing agreement under which ownership of oil remained throughout the period of exploitation with the state oil corporation. In this new form of agreement, foreign corporations perform a participatory role, with the state-owned corporation having dominant control of the operations. Such agreements reflect the shift in the power equations that have taken place within the oil industry.[25] The shift was aided by the formulation of international law

---

[22] It is an interesting point as to whether international lawyers who promote the norm of democracy would concede that concessions and other foreign investment agreements signed by dictators or unrepresentative governments should be considered invalid. It is possible to argue that the norm of self-determination, now having acquired a near *ius cogens* status would invalidate concession agreements signed by unrepresentative rulers.

[23] It would be interesting to speculate whether contracts made in post-Saddam Iraq under the foreign investment law promulgated by the American-instituted administration will be considered valid after a new regime takes over.

[24] For an excellent consideration of the issues that arise in the Australian mineral sector, see Anne Fitzgerald, *Mining Agreements* (2002).

[25] Indonesia was a pioneer in introducing the new arrangements into the petroleum industry. They were widely copied. See S. Rochmat, *Contractual Arrangements in Oil and Gas Mining Enterprises in Indonesia* (1981).

doctrines such as the doctrine on the permanent sovereignty over natural resources. Scholarly views as to the nature of such doctrines may differ.[26] Some regard them as *ius cogens* principles and others as mere *lex ferenda*. But, this argument has been rendered academic. In many states, the principle, once formulated at the international level, has been incorporated in constitutions and in foreign investment codes.[27] Contracts like the production sharing agreement in the oil industry operate on the basis of this principle. The doctrine has operated at three distinct levels. After its formulation at the international level, it has been translated into national legislation in the form of constitutional provisions and foreign investment codes. It has also led to the drafting of contracts which ensure that the host state party has greater control over the process of the exploitation of mineral resources. The production sharing agreement in the oil industry provides the best example. It is futile to argue that the doctrine has no legal substance and is an expression of desirable norms when it has been acted upon so consistently. In the mineral resources industry, which it was principally designed to affect, the doctrine of permanent sovereignty over natural resources reflects a change that is now well established. In any event, it merely asserts a truism in international law that the sovereignty of a state includes control over all persons, incidents and substances within a state unless such control has been removed by treaty.

Though the control of the natural resources sector by foreign corporations was broken, the command of technology and capital that these corporations had makes them significant players in this sector. Nationalisation may have ended direct control. Indeed, modern legislation preserves the natural resources sector to state corporations or, alternatively, to nationally controlled corporations. Yet, alliances with the foreign corporations have been necessary to operate the sector, as these foreign corporations possess the technology and risk capital necessary for the exploration and exploitation of the resources. The interests that multinational corporations create in order to carry out activities in this area need protection and become a focus of the international law on foreign investment. In recent times, one may argue that there has been a discernible swing towards the protection of the interests of foreign investors which is associated with the trends towards liberalisation.

---

[26] For a survey of the different views of the doctrine, see generally Nico Schrijver, *Sovereignty over Natural Resources: Balancing Rights and Duties* (1997); M. S. Rajan, *The Doctrine of Permanent Sovereignty over Natural Resoruces* (1982).

[27] See e.g. Article 12 of the Philippines Constitution and the Constitution of Papua New Guinea.

1.1.2. The plantation sector

In many colonies, plantation sectors were created by European powers. Most of the colonies had operated self-sufficient agricultural economies. The colonial powers used the land that was previously agricultural for the planting of export crops. Thus, in Sri Lanka, tea, rubber and cocoa which were not native to the island were introduced. Vast tracts of agricultural land were converted to the production of these export crops. The changes were effected through large colonial companies which bought up the land and set up vertically organised industries which were responsible not only for the production of these export crops but also their subsequent transportation to and sale in the European markets. The corporations controlled these markets, the tea sector being the classic example. Companies such as Brooke Bond, Liptons and Twinings exerted global control. Long after colonialism ended and the tea estates were nationalised, the control over the markets remained with these corporations. The distribution of these products in the markets of the developed states continued to be controlled by these corporations.

1.1.3. The manufacturing sector

Multinational corporations dominate the manufacturing sector. The sector was initially operated through wholly owned corporations established in the home states of colonial powers. They were, however, different from the modern multinational corporation. Due to lack of speedy means of communications, it was possible for managers at local posts to run the affairs of the corporation by themselves. In the case of the modern multinational corporation, central control through the parent company over its subsidiaries has become a reality due to instant methods of communication. The modern multinational corporation has, as a result, acquired a considerable amount of global power through its integrated networks of production. Different patterns of diversification of production dependent on the sourcing of materials and cheap labour have emerged within the various manufacturing sectors.

It was at one time argued that this network of control of the subsidiaries of multinational corporations, which by the nature of their operations become integrated into the economies of host states, would undermine the sovereignty of these states.[28] Control became a central feature of the

[28] The early literature on multinational corporations showed a preoccupation with this issue. Raymond Vernon, *Sovereignty at Bay* (1971).

conflict between the host states and multinational corporations. There is visible evidence of this struggle for control in the foreign investment legislation of many host states.

In their efforts to maintain control over foreign investment, host states have enacted legislation through which entry of multinational corporations and their subsequent operations are carefully regulated.[29] At the same time, the home states of multinational corporations have argued for a system of open entry and the liberalisation of movement of multinational corporation by arguing for and introducing into investment treaties the right of pre-entry national treatment. This right would enable the multinational corporation to establish a business on the same terms as a national of the host state.[30] The tussle between the right to regulate entry and establishment and complete liberalisation of entry and establishment is a characteristic of the conflict between the different sets of norms. Neither set of norms is dominant. Even in instruments in which liberalisation seems to be dominant, there are sectors which remain subject to regulation.[31]

The interests of host states are generally articulated through the requirement that entry is made into the state through the establishment of a joint venture with a local partner. In sectors in which foreign ownership is restricted to a certain percentage of the market, it is natural that joint ventures reflecting that percentage of participation are formed. Partnership with a local partner ensures that some profits stay at home, the local partner acquires expertise in business as well as technology and, if a state entity is a partner, local control over the investment is effectively assured. Here, the claims made at the global level for the control of the economy have been translated into the national law through legislation.

Multinational corporations, in turn, have responded to these measures with strategies that would ensure that they retained control over their subsidiaries. Requirements of the joint venture legislation are defeated by making partnerships with nominees or with local businessmen who will not insist on exercising their rights of control. Indigenisation measures are similarly thwarted by sale of shares to local persons who are favourable

---

[29] See Chapter 3 below.

[30] A good example is contained in NAFTA and the bilateral investment treaties entered into by the United States.

[31] NAFTA provides the classic example where parties can still close sectors to entry and establishment.

to the continuation of foreign control. There is not always a single winner in this struggle for control.[32]

Prevailing weaknesses in the economy, such as corruption, could be exploited to thwart the purposes of the legislation. There are different views as to whether protection will be given to multinational corporations which violate the internal laws of the host state. In *Shott* v. *Iran*,[33] a tribunal held that the shares purchased through a nominee in violation of the law after the foreign quota of shares had been exhausted cannot be protected. But, there are other awards which indicate that, where there is a climate in a host state that condones illegalities, the law should ignore the illegalities.[34] The latter view seems unacceptable as it promotes through condonation the violation of the host state's laws. It cannot, for example, be argued that the existence of rampant bribery in a state excuses bribery altogether and that the court or tribunal should disregard it.

1.1.4. The financial sector

Financing of foreign investment was not a major problem in the past. Much of the capital was raised in the home states of the multinational corporations in the form of venture capital. But, in recent times, international banks have come onto the scene and are financing the making of foreign investments as well as major projects. The roles these financial institutions play, the forms of transactions used by them and the regulation by both the host and the home state of these transactions fall within the field of the international law of foreign investment. Where the nationality of the bank financing the investment is different from the foreign investor or the multinational corporation, the interests of the bank can be given protection by its home state. As a result, several home states could have claims based on nationality to exert pressure on the host state which acts to the detriment of the foreign investment.

1.1.5. Intellectual property

There was hardly any law on the cross-border transfer of intellectual property at the formative stages of this branch of the law. The law was fashioned in the context of the protection of tangible assets. It is only in recent times that the protection of intangible assets of the foreign investor has come to

---

[32] Thomas J. Bierstaker, *Multinationals, the State and the Control of the Nigerian Economy* (1987).
[33] (1990) 24 Iran–US CTR 203 at 218.   [34] *Biloune* v. *Ghana Investment Centre* (1990).

be discussed.[35] With the industries in the area of information and biotechnology being largely dependent on intellectual property, the protection of such property has become of crucial importance.

The transfer of technology to the host state is regarded as one of the benefits of foreign investment to the host state. The host state has an interest in ensuring that such a transfer does, in fact, take place. The host states insist on such transfer of technology to local personnel in the hope that local skills in the industry could thereby be developed, with a view to local manufacture of the product at some future time. The requirement that foreign investors operate through joint ventures also makes it more difficult to keep technological processes secret within the organisation. These policy changes come at a time when foreign investors prefer to risk technology than capital and equipment in the making of the investment.

The tendency in developing countries to disregard the standards of protection for intellectual property recognised in international conventions makes this an area of concern for developed states. The fact that much of industry in new areas, such as biotechnology, computer science and related fields, will depend on the protection of intellectual property has resulted in developed states requiring greater protection for intellectual property. The dilemma in the area is that these rights are created by local law in each state. The problem then was to induce the local law to ensure that such rights are created and protected in accordance with a desired, external standard.

Capital-exporting states have developed a three-pronged strategy to deal with the problem. The first strategy of taking unilateral measures against recalcitrant states is confined to the United States. Under section 301 of the Omnibus Trade Act, trade sanctions may be imposed on states that do not confer adequate standards of protection against violations of intellectual property rights.[36] The legislation and threats to use it continue

---

[35] The effect of taking over of know-how and similar rights was discussed in the *Chorzow Factory Case* [1928] PCIJ Series A No. 17.

[36] The legislation enables the surveillance of standards of protection of intellectual property in each state by the United States Trade Representative (USTR). The USTR is required by the 1988 amendment introduced by the Omnibus Trade and Competitiveness Act to investigate allegations made by private parties of violations of such property rights in foreign countries. The USTR may adopt a range of measures including the listing of countries, specification of time limits within which offending practices are to be eliminated and, finally, trade sanctions if these violations are not rectified. Determinations are made annually as to violations in reports published by the USTR. States which violate standards are listed. Inclusion in the list amounts to a threat of action by way of trade sanctions in the event the alleged violations are not corrected. The validity of these measures has been

despite the fact that multilateral measures have been successfully instituted in the field.

The second strategy is to include intellectual property rights within the definition of foreign investment and extend the protection of bilateral treaties dealing with investments into the area of intellectual property protection. The pattern in all bilateral investment treaties is to extend the definition of foreign investment to include intellectual property rights. There are also bilateral treaties which specifically deal with the protection of intellectual property, which usually contain standards that are in advance of standards contained in multilateral treaties.[37]

The third approach has been to include the protection of intellectual property through the World Trade Organisation. The WTO instrument, Trade Related Intellectual Property Rights (TRIPS), seeks for the first time to create external standards as to intellectual property rights created by the domestic laws of each member state. This is based on the assumption that international trade distortions occur when such rights are not protected. A high volume of goods incorporating such rights are transferred in the course of international trade or are manufactured within states to be transported to other states. Hence, the argument made by the developed states was that the protection of intellectual property rights is the concern of a regime on international trade.[38] The concept of trade and investment became diffused here because multinational corporations were the purveyors of both trade and investment through technology. Also, technology was used in the manufacture of goods by foreign investors and it was thought proper that such technology should be protected through the same measures.

---

challenged with varying success before GATT and WTO panels. In 1998, a WTO panel held that 301 action was not inconsistent with the WTO because of the commitment of the United States not to use it in a manner inconsistent with the WTO obligations of the United States. The European Union has a similar mechanism but has not been active to the same extent. See M. Bronckers, 'Private Participation in the Enforcement of WTO Law: The New EC Trade Barriers Regulation' (1996) 33 CMLR 299.

[37] Peter Drahos, 'BITS and BIPS: Bilateralism in Intellectual Property' (2002) 4 *Journal of World Intellectual Property* 792. Free trade agreements, negotiated bilaterally also contain provisions on intellectual property protection. See e.g. the United States–Jordan Free Trade Agreement (October 2000).

[38] Bernard Hoekman and Michel Kostecki, *The Political Economy of the World Trading System* (2001), 274–300; Jayashree Wattal, *Intellectual Property Rights in the World Trade Organization: The Way Forward for Developing Countries* (2000); Keith Maskus, *Intellectual Property Rights in the Global Economy* (2000); and Duncan Mathews, *Globalising Intellectual Property Rights* (2003).

The developing countries opposed such comprehensive protection. In their view, the TRIPS agenda was not about free trade but about externalising control over domestically created intellectual property rights through the creation of an international regime with dispute settlement functions. It involved considerable loss of sovereignty over purely internal processes that may have vital economic significance to the state. The industrialised states had already created a sophisticated body of legal principles on intellectual property rights. They were now being universalised. The TRIPS measures were clearly aimed at the developing states and the manner in which they conducted trade and investment. Yet, there was insufficient cohesion among the developing countries to resist TRIPS. Many had already been either coerced into enacting appropriate legislation on intellectual property through the threat of unilateral sanctions or had already done so in the belief that such legislation was necessary to attract foreign investment. Besides, there was a free market mood sweeping the world in the mid-1990s which was generally favourable to the adoption of the instrument. There was also the promise of market access if TRIPS was accepted.[39]

The TRIPS agreement has significance for foreign investment in several ways. Multinational corporations which are required to enter into joint venture alliances with local partners by developing country laws may wish to keep the transfer of technology separate by making separate contracts for this with the locally incorporated joint venture. The technology that is so transferred needs protection as foreign investment as it is made in connection with such investment. The goods that are manufactured may incorporate technology that needs protection. The processes that are employed in extraction or manufacture by a foreign investor also need protection. For a variety of reasons, the TRIPS instrument will impact foreign investment. Initially, where there is a violation of the standards of the instrument, protection will have to be sought from the local courts under the local laws which would have incorporated the TRIPS standards. There is a duty on states to provide adequate enforcement procedures and remedies. Where such remedies are not provided, recourse may be had to the home state which could take the matter to dispute settlement through the WTO processes. This becomes possible largely in situations where the policy of the host state affects intellectual property rights. It is unlikely that situations affecting individual foreign investors could be

---

[39] The Agreement on Textile and Clothing would not have been concluded if TRIPS had not been accepted. These provided for better market access.

construed as involving violations of TRIPS. But, it is possible that there is a duty in the laws of states to take up the cause of individual foreign investors, in which case the WTO system could become the avenue for providing remedies to individual investors.[40] The law under the WTO and its processes has assumed significance for an aspect of foreign investment. If a more comprehensive foreign investment discipline is negotiated, as contemplated in the Doha Declaration of the WTO, then there will be protection given to intellectual property as foreign investment under that discipline.[41] Following investment treaties, the definition of investment will include intellectual property. There will, however, be a resumption of the North–South debate on this issue, before a comprehensive agreement can be accomplished. Developing countries are importers of technology. There will be rent transfers for such technology to developed states, having adverse impacts on economic development.[42] In calculating the benefits of foreign investment to economic development, the costs of technology will have to be factored in.

2. Conflicting economic theories on foreign investment

Theoretical conflicts have had an impact on shaping legal attitudes to foreign investment. Leaving aside the Marxist theories,[43] the conflict is between two extreme theories, one of which maintains that foreign investment is wholly beneficial to the host state while the other maintains that unless a state veers away from dependence on foreign investment it cannot achieve development.[44] There are theories which seek to adopt a middle course between these extreme views. All theories focus attention on the economic development of the host state, particularly the host developing

---

[40] In the United States, it could be argued that there is a duty on the United States Trade Representative to take up the cause of any individual company which suffers harm in international trade.

[41] This is considered further in Chapter 6 below.

[42] Hoekman and Kostecki, *Political Economy*, 294.

[43] In classic Marxist theory, there would be no scope for an international law on foreign investment as there will be no concept of private property which is central to the existence of such law.

[44] The theories are presented in a stark fashion in this section. There are, of course, various nuances in their formulation by different scholars. For the purposes of understanding the effect of the economic theories on the formulation of the law, a stark presentation of the competing theories on foreign investment is preferable. For statements from an economic point of view, see Thomas Bierstaker, *Multinationals, the State and the Control of the Nigerian Economy* (1987), 3–51.

state. Lawyers who favour complete protection for foreign investments rely on theories which emphasise the positive effects of foreign investment on economic development. This view gained impetus during the high point of globalisation when arguments made for the liberal flow of multinational capital had wide acceptance and many legal instruments in the field reflected these views. There was also a formulation of legal principles on the basis that they would promote such beneficial flows of capital. Lawyers holding the opposite point of view argued to the contrary, relying on economic theories which emphasised the deleterious nature of foreign investment on the host economy. They also articulated competing legal principles on the basis of these economic theories. They were not articulated on the basis of any in-depth study of the economic aspects of the problem but were a reaction to what the policy of the law should be, based on assumptions made on superficial understandings of economic views on the subject. The literature on the subject does not reveal any survey made of the economic assumptions on which the law is based. The references to the economic bases of the law are scanty at best and are made as secondary justifications for conclusions already reached. Yet, the conflicting economic theories had a definite impact on the articulation of the legal principles, and it is necessary to have an understanding of these theories.

2.1. The classical theory on foreign investment

The classical economic theory on foreign investment takes the position that foreign investment is wholly beneficial to the host economy. There are several factors which are relied on to support this view. The fact that foreign capital is brought into the host state ensures that domestic capital available for use could be diverted to other uses of public benefit. The foreign investor usually brings with him technology which is not available in the host state, and this leads to the diffusion of technology within the host economy. There is new employment created, whereas, without foreign investment, such opportunity for employment would have been lost. The labour that is so employed will acquire new skills associated with the technology introduced by the foreign investor. Skills in the management of large projects will also be transferred to local personnel. Infrastructure facilities will be built either by the foreign investor or by the state and these facilities will be to the general benefit of the economy. The upgrading of facilities such as transport, health or education for the benefit of the foreign investor will also benefit society as a whole. Focus on these beneficial aspects of the foreign investment flows enables the making of the policy-oriented argument that foreign investment must be protected by international law. Such protection will facilitate the flow of foreign investment and lead to the economic development of less developed countries. It provides a strong, seemingly altruistic policy justification for the protection of foreign investment through the principles of international law. The theory does not explain why, despite all these benefits, there is still state interference with foreign investment.

Events in the recent past have given a great boost to the view that foreign investment brings uniform benefits to developing countries. The dominance of free market theories in the United States and Europe ensured that the classical view on foreign investment dominated thinking on the subject. The process of globalisation was regarded as inevitable due to advances in technology. This view promoted the idea that multinational corporations, which were the harbingers of globalisation, should have unlimited movement around the world and that their investments should be protected so that the process of global integration could be advanced. The new mood was enhanced by the dissolution of the communist states and the much flaunted triumph of capitalism.[45] The 1990s were the heydays of economic liberalism, embodying the classical view on foreign investment. It swept across the world. It was also spread by international economic institutions like the World Bank and the International Monetary Fund.[46] The conditionalities attached to loans granted by such institutions were an effective means of the dispersal of these views. Privatisation, liberalisation and macro-stability are the prescriptions given by these institutions to attract foreign investment which would, it is assumed, contribute to development.

Practical considerations also led to the dominance of the classical view. The financial crisis brought about by defalcations on sovereign borrowings had led to banks being unable to lend money for development projects. Aid as a development policy was frowned upon by the new leaders of the United States and Europe as it was inconsistent with the notions of economic liberalism. With the dissolution of the Soviet Union, new states came into being. They espoused free market ideologies and began to court foreign investment. The only capital that was available was that provided by multinational corporations. There was strong competition among the developing countries and the new states resulting

---

[45] Francis Fukuyama, *The End of History and the Last Man* (1992).
[46] Joseph Stiglitz, *Globalization and Its Discontents* (2002).

from the collapse of the Soviet Union for the available foreign investment capital. The espousal of the classical theory became necessary to demonstrate that the states courting the multinational corporations were receptive to their needs for protection of their capital flows. This accounts for the sudden burst of bilateral investment treaties in the 1990s and the favourable foreign investment laws giving guarantees and incentives to multinational corporations. In the area of international trade, the success of economic liberalism was reflected in the acceptance of the World Trade Organisation with new disciplines relating to intellectual property (TRIPS), services (GATS) and investment (TRIMS) attached to it. This set the stage for greater involvement by the WTO in investment. The Doha Ministerial Conference of the WTO committed itself to the consideration of an investment code attached to the WTO.

Added to this was the attitudes taken by the World Bank and the International Monetary Fund. They made loans conditional on the acceptance of ideas embedded in economic liberalism. The term 'Washington consensus' came to epitomise the notion that the two financial institutions acted in concert with the government of the United States in imposing conditions that were based on notions of economic liberalism. There were theories in international law which were being formulated favouring the instrumental use of international law to favour the interests of the United States and the neo-liberal thrust. In this context, the classical theory on foreign investment which had its base in notions of economic liberalism gained great currency.

Despite all this acceptance of the classical theory, there is no evidence yet that its tenets are based on accurate evidence. Though initial capital inflows may take place through foreign investment, there is evidence that outflows by way of repatriation of profits are greater.[47] Some studies indicate that capital outflows associated with foreign investment may be twice as much as the initial inflows.[48] The presumed advantage that new technology is brought in by the foreign investor may also be untrue as usually technology that has spent its cycle in its state of origin is introduced in the developing states where the product may be new. Consumer tastes are created for products of little social utility. A classic example is the

---

[47] J. R. Oneal and F. H. Oneal, 'Hegemony, Imperialism and the Profitability of Foreign Investment' (1988) 42 Int Org 347.

[48] Cunningham, 'Multinationals and Restructuring in Latin America' in C. Dixon, D. Drakakis-Smith and H. Wads (eds.), *Multinational Corporations and the Third World* (1986), 46.

introduction of breast-milk substitutes by multinational companies and the creation of demand through advertising. The claim that management skills are transferred may also be illusory as higher positions requiring confidence are seldom within the reach of local personnel. The claim that infrastructure facilities are built may also be contested as health and educational facilities that are created are only accessible to the elite within the host state who could afford such facilities. The alliance between the elite of the host state and the personnel of multinational corporations has unhealthy effects on the political life of the state.[49] The absence of regulatory controls over the sudden influx of foreign investment brings about social and economic confusion within the state. Besides, despite the introduction of these policies in countries like Argentina and Indonesia, there seems to have been a worsening of the economic situation. Many African countries have enacted laws that are favourable to foreign investment without seeing any increase in foreign investment in real terms. The foundations of the classical theory have been contested on these various grounds.

Despite the refutable assumptions on which the classical theory of foreign investment is based, it has had a strong hold on the policy underlying the international law on foreign investment. It is maintained by economic power. It is espoused by the international institutions that are controlled by capital-exporting states. Therefore, it finds expression in many international instruments. The preambles to bilateral investment treaties state the belief that the foreign investment flows between the parties will benefit the development of the host parties.[50] They commonly assert that such investment will 'stimulate the flow of capital and technology and economic development of the Contracting Parties'. Since virtually every developing country has made such treaties, this is evidence of the widespread belief in the tenets of the classical theory. The documents sponsored by the World Bank are clearly based on the classical theory. The Convention on the Settlement of Investment Disputes between States and National of Other States (the ICSID Convention) begins with the statement of the belief that provision for the settlement of disputes arising

---

[49] For a review of the literature on the subject and a refutation of the view that foreign investment leads to repressive government, see J. M. Rothger, 'Investment Dependence and Political Conflict' (1990) 27 *Journal of Peace Research* 255.

[50] The basis of such belief has been seriously dented by reports which indicate that there is no evidence at all for such a claim. UNCTAD, *World Investment Report, 2003*, 89. An aggregate statistical analysis does not reveal a significant independent impact by BITs in determining investment flows.

from foreign investments will increase flows of foreign investment. Such flows are stated to be beneficial to the economic development of developing countries. The preamble states that the contracting states agreed on the Convention after 'considering the need for international cooperation for economic development and the role of private international investment therein'. The Multilateral Investment Guarantee Agreement, which provides for the insurance of foreign investment against political risks, was promoted on the basis that it would have 'considerable potential to remove barriers to international investment and give new vigour to the development process'.[51] The World Bank's Guidelines on the Treatment of Foreign Direct Investment issued in 1992 encapsulate the philosophy of the classical theory when it recognises:

> that a greater flow of foreign direct investment brings substantial benefits to bear on the world economy and on the economies of developing countries in particular, in terms of improving the long term efficiency of the host country through greater competition, transfer of capital, technology and managerial skills and enhancement of market access and in terms of the expansion of international trade.

Recent literature emanating from the World Bank takes the view that there is no hard proof to the claim that these instruments do promote foreign investment.

The classical theory, without doubt, provides the policy basis for the formulation of many documents which relate to the international law on foreign investment. It has also influenced the thinking of arbitral tribunals. Thus, for example, an arbitration tribunal asserted in *Amco* v. *Indonesia* that 'to protect investments is to protect the general interests of development and developing countries'.[52] There is implicit in these formulations a belief that all foreign investments are to be protected because they are beneficial to the development goals of the host states. Since only developing states need such development, the further assumption is that the instruments are addressed to the developing states and the law is created for them, thus entrenching the division between developed and developing countries within the international law on foreign investment. The experience of litigation under NAFTA demonstrates that the law on the protection of foreign investment is as relevant to the dealings of investments between developed countries like the

---

[51] I. Shihata, *The MIGA and Foreign Investment* (1988).
[52] *Amco* v. *Indonesia* (1984) 23 ILM 351 at 369 (para. 23).

United States and Canada as they are to investments made in developing countries.

The classical theory also spawned the theory relating to 'economic development agreements'. This theory was that foreign investment contracts made in developing countries, unlike those made in developed countries, promoted economic development and hence should be treated as akin to treaties and protected through international law principles. Despite the obvious fact that the idea is offensive to the notion of equality of states and was quickly given up, vestiges of it can be seen in modern writings.[53]

The classical theory will continue to maintain its vigour in international law due to the support it receives from powerful sources. These include not only capital-exporting developed states and international financial organisations that are controlled by them but also multinational corporations which are themselves sources of power in international relations. They have the capacity to shape the norms of international law not only by lobbying their states but also by exerting private power through private means of law-making. Conservative international lawyers do not concede this, but the subsidiary sources of international law, the writings of publicists and the decisions of tribunals, including arbitration tribunals, are eminently manipulable towards the creation of an international law that applies to foreign investments. The law stated through these low-order sources is passed off as international law.

The uniform belief, that foreign investment leads to economic development, is difficult to accept. There is evidence that, where a multinational corporation integrates its operations through production in a developing country, beneficial results to the economy of the host state take place. But, this may not be the case where a multinational corporation moves in to exploit scarce resources or labour, or exports what are known as dirty industries.[54] Studies, particularly in terms of law, no longer look at the issue of foreign investment in purely economic terms. There are studies which look at the effects foreign investment has on ethnicity within the host state.[55] There are other studies which show concern with the human

---

[53] For an early statement, see J. N. Hyde, 'Economic Development Agreements' (1962) 105 *Hague Recueil* 271; *Revere Copper and Brass Inc.* v. *OPIC* (1978) 56 ILR 258 is entirely based on the theory. For a rejection of the theory, see I. Pogany, 'Economic Development Agreements' (1992) 7 ICSID Rev 1.

[54] Dirty industries are highly pollutive industries which cannot be established in the home state because of stringent environmental laws.

[55] See in particular the work of Amy Chua, *The World on Fire* (2003).

rights and environmental impact of foreign investment. It is futile to dole out economic theories alone as justifications for the formulation of policies on the international law on foreign investment. The opposition is likely to ask whether, even if the economic theories are sound, the political and other considerations should not be taken into account in devising a global policy on foreign investment.[56] The vigour of the classical theory in shaping law has been considerably dented. But, its influence will remain because of its continued espousal by strong states and institutions.

2.2. The dependency theory

The dependency theory is diametrically opposed to the classical theory and takes the view that foreign investment will not bring about meaningful economic development.[57] It was a theory popularised by Latin American economists and political philosophers, though work based on it has been done in other parts of the world.[58] The theory focuses on the fact that most investment is made by multinational corporations which have their headquarters in the developed states and operate through subsidiaries in developing states. The proposition is that the multinational devises global policy in the interests of its parent company and its shareholders in the home country.[59] As a result, multinational corporations come to serve the interests of the developed states in which they have their headquarters. The home states become the central economies of the world, and the states of the developing world become subservient or peripheral economies serving the interests of the home states. Development becomes impossible in the peripheral economies unless they can break out of the situation in which they are tied to the central economies through foreign investment. The resources which flow into the state as a result of foreign investment are seen as benefiting only the elite classes in the developing state, who readily form alliances with foreign capital. This results in human rights

---

[56] One of the reasons for the failure of OECD's effort at bringing about a Multilateral Agreement on Investment was its reliance entirely on economic justifications for the instrument.

[57] For a review of these theories, see R. Peet, *Global Capitalism: Theories of Social Development* (1991), 43–51; B. Hettne, *Development Theory and the Three Worlds* (1988); P. Evans, *Dependent Development: The Alliance of Multinational, State and Local Capital in Brazil* (1979); T. J. Bierstaker, *Multinationals, the State and the Control of the Nigerian Economy* (1987).

[58] For Africa, see Samir Amin, *Unequal Development: An Essay on the Social Formation of Peripheral Capitalism* (1976).

[59] A factor to take into account is that shareholdings are now so diffuse as the shares are traded on exchanges around the world.

violations as conditions favourable to the operations of the multinational corporations will have to be maintained by legislation or force. Indigenisation measures and efforts to exert control by permitting foreign investment through joint ventures are seen as failures. The foreign investor is able to defeat these attempts at control through his alliance with the elite classes.[60]

This theory comes to the exact opposite conclusion that the classical theory comes to in that it holds that foreign investment is uniformly bad. It holds that, rather than promote development, foreign investment keeps developing countries in a state of permanent dependence on the central economies of developed states. Unless a developing state can break out of the situation of dependence, economic development becomes impossible in the state. The panacea that is advanced is to get rid of foreign investment rather than attract it. The theory reflects the long-held animosity to foreign investment in the Latin American states. It is perhaps a natural outcome of the dominance of the United States in the economic life of Latin America.[61]

There has been a sudden *volte face* on this position in Latin America, with many Latin American states now supporting the trends towards liberalisation. This has moved to such an extent that not only have these states participated in the making of bilateral investment treaties but preparations are being made to negotiate a Free Trade Agreement of the Americas which will contain investment provisions. Yet, the theory did influence many nationalisations that had taken place on that continent. Its significance is that it provided a rationale for restructuring the economy excluding foreign investment. In the life of nations, there is a cyclical pattern in which theories lose and regain favour. The force of the theory of dependency within Latin America and outside that continent cannot be entirely written out. It cannot be clearly demonstrated that the adoption of liberalisation has led to progress in Latin America. The current Argentinian economic crisis occurred despite liberalisation. The possibility of the re-emergence of the theory of dependence should not be underestimated. As in the case of economic liberalism, there will be periods of ascendancy and decline for the dependency theory.

---

[60] See D. Bennet and K. Sharpe, *Transnational Corporations versus the State* (1985); for the view that communist states were able to institute controls over multinationals more effectively than capitalist states, see M. M. Pearson, *Joint Ventures in the People's Republic of China: The Control of Foreign Direct Investment under Socialism* (1991), 14–19.
[61] C. Kay, *Development and Underdevelopment in Latin America* (1988).

Dependency theorists see economic development not in terms of flow of resources to the host state but as involving the meaningful distribution of wealth to the people of the state. The appeal of the theory in times when globalisation has created increasing disparities in wealth should be taken seriously. On this view, there cannot be development unless the people as a whole are freed from poverty and exploitation. Development becomes a right of the people rather than of the state. The appeal of the theory to international lawyers attracted by the rights of people over the rights of states is enormous. If a shift does occur towards the recognition of the rights of people, the role of international law in investment protection will require radical rethinking.

The protests against globalisation and its impact on international law evidence a rift that is taking place. The writings of some international lawyers tend towards the view that international law should arise from the will of the people rather than the practice of states. The reaching out of peoples effectively began when opposition mounted to the Multilateral Agreement on Investments (MAI) sponsored by the OECD. This opposition concentrated on the fact that the MAI provided protection to multinational corporations without addressing the environmental and human rights harms that these corporations cause. These protests, effectively interlinked through the new technology of the Internet, then steamrolled into the movement against globalisation. The dependency theory has relevance in that movement in that it symbolises a way in which local interests could be protected against the interests of multinational corporations.

2.3. The middle path

The animosity which is directed at multinational corporations is the basis of theories such as the dependency theory. This animosity has become somewhat dented in recent times. In an age where communism has proved unsuccessful and the superiority of a free market economy to marshal the means of production is gaining acceptance, theories which are hostile to private initiative as the means of generating growth are unlikely to make headway. With increasing privatisation of state companies under way in developed countries as well as developing countries and the progress of the capital markets in most developing countries, there has been a shift away from ideological predispositions towards foreign investment. Many states have seen more wisdom in a pragmatic approach to the problem than in definite ideological stances. The fear that multinationals pose a threat to the sovereignty of developing states has receded with the increasing confidence of the developing states in managing their economies. Multinational corporations have also left behind the role of being instruments of foreign policy of their home states. On occasions they have even formed alliances with developing countries to the detriment of their home states.[62] But, some of the larger multinational corporations are capable of conducting foreign policy for their own benefit.

The reduction of hostility towards multinational corporations was furthered by the studies of the United Nations Commission on Transnational Corporations (UNCTC).[63] While supporting the view that foreign investment through multinational corporations could have harmful results in certain circumstances, these studies showed that, properly harnessed, multinational corporations could be engines that fuel the growth of the developing world.[64] The reports of the UNCTC generated other works on multinational corporations which contributed to the debate on the role of multinational corporations in the 1980s. The debate, no doubt, had an effect in the formulation of legal attitudes to foreign investment in developing countries and fashioned the legal techniques they were to use to control foreign investment. It also had an impact on the forms through which developing countries preferred to receive investments. The attitudes evolved over time. The laws that were shaped by the older attitudes have not entirely been dismantled by those which were shaped by the new attitudes. Each period has left its mark on the domestic laws of the states.

The studies of the UNCTC on the role of foreign investment helped to identify the beneficial as well as the harmful effects of foreign investment. The beneficial effects identified were very similar to those already identified by the supporters of the classical theory of foreign investment. There was definite support for the view that foreign investments made by multinational corporations benefit the local economy through the flow of capital and technology, the generation of new employment and the creation of new opportunities for export income.

While pointing out the benefits brought in by foreign investment, these studies also identified the deleterious effects of foreign investment. For the first time, serious efforts were made to identify the precise types of activity

---

[62] The obvious examples are alliances made by oil companies with oil producing states which may be adverse to their oil importing home states.

[63] This body, now much truncated, functions within UNCTAD and, in a sign of the times, takes a less vigorous position than it used to.

[64] The views expressed by the Commission received support from an influential group of American and European scholars. See, for example, Fred Bergsten, *American Multinationals and American Interests* (1978).

of multinational corporations which could harm the host economy. This enabled the host countries to take regulatory measures to counter harmful practices. They also resulted in efforts to fashion codes of conduct for multinational corporations, thus generating principles, which, though not international law, will have an influence in shaping the course of the development of the law for the future. The underlying theme of the draft codes of conduct was that multinational corporations should avoid certain identifiable conduct which was seen as harmful to the economic development of the poorer states.[65]

Some of the harmful effects these studies identified may be briefly stated. The studies pointed out that multinational corporations defeated the tax laws of states by engaging in transfer pricing. This practice involved fixing an artificially high price for an item permitted to be imported at concessionary rates bought from the parent company. Tax credits were later claimed on the basis of this artificial price.[66] There were practices associated with transfers of technology, widely touted as one of the benefits brought in by foreign investment, which deprived the host economy of the benefits of the transfer. Thus, there were many restrictive clauses introduced into the transfer agreement which prevented the transferee from obtaining the full benefits of the transfer. They were intended to maximise the benefit to the transferor, but their indirect effect was to hurt the host economy.[67] Thus, there were restrictions on the export of the goods manufactured with the technology, grant-back provisions which required that new inventions or adaptations made by the transferee to be given over to the transferor, tie-in clauses which required associated products to be purchased only from the transferor, and similar restrictions controlling the use of technology.[68]

Successive financial crises have also dented the force of the classical view and the liberalisation of entry standards to some extent. Both the Mexican and the Asian financial crises were attributed to the sudden withdrawal of foreign investment, particularly portfolio investment. In the context

[65] See Chapter 6 below for a description of the code of conduct on multinational corporations. The codes have remained drafts. The schism between the different groupings of states left several matters unsettled.

[66] See further Sol Picciotto, *International Business Taxation* (1992), 171–228.

[67] UNCTAD also worked on a code on restrictive business practices which did not progress beyond the draft stage. There is a difference in the strategy of UNCTAD and that of the contemporary discussions on how to grant competence to the WTO over competition.

[68] An effort within UNCTAD to introduce a code of conduct on the transfer of technology proved unsuccessful due to developed country opposition.

of these events, there has been some re-examination as to the forms of foreign investment that would be beneficial and those which would not be.[69]

The studies also indicated that the nature of the technology which was exported was often obsolete and hazardous. The extent of the harm to the environment caused by the export of such technology was identified in these studies, and there have been dramatic examples of the potential harm to both life and the environment that such obsolete technology could cause. The Bhopal disaster, caused by the gas leakage in a plant set up by a multinational corporation, involved colossal damage to life and property. Such instances indicate that multinational corporations often use technology which they are not permitted to use in their own home states in developing states because it is cheaper to do so and there are no regulations or effective supervision to prevent the use of such harmful technology.[70] The need for the control of such export of hazardous activity has been demonstrated often as a result of environmental and other harm caused by multinational corporations.

The benefits which multinational corporations bring are also thwarted by the global practices they adopt to maximise profits. Restrictive business practices they are able to adopt on a global scale prevent the host state from obtaining maximum scope of the export potential for the goods manufactured within its territory. The carving of the world markets into segments in which each subsidiary operates may be beneficial to the multinational corporations but not to the host states, as exports to some areas are thereby prevented. These are problems the host state cannot address by itself. Hence, efforts have been made to construct codes on restrictive business practices. They have not materialised to any significant extent, but efforts to create them also contribute to the growth of an international law on foreign investment. Recent movement has been to include competition as a WTO discipline. This, however, is resisted by many developing

---

[69] Enrique Carrasco and Randall Thomas, 'Encouraging Relational Investment and Controlling Portfolio Investment in Developing Countries in the Aftermath of the Mexican Financial Crisis' (1996) 34 *Columbia Journal of Transnational Law* 531. Both the Mexican crisis in 1994 and the Asian financial crisis in 1997 raised doubts as to unregulated financial flows, at least in short-term capital markets.

[70] The issue has been raised as to whether a home state has responsibility in international law for permitting multinational corporations to set up in other states with defective technology the use of which would not have been permitted in the home state. M. Sornarajah, 'State Responsibility for Harms Caused by Corporate Nationals Abroad' in C. Scott (ed.), *Torture as Tort* (2000), 491.

states, as they see in it an attempt to prize open their markets rather than an effort to help them reduce the restrictive practices of multinational corporations. The introduction of competition law principles into the WTO regime may also not solve this issue as the present indications are that these efforts are intended to introduce such laws at the domestic level.[71]

Once it is conceded that multinational corporations can produce both good and harm to economic development, it was easy to adopt the position that foreign investment should be harnessed to the objective of economic development and must be carefully regulated to achieve this end. The influence of this view, which strikes a middle course, has been significant. There is an indication that many developing countries, which are increasingly enacting regulatory frameworks within which multinational corporations are to function, have taken some leads from this theory.[72] Many developing states have now enacted legislation to set up screening bodies which permit entry to or give incentives to investments which are approved by these bodies. Some have legislation designed to ensure that technology transfers are effected without too many restrictions on their use by the transferee. On the international plane, the theory has been the basis on which codes regulating the conduct of multinational corporations are sought to be formulated. The theory, which accepts that multinational corporations can engineer development, if properly harnessed, challenges many propositions relating to international law which have been stated on the basis of the classical theory. Unlike the classical theory, which favours liberalisation and the freedom of movement for multinational corporations on the assumption that this promotes development, the newer theory requires the recognition of the right of regulation of the foreign investment process by the host state. The classical theory mandated absolute rules of investment protection and their uniform application to all investments. The basis of this position has been shaken by the increasing acceptance of the view that foreign investment should be entitled to protection only on a selective basis. Protection depends on the extent of the benefit it brings the host state and the extent to which it has conducted itself as a good corporate citizen in promoting the economic objectives of

---

[71] At the Cancun Ministerial Meeting of the WTO in September 2003, consideration of the package of issues known as the Singapore issues, which included competition, was deferred.

[72] This is particularly evident in the legislation of Australia, a resource-producing country conscious of environmental protection.

the host state.[73] There is an obligation to abide by the laws and regulations of the host state which are designed to capture the maximum benefits the foreign investment can bring to the host state's economic development. The *quid pro quo* for existing and profiting from operations in the host state for the multinational corporation is that it should ensure that the laws that seek to enmesh its operations with the economic objectives of the state are followed.

A mix of regulation and openness is what is seen as desirable. The heavy regulatory regimes, which existed in the past, have given way to new regulatory regimes based on pragmatism. The strategy of rapid industrialisation desired by developing countries requires capital which only multinational corporations are able to provide. This reality requires the adoption of new policies that show a willingness to accommodate the interests of multinational corporations.

The adoption of legislation based on the middle approach is a visible factor. There is a strong imitative effect in foreign investment legislation. Since there is also competition for the capital of multinational corporations, states want to ensure that their legislation is more open or at least does not lack the features in those of the other states in the region. While incentives to entry are often imitated, there is no desire evinced in such legislation to dismantle existing regulation unless some clearly demonstrable benefit exists. The institution of administrative controls is seen as necessary to enhance the economic objectives of the state in receiving the foreign investment. International law also has to respond to these changes. A uniform view that all investment has to be protected through international minimum standards is no longer a feasible notion, as the practice of states indicates that they do not subscribe to the idea that all foreign investment is entitled to such a minimum standard. The externally imposed minimum standard insulates the multinational corporations without the creation of any corresponding duties. That idea has to be abandoned in view of the competing notions that extend protection only to multinational corporations which act in accordance with the laws and policies of the host states in which they function. In the alternative, such a minimum standard exists only to the extent that the multinational corporation abides by the regulatory standards mandated by the host state. In that context, it would be invidious for a multinational corporation which causes environmental pollution or does similar

---

[73] The idea that an unscrupulous investor is not entitled to protection is coming to be stated in arbitral awards. See *Robert Azinian* v. *Mexico* ICSID Case No. ARB(AF)/97/9.

damage in the host state to seek the protection of the minimum standards of treatment in international law, when there is interference by the state to prevent such conduct. International law itself may impose a requirement of conformity with environmental standards upon actors such as multinational corporations. Compliance with internal laws is a precondition to access. It is also a precondition to the protection that is afforded by international law. These prescriptions may evolve but not without a schism in the law. Already, the evidence of such a schism may be seen in determining when a regulatory interference amounts to an expropriation for which compensation needs to be paid.[74]

3. Actors in the field of foreign investment

In the past, foreign investments were made by individuals or groups of loosely organised associates venturing abroad to make quick profits.[75] It is evident that much of the law on state responsibility for injuries to aliens developed in order to provide protection for such businessmen who operated in foreign countries. Though similar investments could take place in modern times, the larger percentage of investments take place as a result of decisions of multinational corporations to invest abroad. Unlike the old types of foreign investment which were usually of limited duration, the adventurers returning home with their profits once the venture had ended, the new types of investment made by multinational corporations are intended to last for a long period of time. The focus of the law has consequently shifted from the protection of single or groups of individuals to the protection of the process of investment made by multinational corporations.

A related phenomenon is that the areas of trade, which the multinational corporations seek to enter, are within the sole preserve of state agencies or entities in many developing countries. State control of the industry or economic sector is exercised through the medium of these agencies. The wave of privatisation has not swept away the control of the state in the more important industrial and natural resources sectors. The foreign corporation entering a state will often have to do so in association with a state entity. The new laws on foreign investment in many

---

[74] This issue is discussed in Chapter 9 below.

[75] In Scots law, from which the term 'joint venture' is taken, a joint venture originally meant a group of 'adventurers' going together into a business overseas. They went together because the associated risks were greater.

developing countries as well as the former socialist states make this mandatory. It is a technique which enables the state to have continuous control
over the investment. It ensures that its economic goals are restated by its
representatives at the boards of the joint venture corporations through
which the foreign investment is made. This has implications for the law
on foreign investment. Any study of the subject will therefore have to
take into account the role which multinational corporations and state
entities play in foreign investment.[76] There are other actors besides these
two important entities. International institutions enter the fray, usually
to support one or other of the sets of views that are in conflict in this
area. Thus, the World Bank, the International Monetary Fund and the
OECD support generally the views of the developed world that there
should be liberalisation in foreign investment, whereas UNCTAD had the
traditional role of supporting the viewpoint of the developing states. Various non-governmental organisations (NGOs) also play a role. These have
come onto the scene relatively recently as a result of the protests against
environmental depletion and human rights abuses attributed to multinational corporations. They are usually engaged in promoting single issues
but these issues have an impact on foreign investment. A fifth possible set
of actors are private chambers of commerce which may buttress the views
that favour multinational corporations.[77] There are then five principal
groups of actors who have an impact on the international law on foreign
investment. The roles they play need to be examined.

3.1. The multinational corporation

The multinational corporation is a relatively new phenomenon in international trade and investment. Some writers deny this by pointing to large
corporations like the British and Dutch East India Companies, which
operated in the past. Apart from their large size, there is little in common between these old corporations and the multinational corporation
of modern times. The organisational structure of the multinational corporation and the speed with which it can exercise control over its network
of worldwide subsidiaries set the modern multinational corporation apart
from the old colonial corporations.

---

[76] On the role of multinational corporations and the law, see Peter Muchlinski, *Multinational Corporations and the Law* (1995).

[77] The International Chamber of Commerce has had a leading role to play. It has attempted drafts of codes on foreign investment and other instruments relating to the subject.

The threat that the multinational corporation poses to the sovereign state was a preoccupation when multinational corporations first started to invest abroad. Backed by its own immense financial resources as well as the power of its home state which stands behind it, the fear was that the multinational corporation may influence the political course of the states in which it seeks to invest. It could scuttle the economies of weak states simply by relocating its operations elsewhere. The negative aspects of multinational corporations have been the focus of the dependency theory which was considered above. There are positive aspects to it which are emphasised by other theories. Despite this enormous power both for good as well as for harm, the multinational corporation has hardly been recognised as an entity capable of bearing rights and duties in positivist international law.[78] Obviously, this position may have to change, given the reality that it is as dominant an actor on the international economic scene as the state. Many multinational corporations command financial resources that are greater than many states can muster. Large hegemonic powers act to advance the interests of multinational corporations.[79] Within the international law on foreign investment, there is clear indication that multinational corporations possess both rights and duties. There is a clear tendency to hold them responsible for certain types of conduct, though at the moment this is done largely through domestic law. Yet, the recognition of the multinational corporation as a single entity and the recognition of its responsibility for violating international norms is slowly emerging. Though the draft Code on Transnational Corporations, which sought to achieve this, never progressed beyond its status as a draft, the principles it contained may well come to be recognised in the course of time.

Multinational corporations also wield significant power to shape the law on foreign investment to their advantage. Quite apart from wielding influence on their home states to ensure foreign investment protection, they are also able independently to influence the making of legal norms. Their role is an illustration of the fact that private power can be used to formulate norms with claims to be principles of international law. It is possible to argue that investment protection, which was devised through the system of arbitration of investment disputes, had much to do with

---

[78] D. Ijalye, *Extension of Corporate Personality in International Law* (1978); I. Seidl-Hohenveldern, *The Corporation in and under International Law* (1987).

[79] The allegations that the Iraqi war (2003) was fought by the United States at the instance of the large oil and construction companies, if true, supports this possibility.

the impetus given to the idea by multinational corporations and their advisors. These corporations devised the contractual forms on which the elaborate system was built through the argument that foreign investment contracts are akin to international treaties and are hence subject to principles of international law. In this way, the foreign investment contracts were put beyond the reach of the domestic laws of host states.[80] The theory was built on the basis of the low-order sources of international law such as general principles of law, the writings of highly qualified publicists and uncontested arbitral awards. These are manipulable sources. It would not be too far-fetched to argue that they were manipulated in order to secure the protection of foreign investments made by multinational corporations.

Multinational corporations bring about considerable lobbying pressure so that treaties that are favourable to foreign investment protection are brought about. The classical view on foreign investment would perceive multinational corporations as being incapable of anything but good. On the basis of the theory that the advancement of wealth creation, which is the principal reason for the existence of the multinational corporation, brings benefit to all, including those in the developing world, the multinational corporation is perceived as incapable of misconduct. At any rate, the policy justifications for the law protecting the foreign investment of the multinational corporations are made on that basis. That may be the motivating philosophy of the United States and other developed states.[81] As a result, there is a clear coincidence between the interests of the multinational corporation and many developed states.

The power of multinational corporations to ensure that their home states maintain stances favourable to the protection of their global investments is very clear. They are able to secure legislation which ensures that errant states are penalised through withdrawal of aid and other facilities.[82] They are also helped by their home states through international agencies which they control to ensure that states which are hostile to multinational

---

[80] For the development of the theory of internationalized contracts, see further M. Sornarajah, *The Settlement of Foreign Investment Disputes* (2000). See also Chapter 10 below.

[81] The course of the law in the United States in particular has been favourable to corporations, and the dominant thinking is that misconduct on the part of multinational corporations is rare. This is so despite spectacular instances of corporate fraud and misconduct in the United States in recent times. Successful prosecutions of such practices have been rare.

[82] In *Santa Elena v. Costa Rica* (2002), the award discloses the fact that the threat of withdrawal of aid to Costa Rica under the Hickenlooper Amendment played an important role in the dispute reaching arbitration.

corporations are denied privileges conferred by the agencies.[83] The International Monetary Fund and the World Bank are examples of the institutions. Voting in these institutions is weighted according to monetary contributions. The developed states, particularly the United States, have greater strength in making policy in these institutions because of their greater voting power. The International Monetary Fund has instituted measures which would ensure the adoption of a free market philosophy by those states to which it lends. The nature of the power of multinational corporations to exert influence globally in the shaping of the international law of foreign investments, quite apart from their economic and organisational strengths, makes them influential actors in this sphere.

In the field of international relations, the role of the multinational corporation in international politics has been more honestly articulated than in the law. The shift of economic power from states to markets and the role played in markets by multinational corporations has been studied by a succession of scholars.[84] The charge that the law purposefully hides the role of the multinational corporations, yet vests rights in them, but avoids the issue of their responsibility, is one that is difficult to avoid.

3.2. State corporations

State corporations, through which states have entered the sphere of international trade, are also a phenomenon of the twentieth century. They were the principal agencies through which communist states engaged in international trade. Outside communist states, welfare states also came to use state corporations in sectors like health, education, transport and communications where the provision of essential services to the public was regarded as more satisfactorily performed by the state. The state would be motivated not by profit alone but by the need to provide public service.[85] With privatisation of the public sector, state entities may go out of vogue in the developed countries, though there may be rethinking on privatisation in the light of experience. The functioning of state entities ensures that the sectors in which they operate remain monopolies.

---

[83] Joseph Stiglitz, *Globalization and Its Discontents* (2003), 71.

[84] The writings of Susan Strange initiated these studies. Susan Strange, *Retreat of the State: The Diffusion of Power in the World Economy* (1996); Claire Cutler (ed.), *Private Authority and International Affairs* (1999).

[85] The theory was that private companies would not provide services to areas where the provision of services was deemed uneconomical, whereas state corporations would.

State entities continue to play an important role in developing countries. In developing countries, the theory behind the operation of state entities is that profitable sectors of the economy should be operated by the state so that profits will not go into private hands but into the state treasury to benefit the people as a whole. Also, the provision of essential services remains a function of the state. A purported advantage is that the non-profit-making state entity will supply remote consumers whereas a private entity may find such consumers expendable. Laudable though such motives may be, the tendency towards corruption undermines the achievement of such an objective in many states.

State corporations hold monopolies in sectors which multinational corporations seek to enter. The natural resources sector, which has traditionally attracted multinational corporations in search of supplies of these resources for the developed states, is usually controlled by state entities. Since foreign investment codes in most developing countries now mandate foreign investment entry through joint ventures, it becomes inevitable that foreign investment entry into many sectors has to be made in association with these state entities. The benefit of such an entry is that the foreign corporation enters a monopolistic market. It is assured a share of the monopoly profits and a ready source of supply of products or resources.

In a joint venture, the motives of multinational corporations and the state entity will often be in conflict. The multinational corporation is driven by the need for immediate profit. The state entity, on the other hand, has long-term economic objectives of development and seeks to pursue these through the joint venture with the multinational corporation. The synergy that is essential for the success of the joint venture will be lacking in such an association and the potential for conflict is great. The disputes which could arise pose many problems for the law of foreign investment. Unlike the multinational corporations, the state agency has a claim to greater recognition in international law. There are rules of international law which give it a favoured status and make it immune to a degree from the process of domestic courts. The whole issue of the applicability of sovereign immunity to state entities has been thorny, but is now being resolved by the wide acceptance of the rule that such immunity cannot be claimed by a state entity which engages in commercial activity.[86]

---

[86] The subject is now covered by legislation in most states. Such legislation provides for jurisdiction over essentially commercial acts of the state entity. But, difficult problems of characterisation continue to trouble the courts.

But, many doubts still remain as to the scope of the rule and its future clarification by domestic courts, and national practice will contribute to the formation of rules that may clarify matters. But, for the moment, the case law on the subject has been so complex and replete with inconsistencies that it is difficult to argue that the change in the law has made the situation any better.

Multinational corporations have begun to take a long-term approach to the problem. As a result, they may be more willing to take a conciliatory approach to such conflicts. Their self-interest in maintaining oligopolistic positions in world markets may make it desirable from their point of view to seek accommodation of their interests than conflicts. There is also the problem that the state will be willing to assist its entities by enacting laws that will favour its entities in its dealings with multinational corporations if the need for such a course arises.[87] In these circumstances, the position of the multinational corporation becomes tenuous. In the face of an intransigent state, a multinational corporation has little by way of legal weaponry to use, at least while it wants to preserve its relations within the state.

3.3. International institutions

International institutions do not directly act in the sphere but still have a role to play in bringing about rules that affect foreign investment. They are created for specific purposes and foreign investment may fall within their ambit. Thus, the World Bank and the International Monetary Fund are financial institutions which oversee development objectives, flow of funds and other financial matters involving states.[88] The World Bank has played an active role in foreign investment on the basis of the belief that foreign investment flows promote economic development. It expressly subscribes to the classical theory that foreign investment brings such benefits to poorer states that it must be promoted. The promotion largely takes place through legal and other devices that the World Bank has created in order to remove risks to foreign investment in developing countries. These devices are based on the belief that the elimination of political

---

[87] Third World states are not alone in adopting such a course. In *Settebello Ltd v. Bancot Totta & Acores* [1985] 1 WLR 1050, Portugal enacted legislation to help a state entity resile from contracts it was not able to fulfil.

[88] For a more detailed statement of the functions of the World Bank, see Lawrence Tshuma, 'The Political Economy of the World Bank's Legal Framework for Development' (1999) 8 *Social and Legal Studies* 89.

risks to investments that exist in developing states will result in greater flows of foreign investment into these states and lead to their economic development.

The Multilateral Investment Guarantee Agency (MIGA) was created by the World Bank to provide for a scheme of insurance against political risk in developing states. The aim was that the provision of such insurance guarantees will facilitate investment flows. Likewise, the International Centre for the Settlement of Investment Disputes (ICSID) was created in the belief that the provision of neutral arbitration facilities for investment disputes between foreign investors and host states will boost investor confidence in the host states which participate in the ICSID Convention. Such increased confidence will result in flows of investment into these countries. Though these institutions have existed for some years, it is difficult to assess whether they have helped to increase the flow of investments into the developing world. African states which have participated wholeheartedly, virtually creating compulsory jurisdiction in arbitral tribunals including ICSID through investment treaties, have not increased flows of investment in any significant manner.[89] Studies within the World Bank seem to show that there is no correlation between participation in investment treaties and the flow of investments.[90]

The United Nations Commission on Trade and Development (UNCTAD) was created through the endeavours of developing states. Though its original mandate was to address issues of development from the standpoint of the developing countries, it is now a much reduced force due to lack of sufficient backing. Yet, its studies on investment and its various reports and conferences have had an effect in shaping state and other attitudes to issues relating to foreign investment.[91]

---

[89] For the extent of African participation in ICSID arbitration, see Amazu Asouzu, *International Commercial Arbitration and African States* (2001).

[90] Mary Hallward-Driemeier, 'Do Bilateral Investment Treaties Attract FDI? Only a Bit . . . and They Can Bite' (2003); for the text see http://econ.worldbank.org/view.php?type=5lid=29143.

[91] UNCTAD publishes the World Investment Report annually. Its 2003 Report deals with many aspects of the international law on foreign investment. It also has a series of studies on aspects of investment treaties and has published studies on bilateral investment treaties. The now defunct United Nations Commission on Transnational Corporations (UNCTC) was absorbed into UNCTAD, thus giving it competence over studies relating to multinational corporations. It publishes a journal, *Transnational Corporations*. It has completed a series of studies on different aspects of a multilateral agreement on investment. These studies constitute a comprehensive statement of the law in the area.

The WTO is another organisation with an increasing interest in the area of foreign investment. It already has an instrument, the Trade Related Investment Measures (TRIMS), which deals with the prohibition of performance measures adopted in connection with investments. The competence over such measures is acquired on the basis that their employment in investment distorts international trade. TRIMS prohibits the use of certain performance requirements which are considered trade distortive. The General Agreement on Trade in Services (GATS) is more directly involved with foreign investment. It applies also to multinational service providers who establish a commercial presence within the host state and provide services while being present in the host state. It is clear that such providers are indistinguishable from foreign investors. As far as the services sector is concerned, GATS establishes the competence of the WTO over a significant type of foreign investment which will be regulated by a WTO instrument. To the extent that intellectual property amounts to a type of foreign investment, TRIPS (Trade Related Intellectual Property Measures), which contains the WTO regime for intellectual property, also becomes relevant. Existing instruments already provide for wide WTO competence over aspects of foreign investment.

After the OECD efforts at formulating a Multilateral Agreement on Investment failed,[92] there has been a move to establish an instrument on foreign investment within the WTO. The Singapore Ministerial Meeting of the WTO required the issue to be studied and the Doha Ministerial Meeting has sought to hasten the process. The Doha Declaration requires the matter to be looked at in the context of the development dimension and the right to regulation of the economy. There has been resistance to such an instrument from developing states. If such an instrument were to result, WTO competence over foreign investment would be established. The process of acceptance of a discipline on investment, however, will involve a tussle in which non-governmental organisations are likely to play a leading role. At the Cancun Ministerial Meeting in September 2003, developing countries generally opposed an investment discipline within the WTO. A decision was deferred on the package of issues known as the Singapore issues, of which investment is one.

The task of the global institutions have been to promote economic liberalisation around the world. In doing so, they have subscribed to economic

---

[92] This identifies the role of the OECD as an institutional actor. Besides the failed attempt at the MAI, it has played a role in the field by conducting studies on the subject.

models which favour business. The policy interests of the dominant states dictate outcomes within these institutions. As a result, they clash with other interest groups which have non-economic concerns such as equity, justice, the promotion of human rights, the protection of the environment and the advancement of the economic development of the poor.

3.4. Non-governmental organisations

The impact of non-governmental organisations is a new phenomenon. The role that they could play on the international scene was dramatically revealed in their ability to coordinate an international campaign against the acceptance of the Multilateral Agreement on Investment.[93] Their mobilising capabilities were repeatedly revealed in protests against the WTO at Seattle and Cancun, successive World Bank meetings and whenever institutions regarded as being associated with neo-liberal notions met in the Western capitals.[94] Since their first rush onto the international scene was in connection with a foreign-investment-related issue – the scuttling of the MAI – they are likely to continue to play a leading role in determining such issues.[95]

The main plank in their protests against the making of investment codes is that they emphasise protection of multinational corporations without at the same time taking into account the environmental degradation and the human rights abuses that they are capable of. The view that is advanced by the environmental and human rights groups is that a multilateral code on investments should be a balanced one conferring protection on foreign investment but also attributing responsibility when there are violations of environmental and human rights standards associated with them.[96]

It is evident that the non-governmental organisations will have a significant role to play in the future development of the international law

---

[93] Robert O'Brien, *Contesting Global Governance: Multilateral Economic Institutions and Global Governance* (2001).

[94] This is significant as the protests against neo-liberal capitalism did not take place in the developing states but in the capitals of the developed states. One view is that the yawning gap between the rich and the poor had brought the Third World into the developed states in that the poor in the rich world were acting as surrogates for the poor in the developing states. Caroline Thomas, 'Developing Inequality: A Global Fault-Line' in Stephanie Lawson (ed.), *The New Agenda in International Relations* (2001), 71.

[95] For the role of non-governmental organisations in the failure of the MAI, see Sol Picciotto and Ruth Mayne (eds.), *Regulating International Business: Beyond Liberalisation* (1999).

[96] The responsibility of multinational corporations for environmental and human rights violations is dealt with in Chapter 4 below.

on foreign investment. Their role has already helped to shift the law from the protection of multinational corporations to a consideration of their responsibility for misconduct. The construction of such a law on purely economic models without consideration of the social and political dimensions is not possible. NGOs ensure that the social dimension is kept in the forefront of issues. They are also instrumental in developing litigation strategies to test out the possibility of imposing responsibility on parent companies for abuses by their subsidiaries for environmental and human rights abuses in other countries.

3.5. Other actors

There are other actors with an interest in the area. The International Chamber of Commerce has had a long association with the subject. Though a private organisation, consisting of participating chambers of commerce around the world, it was one of the early proponents of an international convention on foreign investment. The Abs-Shawcross Convention it adopted did not receive acceptance. Its arbitration services have been utilised in settling foreign investment disputes. There are other private bodies which study the area.

4. Risks in foreign investment

The risks to foreign investment increased after the ending of the period of colonialism. Whereas in the colonial period, an investor from an imperial state taking assets into the colonies had almost absolute protection, the picture changed dramatically after the independence of the former colonies. Where investment was taken into countries which were not under colonial domination, protection was secured through diplomatic means which often involved the collective exercise of pressure through the threat of force or economic means by the home states of the investors. The possibility for the use of gun-boat diplomacy had been reduced as a result of the outlawing of the use of force by the United Nations Charter and the increasing possibility of condemnation of states which resort to aggression to maintain their positions in world trade and investment.[97]

---

[97] The attack on Egypt following the nationalisation of the Suez Canal in 1957 was perhaps the last instance when the protection of property was given as a justification for an armed attack.

In the absence of protection through the exercise of military power, there has been an increase in the risks to foreign investment in the modern world. Consequently, there has been a search for legal methods of conferring protection upon foreign investments. The analysis of these legal methods of protection is the main focus of the book. But, an understanding of the nature of the risks to foreign investment is a necessary prelude to such an inquiry.

The principal risks to foreign investment come from certain uniform and identifiable forces. The presence of these factors will result from either regime changes or changes to the existing political and economic policies of the host state. Such changes pose a threat to foreign investment. The right of a state to change its economic policy is recognised in modern international law, though that right may now come to be circumscribed by the increasing number of treaties on international investment and trade to which states are becoming parties. Unless so circumscribed, the right to change economic or other policies is an aspect of the sovereignty of states. The Declaration on Principles of International Law Concerning Friendly Relations and Cooperation Among States recognised this right when it declared that 'each state has the right freely to choose and develop its political, social, economic and cultural systems'.[98] The system of government or the economic policies which a state prefers to follow are matters exclusively for the state.[99] The International Court of Justice asserted this right in the *Nicaragua Case* when it stated:[100]

> A prohibited intervention must accordingly be one bearing on matters which each State is permitted, by the principle of State sovereignty, to decide freely. One of these is the choice of a political, economic, social and cultural system, and the formulation of foreign policy. Intervention is wrongful when it uses methods of coercion in regard to such choices, which must remain free ones.

When a state decides to effect changes to its economic policies, there is a potential threat to foreign investment. It is necessary to understand

---

[98] UNGA Res. 2625 (XXV) 1970. Article 1 of the Charter of Economic Rights and Duties of States stated that every state has 'the sovereign and inalienable right to choose its economic system'.

[99] There is, however, an effort made to indicate that international law prefers a democratic system within a state and that rules must be devised in such a manner as to further this goal. Some have gone to the extent of articulating a right to intervene militarily in another state in order to promote democracy. Gregory Fox and Brad Roth (eds.), *Democratic Governance and International Law* (2000).

[100] [1986] ICJ Rpts 186, para. 205.

the underlying causes for a state wanting to make such changes before examining whether the right of the state to effect these changes can in any way be restricted.[101] The first is political hostility to foreign investment, which is generated by ideological inclinations against the influx of foreign investment. The second is a nationalistic concern over the domination of the economy by foreign elements which may result in xenophobic hysteria directed at foreign investors. The third relates to changes that take place globally within an industry. Such changes may be to the disadvantage of foreign investors as they would be required to renegotiate the bargain originally made in the light of the changes. The fourth would be where an incoming government seeks to rewrite contracts made by the previous regime. The fifth situation would be one in which the state finds the fulfilment of the contract onerous in the light of changed circumstances. The sixth would be a deterioration in the general law and order situation in the country which makes the foreign investment a target for attack by groups of dissidents or marauders. The seventh would be where a state feels it necessary to intervene in a foreign investment in order to exercise a regulatory power such as the protection of investment or some economic interest. An eighth would be where there is internal corruption or where a corrupt government has been replaced by a new government. These and other types of risk situations are obviously not mutually exclusive. They often occur at the same time in one state and the resultant threat to foreign investment as a result of this combination is great. But, for the purpose of examination, these risk factors are dealt with separately.

4.1. Ideological hostility

Communist ideology is opposed to private capital and private means of production. With the fall of the Soviet Union, the force of communism has been dented. The remaining communist states like China and Vietnam are experimenting with mixed systems that permit the influx of foreign investment even into sectors of the economy that are controlled by state entities provided the foreign investor makes a joint venture with these entities. Yet, socialism, as distinct from communism, is also averse to property rights and remains a potent force in the politics of most nations. Whenever socialistic notions take hold in a state, a threat to foreign investment and to private capital will arise.

---

[101] Risk analysis in foreign investment is an independent discipline. See e.g. Thomas Brewer (ed.), *Political Risks in International Business* (1985).

In states which are opening their doors to foreign investment, there are still political forces which remain antagonistic to foreign investment either because they are socialist or because they resent the possibility of foreign control of business sectors.[102] Where groups with ideological beliefs opposed to foreign investment come to power, there will be a definite threat to foreign investment. The incoming government will seek the reversal of previous attitudes to foreign investment. It may also want to dismantle the foreign investment which had been allowed into the state by the previous government. It may regard the terms on which entry was permitted as too favourable to the foreign investor and require them to be changed. Regime changes, particularly those ideologically inspired, pose problems for foreign investment.[103] The involvement of multinational corporations in the politics of the host states is largely aimed at forestalling the possibility of unfavourable regime changes.[104] Such involvement itself poses problems, for if a group which the foreign investors opposed comes into power, there will be additional grounds for the group to interfere with the foreign investment.

4.2. Nationalism

Nationalistic sentiments pose a threat to foreign investments. Particularly at times when the host economy is in decline, prosperous foreign investors who are seen to control the economy and repatriate profits will be easy targets of xenophobic nationalism.[105] They are ready targets for opportunistic politicians who may see advantage in such a situation to bring about a change of government. It is also easy to deliver the promise of taking over or divesting ownership of established foreign-owned

---

[102] In India, a combination of nationalism and socialism brings about a situation that is not favourable to foreign investment. It co-exists with other more dominant forces which favour foreign investment.

[103] A recent instance is the fall of Suharto in Indonesia. The incoming government sought to rescind existing contracts, alleging that they were improperly made. The situation resulted in many disputes, some going to arbitration e.g. *Himpurna* v. *Indonesia* (2000) 25 YCA 13.

[104] Codes of conduct usually forbid multinational corporations from interfering in the domestic politics of host states. But, such interference is necessary to ensure that the multinational corporation's interests are represented to the host state. The issue concerns the boundaries of proper and improper interference.

[105] This is by no means a developing country phenomenon. The first work that reviled multinational corporations with xenophobic vigour was written in the context of France. J. J. Servan-Schreiber, *The American Challenge* (1969).

business ventures. It is a popular measure, which would appease nationalistic forces.[106]

Religious fundamentalism is of a like character. The Iranian revolution of 1981 was both nationalist and fundamentalist. It resulted in the taking of US business interests. The Iranian situation illustrates the futility of political manoeuvring to protect foreign investment. In 1952, when the Mossadegh government sought to nationalise foreign-owned assets, it was overthrown by the joint efforts of Britain and the United States. The monarchy, which favoured foreign capital, was reinstated. But, several years later, Iranian nationalism took an even more virulent, anti-American stance. Such virulence may not have been present if not for the earlier interference in the efforts of a milder government. The driving out of US business after the installation of the Ayatollah Khomeini resulted in the Iran–US Claims Tribunal set up to determine the claims of US companies which had suffered damage as a result of the Iranian revolution.

SPP v. Egypt[107] is an arbitration which illustrates the manner in which nationalistic feeling may engineer a foreign investment disputes. The government of President Sadat had relaxed rules on the admission of foreign investment in Egypt. In response to the government's efforts to promote investment in the tourist trade, Southern Pacific Properties Ltd (SPP) entered into an agreement with the Egyptian Government Tourist Corporation to build a tourist complex near the pyramids. The company had commenced building when an outcry arose about the building of such a project so close to a historical monument of the Egyptian people. The matter was raised in Parliament frequently and became a popular issue through which the government could be confronted. After the assassination of President Sadat, the incoming government of President Mubarak found it prudent to prevent the continuation of the building of the complex. The foreign company had to pull out, even though it had begun construction of the project. The dispute resulted in protracted arbitration that took place before several tribunals and the arbitration gave rise to litigation concerning the enforcement of awards in several states.

Nationalistic feeling plays a dominant role in the restriction of the flow of foreign investment in developed states too. The perception of US dominance of Canadian industry has been a thorny issue in the past.

---

[106] As President Mugabe of Zimbabwe showed, existing politicians can retain power by whipping up xenophobic frenzy against those who are seen as foreign and as controlling the economy.

[107] (1992) 8 ICSID Rev 328.

Both in France and in Canada, the possibility that cultural values could be swamped if US entertainment companies were to be given a free rein in these states has been a long-held fear. It is one of the reasons advanced for the failure of the Multilateral Agreement on Investment. Likewise, in the United States, Japanese ownership of real estate and foreign encroachment of traditional industries such as the automobile industry have caused concern. Astute politicians find foreign investment a convenient subject to focus attention upon in order to secure votes.

4.3. Ethnicity as a factor

Alongside nationalistic factors, the role of the ethnic structure of the host state on foreign investment has become a focus of attention.[108] The hypothesis that is worked upon is that in the developing world, foreign investors make alliances with vigorous minorities that control business and thereby provoke a backlash in the majority community which holds political power due to its numerical superiority, particularly in developing countries which operate on democratic principles.[109] This situation of ethnic nationalism poses a threat to foreign investment. The institutions of the free market and democracy are not effectively mediated in developing states, as they are in the developed world. As a result, the potential for risk to foreign investment in these states is enhanced unless there are effective mechanisms that have been set in place which ensure that the demands of the majority ethnic group to a share in the economic benefits of foreign investment are met. It is also relevant to note that in the context of nationalism, foreign investors who prosper in periods of market liberalisation are in the same situation of economically dominant ethnic minorities. When forces of nationalism return to power, they become targets.

---

[108] This has largely been due to the studies of Amy Chua. See e.g. Amy Chua, 'The Paradox of Free Market Democracy: Rethinking Development Policy' (2000) 41 *Harvard International Law Journal* 287; Amy Chua, 'Markets, Democracy and Ethnicity: Toward a New Paradigm for Law and Development' (1998) 108 Yale LJ 1. The thesis is comprehensively stated in her book, Amy Chua, *World on Fire* (2003).

[109] The assumption is that there is a tension between the free market and democracy as the free market makes a few rich whereas democracy gives power to the majority. This tension is reconciled in developed societies through various means, including the creation of welfare facilities, the myth of equal access to avenues of success and tax measures visibly designed to accomplish the redistribution of wealth. Such instruments for mediating the paradox are non-existent in developing countries.

Market liberalisation promoting foreign investment may accentuate problems arising from ethnic nationalism as foreign investors make alliances with the economic elite of states, who usually belong to minority groups. Measures like privatisation, taking place in the context of corruption, visibly enhance the wealth of these minority groups and their allies. Such situations contain the seeds of instability.

Some states, like Malaysia and now South Africa, have sought to deal with the problem through constitutional means ensuring that the majority community has the opportunity of sharing the economic cake in proportion to its size. Such solutions have met with a measure of success. When treaties are made by such states on investment protection, the internal laws, which are no doubt discriminatory, are preserved from being subjected to treaty obligations.[110] In states which have not worked out such an accommodation, the instabilities inherent in the situation pose a threat to foreign investment as the dominance of the alliance between foreign investment and the local entrepreneurial minority groups will become a target of political animosity. Nationalisation of foreign investment often becomes an option in such circumstances.[111]

4.4. Changes in industry patterns

Where there are changes in the industry bringing about a global change in policy, particularly in the ownership patterns within the industry, the foreign investor's interests will suffer uniformly throughout the world. The best illustration of this proposition is afforded by the changes that took place in the oil industry. The oil crisis in the 1970s was provoked by the concerted effort on the part of the oil-producing nations to take over control of the oil industries in their states and to fix the price of oil. Previously, the major oil companies of Europe and the United States had controlled the production of oil in these states. The legal instrument through which entry was made into the oil-producing states was the concession agreement. As explained in the previous chapter, the principal feature of the agreement was that there was a transfer of virtual sovereignty over vast tracts of land which were oil rich for a substantial period of time, often over half a century, to the foreign company to explore for oil and recover

---

[110] It would be difficult to contemplate such states giving national treatment to foreign investors when the laws discriminate between nationals.

[111] Amy Chua, 'The Privatization–Nationalization Cycle: The Link Between Markets and Ethnicity in Developing Countries' (1995) 95 Columbia LR 223.

and market it when found. In return, the host county would get a royalty on the amount of the oil produced.[112] The early concession agreements were made in the colonies or in states which were protectorates of the home states of the companies which obtained the concessions. The power of the home states also guaranteed the stability of the concessions. Legal techniques were not the only determinant of the security of the concession regime.[113]

There were dramatic changes that took place in the industry. With the more representative governments replacing authoritarian regimes that relied on the imperial powers for their continuance, political demands for the cancellation of the concession agreements became strident. On the global level, there were concerted efforts made by the former colonies for the creation of doctrines, which justified the cancellation of the concession agreements.[114] The doctrine of permanent sovereignty over natural resources was proclaimed through a General Assembly resolution and became a means through which this transformation could be effected by law. Military pressure to make the host state abide by the obligations in the concession agreements were no longer feasible as the use of force for such purposes would have attracted the adverse scrutiny of the international community. The concerted efforts made by the oil-producing nations to change the rules of the oil industry and fix the price at which oil would be sold became successful with the formation of the Organization of Oil Producing States (OPEC). The old concession agreements could not withstand these changes. They had to be replaced by other types of agreements. The production-sharing agreement, pioneered by the Indonesian state oil company, Pertamina, became the industry-wide agreement that came to replace the concession agreement, reflecting the changes that had been effected. It passed the risk of oil exploration onto the foreign company and enabled the state oil company to regulate exploitation of the oil and its subsequent disposal.

Where windfall profits result to the foreign investor, the state is likely to intervene and ask for changes to the contract. This will be particularly so where the profits accrue as a result of external events and are not the result

---

[112] Henry Cattan, *The Law of Oil Concessions in the Middle East and North Africa* (1967); A. Z. El Chiati, 'The Protection of Investments in the Context of Petroleum Agreements' (1987) 204 *Hague Recueil* 1.

[113] The point is nicely illustrated by the role of the Anglo-Iranian Oil Company in the politics of Iran. The British and American governments secured the overthrow of the regime that nationalised the company in 1952.

[114] The doctrine of sovereignty over natural resources was the principal doctrine.

of the innovative or other skills of the foreign party.[115] It is interesting to note that Britain and Canada also rearranged existing contracts so that the state could obtain more benefits from the oil produced, when it was realised that the profits accruing to the oil companies were larger than expected.[116] Where windfall profits occur, particularly in the extractive industries, governments will see these profits as being made without any inherent merit on the part of the foreign party. They may be willing to take over such industries themselves so that they may secure all of the profits, particularly if they feel confident of running the business themselves. Alternatively, they may seek other forms of contract, which ensure that more of the profits stay at home. It must be determined in each case whether the rearrangements sought amount to expropriation which should be compensated. Another issue in these circumstances is whether the increase in taxes amounts to an expropriation. Such issues are discussed in Chapter 9 below.

4.5. Contracts made by previous regimes

Incoming governments may wish to change the contracts made with foreign investors by previous governments. This may take place where there are allegations of corruption in the making of contracts[117] or where the legitimacy of the previous government is doubted on objective grounds by the incoming government.

There are occasional instances of disputes arising where a new state has been created in the area in which the contract was to be performed and the new state refuses to accept any notion of succession to the obligations undertaken by the government previously in control of the territory. In these circumstances, as there is no rule of succession of obligations assumed towards individuals, there is no remedy that would be provided in international law.[118] Where a foreign investor makes an investment

---

[115] The dispute in *Aminoil* v. *Kuwait* (1982) 21 ILM 976 provides the classic illustration. The windfall profits were due to the hike in the price of oil brought about by the oil cartel and not due to any inherent superiority in the methods of the foreign investor.

[116] Peter Cameron, *Property Rights and Sovereign Rights: The Case of North Sea Oil* (1983).

[117] A series of arbitration disputes arose involving Indonesia when the government of President Suharto fell. The incoming government alleged that the contracts made during the regime had been secured through corrupt means. Likewise, the contracts made by the Marcos government in the Philippines and the Abbaccha government in Nigeria were regarded as suspect by the succeeding governments.

[118] *Societe de Grande Travaille de Marseille* v. *People's Republic of Bangladesh* (1980) 5 YCA 177.

with an unrepresentative government, the incoming democratic government may claim a right to rescind the contract that had been made by
the previous government by seeking to doubt the legitimacy of both the
previous government and the contract it made.[119] Its credibility to do so
may be greater if the terms are visibly seen to be disadvantageous to the
state. Many international lawyers have claimed that international law has
moved towards the recognition of democratic governance. If this is so,
then uniform application of the view requires that it be extended to contracts made by foreign investors with unrepresentative governments and
that the rule not be confined to provide a justification for military intervention in the affairs of non-democratic states.[120] The issue will arise in
situations such as post-Saddam Iraq as to the validity of the oil contracts
made by the administration set in place by the United States without any
United Nations authority. The contracts made by the administration in
the Iraqi oil industry will suffer from instability as their validity will come
to be questioned.[121]

Contracts made with military regimes will also pose a problem. Quite
apart from the opportunity for capricious takings in such military
regimes, they are unrepresentative and are led by the preferences of the
junta in power. An incoming democratic regime may declare that it is
not bound by the contracts made by the military regime. The extent to
which democracy and self-determination are normative factors affecting
the exercise of power of governments in the conclusion of contracts is yet
to be worked out.[122] One view could well be that the foreign investor
who made the investment agreement with a totalitarian government

---

[119] The validity of the contracts made in Namibia under regimes controlled by South Africa
has been questioned. See C. M. Pilgrim, 'Some Legal Aspects of Trade in Natural Resources
in Namibia' (1990) 61 BYIL 248. See in particular the discussion of the *URENCO Case* at
pp. 266–78. The case arose from Decree No. 1 of the United Nations Council on Namibia
which banned all trade in the natural resources of Namibia made in pursuance of contracts
made during the regime controlled by South Africa.

[120] The rule relating to democratic governance has been discussed largely in the context of the
legitimacy of intervention to promote democracy in the target state. As such, it becomes a
highly contentious doctrine. Those who favour the existence of such a rule do not address
the situation of foreign investment contracts made with totalitarian governments which
may indicate that the norm proposed is not to be uniformly applied but is a covert basis
for undermining governments that states do not approve of.

[121] The situation is similar to the uranium contracts made in Namibia when South Africa
was in control of that country.

[122] A modern instance is *Yaung Chi Oo Ltd* v. *Myanmar* (2003) 42 ILM.

consciously took the risk of its validity being contested by a later democratic government and hence need not be protected. Yet, to the extent that
an incoming democratic government may derive benefits from the investment, there could be a case for the protection of the investment through
international law, particularly in circumstances where such investment
has been shown to be beneficial to the state. In the extractive industries, the case for the invalidity of such contracts may be greater because
an unrepresentative government cannot act on behalf of a people in
whom sovereignty over natural resources resides in terms of international
law.[123]

4.6. Onerous contracts

Foreign investment contracts, which become too onerous to perform,
are also subject to the risk of government intervention. In these circumstances, states will reduce the loss that could be suffered by the state or
the state agency by interfering legislatively with the contract. The facts of
Settebello v. Banco Totta Acores[124] are illustrative. A state-owned shipyard
in Portugal had made a contract to build a large oil tanker. There were
penalty provisions in the contract for late performance. The shipyard
was unable to meet the time limit set in the contract and was in danger
of having to pay a large penalty. The Portuguese government intervened
through legislation and altered the penalty provisions in the contract. The
other party found that it could not have relief in such a situation both
within and outside Portugal.

4.7. Regulation of the economy

The modern state, despite its adherence to an open economy, contains
a substantial amount of regulatory mechanisms which control the economy. In the case of developing countries, the adherence to the middle path,
which has been described above, makes such regulatory control intense.
The scope for interference with foreign investment, which does not
adhere to the policy objectives behind the regulations, therefore increases.

---

[123] This assumes that the doctrine of sovereignty over natural resources forms a rule of
international law. Some have argued that it forms a *ius cogens* norm of international law,
in which case the argument advanced here has greater force.

[124] [1985] 1 WLR 1050.

Regulations are usually implemented through licensing systems and the sanction is the withdrawal of the licence. Without the licence, the rights of operation of the foreign investor in a sphere of activity become inoperative. The role of regulation and the extent to which it is permissible becomes an important issue in the law. Many recent cases have considered the question as to when a regulation is permissible and when such regulation becomes expropriatory so that it has to be accompanied by compensation. Regulation in the field of the environment is the most common cause of disputes.

4.8. Human rights and environmental concerns

The burgeoning law on human rights and environmental protection also creates instability in an area that has been designed particularly in the context of the single objective of the protection of the foreign investment. The creation of competing objectives of protecting human rights and the environment from the abuse of multinational corporations leads to the recognition of the regulatory right of the state to interfere in circumstances where the multinational corporate investor abuses human rights such as labour rights or causes environmental pollution. The increasing recognition of such a regulatory right will undermine the aim of investment protection and require the recognition that a state has the right to intervene in an investment that poses a danger to the environment or involves an abuse of human rights.

With some poetic justice, the disputes that have highlighted the issues of environmental protection have arisen in the context of investments made in the context of NAFTA provisions on investment. They have involved allegations of environmental abuse made by developed states against multinational corporations from the other developed state party to the treaty. In many of them, the issue of whether a regulatory interference to promote environmental interests could amount to a taking of property has been raised. This issue will be considered more fully in Chapter 8 below. For the moment, it is necessary to note that competing concerns of environmental protection and the protection of human rights could trump the interests of investment protection in certain circumstances.[125] This introduces a new element of instability into the international law on foreign investment.

---

[125] This is a situation as yet far off, if the *dictum* in *Santa Elena* v. *Costa Rica*, that even taking for valid environmental reasons has to be compensated, is accepted.

4.9. The law-and-order situation

Instability in the law and order situation in a state also poses a threat to foreign investment. Where the political situation foments animosity against foreigners and targets their property, difficulties would arise. These usually arise when the government is unable to contain marauding mobs and gangs of criminals or where the government itself foments uprisings against foreigners, as the government in Zimbabwe did in 2002 when it felt itself under political threat.[126] Such situations are usually provided for in terms of international law through rules that engage the responsibility of the state where it fails to give protection to the interests of the foreigner from anticipated attacks on his person or property.

5. The sources of the international law on foreign investment

The claims relating to norms of an international law of foreign investment can be accepted as principles of international law only if they are based on an accepted source of public international law. These sources of international law are stated in Article 38(2) of the Statute of the International Court of Justice. It will be useful to indicate the sources available to build up the principles of an international law on foreign investment.

5.1. Treaties

Multilateral treaties are a source of international law, as they evidence an acceptance of a principle of international law by parties to the treaty. There are no relevant treaties among a large number of states which furnish a comprehensive code of law on foreign investment. At the conclusion of the Second World War, there was an effort to create an International Trade Organization, and some of the rules of its charter would have had relevance for foreign investment.[127] But, the effort to create such an organisation was unsuccessful, though such an organisation was created in 1995 in the form of the World Trade Organization. The Abs-Shawcross Convention, essentially a private endeavour with the backing of the International Chamber of Commerce, sought to formulate such a code on foreign investment, It was

---

[126] The government of Mugabe, facing opposition, diverted attention into a scheme for seizing the property of white farmers and handing the property over to the indigenous people.

[127] James E. S. Fawcett, 'The Havana Charter' (1949) 5 YBWA 320.

not accepted by states and is therefore of little precedential value.[128] The code sought to state principles which were entirely favourable to capital-exporting countries, but they were unacceptable to developing states. It was sponsored by Germany in the OECD, but efforts to have it adopted were dropped. The OECD was to attempt a Multilateral Agreement on Investment in the 1990s, but again the attempt met with failure, largely because of dissension within the developed states as well as because of the opposition generated by non-governmental organisations to a code that took into account only the interests of multinational corporations. The only successful convention in the field is the ICSID Convention. But, this is a procedural convention only, setting up a machinery for the settlement of investment disputes through arbitration. The WTO has been assigned the task of preparing an investment discipline by the Singapore Ministerial Meeting. The Doha Ministerial Meeting reiterated the desire to formulate an instrument on foreign investment. But, the nature of the schisms between the states on this issue is already visible. The differences surfaced prior to the Cancun Ministerial Meeting in 2003. The best that can be expected in the area seems to be an instrument like GATS which does not contain binding commitments other than those individually negotiated *ad hoc* by the different states as to sectors of the industry. Generally, the efforts at the making of multinational agreements in the field have served only to indicate the nature of dissension among states as to what the rules on foreign investment at the global level are.

There have been several regional treaties on foreign investment. The strongest provisions are those contained in Chapter 11 of the North American Free Trade Agreement (NAFTA). The provisions of this chapter largely track the model bilateral investment treaty of the United States. It creates a framework for the free movement of investments within the NAFTA region (the United States, Canada and Mexico). The treaty provides for a strong investor–state dispute resolution mechanism, giving the investor a unilateral right to invoke arbitration against the host state. There has been much case law that has been generated under NAFTA, and considerable literature has been generated because much of this case law indicates that NAFTA will provide restraints on the exercise of regulatory powers by states. Since the treaty affects developed states including the United States and Canada, anxieties expressed earlier by developing states regarding restraints on sovereignty are now coming to be expressed by US and Canadian commentators.

---

[128] G. Schwarzenberger, *International Law and Foreign Investment* (1972); Lord Shawcross, 'The Problems of Foreign Investment in International Law' (1961) 102 *Hague Recueil* 334.

There are other regional treaties. The ASEAN Treaty on the Protection and Promotion of Foreign Investment contains strong provisions, but, since only approved investments are protected by the treaty, there is sufficient room provided for regulatory control over the entry of foreign investment. The later ASEAN framework Agreement on Investments, however, creates the concept of an 'ASEAN Investor' and permits freedom of movement within the ASEAN area to the entity or person who falls within the definition of the ASEAN Investor. Other regional treaties, such as the Mercosur Agreement, create similar regional arrangements with protection granted in varying degrees to the foreign investment of the participating regional states. There is an increasing practice to negotiate free trade agreements. Some of them are bilateral and some are regional. These agreements also contain provisions on investment protection. The most spectacular of them, if it comes about, is the Free Trade Agreement of the Americas which would cover the whole of North and South America.

Besides these regional treaties, there are bilateral investment treaties, which at the last count exceeded two thousand. Relying on this impressive number, some have argued that these treaties create customary international law.[129] Though the repetition of the rule in numerous treaties may create customary international law, regard must also be had to the variations in the structure of the treaties in which the rule is embedded. Bilateral investment treaties, though similar in structure, vary as to detail to such an extent that it would be difficult to argue that they are capable of giving rise to customary international law.[130]

5.2. Custom

A widespread custom is a source of international law as it expresses an *opinio juris* within the international community that the principle involved has to be accepted as obligatory. There are few customs in this sense in the field of foreign investment. There is, however, a custom that, when property is taken over by a state, otherwise than in the exercise of its regulatory powers, there must be payment of compensation, though there is still no agreement on the manner in which this compensation is to be calculated.

The developing states have used their numerical strength in the General Assembly to enact resolutions in the area of foreign investments. The

---

[129] The genesis of this view is in F. A. Mann, 'British Treaties for the Promotion and Protection of Foreign Investments' (1982) 52 BYIL 241.

[130] This point is developed further on Chapter 5 below.

extent to which such resolutions can create international law has been a matter of intense debate. The view has been expressed that the principles contained in the General Assembly resolutions constitute 'instant customary international law' in that they are evidence of an *opinio juris* of the international community formed at a solemnly constituted assembly.[131] However, the proposition was initially formulated in the context of, and was confined to, areas that were not occupied by existing legal norms. There is also the view that frequently asserted resolutions of the General Assembly have a law-creating effect.[132] But, developed states would argue that they had established norms in this area through the assertion of claims dependent on them in the past in a consistent manner. Given this fact, the General Assembly resolutions will at best have the effect of articulating a different set of norms that apply in this area. The resolutions on permanent sovereignty over natural resources,[133] on the Charter of Economic Rights and Duties of States[134] and on the New International Economic Order are the major resolutions which have been passed in this area. The resolution on permanent sovereignty over natural resources would be regarded as a mere assertion of sovereign control over natural resources within the territory of the state. It merely asserts a self-evident principle and hence would receive general acceptance in modern international law.[135] The need for the assertion of permanent sovereignty over natural resources was the existence of a theory that had been built up in international law that contracts made by multinational corporations with host states in respect of natural resources were binding and had the force of quasi-treaties. There was a need to displace such doctrines through the assertion of competing, rather self-evident principles.

Efforts have been made to dismiss the resolutions asserted in connection with the New International Economic Order as soft law or as *lex ferenda*.[136] They are supposed to have only a hortatory significance. But, this area is occupied by rules that are built up through arbitral opinions

---

[131] Bin Cheng, 'United Nations Resolutions on Outer Space: Instant International Customary Law' (1965) 5 IJIL 23.

[132] *Nicaragua Case* [1986] ICJ Rpts 14 at 99–100.

[133] GA Res. 1803 (XVII) of 1962.   [134] GA Res. 3281 (XXIX) of 1974.

[135] The assertion that it is a *ius cogens* principle is, however, contested.

[136] In the *Texaco Arbitration* (1977) 53 ILR 389, the arbitrator, Professor Dupuy, characterised the permanent sovereignty resolution as *lex ferenda*. I. Seidl-Hohenveldern, 'Hierarchy of Norms Applicable to International Investments' in W. P. Heere (ed.), *International Law and Its Sources: Liber Amicorum Maarten Bos* (1989), 147 placed General Assembly resolutions 'at the bottom of the scale of rules dealing with international investments'.

and the writings of publicists, in themselves the weakest sources of law. In that context, the relegation of instruments collectively made by states to a status inferior to that of the views of individual arbitrators and writers is merely an expression of a preference for certain views the impact of which on the law cannot be significant.[137]

There are two objections to the relegation of the principles contained in the resolutions to an inferior status. The first is that, to the extent that the resolutions seek to establish exclusive control over economic activity, including foreign investment, within the territory of a state, they assert a generally established proposition of international law. No state, developed or developing, doubts the proposition that it has total control over all economic activity which takes place within its boundaries. This is a self-evident principle of state sovereignty. The need for developing states to assert such a principle was that, though decolonisation ended political dominance, economic dominance by multinational corporations over the former colonial powers continued to persist. The recovery of economic control was achieved through a spate of nationalisations. It was necessary to assert the validity of these nationalisations. The permanent sovereignty resolutions coincided with these takings of the property of foreign investors and the restructuring of the economies of the newly independent states. There was a specific need for these resolutions in the context of what was taking place. Otherwise, the resolutions were stating a rather innocuous principle of state sovereignty with which there can be no quarrel, except that they also affected the laboriously built-up theory that foreign investment contracts had a status in international law akin to treaties. The continuing significance of the resolutions in modern law is that they refute the theory that foreign investment contracts undergo a process of internationalisation that makes them subject to principles of international law or transnational law. The need to attack the resolutions proceeds from the need to preserve this theory of the internationalisation of the foreign investment contract.[138]

Secondly, dismissal of the norms contained in the resolutions as soft law or as *lex ferenda* must presuppose the existence of rules that are based on sounder genesis in the sources of law or a field that is unoccupied by any rules. Neither seems to be the situation. There are competing rules,

---

[137] The writer acknowledges that the same criticism could be made of his views. There is no monopoly on prejudice. But, the objection is to writers who dress their opinions up as scientific truths without acknowledging the selectivity of their exercise.

[138] This theory is dealt with in Chapter 9 below.

such as the notion of an internationalised contract referred to above. These rules are formulated in arbitral awards, often uncontested, and in the writings of publicists, often not unanimous on the point. The test in this situation should be one of opposability of the different sets of norms. The old norms supported by the capital-exporting states seek to set up an international standard of treatment for foreign investment. These norms depend to a large extent on the opinions of individual arbitrators and publicists. They constitute subsidiary sources of international law. The law created by such low-order sources has little weight when juxtaposed to the view expressed by a large number of states in the General Assembly. At the least, the opinions of these states so expressed must have the effect of neutralizing the views stated by mere individuals even in positivist theory. Mere neutralisation of these norms will not be sufficient, as this will create a situation of normlessness. It is therefore necessary to accept the set of norms that is consistent with basic rules of international law. The notion of economic sovereignty, which the General Assembly resolutions seek to support, accords with the principle of state sovereignty. This is the organising principle of the modern international system, though its erosion through progressive rules in the sphere of human rights and the establishment of peace has to be acknowledged. To the extent that the General Assembly resolutions merely assert the principle of sovereignty over territorial incidents, they state the obvious. Except to the extent that the right to control foreign investment has been subjected to treaty control, the state continues to retain the right to control foreign investment. Such a view will not be contested in respect of foreign investment made in a developed state. There is no basis to argue that the situation is somehow different in respect of developing states.[139] The resolutions of the General Assembly merely claim these basic rights for newly independent states. The felt necessity to deal with the situation through treaties that is reflected in current state practice is an acknowledgment of the fact that there has been a failure to create norms favourable to investment protection through weak sources of international law.

The formation of customary principles has been associated with power. The role of power in this area is evident. Powerful states sought to construct rules of investment protection largely aimed at developing states by espousing them in their practice and passing them off as customary

---

[139] In the 1960s, a body of literature did in fact make this distinction, which flies in the face of the doctrine of equality of states, another basic, though fictitious, organising principle of the international system.

principles. They were always resisted. The Latin American states had, for example, resisted US claims to an international minimum standard of treatment of aliens and their property. Nevertheless, the norms that were supported by the developed states were maintained on the basis that they were accepted as custom though that was never the case. The significance of the General Assembly resolutions associated with the New International Economic Order is that they demonstrated that there were a large number, indeed a large majority, of the states of the world, which did not subscribe to the norms maintained by the developed world. After that, it was no longer credible to maintain that there was in fact an international law on foreign investment, though the claim continues to be made simply because of the need to conserve the gains made for investment protection by developed states.

5.3. General principles of law

General principles of law are recognised as a source of law, but the respect accorded to this source is not high as for those discussed above. Positivist legal scholars, who ascribe the rules of international law to the consent of states, treat custom and treaty solely as the significant sources of international law. The limited scope of the role of general principles of law as a source of international law is generally accepted by authorities.

Yet, many claims as to the existence of principles of international law on foreign investment have been based on general principles of law. Thus, much of the support for the payment of full compensation upon expropriation of foreign property is based on arguments relating to notions of unjust enrichment and acquired rights being general principles of law. Similarly, notions of equity are relied on to support similar rules. The principle that compensation must be paid is itself said to be a general principle of law.[140] General principles of law will therefore supply much fodder for arguments in this area of the law. These arguments will have to be evaluated carefully. The capacity of general principles to contribute to the law must be acknowledged. But, it must also be remembered that there is a high degree of subjectivity which attends the use of general principles

---

[140] Thus, in the *Chorzow Factory Case* [1928] PCIJ Series A No. 17, 29, the Permanent Court of International Justice said that 'it is a general conception of law that every violation of an engagement involves an obligation to make a reparation'. The statement dealt with the violation of a treaty obligation but is used indiscriminately to support the payment of compensation in any taking.

of law. It is often easy to demonstrate that arguments based on general principles are intended to support an *a priori* assumption of writers using them.

General principles of law have been used widely by arbitration tribunals in extracting principles applicable to investment contracts. Since there is a systematic pattern in their use by arbitral tribunals and precedents have been built on the basis of past awards recognising general principles, the existence of some general principles, consecrated by long acceptance within arbitral jurisprudence, cannot be denied. Consequently, general principles have acquired a role in the shaping of rules in the area of foreign investment protection. However, tribunals have used general principles in a manner which may not be acceptable to states. They have often selected rules that favour the promotion of investment protection and which are detrimental to the interests of the host state. This result can be explained only on the basis that the present arbitral system is inclined towards investment protection rather than towards the acknowledgment of norms that may favour developing states.[141]

Many examples of the selection of such norms may be given. The most important is the norm relating to the sanctity of contract. This norm denies the right of the state to change a foreign investment contract unilaterally. The notion of sanctity of contract is stated to be a general principle of law. Yet, the principle is taken from nineteenth-century systems of contract law which emphasised freedom of contract and the bargain struck as a result of the exercise of this freedom. The erosion of this doctrine forms the basis of the modern developments in the law of contract.[142] Yet, these developments that undermine the notion of sanctity of contract are ignored and it is stated as a rule of international law, to the exclusion of the exceptions that undermine it in domestic contract systems.

Another example concerns the question as to whether an agreement between a foreign investor and the host state or a host state entity is akin to the *contrat administratif* of French law. Under the French concept, the administrative contract could be changed unilaterally in the public interest. If the parallel between administrative contracts and foreign investment contracts can be drawn and it can be shown that the notion

---

[141] For an interesting sociological work which considers the neutrality of arbitration and the possibility that arbitrators, particularly in the arbitration of foreign investment disputes, may show obvious prejudices, see Yves Dezalay and Garth Bryant, *Dealing in Virtue: International Commercial Arbitration and the Construction of a Transnational Legal Order* (1996).

[142] Patrick Atiyah, *The Rise and Fall of the Freedom of Contract* (1979).

of administrative contract is not confined to French law but is a general principle of law acceptable to all major legal systems, then the argument becomes possible that international law should accept the general principle that unilateral changes to foreign investment agreements in the public interest are permissible in international law. Though there is overwhelming acceptance of the view that administrative contracts are not peculiar to French law, arbitral jurisprudence has refused to accept this principle, favourable to developing states, as a general principle of law.[143] The acceptability of the law based on the subjective selection of general principles will be increasingly subjected to scrutiny and rejection. The norms based on general principles of law are, in any event, weak norms. They cannot resist norms proceeding from sources which rely on consensual processes among states.

5.4. Judicial decisions

Judicial decisions are a subsidiary source of international law. Though stated to be a subsidiary source, the decisions of the International Court of Justice and its predecessor have had an immense influence in shaping the principles of international law. There are three significant decisions of these courts on the area of foreign investment. The first, the *Chorzow Factory Case*,[144] a decision of the Permanent Court of International Justice, remains the basis for any discussion of issues of compensation for the taking of foreign property. The second, the *Barcelona Traction Case*,[145] concerned corporate nationality and the diplomatic protection of shareholders of corporations. The third, the *ELSI Case*,[146] concerned issues as to what amounts to a taking and whether liquidation of a foreign corporation by a court could provide the basis of a claim that there was a denial of justice for which responsibility arose in the state. There are other decisions of the International Court of Justice which have peripheral relevance to the subject.

Arbitral awards made on disputes arising from foreign investment transactions also contribute to the subject, although many of the early awards were made unilaterally and their value is diminished for this reason. Yet, both the awards made by *ad hoc* tribunals as well as those made by

---

[143] See Arbitrator Dupuy in *Texaco* v. *Libya* (1977) 53 ILR 389; for a further consideration of the issues involved, see M. Sornarajah, *The Settlement of Foreign Investment Disputes* (2000).

[144] (1928) PCIJ Series A, No. 17.   [145] [1970] ICJ Rpts 1.   [146] [1989] ICJ Rpts 15.

institutional tribunals, particularly those made by tribunals constituted under the ICSID Convention, provide evidence of possible norms which could be used for the construction of norms of international law.[147]

The decisions of the Iran–US Claims Tribunal also contribute principles which have to be taken into account.[148] There is one view that the awards of the Tribunal will have limited value as the Tribunal was set up by two states, and lacked a control mechanism, and there was already provision for the enforcement of the awards in the Algiers Accord (the instrument providing for the creation of the Tribunal). The precedential value of the Tribunal's awards will have to be considered carefully as the Tribunal was created by treaty and had to apply the treaty's principles to the disputes. The exact terms used in the treaty have significance.

---

[147] See further M. Sornarajah, *The Settlement of Foreign Investment Disputes* (2000).

[148] The jurisprudence of the Tribunal is well served by extensive analysis contained in George Aldrich, *The Jurisprudence of the Iran–United States Claims Tribunal* (1996); and Charles Brower, *The Iran–United States Claims Tribunal* (1998).

3

Controls by the host state

The right of a state to control the entry of foreign investment is unlimited, as it is a right that flows from sovereignty. The entry of any foreign
investment can be excluded by a state. But, a sovereign entity can surrender its rights even over a purely internal matter by treaty.[1] Some regional
and bilateral treaties now provide for the right of entry and establishment
of investments to the nationals of contracting states.[2] Where such pre-
establishment rights are created by treaty, the denial of a right of entry to
any investor from one of the contracting states would amount to a violation of the treaty, unless it can be shown that his investment is not covered
by the treaty.[3] Where the treaty permits both the right of entry and national
treatment after entry to nationals of the contracting states, the right of
control over the investment on the basis that the investment was made by
an alien is totally lost to each of the contracting states. Where such a treaty
applies to the foreign investment, the treaty completely extinguishes the
right of control the state has over the foreign investment, except where
the treaty itself provides exceptions to the situation. It may still be the
case that, in circumstances of necessity, the treaty rights of the foreign
investor could be suspended. Yet, it has to be concluded that such treaties
diminish the right of control which the state has over the foreign investor.
The extent to which different standards of treatment have an impact on
the power of the host state to exercise control over foreign investment is
discussed at the end of this chapter. For the moment it is assumed that, as
in customary international law, unaffected by treaty, the host state has an

---

[1] Thus, in the case of entry by refugees, the Refugee Convention will control the rights of
the refugee, which may be more certain than the rights of an alien. G. S. Goodwin-Gill,
International Law and the Movement of Persons Between States (1978).

[2] The clearest example of this is to be found in the North American Free Trade Agreement
(NAFTA).

[3] There are wide sectoral and other limitations made to the right of entry. Thus, NAFTA permits sectoral limitations and the list of excluded sectors attached by each of the participants
is long.

absolute right of control over the entry and establishment and the whole of the process of foreign investment.

Once an alien enters a state, both he and his property are subject to the laws of the host state. This result flows from the fact that the foreign investor has voluntarily subjected himself to the regime of the host state by making entry into it. The unqualified right to exclude the alien prior to entry becomes somewhat modified after entry as the alien then comes to enjoy a status which is protected by international law.[4] Apart from the treaty protection that may be accorded to aliens, it is difficult to determine the source from which protection for such status is to be drawn. Where conditions are attached to entry, the nature of the status that is protected is varied by the conditions.

The unlimited right of the state to control entry by an alien was stated by the Privy Council in the following terms:[5]

> One of the rights possessed by the supreme power in every state is the right to refuse to permit the alien to enter that state, to annex what conditions it pleases to the permission to enter it and to expel or deport from the state, at pleasure, even a friendly alien, especially if it considers his presence in the state opposed to its peace, order and good government, or to its social or material interests.

This statement, transferred to the situation of the foreign investor, would mean that conditions could be attached to the entry of a foreign investor into a host state. Conditions could also be attached to the manner in which he operates his business. The proposition applies equally to a foreign corporation which makes the investment. The draft code of conduct on transnational corporations states a similar proposition in the following terms:[6]

> States have the right to regulate the entry and establishment of transnational corporations including determining the role that such corporations may play in economic and social development and prohibiting or limiting the extent of their presence in specific sectors.

---

[4] J. Brierly, *Law of Nations* (5th ed., 1963), 276. Brierly suggested that, after entry, the alien is entitled to 'a certain standard of decent treatment'. Others have referred to the same idea as an international minimum standard. The content of that standard is, however, a matter of dispute.

[5] *AG for Canada* v. *Cain* [1906] AC 542 at 546; See also *Schmidt* v. *Secretary for Home Affairs* [1969] 2 Ch 149 at 168, where Lord Denning said: 'At common law, no alien has any right to enter this country except by leave of the Crown; and the Crown can refuse leave without giving any reason.' The common law has been modified by statute.

[6] UNCTC, Proposed Text of the Draft Code on Transnational Corporations, E/1988/39/Add.1 (1988).

Judge Oda stated a similar proposition in his separate opinion in the *ELSI Case*[7] as regards the establishment of companies in foreign states. He observed:

> It is a great privilege to be able to engage in business in a country other than one's own. By being permitted to undertake commercial or manufacturing activities or transactions through businesses incorporated in another country, nationals of a foreign country will obtain further benefits. Yet these local companies, as legal entities of that country, are subject to local laws and regulations; so that foreigners may have to accept a number of restrictions in return for the advantages of doing business through such local companies.

The rule so stated is not a new one. It originates from a rule relating to the power of exclusion of aliens which sovereign states possessed by virtue of their sovereignty. The power of exclusion implies the power to admit conditionally and withdraw the licence to do business where the condition is not satisfied. The rule is universally recognised.[8] The competing trend is based on the idea that there should be no restriction on the flow of foreign investment. This notion can be traced to Vitoria, who spoke of the natural human urge to trade and the need to protect the right of a person to trade wherever he pleases. The United States has made efforts to maintain the notion of free investment flows through its treaty practice. It has a reputation for being a state which has openly admitted foreign investments.[9] Its adherence to such an idea is now to be doubted in view of the Exon–Florio Amendment to the Omnibus Trade and Competitiveness Act of 1988, which enables the President to prevent inflows of investment which threaten national security. There are also sectors of the US economy which are restricted to nationals.[10] The conflict between the liberal idea

---

[7] [1989] ICJ Rpts at 90.

[8] For the United States, see *Elkin* v. *US*, 142 US 65(1892); *Shaffer* v. *Heitner*, 433 US 188 (1977). Ralston observed: 'A nation may by general provisions exclude a certain class of individuals entirely or place limitations upon their admission subject to the duty to inform them of the special conditions of entry when they seek admission.' J. Ralston, *The Law and Procedure of International Tribunals* (1926), 270.

[9] This US policy dates from early times. The first US Treasury Secretary, Alexander Hamilton, articulated the policy in the following terms: 'Foreign capital, instead of being viewed as a rival, ought to be considered as a most valuable auxiliary, conducing to put in motion a greater quantity of productive labour and a greater portion of useful enterprise than could exist without it.' Quoted in C. D. Wallace (ed.), *Foreign Direct Investment in the 1990s* (1990), 1.

[10] The United States makes reservation of these sectors when it makes bilateral investment treaties which grant rights of entry to the nationals of the other contracting state.

of free flows of investment with the notion of sovereign rights of control of entry of investment is evident here. Powerful states, which see benefits in maintaining the stance of economic liberalism, have not been able to adhere to such liberal ideas in their own policies.[11] Economic liberalism has remained an ideal whereas the prerogative power of the sovereign state to exclude aliens or to impose conditions on their entry is an accepted principle of the law.

On the basis of the rule that conditions could be imposed upon alien entry, the whole process of the foreign investment could be controlled by the host state's laws. The law of the host state could specify the legal vehicle through which the foreign investment should be made, the nature of the capital resources that should be brought from outside the state, the planning and environmental controls that the manufacturing plant should be subject to, the circumstances of the termination of the foreign investment and other like matters. While regulating the entry of foreign investment, a state could also seek to attract foreign investment into its territory by holding out incentives attractive to such investors. Increasingly, such legislation takes the form of a code or a single piece of legislation which states all the pertinent rules relating to the making of a foreign investment in a state. Besides facilitating the promotional purposes behind such codes, the existence of a single code enables the foreign investor to acquaint himself with the laws on foreign investment of a state more easily.

A state is not strictly bound by any unilateral commitments it makes at the time of the entry as to the applicability of future changes it makes to its laws unless there are treaty obligations which require the state to honour commitments made to other states as to the treatment of investments made by their nationals. To the extent that they are unilateral promises, they cannot bind the state or create obligations in favour of any third party.[12] Whether contractual commitments made to the effect that future laws will not affect a specific investment will fetter a state's legislative power to extend the law to that investment is, however, a hotly debated issue. As much as an alien who poses a threat to national security after he enters the country may be deported and the threat he poses thereby removed, a foreign investment which proves to be against the national interest may be terminated in accordance with the domestic law. The extent to which

[11] Stephen Neff, *Economic Liberalism and the Law of Nations* (1991).
[12] It must, however, be remembered that in the context of treaties, a unilateral promise to arbitrate has been held to create an obligation to arbitrate.

this right of the state is subject to standards of international law remains a matter of conjecture.[13]

Laws controlling foreign investment are on the increase. Even states which maintain an open policy as regards foreign investment are now beginning to impose restraints on the inward flow of foreign investments. The reason for this lies in the rapid changes that are taking place in the picture of foreign investment flows around the world. The traditional exporters of capital are increasingly becoming recipients of capital. With greater cohesion anticipated in the European common market, there is an increase in the flow of foreign investment into the region in anticipation of these changes. The United States, the major exporter of capital, is now a recipient of massive inflow of foreign investment.[14] Increasing globalisation enables capital to move around the world more rapidly. The scope for such movements undermining the economy of states is great. A succession of economic crises has added to the fear that the rapid withdrawal of capital from states could destabilise their economies. As a result, there is a greater wariness as to foreign investment and an increasing readiness to control them. The picture that emerges is one of ambivalence. On the one hand, there is a desire to attract investment. On the other hand, there is a need to control it. A state seeks to balance these competing functions through its investment laws. Though these are matters which may affect developing countries more, it is likely that all countries will be concerned with such issues.[15]

The shifts in the pattern of investment flows have caused concern among these erstwhile exporters of capital who have realised the need for the control of such inflows so as to prevent their national and business interests being threatened. The example of the Exon–Florio Act in the United States has already been referred to.[16]

There have been moves to widen the scope of this legislation to include the screening of foreign investment entry into the United States. Within

---

[13] One may reason that there must be some objective criteria to assess situations of necessity. But, in the absence of any machinery that can judge this, a state is the arbiter of what situations justify breaking obligations on the ground of necessity. The possibility of the breach being litigated is remote.

[14] Graham and Krugman, *Foreign Direct Investment in the United States* (1991).

[15] Flows of investment into developed countries take different forms such as mergers and acquisitions which are controlled through different regulatory mechanisms such as securities regulations and antitrust laws.

[16] Waite and Goldberg, 'National Security Review of Foreign Investment in the United States' (1991) 6 Florida JIL 191; Baily, Harte and Sugden, 'US Policy Debate Towards Inward Investment' (1992) 26 JWTL 65.

the European Community, a similar result is sought to be achieved through the use of competition laws to ensure that large foreign multinational corporations do not enter and drive out the smaller European firms through the abuse of their dominant position. Merger controls may be used to achieve the similar result of keeping out large foreign firms from the European markets. Many European countries have stringent reporting requirements for foreign investment. It could well be that competition laws could come to be used for similar purposes in the future in developing countries as well. One problem that could be addressed through competition laws in developing countries occurs where entry is made by foreign multinational companies in association with existing large firms in the host state, thereby reducing or eliminating the possibility of any competition within the market. Often, this has significance not only for the market structure but also for the internal political power balance within the state.[17]

The use of foreign investment laws to scrutinise the entry of foreign investment into host states will be increasingly resorted to for various reasons in both developed and developing states. The satisfaction of nationalist lobbies concerned about the increasing control of the economy by foreign states, the perception of some types of investment as being deleterious to the interests of the state, the fear that national companies may not be able to withstand competition from an incoming foreign company which may have superior technology and other resources are reasons for developed states to seek to control the influx of foreign investment. Many developed states have direct legislation on the entry of foreign investment.[18]

In the developing states, there is a similar body of law controlling the influx of foreign investments, though the reasons for such legislation are somewhat different. Socialist states, like China, Vietnam and Cuba, also began to promote the entry of foreign investments in the hope of attracting much needed capital and technology, and have enacted foreign investment codes. The first part of this chapter contains a study of such laws and the objectives behind the legislation enacted by the developing states, including the socialist states.

---

[17] Thus, in Indonesia, studies show that foreign investment often aligns itself with the dominant Chinese business firms within the state. This creates ethno-nationalist problems and focuses hostility on the Chinese minority community.

[18] David Flint, *Foreign Investment in Australia* (1984). The mechanism described largely continues.

There are seemingly incompatible aims sought to be achieved by such legislation. On the one hand, the legislation evidences a desire to attract foreign investment by offering incentives and guarantees against potential risks such as expropriation. On the other hand, the legislation seeks to regulate both the entry and the operation of the foreign investment in the host state. As a result, the role, if any, which international law plays in the process of foreign investment seems restricted. But, it may come to be argued, with increasing vigour in the future, that even these regulatory measures will have to conform to minimum standards and that the violation of these standards will amount to an actionable wrong in international law.[19] In this way, international law will continue to retain its significance for the process of foreign investment.

The techniques and the degree of control adopted in such legislation may differ. But, they all aim to subject the process of foreign investment to the administrative control of the host state. In some legislation, the vehicle through which foreign investment could make an entry is identified. The host state seeks to increase its leverage over the foreign investment by limiting entry through devices over which control could be more easily exercised. Thus, the foreign investment laws may provide that entry may be made only through a joint venture with a local partner and specify the type of shareholding that the foreign party may have. In many instances, the joint venture could be made only with a state entity, thus ensuring that the government policy in a particular industry is given expression at every stage of the venture in which the foreigner participates. The second section of the chapter deals with the legal vehicles which have been devised to ensure that an element of control by the host state or by host state interests is maintained continuously in the working of the foreign investment. Here again, the strategy of the host country would be to ensure the localisation of the foreign investment process by ensuring that the form that is chosen to implement the foreign investment is amenable to local pressure. It seeks to defeat the possibility of the internationalisation of the foreign investment by increasing contacts with the state. The foreign investor would, in turn, seek to incorporate into this form as many international

---

[19] There is an increasing sign of this development in recent litigation. Thus, in *Amco v. Indonesia*, 1 ICSID Reports 589, after a long and protracted arbitration of the dispute, the eventual conclusion was that the manner of the withdrawal of the licence given to the foreign investor was without sufficient due process and that damages should be awarded on this basis. In the *Ethyl Corporation* case, a ministerial announcement as to an environmental measure was the act complained of.

elements as possible to secure his investment by removing it from the scope of the local control devices.

Despite these efforts at regulating any foreign investment which comes into its territory, a state is never fully able to localise the foreign investment. The nature of the process of foreign investment is such that it will always have international elements. There are three important areas of international law which confer protection on the alien and his property. The first relates to the rules of state responsibility for injuries to aliens.[20] There are strong claims that certain minimum safeguards are provided to an alien and that these minimum standards of treatment cannot be violated by the host state. Though, in the past, these minimum standards of treatment were abusively used to provide pretexts for intervention by powerful states and attracted a measure of resentment, in modern times these standards assumed a new form through association with developments in human rights. But, it still remains an issue whether the arguments based on human rights standards have relevance to this field. Many of the claims as to the law in this area related to the extent to which a state owes a duty to protect foreign businessmen and their property from mobs and riots during civil unrest. The extent of the customary law standards that protect the foreign investor and, to that extent, restrict the right of control of the host state are dealt with at the end of this chapter.

The increasing regulatory standards imposed on foreign investment will also result in novel arguments based on state responsibility. These will take the form of seeking a review of the exercise of such regulatory decisions in accordance with certain minimum standards acceptable to international law. It is conceivable that a body of international administrative law dealing with administrative wrongs could be constructed on the basis of new decisions involving such types of wrong. Such a law postulating common standards of procedural protection against the use of the discretionary power of administrative bodies may be discernible in the trade and investment areas. The second area through which international law operates is through rules relating to international trade. Some of the regulations controlling foreign investors, such as the use of local components, may be violative of principles of free trade. There is an effort to include rules on investment within the competence of the World Trade Organization. The instrument on Trade Related Investment Measures (TRIMS), for example, seeks to prohibit performance requirements

---

[20] C. F. Amerasinghe, *State Responsibility for Injuries to Aliens* (1964).

associated with foreign investment.[21] On the other hand, some measures, particularly those on the control of the use of environmentally harmful methods of production, may be justified by movements that have taken place in the sphere of international environmental law.

A third area in which international law restricts the sovereign rights of the host state to impose whatever measure it pleases, relates to the bilateral and regional investment treaties which have increased in number in recent times. It is well accepted in international law that sovereignty over a purely domestic matter could be restricted if there is an international treaty dealing with that matter. Bilateral and regional investment treaties, which are relatively recent efforts at investment protection,[22] seek to impose certain agreed standards of treatment on the foreign investors of the two state parties. The significance of these treaties to the international law on foreign investment is great. At least as between the parties to the treaties, they constitute the law on foreign investment. The treaties have a certain and definite content. The impact of these treaties is dealt with in Chapter 5 below.

The system of absolute regulation based on sentiments hostile to foreign investment has now passed. In its place, there has been instituted a system that is favourable to foreign investment. States are now more accommodating to foreign investment because they believe that such investment could be harnessed to aid in their development. A United Nations report described the trends relating to foreign investment legislation in developing countries in the following terms:[23]

> In the early 1970s, fortified by their strengthened bargaining position as the centres of economic growth and as recipients of investments by transnational corporations in the developing world, most of these countries introduced rigorous regulatory regimes for foreign investment and technology. The basic objective of such regimes was not to discourage or diminish the flow of foreign resources but to regulate them. These regulations provided,

---

[21] Performance requirements are conditions which require the foreign investor to use local components and labour, to export a percentage of the production or to locate in certain areas of the state. These conditions are prohibited in some bilateral investment treaties. On the basis that they distort trade, there is a move to prohibit them through WTO instruments, the TRIMS being an example of such an instrument. If the project to move the MAI into the area of the WTO succeeds, then, performance requirements will probably feature in the new efforts.

[22] They are generally dated from 1957, which was the year of the treaty between Germany and Pakistan.

[23] UNCTC Third Survey, pp. 56–7.

inter alia, for the screening and registration of foreign investment; the prohibition or restriction of foreign participation in specified sectors; the control of take-overs; the restriction of foreign capital to minority holdings in certain sectors; specific regulation of technology agreements; the prohibition of restrictive business practice; and performance requirements for subsidiaries of transnational corporations, such requirements relating to exports and integration with the domestic economy. However, since the mid-1970s, many of these countries have initiated policies and strategies that depart in certain significant respects from these early regimes. These new policies on the whole portray a more flexible and pragmatic approach aimed at facilitating and speeding up foreign investment inflows.

This may represent an over-optimistic assessment of the picture. Much of the regulatory structures that were put in place earlier still remains, despite the fact that the world has moved through a phase of economic liberalism that favoured the movement of foreign investment without restriction. There was a great move towards privatisation, resulting in the selling of state enterprises in the 1990s but there was disenchantment with such measures due to political and other factors. Nationalism, ethnicity and other factors required states to retain a control over the flows of investment into their states.[24] Economics alone does not dictate the outcomes in the law on foreign investment. As a result, at no stage did a law that favours an entirely open economy come about in any state. The weak market structures of developing countries require the state to intervene more consistently and use policy prescriptions to achieve economic objectives. In that context, it is unlikely that the laws will undergo any dramatic change.[25]

In modern times, there is a greater discretion vested in the administrative bodies screening investment entry to permit entry for investments considered desirable on more favourable terms. No state has taken its fervour for foreign investment to the extent of removing any controls on the flow of foreign investment into the host state. Yet, there was heavy competition for investments in the 1990s, which resulted in a competition to ensure that controls were relaxed and greater incentives were given to

---

[24] The role of ethnicity has been widely studied by Amy Chua, who has pointed out the retention of ethnic balances within plural societies has required states to exert control over foreign investment lest such investment upset balances within these societies by making alliances with economically strong minority groups.

[25] The *World Investment Report* (2003), 86–8 indicates three types of regulation in developing countries: attracting investment; channelling it to benefit development; and avoiding harmful effects of investment.

foreign investment. Even in this period, when conditions were favourable
to foreign investment, there was no effort to remove controls over the
influx of foreign investment entirely.

This case-by-case, regulatory approach to foreign investments will have
fresh implications for the protection of foreign investment that enters a
state under such an administrative regime. The foreign investment comes
to be made not only on the basis of a contract of investment as in the
past but also on the basis of licences granted by the regulatory body. The
process of entry ceases to be a private law measure alone and assumes
public law features. Those who have addressed the issue in terms of international law have been preoccupied with the contractual aspects of the
situation. The introduction of public law features into the process of foreign investment entry has consequences which are yet to be analysed.[26]
The response to this new development took several forms. Investment
treaties responded to it by including the licence within their definition of
foreign investment, for it came to be realised that the mere withdrawal of
the licence would nullify the objectives of the foreign investment leaving
the property and ownership of it intact. Hence, it was necessary to redefine
the taking of property to include the cancellation of a licence. Also, there
was a need to introduce into the international law of foreign investment
the same concepts that protected administrative licences in domestic law.
This is seen in the requirement that due process should be provided before
there is a withdrawal of a licence. This requirement began to appear in the
provisions on expropriation in investment treaties as well as in case law
on the subject.[27] It is important to understand the nature of the public
law controls that have been instituted. The change that has been brought
about as a result of the institution of these administrative measures will
affect the claims and arguments that have been made about the rules of
the law of foreign investment in the past. The foreign investor who enters
the host state is estopped from arguing that he entered only on the basis
of the contract of investment as he would consciously have followed the
legal requirements prescribed by the regulations and accepted the conditions that his investment had been subjected to. In these circumstances,
where there has been an administrative interference by the state on the
basis that the foreign investor had not complied with the conditions of

---

[26] Peter Cameron, *Property Rights and Sovereign Rights: The Case of North Sea Oil* (1983);
Terence Daintith, *The Legal Character of Petroleum Licences: A Comparative Study* (1981).

[27] See e.g. *Amco* v. *Indonesia*, where the tribunal held that violation of the due process
requirement prior to cancellation of the licence was the basis of the award of damages.

entry, it would be futile to look upon the situation as a mere breach of the agreement on the basis of which entry was made. Equally, the state cannot capriciously interfere with the investment by cancelling a licence that it had awarded without providing adequate reasons for such a course and giving an opportunity to the foreign investor to explain why those reasons do not apply. From the point of view of investment protection, the creation of machinery to review the adequacy of these reasons through external arbitral tribunals has been the most effective counter to these developments involving the use of discretionary administrative power over foreign investment.

1. Regulation of entry

Until recently, the control of foreign investment was effected, if at all, through immigration laws. There were no specific rules which controlled the influx of foreign investment. In times of war, there was control over enemy businesses and restrictions were imposed on trading with the enemy and on the movement of alien businessmen present within the state.[28] But, these measures were seldom continued into peacetime.[29] Since state sovereignty provides the justification for such measures, there is no reason why such measures could not be continued in peacetime.[30]

In recent times, there has been a rapid movement towards the institution of foreign investment laws on a global scale. In developed countries, nationalism and protectionism have been the motives for the restriction of foreign investments.[31] There is no uniform policy that is maintained. The Canadian experience is instructive. The Foreign Investment Review Act was enacted in response to a report which indicated the dominance of US multinational corporations in the Canadian economy.[32] But, the Canada–US Free Trade Agreement nullified the assumptions on which the legislation was based as it liberalises the flow of investments between the two countries. Canada enacted new legislation in

---

[28] Even in times of war, an alien owed a duty of allegiance to his host state. *De Jaeger* v. *AG of Natal* [1907] AC 326.

[29] Martin Domke, *Trading with the Enemy in World War II* (1943).

[30] The Trading with the Enemy Act was continued in peacetime by the United States against states perceived as hostile states.

[31] Periodically, politicians emerge who seek popularity on the basis of protectionism. See further, for the United States, P. Choate, *Agents of Influence* (1990).

[32] F. P. Waite and M. R. Goldberg, 'National Security Review of Foreign Investment in the United States' (1991) 3 Florida JIL 191.

view of the treaty, but some limited controls over US investments still remain.[33] The North American Free Trade Agreement entrenches that process. But, Canada was one of the early states to withdraw from the negotiations for a Multilateral Agreement on Investment sponsored by the OECD on the ground, among others, that open entry for investments would mean that its cultural industries would be swamped by foreign influences.

Nationalistic sentiments play a role in Australia's foreign investment laws as well.[34] In Europe, the domination of the economy by US multinational corporations is a fear that has engineered indirect legal responses.[35] The United States, despite its avowed allegiance to free market notions, does not permit certain types of investments to enter its territory. Its antitrust laws are used to prevent dominant foreign firms from entry into US markets. The United States has adopted legislation designed to keep out foreign investment inconsistent with its national security.[36] The legality of the measures that are adopted raise interesting questions. These measures are not dissimilar in effect to those adopted by the developing states. Their legality may be considered along with the legality of the measures taken by the developing states.

Many developing states, and more recently the erstwhile communist states of Eastern Europe, now moving towards market economies, have constructed more elaborate methods of foreign investment regulation. The prevailing philosophy in the 1980s was that investment brought in by multinational corporations could be beneficial to the host states, provided such investment could be properly harnessed to the economic development of the host state. But, in the 1990s, the world was caught up in the vortex of economic liberalism for a variety of reasons. The prevailing philosophy was one of liberalisation and privatisation.[37] The laws instituted in the 1980s came to be changed, though not entirely, in favour of the new philosophy of liberalisation. It is for this reason that there is an

---

[33] Raby, 'The Investment Provisions of the Canada–United States Free Trade Agreement: A Canadian Perspective' (1990) 84 AJIL 344.

[34] The fear of Japanese dominance is regarded as a reason for the controls that have been instituted. The Australian economy, however, has been traditionally controlled by foreign interests, British and American. See further D. Flint, *Foreign Investment Law in Australia* (1986).

[35] Reich, 'Roads to Follow: Regulating Direct Foreign Investment' (1989) 43 Int Org 543.

[36] The Exon–Florio Amendment to the Omnibus Trade and Competitiveness Act, 1988.

[37] See Diane Coyle, *Governing the World Economy* (2000) for a view favourable to economic liberalism.

apparent inconsistency within these new foreign investment laws. On the one hand, the laws that have been enacted provide guarantees relating to repatriation of profits and against nationalisation of the property of the foreign investor without payment of compensation. They contain many tax and other incentives in order to entice the foreign investor. On the other hand, these legislations also contain devices to screen the influx of foreign investment and to permit entry only to investment that is considered desirable. They also contain many other regulations which seek to maximise the benefits which foreign investment could bring to the economic development of the host state but which appear to be restrictive of the manner in which the foreign investor could operate within the host economy. The techniques that have been used need to be isolated and examined. First, the nature of the guarantees and incentives are examined, and this is followed by an examination of the types of regulation that control the process of foreign investment. The study is comparative. There is a great deal of similarity in the legislation on foreign investment among developing states, presumably because states imitate the more successful devices used in other states or because they use models suggested by international organisations. Examples are taken from the legislation of the principal states which use the different techniques of foreign investment control.

1.1. Guarantees against expropriation

Legislation on foreign investment usually contains guarantees against the expropriation of the foreign investment without payment of compensation. States with a history of expropriations are especially intent on giving such guarantees so as to remove any fear of expropriation that the investor may have on the basis of this history. Existing and erstwhile communist states are keen to give such guarantees in their legislation to dispel any idea that they still have ideological predispositions towards expropriation. Thus, Article 5 of the Foreign Enterprise Law of China provides the most explicit guarantee possible, and states that in the event of any expropriation full compensation will be paid.[38] This guarantee is intended to remove what the foreign investor fears to be the greatest threat to his investment. Such guarantees are usually given by high-risk countries in the hope that risk perceptions arising from past nationalisations will be counteracted by

---

[38] But the internal laws of China are inconsistent. In the Joint Venture Law (Article 2), it is merely stated that foreign investment will be protected 'according to law'.

the guarantees.[39] Low-risk states obviously have little need to issue such guarantees. These guarantees, along with bilateral investment agreements which are also entered into in large numbers by the same states, have a signalling function. They indicate to foreign investors that past policies relating to foreign investments have undergone dramatic changes.

The value of these unilateral guarantees is disputed in the literature.[40] There are two opposing views. On the one hand, as a matter of internal constitutional law, it would appear that a guarantee given by one government cannot be binding on a succeeding government, particularly if there has been a revolutionary change of governments.[41] It is the latter type of regime change that poses the greatest threat to foreign investment. Where the incoming regime has ideological stances different from those of the previous regime, it is arguable that there has been such a basic change within the state that the promises made by the previous government cannot be binding on the incoming revolutionary government.[42]

[39] The Eastern bloc states converting to an open economy and permitting foreign investment signalled their change in attitudes to nationalisation and the issue of compensation for nationalisation by guaranteeing against nationalisation and promising to pay compensation in the event of nationalisation. Under socialist theory, no compensation needs to be paid in the event of nationalisation. N. Katzarov, 'The Validity of the Act of Nationalisation in International Law' (1959) 22 MLR 639. The new legislation promises the 'actual value of the property' as compensation. See e.g. Article 22 of the Act amending the Enterprise with Foreign Participation Act 1990 of the old Soviet Union. There is stronger language on guarantees in the new Russian legislation on foreign investment. See the introductory note and text in (1992) 31 ILM 397. Article 7 guarantees against expropriation and promises 'swift, adequate and efficient' compensation, a paraphrasing of the Hull standard. A decision as to compensation is to be made by the Russian Supreme Court. States like Myanmar (Burma) and Cambodia also include such guarantees because they are new to the idea of attracting foreign investments and have to signal changes of policy.

[40] The leading text on the subject is A. A. Fatouros, *Government Guarantees to Foreign Investors* (1962). Vagts observed that these guarantees 'seldom have significant legal effect although it is conceivable that they could later disable the country from making various arguments to international tribunals in defense of measures taken against foreign investment'. D. Vagts, 'Protecting Foreign Investment: An International Law Perspective' in C. D. Wallace (ed.), *Foreign Direct Investment in the 1990s* (1990), 102 at 104. But, they have been given effect by arbitration tribunals. *SPP* v. *Egypt* 3 ICSID Rpts 101.

[41] I. Delupis, *Finance and Protection of Investments in Developing Countries* (1987), 27–32. For an Australian case involving later legislative changes to contracts contrary to guarantees given, see *Commonwealth Aluminium Corporation* v. *AG* [1976] Qd 231.

[42] Often explained as changes in the *grundnorm*. According to the theory of Hans Kelsen, all legal systems have a base in a fundamental legal principle which validates all other principles of the legal system. When a revolutionary change takes place, this fundamental or basis norm changes, justifying the making of changes to other legal principles in the system.

On this reasoning, the guarantees that are made in the foreign investment codes have no value or meaning at all except as devices to attract foreign investment.

On the other hand, there is the view that guarantees that are held out to foreign investors do have legal implications, despite regime changes. It is suggested that these guarantees have the effect of indicating a willingness on the part of the state to refer disputes that arise from the foreign investments attracted by the guarantee to an international rather than a national tribunal for settlement. This would be especially so if the guarantee against expropriation is coupled with the promise of dispute settlement by an overseas tribunal. On this view, a unilateral guarantee against expropriation, at the least, provides support for transferring any dispute arising from the expropriation of the foreign investment into an international sphere. It is suggested that it will also ensure that the fact that a guarantee was made would be taken into account in determining the legality of the taking contrary to the guarantee and also in the calculation of damages.

This issue was raised in *SPP* v. *Egypt*.[43] The claimant had entered into an agreement to build a tourist complex near the Egyptian pyramids in response to a heavy investment campaign embarked upon by government agencies after the announcement of the liberalisation of Egypt's foreign investment laws by the government of President Sadat. The building of the complex so close to historical monuments became a political issue. The new government formed after the assassination of President Sadat cancelled the project. The question was raised as to the liability of the government and its tourist agency, which was a party to the agreement. In finding liability, an arbitral tribunal focused upon the fact that guarantees had been given to the foreign investor in attracting him to the country and that the violation of these guarantees must engage the liability of the state. The tribunal referred to the Egyptian investment legislation which stated: 'Projects may not be nationalised or confiscated. The assets of such projects cannot be seized, blocked, confiscated or sequestrated except by judicial procedure.' The tribunal relied on this and other provisions in the legislation to state that, as the 'policy of the law is to accord greater security to the investment', there was justification for an international arbitral tribunal to exercise jurisdiction over the dispute. The conclusion in the award is contestable. The guarantee in this particular award merely referred to the requirement of judicial procedure and not to a review of the

---

[43] (1983) 22 ILM 752.

taking by an international tribunal. Yet, the fact remains that unilateral guarantees are capable of being used at least as subsidiary arguments for exercising arbitral jurisdiction and awarding damages to the foreign investor where such guarantees have been violated.

However, as a matter of strict law, unilateral guarantees against expropriation without full compensation have no international effect. Though unilateral acts of states do have some binding force, the instances in which such binding force has been ascribed to such unilateral acts have related to matters of international concern and have given rise to expectations as to the conduct of the state making the declaration in other states.[44] This cannot be said of unilateral guarantees against expropriation which are directed to the foreign investor alone. The guarantees are addressed to individuals or entities such as multinational corporations which do not have personality in international law; just as treaties cannot be made with those who lack international personality, no obligations can flow from guarantees given to those who lack international personality. The guarantees obviously operate in the context of national law and not in the context of international law.[45]

But, to the extent that capital-exporting states now actively participate in insurance schemes for their nationals investing abroad and in other activities associated with foreign investment, it may be credibly argued that these guarantees are addressed to the home states of foreign investors as well as to the investor, particularly if the schemes were designed to ensure that the premiums payable for investments in the host country making the investments were reduced by the home state as a result of

---

[44] The *French Nuclear Test Case* [1974] ICJ Rpts 253 is cited as authority for a large number of wide propositions in this area. In that case, a unilateral statement made on television by a French minister that France would desist from further tests was used as a peg on which the International Court of Justice could hang its withdrawal from an embarrassing situation.

[45] The issue as to whether estoppel operates to prevent the state from arguing its entitlement to change the law is a possibility. Though estoppel applies in inter-state relations (*Eastern Greenland Case* (1933) PCIJ Series A/B No. 5), there is little authority that it applies in relations between a state and a private entity with no international personality. The validity of the legal commitment given to the foreign party is the crucial issue. In *Oil Field of Texas* v. *Iran*, the question of estoppel was raised, but this specific issue was not argued. On estoppel, see further D. W. Bowett, 'Estoppel Before International Tribunals and Its Relation to Acquiescence' (1957) 33 BYIL 176. In a different context, see T. Nocker and G. French, 'Estoppel: What's the Government's Word Worth?' (1990) 24 Int Lawyer 409. In municipal systems, it is doubtful whether estoppel lies against the government when it acts in the public interest. For the common law, see *Brickworks Ltd* v. *Warrigah Shire Council* (1963) 108 CLR 568.

the guarantees.[46] If this argument is valid, a case can be made out for an obligation to the home state of the investor in situations where the guarantee had not been honoured.

To the extent that expectations were created in the foreign investor by the unilateral guarantee, the guarantee could have an effect on the assessment of compensation where he suffers damage as a result of action by the government contrary to the guarantee. It may also be an argument to support the payment of full compensation on the ground that the foreign investor was inveigled into the state through the guarantee.[47] As a general proposition and as a matter of domestic constitutional law, however, a guarantee addressed to entities such as multinational corporations which have no personality in international law can have no effect in international law other than as a pious declaration of intent.[48]

1.2. Guarantees relating to dispute settlement

Unilateral guarantees relating to the settlement of disputes that arise from a foreign investment by a neutral arbitration tribunal abroad can be seen in the foreign investment legislation of some states. These guarantees are given in the hope that there would be greater flows of foreign investment if impartial methods of seeking remedies in the event of government intervention are made available to the foreign investor.[49] Where a dispute subsequently arises between the state giving such a guarantee and a foreign investor, the dispute could be submitted to arbitration by a foreign arbitral tribunal in accordance with the provision. The theory on which arbitration tribunals have accepted jurisdiction is that the legislative guarantee contains an offer to arbitrate which the foreign investor converts into

[46] A difficulty in maintaining this argument is that the insurance of foreign investment is an internal act of the home state. It is not one which would normally have international significance.

[47] The American Law Institute, *Restatement on Foreign Relations Law* (vol. 2, 199), which states a general principle of just compensation, thus departing from the traditional US stance of prompt adequate and effective compensation, argues that full compensation must be paid where the investment was specifically encouraged or authorised by the state.

[48] The domestic parallel to such guarantees is perhaps the letter of comfort. Such letters are ordinarily intended to provide some support for a course of action without creating any binding obligations on those issuing them.

[49] Examples of this are to be found in the legislation of many African states. The similarity in the forms of such legislation is remarkable. They result either from models or advice provided by international organisations or because of the competition that exists within the region to attract foreign investment.

an agreement to arbitrate by instituting proceedings before the tribunal. He exercises an option under the law available to him, thereby granting jurisdiction on the usual contractual basis to the arbitration tribunal.[50]

There are, however, internal constitutional difficulties with such guarantees. In constitutional systems that feature a separation of powers, it is a contentious issue as to whether the judicial power of decision over a dispute that arises within the territory of the state could be transferred to a foreign tribunal by the legislature in absolute terms in respect of all future disputes.[51] This is a matter that has not been litigated within those states which provide such guarantees. The fact that the local court system is bypassed altogether in matters of vital national concern will also cause political concern. So far, these issues have remained of low visibility. If the legislation containing the guarantee is a nullity in national law, it would be difficult to argue that it should nevertheless have effect on the international plane.

1.3. Tax and non-tax incentives to foreign investors

Many states provide tax holidays and other incentives to foreign investors in order to attract them to invest in their territories. These incentives are usually available only to investors who fall into specified categories such as those who bring in high technology or who locate their regional headquarters in the host state. There is, of course, nothing in international law which prevents the granting of such tax holidays and incentives. Whether such an incentive should be given or not is a matter that lies within the discretion of the state authorities. There is considerable debate as to the usefulness of such incentives in attracting foreign investment.[52]

Tax incentives are a useful way of ensuring that the foreign investor acts in the manner desired by the host government. Thus, for example, tax incentives may be granted where new equipment is purchased to modernise the plant or on condition that some of the shares in the investment are transferred to nationals of the host state. In this way, a state may seek

---

[50] The reasoning was accepted in *SPP* v. *Egypt* 3 ICSID Rpts 101.

[51] The African states providing such guarantees generally operate under models that recognise the separation of powers. In the *Loewen Case* (2003), a judgment of the courts of Mississippi awarding exorbitant damages was alleged to be a taking within the provisions of NAFTA. The case starkly raises the question of whether the appeals system of the United States could be bypassed, and the matter of the propriety of a decision of a US court being brought before a NAFTA tribunal.

[52] For a recent discussion, see UNCTAD, *World Investment Report, 2003*, 123–7.

to achieve an objective indirectly whereas a direct requirement may give the impression of hostility to foreign investment.[53]

The granting of incentives to desirable investors but not to other investors raises the issue of discriminatory treatment. There can be no objection to discrimination based entirely on economic factors. There may be violations of national treatment and most-favoured-nation treatment involved as well. But, provided an adequate basis for the differential treatment, such as the need to attract certain types of technology or to direct the foreign investor into certain channels of production, can be shown, there can be no illegality involved in such discrimination.

Such discrimination between foreign investors maybe opposed on the ground that it distorts international trade. One purpose of tax incentives and other concessions, apart from attracting desirable investment, is to mask the fact that there are performance requirements imposed upon foreign investors. Such performance requirements may also be opposed on the basis that they cause distortions in international trade. There are economic reasons for opposing tax incentives. They may violate provisions of the TRIMS agreement of the WTO. Assuming the incentives are not associated with performance requirements, tax incentives *per se* are permissible in law.

1.4. Screening of foreign investment entry

The ideal of freedom of entry for the purposes of trade was advocated by the old institutional writers like Vitoria and Vattel.[54] The ideal of freedom of trade is now articulated through the institution of the World Trade Organization. The liberalisation of flows of foreign investment is also an articulated goal. Many bilateral and regional treaties made in recent times provide for the right of entry and establishment of foreign investment. These treaties extend national treatment to the pre-entry phase as well, but the right is not recognised as an absolute right as parties to these treaties continue to make wide sectoral limitations as to entry.

---

[53] Margaret Fordham, *Tax Incentive for Investment and Expansion in Singapore* (1992).

[54] Vitoria asserted loftily the fundamental human right which inheres in all men to trade with people of other lands and thus fulfil the human urge to community (*De Indis*, III.5). The cynic would maintain that this lofty pronouncement was meant to promote the right of powerful states to impose their trade on less powerful states. The stance of free flow of investment finds expression in an OECD Code of Liberalization of Capital Movements (1986). This is a non-binding code.

The starting point of the discussion, however, must be the customary international law position that a state, in pursuance of its sovereignty, has the right to refuse entry to any alien. It is well accepted that a state may institute measures to keep out foreign investment that is considered harmful to its interests. The function of screening entry is accomplished through administrative agencies. The administrative agencies may require that a feasibility study be made of the proposed foreign investment indicating the potential benefits of the investment to the local economy. Since many of these states permit entry only through joint ventures and the making of feasibility studies is a sound preliminary exercise even between purely private parties to such joint ventures,[55] the requirement may not seem onerous. But, as in the case of private transactions, disputes could later arise as to the accuracy of the information that was supplied in the course of these preliminary investigations. Unlike in the case of private transactions, the fact that statements made in the feasibility study could amount to misrepresentations may have more severe consequences, at least in the eyes of the public authority that issued the permit to enter. Overzealous representations as to the benefits of the foreign investment made in order to secure entry can easily be reduced into the legal language of misrepresentation and fraud.[56] In its internal law, such misrepresentations may provide justification for interference with the foreign investment agreement.[57] Whether it will also justify the termination of the foreign investment in terms of international law may be a moot question. But, if there was deliberate fraud on the part of the foreign investor, there will be no wrong done to him if there is a termination of privileges that were secured illegitimately. The determination as to misrepresentation should be preceded by a hearing at which the foreign investor has due process rights. Though the latter proposition is based on contestable authority, it is a rule of prudence that a fair hearing should be given to the foreign investor prior to any interference with the foreign investment by state authorities. The protracted dispute in

---

[55] Preliminary negotiations prior to a joint venture formation include exchanges of information relating to each partner's input, the complementarity of the resources that each could supply to the venture and other factors.

[56] See *Azinian* v. *Mexico* (1999) ARB (AF)/97/2.

[57] In *Amco* v. *Indonesia* (1988) 27 ILM 1281, a failure to comply with capitalisation commitments given by the foreign investor was used to justify the cancellation of the permit. But, the tribunal did not pronounce on this justification, being more concerned with the manner of the cancellation of the permit.

Amco v. Indonesia[58] illustrates the difficulties that attend commitments made in the course of preliminary contacts with administrative agencies that screen investments.

The primary task of the administrative agency is to ensure that the foreign investor brings tangible benefits to the host state. The agency will have regard to the impact of the foreign investment on the local economy. It has the task of ensuring that local entrepreneurs are not affected by the entry of a powerful foreign company into an industrial sector.[59] Again, the question of discrimination against a foreign national arises, if such measures are taken before or after entry. But such discrimination must be considered lawful unless there is a treaty commitment to provide national treatment in like circumstances. There are sound economic reasons for excluding foreigners from certain industries. In developing countries, such exclusion is rationalised on the basis that it would be better that basic industries be handled by local entrepreneurs as otherwise a state could be left stranded by a foreign multinational which relocates. Another reason is that the entry of a foreign business giant may stifle the emergence of an entrepreneurial class within the state. Care is therefore taken to ensure that, while high-technology industries which local entrepreneurs cannot handle without help from outside are open to entry to foreign multinationals, low-technology, labour-intensive areas are reserved for nationals. Developed states may also adopt a policy of keeping foreign investors out of certain industries. Industries associated with the production of military equipment are seldom open to foreign interests. This is justified on national security considerations.

---

[58] This flows from the fact there arises a possibility of a denial of justice in the absence of a fair hearing. The extent to which such a hearing should be given for the making of a purely administrative decision is unclear. In *Amco v. Indonesia* 1 ICSID Rpts 209, the tribunal appeared to be inclined to the view that such a hearing should be given even prior to the making of an administrative decision. This is a contestable proposition. Traditionally, a denial of justice should not be found except in the clearest of cases of judicial impropriety. See Judge Tanaka in the *Barcelona Traction Case* [1970] ICJ Rpts 1.

[59] Many investment codes include a list indicating the sectors in which investment by foreign investors cannot be made. Some sectors are reserved for state corporations. Some are reserved for local business people. Some legislation also identifies areas into which foreign investment may enter only in joint venture with local entrepreneurs. The Mexican legislation provides an example. In Mexico, the petroleum sector is reserved for Pemex, a state monopoly. Other sectors are reserved for local business. When Mexico ratified NAFTA, consistent with its domestic laws, it excluded these sectors from the scope of NAFTA which provides for both pre-entry and post-entry national treatment.

There is general acceptance that a state may impose conditions upon the entry of any alien, and such a principle includes conditions imposed upon foreign investors as well.[60] Whatever the position may have been in the past, in times of rapid movements of political and economic refugees, developed states will not be inclined to support a rule that permits unlimited and unconditional access by aliens to their territories.[61] Yet, bilateral and regional investment treaties and WTO instruments such as the GATS will promote the establishment of freedom of entry for foreign investment in the services sector at least in a limited fashion. GATS will permit a 'commercial presence' within the territories of those members who have permitted such a presence in those sectors which have been indicated by member states. As yet, the general rule that states have the right to exclude entry remains substantially unaffected.

There is a rule of non-discrimination on racial grounds. Its application is relevant, particularly after entry is made by the foreign investor. Except in the case where discrimination is clearly directed at an ethnic group,[62] there cannot be any international wrong committed by discriminating between investors or types of investment. Where a state fears economic domination by a particular foreign power and limits the entry of the nationals of that power who are of a distinct racial group, the question may arise as to whether this is racial discrimination.[63] The issue is one which will cause anxiety as the potential violation of a cardinal rule, the rule against racial discrimination, is involved, but the better view is that such discrimination does not amount to racial discrimination.[64] A discriminatory provision based on objective factors or a reasonable cause

---

[60] F. V. Garcia-Amador, L. Sohn and R. R. Baxter, *Recent Codification of the Law of State Responisbility for Injuries to Aliens* (1974), 369.

[61] Whether a distinction must be drawn between the entry of business and the entry of persons is questionable, but there is a definite trend at least in the positions adopted by the developed states to draw such a distinction.

[62] Even this may seem doubtful in the economic sphere. The free movement of persons and goods within regional groupings like the EC depends on nationality and the exclusion of nationals of other states. This discrimination between groups of persons has been held to be lawful.

[63] *Sramek* [1984] YBECHR 294; *Land Sale to Aliens Case* (1973) 77 ILR 433.

[64] This opinion is based on the analogy of the nationalisation measures after the ending of colonialism. Ordinarily, nationalisation measures which are directed against a definable national group are discriminatory. But, nationalisations directed at nationals of the colonial power were aimed at ending the economic stranglehold that the former colonial power had on the economy of the newly independent states and were widely held to be lawful. There may be similar connotations in the trade measures of the United States.

cannot be regarded as violative of the rules against racial discrimination.[65] The situation is akin to nationalisation decrees directed at a specific racial group. The general rule is that such a decree will be unlawful on the ground of racial discrimination. But, if the decree is intended to end the economic dominance of a particular foreign national or ethnic group, there is room for arguing that the rule against racial discrimination is not violated by the decree.

1.5. Requirements of local collaboration

It was a pattern in the states of Eastern Europe, prior to the fall of communism, and in many developing countries to permit foreign investment only in collaboration with a state entity of the host state. This enabled the socialist states which saw the advantages of foreign investment to marry socialist ideology with the admission of foreign investment on the ground that ultimate control over the investment remained with the state. The rationalisation was that state policy was consistently implemented through the presence of the state entity's nominees on the board of the joint venture. This policy persisted in many Eastern European states even after the fall of communism and the advent of free market economics. The model spread to the communist states of Asia, where it still remains the principal method through which foreign investment is made in these countries.[66] There is a widespread preference for collaborative joint ventures as the method for foreign investment entry in many developing market economy states. Ethnicity also has a role to play in the determination of the structures that are preferred. In Malaysia, the preference that is given to *bumiputras*[67] requires that companies are structured in accordance with a prescribed formula as to shareholdings. This mandates that entry is made by foreigners through minority shareholdings in existing

---

[65] Brownlie formulated this proposition in the following terms: 'The fact that the primary criterion involves a reference to race does not make the rule discriminatory in law, provided the reference to race has an objective basis and a reasonable cause.' I. Brownlie, 'The Rights of Peoples in Modern International Law' in J. Crawford (ed.), *The Rights of Peoples* (1988), 1 at 9. Nevertheless, the formulation in the text causes much anxiety to the present writer for the reason that a rule so formulated can be used to cloak racial discrimination.

[66] In China, for a long time, joint ventures were the principal method of foreign investment entry. But, now, wholly owned subsidiaries are permitted, subject to certain conditions. The situation is similar in Vietnam, Laos and Cambodia, the remaining Asian socialist states.

[67] Literally, the children of the land. The Malays are not indigenous to the land. There are the *orang asli* of Malaysia, whom the Malays themselves regard as the indigenous people.

companies or newly established ones. Ethnic policies, rather than economic ones, as well as other political considerations have a role to play in determining the collaborative structures through which entry is made in many states.[68] In developed states, a joint venture structure between local and foreign business is usually not mandatory. Joint ventures may, however, be used for various reasons such as the need to pool resources and technology or the need to diversify the risks of failure involved in the venture.[69]

Foreign investors may themselves prefer joint ventures in developing countries because it diversifies the risk, gives the foreign investor a lower visibility and provides them with a local partner who will often be an effective mediator with the local government. From the point of view of investment protection, the requirement that entry be made through joint ventures accentuates problems. Since the joint venture entity would always be locally incorporated, problems of corporate nationality and shareholder protection will arise. In the context of arbitration, this has posed problems as the question of whether the arbitration is domestic or international arises. Issues of standing before international arbitral tribunals could arise as the host state will consider the joint venture to be its corporate national.[70]

Exceptions to the requirement of entry through local participation are made by some states in circumstances where the multinational corporation is prepared to make a commitment to export the whole or a large percentage of its products, thus earning revenue for the host state and providing employment for its workforce, or where the investor is prepared to locate in areas designated as industrially backward and thus help in the development of those areas. In the former situation, difficulties may arise after entry where export commitments are not kept. In these circumstances, the host state may well terminate the foreign investment as it will be unwilling to permit sales on the local market which it may

---

[68] The literature on foreign investment has assumed economic considerations to be the dominant ones. But, this is not so. In many states, ethnic and political considerations play a more dominant role in determining the policy as to foreign investment.

[69] See further M. Sornarajah, *Law of International Joint Ventures* (1992).

[70] This categorisation is relevant under the ICSID Convention, where arbitration can take place only if the investor is a national of another state. For the case law on this, see Christoph Schreuer, *Commentary on the ICSID Convention* (2001); and M. Sornarajah, *The Settlement of Foreign Investment Disputes* (2000). The categorisation is also relevant for the enforcement of the award because only international awards may be enforced under the New York Convention on the Enforcement of Foreign Arbitral Awards.

have reserved for its own industries. Again, the question of discrimination between nationals and foreign investors could arise, and the answer must be that such discrimination is justified as it is based on economic grounds. It may be unlawful if there is a bilateral investment treaty affirming absolute national treatment even at the pre-entry stage between the host state and the home state of the foreign investor mandating national treatment of the foreign investor. In the absence of such a treaty, there is no international law basis for claiming violation of national treatment.[71]

1.6. Capitalisation requirements

States may require that a foreign investor seeking entry should bring in all the capital or a certain percentage of it from overseas. A state's interest in ensuring that capital is brought from outside by the foreign investor is to prevent him raising capital on the local markets. If he were permitted to do so, local savings that could be utilised for some project of benefit to the state would be absorbed in serving the interests of the foreign investor. The attraction of local investors to invest in shares in a project with a large foreign corporation will divert investment funds that could have gone to finance local entrepreneurs or local projects. There are economic reasons justifying such discriminatory treatment. The obvious one is that an assumed benefit of foreign investment – that it leads to capital flows from outside into the host state – will be nullified if the investor raises his capital on the local markets.

Where a foreign investor agrees to capitalisation requirements and later fails to comply, a right to terminate or otherwise interfere with the foreign investment arises in the host state. This right arises as a matter of the internal law of the host state. The exercise of this right cannot amount to an international wrong provided due process standards have been met. The protracted dispute in *Amco v. Indonesia*[72] involved this issue. In that case, one of the conditions on which the foreign investor was permitted

---

[71] The United States holds out the principle of national treatment for investment as the norm. Thus, President Reagan's Policy Statement on Foreign Investment (9 September 1983) stated: 'The basic tenet for the treatment of investment is the national treatment principle . . . Exceptions should be limited to those required to protect national security.' Whether national treatment is permitted in the United States after the Exon–Florio Amendment is itself doubted. J. E. Alvarez, 'Political Protectionism and United States International Investment Obligations in Conflict: The Hazards of Exon–Florio' (1989) 30 Va JIL 1.

[72] (1983) 23 ILM 354; (1988) 27 ILM 1281.

to participate in the project in Indonesia for building a tourist complex in a joint venture with an Indonesian partner was that he would bring an agreed sum of capital into the country from abroad to capitalise the venture. Under the law, he would have had to obtain certificates from the Bank of Indonesia to show that such capital had in fact been brought into the country. It was alleged that he had not brought in such capital. Though the foreign investor claimed that he had done so, there was no certification to this effect from the Bank of Indonesia. This was used as one of the grounds for the cancellation of the agreement by the administrative agency. The initial ICSID tribunal found for the foreign investor but the award was nullified on the ground that the tribunal had not given sufficient consideration to the issue relating to capitalisation. A fresh tribunal later found for the foreign investor on the ground that a proper procedure had not been followed in the cancellation of the foreign investor's privileges to operate in the country as the decision to cancel was not taken according to due process standards. The tribunal ruled that there had been a denial of justice for which responsibility arose. The ruling gives rise to the necessary conclusion that, if minimum standards of procedural safeguards had been given to the foreign investor before a decision had been taken, the cancellation of the privileges would have been justified. The Indonesian position in challenging the initial award has been explained by Reisman in the following terms:[73]

> Indonesia apparently felt that it had to challenge the award because if a country establishes a programme to induce foreign investment and grants licences on the basis of that programme, but discrepancies of as much as sixteen per cent of the foreign commitment to invest are internationally determined to be irrelevant such that the host government may not terminate the licence, the country will find itself in the position of being unable to enforce its own law.

This situation clearly has significance for considering whether a regulatory interference could amount to an expropriation. Where the foreign investor fails to conform to conditions that were imposed at the time of entry and the investment is terminated as a sanction for such failure, an argument that the interference amounts to expropriation can scarcely be maintained. Prudence would require that such interference be preceded by procedural safeguards.

---

[73] Michael Reisman, 'The Breakdown of Control Mechanism in ICSID Arbitration' (1989) 89 Duke LJ 739 at 774.

1.7. Requirements relating to environmental protection

The host state and its agencies will have regard to the environmental effects of the entry of the foreign investment. There is a belief that multinational corporations often export hazardous technology the use of which will not be permitted in their home states and that they cut costs in developing countries by not including environmental measures that they would have been forced to use in their home states.[74] The Bhopal disaster in India underlined these general fears.[75]

The feasibility studies which are required to be made prior to permission for the entry of the foreign investment usually require that an assessment be made of the environmental impact of the investment. Permission will be denied if the effects on the environment would be harsh. But, environmental standards in many developing countries are not high.

In developed countries, greater emphasis is placed on the effect of the foreign investor's activity on the environment. An investment project or agreement may be cancelled, even after it has commenced, if it can be shown that the harm to the environment is irreversible or outweighs the benefits of the project. Thus, in the dispute concerning sandmining on Fraser Island close to the Great Barrier Reef, the Australian government terminated a concession which had been given to two US corporations to mine sand on the island. The sand contained zircon and rutile. There was no market for these minerals in Australia. An environmental impact study showed that the adverse effects of such sandmining on the environment of the Great Barrier Reef were considerable. The Australian government refused to give customs clearances for the export of the minerals, thus in effect terminating the concessions. The US corporations had spent large sums in setting up the project. Though the United States, the home state of the multinational corporation which had the concession, intervened diplomatically to protest the cancellation of the concession, the Australian government stood its ground. It was willing to have the dispute submitted to the International Court of Justice. The High Court of Australia upheld the validity of the conduct of the Australian government.[76] There is general acceptance that a state has a right to cancel agreements or investment projects which cause significant environmental harm.[77] The right flows not only from the sovereignty of

---

[74] Handl and Lutz, *Transferring Hazardous Technologies and Substances* (1989).
[75] Indian Law Institute, *The Bhopal Litigation* (1989).
[76] *Dillingham-Moore* v. *Murphy Ores* (1979) 136 CLR 1.
[77] *International Bank of Washington* v. *OPIC* (1972) 11 ILM 1216.

the state which permits the state to protect its territory from environmental harm but also from the fact that, in modern international law, a state is a repository of the right to safeguard the environment in the interests of mankind.

But, *Metalclad* v. *Mexico*[78] and *Santa Elena* v. *Costa Rica*[79] may run counter to these views. In the former, a project to construct an underwater waste-disposal system in a Mexican province had been given clearance by the federal government. But, protests occurred at the site because of fears that the construction would interfere with the subterranean streams which supplied water to the people in the vicinity. The provincial authorities refused permission for the construction. The tribunal, constituted under NAFTA, held on the facts that there was a taking and that compensation had to be paid. It is unsettled yet as to how arbitration tribunals will deal with regulatory interference on environmental grounds. There seems to be developing a trend not to take environmental considerations into account.[80] This issue is given more extensive treatment in considering whether interference on environmental grounds by a state with foreign investment could be construed to be a taking of property.

The progressive evolution of the right to a clean environment as a human right and as a norm incorporating higher values may lead to an inflexible right for the state to interfere in order to protect the environment and to regard this interference as not amounting to a taking which is not compensable. But, the right must be exercised on objective grounds. The fact that an environmentally sensitive area such as the Great Barrier Reef[81] is involved makes the proof of objective circumstances much easier. Sophisticated arguments relating to the protection of intergenerational equities could be utilised to justify the state's conduct in these circumstances.[82] But, there is a definite clash here between the protection of the environment and the protection of foreign investment. Arbitration tribunals, which usually accentuate the interests of foreign investors over those of the environment, are prone to decide in favour of investment protection.[83]

---

[78] (2000) 5 ICSID Rpts 209.   [79] (2002) 5 ICSID Rpts 153.

[80] This statement is made on the basis of *Compañía del Desarrollo de Santa Elena SA* v. *Republic of Costa Rica* (ICSID Case No. ARB/96/1), (2002) 5 ICSID Rpts 153.

[81] The Great Barrier Reef is regarded as one of the natural wonders of the world, and is listed under the World Heritage Convention.

[82] Edith Brown-Weiss, *In Fairness to Future Generations* (1989).

[83] *Metalclad* v. *Mexico* (2000) 16 ICSID Rev 538; *Santa Elena* v. *Costa Rica* (2002) 5 ICSID Rpts 153; and *Tecmed* v. *Mexico* (ICSID, 2003) are cases which support this view.

4 cases
Ethyl Corporation.

Provided it is based on objective factors, the state's right to exclude investment that could cause harm to its environment is justifiable. But, it is sometimes difficult to determine whether the motive behind the interference is concern for the environment or whether the interference is a protective measure designed to keep foreigners out of the economy.[84] Where it is clear that the measure is induced by purely economic considerations, it would be difficult to argue that consideration should not be given to this fact. In the cases that have been decided so far, the environmental motive behind the regulation was stated as an afterthought. In the *Methanex Case*,[85] the United States has been constrained to make the argument that measures induced by considerations relating to the health of the society or the environment should not be regarded as a compensable taking.

The interference with a right to proceed with the investment after permission to enter had been granted is more problematic. If the evidence has come to light only after the investment has been made, the present movements in international law will support the view that nothing should stand in the way of the cancellation of the foreign investment project if the threatened harm outweighs the benefits of the investment. Quite apart from the protection of its national interests, the state's interference with the project will be justified in the burgeoning principles of international environmental law. The state will have the weight of rhetoric as well as principle behind it to support such an interference. Despite the pro-investment stances taken in cases like *Santa Elena* v. *Costa Rica*, environmental regulation is permissible and such regulation should not be treated as expropriation in circumstances in which the primary motive for the interference was the protection of the environment.

1.8. Requirements relating to export targets

The strategy of development adopted by developing states has moved away from manufacturing within the state to substitute imports to a strategy of earning income through the export of goods. The model for such development is provided by the newly industrialising states – Singapore, South Korea, Taiwan and Hong Kong – whose export incomes have led to the spectacular growth of their economies. The shift of emphasis from import substitution to export-led growth has made developing countries turn to

---

[84] *S. D. Myers* v. *Canada* (2000) 40 ILM 1408.
[85] The *Methanex Case* is pending before a NAFTA tribunal.

investment by multinational corporations in the hope that they would manufacture and export products from their countries and thus earn foreign exchange. With this aim, there have been efforts made to induce exports by multinational corporations by the conferment of privileges or through tax and other incentives. The requirement of entry in collaboration with a local partner is often dispensed with if the larger percentage of the production is for export. In some states, the export targets are a compulsory condition of entry.

The United States has consistently opposed such export quotas. Its programme of bilateral investment treaties also seeks to eliminate such requirements. It has sought the elimination of such restrictions on foreign investment in the Uruguay Round of the GATT negotiations. The argument was that the imposition of export requirements was distortive of international trade. The Trade Related Investment Measures (TRIMS) that came into existence along with the establishment of the World Trade Organization deals with performance requirements but does not affect export requirements that are imposed.

It is unlikely that countries intent on a foreign-investment-assisted export policy will agree to dispense with export requirements. The imposition of these requirements will accentuate conflicts between the host state and the foreign investor. Foreign investors will find it difficult to meet the requirements that have been imposed in the present conditions. With recession in the world markets and the possibility of protectionist policies against cheap imports from developing countries being implemented by developed countries, there will be difficulties in satisfying the export requirements of the host state.

In addition, multinational corporations themselves adopt a policy of preventing competition among their subsidiaries by carving out geographical markets and preventing export by their subsidiaries into the territories of each other. As a result, export quota requirements will be more difficult to meet. The failure to do so will bring about more conflicts between the foreign corporations and host states. Such conflicts will be difficult to resolve. The state will seek to justify interference with or the termination of the foreign investment on the basis of the non-fulfilment of the terms on which entry was granted to the foreign investor or seek to impose some other form of sanction. The foreign investor, on the other hand, will seek the remedies provided for him under the contract and have recourse to arbitration. As most arbitration tribunals now seek to emphasise the contract on the basis of which entry was made rather than the public law conditions imposed on the entry, the state party may feel aggrieved and refuse to abide by the award, thus exacerbating the dispute. Public law controls over investment are a new phenomenon. Arbitration tribunals are prone to a contractual analysis of the process of foreign investment. They have yet to come to grips with the problem of accommodating these controls with a system which prefers to assimilate the foreign investment agreements to private contracts.

1.9. Requirements relating to local equity

One uniform pattern emerging from legislation on foreign investments in developing countries relates to the requirement that there should be local equity participation in foreign investments. There was rapid divestment of shares in existing foreign investment companies so that local shareholding targets could be achieved when indigenisation measures in states like Nigeria were announced.[86] In Malaysia, too, for reasons of ethnicity, there were structures that were imposed on company shareholdings. The role of ethnicity in shaping policies of foreign investment is largely reflected in the types of company structure that are mandated. Foreign investment has to conform to these structures when it enters a country, ensuring that its corporate vehicle is designed in accordance with the policies mandated by the state in hitherto foreign-owned corporations. Often, the legislation would specify the percentage of the shares that had to be divested and detail the stages and the timeframe within which such divestment was to be effected. Malaysia provides a good example of such laws. It announced its 'New Economic Policy' in 1970, which was to be implemented within twenty years. Within this period, Malaysia wanted to restructure its economy to ensure that foreign nationals participated in the economy only as minority shareholders.

There was to be an equitable participation by all ethnic groups in the economy according to a ratio. It is relevant to note that the equity restrictions are not imposed on economic grounds alone but have political and other motives. Addressing the equity requirements through economic

---

[86] The indigenisation measures adopted in many African countries also had the aim of ensuring the divestment of shares of foreign companies into local hands. The Nigerian indigenisation measures have been widely studied. Fiona Beveridge, 'Taking Control of Foreign Investment: A Case Study of Indigenisation in Nigeria' (1991) 40 ICLQ 302; Tobi, 'Legal Aspects of Foreign Investment and Financing Energy Products in Nigeria' (1991) 14 Dalhousie LJ 5; Osunbor, 'Nigeria's Investment Laws and the State's Control of Multinationals' (1988) 3 ICSID Rev 38; and Thomas Biersteker, *Multinationals, the State and the Control of the Nigerian Economy* (1987).

instruments like investment treaties or WTO instruments is bound to fail as the primary concerns of many states in introducing equity requirements are political rather than economic. The economic considerations may be to create relations based on agreements from which the foreign investor cannot easily withdraw, thus prevent the disruption that relocation by the foreign investor would cause. But, the political motives are the stronger reasons for such requirements. These requirements seek to ensure that the foreign investment meshes in with the national policy to promote the development of groups within the state which have traditionally been disadvantaged. The making of foreign investment alongside the older elite groups will only enhance the divisions within society. For this reason, the laws of many states direct foreign investors into alliances based on ethnicity.[87] Such states are unlikely to accept efforts to dismantle equity requirements based on economic considerations alone.

Strong economic considerations also exist for the insistence that foreign participation in industry could only be made through joint ventures. This enables a more effective transfer of management and technology to the local joint venture partner and, consequently, the maximisation of one of the assumed benefits of foreign investment. It will also ensure that the state's policies are better reflected when decisions as to policy are made. This consideration applies with greater force in industries which are state monopolies whose industrial policy has been clearly laid down.

It is clear that the requirements relating to local equity in new foreign investment ventures bring obvious economic advantages to the host state. Quite apart from the fact that a smaller proportion of the profits will be repatriated abroad, it ensures that the state has a direct or indirect control over the venture. It also ensures that a local entrepreneurial class, which will profit by its association with foreign investors through the acquisition of managerial and business acumen, will emerge. The criticism of these measures is that they give rise to an elite group of local businessmen who form associations with foreign capital and enable governments that are favourable to their business interests to remain in power. Sometimes, it is alleged that this association between foreign capital and the local elite leads to repression and human rights abuses. Indigenisation measures in any state will become less vigorous once the process of indigenisation has been completed and the visible dominance of foreign investment has

---

[87] South Africa provides a recent example.

diminished. The political pressure for such measures will no longer be pressing concerns.

Though measures relating to local equity may have been put in place, the vigour with which they are pursued will depend on several factors such as the sufficiency and willingness of the administrative authorities and the relative bargaining strengths of the state and the foreign party. Where there is a foreign investment project which the state is keen to attract into the country, it will seek to do so, exercising its discretionary powers to overlook the entry requirements. It is the bargaining strength of the foreign investor that will dictate the manner in which the entry requirements are applied to him. Equity requirements are being relaxed in many states in order to achieve other advantages. Increasingly, states permit foreign investors prepared to locate in certain underdeveloped regions of the state or willing to export larger percentages of their manufactured products to set up wholly owned enterprises or to increase their equity ownership considerably. Many states also permit wholly owned enterprises in industries that are new to them and which they prefer to attract.

There have also been efforts to circumvent the requirements relating to local equity participation. The usual method has been to hold shares through a nominee who has the necessary qualifications to satisfy the requirements of local participation. These avenues for circumventing the law are obviously illegal. A foreign national who suffers penal consequences as a result of attempts to circumvent the law has no remedy through any form of diplomatic intervention by his home state. It is also doubtful whether foreign investments made in transgression of the host state's laws are entitled to any protection under international law.[88]

The requirement that entry be made in collaboration with local business has meant that the preferred form of entry was through a joint venture. This is a logical consequence of the measures relating to the indigenisation of the economy. The joint venture has become the most important vehicle for foreign investment in recent times across the world, for various reasons. From the point of view of investment in developing countries, entry regulations have been the most important reason for their formation. Both the joint venture in the manufacturing and mineral sectors as well as the production-sharing agreement in the mineral sector were agreements which were structured with the aim of maximising local

---

[88] *Shott* v. *Iran* (1989) 23 Iran–US CTR 351.

control of the investment. But, as in all foreign investment contracts of long duration, an internal balance between internationalisation and localisation is struck during the bargaining process that precedes the drafting of the agreement. That balance keeps changing, depending on multifarious factors such as fluctuations in the demand for products, political changes in the country and the health of the global economy as a whole.

1.10. Other requirements

There are several other requirements which can be found in the foreign investment legislation of different states. They may be explained as efforts at maximising the benefits of the foreign investment to the local economy. There may be requirements relating to the level of employment of local staff, thus ensuring that the perceived benefits of the transfer of skills to the local labour and management are made a reality. There may be a requirement for local research relating to products and the adaptation of the products to local conditions. There may be a requirement that the processing of minerals should take place locally so that more activity associated with the mineral industry takes place within the state and more value is thereby added to the product within the state before export. The imposition of such requirements could also be justified as based on the sovereign rights of the state to regulate economic activity that takes place within its territory.

As a result of the policies adopted by developing countries towards foreign investment, some new forms of foreign investment which have the flexibility to give effect to larger economic and social policies have emerged. Some of them are dealt with in the next section.

1.11. Regulation and expropriation

It is abundantly clear that foreign investment has to work within the regulatory framework of the host state. Where admission of a foreign investment is conditional, the failure to meet those conditions justifies interference. Where licences need to be obtained and are made conditional, again the failure to meet those conditions justifies the withdrawal of the licences. In all these instances, there can be no doubt as to the domestic legality of the measures if the procedures mandated by the law have been followed. The issue is whether such interference can amount to an expropriation under international law. The basic assumption would be that it would not amount to an expropriation, as the foreign investor was admitted on the condition that local laws are obeyed. This must be the starting point of analysis. The result would vary in accordance, not with customary international law which has nothing to say on the point, except perhaps that it insists on due process prior to interference, but on treaty constraints. The extent to which there are such constraints and the difficulty of determining when regulation crosses the line and amounts to expropriation under treaty provisions are discussed in Chapter 8 below.

2. New forms of foreign investment

Unlike earlier forms of contract which favoured the foreign investor, modern forms of foreign investment contract ensure that the contractual balance favours the host state. The early measures of ensuring such change lacked sophistication. The picture has changed. There is now a greater pragmatism in the manner in which foreign investment is handled, though one must not forget that basic passions such as nationalism and xenophobia are yet dormant and can be aroused by the astute in the pursuit of power. Equally, endemic corruption defeats these aims in many developing states. The prevailing philosophy that foreign investment can be harnessed to serve the economic development of the host state is the basis of some of the regulatory measures that were detailed above. They are based on the recognition that foreign investment is beneficial to the host economy provided there is careful regulation of such investment. In keeping with this philosophy, the preferred forms of foreign investment have also changed. The contractual forms through which foreign investments now enter are more amenable to public control than the earlier forms and are instruments through which state policy on foreign investment could be given expression. To this extent, they are more in the nature of public contracts than ordinary commercial contracts. They are designed to mesh with the regulatory controls that host states seek to exert over foreign investment.

The principal representative forms of foreign investment are the joint venture and the production-sharing agreement, both of which are briefly described below. They are supported by agreements such as the management agreement (which is based on the divorce of ownership from control so that the manager controls a project in return for a fixed sum whereas the profits of the project go to the state), the transfer of technology agreement (where the technology requisite for the project is supplied by the foreigner) and similar devices through which the state is able to ensure that it controls the project and has a larger share of the profits. These new types of foreign investment contract have been described in the literature.

2.1. The joint venture

The joint venture is a collaborative arrangement between two or more businesses to achieve a particular objective or to participate in another fresh project which may be more successfully pursued as a result of their pooling of resources or technology. The spreading of the risk of failure enables the parties to proceed with the project with more confidence whereas bearing the risk alone would have made any of the parties unwilling to embark on it. Two principal forms of joint venture are recognised. One is the partnership joint venture, which is not very different from a partnership in the common law, except that it is formed with a precise project in mind. The second form is the corporate joint venture, where the parties enter into an agreement to incorporate a company through which they will carry out their business objectives. The constitutional documents of the company will reflect the main points on which there is agreement between the parties.

The joint venture, which is a US contribution to commerce, and its use in international business is now widespread. In the developed countries, the joint venture form has been used in many high-technology industries and in particular in industries such as the automobile industry where the scope for international business cooperation is great. It has become popular, apart from the reasons for the popularity in domestic business described above, also for the reasons that penetration of new markets through local business partners is easier, risks are diversified and market information is more readily gained through the local partner.

In developing countries, apart from these reasons, there are the more compelling reasons that foreign investment entry can usually be made only in collaboration with a local partner. If the industry into which entry is sought is a state monopoly, this will mean that the joint venture will have to be made with a state corporation. This has advantages as well as disadvantages from the foreign investor's point of view. One advantage is that the foreign investor will be able to share in monopoly profits in a captive, monopoly market. Another advantage is that the investor will have a link with the state so that matters such as customs clearances, export permits and other administrative matters connected with entry and later with the functioning of the joint venture will be smoother. The disadvantages are that the state will seek to represent its objectives through the state corporation and ensure that its policies are reflected in the functioning of the joint venture. The constant presence of the directors of the state entity at board meetings of the joint venture corporation will provide the means of securing the adequate airing of the state's policy on the direction the joint venture should take. Since state policies will clash with the profit motives of the foreign investor, the situation is tailor-made for conflict. In any dispute, the state will not hesitate to use its legislative and administrative powers to ensure that the joint venture toes the line that it has drawn. The foreign investor will not be able to assert his will in such circumstances. The nature of the control that the foreign investor may be able to exert varies with the nature of the project. Where there is high technology involved and access to it can be gained only through the foreign partner, the role of the local partner will generally be a passive one. Continued utility to the project, as a supplier of finance and technology and as a means of access to markets abroad, is the key to the control that the foreign investor can exert.

In socialist states, joint venture with the state entity is usually compelled by legislation. The situation is similar in sectors of the developing states which have mixed economies. In the mixed economy states, entry can be made in collaboration with private business in the non-public sector of the economy.

2.2. The production-sharing agreement

A change as to the dominant form of contract has also occurred in the oil industry. Previously, the concession agreement was the prevailing form of contract through which the oil industry functioned in the oil-exporting countries. The concession agreement contemplated a passive role for the host state, which was confined to receiving royalties for the oil that was exported. The concession agreement is no longer used as the oil-producing countries have sought greater control over the industry. The new agreement, which replaced the concession agreement, reflects in every way the fact that there has been a shift of power away from the oil companies to the oil-producing states. The production-sharing agreement is based on the concept that the ownership of oil is always in the state and that the state alone has the right to its disposal, a reflection of the principle of permanent sovereignty over natural resources. The risk of oil exploration is borne by the foreign corporation, which is given a licence for the exploration of parcels of areas where there is a prospect of finding oil. When oil is found, the foreign corporation may extract the oil and is given a certain percentage of it, so that it may recover the expenses of the exploration and secure a reasonable profit. The percentage of the oil given to the foreign corporation progressively diminishes as the expenses are recouped by sale until eventually the whole project is taken over by the state oil corporation.

The state retains ownership of the oil, subject to the right of the foreign corporation to its share of production. There is usually provision for joint management of the project with the state oil company.

Both the joint venture agreement and the production-sharing agreement are legal techniques which demonstrate that host states are asserting their power over incoming investments. The amount of power that can be asserted will depend on the relative bargaining strengths of the parties. A state which is desperate for investment is not going to be too assertive in case it scares away such investment, whereas a state which is perceived as a safe state from which profits can be made will seek to optimise the benefits from the foreign investment for itself while ensuring that the foreign investor has adequate incentives for him to remain and do business in that state.

3. Constraints on control: the customary international law

As a general principle, a state may do whatever it pleases on its territory. The modern assertion of such sovereignty in the economic sphere is effected through the principles of economic self-determination and permanent sovereignty over natural resources. The Seoul Declaration of the International Law Association combined these two principles of economic sovereignty by stating that 'permanent sovereignty over natural resources, economic activities and wealth is a principle of international law'.[89] One could argue that such a principle always existed in international law and that the articulation of principles relating to economic self-determination became necessary only in the context of the need to dismantle domestic economic structures in the post-colonial era. The notion of permanent sovereignty is not confined in the resolutions to natural resources but extends to all economic activities of a state.[90] This extension need not be considered dramatic or novel.[91] The right of control over the economic

---

[89] Section 5 of the Seoul Declaration of the International Law Association (1988).
[90] International Law Association, Report of the Sixty–Fourth Congress (1990).
[91] H. Neufeld, *The International Protection of Private Creditors from the Treaties of Westphalia to the Congress of Vienna* (1971), 55.

affairs of the state is one which European states have claimed and exercised consistently. It is a facet of the state's inherent sovereignty to control all people, incidents and objects that are within its territory. Such a right is not confined to European states. On the principle of equality of states, there is no reason why the same right should not be exercised by other states.

But, state sovereignty is subject to the principles of customary and treaty-based international law. The subjection of state sovereignty to these principles may be explained either on the ground that international law is a system of higher law or on the positivist basis that there has been consent of the state to be bound by treaty and customary principles of international law.[92] Developing countries have not denied the relevance of international law to foreign investment. The most controversial document in the area, the Charter of Economic Rights and Duties of States, acknowledges the fact that the rights it articulates are subject to 'the fulfilment in good faith of international obligations'.[93] The chairman of the drafting committee of the Charter has explained that the Charter 'accepts that international law may act as a factor limiting the freedom of the state'.[94] The problem relates to the content of the international law, which limits the host state's treatment of the alien investor. The content of this body of customary law continues to be relevant as it is incorporated into modern investment treaties through treatment standards such as the international minimum standard and the fair and equitable standard of treatment. As to the content of customary law in the area, there are different claims made by different groups of states.

In the area of foreign investments, there is a claim made by capital-exporting countries as to the existence of a body of customary international law, which, if it exists, will limit the state's sovereignty to impose restrictions on foreign investors. The body of customary law relates to an area referred to in the texts as state responsibility for the treatment of aliens. This law imposes standards upon states as to the treatment of aliens who are present in their territories. Whether this body of law forms

---

[92] Compare Malcolm Shaw, *Title to Territory in Africa* (1986), 16, who states: '[C]ompetences associated with the concept of territorial sovereignty may be seen as derived ultimately from the norms of the international legal order itself' with formulations that regard international law as being based on self-limitations of power by states.

[93] Many developing states did not accept Article 2(2)(c) of the Charter of Economic Rights and Duties of States, which expressed the view that matters of nationalisation were for the state to decide.

[94] Jorge Castenada, 'La Charte des Droits et Devoirs Economiques des Etats' (1970) Ann Fr 31.

part of customary international law is questionable as its universality has been denied by some authors.[95] It is undeniable, however, that treaties on foreign investment could limit the state's sovereignty to treat the foreign investor in violation of the treaty standards which protect him. There are no multilateral treaties containing the substantive rules on foreign investment. The existing multilateral treaties have only a peripheral significance. The General Agreement on Tariffs and Trade (GATT) has little relevance to the field. The disciplines attached to the World Trade Organization, especially those on intellectual property (TRIPS), investment (TRIMS) and services (GATS), have considerably greater significance and are considered in Chapter 6 below. There are multilateral agreements relating to the arbitration of investment disputes and the insurance of foreign investment.[96] The extent to which the rules on state responsibility in international law, if they exist, may impact on the requirements and restrictions imposed by the new foreign investment codes are examined in the first section of this chapter. The extent to which the regulatory devices may conflict with customary international law and with GATT and other treaty provisions is examined in the second section of the chapter. The nature of the treaties and other instruments which may affect a state's treatment of foreign investment are dealt with in Chapters 5 and 6.

[95] Guha-Roy, 'Is the Law of State Responsibility for Injuries to Aliens a Part of Universal International Law?' (1969) 55 AJIL 562. More recently, a United Nations report stated:

> The traditional concept of State responsibility as a body of international standards for the protection of individual aliens was questioned when it was perceived as either inequitable or inadequate for the purpose of addressing the concerns of an international community which lacked homogeneity as to political, economic and developmental values and goals. While it cannot be asserted that a new doctrine of state responsibility prevails, it is clear that the traditional concept no longer commands universal support.

There were several American lawyers who viewed the law of state responsibility as partial to the interests of the developed states long before Guha Roy. Thus, Judge Jessup regarded the law on state responsibility as 'an aspect of the history of imperialism or dollar diplomacy'. Lissitzyn regarded it as an example of international law 'developed in response to the requirements of the Western business civilization'. O. J. Lissitzyn, 'International Law in a Divided World' (1963) 532 Int Conc 58. For more recent views, see UNCTC, 'Outstanding Issues in the Draft Code of Conduct on Transnational Corporations', E/C.10/1985/S/2 (1985), para. 53. P. Trimble, 'International Law and World Order' (1990) 42 Stanford LR 811 at 835, regards the law on state responsibility and minimum standards of conduct as having only a regional significance in the Latin American context.

[96] The ICSID and the MIGA Conventions, both sponsored by the World Bank, are discussed in Chapter 6 below.

3.1. State responsibility for injuries to aliens

The rules relating to state responsibility for injuries to aliens contain the body of international law which seeks to confer a standard of treatment of aliens who enter states for various reasons, including the doing of business.[97] They create liability in the host state for failing to observe the prescribed standards in its treatment of aliens. An alien, who leaves his state, carries with him the protection of his state. This rule of diplomatic protection of nationals comes down from early times.[98] It was a less objectionable right than the right to use military force in the protection of nationals, a right which continues to be asserted as a justification for military intervention. The legality of such intervention in modern international law is subject to doubt.[99]

The theory of state responsibility for injuries to aliens rests on the idea that the injury to the alien is an injury to his home state. In effect, it involved a fiction that was used to overcome the deficiency of personality in the alien to take up his own case in an international forum. The fiction involved a stress on the link of nationality between the alien

---

[97] C. F. Amerasinghe, *State Responsibility for Injuries to Aliens* (1964); see also C. Eagleton, *The Responsibility of States in International Law* (1928); F. Dunn, *The Protection of Nationals* (1933); A. Freeman, *International Responsibility of States for Denial of Justice* (1938); F. G. Dawson and I. L. Head, *International Law, National Tribunals and the Rights of Aliens* (1971); F. V. Garcia-Amador, L. B. Sohn and R. R. Baxter, *Recent Codification of the Law of State Responsibility for Injuries to Aliens* (1974); E. Jimenez de Arechaga, 'International Responsibility' in M. Sorensen (ed.), *Manual of Public International Law* (1968), 362; R. B. Lillich (ed.), *International Law of State Responsibility for Injuries to Aliens* (1983). M. Sornarajah, *The Pursuit of Nationalized Property* (1986); and James Crawford, *The International Law Commission's Articles on State Responsibility* (2002).

[98] The rule is usually traced from Vattel.

[99] The threat of such intervention by European powers was the basis of the 'gun-boat' diplomacy practised in early times to bring pressure to obtain advantageous commercial policies for their nationals. In modern times, the protection of citizens continues to be stated as a justification for military intervention. It has been used as a justification for military intervention chiefly by the United States in the cases of its intervention in Puerto Rico, Grenada and Panama. Non-intervention was a principle consistently articulated by Latin American states because of the frequency of interventions in their domestic affairs. See G. Arangio-Ruiz, *The United Nations Declaration on Friendly Relations and the System of Sources of International Law* (1979), 118. For a survey of the international law on military intervention, see L. Damrosch and D. Scheffer (ed.), *Law and Force in the New International Order* (1991), 111–84. However, wide notions of intervention and the use of force are now resurfacing in international law. There are claims that force may be used in order to promote democracy, and that anticipatory force could be used in order to prevent possible terrorist attacks. The events after the intervention in Iraq to overthrow the regime there adds to the uncertainty in the law.

and his state and the notion of injury caused to the state through the medium of the alien as a result of this link. The law was explained by the Permanent Court of International Justice in the following passage:[100]

> [I]n taking up the case of one of its nationals, by resorting to diplomatic action or international judicial proceedings on his behalf, a state is in reality asserting its own right, the right to ensure in the person of its nationals respect for the rules of international law. This right is necessarily limited to intervention on behalf of its own nationals because in the absence of special agreement the bond of nationality between the state and the individual which alone confers upon it the right of diplomatic protection, and it is as part of the function of diplomatic protection that the right to take up a claim and to ensure respect for the rules of international law must be envisaged.

Though the notion that diplomatic protection of aliens and the idea that an injury done to the alien is an injury done to the home state through the medium of the alien have been basic principles of international diplomacy,[101] the scope for abuse of the principle is obvious. The development of these principles is based on unexceptional sources.[102] There is general recognition that there is state responsibility for direct wrongs done to aliens. Yet, there has been considerable tension generated between developed and developing states as to the application of the rules of state responsibility and diplomatic protection in the area of foreign investment. The disagreement has largely been focused on the standard of treatment to be accorded to the alien.

---

[100] *Panevezys–Saldutiskis Railway Case* (1939) Series A/B No. 76, 16.

[101] The rule of mediate injury to the state is also traced to Vattel, who wrote in 1758 that: 'Whoever ill treats a citizen injures the state which must protect the citizen.' E. de Vattel, *Classics of International Law: The Law of Nations or the Principles of International Law* (C. Fenwick trans., 1916); P. Remec, *The Position of the Individual in International Law According to Grotius and Vattel* (1960). Vattel's view was reformulated in the *Panevezys–Saldutiskis Railway Case* by the Permanent Court of International Justice. Vattel had said: 'Whoever ill treats the citizen indirectly injures the state, which must protect the citizen. The sovereign of the injured state must avenge the deed and, if possible, force the aggressor to give full satisfaction or punish him, since otherwise the citizen will not obtain the chief end of civil society, which is protection.'

[102] The principles are constructed through: (1) *Mavrommatis Palestine Concession Case* (1929) PCIJ Series A No. 2, 12, where the Court stated that a state asserts its own rights when it espouses the cause of its national; (2) *Panevezys–Saldututiskis Railway Case* (1939) Series A/B No. 76, where the need for the link of nationality between the state and the national whose right was taken up was stressed; and (3) *Chorzow Factory Case* (1928) PCIJ Series A, No. 17, where restitution as the basis of damages for the wrong done to the national through the violation of treaty rights was stated.

The developed states have maintained that aliens must be treated according to an international minimum standard, which could be a higher standard than that accorded by a host state to its own nationals.[103] This international minimum standard is asserted as a general principle that applies to the treatment of aliens. But, there is a component in this standard that has special relevance to the treatment of foreign investment. The existence of this minimum standard is asserted in investment treaties. Modern arbitral awards have also recognised that there are minimum standards to which the host state should conform in its treatment of foreign investors.[104] The minimum standard is an external standard which enabled developed states to introduce standards of treatment that they expected for their foreign investors but which developing states may find difficult to satisfy. The failure to conform to the minimum standard of treatment created a cause of action against the violating state. Such a violation could be pursued through dispute settlement mechanisms. Most of the cases in which these standards of liability were articulated involved injuries to the person of the alien. The most dramatic cases, such as the *Neer Claim* or the *Roberts Claim*, concerned injuries to the person of the alien, and it was in the context of such injuries that the old rules came to be stated. There was injury directly caused by agents of the state such as soldiers or indirectly caused by mobs. In the latter case, responsibility arose in circumstances where there was negligence in protecting the alien or a wilful disregard of the duty to protect the alien. The extension of the idea to the property of the alien was not the focus of these early cases. Such an extension came much later and became the basis for building up a law on the protection of foreign investment. Thus, a powerful technique was created which could be manipulated to secure the interests of developed states and their foreign investors. The technique, developed in customary practice, is now stated in treaties.

Some developing countries, however, have maintained that an alien is entitled, at the most, to the same treatment as the citizens of the host state. The heyday of a joint position being adopted by developing countries came when the resolutions associated with the New International Economic Order were being debated in the 1970s. The Charter of Economic Rights

---

[103] For a history of the rule, see E. Borchard, 'The Minimum Standard of Treatment of Aliens' (1940) 38 Mich LR 445; A. Roth, *The Minimum Standard of International Law as Applied to Aliens* (1949).

[104] *American Machine Tools* v. *Zaire* 5 ICSID Rpts 11.

and Duties of States articulated this position in clear terms.[105] While adhering to the standard of national treatment, these states also claim that in exceptional instances they could discriminate in favour of their own citizens. Though this conflict in views can be traced back to the writings of Vitoria and Vattel, it was only in Latin American state practice that it had any significance in earlier times. The claim that its citizens were not given an international standard of treatment became a pretext for intervention by the United States in the affairs of Latin American states. Consequently, Latin American states have steadfastly denied the existence of a rule that mandated a minimum standard of treatment for aliens.

After the decolonisation of the African and Asian states, the developed states espoused the view taken by the United States relating to the rule that there was a minimum standard of treatment for alien property. With the ending of colonialism, there was a greater need to ensure that there was a rule-based system of foreign investment protection as force could not be used to settle such disputes as in the past. The newly independent states, like the Latin American states, had denied the existence of a rule mandating a minimum standard of treatment. Asian and African states joined in by contesting the validity of the rule. Some writers from developing countries challenged the very existence of a law on state responsibility in customary international law.[106]

But, the more vigorous challenge to the viewpoint of the developed countries had been mounted earlier by Latin American jurists who, following the lead of Calvo,[107] argued that aliens had only the rights and privileges enjoyed by nationals and can therefore seek enforcement of

---

[105] See in particular, Article 2(2)(c) of the Charter, which contains in effect a restatement of the Calvo doctrine.

[106] Guha-Roy, 'Is the Law of State Responsibility for Injuries to Aliens a Part of Universal International Law?' (1969) 55 AJIL 562.

[107] Carlos Calvo was an Argentinean foreign minister. He was earlier a professor of public international law and wrote a multi-volume text in Spanish on international law. The doctrine was adopted at many Conferences of American States (Washington Conference, 1889; Montevideo Conference, 1933). Its offshoot was the Calvo clause, which gives exclusive jurisdiction over disputes arising from foreign investment contracts to national tribunals. On the Calvo clause, see D. Shea, *Calvo Clause* (1955); K. Lipstein, 'The Place of the Calvo Clause in International Law' (1945) 24 BYIL 130; A. V. Freeman, 'Recent Aspects of the Calvo Doctrine and the Challenge to International Law' (1946) 40 AJIL 131; D. Graham, 'The Calvo Clause: Its Current Status as a Contractual Renunciation of Diplomatic Protection' (1971) 6 Texas ILJ 289; and A. O. Adede, 'The Minimum Standards in a World of Disparities' in R. St J. Macdonald and D. M. Johnston (eds.), *The Structure and Process of International Law* (1983), 1001 at 1003–4.

such rights only before national courts. This doctrine sought to preclude international review of the standard of treatment accorded to the alien by an external body. The principal purpose of the minimum standard rule was the protection of the lives and liberty of aliens in situations of turmoil that frequently occurred in some states or at the hands of unprincipled officials.[108] If it had been used exclusively for such a purpose, there could have been justification for it, but, instead, it became the basis for a system of foreign investment protection which could curb the institution of economic reform by the developing countries. Since Latin America was one of the first areas to be subject to the application of the minimum standard rule, it was logical that opposition to the rule first came from that region.

3.2. The conflict between the United States and Latin American states

The Latin American view that foreign investors are subject to the laws of the host state alone and have no protection through any external standards is a view which has much support in the international law that existed during the period in which the controversy took place. There was clearly no protection envisaged in international law for contracts made by aliens with the host state.[109] Early twentieth-century US writing on the issue supports the view that there is state responsibility for damage caused to the person of the alien or for destruction of the property of the alien by state forces or as a result of negligence by the host state in providing

---

[108] As formulated by Vattel, the rule was intended to apply to situations where the host state had rudimentary forms of government and was not capable of protecting the alien vigorously. The rule served a deterrent function and justified intervention by the home state for the protection of the alien. It may possibly be extended to mob rule or unstable military rule under dictators as prevailed in many Latin American states. Whether the rule applies to modern governments of whatever ideological persuasion may be questioned. M. W. Gordon, *The Cuban Nationalisations* (1973).

[109] The PCIJ had stated in the *Serbian Loans Case* (1929) PCIJ Series A No. 20, that municipal law applies to state contracts with aliens. In the *Panevezys–Saldutiskis Railway Case* (1939) PCIJ Series A/B No. 76, the PCIJ reiterated that 'in principle property rights and contractual rights of individuals depend in every state on the municipal law and fall therefore more particularly within the jurisdiction of municipal tribunals'. The Mexican Claims Commission usually applied municipal law. Surveying the practice of this Commission, Feller observed that 'international law contains no rules for the controversies involving breach of such contracts'. A. H. Feller, *The Mexican Claims Commission 1923–1934* (1935).

protection.[110] But, there is no unequivocal support for the proposition that this rule should be extended to foreign investment protection. These writings contain clear statements that breaches of agreements made by US citizens with Latin American states should not be the concern of the state. The idea of foreign investment protection through the principles of state responsibility is a matter of later development.

Because of the importance of the subject, the authorities which support the proposition that international law mandates a national standard of treatment and no more need to be examined at least briefly. A convenient starting point is the view stated by Sir Henry Strong, the arbitrator in *Rosa Gelbtrunk* v. *Salvador*.[111] The arbitrator observed in his award:

> A citizen or subject of one nation who, in the pursuit of commercial enterprise, carries on trade within the territory and under the protection of the sovereignty of a nation other than his own, is to be considered as having cast in his lot with the subjects or citizens of the state in which he resides and carries on business. Whilst on the one hand he enjoys the protection of that state, so far as the police regulations and other advantages are concerned, on the other hand he becomes liable to the political vicissitudes of the country in which he thus has a commercial domicile in the same manner as the subjects or the citizens of that state are liable to the same.

The statement is simply that, once the alien voluntarily takes a risk of investing in a host state, he must bear the risk of potential injury to his investment and must be satisfied with the same standard of compensation as is given to the nationals of the state who suffer the same fate as he does. It is a potentially sound principle of risk allocation. Ralston, commenting on the *dictum* of the arbitrator, stated that it accorded with the practice of the European states at the time.[112] Ralston also cited a passage from

---

[110] The arbitral and other awards that are used to support the existence of state responsibility for injuries to aliens deal with capricious damage to the person and property of aliens. They do not deal with the taking of property by the state for a public purpose. These cases came later to be used to construct a legal structure for the protection of foreign investment. For representative early cases, see *Neer Claim* (1926) 4 UNRIAA 60; *Chevreau Case* (1933) 27 AJIL 160; and *Zafiro Claim* (1925) 6 UNRIAA 160. These cases, which involved the treatment of individuals in a degrading fashion, are the basis for the construction of an international minimum standard for property protection.

[111] Foreign Relations of 1902, 877.

[112] J. H. Ralston, *The Law and Procedure of International Tribunals* (1926), 271.

the Venezuelan Claims Commission of 1885 which quoted the following view of Fiore with approval:[113]

> Protection is illicit and unjustifiable where it has for its purpose to secure in favour of the citizens residing abroad a privileged position. Strong and powerful governments must not take advantage of their superiority and exaggerate the duty of protection by exercising pressure upon weak governments, in order to compel them to favour their citizens and exempt them from certain obligations or grant them privileges of any nature whatever.

Resort to an external standard was made only in circumstances where the internal conditions in the host state were such that no remedies could possibly be expected from the host state. Cushing was almost apologetic in stating that in such circumstances there was justification for the home state to intervene. He observed:[114]

> As to the exceptions to the general rule, they have grown up chiefly in Spanish America in consequence of the unsettled condition of the new American republics. Great Britain, France and the United States have each occasionally assumed, in behalf of their subjects or citizens in those countries, rights of interference which neither of us would tolerate at home – in some cases from necessity, in others with very questionable discretion or justification.

The passage leaves no room for doubt that interference is an exception to the general rule and was confined to a region and that too when conditions in the state were unsettled. It also accepts that the justifications for such interventions were often questionable and counterproductive. The exception, however, was to consume the general principle by being broadened by later claims made by the United States. However, on every occasion when such claims were made, the Latin American states have objected so that the claims have remained, in the regional context of the Americas, supported only by the consistent practice of the United States. The Latin American states have, almost collectively, been persistent objectors to the formation of any customary practice in the area. It is only in more recent times that they have departed from this practice by entering into investment treaties which acknowledge the competence of foreign tribunals to settle foreign investment disputes.

---

[113] Moore, *Digest*, 2965.
[114] Referred to in the *Sambiaggio Case* (1903), cited in Ralston, *The Law and Procedure of International Tribunals* (1926), 272.

In the writings of Borchard[115] and Ralston,[116] there does not appear to be any support for the existence of an external standard of protection for foreign investment agreements. Their writings cover the first quarter of the twentieth century. Borchard was convinced that contractual claims of aliens against the host state should not be espoused too readily by their home states. He justified this position on the grounds that the alien had voluntarily assumed a risk in contracting with the foreign state and that, 'by going abroad, he submits impliedly to the local law and local judicial system'.[117] These are views solidly based on the principle of sovereignty of states and the right inherent in such sovereignty to control all economic activity within the state by both aliens and nationals. The only exception to the rule that he recognised was the situation where the local law did not provide an adequate remedy because the local judiciary was corrupt or where the remedy that is provided was too remote.

There is little indication that the picture changed in the next quarter of a century. The United States had insisted on an external standard for the treatment of aliens but the Latin American states continued to deny the existence of such a standard. In this situation, there was no way that even a regional norm, let alone an international law principle, could have emerged that there was an international minimum standard for the treatment of foreign investment.[118]

In the context of the relations between the United States and the Latin American states, foreign investment and the claims relating to the international law that protected it were perceived as instruments through which the United States was able to maintain its economic dominance in the region. Foreign investment was seen by Latin Americans as a trojan horse which ensured that American influence could be exerted through the presence of the foreign investment in the various Latin American states.[119] The

[115] E. Borchard, *The Diplomatic Protection of Citizens Abroad* (1915).

[116] J. H. Ralston, *The Law and Procedure of International Tribunals* (1926).

[117] E. Borchard, *The Diplomatic Protectionj of Citizens Abroad* (1915), 285; Brownlie, who later developed a similar proposition, relied on *Home Missionary Society Case* (1920) 6 UNRIIA 42, *Yukon Lumber Case* (1913) 6 UNRIAA 17 at 20 and on Article 4(4) of the Harvard Draft Convention on the International Responsibility of States for Injuries to Aliens. But, there are awards which go the other way. *Schufeldt Claim* (1930) 5 AD 179. *Delgoa Bay Railway Company Case* (1900) 3 Whiteman, *Digest*, 1694, is not a strong case, as the parties had agreed on many issues. *Goldenberg* (1928) AD 542 can be distinguished, as it was a war-time case decided on the basis of a treaty.

[118] F. V. Garcia-Amador, *The Changing Law of International Claims* (1984), 356–61.

[119] C. Lipson, *Standing Guard: Protecting Foreign Capital in the Nineteenth and Twentieth Centuries* (1985).

idea that there were supranational norms which permitted the protection of the foreign investor was anathema to the Latin American jurists who argued that the only protection that existed for foreign investment was to be found in the domestic legal systems of the host states. The United States itself had espoused such a doctrine when it was a recipient of massive capital investment from Europe but had changed its tack when it became an exporter of capital into Latin American states.

It is the conversion of a principle which was designed to ensure the safety and security of aliens into a system of property protection which has generated conflict. Most of the early cases asserting minimum standards of treatment concerned the personal security of the alien and not his property. When dealing with property, these cases extended protection to property on the basis that such protection was a necessary concomitant of personal security. The rules were developed as safeguards against state violence directed at aliens and not as principles of property protection. It was in later times that the rules essentially directed at state violence came to be isolated in order that a system of property protection could be built up. This was resisted by the Latin American states which have consistently argued that interference with property, particularly in pursuance of economic programmes, fell within the domestic sovereignty of the host state.

The tussle that took place between the United States and the Latin American states was globalised after decolonisation through the claim that the position taken by the United States represented international law. The newly independent states of Africa and Asia had joined the Latin American states in denying that the principles of state responsibility for injuries to aliens extends to the protection of direct investments made by aliens. On this point, there is no agreement between developed states and developing states as to what the international law is.[120] At the bilateral level, states have made investment treaties articulating a set of rules, which to a large extent adopt the model of property protection desired by the developed states. But, there is strong resistance at the multilateral level for the adoption of similar treaty instruments, which indicates that developing states are reluctant to give up their collective stance that there is no international law on the subject.

---

[120] This statement must follow from the universalisation of the Calvo doctrine by Article 2(2)(c) of the Charter of Economic Rights and Duties of States. The Article received the support of the vast majority of the developing states.

During the dispute concerning the Mexican expropriations of US property, the Hull formula that prompt, adequate and effective compensation must be paid to the foreign investor upon expropriation of his property had been articulated. The formula articulated what could be described as a component of the minimum standard. But, there was no argument that interference with the alien property itself was unlawful, for the property rights of the alien rested only to the extent of their recognition in the domestic law of the host state. Roth summarised the state of the law on this point in a series of propositions as follows:[121]

> (1) General international law gives aliens no right to be economically active in foreign states. In cases where the national policies of foreign states allow aliens to undertake economic activities, however, general international law assures aliens of equality of commercial treatment among themselves.
>
> (2) According to general international law, the alien's privilege of participation in the economic life of his state of residence does not go so far as to allow him to acquire private property. The state of residence is free to bar him from ownership of all or some property, whether movable or realty.
>
> (3) Whenever the alien enjoys the privilege of ownership of property, international law protects his property in so far as his property may not be expropriated under any pretext, except for moral or penal reasons, without adequate compensation. Property rights are to be understood as rights to tangible property which have come into concrete existence according to the municipal law of the alien's state of residence.

This statement of the law, made in 1949 by an American writer, again recognises the sovereignty of the host state and its laws over any foreign investment. There is protection for property rights acquired under the law of the host state but such rights are dependent on the host state's laws. The author uses the term privilege rather than right of ownership, which, in Hohfeldian terms, has the significance of indicating that the privilege can be withdrawn by the person or entity conferring it. In the third paragraph, there is reference to an international law standard reflecting the US claim that there was an external standard as regards the expropriation of alien property. This may have been due to the influence of the Hull formula. But, the Hull formula had never been accepted by the Latin American states.

---

[121] A. Roth, *The Minimum Standard of International Law Applied to Aliens* (1949), 185–6.

Clearly, there was a credible case for the minimum standard of treatment being applied to the protection of the life, liberty and property of the alien in the unsettled conditions of many Latin American states from state violence or state-condoned mob violence. There was also a case for the extension of the rule to capricious takings of an alien's property by dictators for their own purpose. There was no support, as a matter of customary international law, for the extension of the concept into the economic sphere to include foreign investment agreements. Indeed, it would have been difficult to prove that, at the time state responsibility for the foreign investment was claimed to have emerged, developed states provided equal treatment to aliens in the economic sphere. Developed states maintained many laws which were racially discriminatory. They continued to discriminate on the basis of race well into the twentieth century.[122]

3.3. The content of the international minimum standard

The content of the international minimum standard is difficult to identify. Apart from the rule relating to compensation for expropriation and the settlement of such issues through a tribunal that sits outside the host state, there does not seem to be any other guidance as to what the content of the standard is. The Hull standard of full compensation is regarded as being incorporated into the minimum standard. The assessment of such compensation by a foreign tribunal, and the requirements that expropriation should be non-discriminatory and for a public purpose are said to flow from the international minimum standard. Apart from the rules relating to compensation for expropriation advanced by the developed states, there does not seem to be any other rule associated with the international minimum standard. The later introduction of the 'fair and equitable standard' led to some controversy as to whether it was a higher standard than the international minimum standard.[123] But, this view has not been accepted by the developed states. The NAFTA Commission issued an interpretative statement indicating that the 'fair and equitable standard' as used in NAFTA did not contemplate a higher standard than the international

---

[122] E.g. there were laws in the United States forbidding Japanese from buying real estate. McGovney, 'The Anti-Japanese Land Laws' (1943) 35 Calif LR 61. Australia maintained a white Australia policy until the 1970s preventing non-white entry into Australia for residence, let alone ownership of property.

[123] It was regarded as a higher standard by some. Francis A. Mann, *Further Studies in International Law* (1990), 234–51.

minimum standard recognised in customary international law.[124] The central issue of the content of the international minimum standard outside the context of expropriation has not been faced. Within the context of the rules on expropriation, the issue of whether full compensation represents international law has remained a contested proposition. Though investment treaties increasingly contain references to full compensation, the question whether they contribute to the creation of customary law on the point remains moot.[125] The international minimum standard evolved as a counter to the standard of national treatment articulated in the Calvo doctrine. Its content was largely determined in the course of the debate on expropriation.

Apart from the standard of compensation, the other aspect of the conflict in the standards related to dispute resolution. The adherents of the minimum standard argued that issues relating to expropriation had to be settled in accordance with an external standard applied by international tribunals. The rule was based on the suspicion that domestic tribunals would not provide objective justice to the foreign investor. It was met with the counter that only domestic tribunals or courts had competence to settle such disputes and that, too, only in accordance with the local laws. The emergence of the local remedies rule was, to some extent, a resolution of that conflict.

The local remedies rule requires that, for an international claim to arise from the mistreatment of a foreign investor, there must be a prior exhaustion of the remedies provided to him by the law of the host state.[126] This rule is widely recognised as a rule of international law and asserts the primacy of the domestic law of the host state to provide a remedy to the foreign investor and thereby avoid an international claim. Exceptions to the rule exist. The foreigner does not have to resort to remedies that are illusory or futile on appearance. These exceptions were formulated in the context of Latin American states which were formerly dictatorships, and their significance for modern democratic states is limited. Besides, a denial of remedy by a state is extremely difficult to establish.[127]

---

[124] NAFTA Commission. The issue was raised in some NAFTA awards which conformed with the interpretative statement, once it was issued. The OECD also had earlier stated the view that 'fair and equitable treatment' is a standard which 'conforms in effect to the 'minimum standard' which forms part of customary international law'.

[125] This issue is more fully explored in Chapter 10 below.

[126] On the rule, see C. F. Amerasinghe, *The Local Remedies Rule* (2nd ed., 2002).

[127] In the *ELSI Case*, the International Court of Justice indicated that a denial of justice will not be lightly assumed.

There have been attempts to displace the rule through treaties. The ICSID Convention seeks to do this. Developments under the Convention relating to 'arbitration without privity' seek to further the deviation from the rule. Yet, the logical basis of the rule is such that it continues to have vigour. Rooted in state sovereignty, the soundness of the rule that the initial remedy must lie in the host state's laws cannot be lightly shaken. So, when the OECD's Multilateral Agreement on Investment came to be drafted, the option of remedies was provided, confining the foreign investor to local remedies once he had chosen them. Yet, this result is also not one which is fully consistent with the local remedies rule, which requires the first attempt at dealing with the issue to be granted to the host state. It is when this option fails that customary international law creates an international claim that could be pursued through international tribunals. The rule also serves the purpose of enabling a local tribunal to identify the dispute and to indicate its views as to the available remedies in local laws and how the matter should be disposed of by the local tribunals applying the domestic law. The techniques brought about by treaty devices on dispute settlement undermine this salutary purpose of the rule by giving too great an emphasis to the rights of the foreign investor.

The bulk of the case law on the international minimum standard concerned physical injury to the person of the individual alien and not to damage to his property. The cases that concerned damage to the property of aliens considered damage that took place during social upheavals and revolutionary situations that posed a danger both to life and to property.[128] There was difficulty in extending these cases to situations of taking for the purpose of economic reform. A mental leap was necessary.[129] The extension of the cases to situations of modern strife has been relatively easily accomplished. The category of cases, such as *AAPL* v. *Sri Lanka*[130] involving damage to alien property during civil strife demonstrate this. There is greater difficulty in extending the principles developed in cases like the *Neer Claim*,[131] the *Janes Claim*[132] and the *Roberts Claim*[133] to the modern situation of regulatory controls of foreign investment.

In the early cases of physical injury, the common strand that was developed was that the mere error in investigation or lack of resources to

---

[128] There are few cases of property damage. *British Claims in Spanish Morocco* (1926) 4 UNRIAA 41.

[129] The leap is now being performed through the usual techniques of arbitral awards and writings of 'highly qualified publicists'.

[130] (1991) 30 ILM 577.   [131] (1926) 4 UNRIAA 60.   [132] (1926) 4 UNRIAA 82.

[133] (1926) 4 UNRIAA 77.

investigate personal crimes will not be a sufficient basis for creating state liability. The reconciliation of the conflict between the Calvo doctrine that asserted national sovereignty and the creation of an international standard to overcome state deficiency in offering protection to aliens required a balancing factor. This was found in the emphasis in the cases that something more than mere violation of the domestic law was required for state liability. That additional element was expressed in nebulous language. The *Neer* formula was that 'to constitute an international delinquency, the treatment of an alien should amount to an outrage, to bad faith, to wilful neglect of duty or to an insufficiency of governmental action so far short of international standards that every reasonable and impartial man would readily recognise its insufficiency'. That idea is to be found in all the cases of the period, discussing state liability in times of civil strife. Transferring that idea to the application of regulatory mechanisms affecting foreign investment in modern times is fraught with difficulty. Administrative law standards differ. Ascertaining a common standard will prove difficult. Unless some specific content can be given to the international minimum standard in the modern context, the mere assertion that the standard is not static remains rhetorical.[134]

3.4. State responsibility and developing states

In the Latin American context, it would be difficult to establish that there is a law on state responsibility for economic injuries done to aliens. The states of Africa and Asia were in colonial bondage at the time the conflict arose. They did not therefore participate in the making of any law in the area. Even if the theory that states are born into the world of existing international law and are bound by its principles is accepted,[135] it is difficult to establish that state responsibility for economic injuries to alien investors was recognised as a principle of customary international law. Latin American states as well as African and Asian states must be taken to be persistent objectors to the formation of such customary international law. Given the existence of such a large number of states objecting to the extension of rules of state responsibility into the sphere of foreign investment protection, it is hardly possible to speak of an international

---

[134] See further the discussion in Chapter 7 below.

[135] This is the view supported by D. O'Connell, 'Independence and Problems of State Succession' in W. V. O'Brien (ed.), *The New States in International Law and Diplomacy* (1965), 7 at 12.

law on state responsibility for injuries caused to the foreign investment of aliens by the host state. It is difficult to establish that these principles had emerged without having a basis in the sources of international law. About the only rule for which there is support in customary international law is the rule that some compensation must be paid for the taking of alien property by the host state. But, this rule developed independently of the law on state responsibility as a result of claims and settlements made by states. It arose as a result of the practice of paying compensation for post-war nationalisations.

3.5. The 'noble synthesis'

In view of the conflict between the developed and developing states, there has been a new approach attempted to the issue of state responsibility for injuries to aliens. The new approach seeks to combine the notion of international minimum standard with the evolving standards of human rights. The principal impetus for this approach was given by the reports of Garcia-Amador who was Special Rapporteur to the International Law Commission on the subject of state responsibility.[136] A consequence of this development is that the distinction between the minimum standard and the national standard of treatment has now become obsolete and has been replaced by a human rights standard that may be determined by reference to the documents on human rights.[137] From the point of view of ensuring that the alien has rights such as the right to life, liberty, freedom of expression and free movement, the progress that is said to have been made should be a welcome one. But, the subsequent treatment of the subject of state responsibility in the International Law Commission indicates that the focus had to be shifted away from the difficult issue of state responsibility for injuries to alien investors. When a new draft code

---

[136] The reports are reproduced in Garcia-Amador, Sohn and Baxter, *Recent Codification of the Law on State Responsibility for Injuries to Aliens* (1974). It is not likely that the so-called 'noble synthesis' was intended by the Special Rapporteur to provide a system of investment protection. His later writings on the issue of investments indicate his leanings against such a course. See e.g. F. V. Garcia-Amador, *The Emerging International Law of Development* (1990). Overzealous US glossators on the 'noble synthesis' undermined a worthwhile development in human rights law by attempting to convert it into a scheme for investment protection. It is unlikely that materialism sits well with the idealism involved in the pursuit of human rights objectives.

[137] For developments of this theory, see M. S. McDougall, H. D. Lasswell and Lung Chu Chen, *Human Rights and the World Political Order* (1980), 761–5; R. B. Lillich, *The Human Rights of Aliens in Contemporary International Law* (1984), 17.

was drawn up by the International Law Commission, there was a deafening absence of significant reference to the subject of state responsibility for injuries to aliens.[138] The simple reason for this is that agreement on this area would have been difficult to secure.

Yet, the question remains whether the human rights standards are relevant to the alien's rights of access to economic activity in his host country or to the protection of his economic interests in that country. On this issue, there have been statements made to the effect that the new human rights standard ensures equal access to the alien on the basis that there is a norm of non-discrimination between the alien and the national that has grown up in international law.[139] Such propositions do not bear close scrutiny. The human rights documents prohibit racial discrimination but have nothing to say on the issue of distinctions made between classes of persons identified on non-racial grounds.[140] Identification of and discrimination between groups on the basis of economic disparities and past inequities is in fact the basis of affirmative action policies instituted in the constitutional system of many states.[141] In fact, many of the human rights documents preserve the law that a discrimination could be made between aliens and nationals as far as access to economic activity is concerned.[142] The assertion of rights of establishment has been accomplished through

---

[138] For the new draft, see James Crawford, *International Law Commission's Articles on State Responsibility* (2002).

[139] McDougal, Lasswell and Lung Chu Chen, *Human Rights and World Public Order* (1983), 773.

[140] See also the *Oscar Chinn Case* (1934) PCIJ Series A/B No. 64, which involved a claim by Britain that its national was not given equal treatment with a corporation created by statute by the host state. The claim was rejected. The Court pointed out that equal treatment was required only between entities in the like group. For more on the question of discrimination, see Z. Kronfol, *Protection of Foreign Investment* (1972), 60–1; H. Kurshid, *Equality of Treatment and Trade Discrimination in International Law* (1968), 20.

[141] E.g. the Indian Constitution permits affirmative discrimination in favour of scheduled castes and tribes.

[142] Article 2(3) of the International Covenant on Economic, Social and Cultural Rights justifies the denial of economic rights to aliens, and states that 'developing countries, with due regard to human rights and their national economy, may determine to what extent they would guarantee the economic rights recognised in the present Covenant to non-nationals'. The Convention on the Elimination of All Forms of Racial Discrimination permits discrimination between nationals and non-nationals. Article 1(2) reads: 'This Convention shall not apply to distinctions, exclusions, restrictions or preferences made by a State Party to this Convention between citizens and non-citizens.' See further N. Lerner, *The United Nations Convention on the Elimination of All Forms of Racial Discrimination* (1980), 30: 'The Convention does not interfere in the internal legislation of any State as far as rights of citizens and non-citizens are concerned.'

some investment treaties on a bilateral and regional basis, but the right is not a part of customary international law.[143]

The proposition that there is complete equality between nationals and aliens as to access to economic activity in a host state may be desirable, but at present it does not reflect the position in international law. State practice in both developed and developing countries abounds with examples of discrimination between nationals and aliens as regards ownership of real estate, the practice of the professions, employment in certain spheres and entry into certain businesses.[144] It may well be argued that this position is being encroached upon through treaty law, but it cannot be argued that there is as yet any customary law that requires equal national treatment to be afforded to foreign investors.

Another facet of the argument in seeking to extend the 'noble synthesis' into the area of foreign investment protection is that the right to property is a human right and that this right in the alien is now to be respected so that, where his property is taken over, he must be paid full compensation. The major human rights documents, such as the International Covenant on Civil and Political Rights and the European Convention on Human Rights, do not contain any reference to the right to property. There is a protocol to the European Convention which states it in qualified terms. The case law generated under the provisions on the right to property do not recognise an unqualified right to property. The other human rights conventions which state it do so in qualified terms which recognise the state's right to interfere with property rights in the public interest. In seeking to establish that there is a universal recognition of an unqualified right to property that is basic to make a case, the proponents of the view have scavenged for authority in the most unlikely quarters.[145] The best

---

[143] US bilateral treaties require rights of pre-entry establishment. NAFTA and the ASEAN Framework Agreement on Investment are instances of regional treaties which contain pre-establishment rights. But, they permit wide sectoral exceptions.

[144] See further, B. Sen, *A Diplomat's Handbook of International Law and Practice* (1988), 350, who observes:

> It is now well established that a state may and is free to prohibit or regulate the professional or business activities of an alien even after he is allowed entry into the receiving state. It follows that any professional or business activities carried on by an alien in the receiving state must be in conformity with the local laws, regulations and executive orders as also municipal and other by-laws.

Section 2 of the Declaration on the Elimination of Racial Discrimination clearly permits the making of a distinction between nationals and aliens.

[145] See e.g. R. B. Lillich, 'Duties of States Regarding Civil Rights of Aliens' (1978) 161 *Hague Recueil* 329 at 399–408.

that has been unearthed is a draft prepared by Baroness Elles as Rapporteur to the Sub-Commission on the Prevention of Discrimination and Protection of Minorities and Aliens. The study was directed at the protection of migrant workers, stateless persons and refugees. The definition of 'alien' for the purposes of the study included refugees, stateless persons, those given asylum, migrant workers, workers who had been transported through clandestine trafficking and women transported from their home states for the purpose of prostitution. The report seeks to protect the property rights of such persons. To extrapolate a scheme for the protection of multinational corporations into this effort at the protection of the meagre property of the flotsam of the human race seems illogical. The need to resort to such illogicality is itself an indication of the meagre nature of the support for the extension of the rules of state responsibility for injuries to aliens to the sphere of foreign investment protection. The relevance of any human rights standard is limited. No one seriously argues that human rights to property can be extended to benefit multinational corporations.[146]

Yet, with the onset of neo-liberalism in the 1990s, a property-centred argument has come into vogue. The Lockean concept of property is sought to be universalised. This concept is based on the idea that the protection of property is so central to the organisation of society that it should be protected through the law in absolute terms. In the United States, the argument has constitutional significance. Since the hegemonic power has a tendency to universalise the views it prefers, there will be a definite effort made to ensure that this particular view of the right to property as an unqualified right receives acceptance. There will, however, be difficulties in the way, as the priority of the public interest over private rights of property is generally recognised in regional systems of human rights as well as in other constitutional systems. In US constitutional law, the issue as to when a regulatory taking can be made by the state without payment of compensation remains unsettled. The devising of a test to distinguish between compensable and non-compensable taking of property has eluded most constitutional systems. The attempt to seek solutions for it through US constitutional law which itself has moved through several

---

[146] See K. Hailbronner, 'Foreign Investment Protection in Developing Countries in Public International Law' in T. Oppermann and E. Petersmann (eds.), *Reforming the International Economic Order* (1987), 99 at 105: 'It is doubtful whether humanitarian considerations are relevant in the context of corporate property and foreign investment in general.'

phases will not be successful as different states have different economic priorities and objectives.

3.6. *Damage to property in the course of civil disturbances*

Another area that was being addressed in the case law of the period as well as in the literature was the liability of the host state for damage caused during civil strife or like emergencies that took place in the host states. The volatile nature of the political changes that took place in the Latin American states through insurrections again provided a back-drop for the litigation that took place in relation to such situations. In many cases, damages were claimed for destruction of property by government forces during the quelling of the insurrection. The law was developed largely in the context again of Latin America, though there were cases from outside the region as well.

The starting point of the discussion was that the foreigner must not expect better protection in times of civil or military strife than the citizens of the host state. The assumption was that the foreigner had entered an unstable country voluntarily and must put up with the perilous conditions there. The position that was taken was that the foreigner 'must be held, in going into a foreign country, to have voluntarily assumed the risks as well as the advantages of his residence there'.[147]

Yet, a competing principle or perhaps a large exception to the rule was also emerging, which recognised that, in certain circumstances, there was an affirmative duty to offer protection to the foreign investor in conditions of strife in the country. Two distinct situations were contemplated. The first was where there was destruction during military action by government forces. In these circumstances, there was liability if the action went beyond what was objectively necessary and caused wanton and unnecessary destruction.[148] One has to balance the necessities of the situation under which a military decision has to be made on the spur of the moment and the extent of the destruction caused.

The second situation related to damage caused not by the military forces of the state but by unruly mobs associated with the strife. In some circumstances, these mobs could be associated with the government and hence could be assimilated with the military forces. They could be regarded as extensions of the resources that the government could summon up in

---

[147] *Upton Case* (1903), cited in Ralston, *Law and Procedure of International Tribunals* (1926), 389.
[148] *AAPL* v. *Sri Lanka.*

order to achieve its purpose. In this case, the situation would share the characteristics of the first category. Agency, a key factor in the imposition of state responsibility, is easier to identify where the link between the mob of rioters and the government can be established.[149]

But, where the mob is not so associated with the government of the state, a second rule would apply. This principle was stated in terms of a failure to provide protection when the state knew that there was an imminent danger of such destruction of property by the insurrectionists or by a riotous mob.[150] In these circumstances, there was a duty on the part of the state to provide protection to the foreigner and his property. The standard of diligence is required in these circumstances. The standard would vary as to the intensity of the strife, the resources that could be diverted for the purpose of protection and similar factors. It is obvious that the standards that could be maintained in an ordered society cannot be maintained in a state that is constantly faced with civil disorder. The rule has to be applied with a great deal of sensitivity.

The rules of state responsibility for injuries to aliens which grew up in the context of the causing of injury to the person and property of the alien in a capricious fashion by the host state or the failure to provide adequate protection to alien property developed in the context of Latin American relations. Their universal validity is questionable. Even if they are to be accepted as universally valid, it will be difficult to establish that they extend to the protection of foreign investment. The old rules were made in the context of the taking of real property and physical assets of the foreigner. The modern takings are largely by way of breach of contractual agreements and by the withdrawal of permission to do business. The old law has little to do with takings of property in pursuance of economic programmes. In any event, the law on state responsibility for injuries to aliens that was developed in the Latin American context has been constantly rejected by the Latin American states and subsequently by the African and Asian states so that it is futile to base any arguments on investment protection on principles of state responsibility.

It is for that reason that efforts to resuscitate the notion of denial of justice in recent case law is unfortunate.[151] A denial of justice takes place when

---

[149] The case law on the point generated by the Iran–US Claims Tribunal on this is extensive.

[150] *Sambaggio Case* 10 UNRIAA 534; *Home Missionary Society Case* (1920) 6 UNRIAA 42; C. F. Amerasinghe, *State Responsibility for Injuries to Aliens* (1967), 281–2; Ian Brownlie, *The System of the Law of Nations: State Responsibility* (1986), 162.

[151] Arguments were advanced both in the *ELSI Case* [1989] ICJ Rpts 16 and *Amco* v. *Indonesia* on the basis of a denial of justice. See also *Robert Azinian* v. *Mexico* (1999).

the judicial organs of a state act in an unacceptable manner in the eyes of the world by denying justice to an alien. There is a need for a vigorous rule in this area, but it should not be a rule made to justify property protection in the most extreme of cases.[152] But, to use the rule merely because there has been an administrative interference with property rights is uncalled for. The need for the revival has been largely due to the fact that in most states foreign investment has ceased to be a purely contractual matter and has entered the sphere of public law regulation. Given this transference and given the inadequacy of arguments previously built on notions on contract law to cope with the situation, it has become necessary to address the issue through other means. This accounts for the revival of the notion of denial of justice to be applied in circumstances in which the administrative decisions taken by the host state do not conform to external standards of desirable administration. Quite apart from the difficulties of definition of the concept and the unsettled nature of the scope of the principle of denial of justice, the application of the principle to administrative decision-making is fraught with great difficulties. Standards of desirable administrative practices cannot be imposed by international law on states as much as political philosophies cannot be imposed upon them. It is best to relinquish attempts to build a law on investment protection through notions associated with state responsibility for injuries to aliens and recognise that foreign investment protection is an area distinct from state responsibility for injuries to aliens though it shares some of its features. The better way of constructing the law is through treaties. But, as will be seen, concepts used in treaties refer back to customary international law so that the problem of bridging the gap between the rules of state responsibility and investment protection still remains. A law constructed through alleged custom will be met with the rule that it cannot be binding on persistent objectors. A law bolstered up by general principles, writings of publicists and arbitral awards depends on weak sources and is open to the charge of subjectivity in the selection of sources. The creation of norms of investment protection is best attempted through consensual processes.

There is consciousness among states that the project to build an international law on foreign investment through customary law has been a failure. This accounts for the proliferation of bilateral investment treaties and regional investment treaties. But, these treaties, as will be seen, state

---

[152] This view finds support in the award in *Robert Azinian* v. *Mexico* (1999).

the rules between parties, while still leaving room for adequate manoeu-vrability for control over investments. They cannot create customary international law. The projects to bring about multilateral agreements on investment have been significant failures indicating the variety of view-points that are taken on this issue even among developed states. The law in the area cannot be seen as settled. It contains norms of varying strength. The strength of the norms will also fluctuate with the preferences that are brought about in the ideological, political and economic settings in which they have to operate.

Chapters 5 and 6 below deal with investment treaties. Bilateral invest-ment treaties have grown in numbers, but, contrary to the views of some, despite their numbers, they do not contribute to the creation of custom-ary international law. Rather, they are carefully negotiated compromises between investment protection and sovereign control over foreign invest-ment. Despite the perceived objective of developed states in strengthen-ing the international minimum standard of treatment in these treaties, the treaties do not entirely succeed in achieving that aim at a universal level. They do succeed in ensuring protection as between the parties to the treaties. The attempts at multilateral treaty-making also indicate the entrenched nature of the stances that different states and groupings of states have taken towards this area of the law.

3.7. Validity of conditions on foreign investment

The requirements that are imposed by regulations on foreign invest-ment may now be re-examined in the light of the claims as to rules devised to protect alien interests in customary international law. It will be sufficient to deal with three main types of regulation: (1) those on the screening of foreign investment prior to entry; (2) those requiring local equity participation; and (3) those imposing export quotas. It must be remembered that all these rights may be circumscribed if bilateral, regional or multilateral instruments exist or come about which affect their exercise.

3.7.1. Regulations on screening of foreign investments

The only objection to screening is that it discriminates between foreign investors and nationals. Where there is a pre-entry right of establishment provided by a treaty, screening legislation will not be consistent with the treaty obligations as to national treatment.[153] It is clear that discrimination among aliens before and after entry is permissible, provided it is based on rational economic grounds. The screening of foreign investments and the exclusion of investments that are not beneficial to the host economy rest on such economic grounds and cannot therefore said to be wrongful.[154]

Questions may be raised as to whether foreign investment laws could be designed to keep out nationals of particular states or discriminate between nationals of different states as to entry. The Nigerian decree on foreign investments exempts the application of procedures for screening for nationals of the states of the Organization of African Unity.[155] Nationals of particular states may also be excluded on the basis that there is already a tendency of the economy of the host state to be dominated by the nationals of these states. Unless the discrimination is based on nakedly racial grounds, the discrimination in such instances may, *prima facie*, be lawful as being based on sound economic and political grounds. It is generally accepted that discrimination between categories of persons, where the categorisation is not based on race, is permissible. States also distinguish between their own nationals when it comes to requirements of formation of joint ventures, and mandate that joint ventures be formed in accordance with certain preferential guidelines as to quotas.[156] This, again, is permissible.

A more difficult question relates to the situation where a state discriminates against foreign investors on racial grounds on the basis that foreign investors or nationals belonging to that particular race already dominate the economy of the state and that the influx of more foreign investors of that race would cause resentment within the state and give rise to protests against the investors. For example, Asians were expelled from Uganda and one argument that was made in justification was that they dominated the economy of the state. In Fiji, there is the similar claim that Indians are dominating the economy, though in Fiji the Indians are nationals of Fiji, whereas, in the Ugandan situation, many of the Asians were aliens who were British nationals. In these circumstances, is it possible for a state to enact legislation preventing entry by foreign investors of the particular race or to use screening devices to ensure that they do not

---

[153] Such pre-entry rights of establishment are provided for in US and Canadian bilateral treaties as well as in NAFTA.

[154] In the *FIRA Case*, the GATT compatibility of the Canadian screening legislation was considered and upheld.

[155] Such exemptions given within the context of regional associations are a common feature.

[156] The laws of South Africa and Malaysia contain examples.

enter? The state may be able to justify the exclusion on national security grounds. The presence of the group will lead to protests and instability within the state. There could be economic instability caused if the group of foreign investors were to use their dominance of the economy as a political weapon. The home state of the investors may also use the presence of the investors to exert influence and control over the host state by interfering in its domestic policies. Though these may be justifications, it may be argued that the importance that has come to be attached to the norm against racial discrimination in international relations is such that it must be held to displace such considerations. Yet, there cannot be a blanket rule of such a nature. Much will depend on the exact circumstances of each state's situation. A state should be able to secure its economic independence by ensuring that its foreign investors come from a range of nations. If not, there is a danger that the state could become subject to economic imperialism of one state or of one racial group. Obnoxious though the idea of exclusion on racial grounds would seem, there may be instances where it would be valid. These instances must be carefully limited to those where the state excludes foreign investors on the ground that, if not for such exclusion, there would be dominance of its economy by the citizens of one state or by one racial group. Such a situation, besides causing disquiet internally, could also lead to dependence on an external power, and the latter could utilise this dependence to its advantage.[157] The issue is complicated by the fact that there are two norms of equal cogency at conflict in this situation. One is the norm against racial discrimination and the other is the norm of economic self-determination and independence. How each situation involving such a conflict is to be resolved will depend on the facts of that situation. The argument based on economic self-determination should, however, not be permitted to cloak an obviously racist decision. The strong abhorrence of racial discrimination in modern international relations must be noted.[158] Precedence must always be given to the principle against racial discrimination.

3.7.2. Local equity requirements

These requirements relate both to foreign-owned companies that existed at the time the requirements were introduced as well as to foreign investments that were to enter after the requirements were introduced. In many

---

[157] E.g. as in Iran, before the ouster of the Shah of Iran, where there existed a largely pro-US government, dependent on US business.

[158] Sandra Fredman (ed.), *Discrimination and Human Rights* (2001).

African countries, legislation relating to existing companies was passed first. Such legislation, referred to as indigenisation measures, was intended to ensure that control of existing companies passed into local hands in stages, without causing too much of a disruption to the economy. The indigenisation measures were obviously lawful, as a state has a right to rearrange the structure of its economic life as it pleases. But, there were issues of adequate compensation that could have been raised in connection with such measures. They required the forced divestment of the shares on the local market. Local buyers may not have had adequate capital resources to pay the real value of the shares. In such a case, the foreign company could not have raised the true market value of the shares on the stock exchange. It had no control over the timing of the sale of the shares. Yet, the issues were not raised as the companies were content to stay on and operate as minority partners in the states. Such accommodation on the part of the foreign companies to the altered situation is a feature of the modern foreign investment scene, for withdrawal may mean a loss of access to markets, raw materials and cheap labour and the surrender of existing market advantages to another multinational competitor. This pragmatism is an important factor, which reduces the acrimony in the debate on compensation. A continuing relationship is often more important than monetary compensation in the long-term interests of both the state and the foreign multinational.

Prospective requirements relating to local equity do raise problems of a different kind for international law. Where a corporation enters a state with a commitment progressively to reduce its control by divesting shares to locals, that corporation cannot complain if the host state requires it to abide by its commitments. There can also be few problems relating to the requirement that entry be made with local collaboration. In such instances, there is a voluntary assumption of conditions by the foreign corporation. A state, in pursuance of its sovereignty, is entitled to impose such conditions.

The imposition of conditions relating to the local equity content of the foreign corporation is effected through the public law mechanisms of the host state. Difficult problems will arise when the public authority seeks the termination of the investment on the ground that its conditions have not been adequately met. In these circumstances, the foreign investor would seem to have little safeguard for his interest. Here, the taking or interference with the property would seem to be done in pursuance of regulatory measures of which the foreign investor had sufficient prior knowledge.

A confrontation of this kind occurred in the *ELSI Case*, decided by the International Court of Justice,[159] and in *Amco* v. *Indonesia*, decided by tribunals constituted under the ICSID Convention.[160] In the former case, the state was held to have acted properly, and in the latter case the foreign investor was awarded damages. Yet, the two disputes indicate that the foreign investor's position is one of weakness when a charge of not conforming to requirements made by administrative authorities is brought against him. In these circumstances, the foreign investor seems to have little remedy, if the host state had followed its internal procedures for dealing with the dispute scrupulously and these procedures met generally accepted standards.

In the *ELSI Case*, a US firm had located in Sardinia, a depressed part of Italy. Under Italian law, a foreign company which located in areas which lacked industrialisation was entitled to certain privileges, such as advantages relating government procurement contracts. But, these privileges were not granted to the US company. The company suffered reversals, and the foreign investor wanted to liquidate the company in an orderly fashion. Under the law of the host state, a company which did not possess sufficient capital assets had to be declared bankrupt. When the company announced its plans for an orderly liquidation, the mayor of the city in which it was located temporarily took over administration of the company. His fear was that there would be a loss of employment if the plant was shut down, as contemplated by the company. The Italian courts subsequently held that this requisition by the mayor was unlawful. When the company was finally declared bankrupt and sold, it fetched a price well below the minimum bid that had been set. One question, among other issues, was whether Italy was responsible for the damage caused to the company on the basis that, but for the requisition by the mayor, the investor would have recovered a larger portion of its investment through orderly liquidation. The mayor was a public official who requisitioned the company to ensure that jobs in his city would not be lost and that there would not be industrial strife at the plant. Here, there was an obvious conflict of interest between the mayor whose interest was in the preservation of jobs in his city and the foreign investor whose interest was to recover as much of his initial investment as possible. The International Court of Justice wriggled out of the difficulty by making a factual holding that the company was rushing headlong into bankruptcy at

---

[159] [1989] ICJ Rpts 15.   [160] (1983) 23 ILM 354; (1988) 27 ILM 1281; 1 ICSID Rpts 509.

the time of the requisition and that, therefore, the requisition changed nothing.

It would appear that, if the public authority interfering with an investment acted in a procedurally fair manner and in accordance with the host state's law in applying rules the existence of which were known to the foreign investor, there could be no liability arising in the state. It is, however, unclear whether procedural fairness is a matter of internal law or of external standards.[161] The court was reluctant to find that the mayor had acted in an arbitrary manner, despite the fact that the Italian courts had found illegality in the mayor's conduct. The finding of a denial of justice on the basis of a denial of due process may have been a possibility, but both denial of justice and due process are imprecise notions which the Court has seldom applied. Instead, the Court confined itself to the issue whether there was arbitrary conduct under the relevant treaty between Italy and the United States and found that there was none.

Though the Court was reluctant to use denial of justice as a basis in *ELSI*, in *Amco* v. *Indonesia* an ICSID tribunal awarded damages to the foreign investor on the basis of this doctrine. Here, an issue in dispute was whether the fact that the foreign investor had not capitalised the project in accordance with his commitments to the screening authority justified the termination of the licences required by the foreign investor to operate the project. Such commitments are to be made by the foreign investor prior to entry and the reason for the requirement was to ensure that the foreign investor did bring capital into the state from abroad and did not capitalise the project by raising funds on the local market. There will not be much benefit to the host state by the entry of the investor through capital inflows if he were permitted to raise funds on the local market. The best proof of the fact that there was money brought in from outside under the law was certificates issued by the Bank of Indonesia. It was clear that the foreign investor did not obtain such certificates. On the basis of these facts, the screening authority rescinded the licences that had been granted to the foreign investor to operate in Indonesia. The hotel complex that was being constructed by the investor had earlier been occupied by the Indonesian army, which had some interest in the project because the joint venture partner with whom the foreign investor had fallen out was controlled by an army pension fund.

---

[161] Hamrock, 'The ELSI Case: Toward an International Definition of Arbitrary Conduct' (1992) 27 Texas ILJ 837.

On these facts, the tribunal performed a neat balancing act by holding that damages should be awarded on the basis of denial of justice. The tribunal held that the foreign investor had not been accorded a proper standard of due process. The decision seems unsatisfactory. It would be obvious to any impartial observer that a hearing would have achieved nothing as the foreign investor did not have the certificates from the Bank of Indonesia as to the capitalisation requirements mandated by the law. There was clear evidence that the foreign investor had not capitalised as was required. This gave a right to the public authority to terminate the licences it had given to the foreign investor. On the reasoning of the *ELSI Case*, what was being terminated was an investment in which the investor had rushed headlong into a situation which made the investment ripe for termination. It was only the procedure that was adopted that was irregular. The tribunal focused upon the lack of procedure to find that there was a denial of justice. It is not a step that should have been so lightly taken, for, in modern international law, a finding of a denial of justice is a serious condemnation. The facts in the case did not justify such a condemnation by the tribunal. It is also doubtful whether an arbitral tribunal called upon to decide an investment dispute has sufficient jurisdiction to decide on an issue of state responsibility for denial of justice. This is an issue between the home state of the alien and the host state. Despite the unsatisfactory features of the decision in *Amco v. Indonesia*, it may be inferred from the case that a failure to meet the conditions imposed is a valid ground for interference by the state provided due process standards are met.

Both the disputes and the decisions in them seem to indicate that, as long as standards of procedural fairness had been followed, the termination of an investment in accordance with previously declared law will not give rise to any violation of international law. The finding of denial of justice in the *Amco v. Indonesia* case seems to have been an easy way of solving a tedious dispute that had been around the arbitration scene for a long time, but it is unlikely to provide any satisfaction to the state party which was convinced that it had acted properly. Where measures terminating the investment are taken, the relevant compensation has to be paid. The issue of compensation is dealt with in Chapter 9 below.

3.7.3. Export requirements

The purpose of export requirements has already been explained. They are imposed to ensure that the foreign corporation earns revenue for the host state through exports. Entry is made conditional on the satisfaction of the export requirements. Since they are usually administered by the public authority responsible for the initial entry of the investment, the same problems as to the imposition of sanctions arise as in the non-satisfaction of other requirements for entry. As explained above, as long as minimum standards of procedure have been followed, there could be no violation of international law where the sanctions imposed by the local law, including termination, are taken against the foreign company, subject to the relevant compensation being paid. But, performance requirements, including export requirements, are regarded as trade distortive under the Trade Related Investment Measures (TRIMS) of the WTO and hence their validity under this instrument has to be assessed. Their place in a possible multilateral instrument on investment will also have to be given consideration.

The United States has argued that export controls violate standards of free trade . More specifically, the United States alleges that they violate provisions of the General Agreement on Tariffs and Trade (GATT). Their prohibition through trade instruments is justified on the basis of the same argument. The argument is developed on the following lines:[162]

> Export requirements to the extent that they lead to exports by subsidiaries that would not have occurred in their absence, have effects similar to export subsidies which artificially increase the supply of the affected product in the world markets and displace more efficient home or third country products and exports of the affected product.

The validity of export requirements under GATT were raised in relation to Canadian investment measures under the Canadian Foreign Investment Review Act 1982, which among other things required specific export targets to be indicated when making application for foreign investment entry into Canada. The GATT panel upheld the validity of the requirements under the GATT.[163] But, the United States has continued to press for the reform of this area. As a result, a provision in TRIMS seeks to prohibit export controls.

---

[162] C. N. Ellis, 'Trade Related Investment Measures in the Uruguay Round: The United States Viewpoint' in S. J. Rubin and M. L. Jones (ed.), *Conflict and Resolution in the* US–EC *Trade Relations* (1989). See also C. N. Ellis, 'Foreign Direct Investments and International Capital Flows to Third World Nations: United States Policy Considerations' in C. D. Wallace (ed.), *Foreign Direct Investments in the 1990s* (1990), 1.

[163] Simmonds and Hill, *Law and Practice under GATT* (vol. 3, 1989).

4. Conclusion

It is evident from this chapter that the state has considerable control over foreign investment which arises from its sovereignty. Foreign investment takes place within the state, and it is the prerogative of the state to control it as it pleases. But, that is not a fact that sits easily with the notion of foreign investment as the states of foreign investors as well as foreign investors themselves are considerable bases of power and have an interest in ensuring the protection of foreign investment. Constraints on the power of the state to deal with foreign investments have been progressively built up through customary international law and through treaties. In the course of building such norms of international law, there has been considerable opposition raised by states. These states have, by no means, all been capital-importing states of the developing world. Though in the stage of the formation of customary international law, the world may have been divided into capital-importing developing states and capital-exporting developed states, the division is no longer as clear cut as it was in the past. The United States is the largest importer as well as exporter of capital. It is also the home of the largest and most powerful multinational corporations which export capital around the world. The interests that a state now has to take into account are diverse. It has to protect its national economy and does so on the basis of intense sovereignty-centred notions. It has to further the interests of its multinational corporations and does so by seeking to create internationally valid norms of foreign investment protection. That situation applies to many states, including the larger states of the developing world, like China and India, though internal factors may for the present dictate that they resist international norms. The picture will never remain constant. It is for that reason that it is not correct to speak in terms of a well-established law on foreign investment that is universally acceptable, though the tendency in the law has been to speak in terms of such certainty.

In the diffused world of the present, several ideas and interests interact to shape the law. These ideas and interests constantly fluctuate. In the 1970s and the 1980s, the developing world had a sufficient cohesion, born out of their new release from colonial bondage, to press for new rules on foreign investment. This resulted in the resolutions associated with the New International Economic Order. But, the 1990s witnessed the dismantling of the Soviet Union, the leader of a grouping which had maintained a uniform attitude of hostility to private property. Its existence helped the maintenance of the developing country views which did not by contrast seem as extreme. With the collapse of the Soviet Union, new forces were released. Ideologically, economic liberalism became triumphant. The free market was trumpeted as a panacea to development, and measures for the liberalisation of the movement of capital were set in motion. In this period, the developing world lost its old cohesion. The developing states, short of funds for development, began to scramble for foreign investment, as such investments were the only available funds for development. The World Bank and the International Monetary Fund ensured that funds were conditional on the acceptance of the liberal premises. The law was set on an entirely different course. There was a proliferation of bilateral and regional treaties. There were moves in the OECD to bring about a Multilateral Agreement on Investment (MAI). Upon its failure, there is ongoing effort to transfer the project to the WTO.

But, the picture was to change rapidly. A disenchantment with liberalisation and globalisation set in rapidly. The clashes at Seattle and elsewhere demonstrated that civil society was becoming disenchanted with the idea of profits for large corporations at the cost of global poverty and environmental degradation. The increasing political pressure that these groups applied is beginning to have the effect of diverting the attention of the international law on foreign investment away from the traditional area of investment protection into new areas such as corporate responsibility for environmental degradation and human rights violations. These new issues will have an impact on how the law functions in the future as they are also addressed through norms of international law.

The chapters that follow identify the constraints that have been created successfully or otherwise on the sovereignty of states to deal with foreign investments, which was the subject of this chapter. The following chapter deals with the constraints attempted through customary international law. Chapters 5 and 6 deal with constraints created through bilateral and multilateral treaties on investment.

4

The liability of multinational corporations and home state measures

Unlike in the old law, there is increasing expectation, particularly among developing countries and non-governmental organisations, that home states of multinational corporations should exert control over the activities of their corporate nationals operating overseas. By home country measures, these interest groups mean not only the measures taken to promote the flows of foreign investment into developing countries, but also those that seek to ensure that multinational corporations do not act to the detriment of the host developing states. This chapter concentrates on the latter type of measure.[1] The rationale is that developed states owe a duty of control to the international community and do in fact have the means of legal control over the conduct abroad of multinational corporations. In moral terms, the activities of multinational corporations eventually benefit the home state's economic prosperity. The argument is that it is therefore incumbent on the home state to ensure that these benefits are not secured through injury to other states or to the welfare of the international community as a whole. The early law concentrated only on the protection of foreign investment through the diplomatic intervention of the home state. However, there is now an evolution of the notion that the home state has duties as well as rights in matters relating to foreign investment which require the home state to intervene to ensure that its multinational corporations act in accordance with emerging standards that require their accountability.

This shift in emphasis is due to a variety of factors. First, the international community's accent has been on ensuring that the poorer countries of the world undergo a process of economic development. The instruments fashioned by the developed countries on investment protection

---

[1] Home country measures relating to the promotion of investment flows include the provision of risk insurance, the grant of tax exemptions, the provision of information, etc. They are non-binding in nature, and are unilaterally assumed obligations.

are premised on the notion that investment flows will promote economic development. The objective of economic development underlies all investment treaties and measures. This is confirmed by the fact that the most recent of the documents on the issue of investment in which the international community expressed a policy objective, the Doha Declaration of the Third WTO Ministerial Meeting, stated that the consideration of an investment instrument had to take the development dimension into account. The touchstone by which norms are to be judged concerns whether economic development is in effect promoted by the observance of a particular norm. In that context, it is interesting to note that some developing countries have expressed the view that, if there is to be a WTO instrument on investment, it should contain provisions relating to home country measures to control activities considered harmful to the development of host developing states.[2]

Secondly, there is a new actor in the area – the non-governmental organisation – which wants to have the emphasis shifted from the notion of the protection of multinational corporations to the idea that these corporations owe a duty of good corporate responsibility. The power of the NGOs was demonstrated when they were able to focus international attention on the Multilateral Agreement on Investment. They are presently actively engaged in the debate on whether there should be a WTO instrument on investment. The activities of NGOs have also brought about spectacular litigation strategies that are directed at the recognition of the parent corporation's responsibility for the activities of its subsidiaries in host states.

Thirdly, the issue also arises in the context of bringing about a multilateral code on foreign investment. The discussion has shifted to whether a complete code would require not only the statement of the rights of

---

[2] The paper submitted by China, India, Kenya, Pakistan and Zimbabwe to the WTO Working Group on Investment stated: 'Multinational Enterprises should strictly abide by all domestic laws and regulations in each and every aspect of the economic and social life of the host members in their investment and operational activities. Further, in order to ensure that the foreign investor meets its obligations to the host member, the cooperation of the home member's government is often necessary, as the latter can and should, impose the necessary disciplines on the investors. The home member's government should therefore also undertake obligations, including to ensure that the investor's behaviour and practices are in line with and contribute to the interests and development policies of the host member. It is important that the Working Group addresses the issue of the investors' and home governments' obligations in a balanced manner.' WT/WGTI/W/152 (2003). The document can be accessed on the website of the WTO.

protection of foreign investment that a home state can insist upon for its outgoing foreign investment but the duties and obligations that should accompany such outflows. Thus, the movement in this area has resulted in incremental progress towards the recognition of jurisdiction in the courts of the home states over acts of subsidiaries abroad.

As a result of these developments, a series of duties are coming to be recognised by multinational corporations as well as by their home states. These obligations are dealt with in the first section of this chapter. The chapter then goes on to survey the extent to which the home states of multinational corporations have the power to enforce these obligations and the extent to which there is an obligation to enforce them.

1. Obligations of multinational corporations

While international law has recognised that the assets of multinational corporations could be protected through investment treaties and through customary international law, there has been little movement towards the recognition of the obligations of multinational corporations towards the host states and the communities in which these corporations operate. The fiction that these corporations do not have personality in law has often been used as a reason for the non-development of these rules, though that has not prevented the development of a right in them through treaty for recourse to dispute settlement. The better reason for the absence of obligations may be that firm rules regarding areas in which rules as to obligations may be necessary were areas of recent development in international law. Thus, norms on the area of environmental harm in which there may be a need to impose obligations on multinational corporations are of relatively recent origin in international law. Likewise, the notions of corporate liability for human rights violations have also been slow in evolving. The international rules on bribery have also been slow to evolve. There may be justification in the view that this slow growth was aided by the opposition to the recognition of such liability by corporations which have delayed the formation of binding rules through the formulation of soft law prescriptions.[3]

The identification of the areas of activities in which obligations of multinational corporations could arise has been largely effected through

---

[3] The area of misconduct is full of voluntary codes of conduct.

international instruments. Because of the intense division as to whether these obligations should be enforced against multinational corporations, many of the instruments were aborted and the few that did come about contain soft law prescriptions. The same institutions which argued for multilateral codes on investment protection creating rights in multinational corporations were content with calls for voluntary codes of conduct for multinational corporations.[4] Developing countries on the other hand have consistently called for the recognition of obligations of multinational corporations. The comprehensive statement of the obligations belong to the period in which there was a certain hostility to multinational corporations, and intense study of their conduct in developing states was undertaken by international institutions and other bodies. These concerns were articulated largely in the 1970s and the early 1980s and may be associated with the general trend among developing countries to change the structure of the international law on the area through the New International Economic Order. The United Nations Commission on Transnational Corporations[5] was instrumental in a large number of studies on the issue, and attempted a binding code of conduct on transnational corporations. Because of divisions among the member states, the code remained in draft form only.[6]

Despite its lack of eventual success, the draft code identified the areas in which the activities of multinational corporations could produce harmful effects on host states. Its main emphasis was on development concerns. The use of restrictive business practices and other like practices attracted considerable attention. Involvement in local political disputes and activities so as to benefit groups favourable to foreign business was another issue that was addressed. The avoidance of bribery and other corrupt practices was advocated. There were references to consumer protection and environmental protection. With the decline of the attitude of hostility to foreign investment beginning in the mid-1980s, the efforts to draft such a code were given up and the instruments that came to be made in profusion emphasised investment protection rather than the control of the activities of multinational corporations. The sweep of economic

[4] The OECD, which wanted a multilateral agreement on investment, had drafted a voluntary code of conduct for multinational corporations.
[5] The Commission has since been absorbed into the UNCTAD.
[6] In fact, the different groupings of states had their own drafts. The draft is more fully considered in Chapter 6 below.

liberalism in the 1990s accelerated this tendency. The fervour for controlling multinational corporations became dormant and the need to attract them became urgent. There were soft prescriptions made in this period, such as the recognition of the norm of non-interference in domestic politics,[7] but no hard rules emerged, except in the field of bribery.

During this period, dramatic incidents that illustrated the possibility of the adverse impact of foreign investment on host states occurred. Of them, the most horrendous was the disaster in Bhopal, India, where a gas leak at a plant belonging to Union Carbide, a US multinational corporation, led to a major calamity. The many thousands affected still remain uncompensated. There were other incidents involving environmental degradation and human rights violations which came to light and again focused attention on the issue of the obligations of multinational corporations.[8]

The vigorous pursuit of these concerns regarding the deleterious activities of multinational corporations in the developing world would not have occurred were it not for the rise of non-governmental organisations concerned with human rights, the environment and development as active players on the international scene.[9] Such developments highlight the fact that non-governmental organisations, as well as their targets, the

---

[7] APEC's Non-Bonding Investment Principles (1994) require foreign investments 'to abide by the host economy's laws, regulations, administrative guidelines and policies'.

[8] Starting with Bhopal, there has been an increasing number of major situations which have been recorded in the literature. For other situations, see Human Rights Watch, *The Price of Oil: Corporate Responsibility and Human Rights Violations in Nigeria's Oil Producing Communities* (1999). The litigation against Unocal relating to its operation in Myanmar (Burma) has been dealt with in other chapters. There is concern with the operations of Freeport-McMoran in Irian Jaya. See also George S. Akpan, 'Transnational Environmental Litigation and Multinational Corporations: A Study of the Ok Tedi Case' (paper published by the Centre for Energy, Petroleum and Mineral Law, University of Dundee, Scotland, CP 11/98, 1998) and H. M. Osofsky, 'Environmental Human Rights under the Alien Tort Statute: Redress for Indigenous Victims of Multinational Corporations' (1997) 20 *Suffolk Transnational Law Review* 335. George Akpan's PhD thesis at the National University of Singapore (2003) contains surveys of the field. The issue is raised in F. van Hoof, 'International Human Rights Obligations for Companies and Domestic Courts: An Unlikely Combination?' in M. Castermans-Holleman, F. van Hoof and J. Smith (eds.), *The Role of the Nation State in the 21st Century: Essays in Honour of Peter Baehr* (1998), 47. See also Menno Kaminga and Saman Zia Zarifi (eds.), *Liability of Multinational Corporations under International Law* (2000).

[9] There were other institutions, such as UNCTAD, which had commenced work on the issue. But, at the practical level, the work of the NGOs accelerated concern with the liability of multinational corporations.

multinational organisations, have the capacity to affect the course of events in this area of international law.[10] Most of the obligations that have been created require action by the home states of the multinational corporations or their courts and, for that reason, may be considered under the heading of home state measures and obligations. The creation of responsibility in the multinational corporation is not in itself a home state measure, but, if such responsibility has to be enforced through the intermediacy of the home state's courts, then it would be fair to characterise such responsibility as involving a home state measure. It is necessary to identify these obligations.

1.1. The obligation not to interfere in domestic politics

This is an obligation that arose from the fear that multinational corporations act in host states in such a manner as to ensure that governments or groups favourable to foreign business retain power. Often, the charge is made that the multinational corporation is a proxy on behalf of the home state to ensure that there is a pliant government or that the home state encourages interference to ensure that pro-business governments are elected. The often cited instance is the overthrow of the government of Allende in Chile, which had been democratically elected, by a coup engineered, it is alleged, by foreign business groups with the covert support of a foreign government.

Many instruments now include a prohibition on the involvement of multinational corporations in the politics of the host state. The statements contained in them are usually soft law proscriptions. But, the issue does arise in modern law as to whether there is more direct responsibility in circumstances in which there is involvement of a multinational corporation or home state officers for effecting coups or bringing about changes in the host states' governments. Such changes would favour the multinational corporation's continued activity or favour the home state's policies and goals. The movement towards the direct personal responsibility of the corporation's officers for such activity is yet to be fully explored.[11] Whether there is a direct obligation on the home state to ensure that

---

[10] Their impact on international relations has been studied in various works. See e.g. Robert O'Brien (ed.), *Contesting Global Governance: Multilateral Economic Institutions and Global Social Movements* (2000); Rodney Hall and Thomas Biersteker (eds.), *The Emergence of Private Authority in Global Governance* (2002).

[11] Since the *Pinochet* case, there has been speculation as to the extent of liability for engineering changes of foreign governments.

no regime changes are effected will also remain a matter that will be raised and debated.[12]

1.2. Obligations relating to human rights

There is increasing literature on the obligation of the multinational corporation to abide by human rights standards in the course of its activities in the host state.[13] The obligation includes the duty not to support a regime which abuses human rights in the host state, particularly in circumstances in which such abuse works to the benefit of the foreign investment. The obvious situation relates to labour standards which are maintained to ensure that there is a ready and servile supply of cheap labour to the foreign multinational corporation. The activity in this area by the International Labour Organization has been effective in bringing about instruments which address the issue of adequate safeguards to protect workers from abuse by multinational corporations.[14] More meaningful are the techniques in the area of human rights that have brought about sanctions against abusive practices against both workers as well as people who are affected by the activities of multinational corporations.

---

[12] The situation arose in the Iraq war in 2003, which was about regime change. One argument was that the regime change was effected not because of the threat posed by the government of Iraq but the need to ensure the supplies of oil from Iraq, thus giving a business motive to the war. The extent to which regime changes are permissible for business and investment reasons is raised by the Iraq situation.

[13] On the increasing literature on human rights concerns with the operations of multinational corporations, see M. Lippmann, 'Multinational Corporations and Human Rights' in G. W. Shepaher and V. Nanda (eds.), *Human Rights and Third World Development* (1985); B. A. Frey, 'The Legal and Ethical Responsibilities of Transnational Corporations in the Protection of International Human Rights' (1997) 6 *Minnesota of Journal of Global Trade* 105; and see further D. Weissbrodt and M. Hoffman, 'The Global Economy and Human Rights: A Selective Bibliography' (1997) 6 *Minnesota Journal of Global Trade* 189; M. A. Geer, 'Foreigners in Their Own Land: Cultural Land and Transnational Corporations – Emergent International Rights and Wrongs' (1998) 38 *Virginia Journal of International Law* 331. For a denial of a linkage between human rights violations and multinational corporations, see W. H. Meyer, 'Human Rights and MNCs: Theory Versus Quantitative Analysis' (1996) 18 *Human Rights Quarterly* 368. A survey of the subject may be found in M. K. Addo (ed.), *Human Rights Standard and the Responsibility of Transnational Corporations* (1999); and Nicola Jagers, *Corporate Human Rights Obligations: In Search of Accountability* (2002).

[14] The issue whether such labour standards should form a part of a multilateral code on investments has also been raised. Lance Compa, 'The Multilateral Agreement on Investment and International Labor Rights: A Failed Connection' (1998) 31 Cornell ILJ 683. The draft OECD code recognised the existence of core labour rights.

The direct techniques of liability have been possible in US law because of the existence of the Alien Tort Claims Act, an old statute which makes any act considered a tort in international law actionable in US courts. There has been an explosive burst of litigation against multinational corporations on the basis of this legislation. Though none has so far been successful, the US courts have not yet denied jurisdiction on the ground that the acts complained of were extraterritorial. Though the pleas of sovereign immunity will protect the host state itself from complicity in human rights violations, the multinational corporation which is complicit in the state conduct could be sued for violations of human rights in the US courts. A series of cases has resulted. It is possible to deal only with the principal cases in this chapter, but they are considered fully in the extensive literature that has been generated as a result of the litigation.[15]

The litigation involving *Doe* v. *Unocal*[16] is representative. Here, the allegation in a class action was that Unocal, a US multinational corporation, had participated actively or passively in the torture, forced labour and killings of aboriginal people by Burmese military agents in the land through which the gas pipeline it was constructing for the Burmese government passed. The Burmese government was able to plead sovereign immunity. The focus shifted to the liability of the multinational corporation for being a knowing participant in the alleged activity. This was the theory of litigation in several other cases as well. In all these cases, brought under the Alien Tort Claims Act, the courts have held that there is a basis for jurisdiction though in none of them have they as yet gone on to hold that there could be liability. The link to the parent company in all these situations is that the parent company exercised managerial control and hence had engaged liability for the acts of the subsidiary in the host state in which the human rights violations were being committed. The existence of the parent company within the jurisdiction of the US courts enabled the exercise of personal jurisdiction of the courts over the parent corporations. The Alien Tort Claims Act helps in establishing such jurisdiction but it is not indispensable to the pursuing of the strategy behind

---

[15] Steven Ratner, 'Corporations and Human Rights: A Theory of Legal Responsibility' (2001) 111 Yale LJ 443.

[16] 963 F Supp 660 (1997) (CD Cal); there is an extensive list of cases in which the issue has been considered. *Saro-Wiwa* v. *Shell*, 226 F 3d 88 (2000) (2nd Cir.); *Beanal* v. *Freeport-McMoran*, 969 F Supp 362 (1997) (ED La). The Bush administration does not favour such litigation and has entered *amicus* briefs against such suits. For consideration of these cases, see M. Sornarajah, *The Settlement of Foreign Investment Disputes* (2000); and Nicola Jagers, *Corporate Human Rights Obligations: In Search of Accountability* (2002), 183–96.

such litigation. The corporate structure and the corporate control are important to jurisdiction. The moral justification is provided by the fact that the parent corporation benefits from the misdeeds of its subsidiaries in host states and should therefore shoulder the responsibility for these misdeeds.[17]

In another line of cases involving the association of multinational corporations with past crimes, there is an evident trend towards liability. Thus, the claims of Jewish plaintiffs against IBM and other corporations is based on the allegation that these corporations had helped the Nazi government through furnishing technology and other forms of assistance, during the Holocaust in Germany. Many other corporations such as banks benefited from the Holocaust and are subject to claims on that basis. The litigation strategies that are being formulated in these different strands of cases will coalesce to ensure that there will be jurisdiction and liability in parent corporations in respect of human rights abuses which are committed in other states. The line of cases which establish universal jurisdiction over gross human rights violations such as torture and genocide will enhance the acceptance of such jurisdiction over the parent corporation.[18]

These developments are not confined to the United States. The law in England has recognised jurisdiction in the parent company in respect of asbestos-related disease in a worker occurring in the Rhodesian operations of a subsidiary.[19] There is a similar decision recognising parent company liability in Australia.[20] Dutch cases also seem to be moving towards the recognition of liability.[21] The development of the law does not seem to be based on the existence of any legislation such as the Alien Tort Claims Act but rather on the basis of the need to impose control over

---

[17] Beth Stephens, 'The Amorality of Profit: Transnational Corporations and Human Rights' (2002) 20 Berkeley JIL 45.

[18] Beginning with *Peña-Irala* v. *Filartiga*, 630 F 2d 876 (1980) (2nd Cir.), a string of cases in the United States has acknowledged that universal jurisdiction exists over gross human rights violations. These include, principally, torture and genocide. The *Pinochet* case [1999] 2 WLR 827 adds to the impetus of this line of cases. See, in particular, the judgment of Lord Millett, who argued for universal jurisdiction in situations of torture, even in the absence of any law incorporating conventional norms prohibiting torture in the domestic law. See also A. Bianchi, 'Immunity Versus Human Rights: The Pinochet Case' (1999) 10 EJIL 237.

[19] *Cape* v. *Lubbe* [2001] 1 WLR 1545.   [20] *Dagi* v. *BHP* [1997] 1 VR 428.

[21] Gerrit Betlem, 'Transnational Litigation Against Multinational Corporations in Dutch Courts' in Menno Kaminga and Saman Zia Zarifi (eds.), *Liability of Multinational Corporations under International Law* (2000), 283. The author suggests that the issue of jurisdiction would be easier in civil law jurisdictions.

the activities of the subsidiary through the parent corporation and on the
moral liability of the parent for not exercising sufficient control over the
subsidiary.

But, the efforts to impose liability on the parent or the assumption of
jurisdiction over the multinational corporation on the basis of presence
within jurisdiction will be stoutly resisted by multinational corporations.
Courts have also wavered and have usually withdrawn from the brink of
imposing liability by finding a want of jurisdiction. The issue is treated
as non-justiciable on the basis that finding jurisdiction over corporations
on the basis of mere presence may jeopardise foreign policy interests.[22]
Powerful companies, it has been suggested, may seek the assistance of
the state to invoke such doctrines relating to justiciability in order to
escape scrutiny.[23] But, countering these developments are those that seek
to expand the scope of universal jurisdiction over gross human rights violations such as torture, mass rape and genocide. Where there is complicity
in the multinational corporations in such crimes, credibility will be lost
if courts permit the argument that national interests countervail the need
to permit the establishment of liability over the offending entities. The
general movements in the field of international criminal law may also
come to affect this area in the future.[24]

There are soft law prescriptions relating to the obligation of multinational corporations to respect human rights. But, these prescriptions are
not seen as having much effect and are often smokescreens to show that
some progress is being made in the direction of dealing with the issues.
The bringing about of law with sufficient teeth to deal with these issues

---

[22] Thus, jurisdiction was refused in *Sarei* v. *Rio Tinto*, 221 F Supp 2d 1116 (CD Cal. 2002).

[23] There is litigation in the US implicating ExxonMobil in the human rights violations during the ongoing Aceh separatist rebellion. The judge sought an opinion from the State Department of the United States which, while acknowledging concern with human rights violations, nevertheless stated that the litigation would affect US interests, including interests in the war on terrorism. The Indonesian ambassador indicated that Indonesia will not accept extraterritorial jurisdiction in respect of events taking place entirely in Indonesia. A similar technique has been employed in the litigation against Shell in the Saro-Wiwa litigation. *Saro-Wiwa* v. *Royal Dutch Shell*, 226 F 3d 88 (2000) (2nd Cir.). For the view that such litigation has been dented by current concerns for national security and terrorism, see Melody Saint-Saens and Amy Bann, 'Using National Security to Undermine Corporate Accountability Litigation' (2003) 12 *University of Miami International and Comparative Law Review* 39.

[24] See further, Andrew Clapham, 'The Question of Jurisdiction under International Criminal Law over Legal Persons' in Menno Kaminga and Saman Zia Zarifi (eds.), *Liability of Multinational Corporations under International Law* (2000), 139.

is what is relevant. It would appear that the law is well set on moving in this direction.

1.3. Liability for violations of environmental norms

The movements in human rights have been paralleled in the area of environmental protection. Again, soft law prescriptions exist but are found to be wanting. As in the case of human rights, this too is an area in which non-governmental organisations have been active and have sought to bring about strategies that would ensure that there is liability created in the parent corporations in the home state. The Bhopal litigation that arose out of the gas leak at the Union Carbide factory in Bhopal, India, resulted in failure, but, since then, there have been movements in doctrines that were associated with the case which indicate that there is a developing trend towards the recognition of liability for environmental harm caused by subsidiaries. The basis of the refusal of the courts in the Bhopal litigation to entertain the suit against the parent company was the *forum non conveniens* doctrine which itself has undergone sufficient change so as to accommodate future litigation along the lines that were used in the Bhopal situation.

The focus of the literature has been largely on whether controls instituted by the host state on environmental grounds can be regarded as takings which are compensable.[25] This is an issue that is considered later in this work. At this stage, the question must be raised as to whether, assuming they are takings, the existence of liability for environmental harm will reduce the amount of the compensation payable or even require that compensation in excess of the value of the taking be paid by the multinational corporation where the harm is severe. Certainly, if environmental liability exists, then obviously both eventualities are possible. Initially, these are matters for local tribunals to settle. This factor raises the issue as to whether environmental takings, initially at least, are matters to be considered by arbitral tribunals. Where there is no taking of property

---

[25] J. Martin Wagner, 'International Investment, Expropriation and Environmental Protection' (1999) 29 Golden Gate ULR 465; Thomas Walde and Abe Kolko, 'Environmental Regulation, Investment Protection and Regulatory Taking in International Law' (2001) 50 ICLQ 811; for a general survey, see Gaetan Verhoosel, 'Foreign Direct Investment and Legal Constraints on Domestic Environmental Policies: Striking a Reasonable Balance Between Stability and Change' (1998) 29 *Law and Policy in International Business* 451; Michael Anderson, 'Transnational Corporations and Environmental Damage: Is Tort Law the Answer?' (2002) 41 Washburn LJ 399.

involved, the issue of the liability of the multinational corporation for the environmental harm arises.

The strategy of investors has been to negate environmental laws through stabilisation clauses in the contract which seek to freeze such controls as at the time of entry and exclude the application of later improvements to environmental standards to the investment. The stabilisation clause being a contractual device cannot fetter the legislative sovereignty of the state from extending its control over the investment and ensuring that later standards are applied to the investment. The liability of the foreign investor for environmental harm cannot be excluded by contractual means. The issue for the present, however, is the extent of the obligation of the home state to ensure that its multinational corporations comply with environmental standards in the host states, particularly if these standards are in accordance with the emerging standards of international environmental law.[26] The contention that is advanced here is that, in circumstances in which the environmental harm is prohibited both by the host state's law and by international environmental law, there arises a duty on the part of the home state to ensure that there is compliance by its corporate national making the foreign investment. The duty exists prior to the making of the investment to ensure that the multinational corporation does not take the investment abroad. If it has, the duty continues to ensure that no faulty use of that technology is made or to warn the host state of the potential for harm in the use of the technology. As argued below, there is an obligation on the part of the home state to ensure conformity by its corporate nationals with international law standards wherever the harmful act takes place. The home state, through the link of nationality, has the ability to exercise such control and hence has an obligation to use its powers to ensure compliance.

There is a duty on the part of all states to ensure compliance with standards that are prescribed either in international treaties or in customary international law relating to environmental protection. Home states of multinational corporations have the power of control over these corporations to ensure that they conduct themselves in accordance with the standards in the international law on the environment.[27] There is

---

[26] On the development of international environmental law, see Patricia Birnie and Anthony Boyle, *International Law and the Environment* (2002).

[27] There are loose reporting requirements imposed by home country legislation requiring that the environmental standards employed be indicated, but they are confined to activities in the home state. Efforts are being made to extend their scope to activities in other states. Halina Ward, 'Legal Issues in Corporate Citizenship' (report prepared for the Swedish Partnership for Global Responsibility, 2003), 4.

therefore a duty on the part of the home state to ensure that this is done. The argument that there is state responsibility for failure to do so will be developed in a later section of this chapter.

As in the case of human rights, there has also been an increase in the litigation before the domestic courts of home states alleging violation of environmental standards. The Bhopal litigation was unsuccessful because of the stringent application of the *forum non conveniens* doctrine. But, with new trends resulting in a more liberal application of the doctrine in various jurisdictions, it has become possible to contemplate the imposition of liability on parent corporations for environmental harm that had been caused in host states. These trends will accelerate, giving rise to the establishment of firm principles of liability of parent corporations for environmental harm caused by their subsidiaries.

1.4. The obligation to promote economic development

Whether there is an international law of development or not, the instruments on investment are premised on the assumption that foreign investment promotes the economic development of the states into which they flow. All bilateral investment treaties and regional treaties on investment contain in their prefatory statements that such development takes place as a result of investment flows. It may be implied from this that multinational corporations which take investments into host states should promote economic development or, at the least, do not conduct themselves in such a manner as to deter such development. If there is clear evidence that a multinational corporation had deterred development, there is a possible argument to be made that the rules of investment protection are not applicable to that investment. After all, all investment instruments insist that economic development is the objective of foreign investment. There is, as a result, an implied obligation on the part of the home state to ensure that its corporate nationals, entering a treaty partner's territory, do not act in such a manner as to harm the economic development of the host state. These may include the avoidance of restrictive business practices and corrupt practices.[28] The idea is encapsulated in the notion of good corporate citizenship.[29]

---

[28] Corrupt practices such as bribery are covered by non-binding codes. The effort to draft a code on restrictive business practices that harm development was made by UNCTAD but met with developed country opposition.

[29] On this, see UNCTAD, *World Investment Report, 2003*, 164–6.

2. Extraterritorial control by home states

The subject of extraterritorial control is studied usually from the point of view of US law, as such control is largely practised by the United States. It is fitting for another reason, as the United States is the home of the largest number as well as of the most powerful multinational corporations. Though other states, in varying degrees, exercise extraterritorial jurisdiction, no state does so as extensively as the United States does. Most of the practice of the United States has been to extend its control through legislation or judicial decisions over matters taking place outside the United States but having an impact within its jurisdiction.[30] In some areas, the extraterritorial legislation of the United States has been influenced by nakedly political objectives.

The most studied instance outside criminal enforcement is the extent to which the United States has arrogated to itself the extraterritorial power to enforce its antitrust laws. In 1945, in the *Alcoa Case*,[31] Judge Learned Hand changed the pre-existing view that the Sherman Act, the principal antitrust legislation in the United States, applied only within the territorial limits of the United States. He announced that a conspiracy, made entirely outside the United States, not to export aluminium into the United States so that the monopoly prices fixed by Alcoa could be continued after the expiration of the lawful monopoly obtained through patents, was a violation of the Sherman Act. If the effects of the conspiracy were felt within the United States, the US courts had jurisdiction over such a conspiracy. As long as the conspirators intended or foresaw the effects on US markets, the jurisdictional test was satisfied. The effects rule as to jurisdiction has been followed ever since, despite the fact that it has brought the United States into conflict with other states, many of which have enacted legislation to counter its effects. Unhindered, the US Supreme Court has affirmed the jurisdictional test in *Alcoa* in *Hartford Fire Insurance* v. *California*.[32] These measures do not affect US companies alone but companies belonging to other states as well. But, they indicate that, like Alcoa, which was a US company that had effected the conspiracy through its Canadian subsidiary, it is possible to control US corporations in their activities abroad through the exercise of extraterritorial jurisdiction. It shows that the United States

---

[30] In criminal matters, such extraterritorial legislation is widely employed by most states in common with the United States. But, it is the employment of such legislation in the economic sphere that has brought the United States into conflict with other states.

[31] *US* v. *Aluminium Co. of America (Alcoa)*, 148 F 2d 416 (2nd Cir., 1945)

[32] *Hartford Fire Insurance Co.* v. *California*, 509 US 764 (1993).

has asserted such powers and is not in any way lacking in the power to control the activities of the subsidiaries of its multinational corporations.

There are other areas in which extraterritorial enforcement has been attempted through legislative and executive measures. These include legislation on export controls which prevents not only US parent companies but also their subsidiaries operating abroad from supplying goods to states considered enemies. The use of that power in connection with the construction of the Siberian gas pipeline, to show displeasure towards the Soviet Union for its invasion of Afghanistan, was widely disapproved of by European states.[33] Likewise, there were freezes of the bank accounts of Iran and Libya in US banks operating overseas. More recently, the Helms–Burton Act sought to prevent companies of third states from trading with Cuba, and imposed sanctions against such trade on companies which do trade. The Liberty and Democracy Act sought to do the same regarding companies trading with Libya and Iran. The assumption of such wide and contested bases of jurisdiction has become common in US law. With such wide powers, it would not be credible to argue that the United States, if so mindful, can control the activities of its multinational corporations in host developing states in such a way as not to harm development or environmental interests.

The absence of sufficient standards of corporate governance has become evident in recent times in the United States. The number of recent corporate scandals involving misreporting of accounts and tax frauds by corporations indicate the seriousness of the lack of corporate standards. The repetition of such practices in developing countries could cause the development of their economies great harm. A reason exists to require that the home states of multinational corporations do exercise their undoubted powers to control the activities of their multinational corporations abroad. While the United States and other home states of multinational corporations have done much to emphasise the protection of the investments of multinational corporations, they have done little to ensure that these corporations do not harm the development objectives of the poorer states. Some states have argued that there is in fact an obligation in the home states of multinational corporations to ensure that these corporations do not harm the development objectives of the host states. There seems to be some basis for this argument. At the least, it can be argued that the right of diplomatic protection of these corporations is

---

[33] Vaughan Lowe, 'International Law Issues Arising from the Pipeline Dispute: The British Position' (1984) 27 GYIL 54.

conditional on the multinational corporations conducting themselves in a manner that accords with internationally recognised practices of good corporate citizenship. It can further be argued that there is, as a matter of state responsibility, an obligation on the part of home states to ensure that the subsidiaries of their multinational corporations conduct themselves in a manner that accords with the development objectives of the host states. This obligation involves the prevention of multinational corporations leaving their home states to set up hazardous industries abroad. If they have already set up such industries, it involves the prevention of continued operations through whatever means of control are available. If harm has occurred in a home state, it involves having sufficient laws and providing sufficient means of access to courts to establish the liability of the parent corporation. These may be considered propositions that require further examination.

2.1. State responsibility of home states for failure to control multinational corporations

This section seeks to establish the difficult proposition that a home state of a multinational corporation has a responsibility to ensure that its corporate nationals do not act to the detriment of their host states while abroad. That duty is easier to establish in the case of nationals, but its extension to corporate nationals is more problematic. Yet, the evolving policy objective, at least of some states, is to argue that there should be an obligation on the home state to ensure that there is no deviation in behaviour from development and other objectives that a host state has set for itself, particularly if those objectives coincide with the objectives of the international community. This section tests that proposition, largely in the context of the obligation to observe human rights standards. It begins with a recapitulation of the rules on state responsibility.

2.2. The existing rules on state responsibility

The right to protect nationals abroad, including (indeed, especially) corporate nationals, has been the focus of attention in the literature on international law on state responsibility.[34] It has not focused on the protection

---

[34] Despite the efforts of the International Law Commission to shift the focus to other areas, much of the law on state responsibility developed in the context of alien protection. Leading statements of the law on state responsibility for injuries to aliens can be found in C. F. Amerasinghe, *State Responsibility for Injuries to Aliens* (1965); and R. B. Lillich,

of the nationals of the host state from the abuse of its power by the multinational corporation. This gap has existed in spite of the fact that, in historical terms, the need for protection in the latter situation was more evident. The British and Dutch East India Companies and their likes plundered and pillaged the natives of Asia and Africa with reckless abandon. The native people of Latin America, Australia and elsewhere were brought close to extinction so that their lands could be utilised for mining and other purposes by foreign investors. But, international law, which the European states fashioned, was more concerned with the protection of the interests of these corporations and foreign investment interests than with the protection of their victims. An elaborate structure of rules relating to mediate injuries permitting states to espouse the claims of the foreign investors and requiring the payment of prompt and full compensation was progressively built up.[35]

There is of course a power-based explanation for this situation.[36] The powerful states fashioned rules in order to ensure the protection of the assets of multinational corporations and expatriate plantation owners in the weaker states of the world. No inquiry was made into the issue of whether the exercise of this protection should be conditional on the conduct of the foreign citizen or corporation in the host state. An instructive case for purposes of illustration is the *Schufeldt Claim*.[37] Here, the foreigner had extracted chicle[38] in Guatemala using injurious techniques of

---

International Law of State Responsibility (1983). The earlier drafts on state responsibility prepared by Garcia-Amador concentrated on alien protection which was and is a divisive subject in international law. See F. V. Garcia-Amador *Changing Law of International Claims* (1984).

[35] Its classic statement is in the *Mavrommatis Palestine Concessions Case* (1924) PCIJ Series A, No. 2, 12. The Court said: 'By taking up the case of one of its subjects and by resorting to diplomatic action or international judicial proceedings on his behalf, a State is in reality asserting its own rights – its right to ensure, in the person of its subjects, respect for the rules of international law.' The converse of this is that a developing state should be able to assert its right of protection of its nationals when an alien causes damage in its state and its nationals are not provided relief in the home state of the alien which has his assets and to which he has repatriated the profits of his operations in the host state.

[36] The role of power in rule formation in international law is coming to be studied in recent times. The work of developing country international lawyers in this area predates the new inquiries that are being made. R. P. Anand, *International Law and Developing Countries* (1987); J. T. Gathii, 'International Law and Eurocentricity' (1998) 9 EJIL 184; and M. Sornarajah, 'Power and Justice in International Law' (1997) 1 *Singapore Journal of International and Comparative Law* 28.

[37] (1930) UNRIAA 1079; (1930) 24 AJIL 799.

[38] Chicle is defined in the *Oxford English Dictionary* as 'a gum-like substance obtained from the bully tree (*Mimusops Globosa*) largely used in the United States for the manufacture of chewing gum'.

bleeding the trees. The host state took the position that the trees would have been destroyed if the techniques were continued. The measure taken was for the protection of the industry. The host state advanced this as a reason for the termination of the concession agreement to extract chicle. When the matter went to inter-state arbitration between Guatemala and the United States, the damage caused by the use of injurious techniques was disregarded even in the calculation of damages. Instead, the arbitrator granted damages, among other things, with touching solicitude, for the 'anxiety of mind' caused to the alien. There was much concern for the comfort of the foreign investor, none for the host state or its people. However, such instances of unconcern for the interests of the developing host state led to this power-based notion of state responsibility being resisted by the developing states in several ways. As a result, there has been a significant erosion of the norms contended for by the developed states.[39] Yet, the idea of the responsibility of the multinational corporation or its home state for the damage it may cause to the host state or its people has yet to be fully explored.[40]

It may be useful to reflect on the possibilities within current international law with some idea of how international law looked in times past. Prior to the ascendancy of the power-based notion of responsibility, it would have been easier to establish that there was a duty to ensure that a national did not act to the detriment of the host state whilst abroad. The right of protection of nationals abroad was conditional on the good conduct of the national.[41] There was a forfeiture of protection where a national engages in censurable conduct abroad. Generally, states recognised this by not interfering in support of a citizen who had done wrong whilst abroad.[42] This was a significant acknowledgment of a

---

[39] In the area of foreign investment, many of the norms advanced by the developed states were dented by the forceful articulation of counter-norms by the developing states

[40] This is not to say that this has not been explored to some extent in the evolving responses to global environmental problems. See, for example, the Basel and Bamako treaties on the transfer of hazardous wastes. Yet, the treatment of state responsibility in the literature seldom addresses anything but conventional issues of state responsibility of the *Trail Smelter* variety. See e.g. K. Zemanek, 'State Responsibility and Liability' in W. Lang, H. Neuhold and K. Zemanek (eds.), *Environmental Protection and International Law* (1991), 187.

[41] The older cases are discussed in E. M. Borchard, *The Diplomatic Protection of Citizens Abroad* (Kraus Reprint Co., 1970; original edition, 1915), 718–20.

[42] Thus in the *Pelletier Claim* (1887), discussed in Borchard, *Diplomatic Protection*, 717, the United States refused to espouse the claim of a man shown to have been guilty of slave trading in Haitian waters. Slavery is subject to universal jurisdiction, as is torture. The refusal of diplomatic protection and the trial of the national for the offence may be

link between state responsibility and the conduct of the foreign national, but was there an *active duty* to prevent the nationals from engaging in censurable behaviour? There is indeed authority for the view in older international law that a state becomes responsible to the state which is harmed if the former state was aware of the intention of the national to commit injurious acts against another state and does not prevent him from doing so. So, too, there was a duty on the part of the state to punish a national who committed a crime whilst abroad or to hand him over for punishment. Failure to do so amounted to a tacit approval of his conduct which triggered *ex post facto* responsibility of the state. Jimenez de Arechega and Tanzi stated the position thus:

> The State which becomes aware that an individual intends to commit a crime against another state or one of its nationals, and does not prevent it or the state which extends protection to the offender by refusing to extradite or punish him gives tacit approval to his act. The State thus becomes an accomplice in his crime and establishes a link of solidarity with him: from such relationship the responsibility of the State arises.[43]

Although the Arechaga and Tanzi statement is made on reliance of Grotius, there is other, more positivistic authority which also supports their argument. For example, the United States argued for such a rule in the well-known *Alabama Claim*, in which it successfully claimed compensation in respect of a confederate warship built in Britain.[44] There are also a considerable number of older arbitral awards which recognise similar claims based on the responsibility of a state for not being diligent in controlling the acts of its nationals abroad.[45] Borchard distils the following rule from these arbitrations:

> A long line of cases has established certain qualification upon the non-liability of the government for the wrongful acts of private individuals. These consist in certain manifestations of the actual or implied complicity of the government in the act, before or after it, either by directly ratifying or

---

mandated in these circumstances by modern law. Where there was a taking of the property of an alien in execution of a criminal fine, this was considered a non-compensable taking. Again, the idea is that the alien loses protection in these situations.

[43] E. Jimenez de Arechaga and A. Tanzi, 'International State Responsibility' in M. Bedjaoui (ed.), *International Law: Achievements and Prospects* (1991), 359. They also suggest that 'this theory of state complicity was adopted in several arbitral awards of the nineteenth century and by important writers on the subject'.

[44] (1872) 1 Moore 495.

[45] These are stated in Borchard, *Diplomatic Protection*, 217.

approving it, or by an implied, tacit or constructive approval in the negligent failure to prevent the injury, or to investigate the case, or to punish the guilty individual, or to enable the victim to pursue his civil remedies against the offender.[46]

This law, as summarised by Borchard, underwent a change as power-based and state-centred positivism gained sway over international legal thought. It came to be understood that the state could only be held responsible for the acts of its own organs and not for those of its nationals.[47] In other words, the approach, as described by Borchard, of treating states as having a species of direct responsibility through implied approval disappeared as a general principle of attribution. The modern position is stated in Article 11 of the International Law Commission (ILC) Articles on State Responsibility in the following terms:

> The conduct of a person or a group of persons not acting on behalf of the State shall not be considered an act of the State under international law.[48]

But, significantly, another draft Article, Article 8, does retain some notion of this older idea of the possibility of attribution of a national's conduct to the state itself. This Article contemplates liability for the acts of persons if they were 'in fact acting on behalf of the State' or where they were 'exercising elements of governmental authority in the absence of official authorities and in circumstances which justified the exercise of those elements of authority'. It may be possible to argue that the rules stated by Arechega and Tanzi, and Borchard, could be interpreted as having been retained by Articles 11 and 8 in combination, but there is no indication that the situation was even contemplated in the ILC drafting process with respect to those two draft Articles. The ILC was quite content to go along with the power-based statement which was more concerned with the protection of aliens from injuries by the host state. That being said, the draft Articles do not speak to substantive rules of law but, rather, only to framework principles of responsibility. Thus, it is generally considered that, even as the Borchardian principle of attribution was expunged from the new understanding of the general law of state responsibility,

---

[46] *Ibid.*

[47] Moore, *International Arbitration*, 2082; *Poggioli Case* (1903), in Ralston *The Law Procedure of International Tribunals* (1926), 847; E. M. Borchard, *The Diplomatic Protection of Citizens Abroad* (1915), 217. There are also cases which recognised the liability for the acts of brigands abroad on the basis that there was a duty on the home state to suppress brigandage.

[48] ILC Report (1996), GAOR, 51st Session, Supp 10, 125.

substantive international law continued to lay down positive duties with respect to the protection of foreigners in the classic type of situation in which there is mob violence directed at the alien which the *host state* did not prevent through due diligence.[49] What we now tend to think of as this 'classic' due diligence rule ceased being a general principle of attribution in the law of state responsibility (according to which negligent control and a failure to provide a process for civil remedies was viewed as creating a kind of direct agency relationship between the home state and its national). It was transformed into a specific positive obligation of one branch of substantive law (the law dealing with protection of host states of foreign nationals). In the process, positive duties on the *home state* of these foreigners dropped out of the legal picture – at least in power-based, mainstream international legal thought.

The unprincipled and indeed arbitrary nature of this transformation is apparent. That being so, there would seem to be good reason to argue that substantive international law should be susceptible in light of a policy-based understanding of international law to interpretative development by analogy.[50] While we are quite distant from the old idea of a form of direct responsibility of states for the conduct of nationals abroad, there is no reason why present international law cannot be shaped to extend the substantive duties applicable to the host state of a corporation to the home state of the corporation where the requisite elements of knowledge and control are present. We should therefore not be surprised to find that, recently, challenges to the notion of the one-sided diplomatic protection of the alien corporation through international law despite the atrocious nature of its conduct have (re-)emerged. The idea is back on the table that the home state of a foreign citizen, quite apart from protecting the citizen or corporation, incurs responsibility if it does not prevent him or it from engaging in injurious conduct whilst abroad.[51]

---

[49] The Iran–US Claims Tribunal dealt with many such situations. See *Short* v. *Iran* (1987) 16 Iran–US CTR 76; *Yeager* v. *Iran* (1987) 17 Iran–US CTR 92.

[50] The inadequacies in the treatment of the ILC's definition of attribution in the human rights contexts are dealt with, in a different context, in R. Lawson, 'Out of Control, State Responsibility and Human Rights: Will the ILC's Definitions of the Act of State Meet the Challenges of the 21st Century?' in M. Castermans-Holleman, F. van Hoof and J. Smith (eds.), *The Role of the Nation State in the 21st Century: Essays in Honour of Peter Baehr* (1998), 91.

[51] *Dicta* in the *Nicaragua Case* [1986] ICJ Rpts 4 indicate responsibility of a state for acts of persons wholly unconnected with the state if there was control over these persons. Where there is such control, the persons would be equated with an arm of that state's government. The Court said (para. 109): 'What the Court has to determine is whether or

However, the creation of such responsibility has so far been effected either by way of treaties dealing with specific subject-matter (such as the Basel Convention on the Transfer of Hazardous Waste) or has been unilaterally accepted by some states concerned to regulate the conduct of their corporations abroad. The case for the existence of such liability in general international law is what this chapter seeks to establish.[52] We can gain a better idea of how easily general international law can embrace home state responsibility by noting some specific instances of the acceptance of such responsibility.

Examples of treaty acceptance of such responsibility are to be found especially in the environmental sphere. Thus, for example, the treaties controlling the transport of hazardous waste impose a duty on states to prevent such transport to other states by nationals.[53] Here, a clear treaty obligation arises not to permit citizens and corporations to export

not the relationship of the control to the United States Government was so much one of dependence on the one side and control on the other that it would be right to equate the contras, for legal purposes, with an organ of the United States Government, or as acting on behalf of that Government.' On the basis of this formulation, the existence of control over multinational corporations acting within the home state to the detriment of the interests of the host state or its people could engage the responsibility of the home state. In the human rights context, the principle was extended in *Bosnia Genocide Case* [1996] ICJ 595 where it was suggested by implication that a state becomes responsible if an individual who had committed a violation of the Genocide Convention was under the control of that state. For such a reading, see S. Rosenne, 'State Responsibility and International Crimes: Further Reflections on Article 19 of the Draft Articles on State Responsibility' (1997) 30 NYU Journal of International Law and Politics 145 at 159. *Dicta* in the *Tadic Case* (1997) 36 ILM 908 at 933 contemplate the Yugoslav state's liability for atrocities committed by Serbs in Bosnia. See also *Loizidou* v. *Turkey* (1996) 108 ILR 443.

[52] There is no doubt that, where the state sends its nationals on a mission abroad to inflict damage in another territory, even if the damage is directed at a third party, there is liability. *Rainbow Warrior Case* (1987) 26 ILM 1346. In the *Lockerbie Case*, the specific allegation was that agents sent by Libya had caused the airliner to explode. In both instances, the incidents took place elsewhere but the acts were of agents of the state whose responsibility was alleged. Agency rather than nationality and the intention with which the act was done are the factors in the attribution of responsibility. See also the *Nicaragua Case* [1986] ICJ Rpts 16 for a norm of near-agency for the purposes of the direct attribution of the conduct of rebels in one state to another state supporting those rebels.

[53] The Basel Convention on the Control of Transboundary Movement of Hazardous Wastes and Their Disposal (1989) 28 ILM 657 (in force, May 1992). See also K. Kummer, *International Management of Hazardous Wastes: The Basel Convention and Related Legal Rules* (1995). For the responsibility of flag states for the discharge of waste by ships on the high seas, see B. D. Smith, *State Responsibility and the Marine Environment* (1988); F. Francioni, 'Exporting Hazard Through Multinational Enterprises: Can the State of Origin Be Held Responsible?' in F. Francioni and T. Scovazzi (eds.), *International Responsibility for Environmental Harm* (1991), 275.

hazardous waste to other countries.[54] The law is no longer based on the premise of sovereignty that a developing state can choose to avoid the harm by refusing to accept the waste. It imposes an active duty on the exporting state to ensure that hazardous waste is not sent to other states.[55] But, these treaty obligations still seem to be territorially linked.[56]

The absence of territoriality, however, is not a problem in the emerging international law of human rights which recognises its basic obligations, such as the prohibition of torture, as being owed to the whole of humanity.[57] The meaningfulness of *erga omnes* obligations rests on the idea that state responsibility exists for the violation of any of those obligations which can be directly or indirectly traced to the acts or omissions of the state. The emergence of a duty to prosecute criminals in international law attests the fact that the place of commission of the violation of the obligations is increasingly becoming insignificant.[58] One may argue that the duty becomes more easily established in situations where the criminal is a national of the state. Correspondingly, there is an increasing recognition of a moral, if not yet a legal, duty to prevent the commission of harm injurious to the interests of other states and their peoples. Such a duty is often unilaterally assumed.

The best example of this would be the legislation recently enacted in some states to prevent the organisation of sex tours by their nationals to exploit child prostitutes in foreign states where the problem has become endemic and difficult to control. Here, the problem can only be controlled if both the state from which the tourists originate and those in which child prostitution exists take measures. States like the United Kingdom, Canada and Australia have voluntarily assumed the responsibility of preventing

[54] See generally R. Risillo-Mazzeshchi, 'Forms of International Responsibility for Environmental Harm' in F. Francioni and T. Scovazzi (eds.), *International Responsibility for Environmental Harm* (1991); and R. Lefeber, *Transboundary Environmental Interference and the Origin of State Liability* (1996).

[55] The Fourth ACP–EEC Convention of Lomé (1989); and International Atomic Energy Agency, Code of Practice on the International Transboundary Movement of Radioactive Waste (1990). The texts of both instruments are in B. Kwiatkowska and A. H. A. Soons (eds.), *Transboundary Movement and Disposal of Hazardous Waste in International Law* (1993).

[56] The obligation is on the state to prevent the physical export of material from its territory, not to prevent export by a national who operates overseas. This is done through a licensing system which requires the prior informed consent of the state to which the export is made.

[57] M. Raggazi, *The Concept of International Obligations Erga Omnes* (1997).

[58] G. S. Goodwin-Gill, 'Crime in International Law: Obligations Erga Omnes and the Duty to Prosecute' in G. S. Goodwin-Gill and S. Talmon (eds.), *The Reality in International Law: Essays in Honour of Ian Brownlie* (1999), 199.

their nationals making such sex tours abroad. Though the legislation contemplates punishment after the event, there is a duty to prevent the tours taking place through denial of passports and other means.[59] The state has the means of preventing harm being caused to other states and persons living within other states. There is a duty to prevent such harm. The duty arises not only in terms of morality but also in terms of law. Here, an extraterritorial situation is being controlled by regulating the conduct of nationals abroad. The moral responsibility to control such activities taking place abroad is accepted by the state which uses nationality as the basis for imposing liability on its citizens.[60]

It may be possible to argue that there is not only a moral duty but also a legal duty to take such measures. Beyond the harm caused to children through prostitution itself, the sex tourist is, in the context of sexually transmittable diseases, like a circulating bomb whose conduct can end up harming a wider circle of people than only the children with whom he has 'sex'.[61] There is a duty on the part of his state, which alone has the best means of ascertaining his condition and his proclivities, to prevent the circulation of the person in other states that are less able to deal with the problem.[62] The liability of tourist corporations which knowingly assist in such tours is already provided for in this legislation. The liability of airlines which knowingly carry such tourists must be contemplated. But,

---

[59] Compare the situation of the rugby tours to South Africa during the apartheid regime. It was argued that the state should use its prerogative powers to prevent its national teams from travelling for this purpose.

[60] Compare the refusal by the United States to issue passports to Mormon missionaries as they would preach polygamy abroad, noted in E. M. Borchard, *Diplomatic Protection of Nationals* (1904).

[61] The link between torture and rape is increasingly being made. Sex with children is rape. In the context of a *ius cogens* principle, there would then be a universal obligation to prevent sex tourism involving paedophiles. In terms of the seriousness of the harm to children, it may be useful, in light of the thematic focus of this book on torture as an example of serious human rights violations, to recall the recent confirmation by the European Court of Human Rights that rape constitutes a form of torture at least for women in state custody: *Aydin* v. *Turkey*. Whether or not private acts of 'sex' are to be considered torture under prevailing international law definitions of torture, the important point is that the kind of abuse of power and associated harm is closely analogous when one considers the conditions under which many children 'choose' to prostitute themselves to foreign tourists. Not only does socio-economic reality and their stage of mental development make their choice illusory, but also we should not forget the jail-like circumstances of much prostitution.

[62] The analogy with the reasoning in the *Corfu Channel Case* [1999] ICJ Rpts 4 is clear. In respect of the mining of the Corfu Channel and responsibility for the damage to vessels as a result of such mining, the International Court of Justice held that Albania, the coastal state, was responsible under the law.

what is more important is that states which enact such legislation accept that they have a responsibility to prevent the occurrence of such incidents which directly involve harm to the host state and its people. One may argue that this may indicate a moral responsibility and not a legal one. But, in situations in which the harm prevented is recognised as prohibited by a *ius cogens* principle, it is credible to argue that the responsibility is a legal one.

The above examples[63] clearly demonstrate that, in certain areas, the assumption of responsibility by states for the conduct of their nationals abroad is coming to be accepted. The argument may now plausibly be made that such responsibility must, as a matter of general international law, be recognised in respect of violations of *ius cogens* principles like torture in two situations.[64] The first is where a state knowingly permits its nationals to engage in violations of *ius cogens* principles whilst abroad. The second is where a state gives active assistance to those who are known to violate or are seen as capable of violating such *ius cogens* principles. There are conditions to be satisfied in the traditional law of state responsibility before any liability can be imputed to the state. The manner of the satisfaction of these rules in the situation of imposing responsibility for the acts of multinational corporations is now canvassed. With respect to the first situation, these rules require the existence of a duty and the ability to control the national from engaging in the proscribed behaviour and the failure to satisfy the duty. The elements of this duty to prevent are the subject of section 3 below. With respect to the second situation, it requires the existence of a link that makes attribution of the conduct of the multinational to the state possible. It will be argued that the home state should be deemed to have implicitly adopted or ratified the conduct of the corporate national if that home state fails to provide for some system of civil remedies for the victims of corporate harm abroad. The legal protection created by this failure should be considered as the requisite active assistance or link needed for attribution – the kind of 'implicit, tacit or constructive approval' spoken of by Borchard.

---

[63] There are other examples besides the one indicated here. Thus, the legislation to prevent bribery abroad by nationals (e.g. the Foreign Corrupt Practices Act) may be a similar instance. Here again, there may be a slow evolution of international norms prohibiting bribery which may make it incumbent on home states to act to prevent it. P. M. Nichols, 'Regulating Transnational Bribery in Times of Globalisation and Fragmentation' (1999) 24 Yale JIL 257

[64] There is overwhelming authority for the view that torture is a violation of *ius cogens* principles.

An alternative argument for the responsibility of the home state could be created on the basis of human rights law. There is a definite commitment on the part of all states to prevent the violation of human rights that take place not only within their territories but anywhere. The statements of the rights in the major conventions are not territory-specific.[65] They also provide for liability in states not only in respect of violations which they sponsor but also for violations by private persons, whose acts have been condoned or encouraged by the states.[66] The argument is possible that a state, whose multinational corporations are known to participate in violations of human rights such as torture, condones such violations as a matter of state policy, particularly if they do not take any measures to prevent these violations. A state which profits from the repatriation of the profits which the multinational corporation makes must be credited with the duty to ensure that such profits are made without mass violations of human rights.

2.3. The duty to control nationals abroad

The principles that potentially apply to the control of nationals' conduct abroad are those relating to responsibility in relation to the acts of private citizens that the state was under a duty to control. As noted earlier, this category has grown up largely in the context of cases involving mob violence against a foreigner within the territory of the host state.[67] The

---

[65] E.g. Article 3 of the International Covenant on Civil and Political Rights creates a general duty to 'ensure the equal right of the men and women to the enjoyment of all civil and political rights set forth in the present Covenant', whereas Article 2 contains a statement that is territory-specific.

[66] See Reporters Notes to Article 702, in American Law Institute, *Restatement of the Law: The Foreign Relations Law of the United States* (vol. 2, 167). The notes contemplate the possibility of avoiding responsibility by providing domestic remedies against violations.

[67] This area of the law was recognised in modern times in the *Rainbow Warrior Arbitration* (1990) 82 ILR 499 and in the *Nicaragua Case* [1986] ICJ Rpts 14. In the *Rainbow Warrior*, a Dutch citizen was killed when French agents sank the *Rainbow Warrior*. The damage was to an alien life and property by aliens sent into New Zealand as agents by France. The New Zealand Minister of Justice said: 'What New Zealand was saying to France on this matter was, in effect, that it was a political imperative that decent arrangements be made for compensation for damage suffered in New Zealand but not by New Zealand.' France paid compensation. G. Palmer, 'Settlement of International Disputes: The Rainbow Warrior Affair' (1989) 2 *Commonwealth Law Bulletin* 585. In *Letelier* v. *Chile*, 488 F Supp 665 (1980), state responsibility (of Chile) for the act of its agent in setting off a car bomb which killed a former Chilean ambassador was recognised. The *Pincochet* case also recognised the liability of a head of state (Chile) for acts of torture committed in Spain. The issue of liability of Chile was not raised. But, in *Al-Adsani* v. *Kuwait* (*The Times*,

law relating to liability for agents sent out to commit acts of sabotage or abduction is also relevant.

It is the combination of these two sets of rules which will provide an answer to the issue of home state liability for the acts of a multinational corporation which is associated with torture in a host state. Before dealing with the question of state obligations to control nationals abroad, it should first be noted that *jurisdiction* (i.e. the power or liberty) of a state to control nationals abroad exists in international law. It is relatively common for some legal systems, notably those of civil law countries, to make it a violation of the country's criminal code for a national to commit serious common crimes abroad. Common law jurisdictions tend, as a general rule, to prescribe criminal law rules on a territorial basis.[68] However, it is far less common for states, whatever the nature of their legal systems, to legislate extraterritorially outside the criminal law, with the United States probably being the state most inclined to create legislated exceptions to the presumption of the territorial application of its law. But, even the United States has been selective in the exercise of this jurisdiction. So far, it has exercised such jurisdiction when it has been advantageous to its interests.[69] It has not exercised such jurisdiction on purely altruistic grounds. Claims before courts that environmental legislation applies to the operation of US companies abroad have uniformly failed, the courts interpreting the environmental legislation as having only a territorial application. It is true that the *Unocal* case establishes that judicial jurisdiction to entertain suits against corporations alleging their participation in torture with a government against its own citizens exists in domestic courts.[70] But, in terms of the jurisdictional foundations

---

29 March 1996), the English court recognised that Kuwait could be liable for acts of its agents in Britain if they had caused personal injury to any resident in Britain.

[68] C. Blakesley, 'United States Jurisdiction over Extraterritorial Crime' (1982) 73 *Journal of Criminal Law and Criminology* 1109.

[69] The United States export control legislation applies to corporations operating overseas. Some tax legislation also applies. But, the US courts have consistently held that environmental legislation does not have extraterritorial application.

[70] *Doe I v. Unocal*, 963 F Supp 880 (1997) (CD Cal.); *Doe I v. Unocal*, 27 F Supp 2d 1174 (1998) (CD Cal.). The litigation involved claims that the imposition of forced labour, rape and violence on indigenous people in the remote regions of Burma through which Unocal was constructing a pipeline involved liability of the Burmese state as well as Unocal. The responsibility of the state was alleged on the basis that the army was involved in the atrocities and that of Unocal flowed from complicity in the atrocities. For a description of the litigation in respect of the massacre in East Timor brought in Boston against an Indonesian military officer who had come to the US to study management at Harvard, see R. Clark, 'Public International Law and Private Enterprise: Damages for a Killing in East

of the *Unocal* case, it proceeded largely on the basis that there is universal jurisdiction over *ius cogens* violations of international law such as torture and slavery and not on the basis of nationality, although Unocal is a US corporation. The fortuitous existence of a statute according the US courts jurisdiction, the Alien Torts Claims Act, facilitated the court's assumption of jurisdiction over corporate conduct abroad amounting to breaches of the 'law of nations'. Such legislation does not exist in other states which are home states of multinational corporations.[71]

The issue is whether a state's capacity to control its nationals in respect of their activity abroad must be exercised by a state when the state has knowledge that harm could eventuate to another state or its people. Phrased in this way, it can be seen that the only link that is missing is the absence of a clear positive duty to exercise the jurisdiction to control the conduct of nationals. It is clear that responsibility will arise if there are specific instructions given to nationals to engage in the harmful behaviour abroad.[72] Such instructions in effect create an agency relationship such as is contemplated by draft Article 8 of the ILC Draft Articles on State Responsibility, resulting in the nationals acting on behalf of their state. But, where such instructions are absent, can a state's mere knowledge of the harmful behaviour of its national be sufficient to trigger responsibility if the state fails to do what is necessary to cause the harmful conduct to cease?[73] Finally, how far do the home state's positive obligations go in situations where it is not alleged that the national's employees are the direct agents of harm but rather that the national is benefiting from a foreign state's human rights violations which have been committed in order to advance a joint project involving both the national and that state? In other words, in the situation such as the one in *Unocal*, is there a duty on the part of the United States to prevent Unocal acquiescing in the

---

Timor' (1996) 3 *Australian Journal of Human Rights* 21. The action was based on the Alien Tort Claims Act (1879) and the Torture Victim Protection Act (1992). For environmental litigation, see *Beanal* v. *Freeport-McMoran*, 969 F Supp 362 (1997) (ED La).

[71] A point made by the English courts in another context in *Al Adsani* v. *Kuwait*, *The Times*, 29 March 1996.

[72] The *Nicaragua Case* [1986] ICJ Rpts 4 provides obvious authority. There need not even be the link of nationality; the mere existence of control of a group would suffice. The ICJ held that control over the contras was absent and that state responsibility could not be imputed to the US. Nationality makes control easier to establish, particularly in circumstances where the national's activities are known to the home state and the home state profits from them directly or indirectly.

[73] And, further, is advance knowledge not of actual harm but of the *risk of harm* sufficient to trigger the duty to control the national in order to prevent the harm before it occurs?

Burmese government's torture and rape of local people as alleged in that case?

The argument is that such a duty *can* be constructed under present international law. As already indicated, the intentional sending of nationals or agents abroad to cause harm involves state responsibility. To extend this to situations where there is actual or constructive knowledge that harm will be caused by nationals requires but a small leap in the law. This leap is justified by existing doctrines. There is a general duty in international law not to cause harm to other states. Where a state knows that its national's activities will cause, or are causing, harm to other states or their peoples, it is consistent with this duty that it should prevent such harm. As a matter of general principle, if the state has the right to have its nationals protected abroad, a concomitant duty to ensure that the nationals act in a manner consistent with international norms should be recognised. Additionally, in a situation such as that alleged in *Unocal*, the home state of the foreign investor benefits from the foreign investment through the repatriation of the company's profits. The profits are enhanced by the forced labour that is secured by torture and repression. The fact that the home state itself benefits in this way casts a duty on the state to ensure that the company's profits (which are in a sense also profits for the home state) are not secured through means that violate international norms.

The home state has the ability to ensure that its nationals who operate abroad as foreign investors act in a manner consistent with international norms through the exercise of jurisdiction on the basis of nationality. If tax legislation and other legislation such as antitrust legislation can be extended in this manner, then the creation of a duty to exercise such jurisdiction to secure fundamental norms of international law cannot be regarded as unjustified. Some states reached out in this manner to prevent corruption and bribery in international business by their national corporations even before agreement on multilateral treaties began to be reached under the auspices of regional and sectoral organisations like the OAS and the OECD.[74] The prohibition of bribery has not nearly as much support in international policy as the prohibition of torture. Indeed, in the hierarchy of public policy norms, the prohibition of bribery comes well below the violation of human and environmental rights. The minimum effect of a state being unprepared to prevent the violation of international public policy norms, it must lose its right of diplomatic protection of its

---

[74] Foreign Corrupt Practices Act; see also Article 2 of the OECD Convention on Combating Bribery of Foreign Public Officials in International Business (1997).

nationals. The theory of foreign investment that was articulated in the past justified the protection afforded to business on the ground that the home state made sure that the business practices of the multinational corporations it sent abroad were above board, thereby entitling the state to give the corporate national its maximum protection. This policy fails in situations in which the multinational corporation engages in practices that violate *ius cogens* norms against torture or engages in other practices which violate international public policy.

There must be a satisfaction of the existing rules on state responsibility before a state is subjected to responsibility. As the International Court of Justice stated in the *ELSI Case*, an allegation of state responsibility should not be lightly made.[75] Hence, the rules on state responsibility must be clearly satisfied before an allegation of state responsibility for the conduct of its nationals is raised. Knowledge must be attributable to the home state with respect to the acts of the nationals in question. This will ordinarily be difficult to satisfy as a state cannot know beforehand what its nationals who go abroad seek to do. But, where a multinational corporation, as in the *Unocal* situation, is alleged *currently* to be violating the human rights of peoples abroad, the situation will be sufficiently widely known for the state to have imputed knowledge of the situation. There is not merely a jurisdictional power to control but a duty to control the activities of the national corporation in these circumstances.[76] The issue then becomes one of whether the state took reasonable steps to prevent the harm where advance knowledge of likely harm can be shown or to stop an ongoing violation of human rights.

Returning to the parallel provided by the law on state responsibility for the activities of loosely organised mobs which attack foreigners, the law has been worked out on the basis that, if the state had knowledge of the situation, a duty to protect the aliens is triggered. If a mob attack was foreseeable, then a duty of protection is owed to the alien. State responsibility arises from the failure of the territorial state to provide such

---

[75] *ELSI Case* [1989] ICJ Rpts 15.
[76] In the *Sambaggio Case* (1903) 10 UNRIAA 499, Arbitrator Ralston said: 'Governments are responsible, as a general principle, for the acts of those they control'. Control through the nationality principle of the conduct of multinational corporations is possible, and the United States has used such control in many areas, such as the export of technology. See also Article 30 of the Charter of Economic Rights and Duties of States (1974): 'All states have the responsibility to ensure that activities within their jurisdiction *or control* do not cause damage to the environment of other states or areas beyond the limits of national jurisdiction.' Emphasis added.

protection, liability flowing from the omission to act in a situation where the law creates a duty to act.[77] Even if a standard of strict liability is not the basis of state responsibility, a due diligence fault requirement will be satisfied in these circumstances where there is the existence of the capacity control and the failure to take the steps reasonable in the circumstances to exercise that capacity. Since a capacity to control exists in the home state with respect to a multinational corporation which operates abroad, the same rules can therefore be extended to render home states liable when they are aware of the conduct of their multinational corporate nationals and do not curb such conduct through the means available to the state.

International law requires that there must be an exercise of governmental authority before a state can become responsible. It may be argued that there is no governmental authority in the situation of a multinational corporation whereas there is such authority in the agent who is sent to commit sabotage abroad, as in the *Rainbow Warrior* situation, in which French security agents were sent abroad to sabotage one of Greenpeace's vessels while in port in New Zealand. But international law recognises very clearly that governmental authority may be exercised either by act or omission.[78] Whether or not conduct by omission breaches international law depends on whether there is a positive duty placed by substantive international law on the state (i.e. a duty to act in a certain way and/or with a view to achieving a certain result). Again, the classic mob situation illustrates the way out of this supposed difficulty. The mob is by no means the agent of the government. The requirement of governmental authority is provided in these cases by the failure of the governmental authorities to act in the situation of danger to the alien posed by the mob.[79] It is the failure to exercise due diligence to protect the alien from which governmental complicity in the episode arises. Likewise in the case of the multinational corporation, responsibility arises due to the failure of the state authorities to prevent it from engaging in human-rights-abusive conduct abroad. The

---

[77] *Home Missionary Society Case* (1920) 6 UNRIAA 20; R. Pisillo-Mazzeschi, 'The Due Diligence Rule and the Nature of the International Responsibility of States' (1992) 35 GYIL 46.

[78] It is generally recognised in the law of state responsibility that an omission to act to prevent harm entails responsibility.

[79] *Youmans Claim* (1926) 4 UNRIAA 110; *Zafiro Claim* (1925) 6 UNRIAA 160 (where liability was imposed on the basis that the naval officer did not stop the looting by the mob 'with sufficient promptitude'). This case is relevant to the situation under discussion, as liability was imposed on the basis that an unruly Chinese crew of a privately owned ship that was requisitioned by the United States was let loose to riot in an area of the Philippines that had no civil administration.

theory of liability that has evolved primarily in arbitral case law on mob violence provides the necessary body of general principles for establishing the liability of the home state for the torture and other human rights violations engaged in by multinational corporations. We would do well to remember that the application and development of these principles in some cases also involved the making of leaps in legal reasoning from general principles to concrete contexts no less creative than what is being contended for here.

Some may argue that distance is a constraining factor in the attribution of state responsibility to home states for corporate conduct abroad. In most instances of state responsibility, the state held responsible had caused injury to the alien resident within that state's territorial limits. But, this common *factual situation* of territoriality cannot be understood as having given rise to any *legal* rule that the proximity to the act is necessary. Proximity has never been isolated as a limiting rule by any writer.[80] In any event, it would be completely inconsistent with the willingness of international law to extend responsibility to states for extraterritorial acts of its nationals where there is some direct agency or similar kind of link. For example, in *Short v. Iran*,[81] it was contemplated that, if the Ayatollah Khomeini, who had yet to come to Iran, had instigated hostile acts towards the US nationals resident in Iran whilst still in exile in France, his incoming government would be responsible for the acts. And states have been held responsible for sending forth agents to engage in abduction abroad and for sending saboteurs into another state.[82] It is true that the existing principles of state responsibility will have to be extended creatively to cover state responsibility for corporate misconduct. But, as was argued earlier, if the need and will to achieve a pressing policy objective is to be placed at the centre of the evolution of international law, achieving it by adapting and extending existing law is a legitimate means to do so.

Another challenge might take the form of the question of why there should be state responsibility in these circumstances. This question has

---

[80] Nor have the older cases required that the injurious acts should have taken place on the territory of the state held responsible. E.g. in the *Zafiro Claim* (1925) 6 UNRIAA 160, responsibility of the United States in respect of acts of vandalism of a Chinese crew under the command of a US naval officer in a port city of the Philippines (which was, at the time, not under the control of any authority). The presence of the officer at the scene of the injury was held not to be necessary.

[81] (1987) 16 Iran–US CTR 76.

[82] *Rainbow Warrior* (1987) 26 ILM 1346.

implicitly already been answered. The imposition of state responsibility on the home state is one means of providing for control over the conduct of a multinational corporation whose conduct otherwise remains unregulated in modern international law – and arguably is increasingly unregulated as economic globalisation pressures sap the will and capacity of states to regulate corporate conduct within their borders for fear of losing investment.[83] The paradigm being argued for will throw the onus of control onto home states which are not only able to bear that burden but which also have a moral duty to shoulder it because they and their societies profit from the overseas operations of their multinational corporations. It is clear that they have the ability to control such activity as they have claimed wide extraterritorial powers of control over these corporations in several areas. Home state responsibility will help in the creation of an international law which prevents human rights abuses by these corporations which exert much power and influence over the course of international relations without being subjected to any meaningful control.

Finally, of specific interest to the civil liability theme of the present book is that an important aspect of such state responsibility is that the wrongdoing state then comes under a duty to provide a remedy to the victim. The failure to provide a remedy again leads to an independent basis of state responsibility. To this issue we now turn in the final section of this chapter.

2.4. State responsibility and the duty to provide remedies to victims

It has been demonstrated that state responsibility arises from the breach of a duty to control the human rights violations of a multinational corporation abroad. When such a breach occurs, a duty on the part of the home state to provide a remedy to the victims of its misconduct then arises. More specifically, the contention is that, in the Bhopal or Unocal-type situations, there is an obligation to provide a remedy through the domestic courts by the home state. This again is a contention that initially seems difficult to establish, but, once it is conceded that there is a duty to prevent nationals from causing harm to people in other states, the obligation can be made out as a matter of law.

---

[83] The voluntary codes which exist hardly provide the function of control.

The current paradigm of the duty to provide an effective local remedy is the situation of an alien who suffers injury at the hands of the host state. The duty to provide access to local courts in order to receive an effective remedy is already well recognised in the law.[84] It follows (at least at the level of consistency of the policy justifications underlying the law) that once the primary obligation to prevent harm abroad is accepted as applicable to the home states of multinational corporations, the law must be shaped to ensure that the home state provides a remedy. That is, at least where the home state itself has breached duties to control in situations of adequate knowledge of the corporate national's conduct abroad, the duty to provide a remedy to the victims seems to follow as a matter of basic considerations of justice.

Significantly, the existing law is not a blank slate on this, and in fact contains the kernel of a duty to provide access to the home state's courts whether or not the home state itself bears responsibility for a failure to control the corporate national prior to or during the harm. There is sufficient authority that a state which does not provide a remedy against the wilful harm caused to other states by a national becomes responsible to the state which suffered the harm.[85]

It must finally be noted that the duty to provide a remedy to victims may exist in general international human rights law, quite independently of any argument relating to state responsibility for the state's own involvement in or failure to prevent human rights harms.[86] There is a generic duty to provide remedies for human rights violations.[87] There is a credible argument to be made that there is not only a duty to provide a remedy but that in the case of violations of *ius cogens* norms, like torture committed by nationals abroad, emerging international law recognises a positive duty to prosecute the offenders. If such a positive duty exists, then, it must follow that failure to perform it engages the responsibility of states.

---

[84] C. F. Amerasinghe, *Local Remedies in International Law* (1990).

[85] The rule is usually discussed in the context of the requirement either to punish or to hand over a national who has committed a crime abroad. There is no reason why the rule should not be applied to situations of human rights violations which involve acts like torture, which are considered criminal in most legal systems.

[86] The view is canvassed in R. Pisillo-Mazzeschi, 'International Obligations to Provide for Reparation Claims?' in A. Randelzhofer and C. Tomuschat (eds.), *State Responsibility and the Individual* ((1999), 149.

[87] *Velasquez Rodriguez* (1988) 9 HRLJ 212 (where the Inter-American Court of Human Rights recognised the duty of states to prevent violations and remedy or punish such violations after their commission). Recognition of human rights requires positive action by states including access to courts for remedies.

3. Conclusion

Globalisation is supposed to be moving at a rapid pace, but, historically, the process of globalisation has always been accompanied by a process of fragmentation which involves the withdrawal of people into their own cultures and values in order to face the onset of the global values. This process of fragmentation is seldom studied. The violence which is generated by the clash will be a concern of the future. The potential for violation of human rights in this clash has also been seldom studied. There is a paucity of norms in international law which provided for the control of such violence.

The process of globalisation itself is a power-based process which seeks to secure the rights of business to the detriment of the rights of people. The positivist basis of the rules on state responsibility were formulated so as to enhance this process which stressed the rights of the foreign investor and eclipsed the earlier law which did recognise the fact that responsibility could arise in the home state for the conduct of a national abroad. The draft of the International Law Commission continues this trend by its emphasis on power-based solutions to state responsibility. Yet, the development of an international law of human rights is based on the competing notion of idealism in the law which requires the recognition of the responsibility of the state for the violation of the more basic human rights giving rise to *erga omnes* obligations wherever they take place as long as they can be directly or indirectly be attributed to that state. There is clear evidence of the impact of this competing objective. The progress towards the stabilisation of this norm may be incremental but the signs are that, once a breach is made, the law will quickly develop to ensure this progress, notwithstanding the establishment views stated in the ILC's draft code. Work remains to be done in coalescing the different strands which are moving towards supporting the growth of such a law.

5

Bilateral investment treaties

There was a massive proliferation of bilateral investment treaties in the 1990s. A World Bank study stated that in 1994 there were over 700 such treaties.[1] By the end of the millennium, the figure had moved towards 2,000 treaties. It has now exceeded that mark.[2] Many more are in the process of being negotiated. Obviously, states which participate in the making of these treaties consider them to be necessary for a variety of reasons. Their significance needs assessment. Despite the increase in the number of bilateral investment treaties, there is as yet no possibility of agreeing a multilateral agreement on investment. The reasons for this also need to be explored.

1. Introductory survey

In the 1980s, bilateral investment treaties were considered a rather recent phenomenon in the international investment scene.[3] They seek to set out

[1] Rudolof Dolzer and Margrete Stevens, *Bilateral Investment Treaties* (1995), 1. According to a list of treaties that appears in (1989) 4 ICSID Rev 189, the first bilateral investment treaty was that concluded between Germany and Pakistan in 1959. The list refers to 308 treaties that had been concluded by the end of 1988. The treaties are collected together in a looseleaf publication. ICSID, *Investment Promotion and Protection Treaties* (1983–).

[2] UNCTAD, *World Investment Report, 2003*, puts the figure at 2,153. It has charts pointing to the treaty activity peaking in the mid-1990s and declining in the first years of the new millennium.

[3] For the literature on the subject in the 1980s and the 1990s, see J. Voss, 'The Protection and Promotion of European Private Investment in Developing Countries' (1981) 18 CMLR 363; A. Asken, 'The Case for Bilateral Investment Treaties' in South West Foundation, *Private Investors Abroad* (1981); F. A. Mann, 'British Treaties for the Promotion and Protection of Investment' (1982) 52 BYIL 241; K. Kunzer, 'Developing a Model Bilateral Investment Treaty' (1983) 15 *Law and Policy in International Business* 273; M. S. Bergman, 'Bilateral Investment Treaties: An Examination of the Evolution and Significance of the US Proto-type Treaty' (1983) 16 *NYU Journal of International Law and Politics* 1; D. A. Cody, 'United States Bilateral Investment Treaties: Egypt and Panama' (1983) Ga JIL 491; J. E. Pattison, 'The United States–Egypt Bilateral Investment Treaty: A Prototype for Future Negotiation'

the rules according to which the investments made by the nationals of the two states parties in each other's territory will be protected. Writers are divided as to the effect of these treaties. Some writers believe that these treaties give 'important support for those standards of customary international law which had seemed to be slipping away'.[4] For such an assessment to be made, one must be convinced as to the existence of a customary international law in the field covered by bilateral investment treaties. It is doubtful whether there was much customary international law on the point. The existence of such customary international law is difficult to establish, as a large part of the world community of states objected to the creation of such customary law, particularly during the early decades of bilateral investment treaty practice.[5] It may be claimed

(1983) 16 Cornell ILJ 305; K. J. Vandevelde, 'The Bilateral Investment Treaty Program of the United States' (1988) 21 Cornell ILJ 201; UNCTC, *Bilateral Investment Treaties* (1988); J. W. Salacuse, 'BIT by BIT: The Growth of Bilateral Investment Treaties and Their Impact on Foreign Investment in Developing Countries' (1990) 24 Int Lawyer 655; K. J. Vandevelde, *United States Investment Treaties: Policy and Practice* (1992); 'The Development and Expansion of Bilateral Investment Treaties' (1992) *ASIL Proceedings* 532; Andrew Guzman, 'Why Do LDCs Sign Treaties That Hurt Them? Explaining the Popularity of Bilateral Investment Treaties' (1998) 38 Va JIL 639; K. J. Vandevelde, 'Investment Liberalization and Economic Development: The Role of Bilateral Investment Treaties' (1998) 36 Columbia Journal of Transnational Law 501; K. J. Vandevelde, 'The Economics of Bilateral Investment Treaties' (2000) 41 Harvard ILJ 469; Stuart Gross, 'BITs, Non-NAFTA MITs and Host-State Regulatory Freedom – An Indonesian Case Study' (2003) 24 Michigan JIL 893. A bibliography can be found in (1992) 7 ICSID Rev 231.

[4] E. Denza and S. Brooks, 'Investment Protection Treaties: The United Kingdom Experience' (1987) 36 ICLQ 908 at 912. White seems to agree with this view. G. White, 'The New International Economic Order: Principles and Trends' in H. Fox (ed.), *International Economic Law and Developing States* (vol. 2, 1992). The view was stated by Mann that such treaties contribute to the development of customary international law. F. A. Mann, 'British Treaties for the Promotion and Protection of Investment' (1981) 52 BYIL 241. But, in a later contribution, his enthusiasm for such treaties was somewhat muted. F. A. Mann, 'Foreign Investment in the International Court' (1992) 86 AJIL 92. German lawyers concede that the German treaties (which provide the model for European practice) do not constitute customary international law or even state practice, but show 'that there are reciprocal interests between the investor and the host state leading to a mutually agreed standard of protection'. A. Weber, 'Investments Risks and International Law' in T. Oppermann and E. Petersmann (eds.), *Reforming the International Economic Order* (1987), 36 at 37. The view among US lawyers also seems to be that the treaties contribute to customary law. This is a parochial view based largely on the examination of US treaties. It is summarily dismissed in the preliminary award in *UPS* v. *Canada* (2003), para. 97: '[W]hile BITs are large in number, their coverage is limited . . . and in terms of *opinio juris* there is no indication that they reflect a general sense of obligation.'

[5] The 1960s and 1970s were the heydays of the New International Economic Order through which developing states canvassed a system that stood in opposition to the normative system favoured by the developed states.

that the treaties stabilise practices that have existed and contribute to the creation of customary principles in the area in the future. The opposing view is that the states making such treaties create *lex specialis* as between themselves in view of the uncertain state of the existing international law on foreign investment protection. It is, of course, possible that, if there is a concordance of standards in these bilateral investment treaties, such standards on which there is consistent agreement evidenced by such treaties could become international law. For, it is well established that bilateral treaties could become international law through the fact that they evidence consistent agreement of states as much as multilateral treaties do. They are also evidence of customary practices of states.[6] But, there is so much divergence in the standards in bilateral investment treaties that it is premature to conclude that they give rise to any significant rule of international law.[7] Though the outer shell of bilateral investment treaties looks similar, thus contributing to the claim that they create customary international law, a deeper examination would indicate that the contents of the treaties vary so widely that each must be considered a carefully balanced accommodation reached after negotiation between the parties.[8] These treaties are best seen as creating *lex specialis* between the parties rather than as creating customary principles of international law.[9] Yet, the widespread belief in their significance among international lawyers and the fact that they have the potential for the creation of

---

[6] Shabtai Rosenne, *Developments in the Law of Treaties* (1989), 124: '[T]he law generative role of the international treaty may be its most important function, and its most durable.' But, the law-creating function of bilateral treaties is diminished by the fact that most of them have an impact on domestic legal systems and are prone to be interpreted differently by national courts. Extradition treaties and double taxation treaties are examples. Due to the differences in interpretation, the opportunity for standards emerging from such treaties is reduced.

[7] The present writer took this view in 1986. See M. Sornarajah, 'State Responsibility and Bilateral Investment Treaties' (1986) 20 JWTL 79. Despite the growth in the number of bilateral investment treaties, there has been no reason to change this conclusion. More recent studies also indicate that it is premature to regard these treaties as creating customary law. J. W. Salacuse, 'BIT by BIT' (1990) 24 Int Lawyer 655 at 660, states that the purpose of the treaties was to establish 'specific legal rules' as between the parties.

[8] The US treaties show great similarity. But, US treaty practice does not make international law (or, so one assumes).

[9] *AAPL v. Sri Lanka* (1992) 17 YCA 106. Both the award and the dissent make frequent references to the investment treaty between the United Kingdom and Sri Lanka being *lex specialis*. The award, in particular, contrasted the rules of the treaty with customary principles.

customary principles of international law contribute to the importance of these treaties.

Another feature of bilateral investment treaties is that they are made between unequal partners.[10] They are usually agreed between a capital-exporting developed state and a developing state keen to attract capital from that state. The observation that developing countries make such treaties among themselves does not obscure the fact that one of these countries is an exporter of capital *vis-à-vis* the other.[11] The rationale for the treaty itself is the promise of protection for the capital that is so received. Though the treaty contemplates a two-way flow of investments between the states parties to the treaty, it is usually only a one-way flow that is contemplated and feasible in reality in the context of the disparities of wealth and technology between the two parties. There is an insufficient *quid pro quo* in that the two-way flow that is openly stated as the basis of the treaties is often a fiction. There are interesting problems that arise as a result of this inequality of bargaining power. It is difficult to expect some of the developing countries which are signatories to these treaties to have legal departments sophisticated enough to understand the nuances in the variations in the language that is used in these treaties.[12] There may be a basis for the suspicion that these treaties are signed in the belief that they will result in the inflow of foreign investment. They do not contain any firm obligation on the part of the capital-exporting state to ensure that such flows take place. In the belief that foreign investment flows will be forthcoming, there is a surrender of sovereignty on the part of the state that hopes to receive the capital by way of foreign investment. Sovereignty is ceded as the foreign investment subject to the

---

[10] Salacuse ((1990) 24 Int Lawyer 655 at 663) observed: '[I]n reality, an asymmetry exists between the parties.' See also J. E. Alvarez, (1992) 86 *ASIL Proceedings* 552, where he said: 'BIT partners turn to the US with the equivalent of an IMF gun pointed at their heads; others feel that, in the absence of a rival superpower, economic relations with the one that remains are inevitable. For many, a BIT relationship is hardly a voluntary, uncoerced transaction.' At *ibid.*, p. 555, the treaty is described as 'a one-way ratchet designed to benefit multinationals'.

[11] E.g. when Singapore makes a treaty with Bangladesh, Singapore is seeking to protect the low-technology, labour-intensive industries its foreign investors relocate in Bangladesh. The existence of these treaties do not diminish the fact that there is an inequality in the relationship as there are no mutual flows of investments which take place.

[12] This is particularly so in view of the very unexpected interpretations that are now being placed on the NAFTA provisions on foreign investment. The meaning of the so-called umbrella clauses provides an interesting example of creative extrapolations: *SGS* v. *Pakistan* (2004, unreported).

treaty receives external protection from international dispute settlement mechanisms and is insulated from the reach of the local laws to a considerable extent. Despite this inequality, there is an external validity to these treaties. States which conclude them must be presumed to have intended to be bound by them. It is unlikely that, if any doctrine of unequal treaties does exist outside the field of coercion, it could be applied to the situation of bilateral investment treaties.[13] Bilateral investment treaties are voluntary, and there is no element of coercion involved in their making.[14] The developing state which enters into such treaties does so freely, in the belief that the existence of such treaties will promote the flow of foreign investments from the other contracting state.[15] Unless there is compelling evidence of coercion, one must proceed on the basis that these treaties are voluntarily made. Such evidence may exist where the signing of the treaty is made conditional on the granting of aid, loans or trade preferences.[16]

Before dealing with modern bilateral investment treaties, it is useful to examine the treaties of 'friendship, commerce and navigation' which were the precursors to the bilateral investment treaty. The experience that was gained with these treaties shaped the formulation of bilateral investment treaties.

[13] On unequal treaties, see I. Detter, 'The Problem of Unequal Treaties' (1966) 14 ICLQ 1069, who regarded capitulation treaties entered into between China and European powers as unequal and subject to annulment. Parallels can be drawn between on the one hand the capitulation treaties which insulated European traders totally from the scope of local laws and on the other hand bilateral investment treaties the purpose of which is to insulate foreign investors at least partially from the scope of local laws.

[14] Whether the approach of the United States which has a pre-announced model bilateral treaty from which it does not permit significant variations makes the situation different is an issue that must be raised. The charge that the treaties are unequal may become effective if signing them is made a condition for aid and access to preferential treatment in trade matters and in the granting of aid or loans. In *Santa Elena* v. *Costa Rica*, the award mentions that the dispute was arbitrated under the treaty because of the possibility of aid being refused under the Hickenlooper Amendment.

[15] Nevertheless, suspicions will be raised as to their real nature. Asante skirts close to calling them unequal treaties. Doubts are raised as to whether the nuances in the different terminology that is used are understood by developing country advisers. In some instances, high officials in the developing state are even unaware that such treaties have been concluded. S. K. B. Asante, 'International Law and Investments' in M. Bedjaoui (ed.), *International Law: Achievements and Prospects* (1991), 667 at 675.

[16] OPIC, an insurance scheme established by the US government, does not insure foreign investments flowing into states which do not have investment treaties with the United States. There is evidence in the publications of the World Bank that the Bank promotes investment treaties. Anecdotal evidence suggests that loans are made dependent on signing investment treaties.

2. Treaties of friendship, commerce and navigation

Bilateral treaties for the protection of trading interests have been in existence from early times.[17] The progenitors of the modern bilateral investment treaty were the treaties on 'friendship, commerce and navigation' (FCN) which were concluded from the eighteenth century onwards.[18] The United States concluded such treaties in large numbers with its allies, and many of them have been the subject of both domestic and international litigation.[19] One clear purpose of these treaties is to tie many states of the world to alliances with the United States. The treaties were not confined to commerce. They extended to military matters such as access to ports and navigation through internal waters. The early treaties were designed at a time when commerce was largely restricted to trading in goods by merchants and did not contemplate direct investment by corporations.[20]

The treaties emphasised the protection that should be accorded to individual aliens, as trading was largely done by individuals establishing themselves overseas for the purposes of trade. This may indicate a linkage between trade and investment, a much searched for link in modern times in formulating a thesis that trade and investment are interlinked and must be provided for in instruments attached to institutions that are linked

[17] H. Neufeld, *The International Protection of Private Creditors from the Treaty of Westphalia to the Congress of Vienna* (1971); see also *Sumitomo Shoji America, Inc. v. Avagliano*, 457 US 176 (1982), for a discussion by the US Supreme Court of the history of these treaties.

[18] A treaty between France and the United States concluded in 1778 is reputed to be the first such treaty. See further K. J. Vandervelde, *United States Investment Treaties: Policy and Practice* (1992).

[19] The United States relied on the FCN treaty with Italy for developing many of its propositions as to liability in the *ELSI Case* [1989] ICJ Rpts 15. There were also frequent references to the treaty with Iran in the awards of the Iran–US Claims Tribunal. But, other states' use of these treaties to enable the International Court of Justice to assume jurisdiction over the United States has caused considerable concern. The FCN treaty was used by Nicaragua to bring its case against the United States before the Court in *Nicaragua v. United States* [1984] ICJ Rpts 352. Iran now has a claim regarding the shooting down of a civilian airliner before the Court where jurisdiction is also sought to be established on the basis of an FCN treaty. In *Sumitomo Shoji America, Inc. v. Avagliano*, 457 US 176 (1982), the treaty was used in its defence by a Japanese company charged with discrimination in employment practices.

[20] For the treaty practice of the United States, see Foster, 'Some Aspects of the Commercial Treaty Program of the United States – Past and Present' (1946) 11 *Law and Contemporary Problems* 647; Walker, 'Modern Treaties of Freedom, Commerce and Navigation' (1958) 42 Minn. LR 805; H. Walker, 'Post-War Commercial Treaty Program of the United States' (1958) 73 *Political Science Quarterly* 57; R. Wilson, *United States Commercial Treaties and International Law* (1960).

with trade. The treaties dealt with a variety of matters concerning alien treatment, including freedom of worship and travel within the host state. The FCN treaty contained almost a charter of the rights that the alien was to enjoy in the host state, often listing his due process and procedural rights in the case of arrest and criminal trial. Post-Second World War treaties were more investment-specific, and provided for the making of investments by corporations and for the freedom of establishment in the host state. To the extent that the early FCN treaty was not specific to investment, the FCN treaty may not be the precursor of the modern bilateral investment treaty, but its investment provisions contain many features which are now found in a more refined way in bilateral investment treaties. The wide use of the most-favoured-nation clause in the FCN treaty was taken over in the later bilateral investment treaties. The treaties made after the Second World War provided for national treatment as regards entry and establishment for corporations of the state parties.[21] The dispute resolution mechanisms that are to be found in FCN treaties were considerably strengthened in the later bilateral treaties. The experience of the FCN treaties certainly benefited the bilateral investment treaties which dealt with the more specific needs of foreign investors.

FCN treaties belonged to a different age and contained many features which would not be accepted by many states in modern times. They provided for an unlimited right of entry and establishment of business. They provided early instances of the right to entry and establishment which are now recognised in modern investment provisions such as those in Chapter 11 of the North American Free Trade Agreement and the US bilateral investment treaties. The FCN treaties were undoubtedly measures for spreading the influence of the major powers. They were concluded with smaller, less powerful states, which could be tied to the larger power in the context of the bipolar world that existed at the time the treaties were signed. With changes in the economic and power balances and changes in the internal structure of the states, the FCN treaties came to be used in ways quite unintended by the powerful state which secured the treaty. Thus, the FCN treaty between Japan and the United States, which permits access and establishment in the Japanese market, has come to be used by

---

[21] In *Sumitomo Shoji America, Inc.* v. *Avagliano*, 457 US 176 (1982), it was held that the foreign corporation could incorporate in the host state which was party to the treaty as a result of the freedom of access provided by the FCN treaty, and thereafter it acquires the nationality of the state of incorporation, becoming entitled to the same treatment as other corporate nationals.

Japan for making claims of access to US markets at a time when there was a dramatic change in the economic balance between the two states.[22] Not only is access claimed on the basis of the treaty, but claims are also made as to exemptions from domestic laws such as those on non-discrimination in employment.

Nicaragua has used the dispute settlement provisions of its FCN treaty with the United States to establish jurisdiction in its claims against the United States regarding the military intervention of the United States in Nicaragua's internal affairs.[23] Similar use of an FCN treaty was made by Iran in the *Oil Platforms Case*. The fact that worms may turn and the treaty may be used against the more powerful party will lead to a rethinking of the usefulness of these broadly framed treaties. The past is instructive for the future. It appears that the provisions of the NAFTA dispute settlement procedure are having consequences quite unintended by the parties to the agreement. Several claims have been made against Canada and the United States on the basis of the investment provisions, testing the limits of these treaties, and these developed states are largely taking refuge in the same arguments relating to sovereignty and regulatory control which developing states have made in the past. Apart from this, the FCN treaty has few bases for comparison with the more focused investment treaties of modern times.

3. Reasons for bilateral investment treaties

There were several unsuccessful attempts at multilateral treaties on foreign investment protection.[24] The reasons for the failure of these attempts

---

[22] The arguments based on the treaty bestowing powers on a company to use its own employment practices were used by the defendant Japanese company in *Sumitomo Shoji America, Inc. v. Avagliano*, 457 US 176 (1982). The Supreme Court side-stepped the argument by holding that the Japanese company was a US corporate national as it had incorporated in the United States and that it could, therefore, not claim the treaty rights. This would mean that a Japanese employer, choosing not to incorporate in the United States, could violate US laws against discrimination with impunity. The result was never thought of at the time of the treaty simply because the economic dominance of Japan was not contemplated at the time. In a later case, *Fortino v. Quasar Co.*, 950 F 2d 389 (1991), the right of a Japanese subsidiary to employ Japanese personnel in preference to Americans was recognised on the basis of the provisions of the FCN treaty. The decision has been criticised. S. Mozarsky, 'Defining Discrimination on the Basis of National Origin under Article VII(1) of the Friendship Treaty Between United States and Japan' (1992) 15 Fordham ILJ 1099.

[23] *Nicaragua Case* [1984] ICJ Rpts 352.

[24] See Chapter 6 below. Early attempts are described in G. Schwarzenberger, *Foreign Investments and International Law* (1969), 109–20.

are obvious. The issues that relate to foreign investments made by large multinational corporations give rise to sensitive issues of sovereignty, exploitation of natural resources and internal economic policies. It is unlikely that developing states will commit themselves readily on such issues in a binding multilateral treaty, though developed states will be keen to realise such a treaty. In the decades after decolonisation, the developing states have been striving to bring about a New International Economic Order (NIEO), one facet of which is national control over all foreign investment. Though the vigour of the movement for the NIEO has dissipated, there has been no urgency among the developing states to dismantle the gains that resulted during that period. Hence, it is unlikely that the developing states will surrender their efforts to establish national control as the prevailing general standard by subscribing to a multilateral treaty which strikes at the principle of national control. The efforts at making multilateral instruments on investment will continue, but the possibility of making strong rules in such an instrument remain a distant possibility.

Bilateral treaties, on the other hand, are different in that they are made on an *ad hoc* basis and their ability to give rise to general principles is remote. In addition, such treaties could be negotiated in such a manner as to suit the mutual interests of the parties, whereas a multilateral treaty cannot be. Bilateral solutions become necessary simply because of an absence of a consensus to create multilaterally acceptable norms.[25]

The rules on investment protection became considerably diffuse in the post-colonial era as a result of the developing states' concerted attacks on rules contended for by developed states. Contractual regimes on the basis of which foreign investments were made were being disturbed and replaced by new contractual techniques that were favourable to national control of the investment. The rules of state responsibility and the minimum standards of treatment of aliens were being attacked not only by Latin American states but also by other developing states. The norm of prompt, adequate and effective compensation in the event of the expropriation of foreign property, which had been consistently supported by the developed states, was threatened by a competing notion of appropriate compensation. Whereas the previous tendency had been to create doctrines that favoured the insulation of foreign investment through

---

[25] For a similar view in a different context, see A. Carty, 'Critical International Law: Recent Trends in the Theory of International Law' (1991) 2 EJIL 66.

theories of internationalisation of foreign investment, there were now competing norms such as the doctrine of permanent sovereignty over natural resources, economic self-determination and national control over all economic activities. These norms sought to localise the foreign investment process by vesting control in the hands of the host state. Though much of the acrimony that attended the debate has subsided, the ideas that were generated in the course of the tussle of norms still persist. They led to regulatory legislation in the developing world, controlling the entry of investments and their subsequent operation within the host state. The system of norms so constructed stood in stark opposition to the system of norms that were favoured by the developed states that emphasised the protection of foreign investment.

In this confused state of conflicting norms, bilateral investment treaties provided the parties with the opportunity to set out the definite norms that would apply to the investments their nationals make in each other's territory. It would be wrong to subscribe to the thesis that the treaties stabilised customary international law. If there was a definite conviction as to the existence of customary international law in the area, there would have been little need for such frenetic treaty-making activity on investment protection. There was an absence of significant customary international law in this area simply because it would be difficult to show that there was free consent on the part of all the developing states to the creation of any customary principles in the area. If there was such customary international law, many developing states would regard themselves as persistent objectors who were not bound by the customary law. If there was customary international law on investment protection, there was no need to confirm so many times over what already existed by making bilateral investment treaties. States, which entered into investment treaties, were not engaging in an exercise of such self-stultification, confirming repeatedly what already existed. On the contrary, knowing the confused state of the law, they entered into such treaties so that they could clarify the rules that they would apply in case of any dispute which may arise between them.

The view that there has been an absence of a rapid development of international law to meet the needs of foreign investment was stated by the International Court of Justice in the *Barcelona Traction Case* in the following terms:[26]

---

[26] [1970] ICJ Rpts 3.

Considering the important developments of the last half-century, the growth of foreign investments and the expansion of international activities of corporations, in particular of holding companies, which are often multinational, and considering the way in which the economic interests of states have proliferated, it may at first sight appear surprising that the evolution of the law has not gone further and that no generally accepted rules in the matter have crystallized on the international plane.

There was a need for a rapid development of the law in the area, but such development was not forthcoming because of the conflicts which were inherent in the area of foreign investment. Hence, states had to resort to the second best solution by making bilateral investment treaties to ensure that, as between them at least, there would be definite rules relating to foreign investment. This is a better explanation for the rapidity with which such treaties have come about on the international scene than the explanation that they merely confirm existing customary international law or create new customary international law.

In recent times, the states of the old Soviet bloc, now turning towards a market economy and foreign investment, have begun making bilateral investment treaties with capital-exporting countries. The practice began even when communism was still in place as the Eastern bloc countries were desperately short of capital and looked to foreign investment to provide it. The remaining communist states have also made several investment treaties. China, which announced its 'open door' policy in 1984, signed over 100 such treaties within a short period.[27] Vietnam has also joined the trend. There are also treaties between developing countries.[28] In the case of the remaining communist states and the former communist states, the reasons for this treaty activity may be to dispel perceptions that they are high-risk countries because of past ideological commitments that opposed the influx of foreign investments and the notion of

[27] UNCTAD, *World Investment Report, 2003*.

[28] Two such treaties are the treaties between Singapore and Sri Lanka and between Thailand and Bangladesh. In these treaties, too, it is a one-way relationship that is contemplated, Singapore and Thailand being capital-exporters while Sri Lanka and Bangladesh are recipients of capital. The reason for the flow may be that Singapore and Thailand are relocating the less technology-intensive industries to Sri Lanka and Bangladesh as the latter are sources of cheap labour and also products made in these countries are able to obtain greater access to the markets of developed states due to the generalised system of preferences (GSP). Singapore was removed from the GSP list on the ground that it had become an industrialised country. Developing states which fear such graduation will seek to invest in other less developed countries in the hope of making use of cheaper labour and preferential access terms. They will need protection for their investments.

private ownership of property.[29] The treaties have a signalling function in that they are addressed to the investment community to indicate a major change of policy undertaken by a country in relation to foreign investment.[30]

The sudden spurt of treaties in the 1990s was due to a variety of factors. The lack of funds for economic development consequent upon the loan defaults in the previous years caused sovereign lending by banks to dry up. The flow of aid also dwindled due to recession in the developed economies as well as due to changes of policy. Economic liberalism being the prevailing philosophy in the United States and Europe, there were vigorous efforts made to promote the free market and liberalisation of the international economy. One phenomenon of these trends was the increase in bilateral investment treaties in the 1990s. They were seen as instruments that accomplished liberalisation in the sphere of foreign investment, not because they contained any norms on liberalisation itself but because of the belief that protection of foreign investment increased flows of foreign investment.[31] The flow of foreign investment funds were seen as leading to economic development. The view that securing foreign investment protection through investment treaties facilitated such flows was a reason given for the increase in the number of bilateral investment treaties.[32]

Though the number of these treaties may be increasing, their contents indicate the adoption of a variety of standards depending on the negotiating positions of the different states. The treaties concluded in the 1990s show the vigour of the liberalising tendencies of economic liberalism. Yet, the treaties are disparate as to content. Only US and Canadian treaties provide for pre-entry establishment. The flow of assets of multinational corporations once they had made entry is guaranteed through the provision of a right of repatriation in these treaties. The protection

[29] See K. R. Propp, 'Bilateral Investment Treaties: The US Experience in Eastern Europe' (1992) 86 *ASIL Proceedings* 540.

[30] Thus, the recent Argentinean treaties signal a departure from the Calvo doctrines which that country had adhered to and a policy of assumption of international obligations in respect of investment flows into the country as regards investments from the treaty partners. It is a signal to other capital-exporting states of a willingness to sign similar treaties with them and to be accommodating to foreign investment from them.

[31] Except for US and Canadian treaties, investment treaties seldom accepted pre-entry national treatment as an obligation.

[32] This is an untested hypothesis. South-east Asian states which have received large investments from the United States do not have investment treaties with that country. Stability and other factors have a greater influence on investment flows than do investment treaties.

standards are also intended to promote the flow of foreign investment. Often, the same state will accept varying standards on areas such as compensation for expropriation, the repatriation of profits and the arbitration of disputes that arise. The developed state will seek to extract as much protection for the investor as possible but often concedes the fact that this may not be possible. These concessions are seen in the exceptions to the general propositions contained in the treaties. Thus, the treaty may recognise the right of the foreign investor to repatriate profits, but also contain a provision that in exceptional circumstances, such as a foreign exchange shortage, a state party may restrict repatriation to a percentage of the profits. The developing state will seek to concede as little as possible, ensuring that the treaty is consistent with its foreign investment laws and its national interests. Its interests always lie in giving up as little of its sovereign rights of control over the foreign investment as possible and preserving as much regulatory control over foreign investment as is possible. In the reconciliation of these mutually incompatible aims, vague terms often come to be used in the treaties, making the protection they give to the foreign investors meagre. For this reason, each treaty must be taken as a bargain that has been struck between the parties, depending on their relative strengths and mutual dependence. This may also explain the reasons why the terms in the treaties differ to a considerable extent.

There are also differences that reflect the period in which the treaties were made. The provisions in the early treaties are often less stringent and formulated in nebulous terms. The treaties gather increasing sophistication as the practice develops. Thus, new dispute settlement techniques are tried out, but there is doubt as to whether the full ramifications of the words used were really understood by both parties. There is also the suspicion that the making of the treaties were made conditions for loans and rescue packages that were put together by financial institutions.

The claim is made that these treaties boost investor confidence in the host state and that as a result more investment flows take place. This is an untested claim. It is empirically untestable whether states will receive more investments if they conclude such treaties.[33] Many smaller

---

[33] UNCTAD, *World Investment Report, 2003*, 89: 'An aggregate statistical analysis does not reveal a significant independent impact of BITs in determining FDI flows. At best, BITs play a minor role in influencing global FDI flows and explaining differences in their size among countries.' Similar conclusions are drawn in the World Bank, *World Development Report*, 129: 'Countries that had concluded a BIT were no more likely to receive additional FDI than were countries without such a pact.'

developing states have signed a large number of treaties without witnessing significant inward investment flows. Nevertheless, the principal reasons for developing countries concluding such treaties is the belief that they will lead to greater investor confidence by dispelling any impression of risk associated with the country in the past. States with a record of nationalisation see such treaties as a panacea for their past deeds. Thus, Sri Lanka, after the fall of its socialist government which had embarked on a course of nationalisation, entered into seven treaties in three years, whereas it took Singapore and Malaysia twelve years to accomplish the same number of treaties. There is nothing to show that there were greater investment flows into Sri Lanka than into Singapore and Malaysia as a result of these treaties. In reality, attracting foreign investment depends more on the political and economic climate being favourable to such foreign investment than on the creation of a legal structure for its protection.

The assumption behind the treaties is that the framework for protection they create leads to increased flows of foreign investment. This assumption is coming to be questioned. Institutions, which have assiduously promoted investment treaties, have expressed scepticism of the proposition that there is a correlation between investment treaties and flows of investment. It now seems to take the view that other factors such as political stability and economic circumstances play a greater role in promoting investments.

4. Features of bilateral investment treaties

The structure of different bilateral treaties has a basic similarity. The treaty begins with a prefatory statement as to the aims of the treaty, which are usually the reciprocal encouragement and protection of investment flows between the two states. This is followed by an identification of the types of property which are protected and the nature of the link of nationality to one of the parties that entitles the foreign investor to the protection of the treaty. The standard of treatment to be accorded to the foreign investor is established. The right of repatriation of profits is asserted. There are statements on the nature of the compensation, if any, to be provided to the foreign investor for loss occurring during wars and civil riots. The standard of compensation in the event of a takeover of the foreign investor's property is identified. The procedure for the settlement of disputes arising from the investment by arbitration is stated. These are standard contents in all bilateral agreements. But, there are variations of the statements of the rules that are to be applied as between the parties on each of these areas. To understand these variations, it is necessary to analyse the contents of these treaties separately. The variations indicate the impossibility of customary principles arising from these treaties, however many of them there are.[34]

4.1. The statement of the purpose of the treaty

Every bilateral investment treaty begins with a declaration as to the purpose of the treaty. This is usually stated to be the reciprocal encouragement and protection of investments. The statement disguises the important fact that the flow that is contemplated is in reality a one-way flow of investment from the developed state to the developing state. There is an inequality inherent in the very process of making a treaty between the giver and the receiver. As pointed out earlier, there is an erosion of sovereignty by one party without a corresponding erosion in the other party.

The extent to which this important consideration affects the whole process of making bilateral investment treaties is yet to be analysed, though writers have referred to the asymmetry inherent in the making of such treaties.[35] Sometimes, bilateral investment treaties are secured by the holding out of promises or threats of trade sanctions. Sometimes, the making of the treaty is made a condition for a loan. In this latter case, the problem of inequality becomes accentuated. Though it has not been suggested that these treaties are invalid because of their unequal nature, it is easy to foresee a state, pushed into a corner in an investment dispute, taking this path and arguing that the treaty is invalid. In such circumstances, the better view would be that, despite any argument as to inequality, the treaties, for whatever reason, were freely entered into and are valid. The motive of a state for entering into a treaty does not affect the validity of the treaty. The inequality in the bargaining power of the states is also irrelevant. However, where there had been inducements held out to the weaker state

---

[34] There are no bilateral investment treaties between developed countries. The reference made to the existence of treaties between developing countries does not affect the fact that one of them is an exporter and the other a receiver of foreign investment. Two receivers of foreign investments do not sign such treaties.

[35] Thus, Salacuse, (1990) 24 Int Lawyer 655 at 662, observed:

> A BIT purports to create a symmetrical legal relationship between the two states, for it provides that either party may invest under the same conditions in the territory of the other. In reality, an asymmetry exists between the parties to the BITs since one state will be the source and the other the recipient of any investment flows between the two countries.

for making the treaty, the situation may be different. It would be interesting to speculate as to the effect of the treaty where the level of understanding of the treaty as between the officials of the state was different.[36]

An issue may arise as to whether the prefatory statement creates a positive duty on the part of the capital-exporting state to encourage its investors to take investments to the other party. Such a positive duty is not created by the prefatory clause itself, but there may be a duty on the part of the capital-exporting state to facilitate the making of investments in the host state by giving, at the least, the same assistance and facilities that are given to nationals making foreign investments in other states. Thus, where other investors are permitted to insure with the state insurance scheme for foreign investors, the state could be said to be under a duty to grant insurance to a foreign investor.[37] Where the parties undertake to encourage investment flows in a separate article rather than in the prefatory statement, the duty to encourage flows of foreign investment may be stronger.[38] But, the content of such a duty cannot be assessed as the amount of the investment that should be encouraged under the treaty cannot be quantified. The duty so created is not a positive duty. It is satisfied so long as a state does not impede the flow of investments to the other contracting party.

The prefatory statement usually contains a statement of the beliefs of the parties that the flows of foreign investment between themselves are mutually beneficial to their economic development. One question that may arise is whether the treaty protection will apply to all investments or only to such investments as can be shown to contribute to the economic development of the host state. Can it be argued that the host state can escape its obligations by showing that a particular foreign investment coming from the capital-exporting state did not in fact contribute to its economic development or that it was positively harmful to such

---

[36] Treaty law does not go behind the treaty and examine such issues. The fiction is that states are equal. This is an absurdity when most treaties between developing countries and developed states are made by persons unskilled in international law, on the one side, and a team of sophisticated lawyers and economists, on the other.

[37] Such insurance is not granted if foreign investors invest in states without treaties, which in itself is an inducement for developing states to make such treaties.

[38] Can a state argue that the treaty could be rescinded because this duty has not been satisfied? If so, how can the amount of investment that must be encouraged be quantified? Can a developing country justify its breach of the treaty on the ground that the failure of the developed state party to encourage a sufficient flow of foreign investments was a prior breach which gave it the right to regard the treaty as invalid? These are problems that arise, given the vague nature of some of the provisions of the investment treaties.

development and therefore fell outside the protection of the treaty? Can it be said that the prefatory statement showed that it was never the intention of the parties to protect an investment which did not promote economic development? These questions are yet to be answered. The literature on the subject of bilateral investment treaties is usually laudatory of them and has yet to grapple with issues of this nature. Many writers regard these treaties as instruments of economic liberalism, and, for them, the answer is based on the simple belief that the treaties do promote investments and investments are beneficial to development. The heavy accent on protection forestalls the possibility of such questions being raised.

4.2. Definitions

All the treaties seek to define some of the terms that are used in the treaty and the definitions contained in them have a similarity that will contribute to the understanding of the usage of terms in international investment law. In addition, they also indicate the understanding the states have on issues such as corporate nationality and thereby contribute to the stabilisation of theories that may be evolving in such areas. These are innovative features in the treaties. Some of the common terms that are defined in the treaties are considered below.

4.2.1. Investments

All treaties contain definitions of investments. Investments are usually defined as broadly as possible. They dispel any lingering doubts that may exist from early ideas that intangible property is not property that is protected by international law. Many early texts contain the idea that the intangible property of an alien is incapable of protection by international law, presumably because the creation of intangible property is dependent on the laws of the host state. Rights to intellectual property such as patents, copyright and know-how, which are the intangible assets referred to most often in the context of international investment, vest in a person only to the extent that the local law recognises such rights. Hence, there was a view that the host state had absolute control over intangible property as such rights was dependent on the law of the host state for their recognition. Rights of protection for shareholders were also seldom referred to. These rights were also created by reference to an entity whose existence depended on the law of the state of incorporation. Verdross, writing in 1931, excluded from his definition of property recognised by international law, 'so called literary, artistic and industrial property'.[39] But, increasingly, it came to be recognised that the protection of intangible rights was central to investment protection. The concession agreement which was the principal vehicle of foreign investment in the mineral resources sector created contractual rights which were intangible. The idea that in these contractual situations what was being protected was an intangible contractual right and not the physical assets took time to evolve.[40] A series of cases dealt with the protection of such rights. In *Le Courturier* v. *Rey*,[41] the assets confiscated in France included trademarks. The dispute in the *Carl Zeiss Stiftung* cases[42] litigated in England and elsewhere also concerned trademarks. Many of the new forms of foreign investment contracts involved the transfer of intangible rights. Licensing agreements, management contracts and consultancy contracts had intangible assets as their subject matter. Protection of foreign investment increasingly meant the protection of not only the physical assets of the investor but also the intangible assets that he took into the venture, which were often as or more valuable than the physical assets. It was possible to capitalise new ventures by transferring intangible assets such as technology or know-how to the ventures. Yet, as in domestic law, the original idea that rights in property related to physical property was difficult to shake off.

Bilateral investment treaties leave no room for doubt that they include intangible assets within the definition of property and often spell out the types of intangible assets protected by the treaty. Article 1 of the United Kingdom treaty with Singapore may be taken as representative of the types of property listed as protected by such treaties in some early treaties. The term 'investment' is defined as including: (1) movable and immovable property and property rights such as mortgages, liens and pledges, (2) shares, stocks and debentures in companies and other interests

---

[39] A. Verdross, 'Les Règles Internationales Concernant le Traitement des Etrangers' (1931) 37 *Hague Recueil* 364; see also G. White, *Nationalisation of Foreign Property* (1961), 421–30; in the *Chorzow Factory Case* (1928) PCIJ Series A No. 17, however, much emphasis was placed on the protection of know-how that was transferred in the calculation of the damages claimed by Germany.

[40] See Chapter 1 above. See also Ian Brownlie, 'Legal Status of Natural Resources in International Law' (1979) 162 *Hague Recueil* 255; Nico Schrijver, *Permanent Sovereignty over Natural Resources: Balancing Rights and Duties* (1997). Some treaties show little regard to the notion of permanent sovereignty over natural resources. Thus, the Australia–Vietnam treaty defines property that is protected to include contractual rights 'to engage in agriculture, forestry, fisheries and animal husbandry, to search for, extract or exploit natural resources and to manufacture, use and sell products'.

[41] [1910] AC 262.   [42] [1967] 1 AC 853.

in companies, (3) claims to money or to any performance under contracts having a financial value, (4) intellectual property rights and goodwill, and (5) business concessions including concessions relating to natural resources. But, as treaty practice advances, the definition becomes more refined and seeks to capture new instruments that are associated with the making of investments within the definition of investment.

The US model bilateral investment treaty contains a longer list which includes, besides the five categories listed above, 'licenses and permits issued pursuant to law, including those issued for manufacture and sale of products' and 'any right conferred by law or contract, including rights to search for or utilise natural resources, and rights to manufacture, use and sell products'. These additions are not merely taken out of excessive caution, but are a recognition of the fact that many of the rights which the foreign investor obtains in host states are administrative law rights based on permission to conduct certain activity in the host state. The whole course of the foreign investment may depend on the existence of such public law rights. The investment will cease to be of much value if rights such as the right to export or repatriate profits initially granted are later withdrawn by the administrative agency which grants them.[43] The protection of such acquired rights and privileges is seen as a task of the bilateral investment treaty, and the US model seeks to achieve this by extending the definition of property to include these public law rights acquired under the host state's law in the definition of property. Whether the freezing of a decision taken in pursuance of the exercise of a discretionary power, though feasible in terms of law, is wise in terms of practice remains to be seen. The objection to it is that it excessively curtails the regulatory power of a state. The idea that the first exercise of a discretionary power is binding for all time is one that sits uneasily with administrative practice. Administrative decisions are made by a state having the public interest in mind. Whether a treaty should be able to fetter that discretion will always be a contentious issue. Many states overcome this problem by confining the investments that are protected by the treaty to investments which are made in accordance with their laws and regulations on investment.[44] This introduces even greater subjectivity and uncertainty into the

---

[43] Some of the issues in *Amco* v. *Indonesia* concerned such administrative controls. The fact that the rights of the foreign investor are dependent on administrative decisions has been pointed out in Chapter 3 above.

[44] The formula used in Australian and Indonesian treaties is that only such investments 'made in accordance with the laws, regulations and policies, from time to time in existence' are protected. This introduces indeterminacy into the treaty as a state could remove protection from an investment simply through a change of policy, regulation or law.

treaty as local laws and regulations may be changed. The content of the treaty obligations could be manipulated simply through changes to laws and regulations.

From the point of view of the capital-exporting state, the stance adopted in the US model treaty safeguards the interests of US nationals given the increasing tendency to subject investments to screening and other administrative mechanisms instituted in the host state. The US treaties provide for open entry to US investments as well as for the protection of those investments.[45] But, the host state is unlikely to view the inclusion of the privileges it confers on the foreign investor under its public law as rights that are protected by an international treaty. The effect of the treaty would be to make the public law rights irrevocable once granted. This defeats the very notion of public law rights which are granted with the public interest in mind and become defeasible when they are no longer in the public interest. It is well accepted that any matter that falls within the domestic sphere can be brought within the sphere of international law by making it the subject of a treaty. But, it is unlikely that a state will lightly surrender its public law powers relating to the regulation of foreign investment. The inclusion of these public law rights will mean that rights that are granted in connection with the exploitation of natural resources cannot later be withdrawn without violating the treaty. The extent to which a state is willing to lose its regulatory powers over foreign investment through the creation of treaty rights in the foreign investor lies at the crux of the problem in this area.

In the case of the protection of concession agreements, the consistency of such a position with the notion of permanent sovereignty over natural resources, which some authorities regard as a *ius cogens* principle, will have to be considered.[46] It may well be argued that the removal of public law rights of the host state relating to natural resources has no effect in law on the ground that it is contrary to a *ius cogens* principle.[47] There could be problems regarding other public law rights which the bilateral investment

---

[45] The idea that the right of establishment must be provided for is taken over from the FCN treaties. See note by H. Golsong, (1992) 31 ILM 124. The FCN treaties had political objectives which dominated their economic objectives. The link between politics and investment has always been close but unobserved.

[46] See note 40 above.

[47] A treaty, conflicting with a peremptory norm of international law, is invalidated to the extent of the conflict by Article 53 of the Vienna Convention on the Law of Treaties. There is some authority for the view that the doctrine of permanent sovereignty over natural resources is a peremptory norm of international law. Ian Brownlie, 'Legal Status of Natural Resources in International Law' (1979) 162 *Hague Recueil* 245 at 255.

treaty seeks to ensure the continuity of, once granted. The treaty will remove the discretion of the granting state to interfere with this public law grant for the duration of the treaty. Whether such a freezing of the right created in pursuance of its discretionary power was contemplated by the developing state at the time it signed the treaty is conjectural. There is continuing disquiet expressed as to the extent of the sovereignty that has been unwittingly transferred over inherently sovereign functions through the treaty device.

There is little doubt that bilateral investment treaties contribute to the development of a concept of property in international law.[48] Its identification and inclusion of various types of intangible property is an important step towards the formulation of such a concept. The protection of tangible property was an easy notion to fit into the scheme of alien protection as such property was often taken in by the alien himself. In the case of intangible property, the difficulty was created by the fact that the right to such property depended on the extent to which the domestic law itself recognised it. It is now coming to be recognised that once the right to such intangible property has been acquired under the domestic law of the host state by the alien, the acquired rights could be converted into rights protected by international law through bilateral investment treaties. In the absence of such treaty protection of such intangible rights, the old view that they are rights dependent on the law of the host state and may be extinguished in accordance with the law of the state must still be valid.

But, the philosophical bases of the concept of property that is involved in various bilateral investment treaties differ markedly and influence the manner in which the treaty itself is formulated. The US treaties clearly give expression to a notion of property as an absolute and indefeasible right. Such a view is consistent with US constitutional thinking on the right to property. This notion is a unique product of US history. Transported to the United States, the Lockean notion of property as an indefeasible right of the individual found a hospitable home in the context of the history of a country in which land was cleared by labour and wrested from hostile natives and the elements by personal effort. It is this concept of property which finds expression in US investment treaties and US policies on investment protection which have influenced international law. It is not a notion of property that one finds in the English law. Nor is it to be found in the legal systems of the Commonwealth based on the English

---

[48] In earlier times, there was some doubt as to whether international law had a notion of property. The concept of territory was quite distinct.

law. Like European systems, the common law recognises that the right to property is always defeasible in the public interest. This schism between attitudes to property is reflected in the bilateral investment treaties as well and to a large extent is reflected in the differing attitudes to investment protection. The arbitral awards that are made on the basis of investment treaties will increasingly reflect these different attitudes to property and its protection.

4.2.2. Limitation on the definition of investment

Though investments are defined as widely as possible, many bilateral investment treaties confine the benefits of the treaty only to investments approved by the state parties to the treaty.[49] This limitation, at once, creates two categories of foreign investment originating from the same state party, one which is protected by the treaty because it is approved by the state party which receives the investment, and one which is not because it lacks such approval. Discrimination between investments is inherent in this situation.[50] This category of investment which is not approved by the host state is protected by whatever principles of investment protection there are in international law. Approved investments are entitled to the special protection devised by the treaty regime. The recognition of a distinction between approved investment and other investment itself indicates the *lex specialis* nature of bilateral investment treaties, for unapproved investments are subject to general norms of investment protection, if any exist, whereas approved investments are subject to the treaty regime.[51] The investments covered by the different treaties differ according to

---

[49] This limitation is to be found in the treaties made by south-east Asian states. The treaties of Singapore and Malaysia contain the requirement that the investment must be approved for the purposes of investment. The newer Malaysian treaties offer protection only to investments made in accordance with the 'laws, regulations and policies' of Malaysia. In *Grueslin v. Malaysia* (2000) 5 ICSID Rpts 483, the tribunal ruled that jurisdiction under the treaty could not be invoked by investors who did not have specific approval. The parties who do not qualify as investors or whose investments do not fall within the definition of investments will not be able to invoke the dispute settlement provisions of the treaties. *Yaung Chi Oo Ltd v. Myanmar* (2003) 42 ILM 540.

[50] Such discrimination is based on objective, economic factors and does not offend any norm against discrimination involved in the provision of national treatment to all foreign investors. It is unlikely that racial discrimination is involved in such situations.

[51] This approval procedure proved crucial in *Yaung Chi Oo Ltd v. Myanmar* (2003) 42 ILM 540, where the arbitral tribunal refused jurisdiction on the ground that there was no specific approval in writing as required by the ASEAN Investment Protection Treaty (1987). Also, where the regulatory laws of the state are not adhered to by the investor, he will lose the protection of the treaty, if the treaty had confined protection to investments that ensured conduct according to the regulations of the host state.

definition. In these circumstances, it is wishful thinking to contemplate the possibility of customary international law emerging from these treaties.

The distinction between approved and other investments comes about as a result of the systems for screening foreign investment entry maintained by host state laws. Some states require approval for all incoming foreign investments. Others maintain an open door for all foreign investments but give special privileges only to investments that secure approval. The approval is usually given only to such investments as are considered particularly beneficial to the host state and are subject to the satisfaction of conditions that may be imposed. Difficult problems could arise where the approval is later withdrawn by the state for non-satisfaction of the conditions. Does such withdrawal result in the investment losing the protection of the investment treaty as it will cease to be an approved investment? It would be best that this problem is ironed out by the treaty itself. One solution is to require that such withdrawal of approval is not made except on objective factors and that the investor can resort to domestic tribunals to test whether there was justification for the withdrawal of the approval.

Some treaties seek to meet the situation by treating the right of entry and establishment that is granted by the screening authority as investment rights to be protected by the treaty. It is a neat solution, but it is unlikely to be accepted by states which are keen on devising effective systems of investment screening. The whole object of the system is to keep out investments that do not promote the economic objectives of the state. The termination of investments that are seen to be inconsistent with these objectives will also be seen as necessary for the functioning of the scheme. The subjection of the right of termination to external scrutiny by submitting it to the protection of a bilateral treaty regime will therefore be resisted by many developing states.

In view of these problems, a wider limitation on the type of investment that is subject to the protection of the treaty is emerging. This focuses on the issue of the internal laws and regulations of the host state. The limitation is to provide protection to the investments, however broadly defined, only if they are made according to the laws and regulations of the host state. Some provisions indicate that the investments must continue to function according to the laws and regulations of the host state. Some even contemplate future changes to these laws and regulations and insist that the foreign investment complying with these laws and regulations 'from time to time in existence' alone will qualify for protection. This indicates that many of the treaties which contain such limitations are uncertain as to the types of investment that they protect. For the host state could manipulate this through its own internal laws and regulations. Such treaties contain an internal device which leads to uncertainty. However elaborate their treatment or protection standards may be, the initial statement of the investments covered by the treaties in such uncertain terms makes these treaties quite unstable and subject to the caprices of each state party to the treaty. Such treaties err on the side of preserving the host state's right to regulation without balancing it with the right to protect the foreign investment. Even this short survey demonstrates the disparity as to the types of investment that different treaties protect.

4.2.3. Portfolio investments

In some treaties, portfolio investments are included in the definition of investments. Portfolio investments must be distinguished from primary shares in companies which are the vehicles for the foreign investment.[52] These are not shares that are ordinarily traded.[53] Portfolio investments are instruments connected with companies like shares or unconnected with them like promissory notes and bonds. They are used in order to raise capital for ventures and are freely circulated through stock exchanges or through other markets or means. The argument for the inclusion of portfolio investments is that they are an important means of encouraging capital flows, and that it is in the interests of developing states that their flows should be encouraged. The argument against including portfolio investments is that their inclusion in investment treaties means that the host state owes a duty of protection to unascertainable holders of these instruments whose identities would continuously change. In addition, because of the fact that they can be rapidly pulled out of a state, the value of such investment has come to be questioned in view of the financial crises that have been precipitated through the sudden exodus of portfolio capital. *Fedax* v. *Venezuela*[54] is an interesting decision, in which the domestic holders of promissory notes, who were not entitled to any protection, transferred them to foreign citizens of a state with an investment treaty, who then became entitled to claim against the state

---

[52] As where a foreign investor becomes a shareholder in a joint venture company the creation of which is mandated as the form of entry of foreign investment by the host state.

[53] This distinction is unfortunately not made in some of the literature which asserts, on the basis of the protection of shares in companies like joint venture companies which are the vehicles of foreign investment, that portfolio investment is protected. This is erroneous.

[54] (1998) 37 ILM 1378.

on the basis that the treaty protected portfolio investments. The case illustrates the problems that attend the inclusion of portfolio investments in investment treaties. Policy on portfolio investment varies. As much as there are treaties which include them, there are treaties which expressly exclude portfolio investments.[55] There are widely drafted formulations which clearly take in portfolio investments as much as there are treaties which specifically exclude portfolio investments from their scope.

4.2.4. Corporate nationality and protection of shareholders

The definition of a company in bilateral investment treaties goes against the traditional notions in international law. The general rule relating to the diplomatic protection of corporations making investments in foreign countries was stated in the *Barcelona Traction Case*.[56] According to the International Court of Justice in that case, a corporation has the nationality of the state in which it is incorporated, and only the latter state has the right of diplomatic intervention on behalf of the corporation. This is a rule based in logic, for a corporation cannot have an existence outside the legal system which created it. This rule, however, did not permit the protection of shareholders of companies. In the *Barcelona Traction Case*, the Court denied that Belgium had *locus standi* to maintain an action against Spain to protect the interests of Belgian shareholders of a Canadian company whose investments in Spain had been affected by Spanish judicial and administrative measures. The Court, in reaching this much criticised conclusion, referred to the growth of multinational corporations within the international economy and expressed surprise that there had been little development towards securing greater protection for investments by multinational corporations.

The Court indicated clearly that the technique of protection of shareholders may be found through bilateral and multilateral arrangements on investment protection.[57] The increase in the number of bilateral investment treaties in the 1970s may also be a result of the decision in the *Barcelona Traction Case* which created doubts as to the possibility of the protection of shareholders in the absence of bilateral or multilateral

---

[55] The ASEAN Framework Agreement on Foreign Investment contains an article which specifically excludes its application to portfolio investments.

[56] [1970] ICJ Rpts 1. The separate judgment of Judge Oda in the *ELSI Case* [1989] ICJ Rpts 15 contatins an affirmation of the rule.

[57] Para. 90.

treaties.[58] Shareholder protection was becoming important due to the insistence of many foreign investment codes which limited the entry of foreign investments except through locally incorporated joint ventures formed in association with domestic entrepreneurs or state entities. There has been an increase in the number of such foreign investment codes. This has meant that much of the foreign investment would have to be made without the diplomatic protection of the home states of the foreign investors. The situation had to be remedied and it was remedied to a large extent by a spurt of bilateral investment treaties redefining investments to include intangible property such as shares and including tests of corporate nationality other than incorporation. Again, the departure that these treaties make from customary international law is clear. The treaties remove any doubt that may have existed in customary international law as to shareholder protection by defining investments to include shares. The intention clearly was to include primary shares.[59] The second method through which shareholder protection is effected relates to the definition of corporate nationality. Customary international law shows no inclination to depart from incorporation as the test of corporate nationality.[60]

58 *Barcelona Traction* recognised that there could be treaty protection of shareholders: [1970] ICJ Rpts 1, paras. 54 and 61. Judge Tanaka, in his separate opinion, was willing to regard shares as property (pp. 127 and 134). The technique of regarding shares as property is widely used in bilateral investment treaties. On shareholder protection, see further J. M. Jones, 'Claims on Behalf of Nationals Who Are Shareholders in Foreign Companies' (1949) 20 BYIL 227; C. Staker, 'Diplomatic Protection of Private Business Companies' (1990) 61 BYIL 155; G. Sacerdoti, 'Barcelona Traction Revisited: Foreign-Owned and Controlled Companies in International Law' in Y. Dinstein (ed.), *International Law at a Time of Perplexity: Essays in Honour of Shabtai Rosenne* (1989), 699.

59 This point is made again to assert the view that portfolio investment was never intended by the reference to shares in companies. The history of the inclusion of shares suggests that it was done to get over the problem raised in *Barcelona Traction*.

60 Besides *Barcelona Traction* and the separate opinion of Judge Oda in the *ELSI Case* [1989] ICJ Rpts 15, there are arbitral awards in which incorporation has been held to be the test of corporate nationality. The problem of corporate personality has arisen in arbitral jurisprudence, particularly before ICSID tribunals. ICSID has accepted that, where a foreign investor incorporates his company in the host state, ICSID will not have jurisdiction unless the host state clearly indicates that it was still willing to consider the company as a foreign national. A clear clause of waiver was required. *Holiday Inns* v. *Morocco* (1980) 51 BYIL 123. But, in more recent awards, an inference of waiver has been drawn from the circumstances. *Amco* v. *Indonesia* (1983–90) 1 ICSID Rpts 389. National courts have used incorporation as the test of nationality of foreign companies. *Sumitomo Shoji America, Inc.* v. *Avagliano*, 457 US 176 (1982); *Campagnie Europeene de Petroles* v. *Sensor Nederland BV* (1983) 22 ILM 320. The issue of what amounts to effective management for the purposes of the ASEAN Investment Treaty is discussed in *Yaung Chi Oo Ltd* v. *Myanmar* (2003) 42 ILM 540.

There are technical problems with international protection of such corporations because the corporation itself is a creature of domestic law and depends for its existence on domestic law. It can be destroyed at will by the domestic system which created it. For this reason, international law did not interfere with corporate personality in any significant manner. It was also logical that, since the creation of the corporation depended on the will of the state as expressed in its domestic law, the corporation should have the nationality of the state in which it was created.

Some of the bilateral treaties seek to establish alternative tests of corporate nationality for the purposes of protection under the treaty. They specify that a company incorporated in one contracting party will be protected by the other party provided the seat of control of the company is located in the other contracting party or where there is control or a substantial interest in the company by the nationals of the other party.[61] This alternative test is to be found largely in the treaties made by the European states and by those states which have legal systems based on the civil law tradition. They accord with the *siège social* theory of nationality that has wide currency in the civilian systems.[62] A third type of test is used in the Algiers Accord creating the Iran–US Claims Tribunal, which regarded a corporation as protected only if over half the shares in the corporation are held by nationals of a contracting party and the corporation is controlled by such nationals. This formulation was used to overcome difficult issues where the corporation is controlled by persons holding dual nationality.[63] Some treaties require both incorporation and effective management to be located in the state which is party to the treaty.[64] Australian and Dutch treaties seek to confer protection on companies incorporated in a state

---

[61] Thus, the Singapore–UK treaty provides that a company incorporated in Singapore is to be regarded as a British company if the majority of the shares of the company are held by British nationals. The *siège social* theory of corporate nationality, which attributes nationality to the state of the seat from which the corporation is controlled, is followed in many civil law legal systems. The Netherlands and Denmark use the incorporation test. For Denmark, see *Centros Ltd* v. *Ehverves-og Selskabsstyrelsen* [1999] 2 CMLR 551. Ireland, being a common law jurisdiction, also uses the test of incorporation. It would appear that European Community law is veering towards an incorporation test.

[62] Problems have arisen in EC law on the issue of corporate nationality. For a discussion, see Peter Behrens, 'International Company Law in View of the Centros Decision of the ECJ' (2000) 1 *European Business Organization Law Review* 125.

[63] Extensive case law was generated by the Iran–US Claims Tribunal on this point.

[64] The Philippines treaties contain this formula. The ASEAN Investment Treaty also contains this formula. It was one of the issues considered in *Yaung Chi Oo Ltd* v. *Myanmar* (2003) 42 ILM 540.

other than the party to the treaty in which their nationals have shares. All these different formulations also introduce uncertainties into the area as there is no uniformity in the definition of the protected company. The corporation has the duty to indicate that it is entitled to the protection under the treaty because it was established in the contracting state and it took the investment into the other contracting state.

Depending on the investment laws of the host state party to the treaty, the investment could be made through a wholly owned subsidiary of the foreign corporation or through a joint venture. The treaty would ensure protection for wholly owned subsidiaries of multinational corporations which are incorporated in a host state party and which could easily be identified as a foreign-controlled corporation. The situation in which the multinational corporation invests through the formation of a joint venture in the host state party, however, requires a different solution. The protection of joint venture interests will still remain a problem in many states. The foreign party may have to be the minority shareholder who will not have control over the joint venture corporation.[65] If the shares of the minority foreign shareholders are affected through the procedures prescribed in the internal constituent documents of the joint venture company in accordance with the laws of the host state, there can be little protection given through diplomatic intervention. The fact that the bilateral investment treaty provides protection for shareholdings by including them in its definition of investments may provide an avenue for such protection. In *AAPL v. Sri Lanka*,[66] an ICSID tribunal decided that an appropriately worded bilateral investment treaty will confer protection on a minority shareholder in a joint venture. Such a treaty will protect the shares and other interests in the joint venture company but possibly not the assets of the company.[67]

Though some of the bilateral treaties seek to grapple with the problem raised by corporate nationality, there is no consistency in the solutions adopted by them which could give rise to any uniform principle. One can

---

[65] Though there has been considerable movement away from minority shareholdings, there are states which still insist on control remaining with local entities.

[66] (1992) 17 YCA 106.

[67] [1970] ICJ Rpts 1; the separate judgment of Judge Oda in the *ELSI Case* [1989] ICJ Rpts 15 contains affirmation of this rule. See also *AAPL v. Sri Lanka* (1992) 17 YCA 106, para. 90, where it was held that the physical assets of a company incorporated in a host state are not protected by a bilateral investment treaty as the assets belong to a national of the host state. In such circumstances, the foreign investor can only rely on shareholder protection. [1970] ICJ Rpts at 47.

find a wide array of solutions in different treaties. The Japanese treaty with Sri Lanka uses a test of 'control or decisive influence' in determining corporate nationality but leaves the application of the test itself to the *bona fide* decision of the party in whose territory the investment is made.[68] The practice of even single states varies. Thus, the Singapore–UK treaty defines a British company as a company incorporated in Britain whereas the Singapore–Germany treaty defines a German company as one 'having its seat in the Federal Republic of Germany'. British practice is also inconsistent on this point. Whereas the incorporation theory is preferred in the treaty with Singapore, the UK–Philippines treaty opts for a theory of control when it defines a protected company as one 'actually doing business under the laws in force in any part of the territory of that Contracting Party wherein a place of effective management is situate'. The absence of uniformity of approach in the several bilateral investment treaties to the problem of protecting companies again indicates that they cannot provide the basis upon which common principles or customary law can evolve on the issues of corporate nationality and shareholder protection in international law. They merely represent a consensus of opinion as between the two parties to the agreement as to such issues. They are negotiated in the context of legal preferences shaped by legal attitudes that exist within the legal systems of the different parties to such treaties. Thus, civil law countries have preferred to use the *siège social* theory whereas common law states have approached the treaty negotiations with the understanding that the norm is the test of incorporation. But, even such an explanation of the variations cannot find uniform support, for there are common law countries which have used the *siège social* theory.[69]

In any event, neither test will be meaningful where the laws of the host state make it mandatory that foreign investment can enter only through the incorporation of a joint venture with a local partner or that minority participation must be progressively achieved. In this case, neither test of corporate personality will afford much protection to the foreign investor. The strengthening of protection for shareholders is necessary in such circumstances. But, even this may not provide much relief for the foreign investor in circumstances where the host state takes over control of the

---

[68] Article 12(2) of the Japan–Sri Lanka treaty.
[69] This is particularly so in multilateral treaties where several legal traditions are brought into play. Thus, the ASEAN Treaty on the Protection and Promotion of Investments (1987) uses the test of effective management. Some members of ASEAN (Malaysia and Singapore) are common law states.

company without affecting the shareholding in the company, as where it intervenes to appoint a new management. The company cannot be protected simply because it is a corporate national of the host state and the shareholdings cannot be protected as they have not been affected.[70] A state could also take over management of a company, without affecting the company or its shareholdings.[71] In these circumstances, protection will depend on the manner in which the taking of property is defined in the treaty.

4.3. Standard of treatment

There are a variety of standards of treatment provided for in bilateral investment treaties. They would usually contain one article on treatment standards but that article would identify several different standards of treatment. These include national treatment, fair and equitable standard of treatment, international minimum standard of treatment and full protection and security. Chapter 7 deals with the violation of these different standards of treatment. It is sufficient at this stage to describe the issues which arise in connection with each of these treatment standards.

4.3.1. National standard of treatment

There has been considerable disagreement between states on the question of state responsibility for injuries to aliens. Many Latin American countries and other capital-importing countries have argued for the national standard of treatment of aliens. Article 2(2)(c) of the Charter of Economic Rights and Duties of States articulated the national treatment principle. Capital-exporting states, however, have argued that aliens should be treated in accordance with an international minimum standard. If the national treatment principle is accepted, the protection for the foreign investor will become minimal as a statute that affects property enacted

---

[70] Mann made the point as follows: 'The shares in a company incorporated in a host country are not usually affected by any measures taken there. It is the company itself that is the victim.' F. A. Mann, 'Foreign Investment in the International Court of Justice: The ELSI Case' (1992) 86 AJIL 92 at 100. Technical arguments may be made that such interventions are takings in that they lead to depreciation in the value of shares. But, such arguments contemplate the existence of sophisticated stock markets in the state.

[71] Interference with management of a company is regarded as a taking as it affects the property rights of the foreign investor. This view has been accepted in many arbitral awards. *Revere Copper & Brass Inc.* v. *OPIC* (1980) 56 ILR 258 at 290–3 and 295. There are many awards of the Iran–US Claims Tribunal which considered the issue. These are dealt with in Chapter 8 below.

uniformly to apply to all in the state irrespective of nationality will leave the alien without any remedy in international law.

Capital-exporting states have rejected this view, arguing for a minimum standard of treatment to be accorded to aliens. The recognition of a minimum standard of treatment will permit international scrutiny of the treatment of the foreign investor by the host state. However, unlike in the past when national treatment was rejected altogether because such treatment was in the case of some countries lower than the minimum standard contended for by the capital-exporting states, in modern times national treatment may have its advantages as states reserve many of their economic sectors and privileges to their nationals. In addition, national treatment at the stage of entry is regarded as an important right, as it entitles the foreign investor to a right of entry and establishment in the host state. Treaties which aim at liberalisation contain such pre-entry rights of establishment. The granting of national treatment after entry may confer advantages on aliens as it will grant them the same privileges enjoyed by nationals. For this reason, there is a tendency among developed states to support national treatment as a relevant standard and to approach the issue of international responsibility on the basis of discrimination resulting from the failure of the host state to provide national treatment to the foreign investor. In fact, the violation of national treatment is emerging as a significant cause of action arising from investment treaties.[72]

The existence of a national treatment standard could provide a basis for the argument that performance requirements such as export quotas or local purchase requirements should not be imposed upon the foreign investor, at least after entry has been made. Such requirements are not imposed on local entrepreneurs, and it is to be expected that the national treatment standard would require that it not be imposed on foreign investors as well. National treatment standard may as a result work against the imposition of performance standards unless such performance requirements are exempted from the national treatment standards.[73]

Yet, treaties that refer to national treatment often have specific provisions excluding performance requirements, and often spell out the types

---

[72] Thus, under NAFTA, there are a significant number of cases which have been instituted on the basis of a violation of national treatment, principally between the United States and Canada. See e.g. *S. D. Myers* v. *Canada* (2002) 121 ILR 7; *UPS* v. *CanadaPost*; and *Marvin Feldman* v. *Mexico* (2002) ICSID ARB(AF)/99/1.

[73] *ADF* v. *United States* (2003) is a NAFTA case in which the issue was raised as to performance requirements, in this case the 'buy America' statutes, being a violation of national standard treatments.

of performance requirement that are excluded. The inclusion of national treatment will also mean that the existence of an economically valid reason for the discrimination between nationals and foreign investors may not provide a justification for the discrimination. The trade-related term 'in like circumstances' is used to limit the effect of the national treatment requirement. It is difficult to understand the nature of such a limitation in the context of investment. A large multinational corporation as an investor is never in 'like circumstances' because of its size and vertically integrated global organisation. If this is a basis for discrimination, then the granting of national treatment becomes useless. But, it is the precise reason why the foreign multinational corporations should be discriminated against. There is a dilemma presented by the unthinking extension of notions of trade law into the area of investment. The two areas do not mix that easily. Another exception, again from the trade arena, relates to the exceptions of discrimination based on national security, public health or morals. Again, there is no precedent in investment law relating to the interpretation of these exceptions.

Wide sectoral exceptions are also used, particularly where the treaty provides for pre-entry rights of national treatment and rights of establishment. Thus, in the case of NAFTA, which requires both pre-entry and post-entry national treatment, Mexico incorporated all the sectors that it excludes foreign investment from under its Foreign Investment Law as sectors that are exempted from the obligation of national treatment. The use of a negative list of sectors is a common practice. Thus, for example, the Canada–Thailand investment treaty contains in its appendix the Thai investment laws, which list the sectors into which foreign investment is not permitted and the sectors into which foreign investment is permitted in partnership with its nationals. Where states have investment codes with such negative lists, it is sensible to include that list of sectors as industries that are not subject to national treatment.

National treatment seems a sensible answer in view of the increase of administrative controls over foreign investment. National treatment may, however, rebound on the foreign investor. A harsh measure taken against one's own nationals may be extended to the foreign investor and be justified on the basis of national treatment. For this reason, it is necessary to include other standards of treatment in the treaty.

4.3.2. Fair and equitable standard

Treaties refer to 'fair and equitable treatment' to be accorded to the nationals of the contracting parties. This phrase is vague and is open to different interpretations. The content of this standard has caused much anxiety.[74] It was at one stage thought that the standard was a higher standard than the international minimum standard. But, in NAFTA litigation, the wide interpretation given to the formula resulted in the NAFTA Commission issuing an interpretative note declaring that the fair and equitable standard was no more than the international minimum standard of customary international law. The letters attached to the Singapore–United States Free Trade Agreement also take the position that the term fair and equitable treatment as used in the treaty should be taken to refer to the international minimum standard of treatment. The resulting practice makes the phrase 'fair and equitable treatment' otiose. But, the content of the international minimum standard now has to be spelt out. There is a discussion of this issue in Chapter 7 below.

4.3.3. Most-favoured-nation treatment

The more usual clause that is included comes down from the old FCN treaties and provides for most-favoured-nation treatment, enabling the nationals of the parties to profit from favourable treatment that may be given to nationals of third states by either contracting state. The inclusion of the most-favoured-nation treatment presents the difficulty that the foreign investor could latch onto more favourable treatment provided in past or future treaties. Already, a precedent for this has been established in relation to dispute settlement. It has been held that it is possible for a foreign investor who is protected by an investment treaty with a most-favoured-nation clause to use the better dispute settlement provision in a treaty made by the respondent state with a third state.[75] This would be particularly so where a multilateral or regional treaty comes about. If the state had entered into a multilateral treaty which contains a most-favoured-nation clause, the network of states that could utilise a more favourable provision in a future bilateral investment treaty could become wider. This may be an unintended result against which care must be exercised.

Where a state belongs to a regional organisation, and as a result the state give special privileges to other member states in the arrangement, it will seek to exclude those privileges, extended to its fellow members, from flowing to a state with which it makes a bilateral investment treaty by the automatic operation of the most-favoured-nation clause. This will be

---

[74] UNCTAD, *Fair and Equitable Treatment* (1999).
[75] *Maffezini* v. *Spain* (2000) 5 ICSID Rpts 396.

stated in the treaty itself. It cannot therefore be argued later that measures conferring privileges under these regional arrangement should be conferred upon foreign investors on the basis of the most-favoured-nation clauses.

4.3.4. Full protection and security

The treatment provision also includes provision of 'full protection and security' to the foreign investment. It has been held in arbitral awards that this again adverts to customary law standards which require either that the state's forces should not be utilised to harm the foreign investor's property nor that the state should give protection from violence against the interests of the foreign investor if such violence could be reasonably anticipated.[76]

4.4. Performance requirements

Treaties made by the United States and Canada in particular have sought to do away with performance requirements. These performance requirements are imposed by host states in order to ensure that the foreign investor exports a percentage of his production, buys local products and services, and employs local labour. From the point of view of the developing countries, the imposition of such requirements enhances the value of the foreign investment. Thus, the requirement of export ensures that more foreign exchange is earned for the host state than profits be made for the foreign investor through sales on the local market. Such profits will be repatriated, causing a possible loss to the foreign investor which could be balanced against profits made on exports. Another reason for the export requirement is that it preserves the market for local entrepreneurs. Local entrepreneurs are likely to be driven out of the market if they are to compete with the foreign multinational corporations which would be able to produce at a lower cost. This effect will mean that incipient local industry will be scotched. Export requirements are justified on the basis that such a crowding-out effect will be avoided.[77] Multinational corporations are averse to export requirements, as they require internal competition within the production systems of the multinational corporation. The use of local content requirements will ensure that local products are utilised in the

---

[76] *American Machine Tools* v. *Zaire* (1997) 36 ILM 1531; *Wena Hotels* v. *Republic of Egypt* (2002) 41 ILM 896.
[77] Further see UNCTAD, *World Investment Report, 2003.*

manufacture of products made by the foreign investor and not imported from abroad. The employment of local personnel also ensures one of the presumed advantages of the foreign investment.

But, these arguments are countered by the developed countries on the basis that performance requirements distort international trade. To some extent, the Trade Related Investment Measures (TRIMS) instrument of the WTO is based on the prohibition of performance requirements on the basis of this argument. Unlike TRIMS, which prohibits only trade-related performance requirements, the investment treaties which address the issue of performance requirements seek to prohibit them altogether. The provision of national treatment will also require that these restrictions be done away with as they are not imposed on nationals. Economic literature is not conclusive on whether performance requirements enhance the developmental goals of host states. Though studies concentrate on the trade-distortive effects of such requirements, there are studies which show that the use of performance requirements has ensured the harnessing of the foreign investment to the economic objectives of the host state.[78]

4.5. Repatriation of profits

The main objective of all foreign investment is to make profits and to repatriate those profits to the home state. If repatriation of the profits is prevented by the host state, this purpose of the foreign investor will be frustrated. The protection of the right to repatriate profits becomes an objective of the investment treaties. Many of the treaties contain absolute statements protecting the right of repatriation. This is unrealistic as problems will arise when a contracting party has exchange shortfalls necessitating currency controls. Absolute rights of repatriation are included in treaties in the overzealous belief that such situations will not eventuate. Situations like the Asian financial crisis do occur. When they do, an absolute right of repatriation in a treaty will cause difficulties for the state experiencing the crisis.

Some UK treaties provide that the right of repatriation of profits may be restricted 'in exceptional economic or financial circumstances'.[79] In other UK treaties, there is a requirement that the repatriation of a percentage of the profits (usually 20 per cent) should be permitted every year

---

[78] For policy debates on performance requirements, see UNCTAD, *World Investment Report, 2003*, 119–23.

[79] Not all UK treaties contain such provisions. The treaty with Jamaica is an instance.

in circumstances of foreign exchange difficulties. The UK formulation is preferable. Absolute rights of repatriation cannot bind a state in times of financial stringency. It may be argued that circumstances of financial stringency call for the application of the doctrine of *clausula rebus sic stantibus*, making the provision on absolute rights of repatriation defeasible as a result of the different situation that had arisen. In situations of extreme balance-of-payment difficulties, it could be argued that the general doctrine of necessity suspends the treaty obligation to permit repatriation, at least until the situation improves.

The more realistic approach is to adopt the solution found in the British treaty practice and create an obligation to permit the repatriation of at least a percentage of the profits and the remainder when circumstances permit. The repatriation clause will usually include not only the profits that are made but all other payments such as fees or other entitlements that are paid to the foreign investor and his employees. Again, practice on the right of repatriation varies in the treaties.

Exceptions are sometimes made in relation to delays occurring due to reporting requirements or seizures of assets that may be made by courts to satisfy debtors. These exceptions are provisions that relate to the laws of one of the contracting parties. They are not related to balance-of-payment difficulties that are experienced by developing state parties to such treaties but exceptions that cater to the requirements of the laws of the developed state parties.

4.6. Nationalisation and compensation

Nationalisation poses the greatest threat to foreign investment. Capital-exporting states have sought to circumscribe the right of a state to nationalise foreign property by regarding at least certain types of taking of alien property as unlawful. It is now generally accepted that a state has a right to nationalise foreign-owned property, subject to exceptions. The change from illegality to legality of state takings of alien property had much to do with the fact that the nature of takings had undergone significant change. Whereas previously takings were largely confiscations motivated by the greed of dictators in power or were racially motivated, modern state takings are done in pursuance of economic reforms on the basis of sincerely held ideological views or policy grounds. Though vestiges of the old law still remain to cater for the occasional takings that are racially motivated or motivated by the greed of ruling coteries, modern law tends to regard takings by the state as lawful, unless the contrary can be established. There is broad agreement that the exercise of the right should not be discriminatory and should have a basis in public purpose.

The conditions relating to public purpose and non-discrimination are stated in all bilateral investment treaties, and there can be little doubt that these conditions form part of customary international law. It is such customary law that is reiterated in these treaties. In this respect, the treaties do not create new customary law but reinforce existing customary law as found in the practice of developed states. In modern international law, the force of these exceptions to the legality of nationalisations is somewhat muted, as the subjective view of the state that the nationalisation serves a public purpose is given great weight.[80] A discriminatory nationalisation is illegal, but discrimination may be difficult to establish in circumstances in which there is an ostensible economic reason for the nationalisation, as the state could argue that the economic reason was the predominant reason behind the nationalisation.

The treaties indicate that the provisions relating to expropriation apply not only to outright takings but also to 'creeping expropriation' or the slow erosion of the alien's ownership rights through regulatory measures. Thus, US bilateral investment treaties define expropriation to include 'any measure or series of measures the effect of which would be tantamount to expropriation or nationalisation'. Chapter 11 of the North American Free Trade Agreement, a regional treaty, contains the same formulation. It has received extensive interpretation.[81] In the earlier US treaties, examples are given of such indirect takings. They are: confiscatory taxation, total or partial compulsory sale, and impairment or deprivation of management, control or economic value.[82] Later treaties do not contain such illustrations, presumably in the belief that they are unnecessary or in the belief that they may limit the effect of the language. Indirect taking is regarded as bringing about results akin to a physical taking without actual interference with the property itself. The phrase 'tantamount to a taking' has caused considerable problems. In the context of NAFTA, it has been read as not adding to the meaning of indirect taking. It is another clause in the investment chapter of NAFTA that has become otiose as a result of interpretation. These matters are dealt with in Chapters 8 and 9 dealing with expropriation.

The issue of compensation is controversial, and, on this issue, bilateral investment treaties make law as between the parties but make no

---

[80] *Marvin Feldman* v. *Mexico* (2002) ICSID ARB(AF)/99/1, para. 136.
[81] See further Chapter 8 below.   [82] US–Egypt treaty (1982).

contribution to the formation of common norms of international law. Capital-exporting states, particularly the United States, have steadfastly adhered to the standard of 'prompt, adequate and effective compensation' as the standard of compensation that must be satisfied in the event of nationalisation. The standard would require, at the least, the payment of the full value of the property that had been taken over. The developing countries have collectively articulated the standard of 'appropriate compensation'. This latter standard would be a flexible standard that would permit a state to take into account factors such as the profits made by the foreign investor, the duration of the period during which profits were made and similar factors in assessing the compensation. Developing countries have also expressed the view that the tribunals of the host state should be the sole arbiters of the amount of compensation. Given the existence of this conflict between states, bilateral investment treaties have become the means by which the parties could agree on the standard of compensation that is to be used as between themselves. Some writers advocated the use of bilateral investment treaties to settle the issue of compensation as between the parties, given the uncertainty as to the existence of a standard in international customary law. Thus Eli Lauterpacht, referring to the alleged existence of a customary law standard of 'appropriate compensation', observed:[83]

> The evidently discretionary and objectively unpredictable content of this standard is as good a reason as any for recognising the virtue of the use of specially agreed bilateral treaty standards.

Bilateral investment treaties are not made with the aim of subscribing to the formulation of a uniform standard of compensation but are efforts by the parties to agree on the standard on which they would compensate in the event one of them nationalises the property of a national of the other. The imputation of any more grandiose motive to such treaties is misplaced.

However, heavy reliance is placed on bilateral investment treaties to argue that the standard of prompt, adequate and effective compensation has been reinforced in these treaties. A former legal adviser to the US Department of State relied on bilateral investment treaties to argue that

---

[83] Eli Lauterpacht, 'Issues of Compensation and Nationality in the Taking of Energy Investments' (1990) 6 *Journal of Energy and Natural Resources Law* 241.

the standard of prompt, adequate and effective compensation has been reinforced by these agreements. He observed:[84]

> States have shown their real practice by establishing a network of international treaties. Provisions controlling compensation in expropriation are often contained in bilateral friendship, commerce and navigation (FCN) treaties. In the case of the United States, many of these are with developing nations. They contain provisions calling for compensation in terms equivalent to the traditional standard, although there are slight drafting variations. The history of these agreements indicates that the parties recognised that they were thereby making the customary rule of international law explicit in the treaty language and reaffirming its effect.

The old FCN treaties were drafted before the alternative standards came to be articulated. In the new investment treaties that the United States has made, it appears to have taken an inflexible stance on the issue of compensation and not permitted any 'drafting variations'. Its new bilateral investment treaties require the payment of prompt, adequate and effective compensation and refer to the standard of valuation being 'the fair market value of the expropriated investment immediately before the expropriatory action was taken or become known'.

As regards the treaty practice of other states, the requirement of 'prompt, adequate and effective' compensation is frequently used, but there are departures from the formula in some treaties. In UK treaties, the formula is often used, but there are other formulations as well. It will be too facile to explain these departures as drafting variations, for every state will seek consistency in its practice and there is an obvious advantage to the capital-exporting state in insisting on the standard of prompt, adequate and effective compensation. But, in the UK treaties, whatever formula is used to describe the compensation, there follows a valuation standard stated in a clause which reads as follows:

> Such compensation shall include market value of the investment expropriated immediately before the expropriation became public knowledge, shall include interest at a normal commercial rate until date of payment, shall be made without delay, be effectively realisable and be freely transferable.

It can be argued that this standard of valuation indicates an obligation to pay full compensation.

---

[84] Robinson, 'Expropriation in the Restatement (Revised)' (1984) 78 AJIL 176.

In the treaties to which Singapore is a party, there are wide variations in the statements relating to compensation. The prompt, adequate and effective formula is referred to in the treaties with the UK and Switzerland, but the alternative formula of 'just' compensation is used in the treaties with the Netherlands and Germany. In the treaty with France, the agreement is to pay as compensation, 'the commercial value of the assets on the day of the expropriation'. This formula does not take into account the fact that the value of the property may have depreciated as a result of the earlier announcement of the expropriation. In most Dutch treaties, there is a reference to 'just' compensation. Australia, a relative newcomer to the area of bilateral investment treaties, has been able to secure the inclusion of the prompt, adequate and effective formula in all its treaties. Its treaty with China also contains such a formula. But, its neighbour, New Zealand, was able to secure in its investment treaty with China a formula which simply refers to 'compensation which shall be effectively realisable'. Treaties between developing countries also contain the prompt, adequate and effective formula. Bargaining strengths and negotiating strategies have much to do with the variations that appear in all these treaties. Since the variations are attributable to such strengths and strategies, they cannot be dismissed as 'drafting variations' so as to make them fit an *a priori* conclusion.

The practice that can be analysed will support different claims depending on the predisposition of the person drawing the conclusions. The use of the formula of 'just compensation' in a significant minority of treaties cannot be dismissed as 'drafting variations'. It can also be a compromise formulation adopted by some states in the light of the conflict that has been generated in the area. A writer in the field has pointed out that 'it would seem foolhardy, if the argument that the nineteenth century customary law being recreated by these treaties is pressed too far, to maintain that "just", "full", "equivalent" and "adequate" have exactly the same meaning'.[85]

Quite apart from the relative bargaining strengths of the parties, the period in which the treaty was drafted has relevance. At a time when there is an availability of investment funds, capital-importing states will be reluctant to agree to higher standards of compensation. But, treaties that are concluded at a time when there is a dearth of such capital will contain higher standards such as the Hull formula. The ascendance of a

---

[85] C. F. Amerasinghe, 'Issues of Compensation in the Taking of Property in the Light of Recent Cases and Practice' (1992) 41 ICLQ 22.

free market philosophy in a given period may also favour the acceptance of such a formula. This may explain why the more recent treaties, concluded at a time when there was intense competition for foreign investment and a relatively widespread acceptance of a free market philosophy, contain more frequent references to the Hull standard. So, too, when high-risk states conclude treaties with states having large investment capital, they are likely to include the Hull formula. Thus, China and Vietnam have cast aside their ideological objections and included the Hull formula in many of their treaties simply because they are keen to attract investments and keen to dispel impressions that they are high-risk countries.

There is also a double standard that is apparent in the conduct of many developing states. On the one hand, they maintain stances that oppose the Hull formula in international fora but, on the other, they are busy making bilateral treaties containing the formula. This duplicity can be explained on the basis that, while these states subscribe to a particular norm of international law at the global level, they are nevertheless prepared to accord a higher standard of protection to the nationals of states with which they conclude bilateral investment treaties in the hope of attracting investments. They subscribe to a general standard of appropriate compensation at the international level but are prepared to negotiate higher standards on a case-by-case basis. This may be a pragmatic approach dictated by circumstances. The charge of duplicity may therefore be misplaced.[86]

The inclusion of the Hull standard in treaties between developing states also constitutes a paradox. The explanation for these treaties is that they are not only intended to attract investments from richer developing states but are also aimed at multinational corporations already operating in the state. Thus, a treaty between Singapore and Vietnam is aimed not only at Singaporean nationals and companies which have now acquired the capacity to invest overseas but also at multinational corporations already operating in Singapore. These corporations will have incorporated in Singapore and hence are entitled to the benefit of the treaties as corporate nationals of Singapore. The strategy of a state like Vietnam could well be to attract such corporations through making investment treaties with states like Singapore which have already been able to attract good foreign investments. This constitutes Singapore as an export platform for the region, and Singapore will not be unhappy with the situation as there will be revenue flows moving through Singapore. The treaty may also attract

---

[86] Andrew Guzman, 'Why LDCs Sign Treaties That Hurt Them: Explaining the Popularity of Bilateral Investment Treaties' (1998) 38 *Virginia Journal of International Law* 639.

other multinational corporations to set up in Singapore and then proceed to Vietnam and thereby invoke the protection of the investment treaty. The inclusion of the Hull formula in these treaties is for strategic reasons. Yet, the argument that these treaties stabilise the Hull formula must be seen as having merit, despite the fact that they do not provide any conclusive evidence of the acceptance of the formula as customary international law.

The motives for the inclusion of the Hull formula as well as the variations that appear in the different treaties as to the standard of compensation make these treaties unsafe bases on which to make the argument that they contain evidence that there is sufficient acceptance of the Hull formula to make it part of customary international law. There is a lack of unanimity in the practice of states on the point. It must, however, be conceded that the large majority of treaties contain the Hull standard. But this is no more than about half the treaties that had been concluded in 1992 when the count was last made.[87] The rest have different formulas to indicate the compensation payable. The definite conclusion that these treaties support the Hull formula is untenable.

Besides, many of these treaties in which the Hull formula appears qualify the types of investment that are protected. Thus, quite uniformly in south-east Asian treaties, only 'approved' investments are protected by the Hull formula, if used. This leaves aside the large number of investments which do not have approval. In such a situation, these treaties cannot create customary international law. Likewise, many states, China, Australia and Indonesia included, protect only investments which are made in accordance with their laws and regulations. In the context of these qualifications, the nature of the investments that are protected by many treaties made by large groups of states is so qualified that they cannot meaningfully contribute to any customary practice as to the Hull formula. In these cases, the Hull formula becomes a higher type of standard that protects a desirable type of investment made under the regulations of the host state and not all investments.

The contemporary controversy pertains to the extent to which regulatory intervention can be characterised as a 'taking or an act tantamount to a taking' under the expropriation provision in investment treaties. This issue has displaced compensation as the central issue in expropriation

---

[87] This was the position in 1992. See World Bank Group, *Legal Framework for the Treatment of Foreign Investment* (vol. 1, 1992), 48. But, the newer treaties refer to the Hull formula more frequently so that the proportion may now be different.

law. Some arbitral decisions which have construed the phrase used in the treaties seem to indicate that the regulatory character of the taking is no reason for regarding the taking as non-compensable. This view has created controversy, as it would mean that takings motivated by environmental and other concerns will have to be compensated. There have been reactions against this view. This issue is discussed more fully in Chapter 8 below.

4.6.1. Compensation for destruction during wars and national emergencies

Investment treaties contain provisions for compensation in the event of damage to the foreign investor's property as a result of war, civil unrest or other national emergencies. They provide for national treatment of the foreign investor so that, if nationals of the state are compensated for such losses, then the foreign investor will also have to be compensated on the same standard. The treaties also provide for liability where the armed forces requisition the foreign investor's property or where such property is destroyed by the armed forces. However, liability for such destruction is excluded where the destruction takes place during combat action or was required by the necessity of the situation. These provisions have been used in a dispute involving a national of Hong Kong and Sri Lanka which was submitted for arbitration to the International Centre for the Settlement of Investment Disputes. The award in *Asian Agricultural Products Ltd (AAPL)* v. *Sri Lanka*[88] is the first dispute in which an international tribunal had an opportunity to deal with the provisions of a bilateral investment treaty. It has significance not only for the provision on compensation for damages caused during wars and national emergencies but for bilateral investment agreements generally.

The dispute arose as a result of the destruction of the shrimp culture farm AAPL had established in a joint venture with a local company, as a result of a military action taken by the armed forces of Sri Lanka against Tamil insurgents fighting for a separate state. The tribunal's jurisdiction was based on the provision on dispute settlement in the bilateral investment treaty, again making the award of significance for the development of the law on bilateral investment treaties. It was the first occasion on which an arbitral tribunal exercised jurisdiction on the basis of a provision in a bilateral investment treaty providing for such jurisdiction. The

[88] (1992) 17 YCA 106.

issue was whether the foreign investor was entitled to compensation for the destruction of the property.

The claimant's argument was presented on the basis that the bilateral investment treaty created a higher standard of protection, so that there may even arise strict liability in the event of destruction of foreign investment property. This was rejected by the arbitral tribunal, which held that the inclusion of terms such as 'full protection' in bilateral investment treaties does not refer to any standards higher than the minimum standard of treatment required by general international law. The tribunal then went on to consider whether there could be liability under the provision of the treaty which stated that a party will be liable where the foreign investor suffers losses as a result of his property being requisitioned or as a result of destruction of his property by the armed forces of a contracting party 'which was not caused in combat action or was not required by the necessity of the situation'. The tribunal held that the action taken by the Sri Lankan armed forces leading to the destruction of the foreign investor's property was directed against the Tamil guerrillas and qualified as combat action which attracted the application of the exception to liability. But, the tribunal held that the bilateral investment treaty included the standards of protection of general international law to which the foreign investor could have resort as these standards are incorporated in bilateral investment treaties. The rule that was applied by the tribunal was that, in times of civil conflicts, there was a duty on the part of the host state to confer adequate protection to foreign investment and that the failure to give such protection will engage the liability of the state. This rule was extracted as a proposition of customary international law which formed a part of the bilateral investment treaty. It was on the basis of the failure to provide the protection required by general international law that the tribunal awarded compensation to the foreign investor.

On this reasoning, bilateral investment treaties are *lex specialis* which stand apart from general international law, entitling the foreign investor to the protection of both the standards of general international law as well as the standards contained in the treaty itself. In this case, the two standards worked in tandem, for the foreign investor was able to invoke the protection of the general international law before the tribunal only because the bilateral investment treaty had created jurisdiction in the tribunal. But, an issue which the tribunal failed to answer was whether the tribunal could assume jurisdiction on the basis of the treaty and apply rules that were not stated in the treaty itself. The tribunal was assuming virtually limitless jurisdiction by dealing with the problem through customary international law. A tribunal concerned essentially with investment law could find itself out of its depth when it concerns itself with general international law. Could the tribunal in *AAPL v. Sri Lanka* have looked into the question as to whether the war in Sri Lanka was a war of national liberation and, hence, akin to an international war? Could it then have gone into issues of protection of property under the laws of war? Surely, arbitral tribunals which are constituted for investment disputes are not designed to deal with such problems. Its personnel are not selected on the basis of their competence in these matters.[89]

The award of the tribunal indicates that bilateral investment treaties could raise problems of vital national interests before international tribunals and that sometimes these problems may not be directly involved with the investment. If the fighting of a civil war becomes the concern of an arbitral tribunal that was essentially created to settle commercial disputes, then there is an unexpectedly large genie being released from the bottle. In the civil war type of situation like that in *AAPL v. Sri Lanka*, issues such as the characterisation of the war, the legality of the force used to suppress it and other like matters that may concern the internal sovereignty of the state could have been raised. An issue of investment thus opens the possibility of the conduct of the hostilities being queried by an international tribunal which is not designed to deal with such political matters. The US experience with FCN treaties rebounding to provide jurisdiction for Nicaragua and Iran to score juridical triumphs can be expected to be repeated many more times. This may lead to capital-exporting countries being more cautious in embarking upon bilateral investment treaties. The issue as to whether there is a doctrine of arbitrability which prevents arbitral tribunals constituted to deal with foreign investment disputes straying into other fields over which they have little or no competence is fairly raised in situations like that in *AAPL v. Sri Lanka*.

4.7. *Protection of commitments*

Investment treaties contain clauses which require the parties to keep commitments that are made to each other's nationals. Thus, the treaty between the United Kingdom and the Philippines contains the following clause:

---

[89] For the criticism that personnel on these tribunals have little acquaintance with international law, see C. F. Amerasinghe, 'The Prawn Farm Arbitration' (1992) 2 *Sri Lanka Journal of International Law* 12.

> Each Contracting Party shall observe any obligation arising from a par-
> ticular commitment it may have entered into with regard to a specific
> investment of nationals or companies of the other Contracting Party.

The reference to specific commitments made to the foreign investor may mean that guarantees such as the guarantee against expropriation without compensation or guarantees as to repatriation of profits made in investment codes which are general commitments are not covered by the clause. It may, however, be possible to argue that these general commitments are addressed to the particular foreign investor as well and hence fall within the protection of the clause.

The clause may refer more specifically to the contractual commitments that a state or a public entity like the investment board screening the application of the investor prior to entry may have made in the course of initial contacts with the foreign investor. Liability will arise where these commitments are not met. They could also refer to contractual commitments made to the foreign party. Thus, where there are stabilisation clauses in the contract, it could be credibly argued on the basis of the provision in the bilateral investment treaty that future changes to the law in the host state adverse to the interests of the foreign investor should not be applied to the contract. But, a difficulty with the argument is that such contracts are not made directly by the state. They are made by state entities and the stipulations and guarantees given by the state entity may not bind the state. The state will argue that these guarantees are not binding on it and that the treaty protection does not apply to contractual guarantees made by state entities. But, administrative commitments, such as those relating to the grant of permits necessary to do business effectively, may be protected by this treaty provision. The extent to which the provision will limit sovereign and regulatory powers of the host state is unclear. Unilateral guarantees not to nationalise except on payment of full compensation will be protected by the provision in the investment treaty.

4.8. Dispute resolution

Many bilateral investment treaties make significant progress in the area of the resolution of disputes arising from the foreign investment by specifying arbitration in a neutral forum as the method of resolution of the dispute.[90] There are several different types of clauses creating different

---

[90] Wolfgang Peters, 'Dispute Settlement Arrangements in Investment Treaties' (1991) 22 NYIL 91.

obligations as to such arbitration. At the lowest level, the clauses merely direct the parties to arbitration as a way of solving disputes arising out of foreign investment transactions. In these treaties, there is merely a prescription of arbitration as a method of settlement of the dispute without in any way creating an obligation on the part of the any party to submit compulsorily to arbitration. At the highest level, the treaties entitle the foreign investor to initiate proceedings by himself before an ICSID tribunal. The existence of such provisions in bilateral investment treaties is a major step that has been taken to ensure the protection of the foreign investor by enabling him to have direct access to a neutral forum for the settlement of disputes that could arise between him and the host state. It has been suggested that this technique of permitting the foreign investor to take up his own dispute 'depoliticises' the process, as the dispute does not become a dispute between the home state and the host state. The two states could continue their relations as if the dispute did not affect their mutual relations.[91]

A foreign investor, justifiably in many instances, will not have confidence in the impartiality of the local tribunals and courts in settling any disputes that may arise between him and the host state. Arbitration, in a neutral state before a neutral tribunal, has traditionally been seen as the best method of securing impartial justice for him. Where an international treaty backs him up by creating an obligation on the host state to submit to any arbitral proceedings brought against it by the foreign investor, a major step could be said to have been taken towards investment protection. Bilateral investment treaties take such a step with varying degrees of success. It would, once more, be wrong to say that there is any uniform pattern in the nature of the obligation to arbitrate created by the different treaties. There is no uniform pattern or commitment to arbitrate which emerges from the different treaties. The superficial similarity in many of the provisions is deceptive.[92]

In some treaties, there is a period during which conciliation of the dispute should be attempted prior to arbitration. Treaties concluded by China uniformly contain such a provision indicating the Chinese preference for conciliatory solutions than litigious ones. The requirement of

---

[91] I. Shihata, 'Towards a Depoliticisation of Foreign Investment Disputes: The Roles of ICSID and MIGA' (1986) 1 ICSID Rev 1.

[92] A thorough survey is made in Antonio Parra and Ibrahim Shihata, 'Provisions on the Settlement of Investment Disputes in Modern Investment Laws, Bilateral Investment Treaties and Multilateral Treaties on Investment' (1997) 12 ICSID Rev 287.

a period in which negotiations must be attempted is becoming usual in treaty practice. Unless a time limit is attached to such a requirement to negotiate, the reference to arbitration may be frustrated by the adoption of delaying tactics.

Most dispute settlement provisions in investment treaties refer to ICSID arbitration. The treaties work in tandem with the ICSID Convention in creating jurisdiction in an ICSID tribunal. But, care must be taken to examine each provision so as to discover the precise extent of the commitment to create such jurisdiction. Broches, who studied the provisions containing references to ICSID arbitration, pointed out that the mere references to ICSID in these treaties did not give rise to jurisdiction over individual disputes to ICSID.[93] Whether such jurisdiction is created will depend on the precise words used in the treaty. Broches makes a distinction between four types of arbitration provision in bilateral investment treaties. The first type merely states that the dispute 'shall, upon agreement by both parties, be submitted for arbitration by the Centre'. Such a clause does not constitute consent to arbitration in the absence of an agreement after the dispute had arisen. The second type, which requires 'sympathetic consideration to a request [for] conciliation or arbitration by the Centre', does not amount to consent but, according to Broches, it may imply an 'obligation not to withhold consent unreasonably'. The third type of clause requires the host state 'to assent to any demand on the part of the national to submit for conciliation or arbitration any dispute arising from the investment'. Refusal to assent may amount to an international wrong but the clause itself does not create jurisdiction in ICSID. The fourth type of clause creates jurisdiction in the Centre by giving consent in anticipation of the dispute. This clause, which is usually found in the treaties concluded by the United Kingdom, reads:

> Each Contracting Party hereby consents to submit to the International Centre for the Settlement of Investment Disputes for settlement by conciliation or arbitration under the Convention on the Settlement of Investment Disputes between States and Nationals of Other States . . . any legal disputes arising between that Contracting Party and a national or company of the other Contracting Party concerning an investment of the latter in the territory of the former.

---

[93] A. Broches, 'Bilateral Investment Treaties and Arbitration of Investment Disputes' in J. Schulsz and J. A. van den Berg (eds.), *The Art of Arbitration: Liber Amicorum Pieter Sanders* (1982).

Such a clause creates jurisdiction in the ICSID. Broches is cautious in speaking about the fourth type of clause, and it is best to cite his words as to the effect of such a clause:

> Provisions of this kind, subject to the conditions stated therein and subject further to their compatibility with the Convention, will enable the investor to institute proceedings against the host state before the Centre and may entitle the host state to avail itself of the same remedy against the investor.

An ICSID tribunal assumed jurisdiction on the basis of a provision in an investment treaty for the first time in *Asian Agricultural Products Ltd* v. *Sri Lanka*. The provision in the UK–Sri Lanka treaty on the basis of which such jurisdiction was assumed is a standard type used in UK treaties and has been reproduced above as an example of the fourth type of clause adverted to by Broches. Neither party contested the jurisdiction assumed by the tribunal on the basis of the treaty. Since *AAPL* v. *Sri Lanka*, there have been several instances in which jurisdiction has been assumed by ICSID tribunals on the basis of provisions in investment treaties.[94] There are also NAFTA awards in which jurisdiction was based on the equivalent provisions in that treaty.[95] Whether or not the assumption of such jurisdiction is proper, there is little doubt that many precedents have been established for the assumption of such jurisdiction in several awards.[96]

---

[94] *AMT* v. *Zaire* (1997) 36 ILM 1531; *Tradex* v. *Albania* (1999) 14 ICSID Rev 161; *CSOB* v. *Slovakia* (1999) 14 ICSID Rev 251. Schreur, *Commentaries on ICSID Convention* (2001), 210–23. The amount of litigation before ICSID sky-rocketed after this new basis of jurisdiction, which obviously had existed in the past, was 'discovered' in *AAPL* v. *Sri Lanka*. Commentators on the UK treaties had not adverted to the possibility at the time the UK treaties like the one with Sri Lanka or the Philippines were drafted. Care must be taken to ensure that the investment from which the dispute arises qualifies the conditions that are imposed by the treaty regarding approval, licences, etc. *Yaung Chi Oo Ltd* v. *Myanmar* (2003) 42 ILM 540.

[95] Most NAFTA tribunals, given the strength of the provision on dispute settlement, have rightly assumed jurisdiction on the basis of the provision. Given existing trends, they have not seen it necessary to discuss the issue. When jurisdiction is contested in NAFTA cases, it is not contested on the basis that the provision does not create jurisdiction in the tribunal but on issues pertaining to the standing of the claimant, lack of finality or time bars. *Mondev International* v. *United States* (1999) ARB(AF)/99/2.

[96] The present author expressed disquiet about the situation in M. Sornarajah, 'Power and Justice in International Investment Arbitration' (1997) 14 *Journal of International Arbitration* 103. There have been recent writings which also indicate that the ready attitude of arbitral tribunals to infer jurisdiction from treaties may cause concern as to whether there is in reality consent. In the absence of actual consent, there will be an unwillingness

Many treaties make a reference to the New York Convention on the Enforcement of Foreign Arbitral Awards. It is doubtful whether the New York Convention, which was designed for the enforcement of arbitral awards made in disputes arising from private traders can be easily used to serve the purpose of disputes involving sovereign states. If an obligation to abide by the arbitral award is created by the investment treaty, any reference to the New York Convention must be regarded as a surplusage. There does not appear to have been any awards against states enforced under the New York Convention.

4.9. Arbitration and the exhaustion of local remedies

One further problem which arises in connection with the existence of the arbitration provisions in these treaties is whether, despite the existence of these provisions, there is still a duty on the part of the foreign investor to exhaust all the local remedies provided by the host state before resorting to international arbitration.[97] Some of the arbitration provisions themselves recognise the local remedies rule, which requires the prior exhaustion of all the remedies provided for by the law of the host state before resorting to international remedies. Some impose a time limit and permit the international arbitration after the time limit has espired. The remarks of the International Court of Justice in the *ELSI Case* on whether there is a duty to exhaust local remedies when there is an FCN treaty between the parties is pertinent to bilateral investment treaties as well.[98] The Court observed that the local remedies rule is such a fundamental principle of international law that it cannot be excluded except by express words having that effect. A view has been forcefully stated by Judge Schwebel that the presence of an arbitration clause excludes the need to exhaust local

---

on the part of states to accept the awards that are made. Since the awards are difficult to enforce due to a multiplicity of factors such as sovereign immunity and the act of state doctrine, it would be counterproductive for awards to be made in cases where actual consent by the state is difficult to find. See further Emmanuel Gaillard, 'Commentary' (2002) 18 *International Arbitration* 247 at 249: 'In recent years, around 70 per cent of ICSID cases were based on bilateral or multilateral investment treaties, not a specific agreement. In all other cases, the state therefore consented to ICSID arbitration only by entering into the investment treaty, not by a specific agreement. It is difficult in this context to sustain an argument based on the supposed consent of the state.'

[97] C. F. Amerasinghe, *The Local Remedies Rule in International Law* (1991).

[98] Adler, 'The Exhaustion of Local Remedies Rule after the ICJ's Decision in ELSI' (1990) 39 ICLQ 641.

remedies.[99] It is sufficient to point out that this view sits uneasily with the view of the Court that even a treaty such as an FCN treaty should not be considered as ousting the local remedies rule. Yet, it is sometimes claimed that an arbitration clause in a contract can have this effect. This is clearly not possible. This conclusion is supported by the fact that many bilateral investment treaties, despite providing for arbitration, still require the exhaustion of local remedies. Thus, for example, the UK–Jamaica treaty permits submission of disputes to ICSID arbitration only if 'agreement cannot be reached through pursuit of local remedies in accordance with international law'. There are also treaties which require exhaustion of local remedies but specify a time limit for such exhaustion. These treaties recognise the primacy of the rule of exhaustion and of the jurisdiction of the local tribunals over the dispute but effect a compromise between the competence of the local tribunal and the foreign investor's preference for international arbitration by imposing a time limit for local remedies to be exhausted. This latter type of treaty again confirms the existence of a duty to exhaust local remedies despite the fact that they also make provision for the overseas arbitration of the dispute. There are a very few treaties which expressly provide that local remedies need not be exhausted. This indicates a consciousness that securing the exclusion of the rule is advantageous to the foreign investor. Yet, most of the treaties are silent on this issue. Where the treaty is silent on the question of the exhaustion of local remedies, it may be assumed that the reference to arbitration is subject to the rule.

Where the treaty is silent on the issue, it is imperative that it be interpreted in a manner that least derogates from the sovereignty of the parties to the treaty. The local remedies rule is a recognition of the judicial sovereignty of the state over issues that fall within its jurisdiction. It should not be lightly disregarded. This conclusion is supported by the fact that, in the *ELSI Case*, a Chamber of the International Court of Justice dealt with a similar issue regarding the FCN treaty and observed that it was 'unable to accept that an important principle of customary international law should be held to have been tacitly dispensed with, in the absence of any words making clear an intention to do so'.

The absence of any indication regarding the local remedies rule may simply be due to the fact that its negotiation would have provoked too much controversy and raised all the arguments relating to the Calvo

---

[99] Stephen Schwebel and Gillis Wetter, 'Arbitration and Exhaustion of Local Remedies' (1966) 60 AJIL 484; Stepehn Schwebel and Gillis Wetter, 'Arbitration and the Exhaustion of Local Remedies Revisited' in *Festschrift for Joseph Gould* (1989).

doctrine, which required that foreign investment disputes be decided exclusively by the domestic courts. It is a doctrine that has been universalised through the adoption of Article 2(2)(c) of the Charter of Economic Rights and Duties of States. The local remedies rule was at least a compromise. It is unlikely that capital-receiving states will desire to do away with a rule which was in their interest and which has general acceptance. The local remedies rule should therefore be implied into bilateral investment treaties which are silent on the issue, even where there is provision in them for overseas arbitration of the dispute. It was implied in circumstances where there was provision for the dispute to be decided by the International Court of Justice. There is no reason why it should not be implied in circumstances where there is reference for resolution of the dispute by an inferior tribunal. The fact that an arbitration clause which is supported by treaty obligations still requires the exhaustion of local remedies considerably weakens the view of Judge Schwebel that the mere existence of an arbitration clause providing for settlement of the dispute by an overseas tribunal dispenses with the need to exhaust local remedies. The foreign investor had consciously undertaken the risk of establishing contacts with the legal system of the host state and should not be permitted to remove himself from it merely by inserting an arbitration clause in his contract.

However, the situation is different where the dispute arises directly from a violation of the treaty rather than from a violation of the contract in pursuance of which the dispute arises. Where a treaty violation arises, the dispute may be directly submitted to arbitration, without resort to local remedies. It has also been held that this treaty right cannot be excluded by a contractual provision.[100] This seems to be a sensible distinction. It concedes that the contract and the treaty operate in two distinct realms, the first in national law and the second in treaty law. Where a state has entered into a treaty which gives the automatic right of arbitration to the foreign investor in respect of violations of rights given to him by treaty, it is appropriate that the state should subject the dispute to arbitration. This view is now so established in arbitration practice that it is too late to be contested.

4.9.1. Arbitration between states

The treaties provide that, if disputes were to arise between the two parties, the dispute should be submitted to arbitration. Whether this is a desirable

---

[100] The reasoning is that treaty rights exist independently of the contract.

provision in bilateral investment treaties is doubtful. The inclusion of this provision may make many internal political matters of a state subject to arbitration. The decision in the *Nicaragua Case* demonstrated how an FCN treaty, concerned largely with commerce, could give rise to jurisdiction in an international tribunal over a wide array of matters involving the conduct of foreign policy. The *AAPL* v. *Sri Lanka* case, discussed above, showed how matters involving the conduct of civil and secessionist wars could arise before a tribunal which was created to deal with investment disputes. In the case of a more specific treaty such as the bilateral investment treaty, an arbitration clause may create a wider base of jurisdiction. Since the promotion of conditions favourable to the flow of investments is the stated objective of the treaty, hostile acts that undermine that objective could become arbitrable. This has the potential for creating jurisdiction in an arbitral tribunal created under the treaty to review the policies of a contracting state. The implications of this possibility are as yet unclear. There may be reluctance on the part of more powerful states to conclude treaties with wide language because of such possibilities, but this means not being able to give investments adequate protection. The state will have to balance these factors in deciding whether to conclude such treaties and, if it does so, how restrictive the language it uses should be. There is no perfect treaty which will take all these factors into account.

4.9.2. Subrogation

Modern bilateral investment treaties provide for subrogation of the claims of the foreign investor in the home state. This enables the home state to succeed to the investor's claims against the host state after paying out the claims through the insurance schemes for foreign investments run by the home state. The major capital-exporting nations provide such insurance facilities for corporations which make investments overseas. In a sense, this promotes the outflow of investments. Though it is suggested that such outflows are made for the altruistic purposes of promoting investment flows into less developed parts of the world, the fact is that national interests are served by these outflows. Quite apart from the exported capital earning more than it would if it had stayed home, there is repatriation of profits that will benefit the home state. Where the foreign investment is in the resources field, this assures the home state a ready source of such resources. There is also the fact that extension of investment and trade overseas, does involve the extension of power, and this serves the foreign policy goals of the home state. The facilitation of foreign investment flows through insurance promotes the goals of the home state.

Subrogation of the home state, in place of the foreign investor who had suffered damage and has been paid off by the insurance agency, achieves another goal. It enables the home state to pursue the claims of the foreign investor as if it had suffered the damage. This substitution has a deterrent effect on the host state as it would be loath to tangle directly with a powerful home state. Technically, the home state will have to pursue the foreign investor's claim in exactly the same manner as the foreign investor himself would have. There has as yet been no rush on the part of home states to utilise this procedure. The prejudice it would cause to the diplomatic relations between the two states deters resort to such extreme measures. Subrogation acts as a subtle threat, but it will not be put to extreme use.

4.10. Safeguard provisions and exceptions

Investment treaties usually contain safeguards and exceptions to the standards of protection and standards of treatment that they offer foreign investors. The existence and variety of these safeguards and exceptions themselves defeat any claims as to the possibility of customary international law developing from these treaties. The nature of these safeguards and exceptions in relation to the treaty as a whole and in relation to specific provisions must be carefully scrutinised in order to determine the precise balance that has been struck in each treaty.

The treaty as a whole is affected where the definition of the protected investment is limited by qualifications. It has been seen that some treaties confine protection to investments specifically 'approved in writing' for purposes of protection of the treaty. Others contain formulations such as investments 'made in accordance with the laws and regulations' of the host state or the wider formula, 'made in accordance with the laws and regulations from time to time in existence'. These treaties conserve sovereign rights. The wider preservation of laws and regulations which contemplate the application of future amendments being included considerably weakens the scope of the treaty because of the implied suggestion that the contracting state could simply move an investment out of the scope of treaty protection simply by making a subsequent amendment to its laws on investment. In Indian treaties, this exception is stated in a separate article. Canadian treaties, following the US model, contain an exception relating to the environment, but this provision has been considered to be merely hortatory.

Safeguard provisions are intended to conserve at least a degree of regulatory space. But, such space is preserved more effectively by provisions which are attached to the definition of the investment that is protected. A more effective way to preserve regulatory space is to confine the protection of the treaty only to those investments which conform to the regulatory regime of the host state. Such a limitation also achieves the objectives of economic development as the regulatory framework exists to promote such development. The extent of the regulatory space that can be preserved depends on the ability and bargaining strength of each state.

4.11. Succession of governments and bilateral investment treaties

One important issue that arises in connection with bilateral investment treaties is whether a government of a state different from that which made the treaty could, at a later time, claim that it is not bound by the treaty because it subscribes to an ideology or an economic strategy that is antithetical to foreign investment. The issue could arise particularly where the subsequent government was installed as a result of a revolutionary change. The new government could argue that the investment treaty stands in the way of the implementation of its economic programme as it imposes more stringent requirements such as the payment of immediate and full compensation for the termination of existing foreign investment. The argument could also be made that the revolutionary change was a changed circumstance which justified the termination of the treaty. It is unlikely that such arguments could succeed in the present state of international law. A change of government, even through a revolution, cannot amount to a 'change that radically transforms the obligations under the treaty'.

The situation where the treaty is made by a non-representative government consisting of an elite that has ties with foreign investors and is replaced by a democratic government which seeks to do away with privileges given through treaties and other means to a group of foreign investors is more difficult. There may, in addition to arguments based on changed circumstances, also be an argument based on the fact that the previous government was an undemocratic government making a treaty that did not accord with the general interests of the people. It is unlikely that such an argument, despite the moral merits involved in it, could succeed. It may be possible to make arguments based on self-determination and related principles, but it is unlikely that the law would look beyond the fact that a treaty was made and that its obligations are binding on succeeding governments. If self-determination is taken to include the existence of a freely elected government and thus has the nature of a *ius cogens* principle, there may be room for the argument that a treaty concluded by a coterie in power is not binding on a succeeding government which has a free mandate of the people of the state. But, the notion of self-determination has not developed in international law to cover such a situation. Such arguments, despite their moral merit, may not have legal validity.

5. New concerns in bilateral investment treaties

The globalisation protests against multilateral investment agreements were generated by the fact that these agreements showed little concern for the environmental and human rights interests involved in foreign investment. The charge was that investment agreements focused entirely on the protection of the interests of the foreign investor and did not concern the interests of the international community or the host state in the protection of the values that were of concern to them. These values generally involve the areas of environmental protection, human rights and economic development. The protests against globalisation have also focused attention on these areas. The non-governmental organisations working in these fields have ensured that the criticisms remained vibrant. Though initially made against the Multilateral Agreement on Investment promoted by the OECD, these criticisms have become directed at all types of investment treaty. Those who argue along these lines would want to ensure that the regulatory function of the state in areas such as environmental protection are retained, that the state should have a defence to any claims made by foreign investors on the basis of the protection of its interests and that the state should also have the means of recourse to the same dispute resolution mechanisms provided in the treaty in the event of the violation of its interests. Only the ASEAN Investment Treaty contemplates the possibility of such an action being brought against a multinational corporation. The reaction is justified, for investment treaties have almost solely provided for the interests of multinational corporations without taking into account the possible harm that may be caused by such corporations and the plight of the developing state that stands powerless in the face of this problem. For this reason, the criticisms and the effect they have had in bringing about changes to investment treaties, both regional and bilateral, may be dealt with at this stage.

5.1. *Environmental concerns*

Environmental groups have regarded multinational corporations as having been responsible for pollution caused particularly in developing countries, where environmental standards are lax. As a result of lax laws, multinational corporations see developing countries as havens where they may make profits without having to bear the costs associated with compliance with the strict regulatory standards they face in their home states. NGOs believe that investment treaties deter actions being taken against polluters as the treaties ensure that infringements of existing rights of investors are regarded as expropriations under the treaties.[101] The argument has also been made that investment treaties secure the export of highly polluting industries into the developing world. For this reason, these groups have argued that investment treaties should contain exemptions for interference by host states to protect the environment.

Few investment treaties have responded to this concern. US and Canadian treaties do contain provisions addressing environmental concerns. This provision may also be found in NAFTA. Article 1114(1) of NAFTA reads:

> Nothing in this Chapter shall be construed to prevent a Party from adopting, maintaining, or enforcing any measure, otherwise consistent with this Chapter, that it considers appropriate to ensure that the investment activity in its territory is undertaken in a manner sensitive to environmental concerns.

But, in *S. D. Myers* v. *Canada*,[102] the tribunal, which interpreted this provision, said that its nature was merely 'hortatory'. The tribunal did not consider that the Canadian defence – that Canadian hazardous waste should be disposed of in Canada and not sent across the border into the United States for disposal – had any merit. This view was taken despite the fact that Canada's action to prevent the export of the waste was consistent with obligations under the Basle Convention on the Transboundary Movement of Hazardous Waste. The tendency of tribunals has been to read down the effect of the rare environmental provisions that are to be found in investment treaties, thus preserving the original basis of these treaties as investment protection treaties.

---

[101] This is borne out by cases such as *Santa Elena* v. *Costa Rica* (2002) 5 ICSID Rpts 157.
[102] *S. D. Myers* v. *Canada* (2002) 121 ILR 1.

5.2. Human rights

Again, human rights are seldom, if at all, referred to in bilateral investment treaties. But, violations connected with the suppression of dissent against particular projects initiated by multinational corporations have come to light in recent years. Recent litigation before domestic courts against parent companies of multinational corporations allege violations of human rights committed by agents of those multinational corporations in association with the political elites of developing countries illustrates the extent of the problem. Investment treaties may deter a state from interfering to correct a human rights situation that may have arisen. Often, however, the state, or the elites which control it, are also participants along with the multinational corporation in the violation of the human rights abuse. Succeeding governments may, however, want to remedy the situation but may be deterred from doing so by the fact that such interference may be regarded as an infringement of investor rights under the treaty.

There are few treaties which address this issue. The saving of issues of health, morals and public welfare, a formula that is used in international trade law, has found its way into some investment treaties. But, the scope of the use of the phrase in investment treaties has yet to be determined. In international trade, tribunals have not given the term such a scope as would enable the interests contained in the formula to trump the interests of free trade.[103] There is little room to believe that the situation will be any different when the phrase is considered in relation to investment treaties. The general trend to interpret these treaties as giving primacy to investment protection will probably be continued. But, the seeds of discontent will multiply as a result.

Many states, particularly in Asia and Africa, walk on tightropes when it comes to adopting ethnic policies. Repeated race riots have sundered their economies. Their laws forestall problems by allocating the economic pie in accordance with ethnic policies devised to reduce tension by ensuring that the majority have an economic role. These policies are enforced by legislation.[104] Investment treaties sit uneasily with such social experiments as they contain national treatment standards that may require that the best national standards are given to foreign investors. There is an obvious need

---

[103] See e.g. *The Thai Tobacco Case* (1991) 37 GATT BISD 200, where the ban on cigarettes by Thailand justified on health grounds was given short shrift.

[104] The Malaysians have had such a policy for some time. In South Africa, the land redistribution and other schemes envisage that economic power will be slowly transferred to the hands of the native people of that country.

to remove those provisions favouring the disadvantaged sections of the community from the scope of the investment treaties, but, so far, there have been few efforts made in this regard. The South African treaties attempt this by providing that their affirmative action programmes are exempt from national treatment.[105]

5.3. Economic development

The premise on which investment treaties are made is that foreign investment leads to economic development and that treaties lead to greater flows of foreign investment. Both assumptions are coming to be contested. There is no evidence to show that investment treaties have led to greater flows of foreign investment into states making them. Many states, particularly the least developed states, have liberalised their foreign investment laws and made a large number of investment treaties without witnessing the expected flows of foreign investment.[106] The institutions that were formerly advocating the treaties, now have studies indicating that the evidence that they lead to positive flows of foreign investment is non-existent and conjectural.[107] Since the underlying assumption of the treaties is that flows of foreign investment lead to economic development, there is no reference to economic development in the treaties nor do they contain any meaningful provisions as to the promotion of such economic development. The role of the capital-exporting partner in promoting flows of foreign investment is not stated as an obligation in the treaties, but instead is referred to in permissive language.

But, the movement for the inclusion of development provisions in investment treaties will gather increasing momentum. The Doha Declaration of the WTO Ministerial Meeting, which mandates the study of investment as a possible discipline under the WTO, requires that the issue be studied in the context of development. Such concessions will highlight the need to ensure that investment treaties contain provisions addressing issues of economic development and a movement away from

---

[105] The clause in the South African treaties, after providing for exemptions from national treatment, lists as an exception: 'any laws or other measure the purpose of which is to promote the achievement of equality on its territory or to advance persons or categories of persons, disadvantage by unfair discrimination in its territory'.

[106] Ghana provides the classic example.

[107] Mary Hallward-Driemeier, 'Do Bilateral Investment Treaties Attract FDI? Only a Bit . . . . And They Could Bite' World Bank research paper, 2003, available on the website of the World Bank).

the investment-protective models of economic liberalism to models that contemplate the elimination of the harmful effect of foreign investment while protecting beneficial investment.

The issue of economic development is intertwined with that of corporate responsibility and good corporate governance. It is obvious that a company that does not practice such responsible conduct cannot contribute to the economic development of the host state. Every positive aspect of foreign investment has a negative aspect as well. If foreign investment does bring about the transfer of technology, there is the possibility that such technology is unsuitable because it is not labour-intensive or is obsolete. In addition, it is also the basis on which restrictive practices such as tie-in provisions,[108] restrictions relating to geographical markets and restraint of competition are practised. If there is employment creation, the employment is at lower wage levels and at a cost that bears no proportion to the price of the manufactured goods. If there is infrastructure upgrading, this is usually a cost borne by the host state. Environmental pollution and hazardous technology bring about costs to the host state. When a situation like Bhopal occurs, the costs are too horrendous ever to be redeemed. In that context, the idea of the absolute protection of foreign investment that is offered by current investment treaties sits uneasily with the possibility of adverse effects. In several instances, the entry of foreign investment could have beneficial effects but it could also have the opposite effect. A treaty premised on the notion that all foreign investment is uniformly beneficial is not one based on sound foundations.

5.4. International concerns

Quite apart from the concerns of the host state, foreign investment within a state implicates international concerns as well. It is evident that international law has moved to recognise the fact that matters that fall within the domestic concern of states can implicate international values and that in these situations the international community has a right to ensure that changes are brought about in the domestic situation. The classic modern situation is the movement that has taken place in the area of human rights. No longer can a state claim that gross violations of human rights taking place within its territory are of domestic concern only and do not concern the rest of the international community. The international law

---

[108] These provisions require that goods to be used with the technology be purchased from the transferor only.

on foreign investment has also moved in the same direction, adopting values that it has drawn from associated areas of international law. Though foreign investment is a process that takes place entirely within the host state's territory, the host state cannot avoid the scrutiny of the international community. It cannot avoid the overriding power of international rules over domestic law that justifies the conduct.

There are instances in which international law values have supported changes in foreign investment arrangements and other instances in which these values have been used as a justification for effecting changes in existing foreign investment arrangements. Thus, for example, in *International Bank of Washington v. OPIC*,[109] the blanket measures changing the environmental law were held to justify the breach of a foreign investment agreement. The federal government's interference with a foreign investment contract on the ground that the sand-mining project involved potential damage to the Great Barrier Reef, an area classified under the World Heritage Convention was held to be justified by the domestic courts. Likewise, the creation of a new state through the assertion of self-determination measures was held to rescind obligations arising from a foreign investment contract.[110] Then there are decisions which indicate that obligations are subject to higher values of the international community. If so, the question has to be raised as to whether investment treaties must accommodate these higher values or make reference to them.

But, the provisions of bilateral investment treaties have not been interpreted in that manner at all. In *S. D. Myers v. Canada*, the Canadian argument was that, in requiring Canadian hazardous waste to be disposed of in Canada, Canada was complying with the community values articulated in the Basel Convention on the Transboundary Movement of Hazardous Waste. But, the argument was rejected on the ground that NAFTA provisions on national treatment were violated. In *Santa Elena v. Costa Rica*, the tribunal held that a foreign investment contract to convert a coastal area into a tourist resort had priority over a later decision of the state to preserve the unique wildlife of the region by converting the area into a nature reserve. In *SPP v. Egypt*, the issue was raised as to whether the protection of a cultural site which was listed under the World Heritage Convention justified the termination of a project to build

---

[109] (1972) 11 ILM 1216.
[110] *Société des Grands Travaux de Marseille v. East Pakistan Industrial Development Corporation* (1980) 5 YCA 177.

a tourist complex at the site.[111] These decisions, made under investment treaties, indicate that there is insensitivity to international values in tribunals which obtain jurisdiction over the dispute through the dispute settlement mechanisms in investment treaties.

The issue arises as to whether matters of international concern relating to the environment or human rights are not *ius cogens* principles which trump the rights of foreign investors to unilateral arbitration that are created by investment treaties. The argument can credibly be made that there are some values in international environmental law and human rights law that are so fundamental that the propositions of investment treaties which are designed to protect large multinational corporations should give way to them. There is also room for the further proposition that these issues should not be dealt with by arbitral tribunals that are created under investment treaties which have only a narrow mandate to decide issues that arise from the foreign investment. Instead, tribunals that reflect the interests of the international community as a whole should deal with such disputes. There must be a doctrine of arbitrability created which ensures that issues that concern the international community as a whole should not be disposed of by arbitral tribunals which draw their jurisdiction from the will of only the parties to the dispute before them.

5.5. *Regulatory space and bilateral treaties*

All treaties constrain sovereignty. Investment treaties constrain sovereign rights of control over the intrusive process of foreign investment, which takes place entirely within the territory of the host state. To this extent, the erosion of sovereignty in such treaties is considerable. But, it is trite law that a treaty can control events that are entirely internal and domestic. In Chapter 3 above, it was shown that states have various techniques of controlling foreign investment so that it can promote the development objectives of the state. The issue arises as to whether the right to control investment by the host state is lost as a result of investment treaties. The answer depends on the type of treaty that is made. Where the treaty is of the type that the United States makes, with rights of entry and national treatment, then the erosion of the regulatory space becomes considerable. But, in other treaties, there is always a negotiated balance between the right

[111] This case did not arise under a treaty.

of regulation by the host state and the rights of protection and treatment given to the foreign investor.

Many treaties conserve the regulatory regimes of the host state by confining the scope of the treaty or defining the foreign investment that is protected in a restrictive manner. This point bears repetition. In most south-east Asian treaties, the practice has been to extend protection only to 'investments specifically approved in writing'. This ensures that only investments that are regarded as particularly beneficial to the state are given approval for the purposes of protection. In other treaties, the formula is to extend protection only to investments 'made in accordance with the laws, policies and regulations' of the host state.[112] It is evident that there is a desire to ensure that the regulatory regime plays a role in defining the extent of the treaty protection. It is evident that only investment which conforms to the state's regulatory structure will receive protection under such treaties. Another formulation is so subjective as to tilt the balance entirely in favour of the host state. This contains the subjective formula that the investment that is protected is an investment 'made in accordance with the laws, policies and regulations from time to time in existence'.[113] Such a formulation, while fully conserving regulatory space, deprives the treaty of all its protective content, as the host state could defeat the protection of the treaty simply by changing its laws. The existence of this concern over the conservation of the regulatory space and the manner in which it has been achieved in different treaties indicates that a carefully negotiated balance is struck in every bilateral investment treaty. The conservation of regulatory space is achieved in individual provisions in the treaties through various methods. Thus, the limitations of right of repatriation of capital in times of economic difficulties and of the safeguard provisions in some treaties are examples of conserving regulatory space in specific areas.

6. Conclusion

There has been intense activity in the area of bilateral investment treaties. This activity results from a convergence of factors. Developing states are intent on attracting foreign investment, and there is competition for the investment that is available. In the absence of clear rules on investment protection, capital-exporting states have found it desirable that they

---

[112] The Malaysian model treaty, 2002. A similar formula is used in recent Chinese treaties.
[113] This formulation is widely used in the newer treaties of Australia and Indonesia.

should give as much protection as possible to their investors by negotiating treaties with clear rules. This accounts for their desire to enter into
these treaties. They are preferred by new industrial states which did not
have much influence on the developing states. This accounts for the large
number of treaties which a country like Germany has entered into. The
German treaties also indicate that they have no consistent pattern, again
showing the desire on the part of that state to emphasise more the forming of an investment relationship than the form of the treaty. The wide
divergence in the terms of the German treaties indicates this factor. Given
this wide divergence in the practice of even a single state, it is unlikely
that these treaties can give rise to any significant customary international
law on foreign investment protection. Bilateral investment treaties are *lex
specialis* as between the parties, and they are likely to remain so. It was
once thought that their momentum may be somewhat reduced by the
fact that the nature of the uses to which they could be put have not been
explored yet. Indeed, Vagts pointed out, 'so far as the literature discloses,
BITs have not yet been put to the test so that we do not know how much
they enhance the security of foreign investment'.[114] But, passage of time
has shown that the investment treaties have been very effective in providing relief to the foreign investor. The *AAPL* v. *Sri Lanka* case shows that
such a treaty is effective in conferring jurisdiction on overseas arbitration
tribunals. Since then, the caseload of ICSID has multiplied largely on the
basis of the invocation of jurisdiction on the basis of the provisions in
bilateral investment treaties. The explosion of litigation under NAFTA
also demonstrates that, from the point of view of the foreign investor,
creative litigation strategies can be employed to secure the rights of foreign investors. But, the issue now is whether there has been too rapid a
movement in favour of the protection of the rights of the investor without heeding the interests of the host state and its environmental and other
interests. A reaction will set in if there is further movement in favour of
protection without assuaging the valid concerns of those who argue the
case for environmental protection, human rights and economic development. Unless investment treaties come to reflect a balance between
the rights of the foreign investors and the regulatory concerns of the host
states, their future viability will continue to be contested. This concern will
become particularly acute as evidence keeps mounting that such treaties
do not lead to greater flows of foreign investment into a host state or that

---

[114] Detlev Vagts, 'Protecting Foreign Investment: An International Law Perspective' in C.
Wallace (ed.), *Foreign Investment in the 1990s* (1990) 102 at 112.

they do not necessarily lead to economic development. The question will then be raised more stridently as to why there is so great a surrender of sovereignty in favour of the interests of the foreign investor when the *quid pro quo* that the host state receives is tenuous and uncertain. If the fervour for economic liberalism dies down, the challenges to investment treaties will become more strident.

The proposition that foreign investment flows are beneficial to economic investment is based on the tenets of economic liberalism. It is the assumption that has driven the sudden growth in the number of foreign investment treaties in recent times.[115]

---

[115] For the view that developing states are overwhelmed by economic theories that are formulated in the West, see Ozay Mehmet, *Westernizing the Third World: The Eurocentricity of Economic Development Theories* (1999).

6

Multilateral instruments on foreign investment

If states were in agreement as to the norms that constitute the international law of foreign investment, it would have been possible to bring about a multilateral agreement on foreign investment stating the substantive rules which apply in the area. The fact that no such multilateral agreements exist is due to the existence of conflicting approaches to the problem of foreign investment protection and the existence of contending systems relating to the treatment of foreign investment. Several attempts have been made at bringing about a comprehensive code on foreign investment,[1] but they have resulted in failure simply because of the ideological rifts and clashes of interests that attend this branch of international law. Most drafts have been made with the objective of providing as much protection as is possible to foreign investment. These have been rejected by capital-importing states. The entry into the picture of non-governmental organisations further complicates the picture. They object to multilateral agreements which concentrate on investment protection exclusively without addressing issues relating to environmental degradation or human rights violations associated with foreign investment. Some of these organisations take the view that the development interests of the poor are not addressed through such instruments, which seek only to protect the rights of the rich multinational corporations. The entry of these organisations as major players in the area has further complicated the issue of making such agreements. It is relevant to note that non-governmental organisations which supported the rights of the foreign investors have been active in the field for a longer period of time.[2]

---

[1] The first attempt was the foreign investment provisions in the Havana Charter (1948), which contemplated the establishment of an International Trade Organization. It did not eventuate due to the objection to the provisions by business groups and the eventual refusal of the United States to participate in the process of the establishment of such an organisation. James E. S. Fawcett, 'The Havana Charter' (1949) 5 YBWA 320.

[2] The International Chamber of Commerce is one such non-governmental organisation. In 1972, it drafted Guidelines for International Investments. A private group drafted what

But, voices against confining the drafting of investment treaties to investment protection alone have increased as a result of the growing strength of the environmental and human rights groups entering this sphere.[3]

There have also been instruments which contained rules favouring the interests of the developing states.[4] These have been rejected by the developed states. Most of these came about when there was a movement to curb the power of multinational corporations. There was a period in which these corporations were seen as undermining the sovereignty of states in which they operated. That period also coincided with the movement towards the creation of a New International Economic Order giving greater control over foreign investment to developing states. In that context, codes came to be drafted, especially by a specially created United Nations body, the United Nations Commission on Transnational Corporations (UNCTC). These codes were resisted by the developed states, which put forward their own version of the code. The efforts within the UNCTC to draft a code of conduct did not succeed. The first section of this chapter describes the past efforts at drafting multilateral investment codes.[5]

Among the more recent efforts to draft instruments on investment are the Guidelines on Foreign Investment proposed by a study group of the World Bank and the Multilateral Agreement on Investment (MAI) attempted by the Organisation for Economic Co-operation and Development (OECD). The Guidelines were drafted in 1992. They were non-binding, as the expert group felt that the time was not ripe for a binding

---

came to be known as the Abs–Shawcross Convention. It was espoused by Germany and submitted to the OECD. For a discussion of the draft, see Lord Shawcross, 'The Problems of Foreign Investment in International Law' (1961) 102 *Hague Recueil* 334; for the text, see (1968) 7 ILM 117.

[3] This phenomenon is new. Though these non-governmental organisations have existed for a considerable time, their concern with the investment field probably dates from the organised protests against the OECD's attempt to formulate a Multilateral Agreement on Investment (1995–8). The abandonment of the project is at least partly due to the organised protests.

[4] There was an attempt to draft a code of conduct on multinational corporations by the now defunct United Nations Commission on Transnational Corporations. The attempt failed due to its non-acceptance by the developed states.

[5] The World Bank study lists the multilateral instruments made up to the date of the study. The inclusion of human rights documents in the list is selective. It includes the Universal Declaration of Human Rights and the European Convention on Human Rights. But, the relevance of these documents is confined to the statement of the right to property only. If the right to property is relevant, a fuller list containing the variations on the statements of this right should have been included. For the list, see World Bank, *Legal Framework for the Treatment of Foreign Investment* (vol.1, 1992), 63–72.

multilateral code on investment. This was despite the fact that, in the 1990s, there was a general fervour for the liberalisation of the regime for investments. There was a proliferation of bilateral and regional treaties on investment. The developing countries had for various reasons turned away from the attempt to create a New International Economic Order and were courting foreign investors by granting them high standards of protection both through their domestic law as well as through investment treaties. The OECD, in that context, thought that the time was ripe to push through a binding code on foreign investment. Its project for a Multilateral Agreement on Investment began in 1994 but was soon to run aground as the fervour for liberalisation subsided and the anti-globalisation protests took hold. The MAI became the first target of these protests and was the catalyst enabling the coming together of a diversity of interests opposed to globalisation. Since the failure of the MAI, the focus has now shifted to the World Trade Organization. The Second Ministerial Conference of the WTO, held in Singapore, mandated the consideration of an agreement on investment under the auspices of the WTO. The matter was not considered at the Third Ministerial, in Seattle, where massive demonstrations against the WTO muted consideration of the issue. At the Doha Ministerial Meeting, the decision was made to consider the possibility of taking up the subject of investment, but with the 'development dimension' in mind. By the time of the Cancun Ministerial Meeting in September 2003, a group of developing countries had coalesced. They put together a paper expressing the view that if a multilateral code were to come into existence it should not concentrate solely on the protection of investment. The code should also have regard to the prohibition of misconduct of multinational corporations, the active promotion of investment flows and other matters of interest to economic development. As other issues such as agriculture dominated the meeting, the investment issue was not considered. The investment issue, however, remains alive. The area covered by this chapter is both current and controversial.

1. The international norms on multinational corporations

The study of multinational corporations in international law is rather recent,[6] though they have been actors on the international scene for a long period of time. The major trading companies that existed in Europe,

---

[6] For book-length treatments of the subject, see Peter Muchlinkski, *Multinational Corporations Law* (1995); and Cynthia Wallace, *The Multinational Enterprise and Legal Control: Host State Sovereignty in an Era of Economic Globalization* (2002).

such as the East India Company and the Dutch East Indies Company, though they were not multinational corporations in the modern sense, were the progenitors of imperial rule. The modern multinational corporation is better integrated due to superior means of instant communication and is more cohesive due to integrated modes of production. They are responsible for all the investment flows that take place.[7] The largest of these multinational corporations command financial assets in excess of those controlled by states. Their role in domestic and international affairs cannot be underestimated. As major repositories of power, they advanced rules and codes of conduct which suited their interests. They have the capacity to influence the course of international events and shape principles of international law.

It has been a defect in the theory of international law that this fact has not been accommodated in theoretical constructs of the law. The idea of the open seas was formulated at the behest of trading companies so as to ensure that they had open access to the seas to favour their maritime trading interests.[8] The system of appointing diplomatic agents for the protection of nationals owes its origins to the system of agents appointed by corporations to look after their commercial interests.[9] Colonies were first conquered by corporations before they were attached to an imperial system. State-centred theories of international law have, however, never recognised the fact that trading corporations have been forces within the international system with a capacity to generate international norms of behaviour or, at least, have an influence in the shaping of the forms these rules take. The power of the companies continued long after the imperial states took over from the trading companies and established their sovereignty over the colonies. In the Middle East, oil diplomacy upon which power depended in the twentieth century was pursued as much by the major oil corporations as by their home states.[10] It was evident that the system of investment protection through contractual means was devised largely through the activity of individuals and organisations that were keen

---

[7] Technically, every individual is capable of making foreign investments. At least one modern investment dispute arose from an investment made by a single investor. *Vacuum Salts* v. *Ghana*. But, it is seldom that large investments are made by a single investor, though large multinational corporations are often controlled by single individuals or by families.

[8] It is no secret that Grotius, who is sometimes credited as being a disinterested founder of international law, was in the employ of the Dutch East Indies Company when he formulated the theory of the freedom of the seas.

[9] Arthur Nussbaum, *A Concise History of the Law of Nations* (1954), 125.

[10] Daniel Yergin, *The Prize* (1991).

on protecting the interests of these corporations. The law that was built up was built up through private means of law-making focusing on arbitral awards that result from consensual procedures of decision-making and the writings of scholars who were partial to the building up of a system of investment protection through the instrumentality of international law.

The power of the old trading corporations like the East India Company pale into insignificance when compared with the power of the multinational corporation in the modern world. The old trading corporation was a dinosaur with a small head and a huge body in the sense that actual control over the subsidiaries in far-flung areas could not be exercised by the parent company due to inadequate communication facilities. The control exercised by the parent company over its subsidiaries in the case of a modern multinational corporation is far more effective due to speedier methods of communications and the transferring of assets and personnel. The influence that the multinational corporation can exert on states and on the international community is commensurate with the increase in this power. Many multinational corporations command capital assets far in excess of the states in which they operate. It is not difficult to understand that they can affect trends in both international and domestic politics. The need for the regulation of this private power through the instrumentality of international law is a necessary fact which has not been adequately addressed, largely because the existence of such power itself ensures that no control is brought about.[11] The curtain of positivism provides obvious advantages.

At one stage, developing countries saw the need to control the power of multinational corporations. They sought to influence the United Nations bodies which they controlled to formulate rules of conduct for multinational corporations. These efforts were part of the package to bring about the New International Economic Order. These efforts began at a time when the developing states had sufficient cohesion and sufficient confidence in being able to achieve new rules through their unity. The general belief that multinational corporations were undermining the sovereignty of states also had a hold in Europe at the same time. The dependency theory – that multinational corporations were instrumental in keeping the economies of peripheral states in a state of perpetual dependence – still

---

[11] Through employment of such devices as soft, non-binding codes and heavy advertising campaigns, attention is deflected from the need for control. The very institutions like the OECD which want strong binding measures on foreign investment protection, argue for soft codes for the regulation of the conduct of multinational corporations.

had hold in Latin American states. In that context, it was possible to talk of bringing about binding codes of conduct to regulate the activities of multinational corporations. The circulation of petro-dollars ensured that there was sufficient money available for developing countries. It is in that context that the effort was made by the United Nations Commission on Transnational Corporations (UNCTC)[12] to draft a code of conduct on transnational corporations.

But, the fervour for the New International Economic Order was to diminish. With aid drying up and a loan crisis emerging due to a failure to meet payments on the petro-dollar loans, foreign investment capital became the only available capital for economic development. All developing countries began to compete with each other for the limited foreign investment that was available. Hostility to multinational corporations ended and they began to be heavily courted. Ideological changes also took place with the fall of communism. With the new states resulting from the break-up of the Soviet Union embracing free market notions, the competition for foreign investment among the developing countries increased. The ascendancy of neo-liberalism speeded the process of liberalisation of trade regimes resulting in the formation of the World Trade Organization. Though, in 1992, the World Bank judged rightly that the world was still not ripe for a binding code on foreign investment and brought out a set of guidelines instead, the OECD, just a few years later, embarked upon the framing of a binding Multilateral Agreement on Investment (MAI).

The picture was to change again. The MAI soon became the focus of protests. They were generated largely by human rights and environmental groups which claimed that the instrument focused entirely on the protection of multinational corporations without addressing the fact that they were also responsible for much of the human rights abuses and environmental degradation that takes place around the world. Around that time, there was also growing disenchantment with globalisation, which had been trumpeted as a force that integrated the world and assured human progress.[13] Suddenly, there was discontent with the process. It was seen as

---

[12] The UNCTC was established in pursuance of a study of the problem of multinational corporations. A group of eminent persons was appointed by ECOSOC Resolution 1721 (LIII) to study the problem. The group recommended the setting up of the UNCTC, which was established in 1974. The group justified its continued interest in the issue on the ground that 'certain practices and effects of transnational corporations had given rise to widespread concern and anxiety in many quarters and a strong feeling has emerged that the present *modus vivendi* should be reviewed at the international level'.

[13] George Stiglitz, *Globalization and its Discontents* (2002).

driving a wedge between the poor and rich not only on a global scale but within the developed states themselves. As one commentator put it, the process of globalisation had so divided society on economic scales that the Third World had moved into the first world.[14] The battles that ensued on the streets of Western capitals whenever the economic organisations connected with neo-liberalism met, signalled the growing opposition to the idea of bringing about regimes on foreign investment that gave protection to multinational corporations without controlling their faults. The counter-groups had organised themselves so effectively that they were able to exert sufficient pressure on their governments to pull out of the negotiations of the MAI.

But, the issue of investments has now been moved into the World Trade Organization. It is tasked with the formulation of an instrument on investment which will then be fitted into the existing structure of the WTO with its dispute resolution mechanism. The assurance to the developing world and to the discontents is that the issue of investment will be considered in the context of economic development. The text of the Doha Ministerial Meeting of the WTO assures that this would be done in formulating an instrument. Though work on the process of considering an instrument has begun, there are states which have already come out strongly against the making of such an instrument.

Three principal instruments that have been attempted, all of which resulted in failure, tell the tale of these movements. The first is the OECD's draft code of conduct on multinational corporaitons. The second is the World Bank Group's non-binding guidelines on foreign investment. The third is the OECD's MAI. The present, ongoing effort is to move the issue into the WTO. The following sections describe the principal features of each of these efforts.

2. The UNCTC Draft Code on Multinational Corporations

The UNCTC Draft Code on Multinational Corporations, like the OECD's Multilateral Agreement on Investment, never received acceptance. But, both are important as they indicate the differences that exist between the states and the conception of what the ideal code for investments would be at both ends. Both documents were drafted at the time when the political climate was favourable to their drafting. The UNCTC's Draft Code was

---

[14] Caroline Thomas, *Globalization and the South* (1997).

attempted at a time when there was considerable hostility to multinational corporations and there was a cohesion among developing countries to control foreign investment. The OECD's MAI was drafted a time when the fervour for liberalisation was at its high point, and it came to a halt when it subsided. Both efforts, and the contents of the codes that were drafted, are described in this chapter, along with the intervening attempts. It commences with a description of the UNCTC's Draft Code.

2.1. Description of the UNCTC Draft Code

The final version of the Draft Code contained seventy-three paragraphs. The major provisions of the code may be noted.

2.1.1. The preamble

The preamble to the Draft Code states that the object of the Code is to 'maximise the contributions of transnational corporations to economic development and growth and to minimise the negative effects of the activities of these corporations'. It is clear the code is based on the premise of the report of the Group of Eminent Persons on Multinational Corporations, that multinational corporations may promote economic development provided they are harnessed to the economic goals of the state and provided the negative impacts of their investments are avoided. It thus rejects the classical economic theory on foreign investment, that foreign investment uniformly promotes the economic development of the host state. As a result, the premises on which foreign investment protection has hitherto been built stand rejected. Economic liberalism, which was to gather strength in the 1990s and fuel the move towards the MAI, is also built on the premise that what is good for development deserves protection. The Draft Code contains an implicit rejection of that argument, and therefore presents an ideological counter to the premises on which the developed states have built up their norms on foreign investment protection. The preamble, though not contested by the developed states at the stage of drafting, stands as a rejection of the policy of the developed states in constructing their instruments on foreign investment. It is in marked contrast to other international instruments on investment, such as bilateral investment treaties or the ICSID and MIGA Conventions, which are prefaced by the classical view that foreign investment is uniformly beneficial to economic development.

2.1.2. Definition

There was some early dispute as to the definition of the transnational corporation. The developed states required the inclusion of state corporations in the definition of transnational corporations, whereas developing states preferred that the definition is confined to private corporations. There was no consensus as to the inclusion of state corporations within the definition of multinational corporations.

2.1.3. Respect for national sovereignty

Article 7 of the Draft Code states that transnational corporations shall respect the national sovereignty of the countries in which they operate and the right of each state to exercise its permanent sovereignty over its natural wealth and resources. The succeeding articles flow from the principle of sovereignty. They seek to spell out the fact that the foreign corporation which operates in the territory of the host state should recognise the sovereignty of the host state. They require foreign corporations to accept and abide by the laws of the host state and ensure that they do not act in any way that is inconsistent with the economic objectives of the host state.[15] The sovereignty of the host state is not absolute, for the Code later refers to the duty of the state to fulfil in good faith the international obligations that it has undertaken. The qualification is consistent with the reference to sovereignty in the the other documents associated with the New International Economic Order. Thus, the Charter of Economic Rights and Duties of States also refers to the requirement that international obligations are fulfilled in good faith. But, the content of the international obligations is a matter of controversy. It obviously includes obligations in multilateral and bilateral treaties. But, whether it would include contractual agreements between the transnational corporations and their host states and limitations created by customary international law is a matter of dispute.[16]

The reference to permanent sovereignty over natural resources draws its origin from a long string of General Assembly resolutions which have

[15] Articles 8–10.

[16] S. Tiewul, 'Transnational Corporations and Emerging International Legal Standards' in P. De Waart, P. Peters and E. Denters (eds.), *International Law and Development* (1988), 105 at 113, suggests that it does include limitations created by customary international law. But, there is a reluctance to spell this out in the code itself. Resolution 1803 (1962) on the Permanent Sovereignty over Natural Resources contained the obligation by affirming that 'foreign investment agreements freely entered into by or between sovereign states shall be observed in good faith'.

asserted a state's right to control the exploitation of the natural resources of its territory. The doctrine is too well entrenched now, as a result of its acceptance in constitutional provisions as well as in the new forms of contract that have been devised so as to reflect the host state's right of control. Though contested, there is some serious support in the literature for the rule to be considered as a *ius cogens* principle.

2.1.4. Renegotiation of contracts

An obligation is created to renegotiate contracts where the contractual equilibrium which existed at the time of the contract has been altered by a fundamental change of circumstances.[17] This is a departure from the hoary doctrine of *pacta sunt servanda* upon which developed states have placed so much store in building up a theory of internationalisation of foreign investment contracts.[18] But, renegotiation is more sensible as a technique for avoiding disputes and for ensuring that the relationship remains viable in the context of changed circumstances. There is a growing body of opinion which believes that a renegotiation clause should be read into foreign investment contracts of long duration. The inclusion of the duty to renegotiate in the Draft Code is consistent with this opinion.[19] The inclusion of the duty to renegotiate contracts in the light of changed circumstances is consistent with this opinion. Again, one can see that the genesis of much of the ideas that underlay the Draft Code is in the resolutions that accompanied the New International Economic Order and the writings that supported it. To that extent, there was a definite effort being made to bring about norms opposed to those that had been hitherto articulated in the area.

2.1.5. Non-interference in domestic affairs

There is a duty imposed on transnational corporations not to interfere in the domestic political activities of the host state. They are also not to influence their home states to intervene on their behalf in a manner inconsistent with their obligation under the Charter of the United Nations and

---

[17] Article 12.   [18] On the theory, see Chapter 2 above.

[19] The *Aminoil Arbitration* showed the relevance of changed circumstances and the view that the contract cannot remain unresponsive to changed circumstances. For writings which favour the view that renegotiation should be implied in all foreign investment contracts of long duration, see M. Sornarajah, 'The Supremacy of Renegotiation Clauses in Internationa Contracts' (1988) 6 JIA 97; and Nagla Nassar, *Sanctity of Contracts Revisited* (1995).

the Declaration on Friendly Relations Between States.[20] The inspiration for the articles is the fear on the part of the developing states that transnational corporations will use their economic power to influence domestic politics. There was also the fear that they would induce their home states to interfere with the internal politics of the host states to bring about political climates favourable to them as they did in the past. The role of the old companies in imperial history was well remembered. A contemporary instance of such interference was in Chile, which resulted in the overthrowing of the government of President Allende who nationalised the copper mines without paying compensation. The role of foreign corporations as well as their home states in the military coup that ensued and the replacement of the government by a right-wing dictatorship favourable to foreign business induced a general fear that the situation could be repeated in other states. There was a feeling that reformist governments which seek to institute economic policies that may be unfavourable to foreign business may meet with a similar fate.

The requirement of non-interference is an established principle of international law. In the *Nicaragua Case*,[21] the International Court of Justice rejected the US argument that the growing influence of communist power in Nicaragua was a matter which concerned all the regional states. The Court indicated that it was not permissible under international law for one state to dictate the economic system that another state should possess. This, the Court recognised, is a matter entirely for the internal sovereignty of the state. But, the multinational corporation is already present within the state and often it cannot meaningfully participate in business activities unless it acquires and wields some domestic political influence. It is the degree of such political influence that is the issue. The fear of the developing states is that the influence that is acquired could be used to ensure that governments partial to the interests of foreign investors are maintained in power. There is also the fear that the home state will use the multinational corporation to influence the course of politics in the host state. From the human rights angle, the fear has been expressed that multinational corporations form alliances with local ruling elites and ensure that governments favourable to business are kept in power even through repression. The issue is the right balance between acquiring the necessary influence to function as an effective business organisation in the host state and interfering in the political affairs of the state.

[20] Articles 16–20.   [21] [1984] ICJ Rpts 352.

The Draft Code seeks to recognise the difficulty posed by this issue. It seeks a reconciliation of the conflict by stating that legitimate activities permitted by the laws and regulations of the host state are not forbidden. But, the acquisition of the right type of political influence necessary for the multinational corporation to function is not a matter of law or regulation. The question is not adequately addressed by the Draft Code as it would depend on the circumstances of doing business in each state.

Developed states will be touchy in recognising the rule on non-interference as it is an admission of their past acts of interference through multinational corporations and requires abjuration of future interference. The acceptance of the rule may mean the acceptance of the existence of covert interference in international affairs in the past as well as in the present. States will be unwilling to have such a construction placed on their acceptance of the rule. As regards future involvement, states will not be keen on evolving principles which could be used against them. The issue of the recognition of the rule of non-interference will pose problems.

Yet, it addresses one of the issues that plagued the drafting of the OECD's MAI, that of unconcern for human rights. The rule of non-interference imposes an obligation on the multinational corporation not to assist in the repression of the people by the ruling elite so as to promote business. To the extent that the rule promotes such an interest, it will have appeal to human rights groups which will campaign for the inclusion of such a rule in a code on investments. But, they may desire that the rule be stated as a more active obligation and not be confined to the passive obligation of mere non-interference.

Since the UNCTC Draft Code, the prohibition of interference in domestic affairs by multinational corporations has been taken further by other instruments. But, the latter are largely non-binding codes. The OECD Guidelines for Multinational Enterprises requires as a general policy that the multinational corporation have regard to the laws of the host state and abstain from political activities in the host state.

2.1.6. Abstention from corrupt practices

The use of bribery to achieve the objectives of the multinational corporation has also caused general concern. Several scandals involving multinational corporations indicated that the practice was widespread. The United States passed legislation against the use of bribery by their nationals in the conduct of foreign business, though the enforcement of that legislation has not been pursued due to the feeling that it places US businesses at a disadvantage.[22] Later amendments to this legislation have relaxed the heavy penalties that the original legislation contemplated.

The OECD has formulated non-binding codes on illicit payments. The fact that the codes are non-binding indicates that there is a softer approach to the issue of the corrupt practices of multinational corporations. It is an idea that does not sit well with the increasing clamour for the imposition of responsibility on multinational corporations for their misdeeds. It would appear that institutions of developed states are favouring multinational business by not advocating instruments that impose definite liability for the corrupt practices of multinational corporations. It may smack of double standards that an institution that worked for a binding agreement on investments wants a mere non-binding code of ethics on the corrupt practices of multinational corporations.

Domestic legal systems regard bribery as criminal. But, in developing states enforcement is lax because these states are often ruled by the same elites which obtain the bribes. Contracts tainted by bribery are regarded as illegal.[23] The Draft Code creates a definite duty on the part of multinational corporations to refrain from making payments to public officials as a consideration for the performance of their duties and also requires a register to be kept of payments made to officials.[24]

2.1.7. Economic and other controls

There follows a series of articles which deal with the economic, financial and social controls that the host state could institute in respect of the activities of the multinational corporation. Many of these matters are provided for in other international instruments. These issues include transfer of technology,[25] restrictive business practices,[26] labour

---

[22] The Foreign Corrupt Practices Act, (1977) 15 USC s. 78m.

[23] *Lemenda Trading Co. Ltd* v. *African Middle East Petroleum Co. Ltd* [1988] 1 All ER 513.

[24] Article 21.

[25] On the issue of the transfer of technology, UNCTAD had sought to formulate a draft code which also became bogged down as a result of ideological divisions. The code sought access to technology by developing countries and the elimination of restrictive business practices involved in the transfer of technology such as grant-back and tie-in provisions, geographical divisions of markets and export restraints. For the text of the draft code, see UNCTAD, *Draft International Code of Conduct on the Transfer of Technology*, UN Doc. E/1990/94 (1990).

[26] The effort to identify and provide for the restrictive practices of multinational corporations has met with a degree of success, at least to the extent that a General Assembly resolution on the subject was voted without dissent. See generally, M. Sornarajah, 'Towards an International Antitrust Law' (1982) IJIL 1; J. Davidow and L. Chiles, 'The United States and the Issue of the Binding or Voluntary Nature of International Codes of Conduct Regarding Restrictive Business Practices' (1978) 72 AJIL 247.

relations,[27] transfer pricing, consumer protection[28] and environmental protection. Duties are imposed on multinational corporations to avoid harmful practices in the areas identified.

The imposition of these duties recognises the need for the assertion of corporate accountability of the multinational corporation for harm that is caused in the course of its operations. The major criticism of the OECD's MAI was that its emphasis was entirely on the protection of the multinational corporation without addressing the issue of the multinational corporation's social responsibility and accountability for harm.[29] There is increasing litigation addressing issues of corporate fraud,[30] participation in genocide,[31] participation in torture,[32] and environmental harm.[33] In view of these developments, it would seem hollow that a code on multinational corporations should come to be drafted without addressing the issues of responsibility for harm that is caused during the operation of the foreign investment. The difficulty of combining foreign investment protection with ideas of social accountability is that such protection will be considerably diluted if combined with notions of accountability. But, for that reason, the issues raised cannot be avoided. An instrument that is made on the basis of foreign investment protection alone will lack credibility.

2.1.8. Disclosure of information

There is a broad disclosure requirement that is imposed in the Draft Code. It requires information to be given publicly of financial and other matters relating to the operations of multinational corporations. This may not be too onerous a duty as the company law of most states will require

---

[27] ILO, Tripartite Declaration of Principles Concerning Multinational Enterprises and Social Policy (1977).

[28] There is a General Assembly resolution incorporating guidelines on consumer protection. For the text, see UN Doc. ST/ESA/170 (1986); see also OECD, Guidelines for Multinational Enterprises and the Protection of Consumer Interests (1999).

[29] UNCTAD Series on Issues in International Investment Agreements, *Social Responsibility* (UNCTAD/ITE/IIT/22, 2001).

[30] Particularly after the unearthing in 2002 of the accounting practices of Enron Corporation in the United States.

[31] Anita Ramasastry, 'Secrets and Lies: Swiss Banks and International Human Rights' (1998) 31 *Vanderbilt Journal of Transnational Law* 325.

[32] *Doe* v. *Unocal*, 27 F Supp 2d 1174 (CD Cal., 1998).

[33] *Beanal* v. *Freeport-McMoran*, 969 F Supp 362 (1997); *Jota* v. *Texaco*, 157 F 3d 153 (1998) (2nd Cir.).

such disclosures to be made. Similarly, the duty to make disclosures is now a feature of many foreign investment codes that require that foreign investment should enter through joint ventures. Many of these codes mandate that feasibility studies of the proposed foreign investment projects should be made. Such feasibility reports should contain full disclosure of information.

2.1.9. Treatment of transnational corporations

This section of the Draft Code contains four parts, which seek to recognise duties owed by the host state to the multinational corporation. Its brevity stands in marked contrast to the manner in which the duties owed by the multinational corporation to the host state are set out. It is, no doubt, a concession to the developed states and their demands for a 'balanced code'. The question is whether the concessions go far enough to appease the interests of the developed states. The four matters that are included are: the recognition of international legal rules and principles relevant to the treatment of multinational corporations; the requirement of compensation for nationalisation; jurisdiction; and dispute settlement.

3. The outstanding issues

The Draft Code has been described above. Though consensus had been reached on many of the provisions in the code, there were issues on which no agreement had emerged. These are referred to as the 'outstanding issues' in the successive reports of the Secretary General which have identified and discussed them.[34]

3.1. The relevance of international law

Developing countries have generally rejected the relevance of international law to the making of foreign investments, except where commitments relating to such investments have been created by treaty. The developed states have, however, adopted a strategy of insulating foreign investment from the scope of domestic law, subjecting it to minimum standards of treatment which they claim are required by international

---

[34] UNCTC. *Outstanding Issues in the Draft Code of Conduct on Transnational Corporations,* UN Doc. E/C.10/1985/S/2 (1985).

law. The dispute between the two groups of states has been stated in the following terms:[35]

> The industrialised Western countries insist that the code must unequivocally stipulate the applicability of international law in the relations between the governments and transnational corporations. The developing countries, while recognising that states may have multinational obligations in this area, are reluctant to accept the term 'international law' because of its traditional connotations, and have instead proposed a formula calling for states to fulfil, in good faith, their international obligations in this area. The Western countries have however rejected the term 'international obligations' or 'international legal obligations' on the ground that it does not expressly include obligations founded on customary international law. Some of the developing countries contend with equal fervour that beyond the norms provided in the code, they are unable to recognise 'vague' and 'imprecise' principles of customary international law in the area of foreign investment.

Since the strategy towards foreign investments in the New International Economic Order was to ensure the primacy of host state control, the position of the developing states was to downplay the significance of international law. The argument was that there were no clear doctrines on state responsibility for the treatment of foreign investment because there was opposition, particularly by the Latin American states through the assertion of the Calvo doctrine which asserted the host state's right of control over foreign investment. The socialist states had also resisted the relevance of international law to foreign investment. The resolutions on permanent sovereignty over natural resources as well as the Charter of Economic Rights and Duties of States had also asserted the primacy of host state control. Consistent with this view, the developing states took the position that international law was not relevant to foreign investment. This view was reflected in the early versions of the Draft Code.

A compromise formulation was adopted in the final version of the Draft Code. It is contained in the section of the Draft Code entitled 'General provisions relating to the treatment of transnational corporations'. It stated:

---

[35] Samuel Asante, 'International Codes of Conduct and NIEO' in *Proceedings of the First Yugoslav International Seminar on Legal Aspects of the New International Economic Order* (1986), 245 at 247.

> In all matters relating to the Code, States shall fulfil, in good faith, their international obligations, including generally recognised and accepted legal rules and principles.

This compromise formula will not satisfy the standards of foreign investment protection that developed states seek. The duty is to protect 'international obligations'. Such obligations will not include foreign investment agreements, as international obligations can only arise from agreements between states.[36] The developed states would argue that customary law protects obligations arising from such agreements as well. The compromise formula will apply to multilateral and bilateral treaties on foreign investment protection, but it is not clear whether it applies to the foreign investment agreements themselves. In this sense, the formulation in the Draft Code means very little as there is already an international obligation to fulfil treaty commitments. It does not accept the theory that foreign investment contracts become internationalised and are subject to the protection of customary international law.

Neither does it accept the view of the developed states that there is a body of customary international law that is relevant to the issue of investment protection. It makes reference only to international obligations, though it recognises that such obligations could arise from 'generally recognised and accepted international legal rules and principles'. The reference to 'generally accepted international legal rules' will permit scope for the recreation of the argument as to whether claims relating to the existence of a minimum standard of treatment have such wide acceptance in international law as to amount to 'generally accepted international rules'. The fact is that the existence of an international minimum standard in connection with the protection of aliens generally has been consistently opposed by the Latin American states. It has also been rejected by the developing states as a whole because the context of the protection of the assets of foreigners indicates an absence of the general acceptance required for these rules to be regarded as having any significance for the purpose of this formulation in the Draft Code. The draft, even with the compromise formula, will probably not satisfy the developed states.

---

[36] This interpretation was accepted by a group of experts who met at The Hague to consider the draft code. See *Report on the Hague Summit on the United Nations Code of Conduct on Transnational Corporations* (annexed to UNCTC, *Work Related to the Code of Conduct on Transnational Corporations*, UN Doc. E/1989/28 Rev.1).

3.2. Non-interference in domestic affairs

The inclusion of a provision of non-interference in domestic affairs also proved to be a contentious issue. This provision is not found in later investment agreements, though the APEC Principles on Investments, a non-binding set of guidelines, contained a provision on non-interference in domestic affairs and adherence to the laws of the host state. The OECD Guidelines on Multinational Corporations, another non-binding instrument, also contain a provision on non-interference. But, the UNCTC Draft Code sought to create an affirmative obligation. The formulation had the difficulty that it would have to balance the right of a multinational corporation, which has to integrate itself into the local economy, to function within the ordinary economic and political process of the state and direct interference in influencing the course of government within the state. The final formulation in the Draft Code reads:

> Transnational corporations shall not interfere in the internal affairs of host countries, without prejudice to their participation in activities that are permitted by the laws, regulation or established administrative practices of host states.

It is unlikely that observing 'laws, regulations or administrative practices of the host states' will provide sufficient scope for the exercise of the influence that is necessary to secure the ordinary business advantages a multinational corporation seeks. There is a divergence between the myth system maintained by the 'laws, regulations or administrative practices' which business, both domestic and foreign, should follow in influencing governments and the operational code which demands that other avenues be used in securing these advantages. It is unlikely that the matter can be satisfactorily reduced to a written formula. The general rule of non-interference must be stated, but the drafting of the exception to it is a matter of great difficulty. Too broad an exception will undermine the rule. Too narrow an exception will not satisfy those who insist on its inclusion.

The need for insistence on the rule may diminish as multinational corporations come to be perceived as independent agents acting in their own interests rather than in the interests of their home states. The perception of these corporations as mere purveyors of the interests of their home states will diminish with time when it is seen that they have their own interests to pursue. On occasion, the corporations see advantages in linking themselves with their host states, sometimes even to the detriment of their home states.[37] The importance of the rule is also reduced by the fact that the usual form of entry into most states is through joint ventures with local participation. Where influence is sought to change economic or other policies, the local partner to the joint venture could secure such influence. This would be particularly so where the local partner is a state corporation, in which case the leverage on the government will already exist. The government, in turn, could ensure that the local joint venture partner reflects the policy objectives it has set out for the business. The increase in the number of multinational corporations, the growing ability of the developing states to bargain with them on a competitive basis and the nature of the administrative and other controls that host states have instituted in overseeing the process of foreign investment are trends which will lessen the scope of political and other interference by multinational corporations. These trends may diminish the significance of the rule of non-interference in the future. Developed countries will come to accept the rule of non-interference and developing countries will see little significance in the rule as they will have instituted sufficient internal machinery to ensure non-interference.

Multinational corporations are actors on the international scene and have the capacity and power to influence the policy of governments, particularly their policies on international trade. There appear to be no norms preventing multinational corporations from engaging in such international activity. The question of whether host states could exert pressure upon a subsidiary present within its territory in order to ensure that the parent company does not influence the international policies of its home state in a manner hostile to the interests of the host state is also a matter on which there are no legal norms.

3.3. Permanent sovereignty and international obligations

Another outstanding issue is whether the reference to respect by transnational corporations for the permanent sovereignty of host states over their natural resources should be qualified by reference to international obligations that may have been undertaken in respect of them. As regards treaty obligations relating to natural resources, the need for the rule does not arise as it is well recognised that these rights could be surrendered by treaty between the two sovereign states, unless of course the view that the

---

[37] An extreme instance is the Angolan civil war where Gulf Oil, a US company, was protected by Cuban forces supporting the government from rebels supported by the United States.

doctrine on permanent sovereignty forms a *ius cogens* principle is recognised. Developing states will seek to establish the idea that permanent sovereignty over natural resources is a principle of *ius cogens* in international law and is not defeasible even by treaty. Developed states, on the other hand, resist this view and also insist that international obligations could be contained in the foreign investment contract on the basis of which dealings in the natural resources were commenced in the host state by the multinational corporation. The theory of internationalisation of the foreign investment contract is the basis of this argument, and the preservation of the obligations created by the contract for the duration of the contract is an aim of the developed states. The right to permanent sovereignty is stated in an unqualified manner in the Draft Code, though there is a reference later in the Code to the duty of the host state to respect its international obligations.

4. The regional agreements

4.1. NAFTA

Though there are other regional agreements on investments which had been concluded earlier,[38] the one which has attracted the most attention and provided a model for the OECD's Multilateral Agreement on Investment is Chapter 11 of the North American Free Trade Agreement (NAFTA). The case law that the latter has generated and the extensive commentary it has received makes it the most important of the treaties that have been made in this area.[39] The controversy that has surrounded the making of NAFTA and the jurisprudence that it has generated will have an impact on the development of the law, though it must be kept in mind that NAFTA's provisions are not necessarily repeated in other investment treaties. There must be caution exercised in using the jurisprudence generated by NAFTA for this reason. It would be unfortunate if the principles that are formulated in arbitrations under NAFTA are used in other

---

[38] Of these, the ASEAN Treaty on the Protection and Promotion of Foreign Investment, 1987, is significant in its coverage, in that it involves eleven states, and scope, in that it involves compulsory dispute settlement. The later ASEAN Investment Treaty, introducing the concept of an 'ASEAN Investor', considerably enlarges the scope of the treaty. The 'Asean Investor', defined to include any company incorporated in an ASEAN state, is granted pre-entry rights of establishment and national treatment.

[39] Laura Dawson (ed.), *Whose Rights? The NAFTA Chapter 11 Debate* (2002); Howard Mann, *Private Rights, Public Problems: A Guide to NAFTA's Controversial Chapter on Investor Rights* (2001).

arbitrations without having regard to the precise language that is used in the provisions of Chapter 11 of NAFTA.

NAFTA's provisions on investment are the same as those which appear in the earlier US–Canada Free Trade Agreement.[40] The latter, in turn, are no different from the provisions which appear in the US model bilateral investment agreement. To this extent, NAFTA contains provisions which are preferred by the United States. They essentially embody the investment protection regime which the United States has developed with consistency over many years. The focus therefore has been on ensuring that there is an emphasis on high standards of treatment of foreign investment and its protection. The scope it leaves for sovereign control over foreign investment is limited.

The main features of Chapter 11 of NAFTA may be stated, emphasising its differences from the normal run of bilateral investment treaties. As indicated, the provisions in Chapter 11 are the same as in the model bilateral investment treaty of the United States. NAFTA contains strong treatment provisions. It provides for both pre-entry[41] and post-entry national treatment. It provides for most-favoured-nation treatment and the better of the national and most-favoured-nation treatment standards. It asserts an international minimum standard, and provides for 'full protection and security' of the investment. It provides for the right of repatriation of profits and the transfer of funds associated with the investment. It deals with expropriation, defining it widely to include direct and indirect takings and anything 'tantamount to an expropriation'. It creates strong procedures for securing compliance. Though these procedures are not innovative, as thought by some US writers,[42] the treaty provides for unilateral dispute resolution at the instance of the foreign investor against the host state, if a cause of action is created. It is the first time that a treaty with at least two developed states parties contains such a provision.[43] From this novelty

---

[40] For a record of the anxieties of the Canadian negotiating team in relation to the investment provisions of the treaty, see Michael Hart, *Decision at Midnight* (2001).

[41] Meaning that the treaty creates a right of establishment in the foreign investor.

[42] US writers have referred to the dispute resolution mechanism of providing a unilateral remedy to the foreign investor as innovative. This is not entirely correct. Such remedies have been provided in earlier US investment treaties as well as in UK and other treaties. The first case in which the remedy was invoked related to the UK treaty with Sri Lanka in *AAPL v. Sri Lanka*. It is, however, true to say that it is the first treaty to provide for such a remedy in a treaty that involved two developed states.

[43] One fear is that the concerns and the analysis made in accordance with the constitutional standards of property protection in rich states will drive the law in the future. This may be detrimental to the interests of developing countries where different social and political notions of property may be more appropriate.

proceeds the fact that the focus of much of the case law generated under
NAFTA has dealt with treatment standards and regulatory takings, thus
somewhat shifting the concerns of the law in a new direction. The large
proportion of the case law that has arisen under NAFTA has focused on
whether interference with the rights of the investor on the grounds of
environmental protection could amount to a compensable taking. A view
has been stated that the provisions of NAFTA have reduced the regulatory
powers of the state to such an extent that even the making of non-binding
policies that have an impact on foreign investment through the depreciation of its value could amount to a taking.[44] Such a view has led to
concern among environmental and other groups with the provisions of
NAFTA. The jurisprudence under NAFTA has fed this anxiety. There is
clear controversy as to the impact of NAFTA. The position regarding regulatory taking in the context of the cases under NAFTA as well as other
jurisprudence is considered in Chapter 8 below.

4.2. The ASEAN Agreements

The ASEAN Investment Protection Agreement (1987) is a significant
agreement which creates a system of protection within the ASEAN region.
It also binds the new members of ASEAN, and applies to their existing
investments if specific written consent for such a purpose has been given.
One specific feature of the ASEAN Agreement is that it contemplates the
unilateral right of the host state to invoke the dispute settlement provisions
of the agreement against the foreign investor.

The first tribunal that was set up under the ASEAN Agreement was
in *Yaung Chi Oo Ltd* v. *Myanmar*. The highly dogmatic interpretation
of the requirements of the treaty for the invocation of jurisdiction made
by the tribunal whittles down the possible scope of the treaty. The tribunal also considered the impact of the later ASEAN Investment Treaty,
which sought to liberalise the movement of investment within the ASEAN
region. The aim of the latter treaty was to enable the free movement of
investment assets among the ASEAN states. The tribunal thought that
the provisions of the treaty were 'programmatic', a view that may have
accorded with ASEAN trends in the 1980s but not with the trends towards
liberalisation that were taking place around the world when the ASEAN
Investment Treaty was made. It is unfortunate that the tribunal was not

---

[44] Howard Mann and Konrad Von Moltke, *NAFTA's Chapter 11 and the Environment* (1999).

able to interpret the treaty in accordance with the prevailing mood of the times when the treaty was made. This is a set-back to the development of the law in the ASEAN region.

There are several other regional arrangements of varying sorts but they do not contain the same degree of protection and liberalisation as are contained in NAFTA and the ASEAN agreements.

5. The Multilateral Agreement on Investment

In 1992, a group of experts of the World Bank studied the possibility of a multilateral agreement on investment. But, they thought that the time was not ripe for such an agreement. Instead, they drafted a set of guidelines, the World Bank Guidelines on Foreign Investment.[45] Just a few years later, in 1995, the OECD attempted to draft a multilateral agreement on investment.[46] It was an effort to draft a code among developed countries, and this fact alone makes it unique. NAFTA involved two developed states, but the MAI involved all the members of the OECD. The OECD membership consists of developed states. Some developing states attended the discussions. The strategy was to bring about a multilateral agreement among the developed states and have the developing states accede to it afterwards. Given the ascendancy of neo-liberal tenets in the mid-1990s, it was thought that a code which emphasised those investment protection rules supported by the developed states could easily be drafted among the developed states first and it could then be presented as a *fait accompli* to the developing world. The MAI would then be opened for accession by non-OECD countries. It was also thought that, once finalised, the code could be taken over by the World Trade Organization.[47]

The draft MAI is similar in most respects to the investment provisions of NAFTA.[48] In that sense, it also bears a resemblance to the US

---

[45] The Guidelines are analysed fully in the first edition of this work.
[46] It is generally regarded as having commenced with the G-7 Summit in Halifax in 1995 and ended with the G-7 Summit at Birmingham in 1998.
[47] Though this is referred to, it is difficult to see how the MAI, as drafted, would have meshed in with the WTO. The WTO would, for example, have no competence to deal with such matters as the right of establishment in foreign investors. The OECD was preferred, as the effort of the developing countries in watering down the effect of the Trade Related Investment Measures under the WTO had succeeded. Stephen Canner, 'The Multilateral Agreement on Investment' (1998) 31 Cornell JIL 657 at 656–7. The article also refers to the strategy of final integration of the MAI into the WTO.
[48] Rainer Geiger, 'Towards a Multilateral Agreement on Investment' (1998) 31 Cornell JIL 467, states an official position on the drafting of the MAI.

model investment treaties on which NAFTA was based.[49] It was initially drafted in secrecy.[50] But, when the provisions became widely known, it was immediately the target of attack by environmental and human rights groups which objected to the emphasis on the protection of multinational corporations without providing for protection against the environmental and human rights abuses they were capable of. The latter part of the 1990s saw the emergence of disenchantment with economic liberalism and the force of globalisation to which it had given a free rein. The Asian economic crisis also increased fears that unrestricted liberalisation of the international economy may be harmful. There was a cause needed for the outlet of these feelings and the cause against the MAI was the most opportune one that was available. Opposition to the MAI was galvanised on a global scale through the same forces of instant communication that makes globalisation possible. Disparate groups were able to coordinate opposition to the MAI on a global scale. The mounting dissent affected the governments of Europe and they began to pull away from the project of drafting the MAI. They did not want to displease their electorates.

Quite apart from the impact of the opposition, there were cracks within the developed states as to the rules that the MAI should contain. The conflict between the United States and the European Union over the Helms–Burton Act – which sought to impose secondary boycotts on European and other companies trading with Cuba – was seen as an instance of the United States wanting unilateral rules when it suited its interests. There was also the fear that the advances that had been negotiated within NAFTA may be dismantled if less was negotiated under the MAI. But, there were more direct conflicts such as the desire of Canada and France to protect their cultural industries from US influence. There was a fear that unrestricted access to markets, which the MAI intended to achieve, would lead to the swamping of these industries by the US entertainment industry. There were internal problems rather than the efforts of the non-governmental organisations by themselves which finally scuttled the MAI. Other incidents also added to the rethink of the viability of the MAI from the point of view of each state's own interest.

---

[49] There were differences but they were not substantial. Because negotiations were not completed, the draft contained different alternative formulations. But, the factors which drove both documents were the same.

[50] This is now denied. But, academics found it difficult to get copies when it was being drafted. All contacts with officials concerning the document at the early stages were rebuffed on the ground that the document was secret. This was an early error.

Around the same time, the *Ethyl Case* was decided under NAFTA. It concerned an attempt to ban the use of an additive to petroleum, which was suspected of being pollutive and harmful to humans. The sole manufacturer of the substance in Canada was a US corporation. It sought to bring a suit on the ground that consideration of a ban was tantamount to a taking under NAFTA. The case was seen as NAFTA infringing on the power of states to interfere with foreign investment in order to protect the environment or to act in the interests of the health of the people. More broadly, the case was seen as limiting the sovereignty of the state to perform essential functions relating to the protection of internal values in order to ensure the protection of the interests of the foreign investor. The fears that this case created fuelled the arguments against the acceptance of the MAI.[51]

While the dissension among and within the developed states indicated that fears of losing sovereign control over an intrusive process such as foreign investment underlay the downfall of the MAI, the developing countries would have had even greater problems with the formulations in the MAI. Some developing countries did participate in the discussions as observers. Others offered comments from the sidelines, but, on the whole, there was an absence of developing country participation. But, the objections of the developing countries could be anticipated from the comments made by developing country officials and scholars.[52] The MAI was premised on one view of economic development, that foreign investment was so beneficial that its protection was necessary in order to ensure its flow, which in turn will promote economic growth. One version of the preamble to the MAI spoke of the wish to 'establish high standards for liberalisation of investment regimes and investment protection with

---

[51] The impact of the *Ethyl Case* is stated by Jan Huner, who played a leading role in negotiating MAI, in the following terms: 'Decisive, because some of the points raised by the environmental groups convinced many Negotiating Group members that a few draft provisions, particularly those on expropriation and on performance requirements could be interpreted in unexpected ways. The dispute between Ethyl Corporation and the Canadian government illustrated the point that the MAI negotiators should think twice before copying the expropriation provisions of the NAFTA.' Jan Huner, 'Lessons from the MAI: A View from the Negotiating Table' in Halina Ward and Duncan Brack (eds.), *Trade, Investment and the Environment* (2001), 242 at 248.

[52] A. Ganesan, 'Development Friendliness Criteria for a Multilateral Investment Agreement' (1997) 6 *Transnational Corporations* 139. Chen Huiping, 'Comments on the MAI's General Principles for the Treatment of Foreign Investors and Their Investments: A Chinese Scholar's Perspective' in E. Niewenhuys and M. Brus, *Multilateral Regulation of Investment* (2001), 67.

effective dispute settlement procedures'. That singular vision of foreign investment is not accepted by all developing states. Developing states want to be able to chose between the different models and find one which suits them best. Whereas the institutions controlled by the developed countries have the same prescriptions and conditions for development, each developing country would want to assert its own right to choose the model which it considers best for itself. The regime that the draft MAI sought to impose restricted this choice. That would have made the MAI unpalatable to the developing states.[53]

There were specific provisions in the MAI, which would have been objected to as well. The right of establishment contained in the MAI is at the heart of the liberalisation of investment flows. The provision on national treatment applies to both the pre-entry phase as well as to the post-entry phase.[54] This provision would sit uneasily with the screening legislation which most developing states still maintain. They believe that they should have the right to reject deleterious foreign investment and regulate the investment that is permitted entry so as to maximise and harness the benefits of the investment to the host economy. The opportunity for doing so would be lost if uncontrolled access to foreign investment were permitted. In the treaty practice of a large number of states, specific provisions preserve this right. In south-east Asian treaties, only 'approved' investments are given treaty protection. In the practice of China, Australia and an increasing number of states,[55] only investments made 'in accordance with the laws and regulations of each Contracting Party from time to time in existence' are given protection. Given the existence of this limitation even in the heyday of liberalisation, it is unlikely that the MAI would have made much progress with these states. There were standstill provisions permitting existing sectoral reservations from national and most-favoured-nation treatment and rollback provisions while requiring their eventual elimination. The European Union issued a lengthy list of such sectoral reservations during the negotiations. Most states focused on the telecommunications and transportation sectors. France and Canada

---

[53] For accounts of various interests that opposed the MAI, see Sol Picciotto and Ruth Mayne (eds.), *Regulating International Business: Beyond Liberalization* (1999).

[54] The whole range of activities associated with investment is spelt out, and includes 'establishment, acquisition, expansion, operation, management, maintenance, use, enjoyment and sale or other disposition of investment'. Chapter III on Treatment of Investors and Investments: National Treatment and Most Favoured Nation Treatment, para. 1.

[55] The formula is coming to be used widely. It appears in the more recent treaties of Malaysia and Indonesia.

held out for the total exclusion of the cultural sector. The developed states did not exhibit much unity on this core issue of the MAI.

National treatment after entry is also an important feature of the MAI. Again, this would pose problems for a large number of developing states, as they protect fledgling industry and actively promote local entrepreneurship. A strategy of building up small enterprises within the economy could not be adopted unless extensive sectoral exceptions are made. Developing countries also operate large sectors of the economy through state corporations which are monopolies by definition. Privatisation of state corporations is an aim of economic liberalism, but it is not an aim which appeals to all. There are increasing reservations expressed about the efficiency levels of post-privatisation economic activity even in developed states. There is also a tendency in developing states as well as in developed states to give ethnic groups preferential treatment on the basis of purely political or historical considerations.[56] It would be difficult to accommodate these constitutional preferences with a system of national treatment for foreign investors. These preferences are not driven by economic considerations on which the premises of liberalism rest. It is inappropriate to regard economic factors alone as the driving forces behind policy on foreign investment. There are equitable, historical and other considerations which a state has to accommodate in fashioning policy on foreign investment.

The MAI also prohibits performance requirements. These are widely employed by developing countries. The Trade Related Investment Measures (TRIMS) instrument of the WTO prohibits certain performance requirements. But, it permits those that developing countries usually employ in regulating foreign investment, such as entry through joint ventures, employment of a specific quota of nationals and a minimum level of equity participation. The MAI provided a more comprehensive list of prohibited performance requirements and applied them to a greater range of activities. The MAI prohibited export requirements, the domestic content requirements, domestic purchase requirements, the tying of imports to value of exports, requirements relating to the transfer of technology, territorial exclusivity in export, the compulsory location of research and development activities, the entry of investment through joint ventures and a requirement to hire local personnel. These are all requirements that

---

[56] Reference has already been made to the studies of the role of ethnicity in shaping foreign investment rules. In developed states, like Canada and Australia, such preferential treatment is given to the aboriginal people of these states.

the developing host states wish to impose in the belief that they secure the advantages of foreign investment. The developing countries would have had to dismantle much of their local investment codes in order to accommodate such a long list of prohibitions within their laws. The exceptions seek to secure advantages for developed states rather than to cater for the needs of the developing countries.

The dispute resolution provisions of the MAI are more extensive than those commonly used in investment treaties. They provide for both state-to-state and investor-to-state arbitration. Like other treaties containing provisions relating to prior consent of the host state, the MAI also provides for the prior consent of the contracting parties to arbitration. There is a minor change in that a contracting party may at the time of ratification or accession require the foreign investor to be confined to the remedy of his choice. That is, the foreign investor will have to discontinue other proceedings if he chooses arbitration. This is not a major hurdle from the point of view of the foreign investor as his preferred choice would be arbitration rather than domestic proceedings in the host state. It seems to be a light-hearted parody of something akin to the local remedies rule creating the impression of a disadvantage to the foreign investor.

The MAI included sections containing general safeguards and exceptions. These provisions commence with the statement that they 'shall not apply to Article IV, 2 and 3 (expropriation and compensation and protection from strife)'. The exceptions relate largely to war and public order situations. The fact that such expropriation is saved from even such measures which provide a total justification in customary international law will not prove acceptable to many states. The MAI also avoids the issue as to whether a regulatory interference with foreign investment on environmental or human rights grounds should be considered an exception. The other exceptions deal with the curtailment of financial flows resulting from the investment on balance-of-payment grounds which again contain more stringent standards than are usually contained in bilateral investment treaties.

The MAI failed for a variety of reasons. There have been various assessments of the causes of its failure. The role of the non-governmental organisations is regarded by some as the reason for its failure.[57] Others regard the MAI as not being strong enough, so that the multinational business community did not give it its wholehearted support. If it were any

---

[57] Alan Rugman, 'New Rules for International Investment: The Case for a Multilateral Agreement on Investment (MAI) at the WTO' in Chris Milner and Robert Read (eds.), *Trade Liberalization, Competition and the WTO* (2002), 176.

stronger, the MAI would have failed on its merits. The seeds of the failure of the MAI lay in the fact that there was insufficient agreement within the developed world on the norms of investment protection. France broke off first. The incoming Labour government in the UK was concerned about the non-inclusion of environmental safeguards. Canada joined France in its concern with cultural industries. As much as the NAFTA experience illustrates that the instrument could have a life quite unexpected by the parties and lead to discomfort, the long years of negotiation of the MAI showed the developed states that the rules that they seek to impose on the developing world may prove too onerous to bear when applied to themselves. They could not brook the loss of sovereignty that the MAI entailed. With the failure of the MAI, attention has shifted to the possibility of creating an investment instrument under the auspices of the WTO. The impact of the experience with the MAI will last for a considerable time. The debate is no longer about investment protection alone but about the wider implications it has for globalisation. The move of investment into the WTO will be plagued by the fact that the MAI which was the first target of anti-globalisation protests has now moved into the WTO which was its second target at Seattle. The same coalitions that moved against the MAI are still around and will coalesce to work against the acceptance of any measure that is driven by liberal economic theory on foreign investment alone without taking into account factors such as development, poverty, human rights and the environment.[58]

6. The WTO and foreign investment

The Havana Charter made in 1948 for the International Trade Organization (ITO), which was to have come into existence along with other institutions at the end of the Second World War, contained provisions on investment.[59] Articles 11 and 12 of the Havana Charter dealt with investment. Article 11 of the Havana Charter stated that no member 'shall take

---

[58] M. Sornarajah, 'The Impact of Globalisation on the International Law of Foreign Investment', Simon Reisman Lecture, 2002, Ottawa, published in (2002)12 *Canadian Foreign Policy* 1.

[59] C. Wilcox, *A Charter for World Trade* (1948). The developing countries opposed the provisions on the ground that they articulated the preferred rules of the developed states. C. Lipson, *Standing Guard – Protecting Foreign Capital in the Nineteenth and Twentieth Centuries* (1985), 86–7; Peter S. Watson, Joseph Flynn and Chad Convell, *Completing the World Trading System* (1999), 237–57; Mark Koulen, 'Foreign Investment in the WTO' in Eva Niewenhuys and M. Brus (eds.), *Multilateral Regulation of Investment* (2001), 181. T. Brewer and S. Young, 'Investment Issues at the WTO: The Architecture of Rules and the Settlement of Disputes' (1998) 1 *Journal of International Economic Law* 457.

unreasonable or unjustifiable action' against investment, and assured 'just and equitable treatment'. Article 12 provided members with the right to take appropriate safeguards against foreign investment and 'to determine whether and to what extent and upon what terms it will allow future foreign investment'. This part of the article would have been acceptable to developing countries as it stated basic norms that they later articulated. But, the second part of Article 12 contained the genesis of the developed country position. It stated that 'members undertake to provide reasonable opportunities for investments acceptable to them and adequate security for existing and future investments, and to give due regard to the desirability of avoiding discrimination as between foreign investments'. In the event, the ITO never came into existence.[60] But, the few developing countries that existed at the time objected to the provisions on investment on the ground that they were based on rules preferred by the developed states. The conflict had begun early. The GATT, which was a truncated version of the ITO concerned largely with trade in goods and the elimination of tariff barriers, dealt with investment issues only peripherally. This ensured that international trade law developed separately from international investment law in the intervening period between the ITO and the WTO.

The only issue relating to investment presented to a GATT panel was the challenge by the United States to Canada's Foreign Investment Review Act. This legislation instituted a screening process for incoming foreign investment in Canada. The legislation has many features common to the screening legislation that is used in developing countries. The United States challenged it on the ground that it constituted a GATT violation. The specific challenges concerned the requirements that the foreign investors should export a percentage of their manufactured goods, purchase materials for manufacture from Canadian sources and utilise Canadian resources to manufacture finished products in Canada. The GATT panel found that the GATT did not prevent Canada from exercising its sovereign right to regulate foreign investment. But, it made specific findings. It found that the requirement to purchase Canadian goods to the exclusion of foreign goods was discriminatory as foreign products were given worse treatment and hence violated Article III(4) of the GATT. The panel found against the view that the export requirement violated Article XVII of the GATT. It

---

[60] This was largely due to US opposition. Alfred Eckes, 'US Trade History' in William Lovett, Alfred Eckes and Richard Brinkman (eds.), *US Trade Policy, History, Theory and the WTO* (1999).

did not make a finding on the issue of the local manufacture of products from Canadian materials.

It has been suggested that it was the GATT panel ruling in this case that forced Canada to move away from the policy of the Foreign Investment Review Act to a more permissive policy, which culminated in NAFTA.[61] This is to read too much into the case. The decision did not affect the developing states to any significant degree, as they continued to maintain screening restrictions and performance requirements. There has been no suggestion that these screening devices violated the GATT. The matter was not even tested out and, if the *FIRA Case* was such a success as it is made out to be, there would have been challenges to screening legislation elsewhere.

6.1. Investment in the Uruguay Round

In the Uruguay Round, definite efforts were made to introduce measures relating to investment into international trade. The WTO instruments which affect investment directly and which create competence in the WTO to deal with investment issues are the Agreement on Trade Related Aspects of Intellectual Property Rights (TRIPS), Trade Related Investment Measures (TRIMS) and the General Agreement on Trade in Services (GATS). Other instruments deal with investments indirectly. Thus, the Agreement on Government Procurement requires that there be no discrimination in sourcing materials for purchase by the host government as between foreign investors and local manufacturers. But, the more significant instruments are those which affect investments directly.

6.2. GATS

Of these instruments, the most significant is GATS. It deals with services and defines services supplied by foreign firms within a state as covered by it. Of the four modes of supply that are covered by GATS, one is the provision of services 'through commercial presence' in the territory of a member. This 'commercial presence' could be created through the

---

[61] Christopher Wilkie, 'Origins of NAFTA Investment Provisions: Economic and Policy Considerations' in Laura Ritchie (ed.), *Whose Rights: The NAFTA Chapter 11 Debate* (2002), 7 at 14. Wilkie suggests that the case indicates that 'the artificial divisions between international trade and investment policy would no longer enjoy protection under international rules'. If this was a lesson, it was not learned by developing states which continued with the screening of incoming investments.

establishment of a juridical person or through a branch or office for the supply of services within the territory of a member state.[62] Thus, GATS covers foreign investment in the services sector. It accounts for a large share of foreign investment, and thus establishes WTO competence in a substantial sector of the economy of every member state.[63] GATS considerably liberalises entry barriers in the services sector, which were previously high.

Unlike bilateral and regional investment treaties, which apply a top-down approach in that sectors have to be excluded from standards that are stated, GATS adopts a bottom-up approach requiring the commitments in the services sector to be listed in each member state's schedule. There is, however, an understanding that there would be a progressive liberalisation. The schedules contain sector-specific disciplines.

The core principles of GATS are non-discrimination and national treatment, but these principles are not general in scope.[64] They arise only from specific commitments made by the parties. Though the liberalisation of entry is sought as a target, this does not take place as it does in an investment treaty like NAFTA which requires pre-entry rights of establishment. Access can still be controlled in those sectors not included by the state in its schedule. In that sense, free trade in services is a distant prospect.[65]

National treatment applies only to those service sectors which are listed in each state's schedule, and then only to the extent that no conditions are attached. To that extent, national treatment does not as yet pose a problem for measures that discriminate between foreign investors and local entrepreneurs, unless the state feels confident that competition within the sector is possible and should be promoted by inclusion in its schedule. If the sector is subject to GATS, then there is a prohibition of restrictions on the number of service suppliers allowed, the value of the transaction or assets, the total quantity of service output, the number of persons employed, the type of legal entity through which the service is supplied and limits on foreign equity. These prohibitions will no doubt come to affect regulatory legislation on foreign investment when liberalisation processes advance and more sectors are listed in the schedule.

---

[62] Article 1 of the GATS.
[63] Bernard Hoekman and Michel Kostecki, *The Political Economy of the World Trading System* (2001), 239.
[64] Countries could list exemptions from the general MFN standard.
[65] Bernard Hoekman and Michel Kostecki, *The Political Economy of the World Trading System* (2001), 257–8.

The general most-favoured-nation provision also poses problems. GATS permits members to list exemptions to most-favoured-nation treatment upon entry into force of agreements. The exemptions are to last for no longer than ten years. The exemptions have been explained on the basis that 'an unconditional most favoured nation rule would allow competitors located in countries with relatively restrictive policies to benefit from their sheltered markets while enjoying a free ride in less restrictive export markets'.[66] But, the more pressing issue from the point of view of investment is whether the most-favoured-nation provision applying to GATS, which has a wider membership, can be used to latch onto the advantages that are provided in an instrument like the MAI, NAFTA or even bilateral investment treaties. This would mean that advantageous provisions like the investor–state dispute resolution provisions in investment treaties could come to be used on the basis of the most-favoured-nation clause. This may be another reason for the popularity of exemptions from the most-favoured-nation rule applying to GATS.[67]

GATS is instructive for the making of an instrument on investment. It will be seen as a possible model for such an instrument as the instrument could then be sold to the reluctant members as merely extending an existing instrument which affects investments into the whole of the area. GATS is also seen as a weaker instrument which states could accept, as the exclusion of sectors is permissible. But, this exclusion is time-limited and there may be some exercise of power in ensuring the listing of more sectors. The fear is that, once the breach is made, the breach could be made wider to allow a lot to pass through. It is this fear that will hold back an instrument on investment which is modelled on GATS.

6.3. TRIPS

The Agreement on Trade Related Aspects of Intellectual Property Rights (TRIPS) deals with standards of protection of intellectual property. Since intellectual property is defined as falling within investments in regional and bilateral investment treaties, the link between TRIPS and investment

---

[66] *Ibid.*, p. 253.
[67] Mark Koulen, 'Foreign Investment in the WTO' in Eva Niewenhuys and M. Brus (eds.), *Multilateral Regulation of Investment* (2001) 288. A. Wimmer, 'The Impact of the General Agreement on Trade in Services on the OECD Multilateral Agreement on Investment' (1996) 19 *World Competition* 109.

treaties is clear. TRIPS mandates standards of protection that should be transposed into national law. Intellectual property rights are created in domestic law, and apply within the system which creates it. In that sense, the instrument properly requires that violations of these standards should be addressed through domestic law. It is only a failure to address them in that manner that would result in the violation of the international obligation. Investment treaties, on the other hand, do create international obligations, which protect intellectual property as investment. TRIPS is largely intended to address the problem of piracy, and, to that extent, it is not aimed at investment protection.

The matter may become significant in the context of compulsory licensing. Compulsory licensing was a matter insisted upon by developing states during the TRIPS negotiations, and it was conceded. In the context of drugs, the issue becomes an important one as to whether drugs that are needed could be subjected to compulsory licensing in the host state. It would appear that different answers may flow from the different treaty regimes. Under the TRIPS regime, the case for compulsory licensing could be made out. Under a strong investment treaty regime, the possibility of compulsory licensing amounting to a taking of property becomes a real issue.[68] Under a weaker investment regime, the scope for this is less.[69]

Developing countries are also concerned about the extent to which foreign multinational companies utilise their indigenous knowledge without rewarding its holders. The lack of protection that international instruments provide for such a situation is seen as an instance of unequal treatment that regimes like TRIPS impose upon developing states. The Convention on Biodiversity addresses the issue by seeking to provide protection for indigenous knowledge, but the United States is not a party to the Convention. In the two areas of compulsory licensing of drugs and the protection of indigenous knowledge, there is much opportunity for conflict. The acceptance of TRIPS itself can only be seen as an intrusion that was achieved in the context of the acceptance of economic liberalism as well as the exercise of pressure.

---

[68] For a discussion of these issues, see D'Amato and Hertz, 'Shaping the Trident: Intellectual Property under NAFTA, Investment Protection Agreements and at the World Trade Organisation' (1997) 23 *Canada–United States Law Journal* 261.

[69] Thus, in investment treaties which preserve the laws of the host state being applied to the investment, the possibility of compulsory licensing being considered expropriation is remote.

6.4. TRIMS

The Trade Related Investment Measures (TRIMS) of the Uruguay Round deals directly with foreign investment. It is, however, not a comprehensive document, as it deals only with certain types of performance requirement.[70] The *FIRA Case* had dealt with this issue previously, and established the limited competence of the GATT in issues of foreign investment. The TRIMS agreement is seen as not extending beyond what had been established in that case or as building up on the foundations established in it. It is based on measures involving investments which cause 'trade-restrictive and distorting effects', thus cautiously establishing a link between foreign investment and international trade in goods. TRIMS relates back to the GATT by stating that 'no member shall apply any TRIM that is inconsistent with the provisions of Article III (on national treatment) and Article XI (on quantitative restrictions) of GATT'. The annex to the agreement contains an illustrative list of measures.

The main aim of TRIMS is to prohibit the use of performance requirements. Not all such performance requirements are prohibited, only those that fall within the narrow focus of the limitation provided by the linkage between TRIMS and the old GATT provisions. It is unlikely that there would be an extension of the list of the prohibited performance requirements, as developing countries are opposed to such an extension.

7. An investment regime under the WTO

The existing WTO instruments are piecemeal considerations of aspects of foreign investment. What is proposed by the different WTO Ministerial Meetings is the consideration of a comprehensive instrument under the WTO, and the matter is currently being studied. A Working Group on the Relationship Between Trade and Investment was set up at the Singapore Ministerial Meeting in 1996. The Doha Ministerial Meeting mandated that regard be had to the development dimension of the problem and to the experience of other agencies, in particular UNCTAD. In the light of the rich experience and debate on treaty- and instrument-making that has been attempted so far, the issues that could arise may be anticipated.

---

[70] Eric Burt, 'Developing Countries and the Framework for Negotiations on Foreign Direct Investment in the World Trade Organisation' (1997) 12 *American University Journal of International Law and Policy* 1015; Paul Civello, 'The TRIMS Agreement: A Failed Attempt at Investment Liberalization' (1999) 8 *Minnesota Journal of Global Trade* 97.

This section outlines those issues and will provoke dissent among the participating states.

7.1. The definition of investment

The developing country position would be that only long-term investments should be permitted. This may be more consistent with the Doha mandate, which speaks of 'long-term cross-border investment, particularly foreign direct investment, that will contribute to the expansion of trade'. Such investment would exclude portfolio investment, which though it promotes the liberalisation of capital flows, is nevertheless short term and may be damaging to developing countries. The Asian economic crisis was precipitated by the sudden pull-out of portfolio investment. The Malaysian answer was to institute currency controls. The regulatory ability of the state over portfolio investments will be seen as essential by developing countries. Many developing country instruments, in particular the ASEAN Framework Agreement on Investment, excludes portfolio investment from the definition of investments. There are, however, bilateral investment treaties which include it.[71] It is unlikely that developing countries will agree to the inclusion of portfolio investment in the definition of foreign investment in a WTO instrument, if one were to be made. They would prefer to ensure that only long-term interests or those interests enmeshed into their economies through associations such as joint ventures are given protection.[72] They would also prefer greenfield activity rather than mergers and acquisitions of existing ventures to be protected. The former could be easily accommodated within the existing economic framework whereas the latter will create problems for local entrepreneurs.

The developed countries are likely to favour a broader, assets-based definition of foreign investment, which could include portfolio investments as well. They will prefer a comprehensive definition of tangible and intangible assets which is found in instruments such as NAFTA. But, even NAFTA excludes some assets such as claims to money. The idea that there should be a comprehensive list and that they could thereafter be

---

[71] The arbitral award in *Fedax* v. *Venezuela* (1998) 37 ILM 1378 demonstrates the instability involved in the inclusion of portfolio instruments within the definition of foreign investment.

[72] The IMF definition which defines foreign investment as over a 10 per cent interest in a company may favour their approach.

dealt with on a case-by-case basis in the substantive provisions is not a good one, for, once the door is opened, the bargaining power is lost. The definition of investment itself remains a thorny problem to be overcome at the very outset, as progress cannot be made unless this initial issue is overcome.

7.2. Definition and the preservation of regulatory control

Much of the debate on investment instruments focuses upon the extent to which it is possible to grant liberalisation, treatment and protection to foreign investments on the basis of external standards contained in treaties but, at the same time, ensure that there is regulatory control to protect the host state's interests. It is for this reason that many states define the investment to ensure that only such investments that operate within the framework of their regulatory structure are given the treatment and protection of the treaty. Thus, Australian and Indonesian bilateral investment treaties contain the provision that only investments 'made in accordance with the laws and regulations from time to time in existence' are given the protection of the treaty. China adopts a similar formula. India uses a formula which ensures that the operation of foreign investment is always subject to the laws of India. Thailand often attaches its laws on foreign investment to the treaties it signs.[73] In the practice of most south-east Asian states, only investments 'approved in writing' are given protection by their investment treaties. All this means that the initial screening mechanisms and the conditions they impose as well as other laws, including environmental laws, are preserved and only such investments as operate in accordance with these laws and regulations are entitled to the protection of the treaty. It is unlikely that states which adopt such practices in preserving their regulatory legislation will come to the party if the multilateral instrument does not also preserve the right of the state to regulate foreign investment. The developed states will resent this position for, if regulation were to be permitted, the scope for binding external standards will be significantly eroded. As the Doha Ministerial Meeting stressed that development issues should be approached in a balanced manner, the preservation of the right of regulation in the interests of developing states achieving their economic objectives will achieve importance.

[73] See e.g. the Canada–Thailand treaty.

7.3. Definition of investor

This again is a controversial issue. In the case of natural persons, apart from the issue of double nationality, it does not pose problems. The issue as to whether permanent residents should be included or not is not a major problem, as many developing states do include permanent residents in their bilateral investment treaties as persons whose investments are protected.[74] It is the position of the multinational corporations which is the more important one as the latter make large investments and investment treaties are all about the protection of the investments they make.

Practice differs among states as to the criterion to be used for corporate nationality. States often insist that foreign companies should enter and operate through locally incorporated companies. The company so incorporated then becomes a local corporate national. But, this problem is overcome by the recognition of the foreign interests in the shares of the locally incorporated company. This situation is wrongly considered as protection of portfolio investments in some official publications. All that happens is that the primary shareholdings in the local company are protected. For purposes of ICSID arbitration, the host state will have to acknowledge that the locally incorporated corporation is in reality a foreign company, though an inference as to this is drawn in certain circumstances.

Corporate nationality also becomes a problem, as different legal traditions use different tests for such nationality. The common law jurisdictions use the incorporation test and the civil law jurisdictions use the *siège social* theory. This distinction has come to be reflected in the treaty practice of the different states. Again, in a multilateral agreement, this disparity will be reflected unless states agree upon one test in the interest of uniformity.[75]

7.4. Treatment standards

The WTO essentially has a liberalising mission. In the context of the WTO, it is difficult to envisage an instrument which does not have liberalisation as its ultimate objective. In that sense, the instrument will ultimately, if not immediately, have to provide for pre-entry national treatment. That idea will be stressed by developed states but will not be acceptable to developing

---

[74] See e.g, the model treaty of Malaysia.
[75] This is a larger topic, but space does not permit a longer treatment.

states. It will mean that their screening procedures, based on the view that some types of investment are welfare-reducing and deleterious to developmental goals, could not be maintained. Economic liberalism tends to view all foreign investment as uniformly beneficial and to postulate an even stance relating to their treatment and protection, but this is not a view that finds favour with developing countries which have had a long experience of harmful investments. Those who argue for pre-entry establishment rights point out that, as in the case of GATS, there could be a bottom-up approach adopted with positive lists of sectors open to entry and other conditions attached. But, this is not the preferred approach of developing countries which have usually used negative lists in their investment laws, enabling the exclusion of sectors that are kept for their own nationals and gradually increasing the amount of foreign participation in others. Pre-entry national treatment is used only by the United States and Canada in their bilateral investment treaties. The European states do not use them. It is unlikely that there will be agreement on this issue between the developed states themselves. The standard had to be dropped from the OECD's Multilateral Agreement on Investment. The developing states will resist their imposition. The world is not yet ready for such an idea.

Post-entry national treatment will also present problems. The continued regulation of the multinational corporation after it enters the host state so that it can control its activities is perceived as necessary by developing states. The flow of funds associated with the investment, the protection of local entrepreneurship from competition, the use of local management and labour, the export of products and the utilisation of local raw materials are some of the factors that host states would wish to impose. This raises the issue of performance requirements which will also become unlawful on the additional ground that they violate national treatment standards. Regulatory control will also be affected in that there may be a problem in exercising control over foreign investment without exercising control over local investment. Again, it is unlikely that national treatment will prove acceptable to developing countries. The suggestion that exceptions could be made on the basis of development needs will not prove acceptable, as such exceptions cannot be exhaustive and broad exceptions will not be supported by states which desire national treatment on the ground that the uncertainty which results makes the inclusion of national treatment futile.

It is possible to argue that the introduction of a provision like Article XX of the GATT could solve the problems regarding the preservation of the regulatory framework of the host state. This is unlikely to happen. The uncertainties involved in the interpretation of Article XX have been manifested in the GATT/WTO jurisprudence.[76] The provision for non-trade-related values such as the protection of the environment, national security, the promotion of human rights and labour standards will be objected to as undermining the strength of the protection and treatment provisions of an investment instrument. The introduction of the GATT phrase 'like circumstances' to provide leeway to regulatory schemes is also possible but regulation is seen as a right by most countries and not as an exception to which such terminology as 'like circumstances' applies.[77] The phrase 'like circumstances' is used in later versions of the OECD's MAI, supposedly to permit regulatory discrimination. Towards the end, the negotiators of the MAI recognised the need to 'preserve the necessary scope for non-discriminatory regulation'.

7.4.1. Most-favoured-nation treatment

The inclusion of the most-favoured-nation standard may universalise all the specifically negotiated advantages that are given in bilateral investment treaties and, for that reason, such a move will not find favour with many states.[78] The effects of a multilateral treaty that includes a most-favoured-nation clause are difficult to contemplate as it universalises every provision of every bilateral investment treaty. Its operation will differ from that in the GATT context. In the case of most-favoured-nation standard treatment, the general practice is to exclude from the scope of the clause regional agreements which give partners in regional arrangements preferential treatment. It is uncertain how such an exclusion would fit into a multilateral agreement on investment.

Treatment standards have become important in the NAFTA litigation. This litigation employs strategies using the treatment standards in NAFTA to argue that state regulations violate these standards. The linking of GATT approaches to arguing violations of standards is evident in many of the cases.[79]

---

[76] E.g. the *Thai Tobacco Case* (1991) 37 GATT BISD 200.

[77] These issues are discussed in the context of NAFTA in the separate opinion in *S. D. Myers v. Canada* (2002) 121 ILR 7. They were also considered in the chairman's interpretative package released during the MAI negotiations. OECD, Chairman's Note on Environment and Related Matters on Labour (9 March 1988), DAFFE/MA (98) 10.

[78] In *Maffezzini v. Spain* (2001) 40 ILM 1129, a tribunal held that the better provision of any treaty made by a party will flow through the most-favoured-nation clause in a treaty.

[79] See the undecided *UPS v. Canada* (pending); *Methanex v. United States* (pending); and *S. D. Myers v. Canada* (2002) 121 ILR 7.

7.5. Performance requirements

Only a few GATT-related performance requirements were caught in the TRIMS. The investment instrument that is contemplated will take in a wider variety of performance requirements which in the eyes of the United States are all trade-distortive. The developing countries, on the other hand, believe that certain performance requirements are necessary, and point out that they have been used at various stages of the developed states themselves in their history of development. There are studies which indicate that certain performance requirements were used by the developed states themselves in their progress to development and that it would now be unfair to ban their use by developing states. The issue is still fresh and, despite the practice in US treaties of identifying and proscribing the use of performance requirements, it is unlikely that such a practice will be acceptable to developing countries in a multilateral instrument. India and China have already indicated strong stances on this. An issue akin to performance requirements is that of incentives, which are often tied to performance requirements so as to ensure that these requirements are balanced against each other. Again, views differ as to the economic value of incentives, but it is unlikely that developing countries can be persuaded to forego the granting of such incentives. Incentives, other than tax incentives which are employed by developing states, are given by developed states as well.

7.6. Expropriation

Expropriation has historically been a thorny issue. The expansive views that have been presented in the NAFTA litigation has caused anxiety to developed countries, and developing countries which have been at the receiving end of the stick on these matters will not be happy with the inclusion of definitions of expropriation that are capable of such expansion. With this proviso, developing countries have generally accepted that some appropriate compensation should be paid for any taking effected by the state. The formulation of the provision on expropriation will also be fraught with difficulty.

Any provision on expropriation must now provide safeguards that would ensure the taking of environmental measures. The United States, the principal proponent of the watertight provision, seems to agree with this position as is evidenced by the way in which it is arguing the *Methanex Case*. Its argument seems to proceed on the basis that, where there is a general measure taken to protect the interests of the community through the legislative process, such a measure should not be regarded as an expropriation. The general exception of measures taken to protect the health, morals and the environment that are used in the sphere of international trade will have to be accommodated within the provision. This will take care of the concern of the different groups that have come out in opposition to the formulation of the protection of the interests of multinational corporations without taking into account the concerns of the people of the world for poverty eradication, environmental protection and human rights protection. If this were to happen, the protection aspect of the investment treaty will be considerably weakened.

7.7. Balance-of-payment safeguards

There is a variety of transfer-of-funds provisions which appear in bilateral investment treaties. It will be observed that they vary from strict standards of repatriation of profits favoured by multinational corporations and developed countries to ones which are more accommodating of the balance-of-payment difficulties that could be encountered in the event of an absolute right of repatriation of profits and liquidated assets. Given the succession of economic crises that have buffeted the developing states, it is unlikely that a model favouring an absolute right of repatriation of profits will be acceptable to developing countries or could be said to be in accordance with development objectives. Neither could it be said to fit in with the Doha mandate that the provisions of an investment instrument must take into account the development dimension. The right to regulate capital outflows becomes central to the issue of balance-of-payment safeguards. The imposition of currency controls, which was the Malaysian solution to the Asian financial crisis, was decried by the International Monetary Fund, which had later to accept that it was a possible solution to the problem. The curtailment of this power of regulation cannot be said to promote the development dimension.

7.8. Dispute resolution

This is again a contentious issue. The investment treaties now provide for unilateral remedies to the foreign investor. It is said that this is not possible under the WTO system as only inter-state remedies are made possible under the dispute resolution mechanism. This is used as an argument for multilateral treaties on investment as states will not easily go to bat on behalf of investors unless there are heavy policy implications involved and court the displeasure of other states. This is not entirely true. The United States is the home of the world's largest multinational corporations. They have enormous power to ensure outcomes that are favourable to them. Many of the cases that have been brought before the dispute resolution system of the WTO were clearly brought at the instance of particular multinational corporations. The *Fuji* v. *Kodak* case is an example: it is apparent that the case protected the interests of one multinational corporation, Kodak, but involved no general high policy issue.

The internal laws of the United States also mandate that the United States Trade Representative (USTR) can be compelled by the US courts to take up the claims of any individual investor whose interests have been violated by a foreign state acting contrary to treaty standards. Hence, the USTR will have to institute proceedings before the WTO dispute settlement bodies where a US corporation alleges a violation. The enormous resources of the United States will be brought to bear almost without expense in settling the claims of the multinational corporation. This is a matter that will concern developing states. The same concerns expressed in the case of the United States may also apply in the case of other developed exporters of capital.

8. The right to regulate foreign investment

The right to regulate foreign investment from entry to final liquidation and exit lies at the root of conflicts concerning the making of an investment instrument. It runs through every aspect of the provisions of the instrument from definition to dispute settlement. Customary international law recognised that the entry of foreign investment was entirely a matter for the sovereign prerogative of the state. Liberalising instruments on foreign investment seek to change this aspect. The developed states themselves are disunited on this point. When the OECD's MAI was mooted, France and Canada sought a cultural exception that would have prevented the US entertainment industry from entering these states and dominating their cultural industries. On a wider scale, the objections are even greater. The developing states maintain screening legislation in order to exclude investments they perceive as harmful to their economies. This is a right that is unlikely to be given up.

The regulation of the operation of the foreign investment after entry is also regarded as a right of the host state, as foreign investment, unlike trade in goods is an essentially intrusive activity which takes place entirely within the boundaries of the state. Its regulation is seen as vital by developing countries. Again, during the negotiation of the OECD's MAI, the protests, which came largely from Western non-governmental organisations, were motivated by the fact that the MAI did not have sufficient regard to the protection of the environment and other social concerns such as human rights and labour standards, all of which the multinational corporations were seen as capable of disregarding.

The chairman of the negotiations was conscious of this criticism. He issued a package which was intended to 'achieve a balance between MAI disciplines and other important areas of public policy of concern to MAI Parties and to avoid unintended consequences on normal regulatory practices'. One suggestion was to include preambular sections that would contain references to conventions that contain environmental and labour standards.[80] Preambular provisions are not binding, though they may be of interpretative significance. The need to preserve some scope for non-discriminatory regulation was recognised. An absolute oxymoron of a provision was suggested to accomplish this feat. The provision is worth reproducing, for it demonstrates the draftsman's inability to reconcile the two competing forces of effective protection of foreign investment with the recognition of the right of regulation in the host state. The suggested provision read:

> A Contracting Party may adopt, maintain or enforce any measure that it considers appropriate to ensure that investment activity is undertaken in a manner sensitive to health, safety or environmental concerns, provided such measures are consistent with this agreement.

It is abundantly clear that this provision is practically meaningless. It contains the language of Article XX of the GATT, but in addition to the fact that such language presents difficulties in interpretation, the inconsistency of aims in the provision is obvious. It illustrates the difficulty of marrying the underlying philosophy of liberalisation in an instrument like the MAI with the preservation of the right of regulation. These are difficulties that developed countries faced between themselves in drafting an instrument on investment.

When it comes to the inclusion of the developing countries and the taking into account of the development dimension, as the Doha Declaration

---

[80] In *S. D. Myers* v. *Canada* (2002) 121 ILR 7, Canada unsuccessfully argued that its regulation of the waste disposal industry was supported by the Basel Convention on the Transboundary Movement of Hazardous Waste.

directs, the problems become compounded. For developing countries, the right of regulation lies at the root of foreign investment policy. Most of the domestic laws on foreign investment are premised on this fact. No multilateral investment instrument can come about unless this fundamental inconsistency is resolved. The resolution will prove difficult as no solution will prove acceptable to all groupings of states. The moment for bringing about a solution was at the high point of economic liberalism which has now passed. Until another occasion arises, this effort will remain a hope to be realised. As in the past, efforts will be continued. The issue of the right to regulation will remain a stumbling block that cannot be avoided. The Doha Declaration mandates that the investment solutions should 'reflect in a balanced manner the interests of home and host countries, and take due account of the development policies and objectives of host governments as well as their right to regulate in the public interest'. Finding that elusive balance is what the game is about. The obvious starting point is to ditch the ideas that underlay the OECD's MAI. These ideas were rejected by the developed states which participated in the negotiations and they will be rejected by the developing states, with the non-governmental organisations (a reality of modern international relations) still hovering over the issues. A new approach, sensitive to the needs of development, will recognise the significance of the right to regulation and ensure its meaningful accommodation in the new instrument.

The NAFTA litigation has certainly caused some concern as to whether investment protection has gone too far. The litigation strategies evidence a disregard of the state's right to regulation which discomforts the United States and Canada to such an extent that interpretative devices have been used to ensure that the regulatory rights of the state are not diminished. In that context, it is unlikely that there would be a keenness to draft a comprehensive investment instrument which does not recognise the right to regulate.

9. Conclusion

Each of the eight areas that have been detailed in section's 7.1 to 7.8 above contain concerns to developing countries. The drafting of effective rules relating to these areas will adversely affect the interests of developing countries and diminish their right to regulate foreign investment. If the instrument is inspired by the tenets of economic liberalism, as NAFTA seems to have been, then the diminution of the right to regulation will be near complete. NAFTA does contain exceptions relating to the environment but already tribunals have held that these seemingly wide exceptions have only hortatory significance.[81]

The only way that an acceptable investment instrument can be created that takes into account the Doha prescription relating to the development dimension is to ensure that there is plenty of scope for the right to regulate foreign investment so that a state is given sufficient leeway to harness the foreign investment to its development objectives. This would mean that in the eight areas identified above there must be sufficient flexibility to accommodate the interests of the developing states. But, such flexibility is unlikely to be acceptable to the developed states. The battle-lines are clearly drawn.

---

[81] *Pope and Talbot* v. *Canada* (2002) 41 ILM 1347.

7

Causes of action: breaches of treatment standards

The usual cause of action in investment disputes hitherto had been the taking of property. Though customary international law, it was claimed, recognised an international minimum standard as to the treatment of a foreign investor, the violation of this standard outside the context of the taking of property was seldom discussed. The growth of such a customary law is dealt with in Chapter 4 above, which forms a prelude to the discussion here. That chapter dealt with the manner in which the creation of an international standard was effected and the conflicts which attended it. But, investment treaties have sought to iron out such conflicts and provide certain recognition of treatment standards as between the parties to such treaties. It is only with the spelling out of the different standards of treatment in the investment treaties that the breach of treatment standards has become a distinct head of liability apart from taking of property. In the more recent disputes, the failure to provide treatment according to standards prescribed in investment treaties have become important, especially in the context of Chapter 11 of the North American Free Trade Agreement (NAFTA). The vigour with which disputes have arisen between the two developed country participants in NAFTA largely on the basis of treatment standards and novel theories of the taking of property has opened up new possibilities in the field.[1] Litigation strategies have taken a new turn as creative interpretations have been used to find new arguments, which create liability in foreign investment transactions. Whereas previously the targets of arbitration were developing countries, the new battleground opened up by NAFTA makes two developed states the targets of the mechanisms and legal standards of investment protection they helped to fashion against developing states in the past. Developed states seldom engage in direct takings, but do employ discriminatory and

---

[1] Commentators agree that the extensive use of these provisions against Canada and the United States was unforeseen. D. Price, 'Investor–State Dispute Settlement: Frankenstein or Safety Valve?' (2000) 26 Can–US LJ 107.

protectionist practices against foreign investors. The litigation that has emerged against Canada and the United States has largely focused on the provisions in NAFTA which make arguments possible that such practices are tantamount to takings or violate treatment standards. Both the strategies of litigation that are fashioned as well as the defences that the vaster legal resources of these states employ against them will have an impact on shaping the law in the area. There will be a spill-over effect of this experience into disputes arising from other treaties, which makes the jurisprudence under NAFTA of general relevance. Sophisticated theories of litigation tested out in the context of NAFTA will be extended to disputes involving developing states, which may not have the legal resources to meet these arguments effectively.

The NAFTA provisions on investment closely track the provisions of the model bilateral investment treaty of the United States. There are, however, significant drafting differences.[2] Provisions on treatment standards along similar lines are also to be found in other bilateral investment treaties. Language variations in them will have significance, but the broad content of the standards is generally the same.[3] The law that is created in the context of NAFTA and the debates that take place as a result will have a profound impact on the international law of foreign investment. The tendency to transport the thinking on takings in US constitutional law into the interpretations of NAFTA is strong.[4] There is a likelihood of the jurisprudence that emerges seeping into international law, as similar provisions exist in other bilateral investment treaties. The techniques that are used in NAFTA litigation and the responses to them by arbitral tribunals will influence the decisions that are made by other tribunals. To the extent that NAFTA tribunals state that they are applying standards of international law, there is a likelihood of their decisions affecting the whole corpus of international law in the area. This is despite the fact that NAFTA tribunals caution that their references even to customary law relate only to customary law as between the parties, raising the tantalising possibility

---

[2] Particularly in relation to Article 1105 of NAFTA, which deals with treatment standards.

[3] If they are not, the possibility is raised by the *Maffezini Case* (2001) 40 ILM 1129, that the most-favoured-nation clause in any treaty could be used to entitle a litigant to the better standards in another treaty involving the same treaty partners.

[4] Two US scholars have argued that NAFTA jurisprudence on taking goes beyond the notions of US law. Vicki Bean and Joel Beauvais, 'Global Fifth Amendment? NAFTA's Investment Protection and the Misguided Quest for an International Regulatory Takings Doctrine' (2003) 78 NYULR 30.

of customary international law existing as between just three states of the world.[5] The cross-fertilisation of thinking is already evident in the case law that is emerging.[6] It is for this reason that this chapter is devoted to the study of the failure to abide by treatment standards as creating a cause of action. Causes of action arise not only from the NAFTA provisions but also from the provisions in other investment treaties. Special attention, however, is devoted to the new awards made under NAFTA and the potential impact they have on the law. It must, however, be remembered that, though treatment standards have featured more heavily in the recent NAFTA decisions, they are by no means absent in other types of arbitration. Thus, in *Genin* v. *Estonia*,[7] an ICSID arbitration, the only allegations concerned violation of treatment standards. In other ICSID cases, there are references to violations of treatment standards. But, such references are used to bolster findings relating to taking.[8] Chapters 8–10 below deal with takings of property, which remains the principal cause of action and the issue of compensation for such taking. Though NAFTA perspectives are important on these aspects as well, they can be accommodated under existing viewpoints. This chapter builds upon the earlier consideration of treatment standards in customary international law and is principally concerned with the standards in treaties as well as the interaction of these treaty standards with customary international law. A recapitulation of the customary standards is made before considering the treaty formulation of these standards.

---

[5] See *Mondev* v. *United States* (2003) 42 ILM 85, para. 120; *ADF* v. *United States* (2003), para. 178: 'Thus, it [Article 1105] clarifies that so far as the three NAFTA Parties are concerned the long-standing debate as to whether there exists such a thing as a minimum standard of treatment of non-nationals and their property prescribed in customary international law is closed.' The assumption is that the debate continues for the rest of the world.

[6] It is evident that such cross-fertilisation takes place. The personnel of the arbitral tribunal are usually persons who have experience sitting on other tribunals which deal with investment issues. Thus, members of the Iran–US Claims Tribunal sit on ICSID tribunals and bring over the experiences formed while on the earlier tribunal. This is an inevitable process. The impact of the takings cases decided by the Iran–US Claims Tribunal is beginning to be felt in this area, despite the fact that the wording of the treaty creating the tribunal on takings was different.

[7] (2001) ARB/99/2 (ICSID).

[8] E.g. *Middle Eastern Shipping and Handling Co.* v. *Arab Republic of Egypt* (2002) ICSID ARB/99/6 (12 April 2002), para. 143, where there is a suggestion that a failure to give notice prior to the auction of the investment property amounted to a violation of the fair and equitable standard of treatment.

1. The customary international law standards

In Chapter 4 above, the effort on the part of the United States to create an external standard of foreign investment protection was outlined. The resistance to the creation of such a standard and the assertion of control by national standards by developing states was also examined. Modern tribunals concede the existence of this 'long-standing and divisive debate' between states.[9] Some tribunals have openly acknowledged the fact that two distinct systems existed and that the major tradition pretended that only one existed.[10] The outcome of this was that there was no clear international law standard that had emerged. However, arbitral tribunals had independently created 'law' through their awards asserting the existence of an international minimum standard of treatment of aliens, including foreign investors. The standards created were disputed, for, as long as the collective stances of developing countries supporting the instruments associated with the New International Economic Order remained unaltered through the adoption of a multilateral instrument on investment, there can be no truly international standard relating to the treatment of foreign investment. In the absence of such a treaty, the second best option is to settle the controversy relating to treatment standards as between the parties through regional or bilateral investment treaties. The continuous quest for the creation of external standards through the instrumentality of international law has been carried on through such treaties. The effort to create a multilateral treaty that would have embodied these standards and made them acceptable universally has failed every time it was attempted.

The struggle to create such an international standard of treatment is manifested in several ways. The first is the articulation of the standard in the official positions taken by the developed states. As indicated, these positions have little chance of creating customary practice as there is evidence of resistance to the standard by the developing states. The second is the argument that is continuously pressed that the incorporation of the standards in investment treaties is evidence of customary international law. Again, this is not a tenable argument, as investment treaties are

---

[9] *Mondev* v. *United States* (2003) 42 ILM 85, para. 120: '[I]t is clear that Article 1105 was intended to put at rest for NAFTA purposes a long-standing and divisive debate about whether any such thing as a minimum standard of treatment of investment in international law actually exists.'

[10] See the preliminary award in *UPS* v. *Canada*, para. 90, criticising the Sohn–Baxter codification on state responsibility for not recognising the competing system of state responsibility.

premised on different objectives, and the internal balance that is achieved between sovereign control over investments and the competing notion of the international standards from which there can be no deviation differ from treaty to treaty. It is true that some of the more powerful states are able to secure treaties with very little deviation from their model treaties, but these treaties are too few in number to create customary international law.

The most that can be said is that investment treaties generally recognise treatment standards and some of them refer explicitly to the standards as they exist in customary international law. Thus, they seek to bolster the existence of customary international law standards of treatment the creation and maintenance of which are the avowed objective of most developed states. There is a view that a technique of *renvoi* operates in the area, as reference has to be made to customary international law in order to give effect and meaning to the standards of treatment that are incorporated into the treaties.[11] This view will give the alleged rules of customary international law continuing validity. As a result, an opportunity has been created for arbitral tribunals to interpret these provisions, sometimes creatively, giving rise to further support for the idea of the existence of a customary standard in international law. This interaction takes place largely in the context of the opportunity to interpret appropriate provisions in investment treaties. What follows is an analysis of the different treatment standards in the context of recent arbitral jurisprudence.

2. The violation of national treatment standards

In the age of globalisation and liberalisation, the emphasis has been on national treatment at both the pre-entry and the post-entry phases of investment. The object of national treatment under the Calvo doctrine was entirely different. It evolved as a counter to the external international minimum standard advocated by the United States. The doctrine confined the foreign investor to the standards of the local entrepreneurs. There was an assumption that such standards were lower than those which prevailed in his home state and those which both the foreign investor and the home state would have desired. It is not to be confused with national treatment that is advocated in the more recent investment treaties. In modern international law, the national standard has assumed a much desired form.

---

[11] *AAPL* v. *Sri Lanka* (1991) 30 ILM 577.

At the pre-entry stage, national treatment, if permitted, creates a right of entry into the host state, unhindered by its screening laws, and a right of establishment of business. Post-entry national treatment entitles the foreign investor to be treated equally with national entrepreneurs. It thus becomes an instrument of liberalisation of movement of capital.

The emergence of new meanings that are attributed to old standards of treatment as well as their expansion is what makes the emergence of treatment standards as a new cause of action relevant to the modern law. State responsibility arises from the violation of these standards. Such responsibility is seen not as a static concept but as a continuously evolving one.[12] It is not as if some of the standards had not existed in the past; rather they have been dusted off and given new vigour through philosophical and political underpinnings. The neo-liberalism that motivates the modern investment treaties promotes the free flow of investments around the world. The treaties that are motivated by this philosophy therefore require that all movements of foreign investment must take place without the least amount of restrictions. With that objective, the investment treaties made by the United States and Canada have stressed that there should be free access of foreign investment into the markets of the contracting states. The treaties made by the European states have generally eschewed such an approach, limiting national treatment only to the post-entry phase. Though states have made treaties on the acceptance of national treatment at the pre-investment phase, they have done so on the basis that they could exempt certain sectors from such national treatment. All states, including the United States, have exempted a variety of sectors from the scope of pre-entry national treatment. The idea is that they start with the general proposition regarding free movement of investment but make exemptions of sectors to which the proposition does not apply. It is a technique taken over from trade instruments. The statement of national treatment as applicable to both phases is a change that has been made in these treaties. The change is clearly attributable to the acceptance of neo-liberal views.

Regional treaties have also adopted notions of pre-entry national treatment. Chapter 11 of NAFTA is by no means the only regional investment

---

[12] See *Mondev* v. *United States* (2003) 42 ILM 85, para. 116: 'In particular, both the substantive and procedural rights of the individual in international law have undergone considerable development. In the light of these developments, it is unconvincing to confine the meaning of "fair and equitable treatment" and "full protection of security" of foreign investment to what those terms – had they been current at the time – might have meant in the 1920s when applied to the physical security of the alien.'

treaty that stresses liberalisation as well as the protection of foreign investment. Regional treaties such as the ASEAN Framework Agreement on Investment also contain provisions that seek to confer protection as well as liberalise flows of foreign investment. The latter treaty, for example, seeks to create the concept of an 'ASEAN investor' and ensures that this investor, who could either be a national of an ASEAN member state or a company incorporated within an ASEAN state, freedom of movement within the ASEAN region.[13] Likewise, the Energy Charter Treaty, which is sector-specific, recognises pre-entry rights.

The awards that have been made also show that there is an emphasis on national treatment. The operation of national treatment at the pre-establishment phase has yet to be considered in an award.[14] The creation of such a right will require the dismantling of regulatory legislation which sieves foreign investment to determine whether it will benefit the host state and keep harmful effects such as environmental pollution out. It is clear, however, from the practice of states that have permitted pre-entry rights that many industrial and natural resources sectors could be exempted from such entry rights.

The list of sectors that are excluded by Mexico from the pre-entry national treatment provision of Chapter 11 of NAFTA is long. In the case of ASEAN, the newer members have the right to include sensitive industries in a list and are not under an obligation to open these industries to foreign investment until a future date.[15] But, the technique contemplates a process in which the list of excepted sectors is progressively narrowed. Some treaties fix time limits for the removal of sectors from the list.

National treatment at the post-establishment phase is more common. It has implications for economic development. The granting of special preferences to new industries may not be possible unless exceptions have been made. If ethnic groups within the state are to be given preferences because of positive discrimination programmes,[16] this too may violate national treatment provisions. It would be difficult to formulate such

---

[13] The provisions of this treaty have been interpreted in *Yaung Chi Oo Ltd.* v. *Myanmar* (2003) 42 ILM 430.

[14] The ongoing NAFTA case, *UPS* v. *CanadaPost*, raises issues of pre-entry national treatment.

[15] Specified as 2010 for some, and 2020 for others.

[16] See, for example, Malaysia and South Africa. There are similar programmes for native peoples in Australia and Canada and for 'backward' tribes and castes in India. The South African treaties contain provisions exempting its affirmative action programmes from the scope of national treatment.

exceptions.[17] The constitutional validity of the national treatment of a foreigner may also be a problem in that equal rights are usually conferred by constitutions only on citizens.[18]

National treatment provisions may also have an impact on the imposition of performance requirements.[19] As explained earlier, these requirements are imposed on the foreign investor to ensure that the host state gains the maximum benefit from the foreign investment. Such performance requirements include the requirement that export earnings be made through the export of a percentage of manufactured goods, that local products be incorporated in the manufactured items and that there is employment of local personnel. Some laws also require the foreign investor to locate in prescribed zones or direct that he establishes in regions which are in need of industrialisation. Such requirements are enforced through local laws and regulations, which may have to be disapplied if national treatment is to be provided to the foreign investor. The welfare-enhancing potential of such requirements may be lost if national treatment for foreign investment is to be implemented. Performance requirements are directly prohibited in many treaties, but their violation of national treatment standards could be raised as a ground of liability as well.

Such a situation occurred in *ADF Group Inc. v. United States*.[20] A contention of the claimant, a Canadian company which had contracted for the supply of steel girders to be used in the construction of a highway in the United States, was that the 'use of domestic material' policy mandated by statute was a violation of the national treatment. The supply contract was made with the main contractor for the construction of the highway. The main contract was between the Virginia Department of Trade and a US company. It was a term of the supply contract that the laws on the use of domestic materials be complied with. ADF proposed some of the work on the fabrication of the steel girders produced in the United States to be done in Canada. The Virginia Department of Trade ruled that such fabrication would not be in compliance with the 'buy America' provisions and could not be permitted. The main contract had a 'buy America' clause

---

[17] In some treaties, national treatment is postponed until economic development is reached. But, this is a nebulous formulation which requires later decision as to when such an event occurs.

[18] E.g. the rights under the Indian Constitution are conferred only on citizens. Treaties may confer more favourable rights on foreign investors. In these situations, too, constitutional problems could arise.

[19] The issue is addressed in *ADF v. United States*.

[20] ICSID Case No. ARB(AF)/00/1 (9 January 2003).

which would be violated, and the federal government would not reimburse the state government for the costs of the highway if the provision was violated. A waiver of the provision was refused on the ground that there were local providers of steel fabrication within the United States. As a result, ADF had to incur greater costs by subcontracting the fabrication of the steel. It fulfilled its contractual obligations but brought NAFTA proceedings against the United States on the ground that there were violations of NAFTA standards on national and fair and equitable standards of treatment. But, the tribunal found that there was no violation of the national treatment standard, as all that the regulations required, just as much to US as well as to foreign operators, was that the steel that was to be used in government projects should be fabricated in the United States. On the argument that the requirements were performance requirements as to local content, the tribunal held that, if so, the exception relating to procurements by a state party applied to excuse the state from liability.

There have been several disputes under NAFTA, which have been based on the violation of the national treatment standard at the post-establishment phase. *S. D. Myers* v. *Canada*[21] is a case in which a violation of national treatment was found. It involved an attempt by the Canadian government to prevent hazardous waste being disposed by the claimant's waste disposal system in Ohio in the United States, just across the border from Canada. The government intended to have the disposal done at a Canadian plant in Alberta, far away from the source of the waste. The issue was whether the Canadian policy was in violation of the national treatment provisions of NAFTA. The tribunal held that it was.

Pending cases before NAFTA tribunals invoke the national treatment provision. *United Parcel Services* v. *CanadaPost* is a NAFTA case brought largely on the basis of the violation of the national standard provision. United Parcel Services (UPS), a US provider of courier services, alleges violation of national treatment as CanadaPost, a monopoly provider of postal services, permits its subsidiary which runs a courier service to collect parcels from post offices. This facility is denied to UPS and other courier services and is therefore a violation of the national treatment provision of NAFTA.

The arguments raise interesting issues. The first is that, as a result of national treatment in an investment treaty, the foreign investor is placed on a footing that is not only equal to the host state's citizen but

---

[21] NAFTA/UNCITRAL Tribunal, 21 October 2002.

also superior in that the rights of equal treatment are protected, not by local courts as in the case of the citizen, but by international tribunals. Besides, such rights are protected not in accordance with local laws but in accordance with external standards. This brings in the second issue as to whether rights emanating from the local laws applying to a local situation should be subject to scrutiny by an external tribunal, bypassing the local courts.[22] Thus, the old issue of local remedies is raised. But, the significance here is that the ignoring of the local court system is seen as a violation of the constitution in that a local dispute is taken at once to an international tribunal, without the domestic courts having a chance to speak upon the issues in dispute. The arguments that have been raised, quite apart from the significance of domestic constitutional law to investment treaties, are reminiscent of the old debate as to the place of local remedies in a system of investment protection.[23]

Methanex v. United States is another pending NAFTA case. Its facts are similar to Ethyl but the litigation is premised on the violation of national treatment standards and not on the provision on taking alone. The claimant alleges that the ban on the use of a chemical additive in petroleum on the ground that it was a pollutive substance was motivated by a desire to discriminate in favour of a domestic producer of another chemical additive. Methanex thus raises the issue of national treatment in a direct form. The validity of the discrimination is the basis of the defence that is made to the charge. Methanex also raises the issue of regulatory controls which are addressed to foreign investors. Unlike in the case of the United States, which is the largest of the world's economies, a foreign investor would almost always be the dominant producer in the area of the sector it had entered in a developing country. Where regulatory control has to be exercised, it will almost always be directed at the foreign operator and not at a small-scale national operator. Discrimination based on size is likely to affect foreign investors exclusively. Such discrimination may be necessary in the interests of certain types of regulation such as environmental regulation where the pollution caused by a very large company requires control whereas those of small operators could be absorbed. National treatment therefore works to the detriment of the

---

[22] Or, in the situation of the Loewen Case, whether decisions of local courts should be pronounced upon by foreign tribunals without the appellate processes being exhausted.

[23] Mexico has argued that the local remedies rule is valid in the context of NAFTA. Marvin Feldman v. Mexico (2003) 42 ILM 625, para. 70. Also Loewen v. United States (2003) 42 ILM 811, para. 43. This may presage the revival of the local remedies rule.

exercise of regulatory controls over certain types of activities. Likewise, antitrust concerns are likely, again, if there are competition laws in a developing country, to concern dominant operators. These are more likely to be foreign investors than local companies. Avoidance of liability will require that exceptions be provided for certain types of regulatory interference. But, the prior identification of such exceptions is an impossible task so that they cannot be meaningfully formulated. Too wide an exception will make national treatment meaningless. Too restrictive an exception will not safeguard state interests.

2.1. Performance requirements and national treatment

Performance requirements will also be inconsistent with national treatment. The imposition of performance requirements, as already explained, is necessitated by the host state's desire to obtain the benefits of the foreign investment to the fullest extent possible. The screening laws of host states enable the imposition of these requirements at the time of entry or at a later stage when the foreign investment project has commenced functioning.[24] Many of these requirements constitute the basis of the control that the host state exercises over the foreign investment process.

The requirement that the foreign investor operate only through a locally incorporated joint venture is common in many developing states. So are requirements relating to the hiring of local personnel, the use of local raw materials in the finished product and the export of a percentage of the goods manufactured by the foreign investor.[25] These requirements are intended to ensure the advantages of the foreign investment for the host economy. But, the imposition of these requirements will violate national standards of treatment as they are not imposed on local entrepreneurs. Performance requirements are expressly prohibited in many investment treaties. But, this is unnecessary, as the inclusion of national treatment will have this effect because national treatment will certainly be violated if performance requirements are imposed only on foreign investors. Again, technically, it may be possible to exempt the imposition of performance requirements from the scope of national treatment, but this appears not

---

[24] The imposition of such requirements at a later stage may amount to an act tantamount to a taking on a wide interpretation that the imposition of performance requirements may affect the profit-making capacity of the venture.

[25] In *ADF v. United States* (2003), para. 91, the claimant argued that the 'buy America' policies in the United States were performance requirements prohibited by NAFTA.

to have been done. The states which in their domestic laws impose performance requirements have not addressed this issue in their investment treaties which grant national treatment.[26] But, it is possible to argue that, where the definition of protected investments in a treaty are those investments made in accordance with the laws and regulations of a state, the treaty does not prohibit the imposition of performance requirements through these laws and regulations. Likewise, there could be other strategies adopted to ensure that performance requirements are not covered by the national treatment standards of the treaty.

In *ADF* v. *United States*,[27] the tribunal found that the performance requirement requiring the sole use of steel fabricated in the United States may be a violation of the NAFTA provisions seeking to prohibit performance requirements. But, the tribunal went on to hold that the practice was saved by the exception that such performance requirements may be imposed in cases of procurement contracts by any party. The exception applied equally to procurements made by sub-national entities. The tribunal took a dourly positivistic stance in making an exact interpretation of the terms of the treaty, indicating that there will be a reluctance to expand the scope of national treatment in such a manner as to limit the adoption of regulatory policies by a party. Of course, tribunals could differ as to the approach they take but, in these situations, a strict construction limiting the scope of the treaty to the intention of the parties is justified as it would not upset the balance between liberalisation and regulation which the parties had struck in the treaty.

2.2. National treatment and infant industries

States may want to protect local entrepreneurs from foreign firms which, because of their dominant size and deep pockets, can run them out of business. Infant industry protection ensures that a state has the right to nurse its local industries to a level where they could withstand competition from foreign sources. This has been used as an argument for tariff protection being given to local firms. Most of the developed states practised such protection for their incipient industries at earlier stages of their development. It is used in international trade as an argument that justifies the differential treatment of developing countries. In the case

---

[26] Where the treaties confine their protection to investments made in accordance with the laws and regulations of the participating states, this issue relating to national treatment may not arise.

[27] (2003), para. 161.

of foreign investment, since penetration of the market has already taken place, the need for such protection in the face of competition from the foreign investor may be more urgent. The danger would be that the foreign investor could emerge as the dominant entity within the local market after driving out the weak local competition. The granting of national treatment to the foreign investor will deny the state the ability to protect local business, as such protection will be regarded as involving violations of the national standard of treatment. Again, the issue arises as to whether provision must be made for an exception in the case of states treating foreign investors differently because of the need to protect local industries from the competition of foreign investors. Unless the investment treaty so provides, there will be a violation of the treaty if the protection given to the local industry is not given to the foreign investors as well. A solution would be to exclude sectors which require protection from the scope of the treaty or to preserve regulatory controls relating to competition and similar factors from the scope of national treatment.

2.3. Subsidies, grants and national treatment

Many treaties, including NAFTA, exclude 'subsidies or grants provided by a Party or a state enterprise, including government-supported loans, guarantees and insurance' from the scope of national treatment.[28]

2.4. Ethnicity and national treatment

There will be difficulty in accommodating laws which give preferences to certain sections of the local population with national treatment to foreign investors. Thus, in South Africa, there is a programme to ensure that a certain percentage of the mining sector is controlled by native South Africans. Such laws will be difficult to reconcile with national treatment. They are usually dealt with through the provision of exceptions for such laws.

2.5. Conclusion

The thrust of liberalisation has largely focused on national treatment at both the pre-entry and post-entry phases. But, it would appear that even states that have advocated liberal policies regarding the movement

---

[28] NAFTA, Article 1108(8).

of foreign investment have been reluctant to provide complete national treatment. There is a gap between aspiration and the pragmatic concern that, if fully implemented, national treatment may harm the ability to regulate the economy. That is a concern which is felt by developed countries which, judging by cases like *ADF* v. *United States*, provide for performance requirements and ensure that their programmes are protected through exceptions for government procurement contracts in their treaties. The concern of developing countries in the case of national treatment will be greater as their economies will not be able to withstand competition from foreign investors, unless carefully regulated. For this reason, there will always be a balance maintained between national treatment and the ability to regulate the entry and subsequent operation of the foreign investment. How the balance is struck in the different treaties is a matter that the parties decide and, judging by awards such as *ADF* v. *United States*, the language of the treaties will be construed carefully in determining the extent of the national treatment that is permitted.

3. International minimum standard treatment

Chapter 4 dealt with the division of views among states as to the existence of an international minimum standard of treatment.[29] That division has continued into modern times, and it cannot be said with certainty that there is an international minimum standard of treatment of foreign investment in customary international law, the violation of which results in state responsibility. The content of this international minimum standard as far as foreign investment is concerned is also difficult to identify. But, where there is a treaty on investment which makes reference to an international minimum standard, the treaty conclusively establishes the existence of the standard as between the parties. Thus, in *ADF* v. *United States*,[30] the tribunal said that the relevant provision in NAFTA on the international minimum standard, Article 1105(1), 'clarifies that so far as the three NAFTA Parties are concerned, the long-standing debate as to whether there exists such a thing as a minimum standard of treatment of non-nationals and their property prescribed in customary international law, is closed'.[31] The view is a repetition of what the tribunal in *Mondev*

---

[29] See further Adede, 'The Minimum Standards in a World of Disputes' in R. St J. MacDonald and S. Johnstone (eds.), *The Structure and Process of International Law* (1986), 1001.
[30] (2003), para. 178.
[31] J. C. Thomas, 'Reflections on Article 1105 of NAFTA' (2002) 17 ICSID Rev 21.

v. *United States*[32] had stated. It is an acceptance of the view that there is a customary international law at variance with that claimed to exist by states which have participated in the treaties[33] and have created obligations as between themselves as to the existence of an international minimum standard of treatment. Impliedly, it accepts the possibility of the existence of two sets of customary international law, one recognising the existence of an international minimum standard and the other not. There were few norms of property protection developed as international minimum standards. Most of them dealt with the treatment of the physical person of the alien. The tribunals were conscious of the fact that a gap had to be filled between cases in the first half of the twentieth century which dealt with the protection of the physical person of the alien through the creation of an international minimum standard and the modern treaties which seek to extend that concept to investment protection.[34] The issue will always be whether such a mandate to fill this gap was intentionally given to arbitral tribunals.

Tribunals have asserted that they do have a creative function to perform. They have stated that the concept of an international minimum standard is not a static one but is capable of being developed in a modern context.[35] The difficulty in this approach is whether the tribunal will perform a near-legislative function, which it has consistently stated it does not have,[36] in identifying areas of international minimum standard. The content of the international minimum standard, when it comes to investment protection, will always be problematic. One knows that there is such a standard but what the standard contains and what its modern limits are, are unclear.

There are three instances in which the old cases on state responsibility may provide guidance as to the international minimum standard. These

---

[32] *Mondev* v. *United States* (2002) ICSID Case ARB (AF)99/2. Para. 120 reads: '[I]t is clear that Article 1105 was intended to put at rest for NAFTA purposes a long-standing and divisive debate about whether any such thing as a minimum standard of treatment of investment in international law actually exists. Article 1105 resolves this issue in the affirmative for NAFTA Parties.'

[33] This is certainly the case for Mexico, which has historically opposed the existence of an international minimum standard. Prior to NAFTA, Mexico had not signed any investment treaties.

[34] The *Mondev* tribunal acknowledged that the awards in the 1920s on the basis of which the international minimum standard was built, 'applied to the physical security of an alien'. *Mondev* v. *United States* (2003) 42 ILM 85, para. 116.

[35] This view is stated in *ADF* v. *United States*, para. 180, citing *Mondev* with approval.

[36] NAFTA tribunals have done so when considering the interpretative statement of the NAFTA Commission.

relate to compensation for expropriation, responsibility for destruction or violence by non-state actors and denial of justice. In the context of investment treaties, the relevance of the provision on international minimum standards outside these three areas is to be doubted. Of these three areas, two are separately provided for in almost all investment treaties. Compensation for expropriation forms the centrepiece of any investment treaty. There would usually be a lengthy article stating the circumstances relating to a legal taking and the standard of compensation to be paid for such taking. Responsibility for destruction by non-state actors is also specifically provided for in the provision which requires 'full protection and security'. This leaves only denial of justice, a concept directed at misconduct by the judicial organs of states from which state responsibility arises. It is a nebulous notion which has seldom been the basis of an award, because of the extreme reluctance of tribunals to find that judicial organs of states had acted improperly. The rule has been to require that the judicial impropriety has to be of such a high degree as to shock the conscience. The standard of misconduct is described by using negative superlatives that require an inordinate degree of deviance on the part of the judicial organs of the state before responsibility in the state can arise.[37] There has been a reluctance on the part of tribunals to find such a degree of impropriety as would justify the imposition of state responsibility. One has to struggle to find a role for the international minimum standard stated in treaties. The international minimum standard is then a concept that contains a limitation because treaties limit its meaning to the circumstances in which it was recognised in customary international law as conceived by the major capital-exporting states.

The United State had assiduously built up the idea of an international minimum standard.[38] When confronted with the use of the standard against it, the United States has argued that a claimant alleging the violation of the standard should show the violation of a specific rule of customary international law incorporated in the international minimum standard.[39] Despite the fact that the *Mondev* tribunal was effusive in

---

[37] For a recent statement, see *Azinian* v. *Mexico* (1998) 5 ICSID Rpts 269, para. 102–3.

[38] The international minimum standard can be clearly traced in US practice. The early commentators on the practice supporting such a standard were US scholars. Though its statement in the texts on international law is widespread, it is a doctrine whose roots lie in US practice.

[39] *ADF* v. *United States*, para. 182.

describing the increasing spread of investment treaties, these treaties cannot contribute to the identification of the content of an international minimum standard as none of the treaties seeks to describe the content of this standard.[40] They merely make reference to the standard. The tribunal's assertion that this numerical explosion of treaties must have some meaning hardly gives content to the standard.[41] The number of repetitions of the same notion is immaterial if the content of it is not identified. Emptiness multiplied several times over can still produce only emptiness. The paucity of content in the international minimum standard outside the three areas, two of which are separately provided for in treaties, cannot be rectified by the mere fact of its repetition in a growing number of investment treaties.[42] The fact is that, even in the customary international law, which was developed in cases like the *Neer Claim*,[43] the content of the international minimum standard outside the abuse of the physical security of the alien was minimal. The grafting of the idea into a system of property protection is recent, and the uncomfortable fact is that the content of the standard is yet to be identified. It is unhelpful to suggest that the lapse in the system of identification of a standard can be rectified by having recourse to general principles of law.[44] Neither is it helpful to say that these standards have 'an evolutionary potential'. The question is how they are to evolve and what guidance is to be had from whom as to their evolution. On property protection, it would be extremely difficult for these standards to evolve, from general principles, for, as between the Western legal systems, the principles of property protection vary so markedly that it would be difficult to identify common norms that could be passed off as general principles.

Some tribunals seem inclined to accept the US view, stated in the context of its new-found role as a respondent in litigation involving foreign investment, that when a violation of an international minimum standard

---

[40] This is based on the personal study of African and Asian treaties.

[41] The *Mondev* tribunal said, (2003) 42 ILM 85 at para. 117: 'It would be surprising if this practice and the vast number of provisions it reflects were to be interpreted as meaning no more than the *Neer* Tribunal (in a very different context) meant in 1927.'

[42] The present count puts the number of bilateral treaties at nearly 2,200. UNCTAD, *World Investment Report, 2003*.

[43] (1926) 4 UNRIAA 60. None of the other cases popularly associated with minimum standards involved the protection of property. *Roberts Claim* (1926) 4 UNRIAA 77; *Chevreau Case* (1931) 27 AJIL 153.

[44] The suggestion appears in footnote 176 of *ADF* v. *United States* (2003).

is alleged, there must be a specific violation of the standard that is identified in terms of customary international law. In other words, there is no scope for creating new categories of violation of these standards by tribunals outside existing customary international law. Since the international minimum standard was created almost entirely by the practice of the United States, this view must be given considerable weight. Whatever creative role an international tribunal may have in treaty interpretation, when considering the international minimum standard, there is a limiting factor provided by the alleged rules of customary international law, the existence of which the treaty parties accept.

If not for this limiting factor, arbitrators could adopt expansionary views as to the content of the international minimum standard. Earlier cases such as *Metalclad* v. *Mexico* indicated the potential for such an expansionary view. It is for this reason that Canada and Mexico intervened in later disputes against the United States to support the view that there is a limitation that a specific rule of pre-existing customary international law must be shown to have been violated. There must be a pigeonhole into which the case can fall. The difficulty with this approach is that, outside expropriation, there seems to be no identifiable pigeonhole apart from denial of justice into which an allegation of violation of the international minimum standard could be fitted. The brave face that the *Mondev* tribunal put on the concept not being static sounds hollow if the specific rules of the standard cannot be identified. It is for this reason that the more expansive formulation contained in treaties relating to the 'fair and equitable standard' of treatment, becomes important. They hold out the possibility, as some claimants have argued on the basis of limited academic writing, that it is a standard that is additional to existing standards of customary international law. This view, though originally triumphant, has now been beaten back.

4. Fair and equitable standard of treatment

In modern treaties, a fair and equitable standard of treatment is to be provided to investors and investments in addition to the international minimum standard and full protection and security. The content of this clearly nebulous provision has become a focal point of discussion, particularly as claimants have placed emphasis on this standard of treatment in NAFTA litigation. There are two general views. The first is that the fair and equitable standard does not add anything more to the international minimum standard but merely affirms it.[45] The second is that the fair and equitable standard expands the scope of the international minimum standard by allowing future tribunals to create new standards when the situation demands so that justice may be done for the foreign investor who suffers unfair treatment at the hands of the host state.[46]

The expansive view would mean that any discriminatory measure that the host state adopts could be regarded as offensive to the standard of fair and equitable treatment. This was clearly the approach of the World Bank Guidelines which made reference to the standard.[47]

Until NAFTA, despite the fact that the phrase has been used in a large number of treaties, it had not been analysed by any tribunal because it was not made the basis of any claim. Vasciannie observed, in 1999, that 'the pronounced reliance on the fair and equitable standard in treaties has not been matched by judicial consideration of the meaning of the standard in particular cases'.[48] But, in several of the NAFTA cases, commencing in almost the same year, the phrase has been the focus of the claims. In the early litigation under NAFTA, there was a clear preference for the expansive interpretation of the phrase. This would increase the ability of the NAFTA tribunals to review every act of the state against standards, which do not have a definite content or a reference point against which its validity could be tested. It would enable the tribunals to create new law binding on the parties. The tribunals had set themselves on such a course. In *Metalclad* v. *Mexico*, the absence of transparency in the rules applicable to the circumstances in which licences were granted was said to violate the standard. Expansive language was used as to the obligation to ensure that laws, regulations and administrative rulings are promptly made available

---

[45] Stephen Vasciannie, 'The Fair and Equitable Standard in International Investment Law and Practice' (1999) 70 BYIL 99 at 104. The origin of the phrase is usually traced to the OECD Convention of 1967. The OECD then supported the narrow view and regarded the fair and equitable standard as not distinct from the international minimum standard. OECD, 'Council Resolution on the Draft Convention the Protection of Foreign Property' (1967) 7 ILM 117. But, it took the opposite expansive view when the MAI came to be drafted in 1998.

[46] The most expansionary of these views is the one taken by Francis Mann that it is a standard above and beyond the international minimum standard of treatment and is distinct from any existing international law. This view, stated in 1981, could not have anticipated the manner in which it was later employed in NAFTA litigation. F. A. Mann, 'British Treaties for the Promotion and Protection of Investment' (1981) 52 BYIL 241. Mann's analysis was based on the UK treaty with the Philippines. He spoke of the standard as involving an 'overriding obligation' which not only prohibited discriminatory treatment but embraced within it other standards of treatment as 'specific instances of this overriding duty'.

[47] Guideline III (2).   [48] Vasciannie (1999) 70 BYIL 99 at 162.

to the foreign investor.[49] A British Columbia court reviewed the award at the instance of Mexico. Canada supported the application for review made to the court by Mexico. The British Columbia court ruled that the transparency requirement was not inherent in the Article 1105 formulation of fair and equitable standard by reference to customary international law but was imported from outside the investment provisions of Chapter 11 of NAFTA.[50] The court therefore ruled that there was an excess of jurisdiction in the finding that the transparency requirement was a part of Article 1105's reference to fair and equitable standards. The court also ruled that the finding on treatment also affected the finding on expropriation on the basis of the cancellation of the licence. The court, however, upheld the *Metalclad* tribunal's finding that the Mexican decree involved in the dispute amounted to an expropriation. The decision of the British Columbia court strikes a blow against the expansive interpretation of the standard of fair and equitable treatment. But, events since the judgment have dispelled any possibility of the survival of the expansionary view.

The NAFTA provisions on investment were generally regarded as being aimed at Mexico, the developing country partner in the regional association. The impact of the *Metalclad* award was not as evident as when the NAFTA provisions came to be used against Canada and the United States, challenging their regulatory legislation as inconsistent with the standard of fair and equitable treatment. The reaction of the states was then to secure a limitation on the possibility of tribunals using expansive theories of fairness and equity to scrutinise the validity of their regulatory schemes affecting foreign investment.

S. D. Myers v. *Canada*[51] demonstrated the possibilities of a NAFTA tribunal sitting in judgment over the regulatory schemes of the parties. The case involved Canadian export prohibitions of hazardous waste material for disposal in the United States. S. D. Myers, a US company which alone carried out such waste disposal by exporting the waste to its plants in Ohio, argued that the prohibition was discriminatory and violated both national treatment and the fair and equitable standard of treatment. The

---

[49] Paras. 76 and 99. Mexico failed to ensure a transparent and predictable framework for Metalclad's business planning and investment. The totality of these circumstances demonstrates 'a lack of orderly process and timely disposition in relation to an investor of a Party acting in the expectation that it would be treated fairly and justly in accordance with NAFTA.'

[50] The transparency provision that the tribunal referred to is in Article 1802, which does not form part of Chapter 11.

[51] www.naftaclaims.org.

claimant ascribed the prohibition to the Canadian interest in promoting the Canadian waste disposal industry. The tribunal found a violation of both the national treatment standard and the fair and equitable treatment standard. However, it limited violations of the fair and equitable standard to situations in which there was arbitrary treatment that was 'unacceptable from an international perspective'. The *Myers* tribunal was conscious of the need to limit the scope of the standard to violations of customary international law. It was conscious of the reference to the limiting words in the article – 'in accordance to international law' – when construing the extent of the standard. But, this caution was cast to the winds in *Pope and Talbot* v. *Canada*.[52]

Pope and Talbot v. *Canada* involved consideration of whether the implementation by regulation of a soft-wood lumber agreement between the United States and Canada through permits allocating quotas was a violation of the treatment standards of NAFTA. The tribunal made three separate awards. The first award was an interim award which dealt with issues of whether the right of access to lumber markets in the United States was an investment and whether regulatory measures could amount to expropriation. The tribunal concluded in the interim award that the regulatory measure involved did not amount to an expropriation. That award ruled out a claim on expropriation and left the only possibility of liability to arise from the violation of the treatment standards.

The second award found that the system did not discriminate between domestic and foreign investors. Hence, the regulation did not violate the national standard treatment. It then went on to consider whether Article 1105, which refers to treatment 'in accordance with international law, including fair and equitable treatment and full protection and security', was violated. The issue that arose for interpretation was whether the reference to fairness was over and above the international minimum standard that was required by international law. The tribunal accepted that the language of the article 'suggested otherwise', but that it was possible to read the phrase as requiring a standard higher than the international minimum standard as having an 'additive character'.[53] On this view, the fair and equitable standard would be a higher standard than the international minimum standard.

When it came to the identification of the contents of the standard, the tribunal relied heavily on the policy objectives behind NAFTA, which was

---

[52] *Ibid.*   [53] Para. 110 of the second award.

to 'create the kind of hospitable climate that would insulate [investors] from political risks or incidents of unfair treatment'. One might think that that was also the purpose behind the creation of the international minimum standard as well and of all investment treaties generally. Yet, having created this platform which the tribunal thought was unique to the fair and equitable standard, it went on to hold that existing precedents on the content of the international minimum standard did not contain any limitations on the standard of fairness. After so concluding, the tribunal found that Canada had not breached any obligation except in connection with the 'verification review process' administered by one division. In this respect, the tribunal found that the claimant was subjected to threats, was denied information, was obliged to incur unnecessary expense in obtaining information, was obliged to expend legal fees, suffered as a result of reviews not being conducted in the most convenient place,[54] and suffered loss of reputation in government circles.[55] Such conduct went 'well beyond the glitches and innocent mistakes that may typify the process' and amounted to a violation of the fair and equitable standard. After finding this violation, the tribunal announced that the third award would deal with the issue of the damages to be paid to the claimant.

Prior to the third award,[56] the NAFTA Commission delivered its 'Notes of Interpretation of Certain Chapter 11 Provisions'. It stated that the 'concepts of "fair and equitable treatment" and "full protection and security" do not require treatment in addition to or beyond that which is required by the customary international law minimum standard of treatment of aliens'. The tribunal was, as a result, faced with having to assess the impact of this interpretative note on its second award. The tribunal doubted whether the note was an interpretation or an amendment of the article. It also doubted that it could have retroactive effect. The tribunal reconsidered the interpretation of the fair and equitable standard, and took the view that it could not be a static concept frozen in a manner stated in the *Neer Claim*. But, having said that, it failed to spell out the contents of the new standard, other than repeating the official commentary to the OECD's Draft Convention in 1967 that the standard 'requires at least as good as that accorded by a state to its own investors'. Since this

---

[54] Which in this case was outside Canada in Portland, Oregon.
[55] Second award, para. 181.
[56] The second award was made on 10 April 2001. The note of the NAFTA Commission was released on 31 July 2001. The third award was made on 31 May 2002.

formulation makes the standard no different from post-entry national treatment which is contained in most investment treaties, the inclusion of the standard on the meaning so attributed becomes as much a surplusage as it is to say that it is the same as the international minimum standard. The tribunal reaffirmed its view that the manner in which the verification review took place violated the standards of fair and equitable treatment. Having done so, the damages awarded were paltry, reflecting the expenses involved in the verification review and the expenses of the hearing on interim measures.[57]

The tribunal in *Pope and Talbot* may have made a bold attempt to breathe content into the fair and equitable standard, but it will be opposed by states simply because of the fact that the creators of the standard themselves are faced with the constant threat of their regulatory structures being reviewed by international tribunals. Tellingly, the tribunal in *Pope and Talbot* examined the *travaux préparatoires* of the treatment provisions in NAFTA and found no indication of the meaning attributed to the term by the interpretative note of the NAFTA Commission. The purpose of introducing the fair and equitable standard was clearly to broaden the scope of the standards beyond what was required in the international minimum standard in international law. There was little authority for expanding the scope of the minimum standard beyond the twentieth-century cases, particularly in relation to property protection. It may well be that there was a need felt by capital exporting states to create a more embracing standard to give protection to their investors. But, when the technique of protection was turned against them, the situation became uncomfortable and there was a need for a quick back-tracking, leading to the exposure of the implications of the efforts in *Pope and Talbot*.

It is unlikely that other tribunals will take an expansionist view of the fair and equitable standard.[58] In the ICSID case in which the standard was made the focus of the litigation, the tribunal took the view that was taken by the NAFTA Commission well before the Commission issued its note,

---

[57] The total amount awarded was US$461,566. Canada has sought review of the award before its federal courts.

[58] In the preliminary award in *UPS* v. *CanadaPost*, para. 97, it was stated that the fair and equitable standard was not an addition to the international minimum standard. The interpretative note of the Commission was held not to be necessary to arrive at such a result. The side letters attached to the Singapore–United States Free Trade Agreement indicate that treatment standards are to be read in the light of customary international law. For the text, see http//: www.ustr.gov/new/fta/Singapore/final.htm.

indicating that the Commission was not without any support in law for taking the view it did. *Genin* v. *Estonia*[59] also involved a challenge to the exercise of regulatory control. The allegation was that the revocation of a banking licence violated the fair and equitable standard in the US–Estonia investment treaty, which is similar to Chapter 11 of NAFTA.[60] The tribunal was sensitive to the fact that the regulation took place in a nascent economy unused to the exercise of such controls in a vital economic sector. Once such an approach is adopted, the subjectivities involved in the situation make the fairness standard not a universal standard but a movable standard depending on the circumstances.[61] The tribunal also recognised the primacy of the regulatory laws of the host state and the need for the foreign investor to comply with them. The general provisions of an investment treaty cannot obviously negate the thrust of the specific regulatory laws intended to deal with problems in the economy.[62] The tribunal did not think that discriminatory treatment was always significant, unless of course it could amount to a violation of national treatment.[63] Referring to the content of the fair and equitable standard, the tribunal stated:[64]

> While the exact content of this standard is not clear, the Tribunal understands it to require an 'international minimum standard' that is separate from domestic law, but that is, indeed, a minimum standard. Acts that would violate this minimum standard would include acts showing a wilful neglect of duty, an insufficiency of action falling far below international standards or even subjective bad faith.

Of the three instances given, wilful neglect of duty and insufficiency of action falling below international standards are clearly traceable to the customary international law minimum standard. They are extensions

---

[59] *Genin* v. *Estonia* (2002) 17 ICSID Rev 395.

[60] Chapter 11 is in reality the model investment treaty of the United States cobbled into NAFTA.

[61] To quote: '[T]he Tribunal considers it imperative to recall the particular context in which the dispute arose, namely, that of a renascent independent state, coming rapidly to grips with the reality of modern financial, commercial and banking practices and the emergence of state institutions responsible for overseeing and regulating areas of activity perhaps previously unknown.' Para. 31.

[62] Para. 36.

[63] Para. 51. Citing authority, it suggested that discriminatory treatment by itself did not offend customary international law, though it would violate national treatment. See further *CME* v. *Czech Republic* (2002) and *Lauder* v. *Czech Republic* (2002) available at the website of the Department of Finance of the Czech government.

[64] Para. 50.

of principles in cases like the *Neer Claim* to the situation of property protection. The third – subjective bad faith – is without authority. The tribunal found that the standard of fairness is the same as the minimum standard but it too had difficulty giving content to the two standards. In any event, the tribunal found no violation of any standard of treatment. It accepted the respondent state's explanation that 'the circumstances of political and economic transition prevailing in Estonia at the time justified heightened scrutiny of the banking sector', again affirming the relevance of the context of each situation.

The NAFTA episode is instructive in that states will not permit intrusive supervision of their regulatory mechanisms by international tribunals on the pretext of inquiring into the fairness of the use of the regulation. The approach of the ICSID tribunal in *Genin v. Estonia* indicates that many tribunals will be loath to pass judgment on the regulatory mechanisms and their use. They would prefer to let each state to be the judge of the manner in which such mechanisms are employed, unless there is such a gross violation of procedural norms that shocks the sense of justice.[65] Despite brave assertions that the law on the subject of state responsibility for injuries to aliens has not remained static, there has been little demonstration as to how this law is to be extended to protect foreign investment or what the content of the law is. To merely assert that the tribunals can recognise a violation when they see it, does not take the law any further. Though treaties have used an abundance of standards, the extent of the protection they create is a matter of uncertainty because of the paucity of jurisprudence and the difficulty of identifying the content of these standards. Now that there is a retreat by the two states, Canada and the United States, on assertions of new and expansive standards, the area will probably return to the quiescence of the past. Their attitude, as the principal backers of both the international minimum standard and the fair and equitable standard in treaty practice will deprive the latter standard of any content, if it indeed did have any. In the light of these developments, it would be difficult to view the fair and equitable standard as distinct from the international minimum standard which was created in customary international law largely on the basis of US practice in Latin America. The NAFTA cases also reiterate the idea that the practice that they apply is confined to the region, leaving the old conflicts on the subject alive in the rest of the world.

---

[65] The latter situation would be accommodated within denial of justice.

4.1. Denial of justice

The customary law of state responsibility recognised that the actions of the judicial organs of the state could engage the state in liability if they so exceeded the norms of proper judicial conduct or showed such prejudice as would shock the conscience of the outside world. No ordinary error but an inordinate judicial impropriety was required to engage the liability of the state through the conduct of its judicial organs. This seems to have been well settled in the law on state responsibility. The International Court of Justice in the *ELSI Case* pointed out that it was not the misapplication of a rule of law but the violation of *the* rule of law that engages state responsibility.

In modern law, the idea has been revived in some arbitrations. The *Loewen Case*[66] is the most direct instance where litigation was brought on the basis of a denial of justice. There are other tribunals which have considered whether judicial or quasi-judicial acts of states violated the treatment standards in treaties. The *Loewen Case* is symptomatic of the possible problems of the revival of notions of denial of justice under treaty standards. The more direct argument was that the sum awarded in that case by way of punitive damages was tantamount to expropriation. But, the claimant also alleged that the award of damages was in breach of the treatment standards in NAFTA.

4.2. Due process and administrative irregularity

The notion of denial of justice has also surfaced in the *dicta* and writings on the subject in the form of absence of due process, lack of transparency, absence of good faith and violation of legitimate expectations in exercising administrative functions associated particularly with licences involved in foreign investment.[67] They are usually asserted in the arguments of the claimants but has, on one occasion at least, been upheld by a tribunal. Thus, in *Middle East Shipping and Handling Co. v. Egypt*,[68] the tribunal held that the seizure and auction of the property of the claimant without notification was a violation of the fair and equitable standard and full protection and security required by Article 2.2 of the investment treaty between Egypt and Greece. But, there was also a finding of expropriation,

---

[66] US$600 million were awarded as punitive damages by the Mississippi courts in a civil suit for defamation.

[67] On the good faith requirement, see *ADF v. United States*, para. 116.

[68] (2002) ICSID ARB/99/6, para. 143.

and this seems to have been the sole basis for the award of compensation. The due process that is required for expropriation is distinct from lack of due process which amounts to a violation of a treatment standard.[69] The due process requirement for expropriation is usually specifically provided for in the expropriation provision of the investment treaty.

Another instance of a domestic administrative law principle being used relates to references that are found to legitimate expectations. Such ideas are clearly borrowed from domestic administrative law. The attempt to import into treatment standards the whole body of principles of administrative review into the arbitration of investment disputes through the fair and equitable standard is a visible factor. In *ADF* v. *United States*,[70] arguments were made based on a failure to meet legitimate expectations of the claimant, but the tribunal did not consider the issue, finding that the expectations indicated were not raised by the defendant state.[71] In *Genin* v. *Estonia*[72] too, there are references to lack of procedural safeguards in the exercise of regulatory functions but there were no adverse findings on these grounds. Lack of transparency may be another ground that is advanced as amounting to a violation of the fair and equitable standard.

It is evident that the rules on which liability is being created are not based on international law principles but on notions that are imported from English or US administrative law. These principles cannot be imported into a treaty through a wide interpretation of the fair and equitable standard in investment treaties. In addition, arbitration tribunals were not created under investment treaties to sit in judgment over the manner of the exercise of discretionary power by domestic administrative organs. The tribunal in *ADF* v. *United States* asserted this when it said that the 'tribunal has no authority to review the legal validity and standing of the US measures here in question under the US internal administrative law'.[73]

It would appear that the tribunals are beating back the trend to argue that all administrative irregularity should be regarded as unfairness under the treatment standards. On the odd occasion that the absence of a requirement of notice is stated as a violation of fairness, it is usually provided as

---

[69] *Amco* v. *Indonesia* (1983–90) 1 ICSID Rpts 189 illustrates the situation where due process requirement is not satisfied prior to an expropriation.

[70] (2003) ARB(AF)/00/1.

[71] Para. 189; there were also references to good faith requirements.

[72] (2002) 17 ICSID Rev 395.

[73] *ADF* v. *United States*, para. 190, following *Mondev* v. *US* (2002) ICSID ARB(AF)/99/2, para. 136.

a throwaway addition for a finding based on expropriation but has not yet been an independent ground for awarding damages on the basis of expropriation.[74] It is unlikely that states will accept such an expansive intrusion into their administrative decision-making.

5. Full protection and security

Investment treaties in the provisions on treatment standards include the requirement that the foreign investment should be given 'full protection and security'. This standard has a firmer basis in customary international law as developed by the United States. It has been recognised, in a long series of awards, that the failure to provide protection to an alien who is threatened with violence creates responsibility in the host state.[75] The principles of such customary international law as found in the practice of some states can be taken as being settled. The precedents in the Iran–US Claims Tribunal on this issue are many, and the law was stated in the different cases by the Tribunal on the basis of customary international law. Cases decided by ICSID tribunals in this area are also based firmly on precedents which existed in the past.[76] They do not involve any extension of the law as found in the practice of states. They are based on the existence of a duty of protection to be afforded aliens and state responsibility arising from the failure to fulfil that duty either wilfully or negligently. The standard that is owed is no higher under an investment treaty.[77]

6. Conclusion

The short interlude in experimenting with expansionist views on treatment standards has resulted in these views suffering a setback. Tribunals have now found limiting factors in customary international law, but the content of the treatment standards nevertheless remains uncertain. The fact that the liability arising from treatment standards were tried out

---

[74] *Middle East Shipping and Handling Co.* v. *Egypt* (2002) ICSID ARB/99/6, para. 143.
[75] *Ibid.*
[76] *AMT* v. *Zaire* (1997) 36 ILM 1531; *Wena Hotels* v. *Egypt* (2002) 41 ILM 896. See also the *CME* v. *Czech Republic* (2002), para. 613; and *Lauder* v. *Czech Republic* (2002), decided under the Stockholm Chamber of Commerce Rules. In *Lauder*, para. 54, there was a finding of arbitrary treatment. But, the two awards, on the same facts, are inconsistent on many findings relating to treatment standards.
[77] In *AAPL* v. *Sri Lanka* (1992) 17 YCA 106, the argument that a form of strict liability is created by the investment treaty was rejected.

in litigation involving developed states was fortunate, as the problems involved were exposed quite early. Investment treaty formulations were originally intended to be a sword to be used against developing countries. Their use against developed countries was not foreseen. The nature of the exorbitant claims exposed the extent to which treatment standards could curtail the regulatory powers of the state over foreign investments. Developed states found such restrictions to be unpalatable and reacted with vigour to find guiding principles for their limitation.

The interlude also exposed the democratic legitimacy of arbitral tribunals being able to exercise extensive supervisory control over decisions of judicial and administrative organs of states. Quite apart from being able to review such decisions, which may possibly be explained on some wide interpretation of state consent, tribunals are able to pronounce on issues that transcend the interests of the parties to the dispute and have a wider significance for the international community as a whole. Such issues arise where, for example, a state seeks to regulate environmentally hazardous activity or deal with issues affecting the conduct of a civil war. The extent of the powers with which arbitral tribunals could be vested in these circumstances will remain a moot point and will increasingly come to be questioned. The fact that many of these situations involve developed countries shifts the focus away from developing countries and invites the attention of scholars in the developed world to anxieties that have been raised by developing countries and their lawyers in the past. It is interesting to see that the same sovereignty-centred arguments that were raised by developing country lawyers, with much overt ridicule by developed country lawyers, are now the refuge of those who argue cases for developed state respondents as well as of an increasing band of academic commentators. The birds have come home to roost.

8

The taking of foreign property

What constitutes an act of taking of foreign property in international law was once clear but has now come to be befuddled with difficulty as a result of the progressive expansion of the concept of taking. In the past, the law was discussed in the context of outright takings of the property of the alien. There was no difficulty in characterising the act of physical dispossession as a taking. As the phase of post-colonial nationalisations intended to recover the economy from the control of companies of the erstwhile colonial powers ended, there was a movement away from wholesale takings of industrial sectors to the targeting of specific companies. In developing countries where investments came to be made, there were changes taking place regarding the manner of the entry of foreign investment. There was greater administrative control over investment. The vehicle of foreign investment was often a joint venture company incorporated in the host state. The company became a corporate citizen of the host state and more amenable to its control. The process of foreign investment itself came to be enmeshed in a host of regulations which geared it to economic development objectives and environmental protection. In this context, the ideas of taking had to change. The focus was on the manner of governmental interference with the contracts on the basis of which the original investment was made or on the running of the corporate vehicle through which the investment was made.

In recent times, the controversy has been compounded by the formulations in investment treaties, which refer to three types of taking: direct, indirect and anything 'tantamount to a taking' or anything 'equivalent to a taking'. Previously, the focus of attention in the area was on the issue of compensation and, to a lesser extent, on the question of whether a breach of a foreign investment agreement gives rise to responsibility by itself. The attention has now shifted to the more basic question of what the scope of a taking against which the law, or more specifically the treaty, grants its protection. The problems have been compounded by the fact that the law developed in order to give protection to investments operating in developing countries is now used against developed countries as a result of treaties like NAFTA. With the increase in free trade agreements, the likelihood of developed countries becoming targets of litigation involving takings is likely to increase. As a result, the thinking on takings law in advanced constitutional systems is likely to encroach into this field, which was designed entirely with different motives in mind. This chapter is concerned with the issue as to what acts of the state may be characterised as amounting to taking and with the circumstances in which such taking would be considered unlawful.

Though at one stage of the development of the law, the question of compensation was linked to the legality of the nationalisation, the modern view is that the question of the legality is independent of the payment of compensation. It is recognised that the state has a right to control property and economic resources within its territory to enhance its economic, political and other objectives. Once this right is acknowledged, it must be conceded that the taking of property by a state is *prima facie* lawful. Non-payment of compensation does not make an otherwise lawful nationalisation unlawful.[1] It is generally accepted that a lawful taking creates an obligation to pay compensation, whereas an unlawful nationalisation creates an obligation to pay restitutionary damages. In the calculation of damages for an unlawful nationalisation, the tribunal takes a more liberal view and proceeds on the basis that compensation should be calculated as for any other illegality in international law. However, the issue of compensation for nationalised property is a celebrated cause of controversy among writers on international law. A separate chapter is devoted to the consideration of compensation for the nationalisation of foreign property and damages for unlawful nationalisation.[2] Likewise, a separate chapter deals with the issue of liability arising in international law as a result of a breach of a foreign investment contract.[3]

1. What constitutes taking?[4]

A distinction must be made between confiscation, expropriation and nationalisation of property. The terms are often used interchangeably,

---

[1] The scope for the illegality of an expropriation in modern law is confined to situations where the expropriation was discriminatory or lacked a public purpose.

[2] Chapter 10 below.   [3] Chapter 9 below.

[4] The leading writings on the subject are G. C. Christie, 'What Constitutes Taking of Property in International Law' (1962) 38 BYIL 307; Burns Weston, 'Constructive Takings under International Law: A Modest Foray into the Problem of Creeping Expropriation' (1975) 16 Virginia JIL 103; Rosalyn Higgins, 'The Taking of Property by the State' (1982) 176 *Hague Recueil* 259; Rudolph Dolzer, 'Indirect Expropriation of Alien Property' (1986)

but it is best, for the sake of clarity, that precise meanings be attributed to these terms. Confiscation is the capricious taking of property by the ruler or the ruling coterie of the state for personal gain. This was common in states ruled by dictators and oligarchies. Such takings happen, though less frequently, in modern times.[5] Much of the law on state responsibility was developed in the context of the law relating to the confiscation of property, which had no benefit to the state but helped only to enrich the ruling elite.[6] Unfortunately, the law so developed was extended indiscriminately to other types of taking. Most of the early law was also developed in the context of Latin America. The taking of property by army-ruled states to replenish the personal coffers of military dictators and their coteries must be distinguished from the later taking in that region that was associated with revolutionary zeal to redistribute property. The latter had an economic motive, whereas the former had none. Clearly, there was justification in the view that the confiscatory taking motivated by caprice should be regarded as unlawful. The law that was developed on the basis of confiscation has no relevance to the situation in which a state takes property with the object of effecting an economic programme. Nationalisation referred to a situation in which a state embarks on a wholesale taking of property of foreigners to end their economic domination of the economy or sectors of the economy. This was common in the period after decolonisation when states in Africa and Asia sought to recover control of the economy by taking over the assets of companies controlled from the former colonial powers. Again, the law that was developed in this context had a special flavour and is best confined to the precise period in which these types of taking took place. There is no doubt that ideas that were developed in the context of such takings were carried through to the future. The assertion of national control that was implicit in nationalisation had a continuous force that applies in modern times. The justice-related notions that were articulated cannot be confined in time. Yet, the rhetorical flavour of the law that was developed has little relevance today. There is a temporal quality that attaches to the phenomenon of taking in various periods. In modern times, the law on taking has taken a different turn. The incidents that occur are best described as expropriation which is a specific term that

---

1 ICSID Rev 41; and UNCTAD, *The Taking of Property* (UNCTAD Series on International Investment Treaties, 2000).

[5] *Siderman de Blake* v. *Argentina*, 965 F 2d 699 (1992), where the court suggested that the taking of the property had a 'discriminatory motivation based on ethnicity'. Such takings are clearly illegal.

[6] There were also cases of looting and pillage by mobs or the army for which liability was attributed to the state. *British Claims in Spanish Morocco* (1926) 2 UNRIAA 620.

could be used to describe the targeting of individual businesses for interference for specific, economic or other reasons. Many of them involve the
use of existing regulatory mechanisms. This, of course, does not mean
that takings of the types that were common in the past do not take place
now.[7]

Confiscation in the earlier periods concerned the property of individual traders who had gone overseas in search of wealth and stood powerless
in the face of the organised might of the totalitarian dictators who ruled
some of their host states.[8] The moral dimensions involved favoured the
alien in such circumstances, and the evolution of a law protecting the
interests of the individual trader was justifiable. The picture is quite different in modern times when the foreign investor is often a multinational
corporation, which can often muster greater power than the host state
and is backed by the even greater power of its home state. In this changed
situation, it would be invidious to use the law formulated in the context
of the confiscation of the property of the adventurous individual trader to
cater to the situation of the large multinational corporation of the modern
age.

The early law on taking was worked out in the context of the formative period of the relations between the United States and the Latin
American states.[9] In Latin America, where colonial relationships did not
exist, there was a need for the assertion of norms for the protection of
foreign investment. The United States sought to assert such norms and
the Latin American states resisted their imposition. Some of the Latin
American takings were carried out by elites for their personal benefit,
but some, like the Mexican expropriations of 1917 and 1938, were carried out in pursuance of economic reforms. The US assertions of norms
often did not seek to make a distinction between the two. Both types of
taking were regarded as being in violation of international law, and therefore compensable.[10] The distinction that had to be drawn between these

---

[7] Dictatorial takings may take place in some states even now. The recent case, *Yaung Chi Oo
Ltd* v. *Myanmar* (2003) 42 ILM 430 was argued on the basis that it was such a taking.

[8] There is the issue of whether the voluntary taking of the risk of investing in such states
should be taken into account.

[9] For the view that the rules on minimum standard constitute a regional law, see Philip
Trimble, 'International Law, World Order' (1990) 42 Stanford LR 811 at 835. See also
Charles Lipson, *Standing Guard: Protecting Capital in the Nineteenth and Twentieth
Centuries* (1985).

[10] P. E. Sigmund, *Multinationals in Latin America: The Politics of Nationalisation* (1990).
Arbitral tribunals were in sympathy with takings to effect economic programmes but
glossed over the distinction. See e.g. *De Sabla* v. *Panama* (1934) 28 AJIL 602, where the
taking was effected in pursuance of land reforms. The tribunal stated: 'As the public

types of taking became sharper in the post-colonial period. The states of Asia and Africa had been under colonial domination. In those states which were not, investment protection was achieved through capitulation treaties which ensured that the foreign investor was insulated from the reach of the local law and through the establishment of local regimes of property favourable to the protection of the foreign investor.[11] The development of international norms was not thought to be necessary in these circumstances. Takings in pursuance of economic programmes came to be debated after the Russian revolution. The Eastern bloc states maintained that such taking was non-compensable. In the first half of the twentieth century, there were two regions, Eastern Europe and Latin America, where European attitudes to state taking were questioned. With the independence of Africa and Asia, two more regions were added, and there were four regions in the world which stood outside the European sphere in articulating attitudes to taking which were quite different from those that the European states preferred. Their attitudes to notions of property were also different. Notions of taking differed in accordance with the different philosophical standpoints as to property. In that context, it is futile to suggest that any customary international law could have developed on the point, despite the suggestions of some writers to the contrary.

In modern law, as suggested above, it is best to refer to takings by states as expropriation, as in most instances these takings are carried out for an economic or a public purpose. The term 'nationalisation' should be confined to across-the-board takings that are designed to end or diminish foreign investment in the economy or in sectors of the economy. In dictatorial regimes, there could still be capricious, confiscatory takings

---

statements of its high officials show, it was endeavouring throughout this period to bring order out of a chaotic system of public land administration. In such a period of development and readjustment, it is perhaps inevitable that unfortunate situations like the present one should arise. It is no extreme measure to hold that if the process of working out the system results in the loss of private property of aliens, such loss should be compensated.'

[11] The existence of notions of community of property in native systems was anathema to colonial powers. They soon replaced these notions with notions of individual property ownership. A. G. Hopkins, 'Property Rights and Empire Building' (1980) 40 *Journal of Economic History* 787, quotes a British governor of The Gambia as having said:

On what do the English capitalists rely for their security? Of course on the prestige of English power. On the knowledge that English troops and guns are stationed in different positions along the Gambia – and also I am happy to add on the more civilised and juster notions of the rights of property which the continued presence of Europeans and the spread of legitimate commerce is producing.

but the opportunity for such taking is rare. In the present climate of the world, which is favourable to foreign investment, it is unlikely that nationalisations will occur unless there is some political upheaval resulting in ideological change within a state.[12] Economic nationalism still remains a potent force, and its triumph could still lead to the wholesale nationalisation of foreign investments. Expropriation, the targeting of a specific business, will be the more usual form of governmental interference with which the law has to be concerned. It, in turn, is divided into three principal categories in the modern law. This results from treaty definitions which distinguish between direct and indirect takings and include a third category identified as anything 'tantamount to a taking' or 'equivalent to a taking'. The assumption is that such a definition accepts the existence of three distinct types of expropriation. A view has been expressed that the phrases 'tantamount' or 'equivalent' to a taking do not create a third category because the dictionary meanings of tantamount or equivalent simply require the act to be the same as or similar to direct and indirect takings.[13] But, the fact is that they continue to be used widely in treaties and must at least be taken to expand the meaning of the term 'taking'.

1.1. New forms of taking

In identifying categories of taking, it is necessary to know something of the history. This related, not only to the political circumstances of the different periods, but also to the evolution of ideas as to property and as to control of foreign investment. In the early period, takings involved the direct seizure of physical property, which belonged to the foreign investor. The law was developed in the context of such takings. The period of postcolonial nationalisation also involved direct takings of property. In the period after these spectacular, across-the-board nationalisations, takings of property have been motivated by specific reasons and have been directed against individual corporations. Where such takings are direct, no issue of identification arises. But, a characteristic of taking in the later period was that there was no change effected to the rights of possession of the physical property of the foreign investor. There is a diminution of his property rights that is accomplished without dispossession necessarily taking

---

[12] The last real instance of this was the overthrow of the Shah of Iran and the consequent taking over of US business, resulting in the Iran–US Claims Tribunal. Economic nationalism still remains a potent force and could lead to nationalisation of the whole economy of a state.

[13] *S. D. Myers* v. *Canada* (2002) 121 ILR 7.

place. It is only when the taking is indirect that difficulties arise. There are diverse ways of affecting property interests such that the definition of indirect taking becomes difficult. These types of taking have been identified as 'disguised expropriation',[14] or perhaps to indicate that they are not visibly recognisable as expropriations or as 'creeping expropriations',[15] or perhaps to bring about the slow and insidious strangulation of the interests of the foreign investor. In *Middle Eastern Shipping and Handling Co.* v. *Egypt*,[16] indirect expropriation was described as 'measures taken by a state the effect of which is to deprive the investor of the use and benefit of his investment even though he may retain nominal ownership of the respective rights'. In *Lauder* v. *Czech Republic*,[17] the tribunal stated that such taking 'does not involve an overt taking but effectively neutralizes the enjoyment of property'. It is sometimes referred to as 'constructive taking' so as to emphasise the idea that results akin to taking are produced though externally the situation remains unchanged. Such descriptions, while providing catchy labels for takings outside the obvious situation of direct takings of physical property, do little to further the identification of indirect takings which will attract the application of the international law on expropriation. The best approach to the discussion is to group the types of indirect taking that have been discussed in the literature and the arbitral awards that have dealt with the question. It is this approach which is used in this work. By doing this, an assessment can be made as to the different claims that exist as to the circumstances that qualify as a taking.

The awards of the Iran–US Claims Tribunal have been a fruitful source for the identification of such types of taking.[18] The Iran–US Claims Tribunal dealt with types of taking that took place in the context of a

---

[14] Judge Fitzmaurice in *Barcelona Traction Case* [1971] ICJ Rpts 3.

[15] Rudolph Dolzer, 'Indirect Expropriation of Alien Property' (1986) 1 ICSID Rev 41; Burns Weston, 'Constructive Takings under International Law' (1975) 16 Virginia JIL 103. Creeping expropriation may be more appropriate to denote the slow and progressive measures adopted to initiate attrition of ownership and control rights. See *Tecmed* v. *Mexico* (2003), para. 114, which emphasises that such expropriation takes place 'gradually and stealthily'.

[16] (2002) ICSID ARB/99/6, para. 107. The sentence goes on to equate creeping expropriation with the phrase 'tantamount to a taking' in investment treaties.

[17] *Lauder* v. *Czech Republic*, para. 54. The authorities used for such expansive notions of takings are virtually incestual. Often the arbitrators sat on the different tribunals that made such expansive interpretations and then cite the authorities they create in later arbitrations.

[18] For a survey of the jurisprudence, see George Aldrich, *The Jurisprudence of the Iran–US Claims Tribunal* (1996); Charles Brower, *Iran–US Claims Tribunal* (1998).

revolutionary upheaval, and the propositions the tribunal formulated may not have relevance outside the context of the events that attended the domestic upheaval following the overthrow of the Shah of Iran. Also, one has to be cautious in making any generalisations on the basis of *dicta* in the awards of this Tribunal as its constituent documents gave the Tribunal power to deal not only with direct takings of physical assets but also 'all measures affecting property rights'.[19] It is clear that such a wide definition of taking will not be acceptable in general international law for the reason that many normal activities of states, such as taxation, affect property rights and cannot ordinarily be expected to give rise to claims of expropriation or scrutiny by international tribunals. Also, dispossession was often voluntary because it was unsafe for Americans to stay behind in Iran due to the situation. Since many who previously sat as arbitrators on the Iran–US Claims Tribunal now sit on foreign investment arbitration tribunals, there is a tendency to transfer the ideas developed by the former into other foreign investment disputes. This transference without closer analysis of each situation would be improper, as a wider mandate was given to the Iran–US Claims Tribunal than is generally the case with tribunals deciding with foreign investment disputes. Nevertheless, the guidance provided by the Iran–US Claims Tribunal on many issues relating to taking cannot be ignored.[20] The dissection of ownership rights that was effected in some of the cases decided by the Tribunal will have an impact on future discussions of the subject. The analysis by the Tribunal of property damage caused during mob violence as creating state responsibility will also continue to be valuable in that particular category of liability.

The increase in concern with 'creeping expropriation' in modern literature and arbitral awards is that a state could sometimes diminish property rights without affecting the direct ownership of the investment. Neither is the act of expropriation a single act of finality which either takes away a right or diminishes an interest of the foreign investor. It could be a slow, insidious erosion of such rights and interests set in motion by an initial act and spreading over a course of time. Creeping expropriation takes place within a wide variety of circumstances.

Creeping expropriation can only be described and examples of it catalogued. It cannot be identified through a single principle. The factors that can be isolated are that there is a diminution in the value of the interest of

---

[19] Article 2(1) of the Claims Settlement Declaration (19 January 1981).
[20] The best analysis of the jurisprudence of the Tribunal is to be found in George Aldrich, *The Jurisprudence of the Iran–US Claims Tribunal* (1996).

the foreign investor in the assets and that the time period over which this occurs is often longer than necessary for a single act. But, these are not factors that contribute to the formulation of a single rule that describes the process. Thus, where the management of a company is taken over, the company, its assets and its shareholdings are not affected but the foreign investor's control over the operations of the company is diminished. A similar result follows where a licence to operate is withdrawn or where such a withdrawal restricts or prevents profit-making activities, for example where exports are restricted. With the increase of administrative control over foreign investment, there has been an increase in the use of such techniques of interference with the rights of the foreign investor. The assimilation of indirect expropriation to direct expropriation is seen as crucial, as it builds a platform for analysis of the remedies that are to be provided.[21] Much of the analysis of the law has depended on a dissection of the notion of property.

1.2. The ideas of property

The philosophical underpinnings of property have also become important in the analysis of taking. Roman law recognised the unbundling of property rights into its constituent components.[22] Property was seen not as a single right of ownership but as involving a series of rights relating to its use and enjoyment. The growth of modern law, particularly administrative law, has resulted in the rediscovery of the idea that, when government interference occurs, it targets only some of the rights in the bundle of rights that constitute ownership and thereby reduces the value of the ownership in the property.

The notion of creeping expropriation is based on the unbundling of property rights. Though such a notion was known from Roman times and has been referred to in philosophical writings in England, the concept

---

[21] In *Biloune* v. *Ghana Investment Board* (1993) 95 ILR 183, para. 75, the tribunal held that no distinction should be drawn between direct and creeping expropriation. The decision was followed in the *Metalclad Case* (2000) 5 ICSID Cases 209, para. 108.

[22] The usual Roman law formulation is that ownership constituted *ius utendi, fruendi et abutendi* (the right to use, enjoy and destroy or dispose). It provided the inspiration for the definition of taking in the Harvard Draft Convention on International Responsibility for Injuries to Aliens (1961) 55 AJIL 554. Article 10 of the Draft defines a taking of property as including 'not only an outright taking of property but also any such unreasonable interference with the use, enjoyment, or disposal of property as to justify an inference that the owner thereof will not be able to use, enjoy, or dispose of the property within a reasonable period of time after the inception of such interference'.

became familiar in the case law of the United States in the jurisprudence on the taking of property. It is in the United States – and that too more recently [23] – that the dissection of property into its component rights has been carried out with a high degree of finesse. The issue then becomes one of whether this dissection should be carried into the jurisprudence on taking in international law.

The different types of taking were refined in the awards of the Iran–US Claims Tribunal. One suspects that the analysis, particularly of the US arbitrators who sat on the Tribunal, followed the legal techniques that had been developed in US law. To that extent, the views that were taken in these awards, though based on logical premises, should not be taken as fully reflecting the international law position. To a large extent, they reflected philosophical predispositions to certain views relating to property developed in US law that may not be acceptable in other legal systems. Yet, the fact is that, once made, the sway they have had in the determination of the course of the law has been strong. The precedents have found their way into the awards of other arbitration tribunals.

The precedents that have been generated have a basis in a distinct US theory of property which not only permits the dissection of the concept of property with finesse but also ensures that individual property is protected in more absolute terms than would be the case in other legal traditions. Perhaps because of the fact that in early America, individual property had to be won and defended against odds, this notion of absolute property has become a hallmark of US law.[24] It is widely justified on the basis of the statements of the English philosopher, John Locke, some of whose statements identified the protection of individual property as the central functions of a political society. The thinking is reflected in the US Constitution, which states that there must be just compensation paid when the state takes the property of the citizen. In the formative stages of the United States, the taking of property for the purposes of the state went uncompensated on the theory that the permissible exercise of a

---

[23] The taking jurisprudence in the United States was dormant until the decision of Justice Holmes in *Penn Central* v. *New York City*, 438 US 104 (1978). It became more pronounced only in the 1980s. There was greater latitude shown towards state taking in the formative years of the United States. The experience of the United States in the field must be approached with caution. The tendency has been to foist modern US notions of property onto the international scene.

[24] This is admittedly a contentious statement. The takings jurisprudence in US law does not show sufficient consistency to suggest that the notion of property was not a changing concept.

state's police powers was a necessary feature of government. As the United States progressed into an economic power, there was a re-emergence of the view that there must be just compensation paid whenever a state interfered with the enjoyment of the property rights of the individual.[25] But, when it came to regulatory takings, courts were still reluctant to categorise them as compensable. They refused to formulate a categorical rule. Instead, they preferred a rule which weighed the relevant circumstances of each case to determine whether or not compensation should be paid.[26] In the course of making these judgments, US courts made fine dissections of what constituted these property rights.

This tradition is not reflected in other legal systems. The traditional societies favoured community of ownership of property and would have found notions of individual ownership unacceptable. Western law that was transplanted in colonial times has displaced these traditional notions. Yet, the traditional notions survive in cultural attitudes to property in these communities. Within the traditions of European systems, different notions of property prevail. The competing notion that property must serve a social function and that individual rights are subject to the prior right of society to secure common goals had a wider acceptance in the European systems of law. It is this view that is reflected in the judgments of the European Court of Human Rights. Constitutional systems also indicate a variety of approaches to the protection of property. Canada had much difficulty in fitting a notion of property into its Bill of Rights. The Nigerian Bill of Rights, the model for many Commonwealth constitutions, identifies the circumstances in which the right to property becomes defeasible in the social interest.[27] The African Charter of Human and Peoples' Rights subjects the right to property to the public interest.

Yet, there is a clear project to foster in the international regime, as the centrepiece of foreign investment protection, a theory of absolute protection of foreign investment which sits uneasily with the constitutional systems that are recognised in different parts of the world. In each age of globalisation, the hegemonic power has sought to project its own vision of property onto the world. The United States incorporates in its treaty practice the absolute vision of property protection and works through

---

[25] Again, this is too sweeping a statement. The most recent US Supreme Court decision shows the extent of the disagreement on these issues US law. *Tahoe-Sierra Preservation Council Inc.* v. *Tahoe Regional Planning Agency*, 122 S ct 1465 (2002).

[26] *Palazzolo* v. *Rhode Island*, 533 US 606 (2001); the law was largely developed in the context of real property interests.

[27] For a recent comparative study, see Tom Allen, *The Right to Property in Commonwealth Constitutions* (2000).

international institutions and other means to achieve this purpose.[28] The treaty practice of some states is thus at loggerheads with the constitutional principles of many states. The proliferation of investment treaties which include an absolute concept of individual property rights, especially that of a foreign investor to the exclusion of similar rights for citizens, will provoke internal controversy and lead to the assertion of sovereignty-centred arguments. It will raise the issue as to whether these treaties, made largely by bureaucrats, do not constrain the democratic wishes of the people of the state.[29]

The tendency to dissect the rights that are inherent in the ownership of property may accelerate as a result of decisions made under NAFTA and the US treaties. There are views being expressed that the awards made under NAFTA are more intent on property protection and have constructed more rigorous theories of absolute property rights than even the decisions of US courts.[30] As the same arbitrators and arbitral institutions are often involved in the settlement of other foreign investment disputes, the tendency to use decisions made under NAFTA will ensure that the trends become widespread. As far as taking is concerned, wide theories will be tried out in litigation. Some of them may be accepted in arbitral awards. The *dicta* in the *Metalclad* award illustrate the expansive scope given to expropriation. The tribunal in that case defined expropriation thus:[31]

> [E]xpropriation under NAFTA includes not only open, deliberate and acknowledged takings of property, such as outright seizure or formal or obligatory transfer of title in favour of the host State, but also covert or incidental interference with the use of property which has the effect of depriving the owner, in whole or significant part, of the use or reasonably to be expected economic benefit of property even if not necessarily to the obvious benefit of the host State.

---

[28] The US vision incorporated in its treaty practice has been adopted by Canadian treaty practice, though Canada's internal laws do not contain such absolute visions of property protection.

[29] Canadian scholars such as David Schneiderman have commented on the 'new constitutionalism' that is driven by such treaties. The treaty standards mandate that existing constitutional balances are redrawn to accommodate the new standards of property protection to be afforded to foreign investors who are provided with most-favoured-nation and national standard treatment as well as an external standard provided through customary international law. For the expression of Canadian concerns, see e.g. David Schneiderman, 'Investment Rules and the New Constitutionalism' (2000) 25 *Law and Social Inquiry* 757.

[30] Vicki Bean and Joel Beauvais, 'The Global Fifth Amendment? NAFTA's Invesment Protection and the Misguided Quest for an International Regulatory Takings Doctrine' (2003) 78 NYULR 30.

[31] Para. 103.

The wide definition is by no means confined to awards under NAFTA.[32] The theory of litigation in the *Ethyl Case*[33] and the *Methanex Case*[34] was that any depreciation of the assets of the foreign investor amounted to a taking. They demonstrate the potential that the wide formulation of the provisions in the treaties have. The inclusion of phrases such as 'tantamount to a taking' or 'equivalent to a taking' give rise to the impression that the treaties intend to widen the scope of taking. States will resist the broadening of the definition of taking because of the fact that the legitimate activity of governments may be hindered if overbroad definitions are accepted. The expansionary view of expropriation has already begun to cause concern to the developed states, which now find themselves defendants in expropriation claims based on such broad views on expropriation.[35] As rich countries like the United States and Canada are at the wrong end of the stick, they will contest broad definitions of taking with vigour. As a consequence, in *Pope and Talbot* v. *Canada*,[36] the tribunal upheld the Canadian contention that the phrase 'tantamount to a taking' did not add anything to the concept of taking. The subject is one which no longer concerns developing countries only. It is fortunate that harsh law which could have been developed by maverick arbitrators could now be checked by developed states, who have an interest in doing so. A law that was largely aimed at developing countries now implicates the interests of the developed states as well. It is likely that developed countries

---

[32] Thus, in *Middle East Cement Shipping and Handling Co.* v. *Egypt* (2002) ICSID ARB/99/6 (para. 107), the tribunal defined creeping expropriation as follows: 'When measures are taken by a state the effect of which is to deprive the investor of the use and benefit of his investment even though he may retain nominal ownership of the respective rights being the investment, the measures are often referred to as a creeping or indirect expropriation or as in the BIT, as measures "the effect of which is tantamount to expropriation". As a matter of fact, the investor is deprived by such measure of parts of the value of his investment.'

[33] In the *Ethyl Case*, the claimant company, a US investor in Canada, was the sole manufacturer in Canada of a petroleum additive. A Canadian minister announced in Parliament that he was contemplating a ban on the substance as it was a pollutant. The litigation was brought on the basis that the announcement led to the depreciation in the value of the shares of the claimant company and thereby amounted to a taking. The tribunal upheld jurisdiction, but the dispute was settled as a result of Canada agreeing to pay damages.

[34] The facts of *Methanex*, which has not yet been decided, are similar to *Ethyl* v. *Canada* (1999) 38 ILM 708. Studies showed that the additive that Methanex, a Canadian company, manufactured in California was injurious to health. There was a ban on the manufacture of the additive. The allegation was that the ban amounted to a taking as a result of the effect it had on the internal and overseas sales of the substance.

[35] The United States, in *Metalclad* v. *Mexico* (2001) 40 ILM 55, para. 27, rejected the view that the phrase 'tantamount to an expropriation' created a new category of expropriation.

[36] (2002), http://www.state.gov/s/l/c 3747.htm.

will respond by making the same sovereignty-centred arguments that developing countries have been wont to make when faced with intrusive decisions by international tribunals in this area. It will be an interesting exercise to see whether the arguments the developed countries use in their own defence will succeed when developing countries use them.[37]

Quite apart from the categorisation of taking, one further issue that has become important is the identification of a category of taking described as regulatory taking for which no compensation needs to be paid. The law has always recognised this category. It has always been recognised that ordinary measures of taxation, or the imposition of criminal penalties or export controls do not constitute taking that is compensable. Legislation creating regulatory regimes in areas such as antitrust, consumer protection, securities, environmental protection, planning and land use are more common in developed states.[38] It is well recognised that interference on the basis of such legislation does not constitute compensable taking in situations in which public harm has already resulted or is anticipated. To pay compensation would be to reward a wrongdoer or to recognise an absence of overwhelming public interest in the use of property. These regulatory takings are regarded as essential to the efficient functioning of the state. The problem is to find a rational basis for the distinction between regulatory non-compensable takings and other forms of takings. The new awards indicate that many takings that would earlier have been characterised as regulatory takings are now being subjected to compensation.[39] Thus, in _Santa Elena v. Costa Rica_,[40] the tribunal stated:

> Expropriatory environmental measures – no matter how laudable and how beneficial to society as a whole – are in this respect, similar to any other expropriatory measures that a state may take in order to implement its policies: where property is expropriated, even for environmental purposes, whether domestic or international, the state's obligation to pay compensation remains.

---

[37] The cynic will have regard to the development of the concept of an economic development agreement. A foreign investment agreement made in a developed country is subject to its own law. The same agreement made in a developing country becomes an economic development agreement subject to a supranational law. The distinction was justified on policy grounds.

[38] The exception is stated in the American Law Institute's _Restatement (Third) on Foreign Relations Law_.

[39] _Metalclad_ v. _Mexico_ (2000) 5 ICSID Rpts 209.

[40] (2002) 15 ICSID Rev 72. The passage quoted was cited and followed in _Tecmed_ v. _Mexico_ (2003) ICSID ARB(AF)/00/2.

This blanket statement that compensation is payable for any environmental measure that is taken is unlikely to be accepted even by developed states. The US Supreme Court has decried the possibility of the creation of such a *per se* rule relating to the taking of property. In most states, domestic law would not accept such an absolute statement. The passage articulates a rule for which little authority can be found. The issue has become a hotbed of dispute because of the growth of environmental movements that seek to ensure that interference by states motivated by environmental concerns are not deterred through the characterisation of such interference as compensable taking. The issue as to the distinction between compensable taking and regulatory taking is also considered in this chapter.

The types of taking, other than the obvious situation of a direct taking of physical assets, that could amount to expropriation have been identified in the literature and in arbitral awards. The question as to what amounts to a taking cannot be answered easily. The circumstances in which takings could arise can, however, be described and discussed. They could be grouped as follows for convenience of discussion: (1) forced sales of property; (2) forced sales of shares in an investment through a corporate vehicle; (3) indigenisation measures; (4) taking over management control over the investment; (5) inducing others to take over the property physically; (6) failure to provide protection when there is interference with the property of the foreign investor; (7) administrative decisions which cancel licences and permits necessary for the foreign business to function within the state; (8) exorbitant taxation; (9) expulsion of the foreign investor contrary to international law; and (10) acts of harassment such as the freezing of bank accounts or promoting strikes, lockouts and labour shortages. These different types of taking and their significance to international law are considered below.

All these instances involve conduct by the state. Unless the conduct of those committing the acts is directly attributable to the state, the taking cannot involve state responsibility.[41] In the old law, the cases largely considered the circumstances in which the acts of officials and agents could be attributed to the state. In the modern law, the issue has largely been whether acts of regulatory agencies and sub-national entities such as

---

[41] See *Amco* v. *Indonesia* (1985) 24 ILM 203, para. 158, where the tribunal said: '[A]s a *conditio sine qua non* there shall exist a taking of private property and . . . such taking shall have been executed or instigated by a government, on behalf of a government or by an act which otherwise is attributable to a government.'

municipalities can be attributed to the state. In the case of direct taking, it would be easy to find clear evidence of the link between the state and the taking. In the case of indirect taking, the link may be difficult to find but it must be found, for the requirement of attributability of the taking to the state would not otherwise be satisfied. The law that is being applied is no different from the old law on attributability. The test is whether knowledge and power of control over the regulatory or sub-national body exercising authority over the foreign investment existed but was not exercised so as to protect the interests of the foreign investor.[42]

1.2.1. Forced sales of property

A distinction must be drawn between forced sales of the foreign investment which are brought about by civil unrest or economic downturns and those brought about by a programme of the state such as the indigenisation of the economy. In the former situation, the alien may extricate himself from business difficulties by selling his assets cheaply, or he may abandon his property altogether. It is a situation faced in common by all in business, national and foreigner alike. A state cannot be held responsible for such conduct on the part of the foreign investor.[43] But, if the unrest is engineered by the host state and the violence is directed at the foreign investors for the specific purpose of ensuring that they leave the host state, clearly there is a situation that involves a taking. Where the foreign investor abandons the property or makes a quick sale of the property in these circumstances, there is no voluntary conduct on his part. The conduct is induced by the state. State responsibility could therefore arise in such a situation.

Some of the authority in this area comes from cases where the conduct of the state was motivated by considerations of race. Where there is racial discrimination that motivates conduct, this gives rise to a separate head of liability. However, no comfort is provided to the individual who has suffered as a result. For him, the fact that the taking of his property is a clear illegality in terms of international law provides no better protection than a claim for damages. It could well be that a claim on these grounds is easier to establish if the circumstances show a clear policy of discrimination

---

[42] *Genin* v. *Estonia* (2002) 17 ICSID Rev 395; *Metalclad* v. *Mexico* (2000) 5 ICSID Rpts 209; *Compania de Aguas del Aconquija* v. *Argentina* (2003) ICSID ARB/97/3.

[43] Unless there is some contractual obligation on the part of the state or its organ to protect the property. *United Painting Company Inc.* v. *Iran* (1989) 23 Iran–US CTR 351 at 366–70.

against foreigners of a particular race or group. Illegality flows from the fact that the presence of racial discrimination negates the requirement that a public purpose is necessary for a lawful taking.[44]

The *ELSI Case*[45] contemplates another category of forced sales. Where the rules of a state require that a company facing bankruptcy should be dissolved, the forced dissolution of the alien company will not amount to a compensable taking by the state. The failure had not been brought about by the state but by external circumstances or due to the ineptness of the alien investor himself. In these circumstances, the state has its own interests to protect. In such a situation, the interests of the foreigner were ineluctably being led to a state in which his company must be dissolved and the state merely steps in to protect its own interests by taking over the failing company. In that particular case, there were the interests of the workers of the company and the industrialisation of a depleted area that the state was keen to protect.

There was also pre-existing legislation which permitted state interference in failing companies. In these circumstances, the interference was not considered to be a compensable taking by the state, even though the local courts had held that the administrative measures taken in the interference were not lawful. But, some modern investment treaties protect against the abuse of the process of liquidation.[46] The protection usually appears in the treatment provision of the treaty. There must be a demonstration that the ordinary process of justice attended the liquidation process and that there was nothing that could be seen as a denial of justice. The mere fact that there is a court-ordered liquidation may not provide legitimacy to the taking. The court may be used as an instrument to effect the taking, in which case, clearly, the liquidation could amount to a taking depending on the circumstances.[47]

---

[44] *Osthoff* v. *Hofele*, US Ct Resp App 111 (1950); *Poehmann* v. *Kulmbache Spinneri AG*, US Ct Resp App 701 (1952); and *Zwach* v. *Kraus Bros.*, 237 F 2d 255 (1956) (2nd Cir.) are discussed in the context of forced sales. They arose from expulsions of aliens motivated by racism.

[45] [1989] ICJ Rpts 15.

[46] Thus, the ASEAN Investment Treaty (1987) states that: 'Each contracting party shall, within its territory, ensure full protection of the investments made in accordance with its legislation by investors of the other Contracting Parties and shall not impair by unjustified or discriminatory measures the management, maintenance, use, enjoyment, extension, disposition or *liquidation* of such investments' (Article IV(1), emphasis added).

[47] In *Yaung Chi Oo Ltd* v. *Myanmar* (2003) 42 ILM 540, the claimant had argued that the liquidation proceedings before the Myanmar courts were themselves an act of taking. But, the tribunal did not find on this.

1.2.2. Forced sales of shares

The question whether there could be diplomatic protection and state responsibility where wholly foreign-owned companies incorporated in the host state are taken over has been clouded by problems relating to corporate personality in international law.[48] Such companies, incorporated in the host state, have personality only under the law of the host state and are corporate nationals of the host state. The *Barcelona Traction Case*[49] relied on this proposition when the International Court of Justice denied standing to Belgium to espouse the claims of a company incorporated in Canada and operating in Spain. The much-criticised decision held that Belgium could not espouse the claims of the Belgian shareholders and that Canada alone had the right to protect the company.

The company had been declared bankrupt in Spain and its assets sold. The interests of the foreign and local shareholders in the company were destroyed as a result. The effect of the judgment of the International Court of Justice was that the company could be protected only by the state in which it was incorporated. The interests of the shareholders would thus receive indirect protection but the shareholders themselves could not receive protection directly from the states of which they were nationals. The Court proceeded on the basis that, since there were no adequate rules on the subject of corporate personality in public international law, questions relating to issues on corporations would have to be decided in accordance with the relevant principles of municipal legal systems. There were exceptions to the general rule that there could not be direct diplomatic protection of shareholders. The Court accepted that there could be such protection in circumstances in which the company itself had ceased to exist under the law of the state of the company's nationality and the shares had been divided *pro rata* among the shareholders or in circumstances in which a lifting of the veil was justified as, for example, where there had been an illegal act aimed at the company.[50] Mann summarised the effect of the judgment in the following terms:[51]

---

[48] On corporate nationality, see D. Ijalye, *The Extension of Corporate Personality in International Law* (1971); I. Seidl-Hohenveldern, *Corporations in and under International Law* (1987).

[49] [1970] ICJ Rpts 3; for a discussion of earlier views on the protection of shareholders, see J. M. Jones, 'Claims on Behalf of Nationals Who Are Shareholders in Foreign Companies' (1949) 26 BYIL 225.

[50] Para. 92.

[51] F. A. Mann, 'Protection of Shareholders' Interests in the Light of the Barcelona Traction Case' in F. A. Mann, *Further Studies in International Law* (1990), 217 at 233.

> No rule of customary international law has yet come into existence which
> would confer a right of diplomatic protection on a state merely by reason
> of the fact that the value of its nationals' shareholdings and thus its own
> economic resources suffer damage.

In the three decades that have passed since the judgment, there has been
no evolution of international law which would entitle foreign shareholders of a company to receive protection directly from the state of which
they are nationals except through treaty law.[52] The significance of investment treaties is that they remedy the defects of customary international
law on this point by recognising that shareholders of foreign companies
are protected against government interference through procedures and
remedies that are devised by the treaties. The brave redefinition of property to include shareholdings attempted by Judge Tanaka in the *Barcelona
Traction Case* does not provide the answer. It may reflect the need for protection, but it does not provide a solution to the problem as to whether the
redefinition will also include portfolio investments. Too much of judicial
creativity having regard to teleological factors may provoke dissent.

The International Court of Justice recognised that treaties provide the
answer. The Court observed in *Barcelona Traction*:

> [I]n the present state of the law, the protection of shareholders requires that
> recourse be had to treaty stipulations or special agreements directly con-
> cluded between the private investor and the state in which the investment
> is placed. States ever more frequently provide for such protection, in both
> bilateral and multilateral relations, either by means of special instruments
> or within the framework of wider economic relations.

One possible reason for the increase in bilateral investment treaties is
the need to provide for shareholder protection. These treaties recognise
that shares are included in the definition of treaties.[53] In the absence of
treaty protection, international law does not appear to provide relief to
shareholders of a company whose shares have been affected as a result
of state intervention. But, after *Barcelona Traction*, the UK government
asserted its right to protect the shareholdings of nationals in a foreign
corporation. The rules regarding international claims issued by the UK
government take this view:

[52] Chris Staker, 'Diplomatic Protection of Private Business Companies: Determination of
Corporate Personality for International Law Purposes' (1990) 51 BYIL 155.
[53] Some would specifically include portfolio investments. This has been discussed previously.

> Where a United Kingdom national has an interest as shareholder or other-
> wise, in a company incorporated in another state and of which it is therefore
> a national, and that state injures the company, Her Majesty's Government
> may intervene to protect the interests of the United Kingdom national.

Many bilateral treaties now contain provisions which contemplate the protection of shareholders. They alter the rule in *Barcelona Traction* which is based on the rule that corporate nationality depends on incorporation. The primacy of that rule has been confirmed in later developments.[54]

Shareholder protection becomes important because of the requirement found in host state laws that entry by the foreign investor be made through an incorporated joint venture company formed in association with a local entrepreneur or state company. The foreign partner will usually be only a shareholder of such a company and the protection of his investment in the company would be on the basis that he is a shareholder. The foreign investor or his home state will ordinarily have no status to protect the company or its assets. The only way in which the investment could be protected through international law mechanisms is to confer treaty protection upon the shareholding of the foreign investor.[55] The effect of this would be that, even where the management of the company is taken over as a result of state interference but shareholdings are kept intact, there will be no taking in respect of which the foreign shareholder can invoke protection. This will not be an acceptable result from the point of view of the foreign investor for the profits of the company may diminish considerably in the absence of a vigorous management. It is quite possible that the treaty is widely worded so as to include the right to management and control within the definition of an investment, provided the shareholdings were such as to create management rights in the foreign investor. In any event, investment treaties usually cover contractual rights. This would be so where the foreign investor had made entry through a

---

[54] Corporate nationality features heavily in the jurisprudence of ICSID. Article 25 of the ICSID Convention recognises the incorporation test but permits the state of incorporation to treat the company as a foreign company for the purposes of arbitration. There are many awards dealing with the interpretation of the provision. For a statement of the law, see Christoph Schreuer, 'Diplomatic Protection of Private Business Companies' (1990) 51 BYIL 155.

[55] See *ELSI Case* [1989] ICJ Rpts 15, para. 106: 'While there may be doubt whether the word "property" in Article V, paragraph 1, extends, in the case of shareholders, beyond the shares themselves, to the company or its assets, the Chamber will nevertheless examine the matter on the basis argued by the United States that the property to be protected under this provision of the FCN Treaty was not the plant and equipment the subject of the requisition, but the entity of ELSI itself.'

corporate joint venture. The joint venture contract should have provided for such management and control rights, in which case they will become protected.

Another factor to note is that the shareholder protection that has been evolved through treaties should not be taken to mean that portfolio investments are protected. The developments that have taken place seem to confer protection only upon the primary shareholders and not those down the line to whom the shares may have been transferred. Though no conclusive view can be formed on this, the evolution of the law suggests that there was no intention on the part of the states to create protection for portfolio investments. There are treaties which provide for the protection of portfolio investments.

1.3. Privatisation and forced sales

The present era has witnessed a fervour for privatisation of publicly owned companies in the western world. The same fervour is to be found in many other regions of the world. Since many of the privatisation measures do not restrict shareholdings to foreigners, there are likely to be many foreign investors who will buy shares in the newly privatised overseas public companies. Attitudes to privatisation involve a certain ambivalence, and political parties which have opposed them may reverse the privatisation when the opportunity presents itself. Such a reversal will raise many issues of shareholder protection in developing countries which may find themselves unable to raise sufficient funds to compensate the foreign shareholders adequately if they are to effect the reversal quickly. The reversal can be expected to be effected through forced sales on the local stock markets on which the real value of the shares cannot be raised for the obvious reason that the sales will be confined to the local investors and there will be a flood of the shares on the stock exchange. The question will arise as to whether such forced sales amount to takings or whether the situation is akin to one of interference with portfolio investments in which case the shareholders will have to bear the risk of loss or seek remedies provided by the local law. The buying of shares during privatisation is more akin to the making of a portfolio investment and the answer, resulting from the analogy, may be that there would be no taking by the state in these circumstances.

1.3.1. Indigenisation measures

Indigenisation measures involve a progressive transfer of ownership from foreign interests into the hands of the local shareholders. They were undertaken in many African and Asian countries after they achieved independence to ensure that the termination of political control also meant the termination of economic control and the passing of such control into the hands of local entrepreneurs.[56] One factor that sets indigenisation measures apart from outright takings is that there is no vesting of any property in the hands of the state or the state organ. There is no direct or even indirect enrichment of the government as a result of the measures. Unlike the classic situation of nationalisation where the state takes over a foreign-owned venture and runs it itself or through a state entity, indigenisation measures contemplate the transfer of ownership and control of such ventures into the hands of the local citizenry. There is, however, some authority for the view that there could be a taking by the state even where the state or state entity is not vested with the property that is taken. A second factor is that there may be no change in management control effected by the measures.

The foreign investor may remain in control of his venture and his control may even be desired as the local entrepreneurs may lack the skill to run the business as efficiently at least in the initial stages. When, eventually, the local shareholders displace the foreign managers, the displacement will take place in accordance with the corporate laws of the host state and not through any government fiat. Unless the state itself had bought the majority of the shares, which is unlikely as a purpose of the measures is to diversify the shareholdings among as many locals as possible and build up a local entrepreneurial group, the state seldom exercises control over the internal rearrangements in the control structure of any previously foreign-controlled company.

Yet, the transfer of the ownership is involuntary and the timing of the transfer of the shares in the venture owned by the foreigner is not left to him. As a result, he may not be able to secure the optimum price for his shares. There is no doubt that there is a resemblance to forced sales in indigenisation measures. However, few disputes have arisen from such indigenisation measures, as in the context of the political developments that were taking place in the countries which adopted these measures, the relinquishing of controlling interests in foreign investment ventures was unavoidable. Foreign investors were content to put up with it rather than face a protracted dispute with the host state. They reckoned that they would come out losers in the dispute and prejudice their continued business prospects in the host state. Continuation of links with the host

---

[56] For a description of these measures, see T. Biersteker, *The Political Economy of Indigenisation: Multinational Capital in Nigeria* (1987).

state was a much-prized asset which multinational corporations did not want to lose. There were other strategies and realignments which the foreign investors adopted to maintain their positions in the host states which took such measures.[57] It may also be that home states of foreign investors were reluctant to take issue with the host states as the phenomenon was widespread at a given period of time among newly independent states. There was little to be gained in diplomatic terms in making a stand against such a widespread practice that was brought about by changes which were taking place as a result of the ending of colonialism. The policy behind the indigenisation measures may also have some merit in terms of the goals it seeks to achieve and is sanctioned by the wider idea of economic self-determination. As such, it falls within the regulatory controls a state takes in pursuance of its sovereign rights over economic matters rather than into the category of takings for which the state had to pay compensation. From the state's point of view, the sales took place openly on its stock market and that was the best way of assessing and paying for the value of the shares. Such a view was not based on the reality as a fair price could not be raised for the shares on the local stock exchange.

Both in the *Barcelona Traction Case* and in the *ELSI Case*, there were allegations that the interference in the corporate affairs of the foreign investor was intended to effect a transfer of shares into local hands. Judge Tanaka referred to the allegation of 'hispanicisation' of the company in *Barcelona Traction* but had little to say on whether the technique was contrary to international law. In the *ELSI Case*, there was an effective transfer of the shares of the US-controlled company into Italian hands as a result of the sale in bankruptcy that ended the long conflict between the US shareholders and the Italian authorities. The United States objected to the process by which the transfer took place.[58] Again, the Court avoided pronouncing on the question of whether the requisitioning of the company, which, according to the United States, led to the bankruptcy of the company and its subsequent sale, amounted to indirect expropriation on the basis that the company was failing in any event.

Ethnicity has a role to play in government measures which seek to restructure companies on the basis of their racial compositions so as to achieve a measure of economic equity. In Malaysia, the *bumiputra*

---

[57] Some sought to defeat these measures by buying and holding shares through local nominees or nominee companies. Such practices are obviously illegal. Others sought to maintain influence by entering into management and similar types of relationships with the venture.
[58] Para. 119.

policy was intended to ensure this, and companies had to restructure in accordance with specified ethnic quotas as to shareholdings by each of the races in Malaysia and foreigners were restricted to a percentage of the shareholdings. In South Africa, a similar policy is to be implemented to ensure that the economic cake is shared by the majority native community, whereas foreign investment has traditionally flowed into companies that were owned by the minority groups. Where restructuring is done in order to avoid political conflicts based on past economic inequities, the resultant divestment that takes place could not be regarded as compensable takings. These are general policy measures that apply across the board in order to achieve certain political and economic objectives. Such measures must be considered a part of ordinary business risk. In the case of the Malaysian divestment programme, no argument was made that expropriation was involved.

In *Lauder* v. *Czech Republic*,[59] there is a suggestion that the expropriation should benefit the state or an entity associated with the state. This certainly does not seem to have been a requirement in past expropriations many of which involved land and other reform programmes which did not benefit the state but the people of the state. If the requirement is accepted, measures such as divestment measures do not benefit the state directly and will not amount to an expropriation.

1.3.2. Interference with property rights

There has been a general tendency in international protection of alien property to transfer domestic norms of property protection into the international sphere. The European capital-exporting states found it necessary to promote ideas of individual ownership of property in their colonies and other states into which they exported investments as the security of such investments were achieved by the spread of a uniform notion of property built on notions of sanctity of individual property. But, notions of property do not remain static. Whereas the protection of physical assets were emphasised in earlier times, both the function of property as well as the function of the state have undergone a radical transformation in the European legal systems to require a concept of property that extends beyond the protection of the physical assets.

The view that only an outright take-over of physical assets amounts to expropriation by a state no longer holds. Whereas stress on the physical

---

[59] (2002), para. 57.

nature of property was sufficient to protect ownership in times when there was a *laissez-faire* philosophy, the coming of the welfare state meant an increase in the nature and frequency of state interference with the ownership of individuals. Interference with the exercise of property or ownership rights by the host state could amount to takings which require compensation. Once the jurisprudential fact that ownership itself involves a bundle of intangible rights in relation to property is acknowledged,[60] then it follows that it is not only the outright taking of the whole bundle of rights but also the restriction of the use of any part of the bundle that amounts to a taking under the law. It is necessary to understand the course of developments relating to the concept of property in the municipal systems, in particular of the United States, as the leading capital-exporting states will contend for the transference of the system of property protection in their domestic sphere into the international sphere. There is evidence of such transference in the past.[61] There is evidence that the ideas that are generated in the domestic sphere shape the arguments on the international sphere. The pervasive influence of US jurisprudence on the taking of property is evident in modern discussions on taking in international law. The dominance they will come to have on the jurisprudence generated by arbitral tribunals considering takings under Chapter 11 of the North American Free Trade Agreement is already evident. For this reason, a digression into US and European developments concerning the concept of property is necessary.

1.4. Changing US and European notions of property

Property is constitutionally protected in the United States.[62] This is not so in all states. In Europe, the European Convention on Human Rights did not initially recognise a right to property but the First Protocol to the Convention now recognises such a right. The provisions do not prevent takings by the state, but subject them to the payment of compensation.

---

[60] There are, of course, different explanations of the right to property in municipal systems. There is no indication of a theory of property in international law itself. International law does not create property in an individual. It relies on municipal law for the recognition of property rights.

[61] See G. Lipson, *Standing Guard: Protecting Foreign Capital in the Nineteenth and Twentieth Centuries* (1985), 16–18.

[62] The Fifth Amendment states: '[N]or shall private property be taken for public use, without just compensation.' It is generally suggested that the drafting of the clause was influenced by natural law theories on property rights. Natural law views and positivist views of property clashed in the early cases which dealt with the ownership of slaves. R. M. Cover, *Justice Accused: Antislavery and the Judicial Process* (1975).

There has been considerable case law in the United States in particular which has discussed the issue as to the circumstances in which taking will attract constitutional protection requiring the payment of compensation. The general pattern has been that the US courts showed greater latitude towards state taking when the country was young and needed to create infrastructure through taking private property. There was a greater tendency to hold such takings to be exercises of police power which did not require the payment of compensation. But, as the country progressed, there was a shift towards greater constitutional protection of property rights as a result of which payment of compensation for taking of property came to be increasingly accepted. Though the distinction between taking in the exercise of police powers and taking which required compensation is not clearly drawn, there is a swing towards greater protection of property rights in US law. The tendency towards neo-liberalist notions in modern times makes the swing even more pronounced. The great emphasis placed on the individualist notions of private property are born of the particular experiences of the United States and its espousal of a constitutional philosophy which elevates the protection of individual property rights as a centrepiece of its constitutionalism. This experience may not be repeated in other states.

European notions of property sought to balance the public interest in property use with those of private rights of ownership. They sought to recognise the idea that the interests of the individual in his property may have to be subordinated to those of society at large. The cases on the right to property under the European Convention on Human Rights reflect this difference in attitude. In the Canadian Bill of Rights, the statement of the right of property does not appear at all. In the Commonwealth constitutions, the right to property is stated as being subject to the public interest and not in absolute terms. In Asia and Africa, the traditional systems generally favoured communal ownership of property and played down the idea of individual rights of ownership of property. The concept of the right to property that is sought to be universalised in foreign investment documents and in arbitral awards seems, however, to be an absolute right. To that extent, the universalisation of the idea of the right to property will meet with resistance. Yet, the capital-exporting states found the imposition of an absolute right to property through foreign investment instruments to their advantage and have persisted in that approach.[63]

---

[63] This unity might fail when instruments like NAFTA bring about disputes between the rich states. The schisms in attitudes are beginning to appear between the United States and Canada as to approaches to this area of the law.

The disputes relating to the taking of property have attracted greater and more consistent attention in US law than in any other system. In the context of these decisions, the US courts have dissected property rights into fine categories. Many of these decisions were made in the context of regulatory legislation involving infringements of property rights. The unbundling of property rights and abstract notions of property came to displace physical notions of property.[64] These tendencies sought to entrench ideas that favoured the absolute protection of property through the payment of compensation if interference with the right was necessary.

But, there were competing tendencies that were evident as well. Populist notions which saw property as giving power were also reflected in the law.[65] In addition, there are laws which increasingly affect the enjoyment of property rights in the interests of not only the immediate community but also the international community generally which have been mandated by different conventions on the environment.

These developments favoured the viewing of property as involving a series of intangible rights in relation to property and its use.[66] Infringements of these rights could amount to taking justifying compensation in some circumstances but not in others. The making of the distinction becomes problematic once more.[67] The existing literature on the subject is unhelpful as it merely seeks to study the situation from a US perspective and foist the US solution onto the international scene. It has already been demonstrated that, given the differences in attitudes to property, this solution is hardly one that would meet with general approval. Obviously, infringements of property rights in controlling hazardous or environmentally unsound use of property, in the course of planning decisions and in

---

[64] See T. Honore, 'Ownership' in A. G. Guest (ed.), *Oxford Essays in Jurisprudence* (1961), 107.

[65] Until replaced by market-dominated theories, antitrust laws had a populist basis of interfering with large monopolies and price-fixing cartels. The rationale was that large conglomerations of economic power affected political decisions and were harmful to democracy. Market theories have tended to divert attention from this rationale and look at antitrust laws through the prism of price theory.

[66] The analysis was accelerated by the work of Hohfeld. His positivist analysis of rights ensured that US law viewed property as intangible rights held against others in the community. Rights had correlatives which resided in others. W. Hohfeld, 'Some Fundamental Legal Conceptions as Applied in Judicial Reasoning' (1913) 23 Yale LJ 16.

[67] There is an abundant literature analysing the case law. The leading works are: J. L. Sax, 'Takings and the Police Power' (1964) 74 Yale LJ 36; F. I. Michelman, 'Property, Utility and Fairness' (1967) 80 Harvard LR 1165; R. Epstein, *Takings: Private Property and the Power of Eminent Domain* (1985); and S. R. Munzer, *A Theory of Property* (1990), 442–69.

effecting consumer protection measures or restoring market forces in a situation of imperfect markets are regulatory takings which require no compensation.[68] But the difficulty was in the formulation of a theory that could be used as a predictive device so that there could be guidance as to whether the taking is compensable or not. Here, though several efforts have been made at devising a theory capable of making the distinction, none has been successful.[69]

1.5. The impact on international law

There have been efforts to transfer the changing notions of property law onto the international scene. Such transference is undesirable. The fact is that hegemonic powers have always sought to transfer their domestic law into the international sphere. They have had a measure of success in their efforts. In the present situation, the need for such a transference is felt, due to the increase in administrative controls instituted in the developing countries over the process of foreign investment. These administrative interferences are usually regarded as regulatory in character and as not requiring the payment of compensation. It is to counter this development that the arguments relating to absolute rights of property and the dissection of the different rights to property are made.

From the point of view of property protection, the abstract notion of property as a series of intangible rights has a positive effect in that it makes it easier to protect contractual rights and intellectual property rights. It can be used to accommodate new rights created in connection with ownership such as licences, planning permissions and administrative permissions necessary to operate businesses. The reinterpretation of these rights as constituting property is again a feature of the law both in the United States and in other developed countries.[70] In addition, protection could

---

[68] The theory of Sax that a taking is non-compensable when the state acts as an arbiter in deciding between the public interests and the rights of the owner (for example, in the making of a planning decision) and that it is compensable where it acts in an enterprise function (for example, where it takes over land to build roads) is popular. Sax, 'Takings and the Police Power' (1964) 76 Yale LJ 36. But, it too has limitations. S. R. Munzer, *A Theory of Property* (1990), 459.

[69] The transference from domestic law is itself contestable. A Japanese court in *Tokyo Suikosha v. Tokyo Masonic Lodge Association* (1966) 53 ILR 1, resisted such a transference, noting that there is no principle relating to property among nations to justify its elevation to a principle of international law.

[70] The concept of new property is created on the basis of trends in administrative law. These convert licences, permits and other administrative instruments into property rights, and

be extended to all manner of infringements of the rights of ownership of the foreign investor. The influence of the shift can be seen in US bilateral investment treaties. Thus, the US–Argentina treaty states that 'neither party shall in any way impair by arbitrary or discriminatory measures the management, operation, maintenance, use, enjoyment, acquisition, expansion or disposal of investments'. The formula is repeated in other bilateral treaties made by the United States.[71] A complete range of possible uses of property is covered through an unbundling and spelling out of the package of rights that previously constituted a single bundle. This description of the whole process of foreign investment as being covered by the treatment standards in the investment treaties has become a standard feature of such treaties. One could argue that a series of property rights is spelt out and that impairment of any of those property rights could amount to a taking.

The effort to promote such unbundling of property rights is evident in the awards of the Iran–US Claims Tribunal as well.[72] There were some early arbitral awards where taking was found on the basis of an interference with specific rights of ownership.[73] But, the negative aspect of the development in US law is that it still recognises a category of non-compensable takings.[74] The application of such a notion of non-compensability will have adverse consequences on property protection. Many of the developing

seek to protect their withdrawal through due process safeguards. Charles Reich, 'The New Property' (1964) 73 Yale LJ 733. Administrative law theories owe much to the idea that due process principles now protect interests akin to property from the abusive exercise of discretionary power. The seeping of the ideas of legitimate expectation into arbitration awards is a visible fact. Administrative law notions have been used to give protection to the administrative rights that arise in foreign investment. Such rights are treated as property rights and are included within the definition of foreign investment.

[71] The practice is not confined to the United States. The ASEAN Investment Treaty (1987) uses a similar formulation.

[72] This was established early in the jurisprudence of the Iran–US Claims Tribunal. See *Starret Housing Corp. v. Iran* (1987) 16 Iran–US CTR 112; *Sedco Inc. v. NIOC* (1987) 23 Iran–US CTR 23. Whereas US arbitrators took a liberal view on what amounted to a taking, the Iranian arbitrators sought to justify the takings as necessary under the circumstances and hence not compensable. In some situations, the latter viewpoint prevailed. For example, *United Company Inc. v. Iran* (1939) 23 Iran–US CTR 351 at 366–70, liability was not found on basis of a taking but on the basis of a violation of a contractual duty to take care of the property.

[73] In *Sapphire* (1963) 35 ILR 136, one of the alleged acts of taking was the insistence of NIOC of a right of veto over all aspects of the operation. The Indonesian control measures involved indirect takings and were considered in the literature. Board of Editors, 'The Measures Taken by the Indonesian Government Against Netherlands Enterprises' (1958) 5 Netherlands ILR 227. For other instances, see Whiteman, 8 *Digesti* 980–1016.

[74] The Harvard Draft Convention on International Responsibility, (1961) 55 AJIL 554 at 562, recognised the existence of a category of non-compensable takings. Article 10(5) reads:

countries, after decolonisation, preferred mixed economic systems which provided for state regulation of industry and business. A complete transference of the US notions of property will mean that the notion of non-compensable regulatory takings will have to be transferred to the international plane. But, this is not an idea that has been taken over into the international arena. There has been a selectivity that has generally favoured the interests of transnational corporations. The dilemma, simply, is that, whereas the abstract notion of property rights will afford greater property protection, its counterpart, the notion of noncompensable regulatory takings, will have disastrous effects. The argument that the notion that exists in US law as at present, including the notion of non-compensable regulatory takings, should be transferred will not be accepted by many arbitrators.[75] If it is necessary that guidance must be sought from US law, then the preference of the developing states would be to select an earlier stage of the development of US law at the time when the United States was also undergoing a stage of development. During these early stages, it is evident that the United States did recognise a wider category of regulatory taking which was not compensated.

The issue as to regulatory taking will be fought out among the developed states themselves. If, each time there is an antitrust measure used against a foreign investor, he could allege a taking under some treaty such as NAFTA which needs to be compensated, regulatory measures against foreign investors could become impossible.[76] It is unlikely that there would be such measures taken against developing country investors,

> An uncompensated taking of an alien or a deprivation of the use or enjoyment of property of an alien which results from the execution of tax laws; from a general change in the value of currency; from the action of the competent authorities of the State in the maintenance of public order, health or morality; or from the valid exercise of belligerent rights; or otherwise incidental to the normal operation of the laws of the State shall not be considered wrongful . . .

[75] This may account for the award in *Santa Elena* v. *Costa Rica*, which asserted that all environmental takings have to be compensated. Such a *per se* rule on regulatory takings cannot be found in any domestic system of law. It can only be explained on the basis of the preference for pro-business norms.

[76] An instance of the recognition of this by an arbitral tribunal is to be found in the award of the Iran–US Claims Tribunal in *Islamic Republic of Iran* v. *United States* (1988) 13 Iran–US CTR 173, where, in a dispute relating to the failure to return property belonging to Iran, the tribunal said that the presidential determination preventing the export of the property involved 'the exercise of a sovereign right which is not subject to review by an international tribunal'. But, the court in this case ordered that the property be compensated. The award will not mean that each time the power of preventing exports is exercised there should be compensation paid for interference with contract rights. If it does, there would be interesting consequences in the situations of extraterritorial exercise of the powers under the export control regulations.

as they are not of sufficient size to attract antitrust attention. The Exon–Florio Amendment to the Omnibus Trade Act, whereby the US President has been vested with powers to interfere with the inflow of large foreign investments into the US market on national security grounds, will also result in takings and compensation issues between the United States and states with which it makes treaties. It is possible to argue that the exercise of these powers violate the pre-entry rights of establishment which may be regarded as property rights as well as rights relating to national treatment. The European Community has already protested against the legislation on the ground that 'such action is not subject to judicial review and no compensation is foreseen'.[77] The US view will be that the exercise of the Presidential power under the legislation is regulatory and leads to non-compensable takings.

Features of issues relating to regulatory taking are evident in NAFTA litigation. In *S. D. Myers* v. *Canada*,[78] regulations relating to the processing of hazardous waste was involved. In *Pope and Talbot* v. *Canada*,[79] Canadian timber regulations were involved. In *Methanex* v. *United States*,[80] as in *Ethyl* v. *Canada*,[81] the litigation related to the regulation of substances that were regarded as environmentally unsafe. The issue of regulatory taking will plague the developed states more and will have to be settled in the context of litigation among them.[82]

In *Santa Elena* v. *Costa Rica*,[83] the tribunal addressed the issue of environmental regulation. It held that, where the taking is on environmental grounds, it must still be compensated. The tribunal stated that such expropriatory measures are 'similar to any other expropriatory measures that a state may take in order to implement its policies'. It is unlikely that arbitrators are going to deviate very much from this position. The *Santa Elena Case* itself was forced on Costa Rica through use of the Helms Amendment which threatens withdrawal of aid unless compensation is

---

[77] European Community, 'Statement on US Policy on Foreign Direct Investment' (1992) 31 ILM 467. See also US Treasury Regulations Pertaining to Mergers, Acquisitions and Takeovers by Foreign Persons, effective 21 November 1991, (1991) 31 ILM 424.

[78] NAFTA/UNCITRAL Tribunal, 21 October 2002.

[79] NAFTA/UNCITRAL Tribunal, 26 January 2000.

[80] NAFTA/UNCITRAL Tribunal, 7 August 2002.   [81] (1999) 38 ILM 708.

[82] Some US commentators have expressed the view that the NAFTA tribunals' 'nascent interpretations of Chapter 11 broaden the definition of compensable property interests in several significant ways, extend compensation requirements not only to legislative and administrative changes to the law but also to judicial decisions, and bypass ripeness and exhaustion requirement of the US domestic takings law'.

[83] (2000) 15 ICSID Rev 169 at 192.

paid for expropriated property.[84] The principal position of arbitrators will remain that that there will be little scope for regulatory taking to be pleaded in order to justify non-payment of compensation. *Dicta* to the effect that environmental takings are subject to compensation was followed in *Tecmed* v. *Mexico*.[85]

Yet, regulatory functions are a matter of sovereign right of the host state and there could be no right in international law to compensation or diplomatic protection in respect of such interference. There is already a recognition of such a category of non-compensable taking. The identification of when there is a compensable taking as a result of interference with property rights and when there is non-compensable regulatory taking is fraught with the same difficulties that exist in domestic law. There is, in theory, no reason why a state restructuring its economy cannot argue that there were non-compensable regulatory takings involved in circumstances where property rights were infringed by such restructuring. But, given the present state of the authority, such an argument is not likely to succeed. The authorities seem to divide equally on this issue. The change will occur only when, in the context of disputes between developed states, the absurdity of compensating regulatory taking comes to be recognised and clearer rules are stated to identify what constitutes a regulatory taking. Clearly, every taking motivated by an economic reason cannot qualify as non-compensable. But, where there is a preponderant public interest in the taking, particularly in a situation in which treaty commitments relating to the environment justify the interference with private property interests, tribunals must pause to give adequate consideration to whether the taking is a regulatory taking.

1.5.1. Survey of authorities

Older arbitral awards[86] that are quoted in this context are of little value, for they belong to a period when governments did not play an interventionist role in their economies. They were decided long before the dawn of the welfare state and its assumption of an interventionist role in the marketplace as well as in many spheres of economic and other activity.

---

[84] The tribunal itself provided this information in para. 24.

[85] *Tecmed* v. *Mexico* (2003) ICSID ARB (AF)/00/2, para. 21.

[86] *De Sabla* v. *Panama* (1934) 28 AJIL 602. The takings were in pursuance of land reform. There were internal procedures for securing relief by affected persons. The applicant had not resorted to them. The takings were held compensable. The *Santa Elena* award shows that things have not changed much.

The formulation of the rule that, from the foreign investors' point of view, there is no distinction between such takings and that therefore international law should not make a distinction between the two types of taking is most consistent with investor protection.[87] But, from the point of view of the host state, it could be argued that the foreign investor entered the state voluntarily, knowing the risk of such regulatory laws being applied against him, and that he should bear the risk of such adverse changes as any citizen of the state would. It was implicit in the process of securing admission as a foreign investor that there would be regulation of the foreign investment. Developing states have such legislation in order to ensure that their objectives of economic development are achieved. International law does not question the wisdom of such legislation, as each state has the sovereign power to make such legislation and to ensure that it is obeyed. The issue is simply whether there is an obligation under international law to ensure that there is payment of compensation where there is a taking that is justified on the basis of the regulation.

As long as the regulation was non-discriminatory and not accomplished through abusive processes, there should be an acceptance of the regulation. It should not be the function of international law to insulate the foreign investor from the regulatory regime of the host state's laws. The removal of the regulatory space for the state to control events which may pose dangers for its economic and political structure should never be the function of international law. The provision for the safety and security of its people must constitute the main function of a state. It would be difficult for a law that does not reconcile this interest with those of the foreign investor to find acceptance. To insist otherwise would be to create a regime akin to the regime created by the capitulation treaties of bygone times.[88] Domestic courts, in deciding issues of taking, balance the social benefits behind the taking against the public objectives that are furthered. An arbitral tribunal is incapable of such an exercise. Quite apart from that, many of the issues in the environmental area concern the international community as a whole and are incapable of being settled by an arbitral tribunal that draws its competence from the consent of the two immediate

---

[87] Higgins seems to prefer such a view. R. Higgins, 'The Taking of Property by the State' (1982) 176 *Hague Recueil* 331.

[88] Capitulation treaties ensured that the law of the home state of the alien applied to him while he was in the host state. The treaties were imposed by force and later repudiated as unequal treaties.

parties to the dispute.[89] The democratic legitimacy of a tribunal that is called upon to deal with such issues is suspect. In any event, developed countries, being themselves practitioners of such interference with foreign investment and increasingly being recipients of foreign investment, will not desire such an insulation of foreign investment from the scope of their regulatory laws. The arguments presented by the United States in the *Methanex Case* indicate that there is no desire on the part of developed states to relinquish regulatory control or to have such control restricted by any norm that requires the payment of compensation. The fact that the protection against expropriation is contained in a widely drafted formula in a treaty should not make any difference to these considerations. Many treaties now avoid the problem of regulatory expropriation by defining the investment that is protected in qualified terms so that only those investments that conform to the regulatory laws are given the protection of the treaty. In the recently concluded United States–Singapore Foreign Trade Agreement, an exchange of letters provides that regulatory takings are not to be treated as expropriations.

There is little guidance to be had from the existing authorities on the making of the distinction between compensable takings and regulatory, non-compensable takings in international law. The writings of scholars recognise the existence of the distinction but do not shed much light on the criteria for making the distinction.[90] The older arbitral awards offer little guidance on the more complex regulatory structures that have been devised. In the *Sapphire* arbitration, which involved contracts in the petroleum industry, the state oil corporation was constantly interfering with the operations of the foreign party. It insisted on the right of veto over many decisions that had to be made. This was held to amount to a taking. The arbitrator, Judge Cavin, observed that this 'was a typical case of a squeeze being placed by a state through a state-owned agency against a foreign company'. But, in the changed structure of the petroleum

---

[89] In the *Santa Elena* case, the dispute involved the conservation of an area which was the habitat of a protected species. In *SPP* v. *Egypt*, the dispute concerned the excavation of a site that was protected by the World Heritage Convention. It is true that a dispute could be dressed up so as to include such interests (as seems to have been the case in *Metalclad*, where the protection of rare cacti was stated to be the reason for the cancellation of the project, as an afterthought).

[90] Higgins, who discusses the issue thoroughly, neatly avoids the need for identifying the criteria for the distinction by suggesting that the distinction is not viable and that compensation is due for both types of takings. R. Higgins, 'The Taking of Property by the State' (1982) 176 *Hague Recueil*, 331.

industry in modern times, control of operations by state oil corporations have become so commonplace that such interference can hardly be said to be a taking if the foreign oil company packs up and leaves as the oil company in the *Sapphire* arbitration did. The contractual regime to which the foreign investor agreed would itself usually provide for the exercise of control by the state agency. The complex production-sharing agreements that are drawn up in the petroleum sphere contemplate the continuous supervision and control of the process of exploitation of oil by the state agency. There have been many changes in the different industries and in the attitudes to permissible state interference. It is unlikely that the mere giving of directions by a state agency that controls an industrial sector can amount to a taking. Such expansive notions of taking must be resisted, as regulatory control over economic and industrial sectors by states will otherwise become meaningless. The right of a state to so control sectors must remain a primary rule flowing from its sovereignty.

The more recent awards do not throw much light on the issue. An award of a US tribunal in *Revere Copper v. Overseas Private Investment Corporation*[91] is relevant in this context. The value of the award is diminished by the fact that the tribunal was a domestic tribunal considering the question as to whether the state insurance company ought to pay the claim of a foreign investor who had been subjected to an expropriatory measure.[92] The primary issue before the tribunal was whether the taking satisfied the requirements for the payment of the claim made by the injured investor against the insurance organisation. Yet, the problems involved in the area are illustrated by the facts. The case arose from a concession agreement for the mining of bauxite made by a subsidiary of the Revere Copper Company with the government of Jamaica. The agreement, which was to last for twenty-five years, contained a stabilisation clause that taxes and other financial liabilities on the part of the foreign company would remain as agreed for the duration of the concession. But, the government claimed higher sums as royalties after a few years on the ground of changed circumstances. The company found it difficult to continue operations under the new scheme and closed operations. It then claimed on the insurance agreement which protected it against 'expropriatory action' taken by the

---

[91] E.g. (1978) 17 ILM 1321, discussed by R. Higgins, 'The Taking of Property by the State' (1982) 176 *Hague Recueil* 331–7.

[92] The award was used by the US in its memorial in the *ELSI Case* to support the view that a state's interference with 'the freedom to make rational management decisions' amounted to a compensable taking. Memorial submitted by the USA (15 May 1987) in the *ELSI Case* [1989] ILJ Repts 15, p. 111).

foreign government, and the issue before the tribunal was whether the conduct of the Jamaican government in increasing the royalties by legislation in violation of the stabilisation clause in the agreement amounted to an expropriatory action. There was no direct taking by the government. The claimant had shut the plant down as its continued operation was deemed uneconomic. The tribunal found that there had been a taking by the government. The tribunal observed:

> In our view the effects of the Jamaican Government's actions in repudiating its long-term commitments to RJA [the subsidiary of Revere Copper] have substantially the same impact on effective control over use and operation as if the properties were themselves conceded by a concession contract that was repudiated . . . OPIC argues that it still has all the rights and property that it had before the events of 1974: it is in possession of the plants and other facilities; it has its mining lease; it can operate as it did before. This may be true in a normal sense but for the reasons stated below we do not regard RJA's control of the use and operation of its properties as any longer effective in view of the destruction by government actions of its contract rights.

The tribunal held that the loss of effective control over the operations amounted to expropriation. Effective control of the operations of the company was taken to mean the secure planning on the basis of the stabilisation clause which promised that there will be no change in the operating conditions of the company for twenty-five years. Higgins commented on the award as follows:

> Essentially, the tribunal took the view that – in this particular industry at least – effective control was inseparably linked with a stabilisation agreement. The explanation was offered that without it the risks could not be calculated, because 'what the government did yesterday it can undo tomorrow or next week or next month'. That comes very close to saying that all international contracts for the exploitation of resources are inherently immutable, and that any alteration of them (because it warns that further alteration *could* in principle occur again) takes away effective control; because effective control equals rational decision making based on an ability to calculate the risks.

The tribunal was formulating too wide a rule. Neither its proposition that any interference with the external operating conditions of the contract nor the proposition that the stabilisation clause immunises the contract from the regulatory regimes of the host state can be accepted as a proposition of international law. It is unlikely that international law will admit that fetters can be imposed through contractual arrangements on the sovereign rights of a state to act in its economic interest. As the dissenting opinion pointed out, 'by any reasonable standard what Revere treats as expropriatory is within the proper taxing power of the Jamaican nation'. Attitudes to stabilisation clauses have also undergone significant changes since the opinion in the award was expressed and the notions of immutability conjured up by the tribunal belong to a different period.[93] The power to increase taxation, which is akin to the power to increase royalties, is a regulatory power and the generally accepted view is that the exercise of this power cannot be regarded as a taking in violation of property rights, unless there has been such excessive taxation as would indicate a disguised expropriation.[94]

In Amco v. Indonesia,[95] there was a withdrawal of licences without which the foreign investor could not have operated in the host state. The withdrawal was due to the alleged failure on the part of the foreign investor to capitalise the venture in accordance with the commitments he had given prior to entry. The tribunal did not pronounce on the question of whether the cancellation of the licences amounted to a taking. Instead, the award was based on the procedure followed prior to the cancellation of the licences. The failure on the part of the government organ to follow minimum standards of procedure was held to be a denial of justice and damages were awarded on that basis. The inference that is to be drawn is that there could be an interference with the property rights of the foreign investor in accordance with the law of the host state, particularly in circumstances in which the foreign investor had undertaken obligations as a condition of his entry and does not satisfy those conditions. Minimum procedural safeguards must be followed prior to a finding of non-satisfaction of the conditions. The measures that were contemplated were in the nature of sanctions against breaking commitments and can be rationalised on the ground that the foreign investor had committed a transgression which he could have avoided by honouring his commitments. The cancellation of

---

[93] For example, Aminoil v. Kuwait (1982) 22 ILM 976.

[94] Gudmundson v. Iceland (1960) 30 ILR 253. The European Court was not prepared to accept a 25 per cent tax as confiscatory. Though taxation is included in the lists of indirect expropriation, it will be difficult to maintain that taxation involves expropriation. Many investment treaties provide specifically for situations of excessive taxation. They would require parties to consult in order to settle any dispute but would not treat such taxation as amounting to a taking. Yet, there could be efforts to cloak a taking through the exercise of taxation powers. But, this would be unusual.

[95] (1988) 27 ILM 1281.

the licences was a sanctioning measure which could have been avoided by the foreign investor.[96] But *Amco* v. *Indonesia* does not provide any guidance as to measures taken without any prior indication as to expected conduct.

There have been many awards involving the cancellation of licences since *Amco* v. *Indonesia*. In all of them, it is not the cancellation that is the focus of attention and the basis for the finding of an obligation to pay compensation but the faulty procedure that preceded the cancellation. Thus, in *Metalclad*, the finding was that there was a lack of transparency in the manner in which the licensing system was administered.[97] The finding was later overturned by a Canadian court. In *Middle East Cement Shipping Ltd* v. *Egypt*,[98] again, the absence of notice prior to the cancellation of the licence and the sale of the property of the foreign investor was the basis for liability. It would appear that the inference that, had proper administrative procedure been followed, there would be no liability is a safe one to draw. Licences are often subjected to conditions. Their withdrawal through proper procedure based on a failure to abide by the conditions should not be subject to compensation. Such a situation rewards fault.

One further problem is that decisions in the regulatory field are administrative decisions taken not by the courts of the host state but by executive bodies. Even in advanced administrative law systems, it is recognised that the types of procedural safeguard which should be followed, prior to the taking of these decisions will depend on the circumstances of each situation. The violation of the property rights of individuals is generally expected to be preceded by hearings. But, the situation may well be different where there is a rescission of a licence for non-satisfaction of a condition for in these circumstances no right could have arisen without the satisfaction of the condition. Could a lesser type of procedural protection be sufficient in these circumstances? Could procedural protection be dispensed with where it is clear that there had been no satisfaction of

---

[96] See further *Emanuel Too* v. *United States* (1989) 23 Iran–US CTR 378, where a cancellation of a licence for liquor was revoked for tax reasons. The tribunal held that 'a state is not responsible for loss of property or for other economic disadvantage resulting from *bona fide* general taxation or any other action that is commonly accepted as within the police power, provided it is not discriminatory and is not designed to cause the alien to abandon the property to the state or sell it at a distress price'.

[97] The case cited with approval another award involving licensing, *Biloune* v. *Ghana* (1990) 95 ILR 184. Withdrawals of permits and similar administrative measures are involved in several awards. *Lauder* v. *Czech Republic* (2003); *CME* v. *Czech Republic* (2003); *Middle East Cement Shipping and Handling Co.* v. *Egypt* (2002); *Goetz* v. *Burundi* (2001) 26 YCA 24.

[98] (2002) ICSID ARB/99/6.

the condition? A state should act safely in such circumstances and provide procedural safeguards. Such procedural safeguards are now stated in investment treaties. It must be an assumption that, where these procedural safeguards are satisfied, the taking will be considered a regulatory taking. It cannot be expected that a foreign company which was permitted conditional entry and was subjected to interference because of the non-satisfaction of those conditions could claim compensation for the recission of any licence upon which entry was made.

The *Amco* v. *Indonesia* award seems to envelop the whole area in the formula of denial of justice which is unsatisfactory.[99] The notion of denial of justice was formulated prior to the growth of administrative decision-making and catered for the judicial settlement of disputes. The fact that it has been attempted more frequently in investment cases in recent times does not mean that the fundamental criteria that applied to it have changed.[100] The rule on denial of justice has met with much opposition. The salutary reminder of Judge Tanaka in the *Barcelona Traction Case* that it is 'an extremely serious matter to make a charge of denial of justice *vis-à-vis* a state' must be kept in mind. Whether the notion of denial of justice could be satisfactorily extended to the sphere of administrative decision-making is doubtful. Administrative systems permit decisions to be made without normal procedural safeguards in certain circumstances. What these circumstances are varies over time within each system and the variance between different administrative systems of different states must be enormous.

Within the common law systems, the general tendency has been to ensure that there must be procedural safeguards when the legitimate expectations of individuals are affected by administrative decisions. But, there is no uniform rule on the point. Public interest in the taking of effective and quick decisions may supersede the need for any procedural safeguards. Whether an international court or tribunal should have the power to second-guess the existence of circumstances that will enable the

---

[99] There is also the further question as to whether an arbitration tribunal which derives its jurisdiction from an investment contract can pronounce on the issue of a denial of justice resulting from an administrative act which is a public law act falling outside the scope of the contract. Certainly, an international court could do so when asked to pronounce on an issue of state responsibility, but such competence cannot usually exist in an arbitration tribunal constituted at the behest of an individual party to an arbitration agreement.

[100] For references to it in modern cases, see *Azinian* v. *Mexico* (1998) 5 ICSID Rpts 269; *Loewen* v. *United States* (2003) 42 ILM 811; and *Yaung Chi Oo Ltd* v. *Myanmar* (2003) 42 ILM 430.

administrative decision to be made without the procedural safeguards will remain a moot question.

In certain circumstances, the sanctions that are imposed for non-satisfaction of conditions attached to foreign investments are punitive in nature, and it is well established that the imposition of punitive sanctions do not amount to a taking by a state. The cancellation of a licence for non-satisfaction of a condition does, arguably, have the necessary punitive element. There are many unresolved questions that arise as a result of the transfer of the distinction between regulatory, non-compensable takings and compensable takings to the international sphere. As in the municipal sphere, the fashioning of any meaningful theory to distinguish between the two categories will be a difficult task. Developing states will institute more administrative controls over foreign investment. The need for the making of the distinction will become more apparent. As yet, no conclusive criteria exist in either the domestic or the international systems, apart from the identification of certain obvious regulatory acts as non-compensable. The literature on the subject also does not give much guidance on the issue.

In such a controversy, the nuance in the approach adopted in *Marvin Feldman* v. *Mexico*[101] affords some possibility of accommodating the conflicting interests of the host state and the foreign investor. The case concerned taxation, which, *prima facie*, would be regarded as an instance of non-compensable taking. But, the allegation was that rebates that would ordinarily be granted to an exporter of cigarettes were not granted to the claimant, a foreign company operating an export business in Mexico. Mexico's case rested on the requirement that invoices should be produced for claiming rebates and that the claimant had not produced such invoices.

Faced with this issue, the tribunal admitted that the state had a considerable leeway in regulating its economy and the discomfort caused to the foreign investor should not be dressed up as expropriation. The tribunal observed that 'not all government regulatory activity that makes it difficult or impossible for an investor to carry out a particular business, change in the law or change in the application of existing laws that makes it uneconomical to continue a particular business is an expropriation'. So, too, the reduction of profits as a consequence of regulation cannot be characterised as expropriation.[102]

---

[101] (2003) 42 ILM 625.

[102] Para. 112. The *Ethyl* theory of depreciation of value of shares and the *Methanex* theory of loss of earnings and profits as expropriaton are diminished by the *dictum*. The tribunal

The tribunal consistently spoke of a balance. The conflicting interests in respect of which the balance must be maintained are identified by the tribunal in the following passage:[103]

> The Tribunal notes that the ways in which governmental authorities may force a company out of business, or significantly reduce the economic benefits of its business, are many. In the past, confiscatory taxation, denial of access to infrastructure or necessary raw materials, imposition of unreasonable regulatory regimes, among others, have been considered to be expropriatory actions. At the same time, governments must be free to act in the broader public interest through protection of the environment, new or modified tax regimes, the granting or withdrawal of government subsidies, reductions or increases in tariff levels, imposition of zoning restrictions and the like. Reasonable governmental regulation of this type cannot be achieved if any business that is adversely affected may seek compensation, and it is safe to say that customary international law recognises this.

It is in identifying when the balance is tilted towards the interests of the foreign investor that problems arise. As the tribunal put it, 'it is much less clear when governmental decree that interferes with broadly-defined property rights crosses the line from valid regulation to a compensable taking, and it is fair to say that no one has come up with a fully satisfactory means of drawing this line'.[104] Apart from discrimination and arbitrariness in procedure and the idea that the circumstances should 'rise to a level of violation',[105] there is no further guidance given.

It is possible to construct a picture of when regulation crosses the line to become expropriation. It is clear that any depreciation in the value of the property will be sufficient. That expansive notion, to be found in the litigation strategy in cases like *Ethyl*, will no longer find favour. With the phrase, 'tantamount to expropriation', in investment treaties coming

---

stated: 'Governments, in their exercise of regulatory power, frequently change their laws and regulations in response to changing economic circumstances or changing political, economic or social considerations. Those changes may well make certain activities less profitable or even uneconomic to continue.' The *dictum* will require environmental regulation also to be reconsidered in the *Santa Elena* case.

[103] Para. 103.

[104] Para. 100. The tribunal relied to a large extent on the analysis in the American Law Institute, *Restatement (Third) on Foreign Relations Law* (1987), section 712, comment g. But, this analysis predates the problems relating to environmental regulations that have been the focus of the more recent awards and discussions.

[105] Para. 113.

to be treated as a mere surplusage,[106] the scope for such an argument has diminished considerably. Discriminatory treatment is a criterion for expropriation. But, absence of discrimination was stated to be a requirement for expropriation at all times. In any event, where discrimination in regulatory mechanisms is based on legitimate grounds, the discrimination is regarded as legitimate.[107] The stronger the public purpose behind the regulation, the less is the scope for the regulation being treated as expropriation. A general measure such as an exchange control that uniformly affects all business cannot amount to a compensable taking.[108] This is consistent with the position in most domestic law systems.

The only clear situation where the line between regulation and expropriation is crossed that is disclosed in the existing authorities is where there is an absence of procedural safeguards against the exercise of regulatory powers. In these circumstances, a situation akin to denial of justice prevails. Denial of justice normally applies to the exercise of judicial functions. But, it would appear that, where a discretionary power in a regulatory authority is exercised without procedural safeguards and the absence of such safeguards so transgresses the ordinary sense of justice, liability will arise. It is not every transgression that has this result. The transgression must be of such a kind as to justify international concern.

The starting point must always be that the regulatory interference is presumptively non-compensable. The *per se* rule in the *Santa Elena* award has no place in the law, as it is not supported by any authority, either in domestic legal systems or in international law. That presumption against compensation is strengthened in circumstances where the regulation is in areas of environmental protection or cultural preservation which are of significance to the international community. It is strengthened where the public interests are so dominant as to overwhelm individual interests. It is weakened where there is discrimination that cannot be explained in a legitimate manner. It is weakened also where the exercise is not

---

[106] *Pope and Talbot* v. *Canada* (2002) 41 ILM 1347; *Feldman* v. *Mexico* (2003) 42 ILM 625, para. 100.

[107] *Feldman* v. *Mexico* (2003) 42 ILM 625.

[108] *CMS Gas* v. *Argentina*, (2003) 42 ILM 778, para. 23. The dispute cannot be said to arise from an investment if this happens (see para. 27 of the award). The tribunal said that a state is entitled to follow its own policy choices (para. 29). See also *CME* v. *Czech Republic* (2002), para. 589, to the effect that a general measure cannot be a taking. Where the general measure is applied in a discriminatory manner to a specific investment, this could amount to a taking. The same case supports this view.

accompanied by due process and other procedural safeguards that amount to a denial of justice in terms of international law. The construction of a model of decision-making in the area along these lines is a vital need. The case law that has been developed is in no way inconsistent with such a model.[109] The contrary decisions can be explained on factual and other grounds.[110]

The above analysis is consistent with the side letter on expropriation accompanying the Singapore–United States Free Trade Agreement concluded in 2003. Explaining the provision on expropriation, the letter contains the following paragraph on regulatory takings:

> Except in rare circumstances, non-discriminatory regulatory actions, designed and applied to protect public welfare objectives, such as public health, safety and the environment do not constitute indirect expropriation.

The provision neatly disposes of the possibility of the *per se* rule in *Santa Elena* ever being applied to expropriation under the treaty. The side letter merely states the obvious, and seeks to restore the balance between expropriation and regulation.[111]

It is instructive to compare the situation in international trade law. GATT provisions acknowledge that deviations from market access rules may be made if they are 'necessary' to achieve regulatory objectives.[112] But, the least trade-restrictive alternative reasonably possible should be used. There cannot be arbitrary application of the regulation, nor should it be a disguise for a trade restriction. The final test is one of balancing the values protected by the regulation against the impact of the regulation on trade.

Though such balancing tests may be useful in providing guidance, the starting point of analysis, as indicated, must always be that the state has a right to protect its interests. A tribunal must show reluctance to review the state's assessment of its own needs for the regulation. Unless

---

[109] Cases like *Amco* v. *Indonesia* support this model.

[110] *Santa Elena* may seem to conflict. The *per se* rule in it is clearly in error. *Tecmed* was wrong in accepting the rule. It is not supported by awards such as *Feldman* or *Pope and Talbot*. But, in *Santa Elena*, as in *Metalclad* and *SPP* v. *Egypt*, the environmental and other motives adduced by the state were afterthoughts. So, too, in *S. D. Myers* v. *Canada*, the Basel Convention obligations were *ex post facto* rationalisations of the regulation, thought up at the time of the proceedings.

[111] The notion of balancing is implicit in the *dicta* of the award in *Tecmed* v. *Mexico*, para. 122, which refers to the proportionality between the public interest and the regulatory measure.

[112] Article XX(b) and (d).

there is some strong *prima facie* evidence of abuse, there should be no interference. The fact that the protection of similar values in other states is achieved through similar regulation will add weight to the legitimacy of the regulation of a respondent state. Where clear discrimination exists, the regulation is unlawful. It would also cross the boundary into a taking where the regulation is a disguise for a taking. Here, the issue is as to the primary motive for the interference. As the tribunal in *Feldman* noted, there can be no satisfactory solution proffered to the thorny issue as to when regulation transforms itself into expropriation. Each case has to be considered separately.

2. The exercise of management control over the investment

Interference by the state to take over management and control of the foreign investor's affairs is *prima facie* a taking by the state which should be compensated.[113] The foreign shareholder is entitled to such control and management of his investment or property as he pleases, subject of course to the general laws of the host state. The extent of this exception that the regulatory laws of the host state have a role to play in the determination of the rights of the foreign investor generates considerable problems. The exception may be wide enough, if some views are accepted, to undermine the general rule altogether.

The exception flows from the fact that the host state has interests to safeguard as far as the operation of the investment is concerned. The *ELSI Case* illustrates the nature of the interests of the host state that could be involved. The foreign investor has to operate within the confines of the company and securities legislation of the host state. Interference based on such legislation is fully justified, provided procedures indicated in them satisfy due process standards. There may also be an interest of the host state in ensuring that the workforce of the foreign-owned company is not left without employment as a result of the decisions of the foreign investor. The state has an interest in ensuring that the economy of the area in which the foreign investor operates is not affected by the decisions he makes. The need for the protection of such interests entitles the host state to intervene in the management of the company. In the *ELSI Case* as well as in some of the awards of the Iran–US Claims

---

[113] An editorial comment in the *Netherlands International Law Journal* suggested that the assumption of management control over the Indonesian tobacco plantations amounted to nationalisation.

Tribunal, the conflicts in the interests of the foreign investor and the host state were graphically illustrated. The statement that an interference with management and control of a foreign-controlled company is a taking is only a generalisation that provides a starting point for discussion and no more.

In the *ELSI Case*, the US-controlled company in Italy which was the subject of the dispute between the United States and Italy, was failing. The fact that the company was failing had important consequences under Italian law. Quite apart from issues of bankruptcy, there were requirements in Italian law applying to all companies relating to minimum levels of capitalisation. In modern company law systems, such measures are usually taken by states in order to protect the integrity of stock markets. The state will also have an interest in the effect the failure of a company will have on local employment, particularly if the company was a large one. Such an interest in companies formed by foreign investors is logical, as they usually involve the employment of a large workforce. In the *ELSI Case*, when the foreign company contemplated the dismissal of a part of its workforce, there was widespread industrial action. The state had an obvious interest in ensuring that the dismissals did not lead to unemployment in an already economically depressed part of the country. Bankruptcy proceedings that were later instituted prevented the management from conducting an orderly liquidation of the company, which may have enabled the foreign company to realise a greater value for its assets. Interference in these circumstances in the management and control of the company by the host state was held to be justifiable. The state had a compelling interest in ensuring that the impact on its economy of the failure of the company was reduced or eliminated. The steps it takes to achieve this objective cannot be considered to be such an interference with the foreign investor's management rights as to amount to a compensable taking. Again, a regulatory interference was involved and the approach of the International Court of Justice was not to second-guess whether the interference was necessary.

The analysis which was made of similar problems by the Iran–US Claims Tribunal is in agreement with the view taken, that interference with management and control will not *per se* amount to a taking by the state. Though there are absolute statements of the rule in some of the awards that were made, there are qualifications of the rule in some of the later awards. The disputes, which involved the taking over of the management of US-controlled companies by the Iranian government, concerned companies whose management had fled the country as a result of the anti-American hostility that had been unleashed by the Iranian revolution. The government had then enacted legislation to deal with companies that were left without effective management. The legislation permitted the appointment of managers to companies whose managerial staff had left the country. The legislation could be justified on the basis that the government had to get the economic life of the country back into gear and that one of the ways of doing this was to assume control over the companies that were deserted by their management. But, if such an assumption of control was permanent, then it destroys the rights of the shareholders in the company to appoint a new management, and it may be regarded as a taking. The awards of the tribunals could be reconciled on the basis of this distinction. The awards of the Iran–US Claims Tribunal must, however, be used cautiously, as the Tribunal had a wider mandate regarding what amounted to a taking.

2.1. Cancellation of permits and licences

The cancellation of permits and licences involves a regulatory taking and has been dealt with in that context above. Where licences and permits are necessary to operate in certain sectors of the economy and these licences are withdrawn, the foreign investor's ability to conduct his business will be adversely affected. It could be argued that such measures involve a taking even if they do not affect the ability of the foreign investor to continue with the business or in any way affect the ownership of the property of the foreign investor. In modern investment treaties, such licences are protected, as they fall within the definition of investments.

Technically, the granting of a licence involves the conferment of a privilege in a Hohfeldian sense. There is no vesting of a right in the foreign investor. Where the privilege is revoked, the state is not benefited in any sense. Hence, it would be difficult to say that there had been a taking by the state in situations where there is a revocation of a licence. However, the foreign investor may have to relinquish his business as a result of such a termination and the assets of the business may then vest in some state entity. This will be so where the state entity is a partner in the venture with the foreign investor. In the alternative, it may have to be sold for a lesser price than would otherwise have been the case.

In the administrative law systems in the common law world, there is generally no review permitted for the revocation of licences as they are privileges the conferment of which is entirely at the discretion of the state.[114] There are many awards of arbitral tribunals and claims commissions which have asserted that the withdrawal of licences or the imposition of controls do not amount to the taking of property.[115] Such regulatory takings will fall within the category of lawful takings for which no compensation needs to be paid. It has always been the case that the taking of alien property as a means of the exaction of a criminal penalty is lawful and that such taking need not be compensated as compensation will take away the whole purpose behind the imposition of the criminal sanction.[116]

But, the law stated in these older cases must be reviewed in the light of new developments. In most administrative systems, it is now recognised that cancellations of licences have a significance beyond the withdrawal of a privilege conferred by the state. It withdraws a right that is essential to the earning of a livelihood or the carrying on of business. In these circumstances, the licence gives rise to a legitimate expectation that is protected by due process requirements. The law is increasingly coming to accept that such a withdrawal must not be lightly done without warnings to the licensee to desist from behaviour or to fulfil conditions attached to the licence. It must be preceded by an opportunity for the licensee to explain why the licence should not be withdrawn. In *Amco v. Indonesia*,[117] the several tribunals which dealt with the dispute were unanimous in holding that the due process requirement will be recognised in international law and that withdrawal of foreign investment licences are subject to the rule. The withdrawal of a licence may be considered a regulatory act, particularly where the conditions attached to the licence have not been satisfied. But, the substantive right is subject to procedural regularity. The proper exercise of the substantive right of revocation for non-satisfaction of the condition is not compensable as it is a regulatory act. But, if it is done without procedural regularity, that irregularity gives rise to the duty to pay compensation.

Cancellation of licences on environmental grounds will become more frequent with the increasing concern for the protection of the environment. Such cancellations will often put an end to the foreign investment. They will usually not amount to compensable takings. In *Murphyores Ltd v. The Commonwealth*, a concession had been given for sand-mining on

---

[114] *Murphyores Ltd v. The Commonwealth* (1976) 136 CLR 1.
[115] *Kugele v. Polish State* [1931–2] AD 69; *Claim of Erna Spielberg* (1958) 8 Whiteman, *Digest* 988; and other awards mentioned at pp. 988–9 in the same volume of Whiteman's *Digest*.
[116] A. Freeman, *International Responsibility of States* (1938), 518.
[117] I ICSID Rpts 509.

Fraser Island, close to the Great Barrier Reef, to two US companies. The minerals did not have a local market. They had to be exported. An environmental study found that the sand-mining was harmful to the Great Barrier Reef. The Australian government refused to grant export licences for the export of the minerals. This effectively terminated the operations of the companies. The Australian High Court rejected the claims of the two companies for compensation on the basis that no compensable taking was involved. The Australian government also resisted efforts on the part of the home state of the foreign investor to ensure that compensation be paid to the foreign investor.

The awards in cases like *Amco* v. *Indonesia* and *Middle Eastern Cement Shipping Ltd* v. *Egypt* have found liability not for the cancellation of the permits but for the lack of due process prior to such cancellation. In *Metalclad*, again, it was not the cancellation that triggered liability, but the absence of transparency attending the process. A court of review found the tribunal's view on transparency to be improper. The withdrawal of a licence after following proper procedure is an instance of a non-compensable regulatory taking. The foreign investor would be aware of the circumstances in which the licence is to operate. The cancellation is usually a punitive measure for not abiding by the purpose behind the regulation or the conditions to which the licence is subject. As such, the need for compensation does not arise from this situation, provided procedural safeguards had not been violated. Recent awards have emphasised the need for due process safeguards prior to the cancellation of licences and have deemed cancellations without due process as violations of treatment standards as well as of the expropriation provisions.[118]

2.2. Takings by agents and mobs

This is an area for the application of the rules on state responsibility for injuries to aliens. It has more features in common with confiscatory takings than the type of economic takings which have been considered so

---

[118] Besides *Biloune* v. *Ghana* and *Metalclad* v. *Mexico*, see *Middle East Shipping and Handling Co.* v. *Egypt* (2002) ICSID ARB/99/6, para. 143; *Lauder* v. *Czech Republic; CME* v. *Czech Republic;* and *Goetz* v. *Burundi* (2001) 26 YCA 24. The creeping of administrative law theory into the area is evidenced by these awards. From such awards, it is possible to launch into the whole array of administrative law notions such as legitimate expectations, which has been done in cases like *ADF* v. *United States* and *Tecmed* v. *Mexico*. The present phase of the extension of this area of the law is based on domestic administrative law notions, borrowed largely from common law states.

far. But, having made the point that they are different, it is convenient to consider them here. The rule is that, where there is destruction of property during civil strife or an insurgency, the state is liable for the destruction if it had failed in its duty to protect the property of the foreign investor. It follows that, if there is active participation or instigation of the persons causing the damage by the state or its agents, then responsibility for the damage will arise. It is also clear that there must be a definite link between the perpetrators of the damage and the state or some attributability of the damage to the state through a theory of negligence. These rules have been established through many arbitral awards. They have also been stated in the Draft Code of the International Law Commission on State Responsibility.

The Iran–US Claims Tribunal dealt on several occasions with the situation where property was taken or destroyed by mobs and groups. In all these situations, the essential element was the establishment of the link between the revolutionary gangs and the government which emerged. In the early stages of the revolution, there were several gangs with which the emerging government did not have any links whatever. The Tribunal refused to hold Iran liable for the activities of these gangs. But, when the revolution took hold, groups emerged with links with and authority from the state. Iran was held liable for the acts of these groups.[119]

In the *ELSI Case*, one of the factors focused on by the United States in making its case against Italy was that the occupation of the factory by the workers was promoted by the mayor of the city in which the plant was situated and that he had a sufficient connection with the state to make the state liable for the failure of the company. The court found that the occupation of the factory by the workers was peaceful and that there was no indication that production was affected by the occupation.[120] The inference is that there may be responsibility in the state for the omission, if there had been damage caused by the occupation and it had been condoned by the authorities. In such a situation, the omission to act could have consequences that are akin to a taking. For such a consequence to follow, it must be shown that the disturbance was not an ordinary consequence of the actions taken by the foreign investor himself and that there was a link between the state and the persons whose acts caused the disturbance. Though the existence of a bilateral treaty will enhance the inference of liability arising from the omission to give protection, liability

---

[119] On attrubutablity, see *Yeager* v. *Iran* (1987) 17 Iran–US CTR 92.
[120] Para. 105. At para. 108, the Court said that the dismissal of 800 workers 'could not reasonably be expected to pass without some protest'.

in such circumstances flows from a rule of customary international law on state responsibility. Where an investment treaty exists, the requirement that the foreign investor should be given full protection and security will ensure that the situation is covered.[121] In this case, the matter will be dealt with as a failure to provide the requisite treatment rather than as a taking of property.

Where the armed forces of a state are involved in a taking of property, the attribution of the act to the state is clear. In *Amco* v. *Indonesia*, the taking was effected by the army, but the tribunal held that there was no attributability, as the army was acting in order to further the interests of its own pension fund. In *AAPL* v. *Sri Lanka*, there was destruction of property by the army during hostilities. Liability was based on the state's failure to protect the property. In *Wena Hotels* v. *Egypt*, there was interference by the army. Where the army is involved, the attributability of the act of taking to the state is easier to establish.[122]

2.3. Excessive taxation

Taxation is within the sovereign power of a state. There is no rule in international law limiting the power of a state to impose taxes within its territory.[123] But 'excessive and repetitive tax' measures have a confiscatory effect and could amount to indirect expropriation.[124] A uniform increase in taxation cannot by itself have such an effect. But, where a foreign investment is singled out and subjected to heavy taxation, a clear situation of expropriation can be made out. Such a result may not follow where sufficient justification for such taxation exists. The taxing of windfall profits (i.e. profits which arise without any act on the part of the investor) cannot amount to a taking.[125] Thus, taxation of the oil industry for windfall profits due to price hikes cannot amount to a taking.[126] Where the situation of excessive taxation is dealt with in investment treaties, the mechanism used is joint consultation between the parties as to whether the excessive tax should be permissible.[127] *Marvin Feldman* v. *Mexico* supports the use of a balancing test to deal with the situation where a complainant alleges unfair taxation. This would take into account the objects of the tax

---

[121] *American Machine Tools* v. *Zaire* (1997) 36 ILM 1531.
[122] But see *Yaung Chi Oo Ltd* v. *Myanmar* (2003) ILM 430.
[123] Sol Picciotto, *International Business Taxation* (1992).
[124] World Bank, *Report and Guidelines* (1992) 31 ILM 1375.
[125] *Aminoil* v. *Kuwait* (1982) 21 ILM 976.
[126] See, for the US, *Crude Oil Windfall Tax* (1980), upheld in *US* v. *Ptasynki*, 462 US 74 (1983).
[127] The Canadian treaties use this technique.

measures, the requirements that have to be satisfied if rebates are to be allowed and the need to prevent evasion, and balance these against the interests of the foreign investor to ensure non-discrimination and fairness. Except in certain obvious circumstances, it is unlikely that a charge of unfair taxation would succeed. Many investment treaties deal with taxation separately, requiring that allegations of unfair taxation be dealt with through consultation between the two treaty partners.[128] This removes the area from the scope of the taking provision in the treaty.

2.4. Expulsion of the foreign investor

The expulsion of the foreign investor will amount to a taking if the purpose of the expulsion is the taking of his property.[129] But, where national security or other sufficient grounds exist for the expulsion, this will be different. Objectively reasonable factors for the expulsion must exist if it were to be justifiable on national security grounds. A tribunal which has jurisdiction over the taking on the basis that it is a violation of a foreign investment agreement does not have jurisdiction to pronounce on the human rights issues involved in the taking.[130] This is a sensible idea, for a commercial tribunal has no justification to pronounce upon disputes that do not have a basis in commercial decisions.

2.5. Freezing of bank accounts

The freezing of the bank accounts of a foreign investor could amount to a taking of property in certain circumstances. Where bank accounts are frozen on the grounds that it is necessary to do so in order to investigate a crime or a violation of banking regulations, the interference would be justified. But, where it is done in the process of an expropriation of the property of the foreign investor and as a part of an endeavour to deny him all his property rights, there is a strong case for the view that the freezing of the accounts amounts to a taking.[131]

2.6. Exchange controls

Exchange controls are imposed in order to meet economic crises and prevent the flight of capital from the state. These measures affect the whole

---

[128] Canadian investment treaties adopt this mechanism.
[129] Biloune v. Ghana (1990) 95 ILR 184.   [130] Ibid.
[131] F. A. Mann, Legal Aspects of Money (5th ed., 1992).

economy uniformly and cannot be considered exprorpriation despite the fact that it affects foreign business along with local business. Though there may be a violation of the right to repatriation involved in the imposition of exchange controls, it is now accepted that such controls do not violate the treaty provisions on expropriation. The matter was considered in *CMS Gas Transmission Co. v. Argentina.*[132] The tribunal rightly held that a distinction should be drawn 'between measures of a general economic nature, particularly in the context of the economic and financial emergency and measures specifically directed to the investment's operation'. The making of economic choices cannot be prevented by treaties in these circumstances.

3. Illegal takings

The taking of foreign property by a state is *prima facie* lawful. Such legality is, however, subject to conditions. The taking of foreign property will be lawful only if such taking was for a public purpose and is not discriminatory. There is a duty in international law to pay compensation for the taking of alien property. Non-payment affects legality. But, the standard of compensation which must be paid is a matter of controversy. The controversy relating to the standard of compensation is dealt with in Chapter 9 below. There is a controversial view that a taking in breach of contractual commitments is also unlawful. This view also needs more exhaustive treatment, and is dealt with in Chapter 8 below. There is general agreement that a taking which lacks a public purpose and a discriminatory taking are illegal in international law. Where a taking is done in violation of a treaty, the taking will be considered illegal.

The requirement of a public purpose and the requirement that the taking is not discriminatory are dealt with in this section. The illegality which is attached to a taking in violation of a treaty is also considered. The final section considers the consequences in international law of an illegal taking.

3.1. The taking must be for a public purpose

It is generally conceded that the requirement of public purpose for a taking to be lawful is not much of a limitation in modern times. The origin of the doctrine is probably to be found in the statement of public purpose as

---

[132] (2003) ICSID ARB/01/8, para. 25.

a limitation on the powers of eminent domain by Grotius. *Dicta* in later arbitral awards which are used to support the existence of the limitation are equivocal at best.[133] *Dicta* in some arbitral awards questioned the need for the requirement of public purpose.[134] Writers are divided on the need for the requirement.[135] But, the requirement continues to be stated in all bilateral investment treaties. This may be due to the compulsion to follow a time-tested formula rather than to any conviction that the requirement continues to have any force.[136]

The public purpose limitation may have had some significance in the period when the distinction between confiscation and nationalisation had an importance in the law, for the motive behind the taking was the basis of the distinction. The distinction itself originated at a time when state interference occurred only in exceptional circumstances. Writing in 1941 on the distinction made between types of taking of alien property, a commentator referred to the increasing difficulty of making such distinctions 'especially since states have more and more abandoned the *laissez-faire* conception of their functions and become welfare states interfering daily in all imaginable realms of private activities by all imaginable measures and procedures'.[137] State regulation of private property five decades later is so commonplace that it will be difficult for tribunals sitting outside the state to question the motives behind the taking. Yet, the strength of

---

[133] *Walter Fletcher Smith Case* (1930) 24 AJIL 384 is a leading authority on the point. But, the arbitrator was there referring to an internal requirement of Cuban law. In addition, the taking was found to be for 'amusement and private profit'. As such, it was a confiscation more than an expropriation. *David Goldberg Case* (1930) 2 UNRIAA 901 concerned a military requisition. In *Sabbatino v. Banco Nacional de Cuba*, 193 F. Supp. 375 at 384 (1961), Judge Dimock found the Cuban nationalisation invalid for the want of a public purpose.

[134] *Shufeldt Claim* (1930) 2 UNRIAA 1079 at 1095: '[I]t is perfectly competent for the Government of Guatemala to enact any decree they like and for any reasons they see fit, and such reasons are no concern of the Tribunal.' The PCIJ in the *Oscar Chinn Case* (1934) PCfJ Series A/B, No. 63 at 79 said that the Belgian state 'was the sole judge' of the situation.

[135] G. White, *Nationalisation of Foreign Property* (1961), 150, S. Friedman, *Expropriation in International Law* (1977), 142, and C. F. Amerasinghe, *State Responsibility for Injuries to Aliens* (1967), 138, oppose the need for the requirement. However, the older authors favoured it. B. A. Wortley, *Expropriation, in Public International Law* (1959), 24–5; McNair, 'The Seizure of Property and Enterprises in Indonesia' (1959) 6 *Netherlands International Law Review* 218 at 243; Kunz, 'The Mexican Appropriations' (1940) 34 AJIL 48 at 54.

[136] Interestingly, the Abs–Shawcross Convention, an effort at a multilateral treaty on investment protection, left out the requirement. S. D. Metzger, 'Multilateral Convention for the Protection of Private Foreign Investment' (1960) 9 JPL 40, supported the leaving out of the requirement, but not Schwarzenberger in an article in the same volume of the journal.

[137] J. H. Herz, 'Expropriation of Foreign Property' (1941) 35 AJIL 243 at 251–2.

public purpose may serve to identify whether a taking is regulatory or not.

The requirement is kept alive in the practice of states. Thus, the notes of both the United States and the United Kingdom protesting against the Libyan oil nationalisations refer to the belief of these states that the nationalisations were not motivated by reasons of public utility.[138] These reasons were also pressed before the arbitral tribunals which later came to deal with the disputes arising from the Libyan nationalisations. There is little doubt that the requirement will be used as necessary for lawful nationalisations in the future, but it is unlikely that it will constitute more than a subsidiary, throwaway argument for illegality.

The requirement of public purpose is stated in the American Law Institute's *Restatement on Foreign Relations Law*.[139] But, in the commentary thereto, the significance of the requirement is played down. The commentary reads:[140]

> The requirement that a taking be for a public purpose is reiterated in most formulations of the rules of international law on expropriations of foreign property. That limitation, however, has not figured prominently in international claims practice, perhaps because the concept of public purpose is broad and not subject to effective re-examination by other states. Presumably, a seizure by a dictator or oligarchy for private use could be challenged under this rule.

In the course of the disputes arising from the Libyan nationalisations, the public purpose requirement was given a new lease of life, with the argument that, where a nationalisation is motivated by way of reprisal, it would lack public purpose and should therefore be considered unlawful. In the *BP* award which arose from these nationalisations, Judge Lagegren found the nationalisation to be illegal on the ground that the taking 'clearly violates principles of international law as it was made for purely extraneous political reasons and was arbitrary and discriminatory in character'.[141] But, in the *Liamco* award[142] Arbitrator Mahmassani dismissed the argument based on the requirement of a public purpose in the following terms:

> As to the contention that the said measures were politically motivated and not in pursuance of a legitimate public purpose, it is the general opinion in international theory that the public utility principle is not a necessary

---

[138] For the US statement, see (1974) 13 ILM 767 at 771.   [139] Article 712(1)(a).
[140] Vol. 2, 200.   [141] (1977) 53 ILR 296 at 317.   [142] (1981) 20 ILM 1.

requisite for the legality of nationalisation. This principle was mentioned by Grotius and other publicists, but now there is no international authority, from a judicial or other source, to support its application to nationalisation. Motives are indifferent to international law, each state being free to judge for itself what it considers useful or necessary for the public good . . . The object pursued by it is of no concern to third parties.

These trends accord with the view taken by the European Court of Human Rights in deciding whether the taking had a public purpose or interest. The Court has held that it will not, as a general principle, question the state's view that the taking was in the public interest. The Court said:[143]

The Court, finding it natural that the margin of appreciation available to the legislature in implementing social and economic policies should be a wide one, will respect the legislature's judgment as to what is 'in the public interest' unless the judgment be manifestly without reasonable foundation.

3.2. Discriminatory taking

A racially discriminatory taking is unlawful in international law. The principle against racial discrimination is a *ius cogens* principle of international law. It is odious to international law that nationalisation or any act of state should be based on considerations of race. But, a post-colonial nationalisation which is designed to end the economic domination of the nationals of the former colonial power is exempt from this general rule. Here, nationalisation would be directed at the citizens of a distinct state identifiable by race for the obvious reason that they alone are in control over the economic sectors of the nationalising state. A German court accepted the existence of this exception when considering the legality of the Indonesian nationalisations. It rejected the argument that the nationalisation measures were illegal as they were directed only against Dutch nationals. The court emphasised the fact that the Dutch were the colonial rulers of Indonesia and that they had control over the Indonesian economy.

The equality concept requires only that equals must be treated equally and that the different treatment of 'unequals' is admissible. For the statement to be objective, it is sufficient that the attitude of the former colonial people to its former colonial master is, of course, different from that towards other foreigners. Not only were production facilities in the hands

---

[143] *James v. United Kingdom* (1986) 8 EHRR 123.

of the Dutch for most colonial companies, but these companies dominated the worldwide distribution, beyond the production process, through the Dutch markets.

In the situation dealt with by the German court, there is a justification other than motives of racial hatred involved in the taking. Where racial motives alone are present, the taking cannot amount to a nationalisation. A US case provides an illustration of a purely racially motivated taking.[144] Here, the ruling coterie in Argentina persecuted a family because of their Jewish origin and took over their property after ensuring that the family left Argentina as a result of the torture of the head of the family and threats of further violence. The racially motivated taking in this situation amounted to expropriation and had no economic purpose at all. In these circumstances, the taking becomes illegal and full compensation must be paid for the taking.

In clear cases of racially motivated takings, the illegality will be evident. Thus, in the case of the takings of Jewish property in Nazi Germany[145] or in the case of the takings of the property of Indians in Uganda during the regime of Idi Amin,[146] the racially motivated nature of the takings was clear. The governments themselves did not seek to hide the motives for the takings. But, difficulty will arise where both motives of racial hatred and economic objectives together inspire a taking. It is no easy task to assess which motive is the dominant one, for when economic nationalism is the reason for the taking both motives are present in equal strength. The better view in such circumstances may be to treat the taking itself as a valid taking but to use the taking as the basis of a separate cause of action based on racial discrimination. As a result of movements within international law, it can now be claimed that the violation of the principle against racial discrimination gives rise to a separate cause of action, and it is on this basis that the responsibility of the host state should be pegged in cases where the motives for the taking are not clear.

3.3. Takings in violation of treaties

The *Chorzow Factory Case* concerned a taking in violation of a treaty. The view of the Permanent Court of International Justice was that, in

---

[144] In *Siderman de Blake* v. *Argentina*, 965 F 2d 699 (1992), only one member of the family was a US national, the others being Argentinian. As far as international law was concerned, only the taking of the share of the one member of the family involved state responsibility.

[145] *Oppenheimer* v. *Inland Revenue Commissioner* [1975] 1 All ER 538.

[146] F. Woolridge and V. Sharma, 'The Expropriation of the Property of the Ugandan Asians' (1974) 14 IJIL 61.

circumstances of takings in violation of treaties, restitution was the proper remedy for the international wrong. The general proposition that is drawn from this case, that restitutionary damages is the proper remedy for all nationalisations, is wide of the mark, for the Court was only concerned with a nationalisation in violation of a treaty.

An interesting question that could arise is whether the nationalisation of an investment that is protected by a bilateral investment treaty will be illegal under this rule. Such treaties do not interfere with the right of the state to take foreign property but only seek to specify the manner in which such a taking should be made. Since the treaty itself will provide for the compensation for a taking that is protected by the treaty, the logical answer would be to apply the standard of compensation that is indicated in the treaty itself.

4. Conclusion

Though the law recognised that there could be takings of alien property other than through direct means, the indirect methods of taking have not been identified with any certainty either in arbitral decisions or in the literature. It is unlikely that this deficiency of the law will be cured. The law on alien takings, especially the law on state responsibility arising from such takings, was developed at a time when the state rarely interfered with the marketplace and interference was effected for rather crude purposes such as the self-aggrandisement of ruling cliques. It was easy to identify and stigmatise such takings as unlawful. Investment protection was facilitated by the uniform application of this rule to all types of taking. But, with increasing state intervention in the economy, the maintenance of this rule became unacceptable.

Regulatory takings have brought the tensions in this area to the forefront. The interests of property protection favours a *per se* rule that was accepted in the *Santa Elena* award. But, it is not a rule that can be sustained, not only because of the fact that it is not based on any authority but also because it does not reflect developments in domestic or international legal systems. Domestic legal systems have recognised the need for balancing the competing areas in the situation of every taking. This rule of prudence is transferred into the international sphere by requiring that every situation of indirect taking should be examined as a distinct situation having its own circumstances which must be considered in determining whether it should be regarded as compensable or not. In the international sphere, rules on the environment and human rights have ensured that matters which were domestic are now of universal concern so that a state acting to promote environmental or human rights interests does so to advance universal objectives. In that light, it would be difficult to characterise such regulatory takings as compensable. The increasing tendency among both developed and developing countries to control foreign investments, albeit through different types of regulatory structures, will keep this issue in the forefront of the law in this area. As indicated, this issue has replaced the theory of internationalisation of foreign investment contracts and the debate on compensation – which are dealt with in the following chapters – as the central issue in the area of expropriation of foreign investments.

9

Takings in violation of foreign investment agreements

The view which formerly prevailed was that a taking in violation of a foreign investment contract was illegal.[1] This view has lost support in recent times. But, the existence of an agreement in which the state makes a commitment not to take the property of the foreign investor for a certain period of time has always had some significance in the law. The view is that such agreements are akin to treaties and their violation is unlawful. There is little support for this view in modern times. But, variations of this theme still continue to exist. The argument is sometimes made that the violation of contractual rights enhances compensation. Because the old view still continues to have echoes in modern law, it is necessary to consider the ramifications of the notion that the foreign investment agreement itself has a status in the law and that its violation brings about certain consequences.

Foreign investment agreements are usually the basis on which entry is made into the host country. They are also the basis on which dispute settlement through arbitration is resorted to when parties are in conflict. The bargaining power of the foreign investor is at its greatest at the moment of entry, and he is best able to secure terms favourable to himself. Prudence requires that these terms be reduced to the form of a contract. The agreement secures the basis on which the expectations of the foreign investor are to be protected. But, the agreement also contains an

---

[1] The case for the UK government in the *Anglo-Iranian Oil Company Case* was built up on the basis that, though a state has a right to nationalise, the nationalisation is illegal if it is done in violation of an existing contractual commitment. See the opinion prepared for the drafting of the UK memorandum by Sir Hersch Lauterpacht in H. Lauterpacht, *Collected Papers* (vol. 4, 1978), 25 at 29. The high point of the view was the award of Professor Dupuy in the *Texaco* arbitration. In *Aminoil* (1982) 22 ILM 976, the case for the oil company was built on the view that a taking in violation of the stabilisation clause in the concession agreement was invalid. This view gained support in the separate opinion of Sir Gerald Fitzmaurice in *Aminoil*.

'obsolescing bargain'[2] in the sense that the bargaining power of the foreign investor diminishes as the foreign investment project progresses.
Once the investment has been made and the project is under way, the
foreign investor becomes a captive of the host state. Unless he takes measures to ensure his continuing usefulness to the project, the host state
will seek to change the initial terms on which entry was made by the
foreign investor. The ability of the state to interfere with the foreign
investment is enhanced by the fact that it has the legislative machinery
of the state at its disposal and, at least as far as municipal law is concerned, a theory of legislative supremacy to interfere with any domestic
event.

It is crucial for foreign investment protection that a counterbalancing
theory which neutralises the power of the state to interfere with foreign
investment contracts is constructed. It is an interesting facet of the law that
this counterbalancing theory, which sought to stigmatise a taking in violation of a foreign investment agreement as illegal or, at least, as inviting
the condemnation of the law by requiring the payment of higher compensation, was built up largely through mechanisms devised by foreign
investors and those supporting their endeavours. It is a fiction to say that
international law is a law between states. Power in international relations
is not exercised by states alone but by individuals and conglomerations
of individuals, and the fiction of international law that it is a law between
states merely hid this fact and avoided the scrutiny of these actors. Many
of the legal techniques, particularly in the field of foreign investment, were
created through the exercise of private power.

Capital-exporting states supported the formulation of the theory but
were not direct participants in the initial efforts to build it. To this extent,
this area, at least in its early stages, may evidence a rare instance of an
attempt at private power being used to create public international law.[3]
The sources which were used to create the rules of protection were the

---

[2] R. Vernon, 'International Investment and International Trade' (1966) 2 *Quarterly Journal
of Economics* 80.

[3] It is not suggested that there was a conspiracy to build such a law. Once formulated, the
advantage of the system was perceived by foreign investors and their advisors. The imitation
effect played a role and theory came to be formulated to conserve what was achieved.
Political scientists, unlike lawyers, are not averse to dwelling on the role of private power
in foreign investment protection. It is also instructive to compare the manner in which the
lex mercatoria has been constructed to apply in private international transactions. Again,
the movement is one that has progressed due to the vigour of the support of publicists and
business organisations.

teachings of highly qualified publicists and arbitral awards. They were weak sources, which could be utilised by private power.[4] The capital-importing states, against whose interests the system was created, did not have recourse to any means of countering the creation of these laws.[5] The method of investment protection depended on the nature of the foreign investment contract which initiated the process of foreign investment and the inclusion in it of certain types of clause. The contractual structure on which the theory of foreign investment protection was erected requires examination.

1. Contractual devices for foreign investment protection

There does not appear to have been any rule arising from international concern with liability for breaches of foreign investment agreements until late in the twentieth century. Technically, defaults on debts made by foreign citizens amounted to breaches of contracts, but the manner of the settlement of such disputes was through negotiation, persuasion and finally through military intervention to secure payment. It may be possible to extract a principle that such practices gave rise to a rule that the contract of loan must be honoured, but practice on intervention to extract payment of debts was not so uniform as to give rise to any rule. Latin American states resisted the formation of any rule relating to liability for debts or any rule that military intervention could be justified on the basis of the enforcement of liability for debts.[6]

Writing in 1943, Hackworth stated the US position in the following terms:[7]

---

[4] This is a strong claim to make. It subjects many respected academics to a charge of an absence of neutrality in the pursuit of their disciplines. Such a charge is not intended. The need for investment protection is obvious. The idea that there should be external protection for foreign investment contracts was generated by a genuinely felt need to counterbalance the legislative power of the host state. Given the commitment to notions of sanctity of contract, it would be logical to build up a theory of investment protection through international law. But, the role of private power in accentuating this trend, while it must not be exaggerated, was considerable, for the initial contracts that had to be devised on the basis of building up such protection had to be devised by lawyers for foreign investors. Once the idea took hold, rationalisations of the idea of investment protection came to be made and passed into more serious efforts to formulate theory.

[5] They had to wait until they were powerful enough within the General Assembly to pass resolutions asserting their economic sovereignty.

[6] The Latin American jurists formulated the Drago doctrine, which forbade the use of force to recover debts.

[7] Hackworth, *Digest of International Law* (vol. 5, 1943), 611.

> Generally speaking, the Department of State does not intervene in cases involving breaches of contract between a foreign state and a national of the United States in the absence of showing a denial of justice . . . The practice of declining to intervene formally prior to a showing of denial of justice is based on the proposition that the Government of the United States is not a collection agency and cannot assume the role of endeavouring to enforce contractual undertakings freely entered into by nationals with foreign states.

States were extremely reluctant to intercede in situations of breaches of contract, except where state responsibility arose as a result of denial of justice in the host state. It was recognised that a mere breach of contract to which a state was party did not, *per se*, engage the state in responsibility. In the period after the Second World War, there is clear evidence of an attempt to change this rule. The ending of colonialism and the outlawing of the use of force meant that capital-exporting states could not use military pressure as a means of securing the interests of citizens who had contractual claims against other states. In this state of helplessness, there was a need to develop principles quickly which would ensure that contractual claims could be enforced through some supranational means. It is evident that these means were formulated initially not by the states but by foreign investors and associations favourable to them. It was they who stood in immediate need of protection. By this time, foreign investments were made largely by multinational corporations which had sufficient capacity to act in their own interests.

The early devices relating to the contractual protection of foreign investment were worked out in the context of investments made in the extractive industries, principally the oil industry. In the extractive industries, the usual form of entry was through the concession agreement. The concession agreement involved almost the transfer of sovereignty over whole tracts of land for long periods of time. The agreement ensured total control over the transaction by the foreign investor. These forms of investment were possible only in situations in which the government of the host state was not powerful enough to protest or was subject to the control of the home state of the foreign investor which permitted the situation as it profited from it. The states which granted the concessions were either colonies or protectorates. In some instances, the absolute rulers who controlled their states were dependent on the foreign power to continue their hold on the reins of power. When power came to be transferred to the host states and its people, new techniques of foreign investment had to be devised which would reflect the interests of the host state and involve an internal balance between the interests of the host state and the foreign investor. The change that has come about in the contractual structures also required a reconsideration of the issue of investment protection. Whereas previously, these states would not have dared to court the displeasure of the home state of the foreign investor, the situation had changed. Political and military pressure could not ensure the security of the foreign investor or the supply of the necessary natural resources for the furnaces of European industry. The use of such pressure was unwise due to the anti-colonial sentiments that had been released. In addition, the founding of the United Nations and the outlawing of war by its Charter made the use of military pressure no longer feasible. The Iraqi War of 2003 indicates that there is a weakening of the United Nations system and that the solitary hegemonic power may still use force in order to achieve its ends. Yet, it must still be accepted that there remain constraints on the use of force in modern international law. When such constraints came to be recognised, it became necessary to devise other means to ensure investment protection based on some semblance of legality. This was largely sought to be effected by the construction of a distinct legal system which would give security to existing and future concession agreements. Before examining the construction of this new structure of protection, the basic contractual form on which this elaborate theory was built and the clauses which were used in this contractual form need to be examined.

1.1. The essential clauses

Though the terms of the early concession agreements vary, their core features were similar. They were to last for a long period of time. They were to be immune from interference by the home state during this period. They would contain a stabilisation clause seeking to freeze the law as it was at the time of the entry of the investment and to ensure that later changes to the law did not apply to the concession. They usually contained a choice-of-law clause which would seek to exclude the application of the domestic laws of the host state and subject the contract to some nebulous external standard such as 'general principles of law' or 'standards that prevail within the industry'. The object of the latter technique was to ensure the application of a system which could not be unilaterally altered by the home state as its own laws could have been. In return for the resources extracted, the home state was to receive in return a payment of royalties calculated on the basis of the amount of resources extracted. The later importance of the structure of some of the clauses involved in the concession agreement requires that a more careful study be made of them. It must also be kept in mind that there were many agreements which did not contain all or some of the clauses described here. At this stage, the clauses are described and some of the theoretical difficulties associated with them identified. The use made by them of arbitral tribunals will be discussed thereafter.

1.1.1. The stabilisation clause

The aim of the stabilisation clause was to ensure that future changes in the legislation of the host state did not vary the terms of the contract on the basis of which entry was made. The foreign corporation stood at a disadvantage in any agreement it made with the host state, as the host state had the legislative power to alter any event that took place within its territory or to affect any contractual right or right to property that was located within its territory. Such a power flowed from its sovereignty. It was in the interests of the foreign corporation to neutralise this power. The stabilisation clause was introduced into the agreement to effect this.[8] The basis of the stabilisation clause was that the state was bound by the agreement contained in the clause not to apply any later changes to its law to the particular contract or to alter the terms of the contract directly by legislation. The clause sought to freeze the law of the host state at the time of entry of the foreign investor, and to make the law so frozen, the law that controls the foreign investment. The stabilisation clause is intended to immunise the foreign investment contract from a range of matters, such as taxation, environmental controls and other regulations as well as to prevent the destruction of the contract itself before the contract expires.

Doubts have been raised as to whether a contractual clause can achieve the effect of fettering the legislative sovereignty of a state for a lengthy period of time.[9] The state, in theory, must act in the public good as it perceives it to be at any given time. It may not be possible, as a matter of constitutional theory, for a state to bind itself by a contract made with a

---

[8] Generally, see Esa Paasivirta, 'Internationalisation and Stabilisation of Contracts versus State Sovereignty' (1989) 50 BYIL 315. It has been pointed out that the stabilisation clause is inconsistent with the choice-of-law clause, for the stabilisation clause is an implicit acceptance that the host state's law, in the stabilised form, applies to the contract. A. El Kosheri and T. Riad, 'The Law Governing a New Generation of Petroleum Contracts' (1986) 1 ICSID Rev 259.

[9] In *Aminoil v. Kuwait* (1982) 21 ILM 976, the tribunal suggested that the clause may be valid if limited to a reasonable period.

private party, particularly a foreign party, to fetter its legislative power. It is trite law that a legislature is not bound by its own legislation and has the power to change it. That being so, it cannot be bound by a provision in a simple contract. As a matter of constitutional theory, the stabilisation clause may not be able to achieve what it sets out to do. It may not serve as anything more than a comforter to the foreign investor, who may derive some security from the belief that there is a promise secured from the state not to apply its future legislation to the agreement. This conclusion would hold unless an alternate rationale could be found to give the stabilisation clause greater force. There was a need for a theory which would confer validity on the stabilisation clause by ensuring that its force was derived from some external source that stood higher in the hierarchy of validity than domestic law. The structuring of such a theory was necessary to ensure that the objective behind the stabilisation clause was achieved.

The theory of internationalised contracts sought to achieve this effect. The inclusion of the stabilisation clause was seen as evidencing the intention of the state party to the agreement not to subject it to its domestic law but to subject it to some external system which would ensure the validity of the stabilisation clause and the contract which contains it. The stabilisation clause, along with other clauses which gave rise to such an inference, played an important role in enabling the inference to be drawn that the foreign investment contract was not subject to the domestic law of the host state.

Some examples of a stabilisation clause are apposite. The stabilisation clause involved in the concession agreement between Texaco and Libya which was relevant to the *Texaco* arbitration,[10] read as follows:

> The Government of Libya will take all steps necessary to ensure that the company enjoys all the rights conferred by the concession. The contractual rights expressly created by this concession shall not be altered except by the mutual consent of the parties.

This is not a direct stabilisation clause which spells out that future legislative changes cannot apply to the agreement. But, it creates an obligation to secure the consent of the foreign party before effecting any changes by legislation or otherwise to the contractual regime. It seeks to neutralise sovereignty by creating the need for the consent of the foreign party to changes that are to apply to the agreement. But, since it provides for negotiation between the parties as to changes to be effected to the contract, it

---

[10] (1977) 53 ILR 389.

provides at least an avenue through which the parties could renegotiate and establish a new contractual balance in the light of any new circumstances. To this extent, an indirect stabilisation clausee may not prove as objectionable as a direct stabilisation clause which precludes the making of any changes to the agreement.

A more direct form of stabilisation clause was contained in the contract involved in the *Aminoil* arbitration.[11] It read as follows:

> The Shaikh shall not by general or special legislation or by administrative measures or by any other act whatever annul this Agreement except as provided in Article 11. No alteration shall be made in terms of this Agreement by either the Shaikh or the Company except in the event of the Shaikh and the Company jointly agreeing that it is desirable in the interests of both parties to make certain alterations, deletions or additions to this Agreement.

The fact that the state party agreed to such a wide stabilisation clause is an indication of a promise not to interfere with the working of the foreign investment process during the period of its duration.

After a dispute arises between the foreign investor and the host state, the validity of the stabilisation clause becomes a subject of debate. States have always queried whether such a blanket surrender of sovereignty through what is in effect a contract located under their own laws can curtail their legislative sovereignty. There are two main ways in which the stabilisation clause could be attacked. One is to query the *vires* of the officials who made the contract on behalf of the state party. The contract would usually have been made by officials of a state entity or of some ministry. They would usually lack the powers to commit the state to any definite obligation, particularly the obligation not to use the legislative powers of the state in a particular manner.[12] The second objection to the stabilisation clause is that the legislative powers of a state cannot be fettered by a mere contractual provision, particularly where the exercise of such power is necessary to secure a public benefit. In ordinary terms, both objections have a great deal of validity. These objections are met. The first objection on *vires* is met with the rule which states that, once the contract is made, a state is not permitted to rely on its internal laws to contest its validity. The origins of this rule are obscure. Judge Cavin justified it in the *Sapphire*

---

[11] (1982) 21 ILM 976.
[12] A French court in *SPP Ltd* v. *Egypt* (1983) 22 ILM 752 held that a state does not become a party to a contract merely because officials of a state entity and the minister responsible for the entity signed the contract.

arbitration on the basis that a foreigner cannot be expected to know all the laws of a state. Why a sophisticated multinational corporation with its own in-house legal department should have this privilege when every alien who enters a foreign state is presumed to know and abide by the law of his host state is unclear. The second objection is met with the theory that the foreign investment contract is subject to a supranational system which can bind the local legislature much in the same way that a treaty can bind the state. This observation likens the foreign investment agreement to a treaty, which obviously it is not.[13] In any event, a foreign investment agreement in the natural resources sector has to contend with the principle of permanent sovereignty over natural resources. There is a view gaining strength that this doctrine prevents a foreign investment agreement binding the legislative competence of a state. In any event, the analogy of a foreign investment with a treaty is far-fetched.[14] The foreign investor does not have personality in international law. Some writers have sought to overcome this problem by arguing that the defect of personality in the foreign investor could be cured by the state conferring personality on the foreign investor. This is stretching logic to breaking point. It is far-fetched to argue that the multinational corporation has personality when it suits its interests and that it does not have personality when it does not, as where liability is sought to be imposed on it for misconduct or to institute a code of conduct through international instruments.

But the issue is whether the cumulative effect of other clauses, introduced along with the stabilisation clause, seeking to externalise the agreement will be different. A discussion of this issue must await a consideration of the other clauses.

1.1.2. Choice-of-law clause

The aim of the choice-of-law clause is to ensure that the agreement is not subject to the laws of the host country which can be changed at will

---

[13] Treaties are seldom made with stabilisation clauses. In any event, they are subject to doctrines which make the obligations defeasible due to changed circumstances.

[14] State interference with contracts in the public interest have generally been recognised as valid in English law. As to public contracts, see *Amphitrite* v. *R.* [1921] 3 KB 300. An Australian lawyer has observed that 'the exercise of statutory powers is not inhibited in any way by the prior existence of contractual arrangements which might be detrimentally affected if those statutory powers were to be exercised'. E. Campbell, 'Legal Problems Involved in Government Participation in Resource Projects' (1984) *AMPLA Yearbook* 126 at 144. English courts have recognised foreign legislation interfering with state contracts located within the foreign state's jurisdiction. *Czarnikow Ltd* v. *Rolimpex* [1979] AC 351; *Settebello* v. *Banco Totta & Acores* [1985] 1 WLR 1050.

by the sovereign party. The assumption is that, as in the case of other international contracts, parties have autonomy to choose the law which is applicable to the foreign investment contract. On the basis of party autonomy, the foreign party to the agreement will choose a system other than the domestic law of the host state.[15] The choice of another state's domestic law is possible but will cause affront to the host state. Besides, such a choice will not have the desired effect of subjecting the contract to a system which is higher in the hierarchy than that of the domestic system of the host state. This hierarchical notion is important for the achievement of the strategy of investment protection that is attempted. Another municipal system will have only a co-equal and not a superior force. The choice of international law may be possible, but the theoretical difficulty is that, even if an entity with no status in international law may choose international law as the law applicable,[16] there is no body of international law applicable to contracts between states and foreign private entities. Given this difficulty, the strategy has been to opt for the choice of some nebulous system of supranational principles and indicate the means of the creation of such a system. The formula often is to refer to 'general principles of law'. The assumption is that, because these principles cannot be unilaterally changed by the host state as its domestic law can be, they will provide a measure of protection to the foreign party.

There are two problems with this assumption. The first involves the status of the doctrine of party autonomy. The idea of party autonomy is exalted to a position of near absoluteness in private international trans-actions such as export transactions. But, it may not have the same degree of exclusivity in the case of large transactions which involve state par-ties. The involvement of the state introduces into the contract a party which has to have paramount regard to national interests and give only

---

[15] On party autonomy, see J. D. M. Lew, *The Applicable Law in International Commercial Arbitration* (1978); P. E. Nygh, *Party Autonomy in Private International Law* (1998).

[16] As a matter of private international law, such a choice may be possible. But English law has always required there to be a definite and ascertainable system in which the agreement is rooted. Hence, the choice of equity or an honourable code as the applicable system has been resisted by the English courts. The civil law systems have taken a different attitude to this issue. But, as a jurisprudential proposition, a contract must be founded on ascertainable rules so that the parties may know the extent of their obligations. A system with a variable content can hardly be the basis of a contractual obligation. In *Deutsche Schachtbau- und Tiefbohrgesellschaft mbH* v. *Ras Al-Khaimah National Oil Co.* [1988] 3 WLR 230; [1988] 2 All ER 833, the enforcement of an award involving such a clause was considered. It would appear that there is a move towards regarding concession agreements as *sui generis* in this respect.

secondary importance to the carrying out of the contract. Besides, the nature of the foreign investment contract differs from the types of contract in relation to which the doctrine of party autonomy was developed. Unlike export transactions, which have a uniform degree of contact with several jurisdictions, the foreign investment contract has contact predominantly with the host state. It is of long duration. The carrying out of any major industrial project attracts the application of many regulatory controls, such as those relating to planning, environmental protection, customs controls and similar areas of public law. Such laws are bound to affect a major industrial project being carried out within the state. They will be regarded as mandatory provisions of the law, and it is well accepted in every legal system that mandatory laws cannot be evaded by the mere technique of choosing a foreign law as the law applicable to the contract. It is very unlikely then that party autonomy itself can support the idea that the application of the domestic law to a foreign investment transaction can be excluded altogether by the choice of some nebulous system of law.[17] Much of the case law in this area arose during a time when host states did not have foreign investment codes. Most host states now have sophisticated laws regulating foreign investment, particularly in the natural resources sector.

The second factor is that there are numerous authorities in the first half of the twentieth century identifying the domestic law of the host state as the law applying to the foreign investment transaction. In the *Serbian Loans Case*,[18] the International Court of Justice indicated that international law has no relevance to a transaction involving a state and a private party, and that reference should be made to a municipal system to settle problems arising from such a transaction. It is clear that, at the time of that decision at any rate, the application of any system other than the municipal system of a state to such transactions was contemplated.

There are many other authoritative statements supporting the view that a municipal system, in particular the municipal system of the state party, will apply to the transaction involving the state and a foreign private party. In *Kahler v. Midland Bank*, in 1950, Lord Radcliffe stated that, in the case of a contract between a state and a foreign private party, the state's law 'not merely sustains but, because it sustains, may modify or dissolve the contractual bond'.[19] The view that the host state's law applies was stated in several arbitral awards made in the 1950s. If the law had changed to permit

---

[17] See further M. Sornarajah, *International Commercial Arbitration* (1990) 102–60.
[18] (1929) PCIJ Series A, No. 20.   [19] [1950] AC 24 at 56.

the choice of some other system, then the change must be identified in some concrete fashion. If a rule of international law had emerged on the matter to permit a choice of a system other than that of the domestic law of the host state, its evolution must be identified clearly. The source from which it emerged must be shown with a sufficient degree of precision. This is an onus which may be difficult to satisfy. Whether the onus has been satisfied is discussed below.

1.1.3. Arbitration clause

The third clause, the inclusion of which is said to give rise to an inference that the foreign investment agreement has been subjected to an external system, is the arbitration clause. The arbitration clause is included in the contract so as to allow the choice of a neutral forum for the settlement of disputes which arise from the agreement. The foreign party will not have much confidence in the ability of the courts or other tribunals of the domestic court to settle the disputes that could arise from the contract in an impartial manner. The choice of the domestic court of another state will not be appropriate as there could be problems of sovereign immunity. The choice which is preferred by the foreign investor is an arbitral tribunal which could sit outside the host state and which could be constituted in accordance with the arbitration clause. In older agreements, arbitration clauses made reference to *ad hoc* tribunals. These tribunals could be tailor-made by the parties for the arbitration of the types of dispute that could arise from the contract. In any event, until the creation of the International Centre for the Settlement of Investment Disputes (ICSID),[20] there were no tribunals which had any particular expertise in settling disputes which arose from foreign investment transactions involving states and private parties.

An *ad hoc* tribunal is created in accordance with the procedure for its constitution, stated in the arbitration clause. Since disputes involving state contracts constitute a specialised area of arbitration, it was usual to create *ad hoc* tribunals for the settlement of such disputes. This gave the parties greater freedom in selecting arbitrators as well as the place and procedure of arbitration. It is possible in a contract to refer such disputes to specific arbitral institutions. These institutions are private institutions and do not have any specialisation in the area. ICSID arbitration is exclusively

---

[20] ICSID was created by a World Bank-sponsored convention, the Convention on the Settlement of Investment Disputes between States and Nationals of Other States. The Convention came into force in October 1966.

for disputes arising from state contracts.[21] ICSID is a body created by an international convention. The fact that it was created by sovereign will distinguishes it from private arbitral institutions. It is important to keep this in mind, particularly in view of the fact that these private institutions often arrogate to themselves, without any basis in theory or law, the powers possessed by ICSID.[22]

The arbitration clause should specify the extent of the jurisdiction that is conferred on the arbitral tribunal. The nature of the jurisdiction of the tribunal depends on the clause and the contract that contains it. Where the arbitrator exceeds the jurisdiction so given and makes pronouncements outside the scope of the clause or acts otherwise than in accordance with the clause, the award may be void for excess of jurisdiction. ICSID has its own procedures for annulment of awards made in excess of jurisdiction.

In general arbitral practice, it is accepted that an arbitration clause survives the termination of the contract. The issue is whether this general principle applies to the arbitration of state contracts as well. Where a state seeks to terminate the agreement unilaterally by legislation, at least from the state's point of view, the arbitration clause will be terminated along with the whole contract. The legislative act is an act of sovereignty, and a state which resorts to such an act will rarely concede that the arbitration clause in the contract survives the termination of the contract by legislation. The survival of an arbitration clause after the termination of the contract is possible in a private transaction because the termination is seldom brought about by legislative acts.

---

[21] For a survey of the ICSID Convention, see Joy Cherian, *Investment Contracts and Arbitration* (1975); for recent assessments of ICSID, see M. D. Rowat, 'Multilateral Approaches to Improving the Investment Climate of Developing Countries: The Cases of ICSID and MIGA' (1992) Harvard *ILJ* 103; J. Paulsson, 'ICSID: Achievement and Prospects' (1991) 6 ICSID Rev 380; and S. J. Toope, *International Mixed Arbitration* (1990), 219–62. Clearly, the most important work on the subject now is Christoph Schreuer, *Commentary on the ICSID Convention* (2000). It is, however, very much an official commentary. See also M. Sornarajah, *The Settlement of Foreign Investment Disputes* (2000).

[22] Thus, for example, in *SPP v. Egypt* (1983) 22 ILM 752, a tribunal constituted by the International Chamber of Commerce claimed the power to apply international law as the law applicable to the contract using Article 42(1) of the ICSID Convention as the basis. The fact that the parties to the ICSID Convention gave such a power by the article to ICSID tribunals should not mean that even private tribunals have such a power. An ICSID tribunal is an international arbitral tribunal set up by convention; private tribunals, such as ICC tribunals, are set up by the exercise of party autonomy. In the case of a state contract, one of the parties is a non-sovereign who lacks capacity to constitute an international tribunal in the proper sense.

However, in the case of an arbitration clause referring disputes to ICSID, the position that an arbitration clause in a state contract is effaced by legislation that affects the contract is not tenable. There is an obligation created by the ICSID Convention to submit disputes to ICSID for settlement. The fact that the contract was terminated by legislation cannot mean that an international obligation was extinguished. Legislation cannot have such an effect. In the case of a reference in the arbitral clause to ICSID, the survival of the arbitration clause, even after the termination of the contract by whatever means, is protected by an international obligation created by treaty. The situation may be otherwise in the case of *ad hoc* arbitration or references to private arbitral institutions. This fact accounts for the failure of state parties to appear before such arbitral tribunals and for the fact that, in most cases, *ad hoc* arbitral tribunals have had to proceed to an award unilaterally. Yet, in the case of *ad hoc* tribunals as well as other institutional tribunals, an obligation to arbitrate despite the extinction of the foreign investment by legislation could arise where that obligation is supported by a bilateral or regional investment treaty.[23]

But, arbitrators do not accept the distinction that is made in the last paragraph between ICSID arbitration and other types of arbitration. Instead, they argue that the arbitration clause survives the termination of the contract to create jurisdiction in the arbitral tribunal, whether or not the arbitral tribunal is an *ad hoc* tribunal or one created by treaty. The proposition was stated in the following terms by Arbitrator Mahmassani in the *Liamco* award:

> It is widely accepted in international law and practice that an arbitration clause survives the unilateral termination by that state of the contract in which it is inserted and continues in force even after that termination. This is a logical consequence of the interpretation of the intention of the contracting parties, and appears to be one of the basic conditions for creating a favourable climate of foreign investment.

This is a sound proposition as far as private international arbitrations are concerned. The validity of the proposition has been established beyond doubt as far as such arbitrations are concerned by Judge Schwebel in no uncertain terms in a long survey of arbitral practice.[24] But, whether it applies in circumstances where a contract located in a state is absolutely extinguished by legislation still remains a moot point. For, unlike private

---

[23] See e.g. *Yaung Chi Oo Ltd* v. *Myanmar* (2003) 42 ILM 540.
[24] Stephen Schwebel, *International Arbitration: Three Salient Problems* (1986).

contracts which are broken by the choice of private parties or terminated by other external events, the act which terminates a concession agreement is a public act of a sovereign state. A sovereign state which decides to perform that public act will seek to destroy the contract, arbitral clause and all. In these circumstances, it might be too facile to argue that the arbitral clause survives the unilateral termination of the agreement by the legislative act of the state, unless it is protected by a treaty. States certainly do not seem to think so, for they seldom appear before arbitrators who seek to establish their jurisdiction on the basis of the survival of the arbitration clause. The point remains at least a moot one for the moment. It must, however, be conceded that a reference to an ICSID tribunal is kept alive by the operation of the treaty provision on the arbitral clause. The same would apply where there is an international obligation created by an investment treaty which protects other forms of arbitration.

Given the structure of foreign investment contracts and the fact that it involved states and foreign parties, an elaborate theory of foreign investment protection was created by arbitral tribunals and writers who supported its creation. Put simply, the contract that is concluded between the state and the foreign party goes through a transmogrification which enables it to levitate out of the sphere of the domestic law of the host state into a higher plane of supranational law, variously identified as transnational law, general principles of law and international law. This near-mystical effect is achieved on the basis that the inclusion of clauses, such as the stabilisation clause, a choice-of-law clause and an arbitration clause, which are aimed at establishing external points of contact for the contract, justifies this change. It is this theory of the internationalisation of state contracts on which contractual techniques of foreign investment protection depend to which attention must next be turned.

ICSID arbitration must, once more, be treated differently for purposes of discussion. The ICSID Convention itself elevates a contract which contains an arbitral clause referring disputes to ICSID to a different level. Likewise, the significance of investment treaties is that they do effectively provide a foreign investor with a variety of protection in situations requiring dispute settlement, depending on the precise wording in the provisions of each treaty.

2. The internationalisation of state contracts

The removal of the foreign investment transaction from the sphere of the host country's law and its subjection to an immutable, supranational system is seen as essential for the protection of foreign investment under the theory of internationalisation. The contract acquires stability as it is removed from the legislative control of the state authority and its other sovereign powers. This neutralisation of the power of the state to change the contract is seen as essential to the stability of the foreign investment contract. It is an idea which also contains the seeds of conflict. It is futile to expect a state not to interfere at some stage with the conduct of a transaction which takes place essentially within its territory, involves substantial income and endures over a long period of time. Yet, the formulation of the theory and the nature of the authority which supports it must be examined with care.

2.1. The origin of the theory of internationalisation

The origin of the theory of internationalisation is firmly rooted in three early arbitral awards made in disputes arising from three concession agreements involving petroleum resources and some writings of scholars.[25] In the hierarchy of norms of international law, the awards of arbitral tribunals or the writings of highly qualified publicists are not significant sources of law, and any theory of international law entirely based on such sources will be tainted with the weakness of the sources on which it is built. The same could be said of the writings of highly qualified publicists that emerged during and after this period supporting the techniques that were used in these arbitrations to externalise the state contracts.

In each of the three arbitrations, there are *dicta* that, ordinarily, the law applicable to the concession agreements will be the law of the host

---

[25] It is possible to find old arbitrations in disputes arising from state contracts in which the arbitrator used external standards as an added justification to support conclusions he had arrived at on the basis of the host state's law. However, they do not provide authority for the exclusive application of external standards. Thus, in the *Delgoa Bay Railway Case* (1900), 3 (reported in H. Whiteman, *Damages in International Law* (vol. 3, 1976), 1694), the dispute arose from an agreement to build a railway in a Portuguese-held territory. The arbitrator found Portuguese law to be the applicable law, but also stated that Portuguese law 'did not contain any particular provision on the decisive points that would depart from general principles of the common law of modern nations'. Also, in referring to the principles of damages, there is mention of 'universally accepted principles'. In the *Schufeldt Claim* (1930) 5 AD 179, 24 AJIL 799, the law of Guatemala, which was the state party to the agreement, was applied, but there was reference to the fact that the relevant law was the same in all legal systems. Such references are not efforts at creating a universal system applicable to state contracts but merely efforts on the part of the tribunals to show that their award should be accepted as it accords with conclusions that would have been arrived at by applying the legal systems of the other party or any other legal system.

state in whose territory the transaction is located. None of the concession agreements involved contained an express choice-of-law clause. Applying ordinary techniques of conflict of laws, the arbitrator in these circumstances will have to infer the law applicable to the agreement by looking at the state with which the contract had its closest connection. The use of such a technique would lead to the inescapable conclusion that the law applicable was the law of the host state. The resources which were the subject matter of the agreement were located and the contract was performed in the state. The arbitrators conceded this point. Thus, in the *Qatar* arbitration,[26] the arbitrator, Sir Alfred Bucknil, said that the subject matter of the contract, together with the fact that the state was party to the contract, made Islamic law applicable to the contract. In the *Abu Dhabi* arbitration,[27] Lord Asquith said:

> This is a contract made in Abu Dhabi and wholly to be performed in that country. If any municipal system of law were applicable, it would, *prima facie*, be that of Abu Dhabi.

The arbitral tribunal in the *Aramco* arbitration[28] reached a similar conclusion. Professor Sauser-Hall, who was the arbitrator, observed:

> The law in force in Saudi Arabia should be applied to the content of the concession because this state is a party to the agreement, as grantor, and because it is generally admitted, in private international law, that a sovereign state is presumed, unless the contrary is proved, to have subjected its undertakings to its own legal system. This principle was mentioned by the Permanent Court of International Justice in its judgment in the *Serbian Loans Case*.

There was unanimity in these arbitral awards that the law applicable to the concession agreements should be the law of the host state. It was a conclusion indicated by the state of authority in the 1950s when these awards were made.

But the arbitrators argued that Islamic law, which would have otherwise applied as the domestic law of the host state, was not sophisticated enough to deal with transactions involving exploration for oil. At that time, there does not seem to have been any legal system considered mature which contained any law on petroleum contracts either. The law would have had to be created by analogy.

---

[26] (1953) 20 ILR 534.   [27] (1951) 18 ILR 144.
[28] (1958) 27 ILR 117. For a fuller discussion of the change attempted, see M. Sornarajah, *The Settlement of Foreign Investment Disputes* (2000).

Instead, there was much work done by the European Arabists to establish that Islamic law did not contain any principles on petroleum contracts.[29] The proposition is now contested by Middle Eastern experts on petroleum law.[30] There was no law specific to petroleum contracts in European law either. The law had to be constructed by analogical reasoning, and this could well have been done with Islamic legal principles too. But, after having come the conclusion that Islamic law will not apply, the arbitrators concluded that, in the absence of any relevant principles in the domestic law, they should apply general principles of law to fill the lacunae.

There were important academic writings which also began to support the thesis that, in situations in which there was an absence of any law in the host state, general principles of law could be used to fill the lacunae. The most significant of these writings was an essay written by Lord McNair, who supported the application of general principles to concession agreements.[31] Lord McNair was careful to confine his view to the situations in which the law of the host state lacked any significant principles which would apply to the agreement.[32] But, he was taken by others as supporting a wider proposition that general principles of law applied to concession agreements because the transnational nature of the agreements warranted the application of such neutral principles. Since general principles of law were a source of public international law, an easy transference was possible to the formulation of the rule that contracts between states and foreign private parties were subject to public international law.

A European writer, Verdross, claiming to be the initiator of the theory, suggested that foreign investment contracts with states were quasi-international agreements akin to international treaties and that international law applied to such agreements.[33] There was an array of writers

---

[29] J. N. D. Anderson and N. J. Goulson, 'The Moslem Ruler and Contractual Obligations' (1958) 33 NYULR 917, however, argued that there was, in fact, Islamic law on the issue and that it supported sanctity of contract.

[30] El Chiati, 'Protection of Investment Agreements in the Context of Petroleum Agreements' (1987) 204 *Hague Recueill* 1.

[31] Lord McNair, 'The General Principles of Law Recognised by Civilised Nations' (1957) 33 BYIL 1.

[32] Thus, it is clear from passages in the article that Lord McNair was addressing situations in which, if the normal rule that the host state's law is applied, the situation would result in the contracts being governed by a 'system of law which had not yet been developed to deal with this particular type of transaction' ((1957) 33 BYIL 1 at 4).

[33] A. Verdross, 'Quasi-International Agreements and International Economic Transactions' (1964) 18 YBWA 230.

who followed suit, making the claim that international law applied to agreements between states and foreign private parties.[34] One aspect of the theory was dependent on the characterisation of such transactions as economic development agreements. This idea depended on the policy reason that transfers of wealth to developing countries were beneficial to these countries. It was further argued that the entirely altruistic reasons, namely, economic development, for which foreign investments are made are worthy of protection by international law.[35] This aspect of the formulation of the theory, though it continues to be advanced in modern writings, can be dismissed as without any merit. No one seriously suggests that agreements made with developed nations are subject to anything other than the law of the state. It would be offensive to the notion of the equality of states to suggest that the same principle does not apply to agreements made with developing countries. To overcome this difficulty, it is argued that agreements made in developing countries are different as they are intended to lead to the development of the host states. The idea that foreign investment is motivated by altruistic motives of developing the economy of the host state is such an absurdity that it can hardly be the basis of any rule that deserves even a casual consideration. Transnational corporations which make overseas investments are not charitable institutions doling out largesse but are companies in search of profits which could be distributed among their shareholders. The argument based on the view that they bring benefits to the developing states only shows the paucity of justifications possessed by international lawyers, all of whom, of course, will claim a high degree of rectitude, scholarship and impartiality, in formulating theories to advance the cause of foreign investors belonging to their states.[36]

There are obvious defects with the theory that international law could apply to foreign investment transactions. The foreign party to the transaction, at least in the eyes of positivist international lawyers, does not have sufficient personality in international law to enter into relations with a

---

[34] P. Weil, 'Problemes Relatifs aux Contrats Passes entre un Etat et un Particulier' (1969) 128 *Hague Recueil* 95. For a discussion, see S. J. Toope, *International Mixed Arbitration* (1990), 75–90.

[35] J. Hyde, 'Economic Development Agreements' (1962) 105 *Hague Recueil* 271. For recent support, see G. T. Curtis, 'The Legal Security of Economic Development Agreements' (1988) 29 Harvard ILJ 317; but see I. Pogany, 'Economic Development Agreements' (1992) 7 ICSID Rev 1. For the rejection of the argument based on economic development agreements by an arbitral tribunal, see *Amoco International Finance Co. v. Iran* (1987) 15 Iran–US CTR 189.

[36] See S. J. Toope, *International Mixed Arbitration* (1990), 82–4, who also rejects the notion of economic development agreements as having no merit.

state or be a possessor of rights in international law. There may come a time when international personality may broaden to include multi-national corporations, which are significant actors on the international economic scene, but no serious writer on the subject had recognised, at the time the theory was formulated, that such an evolution had already taken place. It is evident that private power does possess sufficient instruments through which it could assert itself in the realm of international law, even in periods where positivism held sway and emphasised the idea that international law was based entirely on the consent of states.

Another defect in the theory that international law applies to foreign investment transactions is that there is no body of international law on the subject of state contracts. The notion that general principles of law could be used to supply the lacunae is hardly an answer to this criticism. The extraction of law on the basis of such a weak source of law in such a controversial area is unsatisfactory. The principles which have been extracted have been challenged as being based on subjective choices of individual arbitrators and scholars predisposed to building up a system of investment protection. There is also a selective use of principles. Thus, the often advocated proposition relating to sanctity of contract, enshrined in the phrase *pacta sunt servanda* and advocated by the proponents of the theory of internationalisation, is not reflected in any major system of contract law in an absolute manner. In every contract system, absolute sanctity of contracts has given way to conflicting principles relating to the protection of the weaker party to the contract. There has been an increase in the number of vitiating factors the law of contract recognises, based on the acceptance of the idea that the law should take into consideration the relative bargaining strengths of the parties.[37] In the light of these developments, the maintenance of a doctrine of nineteenth-century contract law that contracts have sanctity and the transference of this doctrine without taking account of the fact that the exceptions to it in modern law have increased significantly is an exercise in partiality. The search for general principles of contract law, even if possible, has not been attempted in an impartial manner but in a manner that is designed to promote the interests of investment protection to the detriment of the interests of the host state.[38]

---

[37] For developments in the English law, see J. Cartwright, *Unequal Bargaining: A Study of Vitiating Factors in the Formation of Contracts* (1991).

[38] Christine Gray, referring to remedies given by arbitral tribunals, made the point that there has been no systematic borrowing by arbitral tribunals from municipal law or a coherent theory on which such borrowing rested. C. Gray, *Judicial Remedies in International Law* (1990), 7. One may go further and suggest that expediency has been the main factor in

Besides, the foreign investment contract has now ceased to be a private law agreement to which general principles of the law concerning private contracts could be extended. There has always been an effort to counter the making of an analogy between state contracts and private contracts by pointing out that the state contract was more akin to administrative contracts. Obligations arising from administrative contracts were defeasible in the public interest. Unfortunately, the early efforts concentrated on pointing out the similarities between state contracts and the *contrat administratif* of French law. Since French law developed a law on administrative contracts quite early, the comparison was a natural one to make. This argument was, however, rejected on the ground that the *contrat administratif* was a peculiarity of French law. Hence, it was argued, the principle could not be regarded as a general principle of international law.[39] The idea that a contract made by a state is defeasible in the public interest is demonstrably common to all legal systems.[40] This, again, is an illustration of the selectivity of the arguments used by the scholars who support the theory of internationalisation of contracts.[41]

Whatever the position may have been in the past, recent developments in legal systems indicate that there has been a rapid development of the notion of administrative contracts in all major legal systems.[42] There is a more credible basis now than before to argue that contracts made by states with private parties are universally recognised as defeasible in the

---

the choice of municipal law principles. They are chosen from specific legal systems when support can be found for the view of the arbitrators in analogies from these systems. For the view that an improper choice of general principles amounts to an excess of power on the part of the tribunal, see E. Paasivirta, *Participation of States in International Contracts* (1990), 64.

[39] Thus, in *Texaco* (para. 57), Arbitrator Dupuy, a distinguished French professor of international law, suggested that 'the theory of administrative contracts is somewhat typically French' and that it should not be accepted as forming part of international law. But, Professor Bernard Audit of the University of Paris has rejected the view that the idea is French. B. Audit, *Transnational Arbitration and State Contracts* (1988), 108. He observes: 'These arguments make the form unduly prevail over substance. Comparative law indicates that everywhere contracts concluded by public authority are not altogether governed by the same regime as purely civil contracts.'

[40] S. J. Toope, *International Mixed Arbitration* (1990), 73; E. Paasivirta, *Participation of States in International Contracts* (1990), 194–5.

[41] There was greater receptivity to the view that administrative contracts are recognised generally in most legal systems in *Aminoil* (1982) 21 ILM 976 at 1022, and in *BP* (1977) 53 ILR 976 at 349.

[42] Arghyrios Fatouros, 'The Administrative Contract in Transnational Transactions: Reflections on the Uses of Comparison' in *Ius in Privatum: Festschrift für Max Rheinstein* (vol. 1, 1969), 259.

public interest and that no illegality can be attached to its breach by the state provided it can demonstrate a public purpose for the breach.

Quite apart from this analogy of foreign investment contracts to administrative contracts in municipal systems, the foreign investment contract itself has undergone an important transformation. The nature of the foreign investment agreement is increasingly taking on a public law character in both developed and developing countries. Writers have noted that petroleum agreements that are entered into in Europe are based more in public law than in private law.[43] The production-sharing agreements which are the model universally employed by developing countries permit constant supervision of the whole process of oil exploration and sale by the state oil corporations. In the other areas of foreign investment, the increasing institution of screening of investment entry and other administrative controls over the whole process of foreign investment makes the area more one of administrative law than one of pure contract law. Theories that have been built in the past on the basis of contract may be inapposite to deal with the encroachments that administrative law has made into the process of foreign investment. The theory of internationalisation which is contract-centred may be a casualty in these developments. This theory will be unable to accommodate the modern developments satisfactorily. Despite these theoretical problems, the theory of internationalisation continues to be accepted in arbitral jurisprudence and in the writings of publicists.

The more extreme variety of the theory of internationalisation is that the very nature of the foreign investment contract gives rise to the inference that it is subject to a supranational system of law.[44] Whereas the less extreme version will look to the existence of clauses such as a choice-of-law clause indicating the subjection of the contract to general principles of law and an arbitration clause indicating dispute settlement by a foreign tribunal as factors giving rise to an inference that the parties had an intention to internationalise the contract, the extreme theory infers internationalisation merely from the nature of the contract.

The argument that is advanced is that the foreign investment transaction has contacts with several states besides the host state. The capital

---

[43] See R. W. Bentham, 'The International Legal Structure of Petroleum Exploration' in J. Rees and P. Odell (eds.), *The International Oil Industry* (1987), 57. He pointed out that, in the UK, petroleum licences are part contracts and part instruments of public law (*ibid.*, p. 61). The situation is similar in the case of Norwegian oil contracts, which include express clauses permitting changes by legislation.

[44] *Revere Copper & Brass Inc.* v. *OPIC* (1978) 17 ILM 1321.

for the project may have been raised from banks in several countries. The shareholders of the multinational corporation which makes the agreement may be nationals of different states. The argument states that, in these circumstances, the relevant law cannot be only that of the host state. It must be international law or some supranational system. In these circumstances, even if there is an express choice of law which indicates the applicability of some other law, that express choice must give way to the application of international law as the proper law of the agreement. The reasoning was that in view of the enormous capital risks involved in the project, it was unlikely that the foreign investor would have consciously subjected his investment to the laws of the host state.[45] The less extreme version of the theory states that, even if the host state's law is the relevant law, it is still subject to the standards of international law, so that, if it conflicts with the standards of international law, it must give way to these standards.[46]

The result of this internationalisation has important consequences. The arbitral tribunals which formulated the thesis have identified these consequences. The first is that the host state cannot thereafter rely on its own laws to argue that the agreement is a nullity. The rule was stated in the *Sapphire* arbitration by Judge Cavin.[47] The assumption that was made was that a foreign multinational corporation could not be expected to acquaint itself with all the laws and regulations of the host country that would apply to the agreement. This is a fascinating assumption, given that a multinational corporation has all the resources and expensive advisers to do the necessary research. Besides, like any alien or alien entity, it had entered the state voluntarily and should acquaint itself with and obey all the laws of that state like any other alien. That is a basic principle of international life. Somehow it does not seem to apply to multinational corporations, for the self-evident proposition has had to be stated in guidelines and in treaties. But, it is the rule stated by Judge Cavin which has become the accepted one. The rule that has been formulated has now passed into the Swiss legislation on international commercial arbitration.[48] An explanation of

---

[45] The arbitrations which form the basis of this extreme theory of internationalisation are the *Sapphire* award (1964) 35 ILR 136; *Texaco* v. *Libya* (1977) 53 ILR 389; *Revere Copper Inc* v. *OPIC* (1978) 17 ILM 1321; and *Elf Aquitaine* v. *NIOC* (1982) 11 YCA 112.

[46] *Aminoil* v. *Kuwait* (1982) 21 ILM 976; *SPP* v. *Egypt* (1982) 22 ILM 752.

[47] (1963) 35 ILR 136.

[48] Section 177 of the Act on International Commercial Arbitration. Judge Cavin, who was arbitrator in *Sapphire* (1963) 35 ILR 136, was a distinguished Swiss judge and jurist. A connection is not suggested. The rule was probably derived from the rule in the law

the rule suggests that it has a basis in good faith. It is difficult to accept such an explanation. If the agreement was defective under the host state's law and the foreign party knew or ought to have known of the defect, it is hardly possible to argue that the agreement should be regarded as valid on the basis of good faith.[49] It is basic to all legal systems that aliens entering a state should abide by the laws of the state. If it were otherwise, aliens could transgress the law, particularly the criminal law, of a state and escape liability by pleading ignorance. Legal systems cannot permit such a defence to aliens. Similarly, it should be expected that an alien corporation, particularly a multinational corporation, which usually does not lack access to good legal advice, should know of the capacity of the party with which it seeks to conclude agreements.[50] Such agreements are based on the law of the host state. State entities, which are usually the parties to such agreements, are created by legislation which is publicly available, and the extent of the powers of these corporations can be easily ascertained by looking at the legislation. Legal instruments on foreign investment increasingly recognise the duty of the foreign investor to abide by the laws of the host state.[51] However, secret instructions or regulations concerning the limitations on such powers will not bind the foreign party.

The second principle that is created relates to the immutability of the foreign investment agreement. When the theorists supporting internationalisation argue that international law or general principles of law or some other supranational system applies to foreign investment agreements, the only norm of law that they are all able to identify is *pacta sunt servanda*. Its application is made to rest not on the assimilation of foreign investment agreements to treaties, which assimilation has been demonstrated to have an inadequate theoretical basis; instead, it is claimed that

---

of treaties that a state cannot rely on its internal law to establish that it did not have competence to enter into the treaty, if all the external formalities of treaty-making have been satisfied.

[49] See C. J. Olmstead, 'Economic Development Agreements' (1961) 49 California LR 607, who states that the position in these circumstances is similar to the *ultra vires* contracts of corporations in domestic law. Inconvenient views such as this are conveniently ignored by writers who support the theory of internationalisation or are dismissed as tendentious.

[50] The draft United Nations Code of Conduct for Transnational Corporations makes it mandatory for multinational corporations to abide by the law of the host state. It is to be inferred from the provision that such a corporation has an understanding of the laws of the host state. A recent arbitral award, *Biloune* v. *Ghana Investment Centre* (1989, unreported) contains the unfortunate suggestion that the letter of the law can be overlooked in the light of practice (para. 80).

[51] See e.g. the APEC Guidelines on Foreign Investment.

the norm is a general principle of law. Those who support the view that international law applies to such agreements will argue that it is a rule of international law, as general principles are a source of international law.

There are several difficulties in accepting *pacta sunt servanda* as a general principle of law. Contractual sanctity may have been the basis of agreements in nineteenth-century law, but both it and the notion of absolute free will as the basis of contract law has been subjected to challenge in the twentieth century.[52] Quite apart from the statutory erosion of the notion of free will, there are other notions such as inequality in bargaining power, economic duress and equitable estoppel which have affected the traditional notions of contractual sanctity. The passing-off of the sanctity of contract as an inflexible norm of contractual systems is contestable. Again, there seems to be a selection of principles to favour the building up of a system of investment protection. A system of investment protection built on such questionable premises can hardly provide adequate protection for foreign investors.

Besides, there are general principles which apply to state contracts which may, in effect, work against the notion of sanctity of contract. The notion of sanctity of contract is taken from laws applicable to private contracts, whereas foreign investment agreements are public contracts concluded with a state or a state agency vested with a monopoly so that it can promote the interests of the public and the state through trade and industry. It is a notion common to all major legal systems that contracts concluded by states or state entities are subject to the public interest and that a state may terminate such contracts if the public interest so requires. This idea was dismissed as a peculiarity of French law, but a French lawyer has pointed out that the defeasibility of state contracts in the public interest is a notion that is common to all legal systems.[53] If that proposition is accepted, then the idea of sanctity of contract will have to give way to the idea of the defeasiblity of state contracts in the public interests. The elevation of general principles of law to the status of international law of investment protection may rebound against the interests of those seeking to internationalise the foreign investment agreements as there could be a discovery of equally cogent principles contrary to the notion of sanctity of contract on which these theorists seek to rely so heavily.

The application of international law does not secure the foreign investment agreement to the extent desired by the proponents of the internationalisation theories. The proponents of the theory rely on static notions

---

[52] Patrick Atiyah, *The Rise and Fall of the Freedom of Contract* (1979).
[53] B. Audit, *State Contracts and Transnational Arbitration* (1988).

of international law and seek to ignore the strides that international law has taken in devising doctrines which seek to confer protection on the economic interests of the developing state. International law has also moved into areas such as environmental protection, economic development and human rights which impact on the protection of investments by multinational corporations and question whether the emphasis on protection accords with other interests of the international community. If international law does indeed apply to state contracts, it is obvious that any state contract which conflicts with any fundamental norm of international law will be invalid.[54] If this is so, then the notion of immutability of contracts will conflict with emerging principles of economic sovereignty and international development law and will, to that extent, be invalid. The rapid growth of an international environmental law imposes duties on multinational corporations not to violate the standards contained in them. They support the regulatory controls exercised by the state to ensure environmental protection. The clash in this area has become particularly acute.[55] Arbitrators should not be one-sided and select only those norms of international law which promote investment protection. Likewise, norms of the international law on development will have to be addressed. Thus, the principle of economic self-determination is an offshoot of the notion of self-determination which in itself is a principle enshrined in the United Nations Charter and elevated, at least by a group of writers, to a principle of *ius cogens* in modern international law. One of the offshoots of the principle of economic self-determination is the doctrine of permanent sovereignty over natural resources. The latter doctrine, though regarded by some as a weak principle because it is contained in a General Assembly resolution, is regarded by many to be in itself a *ius cogens* principle. The latter view seems to be more cogent, for the principle itself logically flows from the notion of territorial sovereignty which forms the basis of the international legal order. The idea of state sovereignty and non-interference with the exercise of sovereignty has been asserted consistently. The International Court of Justice asserted the proposition that a state can choose the economic ideology it prefers without interference by other states.

The detailing of the economic aspects of sovereignty by both the International Court of Justice and the General Assembly in numerous

---

[54] The point is made by Olmstead, 'Economic Development Agreements' (1961) 49 California LR 607, who instances a state contract to engage in slave trade and observes that such a contract will be invalid as being contrary to basic norms of international law.

[55] *Metalclad* v. *Mexico* (2001) 40 ILM 55; *Santa helena* v. *Costa Rica* (2002) 5 ICSID Rpts 157.

resolutions emphasising the right of total control over the running of the economy and the management of the resources considerably diminishes the argument that the application of international law to foreign investment contracts provides protection to such contracts. The contrary may, in fact, be the case.

It may be argued, as in fact has been done, that these contrary norms are weak norms or are at best *lex ferenda*. But, the difficulty with this argument is that the notion of internationalisation and the extraction of *pacta sunt servanda* also rely on the weakest norms of international law. The theory of internationalisation relies on the writings of publicists, (and the publicists are by no means in agreement on the point) and on a few, usually uncontested, arbitral awards. Both are weak, manipulable sources and, indeed, the suspicion that they are mercenary sources cannot be avoided easily.[56] The notion of contractual sanctity, which has been demonstrated not to be an absolute principle in modern contract systems, depends on general principles of law which are also a weak source of law. A contractual system of investment protection constructed on the basis of weak norms which are contested by other weak norms cannot inspire much confidence.

A third facet of internationalisation relates to the remedy that is provided. Since the assimilation of the foreign investment contract to a treaty between states is the basis of the theory of internationalisation of foreign investment agreements, it is claimed that an arbitral award before which a dispute involving a breach of the agreement is brought, has the power to order specific performance of the agreement.

Specific performance in these circumstances will appear to be an illusory remedy, especially for an arbitrator to grant. For, short of the use of military power, which an arbitrator does not have at his disposal, an order for specific performance cannot be executed. Even in the cases of breaches of international treaties, the normal order is for damages. Specific performance is seldom ordered by international courts, except in the case of territorial disputes where the order that territory be transferred to the rightful owner can be the only means of solving the dispute.[57] Yet, in

---

[56] The study of international arbitration by two Canadian scholars, Dezalay and Bryant, seeks to confirm this. See their book, *Dealing in Virtue: International Commercial Arbitration and the Construction of a Transnational Legal Order* (1996).

[57] C. Gray, *Judicial Remedies in International Law* (1990), 16–17. Though initially confined to treaty and contractual obligations, her discussion tends to the general view that such orders cannot be made against governments. This cannot stand as an unqualified proposition. Specific performance can be the only remedy in territorial disputes. *Temple of Preah Vihear*

the case of foreign investment disputes, the exorbitant claim is made that the arbitral tribunal can order specific performance. The only reason for this is that it could facilitate the pursuit of the fruits of the concession that has been taken over through the domestic courts into whose jurisdiction such property is later taken.[58] Here again, theory is twisted to suit the convenience of foreign investment protection.

The theoretical objections cannot be overcome merely by defining the supranational system applicable as some system other than public international law. Some authorities, when faced with the difficulty of applying public international law, have suggested the evolution of some intermediate system such as transnational law to apply to foreign investment contracts. This suggestion recognises the theoretical difficulties in applying international law to the contract and hence is a rejection of the notion of internationalisation. But, the attempt to construct a separate regime has been unsuccessful, for these writers also have to rely on general principles of law to quarry the principles applicable to the agreement. This, it has been shown, depends entirely on the subjective prejudices of the persons seeking to extract the general principles applicable to the agreement. The problem with the construction of a transnational law to apply to such foreign investment agreements is the identification of a juridical base for the system. Without the consent of states, such a system cannot be established. The system at present exists only in the imaginings of writers partial to its creation.

2.2. The ICSID Convention and international law

Arbitration under that convention is distinct and should not be confused with *ad hoc* arbitration or with arbitration conducted by private arbitral institutions. Yet, the confusion is frequently made. ICSID, as indicated above is a specialist organisation tasked with the settlement of investment disputes and, unlike other arbitral tribunals, operates on the basis of an international convention. Its juridical status is as an international institution, whereas other arbitral tribunals are either private bodies, creatures of single sovereigns or of the immediate parties to a dispute as in the case

---

Case [1982] 1CJ Rpts 1. But, it is difficult to extend specific performance to areas outside territorial disputes. It would be too artificial to assimilate a dispute relating to a concession agreement involving land to a territorial dispute.
[58] See M. Sornarajah, *Pursuit of Nationalized Property* (1985).

of *ad hoc* tribunals. In the area under discussion, reference is frequently made to Article 42(1) of the ICSID Convention, which reads as follows:

> The Tribunal shall decide a dispute in accordance with such rules of law as may be agreed by the parties. In the absence of such agreement, the Tribunal shall apply the law of the Contracting State party to the dispute (including its rules on the conflict of laws) and such other rules of international law as may be applicable.

Clearly, the article contemplates the relevance of international law to the resolution of disputes by the ICSID tribunal. But, the use of the technique of choice of law is conferred on a tribunal created by an international convention by its member states. Whatever the interpretation of the article may be, the mandate is given by the states which are parties to the Convention to the tribunal created by the Convention to apply the particular technique of choice of law created by the article. It is not a mandate that is given to private tribunals. A tribunal constituted by the International Chamber of Commerce, a private body which is in no way akin to the ICSID which is created by the will of sovereign states, referred to Article 42 in justifying its use of the same choice-of-law technique as contained in that article. In their rush to pretend to greater powers than they really possess, these tribunals seem to sacrifice principle and rush headlong into areas into which they have no mandate to trespass. They can hardly be regarded as bodies capable of deciding on issues relating to the declaration or application of principles of international law.

As much as it is an error for tribunals not created by an international convention to imitate the powers of ICSID, it is also an unwelcome development that in many ICSID arbitrations an effort is being made to marry ICSID jurisprudence with the internationalisation theory. This effort is clear in awards like *Benvenuti and Bonfant* which are based on the theory of internationalisation.

The ICSID Convention has sought to establish a system which remains neutral and finely balanced between the interests of the foreign investor and the host state. It requires the initial consideration of the domestic laws of the host state. It may be that this was a disguised effort to get developing states to agree to the Convention. If so, this would be to attribute improper motives to the framers of the Convention. The ordinary meaning of the words in the article do require that primacy should be attached to the domestic laws of the state party to the dispute. But, there has been an undisguised effort to tilt the law towards the internationalisation theory. Examples of this trend include: the greater willingness to find jurisdiction in the face of problems presented by corporate personality; regarding unilateral guarantees as indicating support for assuming jurisdiction; the use of denial of justice as a basis for damages even though there may be jurisdictional problems of awarding damages on this ground; and a willingness to be involved in matters of war and peace to give relief to the foreign investor. The alacrity with which ICSID tribunals are willing to find jurisdiction from bilateral investment treaties is another feature which will bring the ICSID system into contention. Though at the high point of liberalisation that the world has gone through in the last decade, these trends are in keeping with the times, a backlash will set in once the fervour for liberalisation subsides.

ICSID tribunals have also subscribed to the theory of internationalisation by taking the view that the reference to international law gives that system a supervisory role.

2.3. Lex mercatoria and state contracts

A new avenue of enabling the protection of foreign investment through the creation of international norms has been opened up through the avenue of international commercial arbitration of private transnational business disputes. In such arbitration, lex mercatoria is recognised as a body of rules which could be applied to international commercial transactions. There is no accepted definition of lex mercatoria, but it generally refers to a body of commercial rules that are applied frequently by international arbitrators who short-circuit the need for determining the law applicable to the dispute by discovering a commercial legal principle which is a common denominator to all the possible legal systems applicable to the dispute or discovering some trade usage or custom that may be relevant, and converting that into a legal principle. The argument is that, as a result of an accumulation of arbitral awards and the consistency with which arbitrators have adopted certain doctrines, a system of law applicable to transnational business disputes has now been created. There are many defects with this thesis. It has been pointed out that lex mercatoria does not have any principles that are clearly identifiable and the ones that have been stated as principles of the system are so obvious that they could have been used without any resort to such a nebulous theory. The sources from which the law is to emanate and the ease with which private bodies may foist principles of law onto the whole international community made scholars wary of the theory. There are no objective criteria by which the principles of this so-called legal system can be identified and no benchmark by which it could be tested except its acceptance by a select group of European arbitrators and scholars who promote it through their incestuous writings. The steadfast tradition in the English law of resisting *lex mercatoria*, on the ground that it creates a system of private justice dependent on individual notions of what the law is, seems to be on the wane.[59]

The relevance of this development in the field of private international commercial arbitration and the distinct field of the arbitration of disputes arising from state contracts is that there seems to be an effort to coalesce the ideas of *lex mercatoria* and the idea of the internationalisation of state contracts and the application to it of a supranational system of law. The unity is seen in the manner of the extraction of the norms of both systems. General principles of law and arbitral awards form a substantial basis for both *lex mercatoria* and the use of a supranational system for dispute resolution in state contracts. The writers who favour the creation of both systems appear to come from the same stable. There is seen to be an advantage in seeking to bolster both systems together as the same private power centres in the international arbitral systems support the creation of both principles.

However, both systems are characterised by the same defects. They depend on uncertain norms. The few arbitral awards which purport to apply the system come out with rules like good faith which could have been applied without resort to any convoluted notion like *lex mercatoria*. Both contain the idea that a small group of persons could foist a system on the whole world by an esoteric process that others are not privy to. The claim is that, as a result of an accumulation of arbitral awards and the consistency with which arbitrators have adopted certain doctrines, a system of law applicable to transnational business disputes has now been created.

The relevance of this development in the field of private international commercial arbitration and the distinct field of arbitration of disputes arising from state contracts is that there seems to be an effort to coalesce the ideas of *lex mercatoria* and the idea of the internationalisation of state contracts and the application to it of a supranational system of law. The unity is seen in the manner of the extraction of the norms of both systems. General principles of law and arbitral awards form a substantial basis for both *lex mercatoria* and the use of a supranational system for dispute resolution in state contracts. The writers who favour the creation of both systems appear to come from the same stable. There is seen to be an

---

[59] Its best representations were in the writings of Lord Mustill on the subject.

advantage in seeking to bolster both systems together, as the same private power centres in the international arbitral systems support the creation of both principles.

2.4. Umbrella clauses and internationalisation

There has been revived interest in the internationalisation theory as a result of two recent awards involving the so-called umbrella clauses in investment treaties.[60] These are provisions towards the end of some investment treaties containing a catch-all statement that conditions and privileges that are negotiated by the parties to an investment agreement will be protected by the treaty. This provision, which has generally been ignored by commentators from the inception of these treaties, has been given special significance in the process of arguments in the two recent awards. The two awards, however, take somewhat differing approaches to the question of the interpretation of the clauses as they appear in the treaties.

The argument that the umbrella clause has significance was roundly rejected by the award in *SGS v. Pakistan*. The matter was left more open in *SGS v. Philippines*. It is difficult to see how a clause, hitherto regarded as insignificant, can have the effect of enhancing the obligations contained in contractual documents. As the award in *SGS v. Pakistan* points out, if such an extensive meaning was to be given to the clause, it would render the carefully negotiated provisions of the investment treaties nugatory. Besides, the idea that a yet-to-be-identified multinational corporation, which lacks international personality, could create fresh international obligations in a state through a contract lacks a theoretical basis in international law which carefully regulates the extent to which rights may be created in third parties, normally states, to treaties. Lengthy statements are made on this subject on the basis of little study of the theoretical implications of the expansive propositions that are advanced on the basis of clauses that seem to create only rights between the parties.

3. Conclusion

The attempt to create an international law on investment protection through purely private means did succeed to a large extent, despite the fact that its theoretical foundations were slim. It indicates not only the power

---

[60] *SGS v. Philippines*, ICSID Arbitration 02/1, Award of 29 January 2004; *SGS v. Pakistan*, ICSID Arbitration 01/13, (2004) *ICSID Journal* 307.

of the multinational corporations to create law but also the existence of avenues through which international law can be used as an instrument of private power through weak sources of law such as the awards of arbitral tribunals and the writings of 'highly qualified publicists'. The role of the latter, who are but individuals with partialities to certain views either because they believe firmly in it or because it is lucrative to do so, requires a view of international law in terms not of a scientifically neutral discipline but as a manipulable device which serves the interests of power.

The episode relating to internationalisation continues in the sense that there are still awards that are made purely on the basis of the theory. But, the opportunity for such awards is receding, largely because there are more sophisticated and theoretically sounder bases for the invocation of arbitration for the settlement of foreign investment disputes. Whereas, in the past, the invocation of arbitration was based on the consent of the parties expressed through a clause in a foreign investment agreement, increasingly arbitration in the field of foreign investment has become treaty-based. The role of investment treaties in promoting arbitration has been instrumental in the increase in the number of arbitrations in this area, particularly ICSID arbitrations. While the treaties provide a sounder jurisdictional foundation for the arbitral tribunals, the law that is sought to be applied still continues to be 'international law' represented by the solitary principle of *pacta sunt servanda*. It has been demonstrated that this carry-over from the internationalisation theory also has insecure foundations. But, it would not create even a dent to point this out, as the trends in the field are such that it is not theory which matters but the pragmatism dictated by power and self-interest.

10

Compensation for nationalisation of foreign investments

Compensation for nationalisation of foreign investment is a topic steeped in controversy. Opinions expressed as to the need for compensation have ranged from the payment of full compensation, a concept which includes consideration of future profits the investment would have made, to the payment of no compensation at all. The acuteness of the conflict was evidenced by the division that occurred within the academic and official quarters as to the statement of the rule on the standard of compensation in the American Law Institute's *Restatement (Second) of the Foreign Relations Law of the United States* and in the various awards of the Iran–US Claims Tribunal. The issue has remained dormant in more recent times, attention being shifted to issues such as the scope of taking and the meaning and extent of regulatory taking. Another feature is the attempt to shift the focus of the controversy by articulating standards of valuation. The topic will remain of great interest, despite the fact that there have been few spectacular nationalisations in recent times. The need for foreign investment and the inadequacy of foreign capital to supply this need keeps such activity dormant. Given this context, states will not seek to spoil their record of stability by engaging in any spectacular nationalisations. But, bouts of nationalism will occur in cyclical patterns in the history of nations. When the present philosophy of investment-led growth gives way to some other philosophy inimical to continued dependence on foreign investment, there will once more be hostility to foreign investment. Such hostility is all the more likely because many of the fund- and aid-giving organisations have imposed conditions which require the liberalisation of the entry of foreign investment as a requirement for the granting of such aid. When hostility to these measures gathers momentum, foreign investment may suffer and nationalisation may once more come into vogue. For these reasons, the issue of compensation for nationalisation, though dormant now, could become, once more, a hotly debated issue in the future.

The relevance of the issue will continue as the notion of taking expands. Where expanded notions of taking become accepted, the compensation issue will again become significant.

Because of the controversial nature of the subject, the method of treatment of the subject which is adopted in this chapter is different. The discussion is based on the acceptance of the fact that there is no clear principle as to compensation for nationalisation in international law at the present time. Though most investment treaties require the payment of full market value as compensation, there is as yet no sufficient uniformity of practice to indicate a set pattern on this matter. For this reason, the different claims that have been made as to what the law is are stated and the support for them in the authorities is assessed. The strength of the different claims will appear as a result of the adoption of this technique. Some of the claims can then be discarded. The final process of elimination will be to examine the extent to which the remaining claims accord with or further the objectives of the international community. It must be stressed that the discussion relates to *lawful* nationalisation. Where nationalisations are unlawful, for example, where they are motivated by racial discrimination or are by way of reprisals, different considerations would apply, as international wrongs are involved. The rectification of these international wrongs, as was pointed out in the last chapter, justifies the assessment of damages on other considerations.

It is necessary to point out at the outset that the sources on which the competing claims to the standard of compensation are based are weak sources of international law. It is often pointed out that the claims to the new standards of compensation are based on weak norms or on 'soft law'. The sources on which the claims to the traditional standard of full or adequate compensation are based are by no means capable of producing hard law. The traditional claims are based on arbitral awards, which are often uncontested, and on the writings of jurists. They are weak, subsidiary sources of law. It has already been pointed out that the view that investment treaties bring about customary international law in the area on any point including that of compensation is a fallacy. The competing and relatively new claims are also based on a few arbitral awards, resolutions of the General Assembly of the United Nations as to whose law-making competence there have been doubts and an increasing body of writings of jurists. It is a facet of this area of the law that it is based on weak norms, and it does not help in the clarification of the law that supporters of the different claims refer to the weakness of the sources on which other claims are made, for all the claims are based on the weakest of the sources known to international law.

1. The competing norms: the views of the capital-exporting states[1]

The area of compensation for nationalisation is acknowledged to be one of the most controversial areas of international law. In an earlier period, there was a certain concordance in views so that it could be asserted that a head count of scholars showed a preponderant support for the view that full compensation should be paid upon nationalisation of foreign property. This was largely because the writers on the subject were European or American. The views of Latin American and other writers who opposed this view seldom came to light or were given prominence. But, since then, there has been a diversity of views expressed even within Europe and the United States. It cannot be asserted with any confidence that preponderant opinion favours one particular norm. This is evident simply by looking at the position in the United States, where the official position has consistently been that full compensation must be paid on nationalisation of foreign investment, but where academic opinion has been keenly divided. The authorities supporting the different claims are examined first, before deciding on the position which best reflects contemporary international law.

1.1. The claim that 'prompt, adequate and effective' compensation must be paid

The claim to full or adequate compensation is supported by the majority of capital-exporting states, for the obvious reason that it affords the best protection for the capital which leaves these states as foreign investment. If the full value of the property which is subject to the expropriation and the anticipated earnings of the foreign investment are immediately replaced in currency which is convertible, the foreign investor will not have suffered in any material sense and the capital can be reinvested elsewhere or brought back home. The interest in the capital as well as in the national

---

[1] This is an old-fashioned distinction. The erstwhile capital-exporters are now massive recipients of capital, the United States being the obvious example. Yet, the distinction is useful in explaining the division of views, which are still largely on the basis of a divide between developed and developing countries.

who takes it abroad makes it sensible from the point of view of the home state to hold out for what is the best possible solution from its point of view as the norm of international law. The formula of 'prompt, adequate and effective compensation' was first used by Secretary of State Cordell Hull during the Mexican expropriations and is generally referred to in the literature as the 'Hull formula'. The Mexican expropriations themselves were intended to achieve land reform in that state. One important factor was that the communication by Hull did not characterise the expropriations as illegal.[2] To this extent, the communication amounts to the relinquishing of older views relating to the illegality of takings and an acceptance of the emerging view that takings by the state in pursuance of economic objectives are lawful.[3] But, he insisted that even such lawful expropriation must be accompanied by the payment of full compensation. The communication did not refer to payment of compensation as being a condition precedent to the legality of the expropriation. Whereas previously, there was a view that expropriation may be unlawful in the absence of compensation, the change of opinion was that the socially utilitarian motive made the expropriation lawful in itself but that there should be payment of compensation following such an expropriation. It is this change of opinion as to the legality of expropriation measures which makes the use of precedents as to the standard of compensation from an earlier period suspect.

The view has been stated that it makes no difference to the standard of compensation whether the expropriation is lawful or unlawful. Such a view cannot rest on logical foundations, for every legal system must necessarily make a distinction between damages arising from lawful and unlawful acts. There must be a distinction between a wrong or injury which requires compensation by way of remedy and a justifiable act which

---

[2] For the Mexican expropriations and the exchanges between the governments on the nature of the compensation that should be paid, see Whiteman, 8 *Digest* 1020; and Hackworth, 3 *Digest* 657. The Foreign Minister of Mexico had written to Hull: 'My Government maintains that there is in international law no rule universally accepted in theory nor carried out in practice, which makes obligatory the payment of immediate compensation nor even deferred compensation for expropriations of a general and impersonal character like those which Mexico has carried out for the redistribution of land.' Hull replied: 'Under every rule of law and equity, no government is entitled to expropriate private property, for whatever purposes, without provision for prompt, adequate and effective compensation.'

[3] In his note to the Mexican ambassador on 3 April 1940, Secretary Hull stated: '[T]he Government of the United States readily recognizes the right of a sovereign state to expropriate property for public purpose.' Whiteman, 8 *Digest* 1020. What is done in pursuance of a right cannot be unlawful.

requires that any person who has been adversely affected as a result is recompensed through the payment of money. Admittedly, the distinction between lawful and unlawful takings is difficult to make except in the cases where there had been a clear lack of a public purpose or the taking was racially discriminatory. However, if the law makes it lawful for a state to nationalise and makes certain types of taking unlawful, that law must also ensure that there is a distinction to be drawn in the awarding of damages.

Christine Gray points out in her study on judicial remedies that, though the distinction between legal and illegal acts causing harm exists, the nature of the distinction as to the award of damages in respect of the two categories of act have not been stated with clarity anywhere.[4] This is a matter which requires attention and will be examined in the course of the discussion of the different claims. The types of authority which support the norm of full or adequate compensation may now be looked at. The sources of law as stated in the Statute of the International Court of Justice will be looked at to determine the nature of the support they provide to each claim. Another problem in relation to full compensation is that full compensation has not been defined.[5] It is not confined to the market value of the property. There are loose formulations that full compensation means the awarding of *damnum emergens* and *lucrum cessans*, meaning that the value of the property as well as future profits must be paid. The formulation itself is imprecise. The absence of a firm definition of full compensation enables writers to project authorities to fit their own theories as to what is full compensation. The calculation of damages is an area that needs to be examined separately.

1.1.1. Treaties

There are no multinational treaties on the question of investment pro-tection.[6] Of the several failed efforts to draft a multilateral agreement, the last was in 1998, when the OECD attempted a multilateral agreement

---

[4] C. Gray, *Judicial Remedies in International Law* (1990), 179–80.

[5] Gray, *ibid.*, p. 19, pointed out that full compensation 'has no single, locally determined, fixed meaning. This rather obvious point needs to be made only because there is a temptation facing writers in this area to choose between cases on the basis of their preconceptions as to what is meant by full compensation.'

[6] There are several guidelines and draft conventions. The World Bank Group in its survey of these documents found that the Hull formula 'is contained in only one of the multilateral documents reviewed'. World Bank Group, *Legal Framework for the Treatment of Foreign Investment* (vol. 1, 1992), 88.

on investment. In considering whether treaties give rise to any customary international law in this area, the tribunal in *United Parcel Services* v. *Canada* stated that 'the failure of efforts to establish a multilateral agreement on investment provides further evidence of the lack of a sense of obligation' in the various types of investment treaty to create customary international law in this area.[7] The payment of compensation for takings would have been the most central factor if any multilateral treaty had come into being.

The failure of the attempts at the formulation of such conventions indicates the absence of any consensus among states on many issues of foreign investment protection, including the standard on which compensation must be paid for nationalised property. The Economic Agreement of Bogota (1948) contained a clause requiring full compensation upon nationalisation. But, eight signatories entered reservations to it. The draft OECD convention (1967) contained the traditional limitations on nationalisation and required the payment of full compensation. The later 1998 draft also contained a provision that included the formula of prompt, adequate and effective compensation. But, this draft was made by developed states which would generally have subscribed to the formula reflecting full compensation. The failure of the multilateral efforts demonstrates that there is no identity of interests between the capital-exporting states and the capital-importing states on the issue.

There are several bilateral investment treaties which contain references to adequate compensation. The older friendship, commerce and navigation (FCN) treaties as well as the newer bilateral investment treaties contain references to the standard, but the terminology used is not uniform.[8] Consistent acceptance of a norm in bilateral treaties could convert

---

[7] Award on Jurisdiction, 22 November 2002. The award is available on various websites.
[8] The US FCN treaties containing references to the standard of full compensation are listed in Whiteman, 8 *Digest* 1018. For the bilateral investment treaties and their treatment of the standard of compensation, see Chapter 7 above. UK practice is not uniform. The treaty with Tunisia simply refers to the payment of 'compensation' without a qualifying adjective. Treaties with Antigua and Barbuda (1987), Poland (1988), Guyana (1989) and Hungary (1988) use the Hull formula. The treaty with Bolivia refers to 'just and effective' compensation. But, these formulations are usually followed by a reference to the requirement to pay 'the market value of the property expropriated immediately before the expropriation became public knowledge'. Dutch treaties usually refer to 'just' compensation and are followed by references to the requirement to pay the 'genuine value' of the investment. The practice of China diverges markedly. The market value formula is used in the treaty with Australia (1988), but in the treaty with New Zealand concluded the same year there is merely a reference to compensation without a qualifying adjective. The later treaties made in the 1990s contain more references to the Hull standard but no rule can still be extracted as a general principle. Some of these treaties confine the type of investment that is

that norm into a principle of international law. But, it is unlikely that such a view can be taken of bilateral investment treaty provisions on compensation. It has already been pointed out that the divergence in the standards used and the fact that many of them provide for valuation of compensation to be made by national authorities make the possibility of such treaties creating a norm as to the standard of compensation remote. One reason for the rapid accumulation of bilateral investment treaties is that, as the norms relating to compensation became diffused due to different formulations of the standard of compensation, parties to the investment treaties seek to formulate a binding standard as between themselves. The formulation that is finally included in the treaties on such matters as compensation reflects the compromise the parties had arrived at after negotiations. If this view is correct, then the chances of the standards stipulated in these treaties ripening into propositions of customary law are remote. Besides, many bilateral treaties heavily qualify the types of investment that are protected. In these circumstances, it is clear that, even where the provision on full compensation appears in a treaty, it does not protect all investments but only those of the type that qualifies for protection under the treaty. In the 1990s, there was a sudden growth in the number of these treaties. But, the mere increase in numbers affords no solution as to whether customary international law was created. Expediency and the need to attract foreign investment rather than a clear conviction seem to have been the reason for stating the rule on full compensation rather than any conviction that it represents a rule of law. As a result, the conclusion that there is no treaty law supporting a general norm of full compensation is inevitable.

1.1.2. Customary practice

Customary practice is not uniform as to the payment of full compensation on nationalisation. The Hull standard was resisted by Mexico when it was formulated.[9] The former communist states objected to the formula on ideological grounds. The Latin American states have consistently objected to the standard, though there are signs that many states are willing to subscribe to the standard in bilateral investment treaties. There

---

protected by qualifying the investment. Thus, many of the south-east Asian treaties protect only approved investments or investments made in accordance with laws and regulations. To extract rules by finding the common denominators in them is an impossible task.

[9] Mexico, the state whose expropriations led to the formulation of the Hull standard, participates in NAFTA, which uses words that are similar to the Hull standard. Sensitivities perhaps necessitated the avoidance of the use of the formula, but the result arrived at is the same.

has been ambivalence within developing states as to the standard which they would support. Individually, some of them have subscribed to the standard of full compensation in bilateral investment treaties, though collectively they have promoted different standards at the multilateral level.

There is no indication in modern practice of full compensation ever having been paid as compensation for nationalisation. States which have firmly held on to the standard of full compensation have accepted less than full compensation.[10] Nowhere is this more evident than in the settlement of compensation disputes through lump-sum payments. Though there are strenuous efforts made by some scholars to argue in support of the extreme view that the lump-sum settlement agreements did not deviate from the standards of full compensation, it is difficult to demonstrate that these agreements were not based on the acceptance of only partial compensation. The general tendency of those who seek to support the payment of full compensation is to underplay the relevance of these treaties.[11] The preponderant view is that they have nothing to contribute to the formation of any international law. Thus, the Iran–US Claims Tribunal stated in *Amoco Finance*:

> As a rule, state practice as reflected in settlement agreements cannot be considered as giving birth to customary rules of international law, unless it presents specific features which demonstrate the conviction of the state parties that they were acting in application of what they considered to be settled law. The provisions of such an agreement, indeed, are the outcome of negotiations in which many motivations other than legal ones may have prevailed.

---

[10] The United States, for example, accepted less than full compensation in the Marcona nationalisation. G. Gantz, 'The Marcona Settlement: New Forms of Negotiation Compensation for Nationalized Property' (1977) 71 AJIL 474.

[11] Lillich and Weston are in a minority when they support the contrary view. R. B. Lillich and B. Weston, *International Claims: Their Settlement by Lump Sum Agreements* (1975), 35. There is a 'truly extraordinary consistency in these agreements' in favour of full compensation. See also Lillich and Weston, 'Lump Sum Agreements: Their Continuing Contribution to the Law of International Claims' (1988) 82 AJIL 69. The only consistent theme in these agreements is that they involved the acceptance of partial compensation. M. Sornarajah, *Pursuit of Nationalized Property* (1986), 214–17. The overwhelming majority of writers support the view that partial compensation was the basis of these agreements. V. Pechota, 'The 1981 US–Czechoslovakia Claims Settlement Agreement: An Epilogue to Post War Nationalization and Expropriation Disputes' (1982) 76 AJIL 639. C. F. Amerasinghe, 'Issues of Compensation in the Taking of Alien Property in the Light of Recent Cases and Practice' (1992) 41 ICLQ 22 at 28; R. Dolzer, 'New Foundations of the Law of Expropriation of Alien Property' (1981) 75 AJIL 553 at 560; I. Seidl-Hohenveldern, Book Review (1991) 38 GYIL 592, who takes the view that lump sum agreements are not based on full compensation and that the home state should top up the balance.

Lump-sum settlement agreements are an embarrassment to those who argue that there is a customary law which requires full compensation for nationalisation. These agreements demonstrate that states have settled claims arising from expropriation otherwise than on the standard of full compensation. To the extent that many of them were concluded with the former communist states of Eastern Europe, they constitute a rejection of the communist position that no compensation needs to be paid on nationalisation. They also support the claim that some compensation must be paid on expropriation, though they leave open the issue of the exact standard on which the compensation is to be paid. It is safe to conclude that there is no customary practice supporting the norm of full compensation for expropriation. The capital-exporting countries have articulated such a norm as a negotiating stance, and have been consistent in supporting it. But, it has not received such a generality of acceptance as to be regarded as an international practice that has matured into a rule of international law. The efforts to argue that bilateral investment treaties create custom have already been examined and found to be wanting. They do not create any custom on the question of the standard of compensation for expropriation.[12]

1.1.3. General principles of law

The strongest sources of international law, treaty and custom, have contributed nothing to the formation of any definite principle on the issue of compensation for expropriation of property. The claims as to the existence of a law have had to rely entirely on weak sources of international law, such as general principles of law, decisions of arbitral tribunals and the writings of publicists. The first of these are manipulable according to subjective preferences and the latter two are themselves expressions of the subjective preferences of arbitrators and writers.

General principles of law are a weak source of international law. Their weakness is accentuated by the common tendency to select a proposition from a few national systems and argue that they constitute a general principle, which should be treated as international law. Thereafter, like-minded scholars seek to achieve this conversion through constant repetition. This is a phenomenon which frequently occurs in international investment law. The selectiveness involved in the technique is illustrated

---

[12] In a study of 154 cases of expropriation, Sunshine found that the general practice was to apply the net book value concept. The Hull formula and alternative formulas were used as bargaining counters but never adhered to. R. B. Sunshine, *Terms of Settlement in Developing Countries' Nationalization Settlements* (UNCTC, 1981).

by the fact that often the choice of the principle is restricted to a particular period in the history of the legal system or the principle is chosen and the exceptions to it in the legal systems are jettisoned. The general principles which are used in this area consist of equitable principles of unjust enrichment and acquired rights and the principle of the right to property the violation which requires the payment of full compensation. Another, more recent, source in which general principles supporting the payment of full compensation is sought are the foreign investment codes of different states.

1.1.4. Unjust enrichment

The two principles which are frequently chosen to support the norm of full compensation are unjust enrichment and acquired rights. In the case of unjust enrichment, which as an equitable principle receives wide acceptance in legal systems, the argument is that, since a state is enriched as a result of its taking of foreign property, it must repay to the alien owner as compensation a sum which reflects the extent of the enrichment. This sum, it is suggested, is the full value of the property which had been taken. The focus is to be on the act of expropriation alone. There is a discarding of the prior relationship between the parties or of the nature of the profits which accrued from the investment to the foreign investor. What is made solely relevant is the value of the property at the time of the taking. The argument is that it is this value which has to be paid as compensation.

The principle of unjust enrichment may not work in this manner. It is an equitable principle, and, where it is applied, many legal systems require that the whole course of the relationship between the parties must be taken into account in the determination of the equitable relief which is to be accorded to the party that suffered damage. In contract law and property law where the principle is recognised, it is not recognised as being applicable only by reference to the single act causing injury but as applying only after a nice analysis of the benefits and costs attending the whole course of the relationship had been made.[13] Unjust enrichment

---

[13] F. Francioni, 'Compensation for Nationalization of Foreign Property: The Borderland of Law and Equity' (1975) 24 ICLQ 255. W. Friedmann, *Changing Structure of International Law* (1962), 207, argued that the 'history of the economic-political relations between the parties' should be taken into account in considering unjust enrichment. See D. Dicke, 'Taking of Foreign Property and Compensation' in T. Oppermann and E. Petersmann (eds.), *Reforming the International Economic Order* (1987), 62 at 73–9, for a comparative study of legal systems on the issue of unjust enrichment and the conclusion that 'unjust enrichment as an argument points both ways'.

cannot uniformly support full compensation when applied to a situation of expropriation. It will support less than full compensation when the past benefits of the investment had weighed heavily in favour of the investor. It may support more than full compensation in situations in which the foreign investment is relatively new, had been enticed into the host country and had involved the transfer of assets and technology which would not otherwise have been obtained by the host state.[14] An equitable principle like unjust enrichment lends only equivocal support to full compensation. While there could be full compensation in appropriate circumstances, in other circumstances it could produce results varying from no compensation to less than full compensation.

1.1.5. Acquired rights

There is doubt as to whether the doctrine of acquired rights forms a part of international law at all. Rights are acquired under domestic law. The significance of international law to such rights, except when there is a treaty protecting them, is theoretically a difficult concept to fit into the scheme of international law. If it can be fitted in, the doctrine of acquired rights also does not provide any firm support for full compensation. The rights have to be vested under the municipal law of the host state, and one problem is that the municipal law which vests those rights should also be able to destroy them without reference to other legal systems.[15] The doctrine of acquired rights is also an equitable doctrine. To the extent that it is relevant to the assessment of compensation, it will, like other equitable doctrines, require that the equities involved in the whole course of the relationship between the parties be looked at in the determination of the compensation that is to be paid.[16]

Unjust enrichment and other equitable doctrines operate in the context of private law in domestic legal systems. They cannot be readily transported into an area in which public law features dominate. Rights, which

---

[14] See *Sola Tiles* v. *Iran* (1987) 14 Iran–US CTR 223 at 237.

[15] D. O'Connell, *International Law* (vol.1), 305, stated that acquired rights 'cannot be cancelled without full satisfaction of the equities attaching to them'. On acquired rights, see G. White, *Nationalization of Foreign Property* (1961), 13–16; Kaeckenbeck, 'The Protection of Vested Rights in International Law' (1936) 17 BYIL 1; McNair, 33 BYIL at 16; and J. P. Lalive, 'The Doctrine of Acquired Rights' in South Western Legal Foundation, *Selected Readings on the Protection of Foreign Investments* (1964). The argument relating to acquired rights continues to be used in modern arbitral awards, e.g. *Amco* v. *Indonesia* (1983–90) 1 ICSID Rpts 189.

[16] F. Francioni, 'Compensation for Nationalization of Foreign Property: The Borderland between Law and Equity' (1975) 24 ICLQ 255.

are acquired through the exercise of public law, are generally recognised to be defeasible in the public law systems of major states.[17] So too, the principle of unjust enrichment is seldom the basis of compensation for property acquired under legislation permitting such acquisition for the purpose of development in the public interest. The relevance of these doctrines to the debate on expropriation is contestable. Even if relevant, they do not uniformly support a norm of full compensation. Equitable considerations can be used to support less than full compensation. There have been attempts on the part of some arbitral tribunals to do so.[18] Equity is a double-edged sword and its use can have undesired results for those who invoke it.

1.1.6. Right to property

The argument is sometimes made that the investment codes and constitutional provisions of a large number of states provide support for the existence of a right to property and for the payment of full compensation in the event of nationalisation in violation of such a right.[19] There is little evidence that there is such a widespread and unqualified recognition of the right to property in the constitutional systems of even the capital-exporting states on which any certain principle of international law can be based. At the international and regional levels, the various human rights documents do not accept a right to property without qualifications which justify interference in the public interest. Likewise, where references are made to property rights in the constitutions of states, they are usually defeasible in the public interest. In many instances, it would be uncertain whether these constitutional safeguards give protection to the property of foreigners as they are contained in statements of the rights of citizens.

---

[17] It can never be seriously argued that the right of permanent residence granted to an alien cannot be taken away by the state, though it is also an acquired right. Thus, Ian Brownlie, *Principles of Public International Law* (6th ed., 2003), 533, in rejecting arguments based on acquired rights, observed:

> The argument based upon acquired rights could be applied to a number of reliance situations created by the host state by the grant of public rights such as citizenship or permission to reside or to work. The distinction drawn by partisans of responsibility in contract situations between loan agreements, concessions and other contracts is unsatisfactory. Why do they prefer their reasoning only in certain contract or reliance situations?

[18] E.g. the Iran–US Claims Tribunal in *Phillips Petroleum* (1989) 21 Iran–US CTR 79, citing in support the *Aminoil* award (1982) 66 ILR 518.

[19] Clagget in Lillich, *Valuation of Nationalized Property* (vol. 4, 1987).

In jurisprudential terms, it will be difficult to establish the right to property as a fundamental right even in Western systems. An examination of the philosophical basis of the right to property made by a US scholar contains the following conclusion:[20]

> Under serious scrutiny, there is no right-based argument to be found which provides an adequate justification for a society in which some people have lots of property and many have next to none. The slogan that property is a human right can be deployed only disingenuously to legitimize the massive inequality that we find in modern capitalist countries.

It is doubtful that there is any greater respect for the right to property in the non-capitalist systems.[21] But, taking Europe alone, it will be difficult to demonstrate that there is such an absolute recognition of the right to property that its violation must be followed by the payment of full compensation. The European Court of Human Rights has produced some case law on the right to property in the First Protocol to the European Convention on Human Rights.

The non-inclusion of the right to property in the main text of the Convention itself is significant. The Convention was drafted immediately after the Second World War, and many European states felt that the economic reorganisation that had to take place after the ravages of the war would be impeded by the recognition of a right to property in the Convention.[22] This explains the absence of a provision on the right to property in the Convention. A right to property was included later in the First Protocol to the Convention. In the drafting committee of the Protocol, there was considerable dispute as to whether there was a duty to pay compensation when property was expropriated in the public interest. Some of the European governments did not relish the prospect of their economic programmes being subjected to the scrutiny of a supranational court. It is a feeling which developing countries would share. The present statement of the right to property in the First Protocol is qualified in many ways. It reads:

---

[20] J. Waldron, *The Right to Private Property* (1988), 3.

[21] Communist systems are based on the rejection of the right to property. Philosophical attitudes to property in states influenced by non-materialistic religions are bound to be different. For an interesting account of Maori views on property, see A. Frame, 'Property: Some Pacific Reflections' (1992) 22 *New Zealand Law Journal* 21.

[22] For the drafting history, see W. Peukert, 'Protection of Ownership under Article 1 of the First Protocol of the European Convention on Human Rights' (1981) 1 *Human Rights Journal* 36 at 38–42; E. Schwelb, 'The Protection of the Right to Property of Nationals under the First Protocol to the European Convention on Human Rights' (1964) 13 AJCL 518 at 533–40.

> Every natural or legal person is entitled to the peaceful enjoyment of his possessions. No one shall be deprived of his possessions except in the public interest and subject to the conditions provided for by law and by general principles of international law.

The interpretation of this provision by the European Court does not indicate a belief that the right to property is absolute in any sense. European states have had many socialist governments which embarked on programmes of nationalisation of the property of their citizens or have encroached on the property rights of citizens in the social interest. Since the Protocol refers to international law standards, the Court has had to take international law standards, particularly those relating to compensation, into account in applying the law in the cases generated by challenges to the takings effected by European governments. The case law of the Court indicates that the right to property 'has lost its inviolability' in European law. It will be sufficient to indicate this erosion by referring only to the manner in which the issue of compensation has been dealt with in European law.

In *Lithgow*, which involved the taking of an aircraft industry belonging to a British subject by the UK government, the issue of the standard of compensation in international law arose. Since there was a reference to international law standards in the Protocol, the applicant argued that international law required the payment of full compensation. In presenting arguments to the Court, counsel for the European Commission denied the existence of such a standard in international law. He stated his view on the public international law position as to the standard of compensation as follows:[23]

> [T]he European states would seem to have a more or less coherent view, according to which public international law requires the payment of at least appropriate compensation where foreign property is being taken. As to the practice it is extremely divergent. I am not aware of one single case where, for nationalization of whole industries, full compensation was paid by the nationalizing state to the foreign owners, without special investment treaties being applicable. In most cases of nationalization, lump-sum agreements were reached clearly below the value of the assets taken. At least for large scale nationalization, the notion of sovereignty over natural resources and freedom of decision over the economic order may easily come into conflict with a claim of full compensation.

[23] *Lithgow* (1986) 8 EHRR 329.

The Court did not go into great detail on this issue. But, it did indicate that it will not interfere with the decision of the state as to the question of compensation, unless the state's decision as to the amount of compensation that was payable was 'manifestly without reasonable foundation'.[24]

On the issue of compensation, the general view taken by the Court is that, where the taking by the state is for a public purpose, the extent of the public purpose will affect the amount of compensation. Compensation becomes relevant to the Court in considering whether a fair balance was struck between the public interest in the taking of the property and the protection of the individual owner's right to the property. There is a utilitarian notion at play. The individual interest in securing compensation will diminish according to the strength of the justification for the taking provided by the public purpose. Compensation on this theory represents a balance struck between the individual interest and the public benefit which results from the taking. Payment of less than full compensation is justifiable where economic reform is the aim of the taking. The Court explained its position in the following terms:[25]

> Clearly, compensation terms are material to the assessment whether a fair balance has been struck between the various interests at stake, and notably, whether or not a disproportionate burden has been imposed on the person who has been deprived of his possessions. The Court further accepts the Commission's conclusion as to the standard of compensation: The taking of property without payment of an amount reasonably related to its value would normally constitute a disproportioned interference which could not be considered justifiable under Article 1 [of the First Protocol]. Article 1 does not, however, guarantee a right to full compensation in all circumstances. Legitimate objectives of 'public interest', such as pursued in measures of economic reform or measures designed to achieve greater social justice, may call for less than reimbursement of full market value. Furthermore, the Court's power of review is limited to ascertaining whether the choice of compensation terms falls outside the State's wide margin of appreciation in this domain.

In the United States, where one would expect property protection to be stronger because of its history and traditions, the picture is no different. Though there is constitutional protection for the right to property, the

---

[24] *Ibid.*, p. 373.

[25] *James* (1986) 5 EHRR 35 at 147; Lithgow (1986) 8 EHRR 329; see also *Sporrong and Lonnroth v. Sweden* (1983) 5 EHRR 35 (paras. 69 and 73); G. Cohen-Jonathan, *La Convention Europeenne de Droits de l'Homme* (1989), 526–7.

formulations are in less than absolute terms. The amount of compensation which is to be considered 'just' in the circumstances of state taking has been considered to be a factor in balancing individual rights and the public interest. The views taken in the United States on the issue closely parallel the balancing of factors adopted by the European Court.[26]

It could be that the US view has undergone several changes, with the public interest being dominant when the United States was in a stage of development. In this phase, infrastructure upgrading would have required that there be interference with private property, and the courts justified such interference as necessary in the public interest and as requiring no or lesser compensation. But, progressively as development was achieved, there may have come about a greater stress on individual property rights. This course of development indicates that in any given society a balance has to be struck between individual rights in property and the public interest and that balance can only be struck by each state having regard to its own developmental needs.

The regional documents on human rights in Latin America and Africa do not state the right to property in absolute terms. They have regard to the social function of property and state the right as subject to the public interest. Article 21 of the American Convention on Human Rights, after referring to the right to property, states that 'the law may subordinate such use and enjoyment to the interest of society'. It refers to the payment of 'just compensation' for the taking of property. Article 14 of the African Charter on Human and Peoples' Rights guarantees the right to property, but permits encroachment in the public interest. It makes no reference to the payment of compensation for the taking of property. The European Convention also makes no express reference to the payment of compensation, but the European Court has inferred the requirement.

The developments in the national and regional systems should be reflected in international law. If the notion of general principles must be applied in the area, it should not be selectively applied so as to support the norm of full compensation. Conclusions should not be drawn from abstract and unexamined claims that there is a universally recognised right to property. There is no case for an absolute right to property in any municipal, regional or international system. Taking only the Western legal systems into account, the notion of property always had a social content in

---

[26] See further B. Ackerman, *Private Property and the Constitution* (1977); and *Hawaii Housing Authority v. Midkiff*, 467 US 229 (1984), cited with approval by the European Court in *James v. United Kingdom* (1986) 5 EHRR 35, para. 40.

these systems. The notion of *res communes* was taken from the Roman law into international law by Vattel and other institutional writers. In modern European law, the social function of property has made deep inroads into the individual's right to property. European legal systems do not provide a source from which an absolute right to property can be imported into international law through general principles of law. In any event, there is no unanimity of treatment in national systems. Following Roman law, the European systems recognised that it was necessary to hold property for the common good and that private property was a man-made institution to serve individual needs. The Canadian Bill of Rights avoids stating a right to property. Constitutional systems within the Commonwealth state the right in a highly circumscribed fashion. As such, it would be difficult to argue that the right to property is a general principle recognised in law.

In international law, the growth of the law of development will introduce a concept which stipulates that the collective interests of peoples should take precedence over individual rights of ownership. The principle of permanent sovereignty over natural resources is conducive to the evolution of such an attitude to property in international law. The idea that the right to property could be used to support a claim to full compensation is based on insecure foundations.

1.1.7. Foreign investment codes

Investment codes are designed to attract foreign investors as well as to state the conditions on which foreign investment will be permitted entry into the host state. In such codes, a statement of the norm of full compensation could be expected, as this would be most attractive to foreign investors. Even in these codes, there is an absence of uniformity on the standard of compensation. While some investment codes contain the promise of payment of full compensation in the event of expropriation, there are others which do not contain such promises. In some, the promises relating to compensation are ambivalent at best. Thus, the Indonesian code recognises the state's right to nationalise alien property and promises to pay compensation 'in accordance with the rules of international law'. Much is going to depend on the state's appreciation of what international law on the point is. The Thai Investment Promotion Act contains a blanket undertaking not to expropriate a foreign investment which has been promoted by the government under the legislation. The Chinese Joint Venture Law accords the foreign party to the joint venture protection 'in accordance with the law'. There is much disparity in the promises which are made as to the compensation which is payable in the event of expropriation. Such disparity can hardly be the basis of general principles. The nature of these promises also deprives them of much legal significance. They are unilateral promises which are not binding on the state. There is little internal machinery provided for the enforcement of the rights which are provided in the investment codes. They are merely expressions of how the state hopes to act towards the foreign investor in the event of expropriation, and cannot form the basis of building up any norm of international law. These unilateral guarantees are akin to invitations to treat in the common law of contract and cannot be converted into obligations in law or the basis of the creation of principles of law.

The weakness of general principles of law as a source of international law has been frequently commented upon by scholars. It is futile to build any firm norm of international law in an area as controversial as compensation for expropriation of foreign property on the basis of general principles of law alone. The exercise is bound to attract charges of partiality simply because the approach to property protection in the different legal systems is so diverse that it would be difficult to extract principles that are common to all legal systems. With the crumbling of ideologically oriented legal systems and the building of market economies, common principles of property protection may evolve in the future, but at present it would be difficult to say that there is such commonality among legal systems that the payment of full compensation is a general principle of law.

The vigour of neo-liberalist tendencies in the last decade has given rise to the impression that the absolute right to property has triumphed over other, competing notions of property. But, this is an illusory notion. Despite the fact that there are treaties which seek to act on such a premise and arbitral decisions which are based on the acceptance of such an ideology, there is no clear trend which has indicated the victory of one vision of property over another.[27]

1.1.8. Decisions of courts and tribunals

Decisions of courts, both international and domestic, as well as awards of tribunals may be evidence of the existence of international law principles. The subsidiary nature of the role of such sources is obvious. There is no system of precedent in international law. The statement of the principle by a court will provide evidence of the existence of a principle of international law and the strength of the evidence will depend on the prestige of the court. In many of the instances in which arbitral

---

[27] See further M. Sornarajah, 'The Clash of Globalizations and the International Law on Foreign Investment' (2003) 10 *Canadian Foreign Policy* 1.

tribunals have pronounced on the issue of compensation, the arbitration proceeded with no participation by the state and the awards was made by a single arbitrator.[28] In such circumstances, the award can hardly be regarded as anything more than the opinion of a single person on the dispute, formed without the state's case being presented before him. It is best therefore to approach the subject hierarchically, with the international courts being given precedence over arbitral tribunals and national tribunals.

1.1.9. International courts

The only occasion on which an international court had to pronounce on a taking by a state arose in the *Chorzow Factory Case* before the Permanent Court of International Justice.[29] The case is the source of all manner of wisdom in this area of law. The case is taken as supporting the claim of full compensation as including the market value of the property as well as future profits that could have been earned from the investment. In several awards of the Iran–US Claims Tribunal, the case is used as support for the norm of full compensation.

But the use of the *Chorzow Factory Case* in this manner is unjustified. The case itself was concerned with a taking which was held by the Court to be illegal as it was a taking in breach of a treaty. The propositions in that case are concerned with illegal takings and not with expropriations which are considered lawful in modern international law. This will appear from the examination of the facts of the case.

A German company established a nitrate factory at Chorzow in Upper Silesia in pursuance of an agreement it made with the German government in 1915. In 1919, the land and the factory were sold by the German government to another German company. The first company still managed the factory. Upper Silesia passed into Polish hands after the Treaty of Versailles. In 1922, a Polish court declared the registration of the second company to be void and that the land on which the factory stood was to be transferred to the Polish treasury. A Polish ministerial decree vested management of the factory in a Polish official.

The issue which was presented to the Permanent Court of International Justice in 1926 was whether the taking over of the factory contravened

---

[28] On the possibility of bias by arbitrators in disputes arising from state contracts in favour of the views of capital-exporting states, see S. J. Toope, *International Mixed Arbitration* (1990), 346.

[29] (1928) PCIJ Series A, No. 17.

the provisions of the Geneva Convention of 1922 between Germany and Poland. Article 6 of the Convention stated that Poland may expropriate major industries in Polish Upper Silesia but that it should not liquidate the rights of individual German nationals or companies in this region. The Court held that the taking of the factory was a violation of this treaty. The Court said that the Convention itself made certain expropriations lawful and others unlawful and that the expropriation of the factory fell within the category of unlawful expropriations under the treaty. It is clear that the case concerned expropriations which were considered unlawful because they constituted violations of a treaty.

After the judgment of the Court in 1926, negotiations took place between Germany and Poland for the restitution of the factory or, if this was not possible, for indemnity. It is clear that at this stage of the negotiations, the parties to the dispute themselves contemplated the possibility of restitution. When the negotiations proved unsuccessful, Germany claimed damages for the expropriation in a fresh claim before the Court. The German claim itemised the manner in which damages were calculated and did not include a claim for lost profits. The only claim relating to the future was the claim for an order preventing exports from the factory to certain countries. This aspect of the claim was refused by the Court. The Polish objection to the jurisdiction of the Court was overruled in 1927, and the Court pronounced on the merits of the case in 1928.

The Court reiterated the fact that it was not dealing with a lawful expropriation when it observed:

> The action of Poland which the Court has judged to be contrary to the Geneva Convention is not an expropriation – to render which lawful only the payment of fair compensation would have been wanting; it is a seizure of property rights and interests which could not be expropriated even against compensation . . . It follows that the compensation due to the German government is not necessarily limited to the value of the undertaking at the moment of dispossession, plus interest to the day of payment. This limitation would only be admissible if the Polish government had the right to expropriate, and if its wrongful act consisted merely in not having paid to the two companies the just price of what was expropriated; in the present case such a limitation might result in placing Germany and interests protected by the Geneva Convention, on behalf of which interests the German government is acting, in a situation more unfavourable than that in which Germany and these interests would have been if Poland had respected the said Convention.

It should be clear to any reader of this passage that the Court was dealing with unlawful takings in violation of a treaty and not with takings which could have been rendered lawful by the payment of fair compensation. The passage indicates the Court's view that at the time of the decision the law considered the payment of compensation as an element of a lawful expropriation. The use of the case to support a blanket proposition that full compensation is due for all takings is clearly based on a misreading of the case.

The Court addressed the principles relating to damages for unlawful taking in a separate passage. The passage leaves no room for doubt that the Court was setting out the principles for damages for unlawful takings. The passage reads:

> The essential principle contained in the actual notion of an illegal act – a principle which seems to be established by international practice and in particular by the decisions of arbitral tribunals – is that reparation must as far as possible wipe out all the consequences of the illegal act and re-establish the situation which would, in all probability, have existed if that act had not been committed. Restitution, in kind, or, if this is not possible, payment of a sum corresponding to the value which a restitution in kind would bear; the award, if need be, of damages for loss sustained which would not be covered by restitution in kind or payment in place of it – such are the principles which should serve to determine the amount of compensation due for an act contrary to international law.

The Court also relied on the policy reason that the whole purpose of the treaty was to retain the *status quo* which existed as to property ownership. This was a matter protected by treaty, and the only way that the object of the treaty could have been ensured was through restitution of the property. Since that was not possible, the Court ordered damages which could have put the previous owner in a situation akin to his position prior to the taking. The case also illustrated the fact that, even in a clear situation of a treaty violation, the Court did not consider specific performance, despite the fact that the object of the treaty could have been best achieved by such an order.

It would be unnecessary to go on reiterating the point that the Court was not at all stating the principles applicable to the lawful taking of alien property if not for the fact that the case has, despite the clear language of the Court, mysteriously been construed to apply to all types of taking by states, despite the clarity with which the propositions were formulated by the Court. Another broad inference that is made is that the case contains *dicta* permitting the claiming of future loss. Germany did not make any claims for future loss. The only forward-looking claim that Germany made related to a request that the Court make an order prohibiting exports to certain countries. The basis of this claim was that there could be persons in the factory acquainted with the secret processes of the German owners which would enable the company to compete more effectively on the foreign markets with the German owners. The Court refused to make such an order, characterising the claim as insufficiently proven and as 'falling within the head of possible but contingent and indeterminate damage which, in accordance with the jurisprudence of arbitral tribunals, cannot be taken into account'. After having stated the bases on which damages were to be assessed, the Court appointed a group of experts to assess the value of the property. The significance of this procedure, for claims that are later made on the basis of principles of valuation, should not be overlooked. Legal principles must first be laid down and damages assessed on the basis of such principles. It should not be the case that accountancy principles of valuation dictate which legal principles are relevant. In the event, in the *Chorzow Factory Case*, no valuation was made, as the parties settled the dispute.

The manner in which the case has been utilised in subsequent times is a sad commentary on international law academia. Faced with a paucity of authority that supports full compensation, the case has been utilised improperly by the proponents of full compensation to support their claim. It should be obvious to anyone reading the judgment of the Court that the Court sought to apply full compensation not to all instances of expropriation but only to those unlawful expropriations, such as those in breach of a treaty, to which restitutionary principles will apply.

Unfortunately, the *Chorzow Factory Case* has become the authority for a multitude of claims ranging from full compensation to fair and just compensation, which are terms used in the judgment. It illustrates that terminology has been a problem that has befuddled the law in this area. There are many difficult features in the judgment. But, despite these difficulties, it is difficult not to agree with the assessment of the case made by Judge Baxter who observed that the *Chorzow Factory Case*, 'so often resorted to as the source of wisdom on legal remedies for the taking of property', spoke of restitution only in the case of expropriations in violation of treaty commitments.[30]

---

[30] Foreword to R. B. Lillich (ed.), *The Valuation of Nationalized Property* (Vol. 1, 1987), vii; compare F. Francioni, 'Compensation for Nationalization of Foreign Property: The

Support for full compensation is to be found in the individual opinions of judges of the International Court of Justice in some later cases. For example, unequivocal support for full compensation is to be found in the dissenting judgment of Judge Carneiro in the *Anglo-American Oil Company Case*.[31] Judge Carneiro argued that full compensation for expropriated property must be made, as such a rule is a 'prerequisite of international cooperation in the economic and financial fields'. His view is based on the policy grounds that the flow of much-needed capital would be reduced if the norm of full compensation were not recognized, and not based on any examination of precedents.[32]

In the *Barcelona Traction Case*,[33] Judge Gros, in a separate opinion, made the statement that 'any nationalizations of a regular kind would have been accompanied by compensation'. But, the *dictum* must be limited to the situation that was being discussed. The judge had earlier pointed out that the 'opponents in the present case are two states whose economic and legal conceptions are the same'. Clearly, the statement was intended to be restricted to a regional standard that was to be applied to two European states with similar legal cultures.

1.1.10. Awards of arbitral tribunals

The awards of arbitral tribunals stand in an even more inferior position to decisions of the International Court of Justice as sources of international law. Arbitral tribunals are constituted by the agreement of the parties to the foreign investment contract one of whom is not a state, and often the awards that they make are unilateral in that the state party does not appear before them or recognise their jurisdiction. More recently, the International Centre for the Settlement of Investment Disputes has been set up as a specialised body which deals with investment arbitration.

Borderland of Law and Equity' (1975) 24 ICLQ 255 at 260, who observed: 'The case, often referred to as a decision which sanctioned the illegality of legislation having the effect of terminating foreign acquired rights, was strictly confined to a fact situation characterized by an ad hoc treaty that in itself imposed an obligation on Poland not to expropriate German assets and activities.'

[31] *Anglo-American Oil Company Case* [1952] ICJ Rpts 93 at 151.

[32] Judge Carneiro observed (para. 15): 'When there are so many countries in need of foreign investment for their economy, it could be a mistake to expose such capital, without restriction or guarantee, to the hazards of the legislation of countries in which such capital has been invested.' The *dictum* of Judge Carneiro is incorrectly passed off as a *dictum* of the International Court of Justice in R. B. Lillich (ed.), *The Valuation of Nationalized Property* (1987), vol. 4, 174.

[33] *Barcelona Traction Case* [1970] ICJ Rpts 3 at 274.

The scope for awards made by this body as well as by *ad hoc* arbitral tribunals has increased ever since the possibility of tribunals exercising jurisdiction on the basis of treaty provisions has come to be accepted. As a result, an increasing number of awards have been made. Despite this, the precedential value of these awards is not great. The awards that are so made reflect only the opinion of the arbitrators as to what the law is, and the weight these opinions carry depends on the eminence of the persons making them. It may be argued that the opinions of these tribunals have less weight than the views of publicists, as publicists take independent views as to what the law is whereas arbitrators on tribunals are motivated by other considerations such as the settlement of the dispute before them in an amicable or pragmatic fashion. The views that are expressed by these tribunals must therefore be approached with caution.

Full compensation was awarded by several tribunals established before the Second World War. These awards have continued to influence modern practice and deserve consideration. In the *Delgoa Bay Case*,[34] the tribunal awarded full compensation for the breach of a contract to build and operate a railway in a Portuguese-controlled area in southern Africa. A company formed in Portugal had raised capital for the purpose of constructing the railway. Many foreigners had contributed to the capital. The Portuguese took over the completed railway line without paying any compensation. The home states of the foreign investors and Portugal decided to submit the dispute as to compensation for the taking to an arbitral tribunal. The tribunal, in settling the dispute, applied Portuguese law, which, according to the tribunal, did 'not contain any particular provision on the decisive points that would depart from the general principles of the common law of modern nations'. The damages awarded included not only the value of the rights that were affected but also future profits.[35] The outcome is supportable simply because of the fact that the state party responsible for the breach obtained valuable property in a part of the world that was just opening up to commerce. The state itself did not have the capital or the expertise to build the railway. The foreign party had raised the capital and constructed the railway through difficult terrain. If the state was to put an end to the venture on some frivolous ground, then it should pay for what it takes. Here, payment of more than the immediate

[34] Whiteman, 3 *Damages* 1694 (1900).

[35] The tribunal stated that it was awarding damages according to 'the universally accepted rules of law, the *damnum emergens* and the *lucrum cessans*: the damage that has been sustained and the profit that has been missed'. The tribunal considered as an extenuating circumstance the failure of the company to indicate the time required to complete the railway.

value of the property is fully justified for otherwise states may entice foreign investors into their countries, allow them to build a project and then throw them out without any adequate recompense. There are punitive and sanctioning factors involved in the assessment of compensation, and one would have to accept the view both on policy as well as on legal grounds that the payment of more than full value as damages would be justified in these circumstances. The immorality involved in the conduct of the state may justify the treatment of cases such as this as akin to illegal takings. The types of situation like those that arose in the *Delgoa Bay Case* must be distinguished from other takings and they justify the payment of full compensation.

Full compensation was awarded in the *Schufeldt Claim*[36] on the basis of *damnum emergens* and *lucrum cessans*, a formula that has been taken to mean full compensation. The law which was applied was Guatemalan law, the law of the host state, which was held to be similar to all systems of law. In the *Lena Goldfields* arbitration,[37] the foreign concessionaire had been invited into the country by the state to prospect and mine gold. Here, again, full compensation was granted. In all these awards, there were contracts involved. Both in *Schufeldt* and in *Lena Goldfields*, there was a clear suggestion that a taking in violation of the concession agreement was an illegality. If such illegality had been the basis of the awards, their relevance in modern law is limited, as modern international law does not regard takings in violation of contracts as unlawful. Another factor which causes disquiet about these early awards is that the use of arbitration in these cases to be a means of settling disputes between clearly unequal parties in a diplomatic manner and the arbitrators seemed to have approached their task with this purpose in view.

In the post-Second World War arbitrations, there continued to be an espousal of full compensation in the awards of several arbitral tribunals. But, some of the awards given in the 1970s show a movement away from the standard of full compensation. In the *Texaco* and *BP* awards, which involved Libyan nationalisations effected after the Arab–Israeli war and were said to be retaliatory measures against the US for supporting Israel, there was reference to full value, but in both instances the arbitrators had found that there was illegality in the takings by the state. In *Texaco*, the

---

[36] Whiteman, 3 *Damages* 1652(1930).

[37] *Ibid.*, p. 1737; A. Nussbaum, 'The Arbitration Between the Lena Goldfields Ltd and the Soviet Government' (1950) 36 Cornell LQ 31. Another case of relevance is *Goldenberg & Sons* v. *Germany* [1927–8] AD 542. It concerned a requisition of tin that was in transit to Romanian buyers prior to Romania's entry into the war. The claim was based on the Treaty of Versailles. The tribunal held that full compensation must be paid.

remedy sought and awarded was restitution of the property, presumably to facilitate a strategy of pursuing Libyan oil through domestic courts into whose jurisdiction the oil is taken. *Texaco* is a heavily criticised award in which the arbitrator espoused theories which were totally beneficial to the claimant and bent the law in order to provide the remedy sought by the claimant. In *BP*, after finding illegality on the grounds of reprisal and want of public benefit, the arbitrator held that the 'claimant is entitled to damages arising from the wrongful act of the respondent'.[38] In the other arbitration arising from the same series of nationalisations, *Liamco*, the arbitrator held the nationalisations to be valid and did not accept full compensation as the standard. He referred to the earlier arbitral awards, which had favoured the standard of full compensation, and held that these awards were not good precedents in modern law as they were decided at a time when expropriations were considered illegal. He then observed that, though the Hull formula may have been valid at an earlier time, it had now been replaced by the requirement to pay 'convenient and equitable compensation'. The arbitrator identified the factors which had brought about these changes, and held that under the new criteria the inclusion of future profits in the compensation payable would not be justified.

In the *Aminoil* arbitration, too, the tribunal did not hold that full value must be paid as compensation. The tribunal made an interesting distinction between states which want to break out of the hold of foreign investors entirely and those which welcome foreign investment. The purpose of the distinction was to hold the latter group of states to a higher standard of compensation. Kuwait was held to belong to the latter group of states. The parties had agreed that if compensation was to be awarded the legitimate expectations of the parties should be taken into account. The tribunal also took into account 'the reasonable rate of return' from the investment. It may be difficult to conclude that the standard of compensation which was used by the tribunal was full compensation.

It is clear that the *ad hoc* arbitral tribunals which have decided issues of compensation have not adhered to a single standard of compensation. In more recent times, there is a clear indication that expropriations are normally lawful and that full compensation may not be the general proposition with which to start the analysis of the compensation payable to the foreign investor.

---

[38] (1977) 53 ILR 296 at 355.

ICSID tribunals   ICSID tribunals are set up under the Convention for the Settlement of Investment Disputes. Unlike *ad hoc* tribunals, they function within the context of an international treaty. The Convention requires the tribunal to apply the law of the host state and international law to the dispute in the absence of an express choice of law by the parties. Though the interpretation of Article 42(2) which deals with the applicable law in the absence of express choice is a difficult issue, it is generally agreed that it gives primacy to the law of the host state. For this reason, ICSID tribunals do not apply international law but apply the domestic law of the host state in assessing damages owed to the foreign investor. Thus in *AGIP v. Congo*,[39] the tribunal purported to apply Congolese law in holding that Congo had to indemnify the loss suffered as well as the future profits lost as a result of the taking. The same standard was used in *Benvenuti et Bonfant v. Congo*.[40] Since the tribunals have not indicated clearly whether they were applying domestic law or the law of the host state, the practice of these tribunals is of limited assistance.

Since the possibility of assuming jurisdiction on the basis of the dispute resolution provisions of investment treaties came to be recognised, the case load of ICSID has increased significantly. In these awards, the tribunals have applied the treaty provisions on compensation. These treaty provisions, consistent with the philosophy in treaties that provide for high standards of protection of investments, specify that full compensation must be awarded in the event of an expropriation. The tribunals have complied with these treaty prescriptions. To that extent, the rule applied was treaty-based and the extent to which they would contribute to the formation of any customary principle remains a matter of conjecture. It can be argued that the treaties contribute to customary law, but it has been pointed out that such an argument is flawed.

Iran–US Claims Tribunals   There is a rich body of awards generated by the Iran–US Claims Tribunal. The Tribunal was set up after the Iranian crisis which led to the overthrow of the Shah and the consequent exodus of US business from Iran. The Tribunal was set up under the Algiers Accord and was to hear the claims which US businessmen had against Iran. Many of these businessmen had been forced out of Iran as a result of the anti-American hostility that had been generated by the revolution. The exact nature of the contribution a tribunal created by two states, which had

---

[39] (1982) 21 ILM 726.   [40] (1982) 21 ILM 740.

prescribed the manner in which it was to act, given it a wide mandate and provided the means of enforcement of the award through the funds that had been frozen by the United States, has been a subject of debate. Some argue that the relevance of the work of the Tribunal to international law is limited because of the special circumstances in which it was created and because of the wide nature of the powers given to it. Others, however, point to the diverse nature of the problems that the Tribunal confronted and regard it as a rich storehouse from which principles on international business transactions could be quarried. The relevance of the decisions of the Tribunal to the general problem of nationalisations is limited by the circumstances in which they took place. They were motivated by hostility to US nationals, took place in the context of a revolutionary change and involved takings that were not associated with any economic programme. The takings took place in circumstances in which the continuation of US business in the country would have ended in any event, as such a continuation was fraught with dangers and difficulties. The value of the awards as precedents for large-scale expropriations in pursuance of economic programmes may be limited. The treaty setting up the Tribunal also gave it a wide remit to deal with all 'measures affecting property rights'.[41]

In any event, the jurisprudence of the Tribunal on compensation for nationalisations is ambivalent. The debate on the issue surfaced among the arbitrators on the Tribunal. The US arbitrators uniformly supported the norm of full compensation. The European arbitrators, who were the neutral arbitrators on the panel, also gave some qualified support to this norm. Though they supported the norm of full compensation, they regarded it only as a principle with which to start the inquiry and took several factors into consideration in reducing the compensation which was finally awarded so that on inspection it would appear that full compensation was never awarded by any of the individual tribunals. The Iranian arbitrators articulated norms which were favoured by the developing countries. They generally took the view that compensation was always due on expropriations or the taking of foreign property but that this requirement was satisfied if the net value of the property was paid as compensation. The response of the arbitrators to each other's views, sometimes in acrimonious terms, served only to highlight the divisions in the field.

---

[41] For an assessment, see Maurizio Brunetti, 'The Iran–US Claims Tribunal, NAFTA Chapter 11 and the Doctrine of Indirect Expropriation' (2001) 2 Chicago JIL 203, who argues for the continuing significance of the jurisprudence of the Iran–US Claims Tribunal under later treaties.

The US arbitrators asserted the Hull formula and the Iranian arbitrators rejected it.

There does not seem to be unqualified support for any definite standard of compensation, though there was acceptance that compensation was payable upon the taking of alien property. The leading awards involving the question of compensation for nationalisations should be examined. They are interesting for the reason that they indicate the range of views that could be taken on the issue of compensation for nationalisation as well as for the progressive evolution within the Tribunal of attitudes to the issue. Amusingly perhaps to an outside observer, they also show that the same authorities could be used by different jurists to support different propositions and arrive at different conclusions. This conclusion will also apply to the awards of the individual tribunals. Some have already begun viewing the awards as a victory for the standard of full compensation. Others are more circumspect in their analysis of the views of the tribunals on the issue of compensation.[42]

The first case in which the issue of compensation for the taking of alien property was considered by the Tribunal was *American International Group, Inc. v. Iran*.[43] The case involved the taking of the equity interest of the US claimant in an Iranian insurance company. The taking was consequent upon the expropriation of the whole of the insurance industry in Iran. The claimant asked for full compensation and required that the business be valued as a going concern. On this basis, compensation would have included a sum for lost profits as well as the book value of the assets. Iran, however, maintained that compensation must be the book value of the assets which were taken. The Iranian view was rejected. But, in calculating the compensation, the Tribunal took into account factors such as the effect of the economic and political changes that had taken place in Iran that would have affected the future profitability of the business. The compensation which was awarded was almost one-quarter of the amount claimed by the foreign party. In view of the factors that the Tribunal took into account in calculating compensation, it may be possible to argue that what was awarded by the Tribunal was less than full compensation. In any event, the Tribunal's approach to the determination of the law seems flawed. Its view that the standard of damages for both legal and

---

[42] There is now a substantial body of literature on the subject. R. Khan, *The Iran–US Claims Tribunal* (1990); J. Westberg, *International Transactions and Claims Involving Government Parties – Case Law of the Iran–United States Claims Tribunal* (1991); M. Pellonpaa and M. Fitzmaurice, 'Taking of Property in the Practice of the Iran–United States Claims Tribunal' (1988) 19 NYIL 53.

[43] (1983) 4 Iran–US CTR 96.

illegal takings is the same is not an accurate statement of the law, and it is contestable whether account should be taken of the future profitability of the company in assessing compensation for what was found to be a lawful act of expropriation. The Tribunal cited no authority for its view that market value was the correct basis of compensation for the lawful expropriation of foreign property. There are later awards of the Tribunal which state that future loss is not an element in compensation for the lawful taking of foreign property by a state. Arbitrator Mosk, who would have probably liked to see the claim awarded in full, characterised the award as a 'compromise solution' in his separate opinion. He indicated a preference for basing the award on the Treaty of Amity rather than on the customary international law which the Tribunal said it was applying.[44]

INA Corporation v. *Iran*[45] also involved the expropriation of an insurance company. The Tribunal characterised the expropriation as 'a classic example of a formal and systematic expropriation by decree of an entire category of commercial enterprises considered of fundamental importance to the nation's economy' and clearly regarded such expropriation as falling within a special category.[46] It pointed out that the law on this category of expropriation had undergone a change. It observed:

> In the event of such large-scale nationalization of a lawful character, international law has undergone a gradual reappraisal, the effect of which may be to undermine the doctrinal value of any 'full' or 'adequate' (when used as identical to 'full') compensation standard as proposed in this case. However, the tribunal is of the opinion that in a case such as the present, involving an investment of a rather small amount shortly before the nationalizations, international law admits compensation in an amount equal to the fair market value of the investment.

The Tribunal was here concerned with customary international law and made the interesting distinction between large and small investments and investments made shortly before the nationalisations and those that had existed for a long time previously. However, it did not have to apply these distinctions, as it found an alternative basis on which to peg the standard

---

[44] Arbitrator Mosk pointed out that full compensation was justified, as the investment was made with the encouragement of the Iranian government and was not made in a quasi-colonial context and did not have an adverse effect on Iran (p. 117). He provided authority for the view of the tribunal by citing the *Chorzow Factory Case* and the *Norwegian Ship Owners' Claims*.

[45] (1985) 8 Iran–US CTR 373.

[46] *Ibid.*, p. 378; it also regarded such a measure as 'among [the] risks which investors must be prepared to encounter'.

of compensation in the Treaty of Amity between the United States and Iran. The Treaty required the prompt payment of 'just compensation' and defined such compensation as representing the 'full value' of the property taken. The Tribunal read such value as involving the 'fair market value of the shares'.[47]

In a separate opinion, Judge Lagergren had more to say on the issue of compensation. It is clear that the award already reflected his thinking but his own views were made clear in a separate opinion. As an experienced arbitrator who had made earlier awards on the issue of foreign investment contracts,[48] his views are entitled to respect. He confined full compensation to expropriations which were unlawful. He then referred to the Hull standard and its rejection by Sir Hersch Lauterpacht in his 1955 edition of *Oppenheim's International Law* on the ground that, where a state nationalises in order to effect far-reaching economic reforms, the payment of partial compensation may be sufficient. He then referred to Resolution 1803 (XVII) of the United Nations General Assembly on Permanent Sovereignty over Natural Resources which referred to 'appropriate compensation' as the standard of compensation, and said that this standard is one of 'inherent elasticity'. He observed:

> Whether this standard is more correctly characterized as an exception to a still subsisting – though admittedly shrinking – Hull doctrine, or as evidence of a more general tendency towards the wholesale displacement of that doctrine as the repository of the opinio juris, is still the subject of debate. But the latter view appears by now to have achieved a rather solid bias in arbitral decisions and in writings.

He concluded his opinion with the following passage:

> [A]n application of current principles of international law, as encapsulated in the 'appropriate compensation' formula, would in a case of lawful large-scale nationalizations in a state undergoing a process of radical economic restructuring normally require the 'fair market value' standard to be discounted in taking account of 'all circumstances'. However, such discounting may, of course, never be such as to bring the compensation below a point which would lead to 'unjust enrichment' of the expropriating state.

---

[47] Fair market value was defined as 'the amount which a willing buyer would have paid a willing seller for the shares of a going concern, disregarding any diminution of value due to the nationalization itself or the anticipation thereof, and excluding consideration of events thereafter that might have increased or decreased the value of the shares': *ibid.*, p. 380.

[48] He was arbitrator in BP v. *Libya* (1977) 53 ILR 296 and in the *Argentine Bribery Case* (1963) ICC Case No. 1110.

It might also be added that the discounting often will be greater in a situation where the investor has enjoyed the profits of his capital outlay over a long period of time, but less, or none, in the case of a recent investor such as INA.

The principles which were thus explained in the separate opinion of Judge Lagergren undoubtedly shaped the view in the award in the case that large-scale nationalisations intended to effect an economic restructuring may not be accompanied by full compensation. This was making a departure from the Hull formula. The US arbitrator, Judge Holtzmann, quickly responded by characterising this statement as an *obiter dictum*, as indeed it was, for the award rested on the standard of compensation referred to in the Treaty of Amity. He then pointed out that the passage was the 'hook' on which Judge Lagergren had hung his separate opinion that 'international law no longer favours full compensation'. He then made efforts to stabilise the official US position that 'appropriate compensation' meant 'full compensation'.[49] The dissenting opinion of the Iranian arbitrator, Judge Ameli, tends to favour the view of Judge Lagergren that the norm of full compensation no longer represents an absolute standard.

In *Sedco Inc.* v. *NIOC*,[50] the issue of the standard of compensation was addressed again. The claimant relied on the Treaty of Amity and alternatively on customary international law to claim full compensation as represented by the full market value of the property. The Tribunal started with the proposition that, prior to the Second World War, the payment of full compensation was the norm. One could take issue with this premise, as the Hull formula was not accepted by Mexico as representing the customary international law and there was no confirmed practice to show that there was any customary principle that had matured into law prior to the War. The Tribunal then stated that the issue was whether practice has changed this norm. It found the evidence provided by the lump-sum settlements inconclusive as these were diplomatic settlements induced by external constraints such as the need to restore trade relations and do not necessarily involve *opinio juris*. Bilateral investment treaties also carry 'the same evidentiary limitations as lump sum agreements'. The

---

[49] Judge Holtzmann used the *Chorzow Factory Case* to support full compensation, and pointed out that, in *Texaco*, restitution was awarded, without mentioning that both involved prior findings of illegal takings. There is extensive reference to arbitral awards and to writings, though the writings are selective. Lauterpacht's view is regarded as *lex ferenda*.

[50] (1986) 10 Iran–US CTR 181.

tribunal was prepared to treat Resolution 1803 as reflecting the current international law. It took the view that the resolution applied to 'formal systemic large-scale nationalizations' but not to a 'discrete expropriation of alien property'. In the latter case, full compensation should be awarded. Judge Brower's separate opinion, following the practice adopted by the US arbitrators on the Tribunal, sought to reiterate the norm of full compensation.[51] The award in *Sedco* establishes the view formulated in earlier awards that individual expropriations of smaller projects should carry full compensation, though the norm of full compensation for large-scale nationalisations have undergone a change.[52] Again, the award does not hold out authority for an unchanged, general principle that there is a duty to pay full compensation upon expropriation. The value of the distinction drawn in the award must be doubted. The award seeks to preserve full compensation for small-scale, single-industry nationalisations, while recognising that in the light of modern authority full compensation for large-scale nationalisations is not maintainable. There are several problems with such a formulation. First, it does not specify how small the industry would have to be to qualify. Secondly, the era of full-scale nationalisations was the period following decolonisation. The effort is to contain the developments in the field to a specific period and continue as if nothing has happened in the area to change the norms outside this category which has now become largely redundant. The norms that were formulated in the period after decolonisation were not restricted in this manner.

There then followed a series of awards which involved smaller claims. In these awards, the individual tribunals regarded the standard applicable as full compensation, but, in calculating the compensation, the tribunals took into account factors such as the changes that had taken place in the Iranian economy as a result of the revolution and the effects it would have on the value of the shares and the property involved. In *Tams* v. *Tams-AFFA*,[53] full compensation was regarded as the standard of compensation on the basis of the Treaty of Amity as well as customary international law for the taking over of an engineering and consultancy firm. The takeover

---

[51] In a well-crafted award, Judge Brower effectively states the US case for full compensation.

[52] No criteria have been devised for large-scale nationalisations. The distinction between the two has not been adequately explained. An across-the-board nationalisation of foreign property will obviously qualify, as presumably would an industry-wide nationalisation. There will be problems with selective nationalisation. Where a dominant foreign firm within an industry is taken over, it does not necessarily follow that full compensation must be paid.

[53] (1984) 6 Iran–US CTR 219.

was found to have been effected through interference with management control. The situation was different from a nationalisation effecting economic reform. In *Phelps Dodge Corporation* v. *Iran*,[54] the claimant had controlling shares in a company for the manufacture and distribution of wire and cable products which was taken over. Full compensation was held to be the standard, but in calculating it the Tribunal 'could not properly ignore the obvious and significant negative effects of the Iranian Revolution' on the business prospects of the company. The sum that was awarded as compensation was the sum that was shown to have been invested originally in the company. In *Sola Tiles Inc* v. *Iran*,[55] where the taking was through interference with management control of a corporation in which the claimant had shares, the claimant based his case on general principles of law, but the Tribunal pointed out that the Treaty of Amity forms the background against which the tribunal would decide the case. This demonstrates a difficulty with the awards of the individual tribunals in general as it is difficult to determine when a tribunal was basing its award on customary law and when it was basing its award on the principles of the Treaty of Amity which it regarded as *lex specialis* as between the parties. The Tribunal took the view that, though there was an increasing reference to 'appropriate compensation' as the standard of compensation, this change of terminology did not indicate a change from the standard of full compensation and going concern value as representing the method of valuation. In assessing the value of the property, the Tribunal took into account the fact that the market for the type of high-quality tiles that the company manufactured had vanished after the revolution. The compensation awarded was almost one-sixth of what was claimed. The explanation of the change from adequate compensation to appropriate compensation – that is was a mere terminological convenience in the award – is too facile. It is, once more, a technique to conserve the claims of the capital-exporting states in the face of the contrary claims which have been made by the capital-importing states.

Thomas Earl Payne v. *Iran*[56] involved the taking of a small business providing high-technology services and sales of electronic equipment. The takeover was effected through interference in the management of the company. The standard of compensation was held to be the one stated in the Treaty of Amity. Though the claim was for US $3 million, the Tribunal took into account the fact that the company would have lost much of

---

[54] (1986) 10 Iran–US CTR 157.   [55] *Ibid.*   [56] (1987) 12 Iran–US CTR 3.

its government-related business after the revolution and other relevant circumstances. It awarded a sum of US $90,000 as the 'fair value' of the claimant's share in the business. Though the tribunals did not themselves make the distinction, *Phelps, Payne* and *Sola Tiles* represent takings of smaller one-man businesses by indirect means such as interferences with management control. The tribunal was inclined to be more liberal towards such claimants and grant them somewhat close to the standard of full value though never close to full compensation. Where small, one-man operations are concerned, an atavistic view that makes the law come closer to its historical roots in protecting individual businessmen who ventured overseas to invest is permissible. As much as the law makes a distinction between large-scale and small-scale nationalisations, it is also permissible to make a distinction between investments made by one-man operations and multinational corporations. The views of the Tribunal may be taken as indicating that giving greater protection to the former is justifiable.

In some later awards, there were takings which could have been regarded as efforts on the part of the government to make economic reforms in industrial sectors. The awards in these cases do not show the same certitude as to the standard of compensation applicable. They show a reversion to the old view that the requirement to pay full compensation becomes considerably diluted and even substituted altogether by a different standard where the taking was for the purpose of effecting economic reform. *Amoco International Finance Corporation* v. *Iran*[57] involved the breach of an agreement between the claimant and the National Iranian Oil Company that was to last for thirty-five years and provided for the organisation of a joint stock company to extract petroleum-related products. There were several ancillary agreements concluded at the same time. The agreements were terminated by the Single Article Act Concerning the Nationalizations of the Oil Industry of Iran. The legislation sought to effect an industry-wide nationalisation. The claimant argued that the nationalisation was illegal on several grounds. The Tribunal rejected all the alleged grounds of illegality. In the process, it pointed out that there had been 'a very important evolution in the law . . . with the progressive recognition of the

---

[57] *Amoco International Finance Corporation* v. *Iran* (1982) 1 Iran–US CTR 493; Chamber Three: Virally (Chairman), Brower and Ansari (Members). Brower filed a concurring opinion and Ansari dissented in part. For comments on the case, see D.W. Bowett, 'State Contracts with Aliens: Contemporary Developments on Compensation for Termination or Breach' (1988) 59 BYIL 49. Judge Virally has been associated with several arbitrations involving state contracts. See A. S. El-Kosheri, 'Quelques Reflexions a Propos d'un Texte Inedit de Michel Virally' in *Melanges Michel Virally* (1991), 297.

right of states to nationalise foreign property for a public purpose'. The *Chorzow Factory Case* was used by both parties to support different contentions as to the standard of compensation. The Tribunal therefore had to embark on determining the exact meaning of the decision in that case. The Tribunal held that the case dealt with unlawful expropriations and used restitution as the basis of damages for such takings. Since the Court had said that restitution in the case of unlawful takings is 'not necessarily limited to the value of the undertaking at the moment of dispossession', the Tribunal drew from this a consequence of 'paramount importance' that 'the compensation to be paid in the case of a lawful expropriation (or of a taking which lacks only the payment of a fair compensation to be lawful) is limited to the value of the taking at the moment of the dispossession'. It is not possible to award loss of future profits (*lucrum cessans*) in respect of lawful expropriations. This finding undermines the existence of a uniform requirement of full compensation for all expropriations and subverts the conventional wisdom that the *Chorzow Factory Case* provides the remedy of restitution equally to all types of nationalisation. The Tribunal stated this proposition in the following terms:[58]

> The difference is that if the taking is lawful the value of the undertaking at the time of the dispossession is the measure and the limit of the compensation, while if it is unlawful, this value is, or may be, only a part of the reparation to be paid. In any event, even in case of unlawful expropriation the damage actually sustained is the measure of the reparation, and there is no indication that 'punitive damages' could be considered.

The Tribunal pointed out that all the awards that have been cited to support full compensation had involved unlawful takings. The award punches a large hole in the case of those who support the Hull standard.

The jurisprudence of the Iran–US Claims Tribunal does not support the standard of full compensation in any meaningful sense. Though some commentators have drawn the conclusion that it does, a deeper examination of the awards do not lead one to such a conclusion. The US arbitrators strenuously tried to maintain the Hull standard, and equally the Iranian arbitrators held that the modern standard is one of appropriate compensation and generally favoured the payment of book value as compensation. The neutral arbitrators did not favour full compensation in all circumstances. While indirect takings, particularly of ongoing small businesses run by individuals by the ousting of management, resulted in awards of full compensation including sums for lost future profits, direct

[58] (1982) 1 Iran–US CTR 493.

nationalisations of whole industries in pursuance of what was considered economic reform did not result in awards of full compensation. Where future profits were awarded, it was recognised that such profits will be negligible in the context of the regime change and the hostile climate towards foreign investment which had been generated. One difficulty that analysts of the awards will have is to determine when the tribunals were making awards which were based on the Treaty of Amity which was uniformly considered to be *lex specialis* between the parties by all the tribunals and when it was making an award based on customary international law. The tribunals often recognised the interplay of the standards in their thinking. This failure to indicate a clear basis of the awards will diminish the utility of the awards as sources of customary law. The awards, which have generally reflected the views of the neutral arbitrators, have shattered many myths that have surrounded the issue of compensation. The *Chorzow Factory Case*, as the fountain of wisdom on matters of compensation for all expropriations, has been turned off and spurts only at half-strength as it has rightly been confined to unlawful takings. The view that illegality could arise from a mere breach of contract was also scotched. But, the tribunals were ambivalent on many issues. They reached decisions largely on the basis of compromise, particularly in the area of compensation for nationalisations and in the assessment of compensation. When the dust settles and the precise impact of these awards comes to be assessed, it will become apparent that one can cull from them statements in the awards as authority to support a diversity of views.

The general conclusion that has to be drawn from a study of arbitral awards dealing with the issue of compensation for nationalisations is that they do not support the norm of full compensation except in circumstances in which there had been a prior finding of illegality in the taking of the property.[59] Writers in the field have indiscriminately used the awards on unlawful expropriations to apply to the whole field of state takings. One merit of some of the awards made by the tribunals is to set the law straight by making a meaningful distinction between the two types of taking and also by rationalising the calculation of compensation in respect of the two types of taking. The awards also illustrate how men of obvious eminence could use the same authorities to arrive at different

---

[59] Abi-Saab rejects the awards which support full compensation in strong terms. He observed: '[A]part from the fact that these awards were not handed down by international tribunals properly so called, they do not sufficiently converge in language, in reasoning or in actual results to be really relevant as evidence of a consolidating trend.' G. Abi-Saab, 'Permanent Sovereignty over Natural Resources and Economic Activities' in M. Bedjaoui (ed.), *International Law: Achievements and Prospects* (1991), 597 at 613.

decisions. The explanation for this phenomenon may lie in the fact that the issue of compensation for nationalisations is approached with certain predispositions towards solutions. In the case of the US and Iranian arbitrators, these predispositions were obvious. In the case of the neutral arbitrators, some of whom had written extensively in related areas, the opportunity to sit on the Tribunal enabled an airing for their academic views. Apart from demonstrating the absence of any conclusive law on the question, the awards of the tribunals may have achieved little towards the clarification of the legal position on compensation for nationalisations.

1.1.11. National courts

Domestic courts which have considered the question of the validity of foreign nationalisations without sufficient compensation did not regard the inadequacy of compensation as a ground for holding that the nationalisations were invalid. The only exception is *dicta* in a decision of a West German court which held that the nationalisation of the copper mines in Chile without payment of any compensation at all was invalid.[60] The latter case involved no payment of compensation and cannot be regarded as a pronouncement on the adequacy of compensation.

Two of the highest courts of common law, the English House of Lords and the US Supreme Court, have both held that there was no international law position on the standard of compensation. The House of Lords in *Williams and Humbert* v. *W. & H. Trademarks*[61] held that a Spanish decree on nationalisation of the property holdings of a family could not be questioned before the English courts on the ground that adequate compensation was not paid. Lord Templeman's speech indicated that, in modern law, attitudes to property have changed significantly, and that the state's right to nationalise has received general recognition. The issue of compensation had to be assessed in the light of these changes. The US Supreme Court in the *Sabbatino Case*[62] reached a similar conclusion.

The US Court of Appeals (Second Circuit) made a survey of developments in the field in *Banco Nacional de Cuba* v. *Chase Manhattan Bank*.[63] The court held that the failure to pay any compensation at all would be a violation of international law, but that it was unclear as to what the standard of compensation prescribed by international law is. The court said:

---

[60] *Sociedad Minera el Teniente SA* v. *Aktiengesellschaft Nordeutsche Affinerie* (1973) 12 ILM 251.
[61] [1986] AC 368.   [62] 376 US 378 (1964).   [63] 658 F 2d 875 (1981).

It may well be the consensus of nations that full compensation need not be paid 'in all circumstances', and that requiring an expropriating state to pay 'appropriate compensation' – even considering the lack of precise definition of that term – would come closest to reflecting what international law requires. But the adoption of an 'appropriate compensation' requirement would not exclude the possibility that in some cases full compensation would be appropriate.

The European Court of Human Rights is a regional court and as such enjoys more respect than national courts. In the *Lithgow Case*,[64] it had to decide the interesting question of whether the taking of property without payment of full compensation was a violation of the right to property protected by Article 1 of the First Protocol to the European Convention on Human Rights. Article 1 makes reference to standards of international law, and the views of the Court have relevance to the standards of compensation in international law. The Court took the view that the decision of the state to nationalise and the amount of compensation it decides to pay are intertwined and that the Court will not question the amount of compensation which is eventually paid unless it is manifestly unreasonable. The Court said:

> A decision to enact legislation will commonly involve consideration of various issues in which opinions within a democratic society may reasonably differ widely. Because of their direct knowledge of their society and its needs and resources, the national authorities are in principle better placed than the international judge to appreciate what measures are appropriate in this area and consequently the margin of appreciation available to them should be a wide one. It would, in the Court's view, be artificial in this respect to divorce the decision as to compensation terms from the actual decision to nationalise, since the factors influencing the latter will of necessity influence the former. Accordingly, the Court's power of review in the present case is limited to ascertaining whether the decisions regarding compensation fell outside the United Kingdom's wide margin of appreciation; it will respect the legislature's judgment in this connection unless that judgment was manifestly without reasonable foundation.

With the exception of *dicta* in the West German case, which was concerned with a situation in which no compensation at all was paid and is therefore distinguishable, there are no decisions of national courts which support the view that full compensation is required in international law. These

---

[64] (1986) 8 EHRR 329 at 373.

courts have reached that conclusion, despite the fact that the executive branches of these states have traditionally supported full compensation.[65] The judicial branches which have had to make an impartial assessment of the legal position have, however, pronounced that the norm of full compensation does not represent modern international law.

1.1.12. Writings of publicists

The writings of highly qualified publicists are regarded as subsidiary sources of law. Who a highly qualified publicist is, is nowhere defined. In an area of controversy, there will be much subjectivity in the choice of such persons. In the course of the life of the Iran–US Claims Tribunal, many counsel who represented clients on both sides as well as arbitrators have written on the issue of compensation for nationalisations as well as on other matters arising from the disputes before the tribunals. Those involved have also written books from different perspectives on the record of the work of the Tribunal. It would be a pity if their views are given independent weight even though they appeared in journals of diverse quality. If such weight were to be given, there would be great difficulty in distinguishing between the highly qualified publicist and the hired gun. It is an unfortunate facet of the whole law on foreign investment that writers have had the inclination by training or by preference to pursue certain interests.[66]

In the past, there was a practice of head-counting to show that the majority of the scholars favoured full compensation for nationalised property. There was hardly any meaningful writing emerging from the developing countries in the period before and after the Second World War. The debate took place in this period largely among Western scholars among whom a significant and increasing number began to move away from the norm of full compensation.

[65] One recent feature of case law is the increase in litigation against a state which settles investment disputes otherwise than in accordance with the norm of full compensation. But, so far, no claims against the state have been allowed. For a survey, see M. Leigh and J. A. Swindler, 'Constitutional Restraints of Foreign Economic Sanctions' in R. J. Ellings (ed.), *Private Property and National Security* (1991), 31. In England, the issue has been raised as to whether there is a duty on the part of the state to espouse the claims of its nationals who had suffered expropriation abroad. The issue was left open in *R. v. Secretary of State for Foreign Affairs, ex parte Pirbhai* (1984) 129 SJ 56. See also *Mutasa v. AG* [1979] 3 All ER 257.

[66] The present writer does not claim to be an exception.

When the New International Economic Order (NIEO) came to be artic-ulated, the division among Western international lawyers became clearer. The General Assembly resolutions on NIEO make reference to appro-priate compensation as the standard of compensation. These resolutions focused attention on the controversy, and writers began to take stances on the issue. There was also an emerging body of writing from devel-oping country international lawyers supporting norms other than full compensation.

In the United States, the division of opinion between the supporters of full compensation and those who argue that the standard does not reflect modern international law became polarised when the American Law Institute sought to recognise that there has been a movement away from full compensation in its *Restatement of the Foreign Relations Law*. Professor Oscar Schacter, who was on the panel drafting the *Restatement*, has stated in his Hague lectures his understanding of the position as follows:

> Advocates of the Hull formula often characterize it as a traditional rule of international law. The record does not support this. No international judicial or arbitral tribunal, before or after 1938, has declared the 'prompt, adequate and effective' payment formula to be generally accepted inter-national law. The leading European scholars, De Visscher, Lauterpacht,[67] Rousseau, have concluded that state practice does not support that stan-dard. The Institut de droit international reflected these views in a resolution adopted in 1950_ and numerous studies in Europe and the United States have confirmed these conclusions with detailed evidence. I draw atten-tion to the European and American studies to show that the opposition to treating the Hull formula as customary law does not come only from the 'third world'. Even in the United States, where the executive and leg-islative branches have sought to affirm the Hull formula as accepted law, the courts – including the Supreme Court – have noted the disagreement among states and have declined to find the prompt, adequate and effective standard to be customary law. The Restatement of Foreign Relations Law adopted in 1965 by the American Law Institute considered that the formula

---

[67] Sir Hersch Lauterpacht was the most significant of the writers to move away from the standard of full compensation. In a passage which appeared in his edition of *Oppenheim's International Law* (8th ed., 1952), 352, he suggested that the standard of full compensation was not applicable to nationalisations that took place in the course of economic reorgan-isation. The passage is missing from the new edition of Oppenheim edited by Sir Robert Jennings and Sir Arnold Watts (*Oppenheim's International Law* (9th ed., 1992)). In the new edition, it is conceded that the issue of compensation is an unsettled area of the law.

was qualified by 'what is reasonable in the circumstances' and it noted that
'less than full value' or 'fair market value' was acceptable in certain cases (for
example, land reform). The revised Restatement of 1987 does not consider
the Hull formula as internationally accepted law.

There is an increasing tendency among text writers to move away from
the standard of full compensation as a uniform standard of compensation for nationalised property. The current edition of Oppenheim's text
recognises the existence of the conflict as to the standard of compensation
and is not partial to any view on the issue.[68]
The survey of the traditional sources of international law that have
been made shows that there is no support in them for the standard of full
compensation for nationalisation. One has to be a committed advocate
to a cause that is furthered by the claim to full compensation to believe
that it does represent the norm of international law. Even then, support
for the norm of full compensation can only be found in the weakest
sources of law – the decisions of some tribunals and the writings of some
publicists. The decisions of tribunals do not always provide clear evidence
and have to be interpreted as favouring full compensation. Some are old
and were made in an age in which nationalisations were uncommon. The
writings of publicists do not provide unequivocal support for a standard
of compensation. Even as a proposition of law formed at a time when
state intervention in economic life was non-existent, it would be difficult
to establish that there was evidence to regard full compensation as a norm
of international law. In modern times, where such intervention is generally
recognized as valid, there is no evidence that can be found limiting the
right of a state to nationalise except on the payment of full compensation.
Given the absolute weakness of the sources supporting the norm of full
compensation, it is safe to conclude that, if there is a stronger norm based
on even a slightly firmer base in the sources of international law, it would

---

[68] Sir Robert Jennings and Sir Arthur Watts, *Oppenheim's International Law* (9th ed., 1992),
921. At *ibid.*, p. 922, referring to the Hull standard, the editors state: 'There is . . . a
question whether those elements constitute a separate and necessary part of the standard
of compensation required by international law, or whether they are just considerations to be
taken into account (perhaps along with others) in assessing whether compensation satisfies
some much broader standard such as that it be "just", "equitable" or "appropriate". Papers
in a German symposium also note the deviations from the Hull standard: T. Opperman
and E. Petersmann (eds.), *Reforming the International Economic Order* (1987), 40 (Weber);
ibid., p. 78 (Dicke); and *ibid.*, p. 115 (Hailbronner). For a Dutch rejection of the Hull
standard, see W. D. Verwey and N. J. Schrijver, 'The Taking of Foreign Property under
International Law: A New Legal Perspective?' (1984) 15 NYIL 3 at 20.

displace the norm of full compensation. It is necessary to examine whether there are any such norms.

2. The competing norms

Newly independent capital-importing states and other states whose economies were dominated by foreign corporations have refused to accept the norm of full compensation. The erstwhile Communist states of Eastern Europe held on to the consistent Marxist philosophy that nationalisation did not require the payment of any compensation. Leaving aside these ideologically inspired stances, which also contributed to the undermining of the norm of full compensation as they evidence the fact that a significant group of states for a long period of time did not accept the norm of full compensation, there were other stances taken by developing states which amount to state practice and constitute rejection of the norm of full compensation. The claim that has been advanced by these states, which has the greatest acceptance, is that only appropriate compensation need be paid upon nationalisation. Before discussing this claim, which now commands the widest support, some of the other claims inconsistent with the norm of full compensation are examined briefly.

2.1. The claim that it is permissible to deduct past excess profits from compensation

This claim was made by Chile during its copper nationalisation in 1971. The Chilean statute nationalising the interests of US copper companies, Kennecott and Anaconda, enabled past excess profits made by the two companies to be taken into account in calculating the compensation due to the companies. The tribunal that made the valuation decided that the corporations had made excess profits greater than the present value of the assets of the companies and that no compensation was therefore due them. No indication was given as to the valuation procedures adopted by the Chilean authorities.[69]

---

[69] For discussions of the Chilean copper nationalisations, see R. B. Lillich, 'The Valuation of Copper Companies in the Chilean Nationalization' (1972) 66 *ASIL Proceedings* 213; J. Rohwer, 'Nationalization – Chilean Excess Profits Deduction' (1973) 14 Harvard ILJ 378; A. N. Heibein, 'The Chilean Copper Nationalization: The Foundation for the Standard of Appropriate Compensation' (1974) 23 Buffalo LR 765; and F. Orrego-Vicuna, 'Some International Law Problems Posed by the Nationalization of Copper Industry by Chile' (1973) 67 AJIL 711. D. Dicke, 'The Taking of Foreign Property and the Question of Compensation' in T. Oppermann and E. Petersmann (eds.), *Reforming the International*

Before the controversy could be pressed any further, the Chilean government of President Allende was replaced in a coup which was alleged to have been inspired by the United States. The claim, nevertheless, remains an interesting proposition. It is a claim that is supportable as a matter of strict equity: if a foreign corporation had exploited a situation to its maximum advantage and reaped inordinate profits, the termination of the situation should not result in additions to that profit in the form of compensation. The idea that windfall profits should be shared with the state in the case of mineral resource exploitation receives support from the *Aminoil* award. Where *quantum meruit* principles are applied in fashioning a remedy, the past inordinate profits made by one of the parties is always relevant. But, the problem is to ensure that the state making such a claim is making an honest calculation. One problem with the Chilean claim was that the basis on which the state made the claim for the deduction of excess profits was never disclosed for objective scrutiny. Another is that the state or its authorities should not have had some complicity in permitting the foreign company to make the excess profits, as it may not be equitable for the company to have to pay what had previously been condoned by the state. Where the local elite collaborated in the exploitation, it would be difficult to assess how much of the profits were repatriated and how much were retained at home. In addition, condonation and ratification of the situation by the former government may prevent the situation being used by a later government.[70] But, as long as the claim to compensation is based on equitable notions such as unjust enrichment, fairness will require that the state also be permitted to take into account the past excessive profits made by the foreign company. In appropriate circumstances, the claim that excess profits should be deducted from the compensation payable does remain a valid proposition.

2.2. The claim that the taking is a 'revindication' for which no compensation is necessary

Such claims were made by Peru during the La Brea y Parinas dispute and the nationalisation of Gulf Oil in Bolivia.[71] The latter dispute was

Economic Order (1987), 63 at 78, gives qualified support to the Allende principle on the basis of unjust enrichment.

[70] In many instances, Latin American dictators and ruling cliques worked together with foreign investors in making huge profits out of resource exploitation. G. Coronel, *The Nationalization of the Venezuelan Oil Industry* (1984), 8.

[71] D. B. Furnish, 'Peruvian Domestic Law Aspects of the La Brea y Parinas Controversy' (1970) 89 Kentucky LJ 351; D. B. Furnish, 'Days of Revindication and Dignity: The Petroleum

settled in a remarkably amicable fashion, the emphasis being largely on the agreement that normal commercialisation of hydrocarbons destined for export will continue through the agency of Gulf Oil. Both incidents involved the claim that the land subject to the concession could be taken over without compensation and that the investor should be entitled only to the value of the machinery and other assets. Bolivia insisted on deducting from the net value of the investment the taxes that were owed and the value of the minerals extracted from the land.[72] Revindication is a claim that is couched in emotive language. Its only legal significance may be to ensure that past malpractices which the foreign corporation adopted in exploiting resources could be taken into account in calculating compensation. There could be a punitive measure included in the assessment of compensation. In the *Aminoil* dispute, Kuwait argued that the exploitation practices of the claimant were harmful and that the damage thereby caused should be set off against the compensation that was due. The tribunal avoided pronouncing on the validity of this claim by its finding on the facts that the exploitation practices were not improper. But, future claims along these lines will continue to be made. Where the taking is based on the state's belief on objective grounds that the practices adopted in the exploitation of natural resources were harmful to the environment or depleted the resources unnecessarily, there is room for argument that this factor should be taken into account in assessing compensation.

2.3. The claim that appropriate compensation should be paid

This claim received unanimous support in Resolution 1803 of the General Assembly. There has been some effort to explain the use of 'appropriate' as meaning 'full' compensation. Short of rewriting English (and American) dictionaries, such an effort to give unnatural meanings to words must be dismissed as a feeble effort motivated only by an interest in keeping the norm of full compensation alive.[73] There was a clear effort made in the resolution to change the existing norms of

---

Expropriations in Peru and Bolivia' in R. B. Lillich (ed.) *The Valuation of Nationalized Property* (vol. 2, 1975), 55.

[72] (1968) 7 ILM 1201; (1969) 8 ILM 264.

[73] The drafting history of the resolution indicates that the formulation was a compromise, the capital-exporting nations agreeing to the use of 'appropriate' provided there was a reference to international law as providing the standard. But see Stephen M. Schwebel, 'The Story of the UN's Declaration of Permanent Sovereignty over Natural Resources' (1963) 49 ABAJ 463; and Ambassador Stevenson's letter in (1963) 57 AJIL 406.

international law relating to compensation for nationalisation and the usage of the word was intended to signal that change. The resolution referred to 'appropriate compensation in accordance with international law', thereby indicating that international law provided the standard as to what was appropriate. The resolution did not deny the relevance of international law as a controlling factor in determining the appropriate compensation.

Later resolutions in the General Assembly do not reflect such a compromise. Resolution 3171 (XXVII) seeks to give each state the sole right to determine the 'amount of possible compensation'. The resolution on the New International Economic Order seeks to assert national competence in determining the amount of compensation. The resolution on the Charter of Economic Rights and Duties of States requires that 'appropriate compensation be paid ... taking into account the relevant laws and regulations and all circumstances that the state considers pertinent'. There were similar resolutions enacted in other United Nations agencies.[74] These resolutions were passed without the support of the capital-exporting states. Leaving aside the debate as to whether resolutions of the General Assembly have a law-creating effect, these resolutions, at the least, indicate a desire on the part of the states to reject full compensation as the standard of compensation. The draft Code of Conduct on Transnational Corporations also contains a similar formula.

In this context, the resolution that has received the most support will provide a basis upon which the law can be formulated as it represents a will that is common to all members of the international community. The view that General Assembly resolutions are generally not law-creating and that they are at best expressions of *lex ferenda* may be swept aside for in a field that is occupied largely by the inconsistent practice of a few states and the opinions of tribunals and writers – weak sources of law to say the least – it will be possible to postulate a norm built on the collective view of nations as best representing the law.

Appropriate compensation is a reference to a flexible standard which could range from the payment of full compensation, the amount of future profits lost, to the payment of no compensation at all in circumstances where the foreign investor had visibly earned inordinate profits from his investment and the host state had no benefits at all from it. The relevance of international law to the assessment of compensation continues.

---

[74] See, for example, UNCTAD Resolution 88 (11), which states that it is 'for each state to fix its compensation'.

The resolutions associated with the New International Economic Order are founded on appeals to justice and equity which are supranational concepts and are rooted in international law. It must therefore be conceded that any compensation must meet with supranational standards of appropriateness and be justifiable in terms of objective justice and equity.

The scope for full compensation in the earlier sense has considerably diminished in modern times. If full compensation did not have a basis in the past practice of states, recent practice indicates a total rejection of such a standard. Partial compensation seems to be the generally preferred solution. The Indian nationalisation of the oil installations of Burmah Shell in 1976 resulted in the payment of partial compensation.[75] Ceylon, which took over oil companies in 1964 and tea estates in 1976, paid only partial compensation. African nationalisations have also involved the payment of only partial compensation. Thus, Rood, after a survey of the compensation practices of African states, concluded:[76]

> The compensation promised or paid for the take-overs of foreign property in British Africa falls far short of what the former owner thinks is due. Fair market value, valuation based on capitalized earnings and effective compensation are distant ideals; reality is likely to be partial payment, a vague promise of something in the future or a statement of good intentions by the government.

Latin American practice seems uniform in the payment of some compensation but not full compensation. The settlement of the Marcona nationalisation dispute between Peru and the United States is a case in point. The dispute was settled by the conclusion of a lump-sum settlement agreement. Though the United States interpreted the agreement as involving adequate compensation, the agreement does not provide for monetary compensation equalling the value of the property taken. The emphasis was on the continuation of the relationship between the foreign investor and the host state.[77] Though partial compensation has been the normal practice, the notion of appropriate compensation is flexible enough to provide that full compensation should be paid in certain circumstances.

---

[75] Burmah Shell Act 1976.

[76] L. Rood, 'Compensation for Takeovers in Africa' (1977) 11 *Journal of International Law and Economics* 521; D. Ijalye, 'Multinational Corporations in Africa' (1981) 171 *Hague Recueil* 1.

[77] D. Gantz, 'Marcona Settlement' (1977) 71 AJIL 474.

It is possible in the context of the acceptance of appropriate compensation to account for the case law that has been generated so far as to compensation for takings of foreign property by states. In the analysis that follows, all takings of foreign property and not only nationalisations are included. It is possible to identify five major categories.

2.3.1. Categories of takings for which damages rather than compensation must be paid

In the case of an illegal taking, the state must pay damages calculated on the basis of effecting a *restitutio in integrum*. The obvious instances of this would be where the taking is in violation of a treaty obligation owed to the home state of the foreign investor or where there had been a taking motivated by racial discrimination. The limitation of public purpose is of diminishing significance but the absence of a public purpose will help to establish racial discrimination as a ground of illegality. Where there has been an illegal taking, the classical position that the claimant must be paid both *damnum emergens* and *lucrum cessans* remains unaffected.

Christine Gray referred to the difficulty in distinguishing between the consequences of an illegal and a legal nationalisation in the present state of the law. The meaningful distinction is to ensure damages in the case of an illegal nationalisation which will include both present and future loss, whereas in the case of a legal nationalisation there is compensation which is payable by the state. Future loss has no role to play in the assessment of the compensation, as the state has a present right to terminate the venture.[78] The legality of the nationalisation depends on the recognition of that present right. Future loss which flows from the termination of the venture as a result of the exercise of the right is legally insignificant. In assessing present loss, there is a need to take into account a whole range of factors such as the nature of the past relationship between the parties, the extent of the profits made by the foreign investor, the duration of the investment, the legitimate expectations of the foreign investor and other like factors.

---

[78] D. W. Bowett, 'State Contracts with Aliens: Contemporary Developments on Compensation for Termination or Breach' (1988) 59 BYIL 49 at 63: '[T]he correct principle is believed to be that loss of future profits, whilst a legitimate head of general damages for an unlawful act, is not an appropriate head of compensation for a lawful taking.' See also M. Pellonpaa and M. Fitzmaurice, 'Taking of Property in the Practice of the Iran–United States Claims Tribunal' (1988) 19 NYIL 53 at 123–7.

2.3.2. Categories of lawful takings for which full compensation must be paid

Full compensation must be paid in circumstances in which the foreign investor was invited by the host state to undertake a project which could not have been completed without his investment in resources and technology and the investment is taken over before the investor could receive any profit by his investment. Here, there is an element of fraud in the conduct of the host state which apart from the equities of the situation justifies the payment of full compensation, which could include some element of future profits as a punitive measure. But, ordinarily, the taking of such punitive measures is not the function of an international arbitration. Where legitimate expectations had been created in the foreign investor by the conferment of guarantees and the inclusion of stabilisation clauses, the case for awarding full compensation will be strengthened. Cases which approach this paradigm situation will justify the payment of full compensation or near full compensation. The nature of the invitation held out to the investor and the period for which the investor was permitted to function prior to the taking are important factors. The greater the enticing efforts on the part of the host state and the shorter the period after the investment was beginning to bear profits before the taking, the greater is the justification for the payment of full compensation. The nature of the guarantees given against nationalisation and the absence of alternative sources from which the host state could have obtained the same type of skills or investments for the project concerned will also add to the case for full compensation.

2.3.3. Full compensation must be paid where there is a one-off taking of a small business

Here, the principle of allocation of risk will require the state which benefits by the takeover and can better absorb the risk should pay. The public benefits accruing from the takeover of a small business are unlikely to be high, and the motives for the taking cannot be clearly justified on an economic basis. This type of taking shares features with the confiscatory takings of the past. There is also justification for the payment of full compensation where a state had held out incentives to a foreign investor and had taken over the investment at the stage in which it was about to yield profits.[79] Where the state had created legitimate expectations of settled

---

[79] *Aminoil* (1982) 21 ILM 976, which makes the distinction between states which actively seek foreign investment and states which do not. In the case of the former, there is an expectation

profits for a course of time, this factor too will indicate full compensation. The nature of the guarantees given and the absence of alternative sources from which the foreign investment could have been drawn are factors to be taken into account in considering whether full compensation should be permitted.[80]

2.3.4. Full compensation need not be paid as part of a full-scale nationalisation of a whole industry

Full compensation need not be paid where there is a full-scale nationalisation of an industry as a part of economic reform. There is overwhelming authority supporting a norm of partial compensation in situations in which there is a full-scale nationalisation programme as a part of economic reform.[81] Much of the post-Second World War nationalisations were effected in pursuance of such programmes which were designed to end the dominance of the erstwhile imperial powers of the economies of newly independent countries. The notion of appropriate compensation was articulated in the context of such programmes. Some believe that the need for the norm has ended now that such dominance has ended. Others believe that such dominance continues to be exercised through the network of multinational companies.

The relevance of this norm will continue. Nationalisations will be a cyclical phenomenon. For various reasons, the climate at present is favourable to foreign investment. The shortage of foreign investment, the belief that foreign investment will lead to economic growth and the fact that

that they will favour strong norms of foreign investment protection and hence compensation must be calculated on a basis which 'warrants the upkeep of a flow of investment in the future.' E. Jimenez de Arechaga, 'State Responsibility for Nationalization of Foreign Owned Property' (1979) 11 NYUJILP 179, regarded the stabilisation clause as relevant for the assessment of compensation as did the tribunal in *Aminoil*.

[80] The classic instance of this is the situation in the *Delgoa Bay Case*, where capital and technology for the building of a railway was procured from abroad with the promise that the profits of the railway could be enjoyed by the foreign investor. Also *Starrett Housing Corp. v. Iran* (1987) 16 Iran–US CTR 112, where a housing project nearing completion was taken over.

[81] Authority for this category comes largely from the General Assembly resolutions associated with the New International Economic Order and the writings of scholars like Sir Hersch Lauterpacht. The strategy adopted in the World Bank Guidelines is to accept the norm but confine it to the past nationalisations which effected wholesale economic reforms and state that these circumstances will 'rarely occur and may be expected to become uncommon in the future'. World Bank, *Legal Framework for the Treatment of Foreign Investment* (vol. 2, 1992), para. 48. This overlooks the fact that the claims to the New International Economic Order were made long after the post-colonial and post-war nationalisations.

trade, lending and aid are tied to developing countries maintaining a favourable stance towards foreign investment, are all responsible for this climate. The picture may change after a period when foreign investors have become stabilised in the host states. Nationalistic feelings will be aroused when the dominance of foreign corporations becomes evident. Ideological or economic attitudes to foreign investment may change. When that happens, we may expect a fresh bout of nationalisations. In these circumstances, the claim that such nationalisations could be effected through the payment of appropriate compensation will become relevant. States could then assimilate the nationalisations they effect to the post-war or post-colonial nationalisations.

2.3.5. Partial compensation

Partial compensation is justified where the past practices of the foreign investor were harmful to the host state or where there had been inordinate profits made from the investment. The duration of the foreign investor's stay in the host state is always relevant. If his profits had recompensed the investment initially made, the relevance of full compensation to him diminishes correspondingly to the extent of the profits. This will be particularly so where the ending of the investment is for reasons that the investor had adopted bad industry practices in the past or where he had made inordinate profits. In these circumstances, there must be objective evidence of the allegations made by the state. It would be improper to argue that no compensation need be paid on this ground. There is immediate benefit to the host state as a result of the taking of the assets of the foreigner which is a circumstance that usually justifies the payment of some compensation.

The five categories discussed above are merely guidelines as to how the notion of appropriate compensation is to be applied consistently with the past practice of states. It also helps to show that the past practice of states is consistent with the norm of appropriate compensation and that it is this norm which incorporates within it the notions of full compensation for certain types of takings and partial compensation for others which best represents modern international law.

3. Valuation of nationalised property

The method of valuation of property has been considered in some recent arbitral awards. No consistent pattern has emerged as to methods of valuation. Valuation is a secondary issue. The primary issue is the standard according to which the law requires compensation to be made. Methods of valuation should not be the means by which the tail is made to wag the dog. In the *Chorzow Factory Case*, the Permanent Court of International Justice appointed a committee of experts to value the property after itemising the heads upon which damages could be awarded for the illegal nationalisation that was involved in the dispute. The identification of the legal basis on which damages or compensation should be awarded was the first step adopted by early tribunals.

The method of valuation was also discussed in the awards of the Iran–US Claims Tribunal and in some of the more recent awards of ICSID tribunals. In many of the awards of the Iran–US Claims Tribunal, the standard of compensation was held to be as stated in the Treaty of Amity between Iran and the United States. Valuation was often based on the standard in the Treaty. No conclusion of general relevance can be drawn from the valuation practice of the Tribunal.

There is now an accumulation of literature on the subject.[82] Much of the literature is aimed at projecting theories into methods of valuation used by arbitral tribunals, often despite the fact that the arbitral tribunals did not themselves disclose the method they used. There has emerged an unnecessary conflict on the subject. Valuation is an objective process. It should not be permissible for standards or theories of compensation to be built in through valuation principles. If there are technical problems of valuation, a tribunal can always obtain expert help in making the valuation. Valuation is not the main issue of controversy. Once a tribunal arrives at the standard of compensation, the value of the compensation payable according to that standard can be assessed with the help of experts, if need be. After reiterating the cautionary statement that these principles should not be the means of reintroducing standards of compensation through the back-door and that they are secondary to the finding of the compensation standard applicable to the dispute, some of the standards which have been used may be stated. There are three principal methods, which are discussed below.

---

[82] E. Penrose, 'Nationalization of Foreign-Owned Property for a Public Purpose: An Economic Perspective on Appropriate Compensation' (1992) 55 MLR 351; W. C. Lieblich, 'Determining the Economic Value of Expropriated Income Producing Property in International Arbitrations' (1991) 8 JIA 59; S. K. Khalilian, 'The Place of Discounted Cash Flow in International Commercial Arbitrations' (1991) 8 JIA 31; P. D. Friedland and E. Wong, 'Measuring Damages for Deprivation of Income Producing Assets: ICSID Case Studies' (1991) 6 ICSID Rev 400; and E. Lauterpacht, *Aspects of Administration of International Justice* (1992), 130–6.

The first method is book value. According to a study initiated by the United Nations Commission on Transnational Corporations, book value is the method of valuation most used in assessing the value of property.[83] The book value of assets represents the difference between the corporation's assets and liabilities as stated in the accounts books. This method of valuation was widely used in the petroleum nationalisations that took place in the 1970s, though the companies which were taken over were going concerns. Where the expropriation is lawful and therefore where the award of *lucrum cessans* is not permissible, book value should be the method of valuation used.

The second method of valuation is market value. This method of valuation was favoured by those who argued for the Hull standard of compensation. All writers who have rejected the Hull standard have rejected the market value as the applicable method of valuation. Market value takes future profitability into account. Such a valuation is permissible only if an award can be made on the basis of both *damnum emergens* and *lucrum cessans*. The overwhelming view is that such a standard of compensation is possible only where there is an illegal taking of foreign property.

The third method of valuation is the discounted cash flow method. This is a new basis introduced to stem the tide running strongly against the market value method. This method requires the projection of the future receipts expected by the enterprise after deducting the costs associated with the making of the receipts. The World Bank Guidelines state that this is the method which should be applied where the company that is taken is a going concern. This introduces standards of compensation through the back-door and makes the distinction between lawful and unlawful takings meaningless. To the extent that the method requires future factors to be taken into account, those who seek its application must show that the taking involved was an unlawful taking.

4. Conclusion

The issue of compensation for the nationalisation of foreign property provides fascinating insights into how international legal principles are

---

[83] A study of 174 nationalisations effected in the 1970s showed that the general practice was to apply the book value concept, though companies asserted fair market value, going concern value and replacement costs as the standards on which valuation should be made. R. B. Sunshine, *Terms of Compensation in Developing Countries' Nationalization Settlements* (UNCTC, 1981).

shaped. The principle that nationalisation was illegal was formulated at a time when takings by the state of the property of individual aliens for the self-aggrandisement of the ruling cliques was the normal situation of state takings. The issue of compensation was discussed in the context of this situation. But, when the normal situation of state takings became one of takings with the aim of restructuring the economy, the law underwent a change. This change was brought about by the challenges made to the existing claims relating to compensation by developing states which were in the process of restructuring their economies after the ending of colonialism. That challenge enfeebled the claim relating to full compensation considerably. The manner in which it was displaced by a new formula of appropriate compensation provides an illustration of international law-making. Given the existence of two conflicting norms, decision-making authorities within the international community had to quickly refashion the law on newer lines. The solution adopted preserves the norm of full compensation but also accommodates the view that such full compensation need not always be paid and that each situation must be approached on a case-by-case basis.

In the light of the controversy relating to the standard of compensation, the best solution that could be hoped for in the present state of international law is for states to settle the issue of compensation through bilateral investment treaties and agree upon the standard of compensation between themselves. This strategy is being increasingly resorted to. Where such a treaty exists, the standard referred to in the treaty is conclusive. Since nationalisation presents the greatest risk to foreign investment and the most controversial issue in the law of foreign investment relates to the standard of compensation, it is sensible to resort to this solution to the problem.

BIBLIOGRAPHY

Books

Ackerman, B., *Private Property and the Constitution* (1977)

Addo, M. K. (ed.), *Human Rights Standard and the Responsibility of Transnational Corporations* (1999)

Aldrich, G., *The Jurisprudence of the Iran–US Claims Tribunal* (1996)

Allen, T., *The Right to Property in Commonwealth Constitutions* (2000)

Amerasinghe C. F., *State Responsibility for Injuries to Aliens* (1967)
   Local Remedies in International Law (2004)

Amin, S., *Unequal Development: An Essay on the Social Formation of Peripheral Capitalism* (1976)

Anand, R. P., *The Afro-Asian States and International Law* (1978)
   International Law and Developing Countries (1987)

Arangio-Ruiz, G., *The United Nations Declaration on Friendly Relations and the System of Sources of International Law* (1979)

Atiyah, P., *The Rise and Fall of the Freedom of Contract* (1979)

Audit, B., *Transnational Arbitration and State Contracts* (1988)

Bedjaoui, M. (ed.), *International Law: Achievements and Prospects* (1991)

Bennet, D. and K. Sharpe, *Transnational Corporations Versus the State* (1985)

Bergsten, F., *American Multinationals and American Interests* (1978)

Biersteker, T., *Multinationals, the State and the Control of the Nigerian Economy* (1987)
   The Political Economy of Indigenisation: Multinationals, the State and Local Capital in Nigeria (1987)

Birnie, P. and A. Boyle, *International Law and the Environment* (2002)

Borchard, E. M., *The Diplomatic Protection of Nationals* (1904)
   The Diplomatic Protection of Citizens Abroad (Kraus Reprint Co., New York, 1970; original edition, 1915)

Bradlow, D. D. and A. Escher (eds.), *Legal Aspects of Foreign Investment* (1999)

Brewer, T. (ed.), *Political Risks in International Business* (1985)

Brian, W. V. (ed.), *New States in International Law and Diplomacy* (1965)

Brierly, J., *Law of Nations* (5th ed., 1963)

Brower, C., *The Iran–US Claims Tribunal* (1998)

Brownlie, I., *The System of the Law of Nations: State Responsibility* (1986)

Brown-Weiss, E., *In Fairness to Future Generations* (1989)

Bulajic, M., *Principles of International Development Law* (1992)

Calvo, C., *Le Droit International* (vol. 6, 5th ed., 1885)

Cameron, P. D., *Property Rights and Sovereign Rights: The Case of North Sea Oil* (1983)

Cartwright, J. J., *Unequal Bargaining: A Study of Vitiating Factors in the Formation of Contract* (1991)

Castermans-Holleman, M., F. van Hoof and J. Smith (eds.), *The Role of the Nation State in the 21st Century: Essays in Honour of Peter Baehr* (1998)

Cattan, H., *The Law of Oil Concessions in the Middle East and North Africa* (1967)

Chayes, A., T. Ehrlich and A. F. Lowenfeld, *International Legal Process* (1969)

Cherian, J., *Investment Contracts and Arbitration* (1975)

Choate, P., *Agents of Influence* (1990)

Chua, A., *World on Fire. How Exporting Free Market Democracy Breeds Ethnic Hatred and Global Instability* (2003)

Cohen-Jonathan, G., *La Convention Europeenne de Droits de l'Homme* (1989)

Coronel, G., *The Nationalization of the Venezuelan Oil Industry* (1984)

Cover, R. M., *Justice Accused: Antislavery and the Judicial Process* (1975)

Coyle, D., *Governing the World Economy* (2000)

Crawford, J. (ed.), *The Rights of Peoples* (1988)

    The International Law Commission's Articles on State Responsibility (2002)

Daintith, T., *The Legal Character of Petroleum Licences: A Comparative Study* (1981)

Damrosch, L. and D. Scheffer (ed.), *Law and Force in the New International Order* (1991)

Dawson, F. G. and I. L. Head, *International Law, National Tribunals and the Rights of Aliens* (1971)

Dezalay, Y. and G. Bryant, *Dealing in Virtue: International Commercial Arbitration and the Construction of a Transnational Legal Order* (1996)

Dinstein, Y. (ed.), *International Law at a Time of Perplexity: Essays in Honour of Shabtai Rosenne* (1989)

Dixon, C., D. Drakakis-Smith and H. Wads (eds.), *Multinational Corporations and the Third World* (1986)

Doimi di Delupis, I., *Finance and Protection of Foreign Investment in Developing Countries* (1987)

Dolzer, R. and Marguerite Stevens, *Bilateral Investment Treaties* (1996)

Domke, M., *Trading with the Enemy in World War II* (1943)

Dunn, F. S., *The Protection of Foreign Nationals* (1932)

Eagleton, C., *The Responsibility of States in International Law* (1928)

El-Kosheri, A., *The Law Governing a New Generation of Petroleum Contracts* (1986)

Ellings, R. J. (ed.), *Private Property and National Security* (1991)

Epstein, R., *Takings: Private Property and the Power of Eminent Domain* (1985)

Fatouros, A. A., *Government Guarantees to Foreign Investors* (1962)

Feller, A. H., *The Mexican Claims Commission 1923–1934* (1935)

Fitzgerald, A., *Australian Mining Law* (2002)

Flint, D., *Foreign Investment Law in Australia* (1986)

Ford, A. W., *The Anglo-Iranian Oil Dispute* (1954)

Fordham, M., *Tax Incentive for Investment and Expansion in Singapore* (1992)

Fox, G. and B. Roth (eds.), *Democratic Governance and International Law* (2000)

Fox, H. (ed.), *International Economic Law and Developing States* (vol. 2, 1992)

Francioni, F. and T. Scovazzi (eds.), *International Responsibility for Environmental Harm* (1991)

Freeman, A., *The International Responsibility of States for Denial of Justice* (1938)

Friedmann, W., *Changing Structure of International Law* (1962)

Fukuyama, F., *The End of History and the Last Man* (1992)

Garcia-Amador, F. V. *Changing Law of International Claims* (1984)
  The Emerging International Law of Development (1990)

Garcia-Amador, F. V., L. Sohn and R. R. Baxter, *Recent Codification of the Law of State Responsibility for Injuries to Aliens* (1974)

Gilpin, R., *The Political Economy of International Relations* (1987)

Goodwin-Gill, G. S., *International Law and the Movement of Persons Between States* (1978)

Goodwin-Gill, G. S. and S. Talmon, *The Reality in International Law: Essays in Honour of Ian Brownlie* (1999)

Gordon, M. W., *The Cuban Nationalisations* (1973)

Gowlland-Debbas, Vera, *Multilateral Treaty Making* (2000)

Graham, E. and Paul Krugman, *Foreign Direct Investment in the United States* (1991)

Gray, C., *Judicial Remedies in International Law* (1990)

Hahn, H. J., G. Kegel and K. R. Simmond (eds.), *International Law and Economic Order: Essays in Honour of F. A. Mann* (1997)

Hall, R. and T. Biersteker (eds.), *The Emergence of Private Authority in Global Governance* (2002)

Handl, G. and R. E. Lutz, *Transferring Hazardous Technologies and Substances* (1989)

Heere, W. P. (ed.), *International Law and Its Sources: Liber Amicorum Maarten Bos* (1989)

Himawan, C., *The Foreign Investment Process in Indonesia* (1980)

Hoekman, B. and M. Kostecki, *The Political Economy of the World Trading System* (2001)

Hossain, K., *Law and Policy in Petroleum Development* (1979)
  (ed.), *Legal Aspects of the New International Economic Order* (1980)

ICSID, *Investment Promotion and Protection Treaties* (1983)

Ijalye, D., *The Extension of Corporate Personality in International Law* (1978)

Indian Law Institute, *The Bhopal Litigation* (1989)

Jennings, R. and A. Watts, *Oppenheim's International Law* (9th ed., 1992)

Jessup, P., *The Use of International Law* (1959)

Kay, C., *Development and Underdevelopment in Latin America* (1988)

Khan, R., *The Iran–US Claims Tribunal* (1990)

Krasner, S., *Structural Conflict: Third World Against Global Liberalism* (1985)

Kronfol, Z. A., *Protection of Foreign Investment. A Study in International Law* (1972)

Kummer, K., *International Management of Hazardous Wastes: The Basel Convention and Related Legal Rules* (1995)

Kurshid, H., *Equality of Treatment and Trade Discrimination in International Law* (1968)

Kwiatkowska, B. and A. H. A. Soons (ed.), *Transboundary Movement and Disposal of Hazardous Waste in International Law* (1993)

Lang, W., H. Neuhold and K. Zemanek (eds.), *Environmental Protection and International Law* (1991)

Lauterpacht, E., *Aspects of Administration of International Justice* (1992)

Lauterpacht, H., *Collected Papers* (vol. 4, 1978)

Laviec, P., *Protection et Promotion des Investissements: Etude de Droit International Economique* (1985)

Lee, L. T., *Consular Law and Practice* (1991)

Lefeber, R., *Transboundary Environmental Interference and the Origin of State Liability* (1996)

Lerner, N., *The United Nations Convention on the Elimination of All Forms of Racial Discrimination* (1980)

Lew, J. D. M., *The Applicable Law in International Commercial Arbitration* (1978)

Lillich, R. B., *International Law of State Responsibility for Injuries to Aliens* (1983)
    The Human Rights of Aliens in Contemporary International Law (1984)
    (ed.), *The Valuation of Nationalized Property* (1987)

Lipson, C., *Standing Guard: Protecting Capital in the Nineteenth and Twentieth Centuries* (1985)

MacDonald, R. St J. and D. M. Johnstone, *The Structure and Process of International Law* (1986)

Mann, F. A., *Further Studies in International Law* (1990)
    Legal Aspects of Money (5th ed., 1992)

Maskus, K., *Intellectual Property Rights in the Global Economy* (2000)

Mathews, D., *Globalising Intellectual Property Rights* (2003)

Mayall, J., *Nationalism and International Society* (1994)

McDougall, M. S., H. D. Lasswell and Lung Chu Chen, *Human Rights and the World Political Order* (1980)

Muchlinski, P., *Multinational Enterprises and the Law* (1995)

Munzer, S. R., *A Theory of Property* (1990)

Neff, S., *Economic Liberalism and the Law of Nations* (1991)

Neufeld, H., *The International Protection of Private Creditors from the Treaty of Westphalia to the Congress of Vienna* (1971)

Nygh, P. E., *Party Autonomy in Private International Law* (1998)

O'Brien, R. (ed.), *Contesting Global Governance: Multilateral Economic Institutions and Global Social Movements* (2000)

O'Brien, W. V. (ed.), *The New States in International Law and Diplomacy* (1965)

O'Connell, D. P., *International Law* (2nd ed., vol. 1, 1970)

Oppermann, T. and E. Petersmann (eds.), *Reforming the International Economic Order* (1987)

Paasivirta, E., *Participation of States in International Contracts* (1990)

Pearson, M. M., *Joint Ventures in the People's Republic of China: The Control of Foreign Direct Investment under Socialism* (1991)

Picciotto, S., *International Business Taxation* (1992)

Picciotto, S. and R. Mayne (eds.), *Regulating International Business: Beyond Liberalisation* (1999)

Pritchard, R. (ed.), *Economic Development, Foreign Investment, and the Law. Issues of Private Sector Involvement, Foreign Investment and the Rule of Law in a New Era* (1996)

Raggazi, M., *The Concept of International Obligations Erga Omnes* (1997)

Rajan, M. S., *Sovereignty over Natural Resources* (1978)

  The Doctrine of Permanent Sovereignty over Natural Resources (1982)

Ralston, J., *The Law and Procedure of International Tribunals* (1926)

Randelzhofer, A and C. Tomuschat (eds.), *State Responsibility and the Individual* (1999)

Reisman, M., *The Breakdown of Control Mechanism in ICSID Arbitration* [1989]

Remec, P., *The Position of the Individual in International Law According to Grotius and Vattel* (1960)

Rochmat, R., *Contractual Arrangements in Oil and Gas Mining Enterprises in Indonesia* (1981)

Rosenne, S., *Developments in the Law of Treaties* (1989)

Roth, A., *The Minimum Standard of International Law Applied to Aliens* (1949)

Rubin, S. J. and R. W. Nelson, *International Investment Disputes: Avoidance and Settlement* (1985)

Rubin, S. J. and M. L. Jones (ed.), *Conflict and Resolution in the US–EC Trade Relations* (1989)

Schachter, O., *International Law in Theory and Practice* (1990)

Schreuer, C., *Commentary on the ICSID Convention* (2001)

Schrijver, N., *Permanent Sovereignty over Natural Resources: Balancing Rights and Duties* (1997)

Schulsz, J. and J. A. van den Berg (eds.), *The Art of Arbitration: Liber Amicorum Pieter Sanders* (1982)

Schwarzenberger, G., *Foreign Investment and International Law* (1969)

Schwebel, S., *International Arbitration: Three Salient Problems* (1986)

Scott, C. (ed.), *Torture as Tort* (2000)

Seidl-Hohenveldern, I., *The Corporation in and under International Law* (1987)

Sen, B., *A Diplomat's Handbook of International Law and Practice* (1988)

Servan-Schreiber, J. J., *The American Challenge* (1969)

Shaw, M. N., *Title to Territory in Africa* (1986)
   International Law (4th ed., 1997)

Shea, D., *Calvo Clause* (1955)

Shepaher, G. W. and V. Nanda (eds.), *Human Rights and Third World Development* (1985)

Shihata, I., *The MIGA and Foreign Investment* (1988)

Sigmund, P. E., *Multinationals in Latin America: The Politics of Nationalisation* (1990)

Simmonds, K. R. and B. H. W. Hill, *Law and Practice under the GATT* (vol. 3, 1989)

Sklair, L., *The Transnational Capitalist Class* (2001)

Smith, B. D., *State Responsibility and the Marine Environment* (1988)

Smith, D. and L. Wells, *Negotiating Third World Mineral Agreements* (1975)

Sornarajah, M., *The Pursuit of Nationalized Property* (1986)
   International Commercial Arbitration (1990)
   The Law of International Joint Ventures (1992)
   International Law on Foreign Investment (1994)
   The Settlement of International Disputes (2000)
   The Taking of Property (UNCTAD Series on International Investment Treaties, 2000)

Stiglitz, J., *Globalization and Its Discontents* (2003)

Sunshine, R. B., *Terms of Compensation in Developing Countries' Nationalization Settlements* (UNCTC, 1981)

Toope, S. J., *International Mixed Arbitration* (1990)

United Nations Commission on Transnational Corporations, *Bilateral Investment Treaties* (1988)

Vandervelde, K. J., *United States Investment Treaties: Policy and Practice* (1992)

Vattel, E. de, *Classics of International Law: The Law of Nations or the Principles of International Law* (C. Fenwick, trans., 1916)

Vernon, R., *Sovereignty at Bay* (1971)

Vitoria, F. de, *De Indis et de Jure Belli Reflectiones*

Walde, T. W. (ed.), *The Energy Charter Treaty* (1998)

Waldron, J., *The Right to Private Property* (1988)

Wallace, C. D. (ed.), *Foreign Direct Investment in the 1990s* (1990)

Wattal, J., *Intellectual Property Rights in the World Trade Organization: The Way Forward for Developing Countries* (2000)

Westberg, J., *International Transactions and Claims Involving Government Parties – Case Law of the Iran–United States Claims Tribunal* (1991)

White, G., *Nationalisation of Foreign Property* (1961)

Whiteman, H., *Damages in International Law* (vol. 3, 1976)

World Bank, *Legal Framework for the Treatment of Foreign Investment: Survey of Existing Instruments* (vols. 1 and 2, 1992)

Wilson, R., *United States Commercial Treaties and International Law* (1960)

Yergin, D., *The Prize: The Epic Quest for Oil, Money, and Power* (1991)

Articles

Abi-Saab, G., 'Permanent Sovereignty over Natural Resources and Economic Activities' in M. Bedjaoui (ed.), *International Law: Achievements and Prospects* (1991)

Adede, A. O., 'The Minimum Standards in a World of Disparities' in R. St J. Macdonald and D. M. Johnston (eds.), *The Structure and Process of International Law* (1983)

Adler, M., 'The Exhaustion of Local Remedies Rule after the ICJ's Decision in ELSI' (1990) 39 ICLQ 641

Akpan, G. S., 'Transnational Environmental Litigation and Multinational Corporations: A Study of the Ok Tedi Case' (paper published by the Centre for Energy, Petroleum and Mineral Law, University of Dundee, Scotland, CP 11/98, 1998)

Alexandrowicz, C. H., 'The Afro-Asian Nations and the Law of Nations' (1968) 123 *Hague Recueil* 117

Alvarez, J. E., 'Political Protectionism and United States International Investment Obligations in Conflict: The Hazards of Exon-Florio' (1989) 30 *Virginia Journal of International Law* 1

Amerasinghe, C. F., 'Issues of Compensation in the Taking of Alien Property in the Light of Recent Cases and Practice' (1992) 41 ICLQ 22

'The Prawn Farm Arbitration' (1992) 2 *Sri Lanka Journal of International Law* 12

Anderson, J. N. D. and N. J. Goulson, 'The Moslem Ruler and Contractual Obligations' (1958) 33 *New York University Law Review* 917

Anderson, M., 'Transnational Corporations and Environmental Damage: Is Tort Law the Answer?' (2002) 41 *Washburn Law Journal* 399

Anghie, A., 'Francisco Vitoria and the Colonial Origins of International Law' (1996) 5 *Social and Legal Studies* 256

Asante, S. K. B., 'International Law and Investments' in M. Bedjaoui (ed.), *International Law: Achievements and Prospects* (1991)

Asken, A., 'The Case for Bilateral Investment Treaties' in South West Foundation, *Private Investors Abroad* (1981)

Baily, D., G. Harte and R. Sugden, 'US Policy Debate Towards Inward Investment' (1992) 26 JWTL 65

Bean, V. and J. Beauvais, 'Global Fifth Amendment? NAFTA's Investment Protection and the Misguided Quest for an International Regulatory Takings Doctrine' (2003) 78 *New York University Law Review* 30

Behrens, P., 'International Company Law in View of the Centros Decision of the ECJ' (2000) 1 *European Business Organization Law Review* 125

Bentham, R. W., 'The International Legal Structure of Petroleum Exploration' in J. Rees and P. Odell (eds.), *The International Oil Industry* (1987)

Bergman, M. S., 'Bilateral Investment Treaties: An Examination of the Evolution and Significance of the US Prototype Treaty' (1983) 16 *New York University Journal of International Law and Politics* 1

Beveridge, F., 'Taking Control of Foreign Investment: A Case Study of Indigenisation in Nigeria' (1991) 40 ICLQ 302

Bianchi, A., 'Immunity Versus Human Rights: The Pinochet Case' (1999) 10 EJIL 237

Blakesley, C., 'United States Jurisdiction over Extraterritorial Crime' (1982) 73 *Journal of Criminal Law and Criminology* 1109

Borchard, E. M., 'The Minimum Standard of Treatment of Aliens' (1940) 38 *Michigan Law Review* 445

Bowett, D. W., 'Estoppel Before International Tribunals and Its Relation to Acquiescence' (1957) 33 BYIL 176

Broches, A., 'Bilateral Investment Treaties and Arbitration of Investment Disputes' in J. Schulsz and J. A. van den Berg (eds.), *The Art of Arbitration: Liber Amicorum Pieter Sanders* (1982)

Bronckers, M., 'Private Participation in the Enforcement of WTO Law: The New EC Trade Barriers Regulation' (1996) 33 CMLR 299

Brownlie, I., 'Legal Status of Natural Resources in International Law' (1979) 162 *Hague Recueil* 245

  'The Rights of Peoples in Modern International Law' in J. Crawford (ed.), *The Rights of Peoples* (1988)

Brunetti, M., 'The Iran–US Claims Tribunal, NAFTA Chapter 11 and the Doctrine of Indirect Expropriation' (2001) 2 *Chicago Journal of International Law* 203

Campbell, E., 'Legal Problems Involved in Government Participation in Resource Projects' (1984) *AMPLA Yearbook* 126

Carrasco, E. and Thomas R., 'Encouraging Relational Investment and Controlling Portfolio Investment in Developing Countries in the Aftermath of the Mexican Financial Crisis' (1996) 34 *Columbia Journal of Transnational Law* 531

Carty, A., 'Critical International Law: Recent Trends in the Theory of International Law' (1991) 2 EJIL 66

Castenada, J., 'La Charte des Droits et Devoirs Economiques des Etats' (1970) 16 *Annuaire Francais de Droit International* 31

Cheng, B., 'United Nations Resolutions on Outer Space: Instant International Customary Law' (1965) 5 *Indian Journal of International Law* 23

Christie, G. C., 'What Constitutes Taking of Property in International Law' (1962) 38 BYIL 307

Chua, A., 'The Privatization–Nationalization Cycle: The Link Between Markets and Ethnicity in Developing Countries' (1995) 95 *Columbia Law Review* 223

'Markets, Democracy and Ethnicity: Towards a New Paradigm for Law and Development' (1998) 108 *Yale Law Journal* 1

'The Paradox of Free Market Democracy: Rethinking Development Policy' (2000) 41 *Harvard International Law Journal* 287

Clark, R., 'Public International Law and Private Enterprise: Damages for a Killing in East Timor' (1996) 3 *Australian Journal of Human Rights* 21

Cody, D. A., 'United States Bilateral Investment Treaties: Egypt and Panama' (1983) 13 *Georgia Journal of International and Comparative Law* 491

Compa, L., 'The Multilateral Agreement on Investment and International Labor Rights: A Failed Connection' (1998) 31 *Cornell International Law Journal* 683

Cunningham, H., 'Multinationals and Restructuring in Latin America' in C. Dixon, D. Drakakis-Smith and H. Wads (eds.), *Multinational Corporations and the Third World* (1986)

Curtis, G. T., 'The Legal Security of Economic Development Agreements' (1988) 29 *Harvard International Law Journal* 317

Denza, E. and S. Brooks, 'Investment Protection Treaties: The United Kingdom Experience' (1987) 36 ICLQ 908

Detter, I., 'The Problem of Unequal Treaties' (1966) 14 ICLQ 1069

Dicke, D., 'Taking of Foreign Property and Compensation' in T. Oppermann and E. Petersmann (eds.), *Reforming the International Economic Order* (1987)

Dolzer, R., 'New Foundations of the Law of Expropriation of Alien Property' (1981) 75 AJIL 553

'Indirect Expropriation of Alien Property' (1986) 1 ICSID Rev 41

Editorial, 'The Measures Taken by the Indonesian Government Against Netherlands Enterprises' (1958) 5 *Netherlands International Law Review* 227

El-Chiati, A. Z., 'The Protection of Investments in the Context of Petroleum Agreements' (1987) 204 *Hague Recueil* 1

El-Kosheri, A., 'Quelques Reflexions a Propos d'un Texte Inedit de Michel Virally' in *Melanges Michel Virally* (1991)

El-Kosheri, A. S. and T. Riad, 'The Law Governing a New Generation of Petroleum Agreements' (1986) 1 ICSID Rev 259

Ellis, C. N., 'Trade Related Investment Measures in the Uruguay Round: The United States Viewpoint' in S. J. Rubin and M. L. Jones (eds.), *Conflict and Resolution in the US–EC Trade Relations* (1989)

'Foreign Direct Investments and International Capital Flows to Third World Nations: United States Policy Considerations' in C. D. Wallace (ed.), *Foreign Direct Investments in the 1990s* (1990)

European Community, 'Statement on US Policy on Foreign Direct Investment' (1992) 31 ILM 467

'US Treasury Regulations Pertaining to Mergers, Acquisitions and Takeovers by Foreign Persons' (1991) 31 ILM 424

Fachiri, A. P., 'Expropriation and International Law' (1925) 6 BYIL 159

Fatouros, A., 'The Administrative Contract in Transnational Transactions: Reflections on the Uses of Comparison' in *Ius in Privatum: Festschrift fur Max Rheinstein* (vol. 1, 1969)

Fawcett, J. E. S., 'The Havana Charter' (1949) 5 YBWA 320

Foster, D., 'Some Aspects of the Commercial Treaty Program of the United States – Past and Present' (1946) 11 *Law and Contemporary Problems* 647

Frame, A., 'Property: Some Pacific Reflections' (1992) 22 *New Zealand Law Journal* 21

Francioni, F., 'Compensation for Nationalization of Foreign Property: The Borderland of Law and Equity' (1975) 24 ICLQ 255

Freeman, A. V., 'Recent Aspects of the Calvo Doctrine and the Challenge to International Law' (1946) 40 AJIL 131

Frey, B. A., 'The Legal and Ethical Responsibilities of Transnational Corporations in the Protection of International Human Rights' (1997) 6 *Minnesota Journal of Global Trade* 105

Friedland, P. D. and E. Wong, 'Measuring Damages for Deprivation of Income Producing Assets: ICSID Case Studies' (1991) 6 ICSID Rev 400

Furnish, D. B., 'Peruvian Domestic Law Aspects of the La Brea y Parinas Controversy' (1970) 89 *Kentucky Law Journal* 351

'Days of Revindication and Dignity: The Petroleum Expropriations in Peru and Bolivia' in R. B. Lillich (ed.), *The Valuation of Nationalized Property* (vol. 2, 1987)

Gaillard, E., 'Commentary' (2002) 18 *International Arbitration* 247

Gantz, G., 'The Marcona Settlement: New Forms of Negotiation Compensation for Nationalized Property' (1977) 71 AJIL 474

Gathii, J. T., 'International Law and Eurocentricity' (1998) 9 EJIL 184

Geer, M. A., 'Foreigners in Their Own Land: Cultural Land and Transnational Corporations – Emergent International Rights and Wrongs' (1998) 38 *Virginia Journal of International Law* 331

Goodwin-Gill, G. S., 'Crime in International Law: Obligations Erga Omnes and the Duty to Prosecute' in G. S. Goodwin-Gill and S. Talmon (eds.), *The Reality in International Law: Essays in Honour of Ian Brownlie* (1999)

Graham, D., 'The Calvo Clause: Its Current Status as a Contractual Renunciation of Diplomatic Protection' (1971) 6 *Texas International Law Journal* 289

Guha-Roy, S., 'Is the Law of State Responsibility for Injuries to Aliens a Part of Universal International Law?' (1969) 55 AJIL 562

Guzman, A., 'Why LDCs Sign Treaties That Hurt Them: Explaining the Popularity of Bilateral Investment Treaties' (1998) 38 *Virginia Journal of International Law* 639

Hailbronner, K., 'Foreign Investment Protection in Developing Countries in Public International Law' in T. Oppermann and E. Petersmann (eds.), *Reforming the International Economic Order* (1987)

Hamrock, K. J., 'The ELSI Case: Towards an International Definition of Arbitrary Conduct' (1992) 27 *Texas International Law Journal* 837

Heibein, A. N., 'The Chilean Copper Nationalization: The Foundation for the Standard of Appropriate Compensation' (1974) 23 *Buffalo Law Review* 765

Herz, J. H., 'Expropriation of Foreign Property' (1941) 35 AJIL 243

Higgins, R., 'The Taking of Property by the State' (1982) 176 *Hague Recueil* 259

Hohfeld, W., 'Some Fundamental Legal Conceptions as Applied in Judicial Reasoning' (1913) 23 *Yale Law Journal* 16

Honore, T., 'Ownership' in A. G. Guest (ed.), *Oxford Essays in Jurisprudence* (1961)

Hoof, F. van, 'International Human Rights Obligations for Companies and Domestic Courts: An Unlikely Combination?' in M. Castermans-Holleman, F. van Hoof and J. Smith (eds.), *The Role of the Nation State in the 21st Century: Essays in Honour of Peter Baehr* (1998)

Hopkins, A. G., 'Property Rights and Empire Building' (1980) 40 *Journal of Economic History* 787

Human Rights Watch, *The Price of Oil: Corporate Responsibility and Human Rights Violations in Nigeria's Oil Producing Communities* (1999)

Hyde, J. N., 'Economic Development Agreements' (1962) 105 *Hague Recueil* 271

Ijalye, D., 'Multinational Corporations in Africa' (1981) 171 *Hague Recueil* 1

Ittersum, M. van, 'Profit and Principle: Hugo Grotius, Natural Rights Theories and the Rise of Dutch Power in the East Indies' (PhD thesis, Department of History, Harvard University, Cambridge, MA, 2002)

Jimenez de Arechaga, E., 'International Responsibility' in M. Sorensen (ed.), *Manual of Public International Law* (1968)

'State Responsibility for Nationalization of Foreign Owned Property' (1979) 11 *New York University Journal of International Law and Politics* 179

Jimenez de Arechaga, E. and A. Tanzi, 'International State Responsibility' in M. Bedjaoui (ed.), *International Law: Achievements and Prospects* (1991)

Jones, J. M., 'Claims on Behalf of Nationals Who Are Shareholders in Foreign Companies' (1949) 26 BYIL 225

Kaeckenbeck, N., 'The Protection of Vested Rights in International Law' (1936) 17 BYIL 1

Katzarov, N., 'The Validity of the Act of Nationalisation in International Law' (1959) 22 MLR 639

Khalilian, S. K., 'The Place of Discounted Cash Flow in International Commercial Arbitrations' (1991) 8 *Journal of International Arbitration* 31

Kunzer, K., 'Developing a Model Bilateral Investment Treaty' (1983) 15 *Law and Policy in International Business* 273

Lalive, J.-P., 'The Doctrine of Acquired Rights' in South Western Legal Foundation, *Selected Readings on the Protection of Foreign Investments* (1964)

Lauterpacht, E., 'Issues of Compensation and Nationality in the Taking of Energy Investments' (1990) 6 *Journal of Energy and Natural Resources Law* 241

Lawson, R., 'Out of Control, State Responsibility and Human Rights: Will the ILC's Definitions of the Act of State Meet the Challenges of the 21st Century?' in M. Castermans-Holleman, F. van Hoof and J. Smith (eds.), *The Role of the Nation State in the 21st Century: Essays in Honour of Peter Baehr* (1998)

Leigh, M. and J. A. Swindler, 'Constitutional Restraints of Foreign Economic Sanctions' in R. J. Ellings (ed.), *Private Property and National Security* (1991)

Lieblich, W. C., 'Determining the Economic Value of Expropriated Income Producing Property in International Arbitrations' (1991) 8 *Journal of International Arbitration* 59

Lillich, R. B., 'The Valuation of Copper Companies in the Chilean Nationalization' (1972) 66 *ASIL Proceedings* 213

'Duties of States Regarding Civil Rights of Aliens' (1978) 161 *Hague Recueil* 329

Lillich, R. B. and B. Weston, 'Lump Sum Agreements: Their Continuing Contribution to the Law of International Claims' (1988) 82 AJIL 69

Lippmann, M., 'Multinational Corporations and Human Rights' in G. W. Shepaher and V. Nanda (eds.), *Human Rights and Third World Development* (1985)

Lipstein, K., 'The Place of the Calvo Clause in International Law' (1945) 24 BYIL 1

Lissitzyn, O. J., 'International Law in a Divided World' (1963) 532 *International Conciliation* 58

Malanczuk, P., 'Multinational Enterprises and Treaty-Making – A Contribution to the Discussion on Non-State Actors and the "Subjects" of International Law' in V. Gowlland-Debbas (ed.), *Multilateral Treaty Making* (2000)

Mann, F. A., 'British Treaties for the Promotion and Protection of Investment' (1981) 52 BYIL 241

'Foreign Investment in the International Court of Justice: The ELSI Case' (1992) 86 AJIL 92

McGovney, D. O., 'The Anti-Japanese Land Laws' (1943) 35 *California Law Review* 61

McNair, Lord, 'The General Principles of Law Recognised by Civilised Nations' (1957) 33 BYIL 1

Metzger, S. D., 'Multilateral Convention for the Protection of Private Foreign Investment' (1960) 9 JPL 40

Meyer, W. H., 'Human Rights and MNCs: Theory Versus Quantitative Analysis' (1996) 18 *Human Rights Quarterly* 368

Michelman, F. I., 'Property, Utility and Fairness' (1967) 80 *Harvard Law Review* 1165

Mozarsky, S., 'Defining Discrimination on the Basis of National Origin under Article VII(1) of the Friendship Treaty Between United States and Japan' (1992) 15 *Fordham International Law Journal* 1099

Nichols, P. M., 'Regulating Transnational Bribery in Times of Globalization and Fragmentation' (1999) 24 *Yale Journal of International Law* 257

Nocker, T. and G. French, 'Estoppel: What's the Government's Word Worth?' (1990) 24 *International Lawyer* 409

Nussbaum, A., 'The Arbitration Between the Lena Goldfields Ltd and the Soviet Government' (1950) 36 *Cornell Law Quarterly* 31

O'Connell, D. P., 'Independence and State Succession' in W. V. Brian (ed.), *New States in International Law and Diplomacy* (1965)

OECD, 'Council Resolution on the Draft Convention for the Protection of Foreign Property' (1967) 7 ILM 117

Olmstead, C. J., 'Economic Development Agreements' (1961) 49 *California Law Review* 621

O'Neal, J. R. and F. H. O'Neal, 'Hegemony, Imperialism and Profitability of Foreign Investment' (1988) 42 *International Organization* 347

Orrego-Vicuna, F., 'Some International Law Problems Posed by the Nationalization of Copper Industry by Chile' (1973) 67 AJIL 711

Osofsky, H. M., 'Environmental Human Rights under the Alien Tort Statute: Redress for Indigenous Victims of Multinational Corporations' (1997) 20 *Suffolk Transnational Law Review* 335

Osunbor, O., 'Nigeria's Investment Laws and the State's Control of Multinationals' (1988) 3 ICSID Rev 38

Paasivirta, E., 'Internationalisation and Stabilisation of Contracts Versus State Sovereignty' (1989) 50 BYIL 315

Palmer, G., 'Settlement of International Disputes: The Rainbow Warrior Affair' (1989) 15 *Commonwealth Law Bulletin* 585

Pattison, J. E., 'The United States–Egypt Bilateral Investment Treaty: A Prototype for Future Negotiation' (1983) 16 *Cornell International Law Journal* 305

Paulsson, J., 'Arbitration Without Privity' in T. W. Walde (ed.), *The Energy Charter Treaty* (1998)

'ICSID: Achievement and Prospects' (1991) 6 ICSID Rev 380

Pechota, V., 'The 1981 US–Czechoslovakia Claims Settlement Agreement: An Epilogue to Post-War Nationalization and Expropriation Disputes' (1982) 76 AJIL 639

Pellonpaa, M. and M. Fitzmaurice, 'Taking of Property in the Practice of the Iran–United States Claims Tribunal' (1988) 19 NYIL 53

Penrose, E., 'Nationalization of Foreign-Owned Property for a Public Purpose: An Economic Perspective on Appropriate Compensation' (1992) 55 MLR 351

Peters, P., 'Dispute Settlement Arrangements in Investment Treaties' (1991) 22 NYIL 91

Pilgrim, C. M., 'Some Legal Aspects of Trade in Natural Resources in Namibia' (1990) 61 BYIL 248

Pisillo-Mazzeshchi, R. 'Forms of International Responsibility for Environmental Harm' in F. Francioni and T. Scovazzi (eds.), *International Responsibility for Environmental Harm* (1991)

   'The Due Diligence Rule and the Nature of the International Responsibility of States' (1992) 35 GYIL 46

   'International Obligations to Provide for Reparation Claims?' in A Randelzhofer and C. Tomuschat (eds.), *State Responsibility and the Individual* (1999)

Pogany, I., 'Economic Development Agreements' (1992) 7 ICSID Rev 1

Price, D., 'Investor–State Dispute Settlement: Frankenstein or Safety Valve?' (2000) 26 *Canada–US Law Journal* 107

Propp, K. R., 'Bilateral Investment Treaties: The US Experience in Eastern Europe' (1992) 86 *ASIL Proceedings* 540

Raby, J., 'The Investment Provisions of the Canada–United States Free Trade Agreement: A Canadian Perspective' (1990) 84 AJIL 344

Ratner, S., 'Corporations and Human Rights: A Theory of Legal Responsibility' (2001) 111 *Yale Law Journal* 443

Redfern, A., 'The Arbitration Between the Government of Kuwait and Aminoil' (1984) 55 BYIL 65

Reich, S., 'Roads to Follow: Regulating Direct Foreign Investment' (1989) 43 *International Organization* 543

Reisman, M., 'The Breakdown of Control Mechanism in ICSID Arbitration' (1989) 39 *Duke Law Journal* 739

   'The View from the New Haven School of International Law' (1992) 86 *ASIL Proceedings* 118

Robinson, D., 'Expropriation in the Restatement (Revised)' (1984) 78 AJIL 176

Rohwer, J., 'Nationalization – Chilean Excess Profits Deduction' (1973) 14 *Harvard International Law Journal* 378

Rood, L., 'Compensation for Takeovers in Africa' (1977) 11 *Journal of International Law and Economics* 521

Rosenne, S., 'State Responsibility and International Crimes: Further Reflections on Article 19 of the Draft Articles on State Responsibility' (1997) 30 *New York University Journal of International Law and Politics* 145

Rothger, J. M., 'Investment Dependence and Political Conflict' (1990) 27 *Journal of Peace Research* 255

Rowat, M. D., 'Multilateral Approaches to Improving the Investment Climate of Developing Countries: The Cases of ICSID and MIGA' (1992) *Harvard International Law Journal* 103

Sacerdoti, G., 'Barcelona Traction Revisited: Foreign-Owned and Controlled Companies in International Law' in Y. Dinstein (ed.), *International Law at a Time of Perplexity: Essays in Honour of Shabtai Rosenne* (1989)

Salacuse, J. W., 'BIT by BIT: The Growth of Bilateral Investment Treaties and Their Impact on Foreign Investment in Developing Countries' (1990) 24 *International Lawyer* 655

Sax, J. L., 'Takings and the Police Power' (1964) 74 *Yale Law Journal* 36

Schneiderman, D., 'Investment Rules and the New Constitutionalism' (2000) 25 *Law and Social Inquiry* 757

Schreuer, C., 'Diplomatic Protection of Private Business Companies' (1990) 51 BYIL 155

Schwebel, S. M., 'The Story of the UN's Declaration of Permanent Sovereignty over Natural Resources' (1963) 49 ABAJ 463

Schwebel, S. M. and G. Wetter, 'Arbitration and Exhaustion of Local Remedies' (1966) 60 AJIL 484

'Arbitration and the Exhaustion of Local Remedies Revisited' in *Festschrift for Joseph Gould* (1989)

Schwelb, E., 'The Protection of the Right to Property of Nationals under the First Protocol to the European Convention on Human Rights' (1964) 13 AJCL 518

Seidl-Hohenveldern, I., 'Hierarchy of Norms Applicable to International Investments' in W. P. Heere (ed.), *International Law and Its Sources: Liber Amicorum Maarten Bos* (1989)

Book Review (1991) 38 GYIL 592

Shawcross, Lord, 'The Problems of Foreign Investment in International Law' (1961) 102 *Hague Recueil* 334

Shihata, I., 'Towards a Depoliticisation of Foreign Investment Disputes: The Roles of ICSID and MIGA' (1986) 1 ICSID Rev 1

Sornarajah, M., 'State Responsibility and Bilateral Investment Treaties' (1986) 20 JWTL 79

'Power and Justice in International Investment Arbitration' (1997) 14 *Journal of International Arbitration* 103

'Power and Justice in International Law' (1997) 1 *Singapore Journal of International and Comparative Law* 28

'South East Asia and International Law – State Responsibility and Sex Tours in Asia' (1997) 1 *Singapore Journal of International and Comparative Law* 414

'Neo-liberalism and International Law on Foreign Investment' in T. Anghie and B. Chimni, *Third World in International Law* (2003), 181

'The Clash of Globalizations and the International Law on Foreign Investment' (2003) 10 *Canadian Foreign Policy* 1

Staker, C., 'Diplomatic Protection of Private Business Companies: Determination of Corporate Personality for International Law Purposes' (1990) 51 BYIL 155

Stephens, B., 'The Amorality of Profit: Transnational Corporations and Human Rights' (2002) 20 *Berkeley Journal of International Law* 45

Thomas, C., 'Where is the Third World Now?' in P. Wilkins and C. Thomas (eds.), *Globalisation and the South* (1997)

Thomas, J. C., 'Reflections on Article 1105 of NAFTA' (2002) 17 ICSID Rev 21

Tobi, N., 'Legal Aspects of Foreign Investment and Financing Energy Products in Nigeria' (1991) 14 *Dalhousie Law Journal* 5

Trimble, P., 'International Law, World Order' (1990) 42 *Stanford Law Review* 811

Tshuma, L., 'The Political Economy of the World Bank's Legal Framework for Development' (1999) 8 *Social and Legal Studies* 75

Turrell, R. V., 'Conquest and Concession: The Case of the Burma Ruby Mines' (1988) 22 *Modern Asian Studies* 141

Vagts, D., 'Protecting Foreign Investment: An International Law Perspective' in C. D. Wallace (ed.), *Foreign Direct Investment in the 1990s* (1990)

Vandevelde, K. J., 'The Bilateral Investment Treaty Program of the United States' (1988) 21 *Cornell International Law Journal* 201

'The Development and Expansion of Bilateral Investment Treaties' (1992) 86 *ASIL Proceedings* 532

Vasciannie, S., 'The Fair and Equitable Standard in International Investment Law and Practice' (1999) 70 BYIL 99

Verdross, A., 'Les Règles Internationales Concernant le Traitement des Etrangers' (1931) 37 *Hague Recueil* 364

'Quasi-International Agreements and International Economic Transactions' (1964) 18 YBWA 230

Verhoosel, G., 'Foreign Direct Investment and Legal Constraints on Domestic Environmental Policies: Striking a Reasonable Balance Between Stability and Change' (1998) 29 *Law and Policy in International Business* 451

Vernon, R., 'International Investment and International Trade' (1966) 2 *Quarterly Journal of Economics* 80

Verwey, W. D. and N. J. Schrijver, 'The Taking of Foreign Property under International Law: A New Legal Perspective?' (1984) 15 NYIL 60

Voss, J., 'The Protection and Promotion of European Private Investment in Developing Countries' (1981) 18 CMLR 363

Wagner, J. Martin, 'International Investment, Expropriation and Environmental Protection' (1999) 29 *Golden Gate University Law Review* 465

Waite, F. P. and M. R. Goldberg, 'National Security Review of Foreign Investment in the United States' (1991) 6 *Florida Journal of International Law* 191

Walden, J., 'International Petroleum Cartel – Private Power and the Public Interest' (1962) 11 *Journal of Public Law* 64

Walker, H., 'Modern Treaties of Freedom, Commerce and Navigation' (1958) 42 *Minnesota Law Review* 805

'Post-War Commercial Treaty Program of the United States' (1958) 73 *Political Science Quarterly* 57

Ward, H., 'Legal Issues in Corporate Citizenship' (report prepared for the Swedish Partnership for Global Responsibility, 2003)

Weber, A., 'Investments Risks and International Law' in T. Oppermann and E. Petersmann (eds.), *Reforming the International Economic Order* (1987)

Weil, P., 'Problemes Relatifs aux Contrats Passes Entre un Etat et un Particulier' (1969) 128 *Hague Recueil* 95

Weissbrodt, D. and M. Hoffmann, 'The Global Economy and Human Rights: A Selective Bibliography' (1997) 6 *Minnesota Journal of Global Trade* 189

Weston, B., 'Constructive Takings under International Law: A Modest Foray into the Problem of Creeping Expropriation' (1975) 16 *Virginia Journal of International Law* 103

Williams, J. Fischer, 'International Law and the Property of Aliens' (1928) 9 BYIL 20

Woolridge, F. and V. Sharma, 'The Expropriation of the Property of the Ugandan Asians' (1974) 14 *Indian Journal of International Law* 61

Zemanek, K., 'State Responsibility and Liability' in W. Lang, H. Neuhold and K. Zemanek (eds.), *Environmental Protection and International Law* (1991)

INDEX

seas, 190, 272
Seattle Meeting, 3, 74, 168, 271
self-determination, 42, 135, 161, 213,
    427
Seoul Declaration, 135
sex tours, 191–3
shareholders' rights
    bilateral treaties, 228–33
    forced sales, 361
    privatisations, 364–8
    property rights, 229
    protection, 10–11, 95
    recognition, 220
Shell, 178
ship waste, 190
siège social theory, 230, 232, 306
Singapore
    bilateral investment treaties, 217,
        243
    BIT with Bangladesh, 207
    BIT with France, 243
    BIT with Germany, 232, 243
    BIT with Netherlands, 243
    BIT with Sri Lanka, 214
    BIT with Switzerland, 243
    BIT with UK, 221–2, 232, 243
    BIT with US, 236, 337, 377, 386
    BIT with Vietnam, 244–5
    common law regime, 232
    definition of investments, 225
    export targets, 126
    expropriation, 243
    success, 2, 24
Singapore issues, 63, 73
slave trading, 184, 186
socialism, 77, 111
socialist states, 102, 120, 134, 284
Soros, George, 27
sources of law
    arbitral opinions, 90, 92
    compensation for expropriation, 436
    custom. *See* customary law
    general principles of law, 93–5, 443,
        452
    generally, 87–96
    jurisprudence, 95–6
    publicists' writings, 474–7
    treaties. *See* treaties

South Africa
    affirmative actions, 262
    bilateral treaties, 262
    ethnicity, 81, 129, 261, 321, 327, 367
    joint ventures, 160
    rugby tours, 192
South Korea, 126
sovereign immunity, 70–1, 176
sovereignty. *See* state sovereignty
sovereignty over natural resources
    bilateral treaties, 221
    and compensation, 465–6
    and concession agreements, 223–4
    principle, 90, 213, 284
    Seoul Declaration, 135
    UNCTC draft code, 277–8, 287–8
    UNGA resolutions, 1, 82
    weak principle, 43, 427
Soviet Union, 52–3, 167–8, 183
Spain, 472
specific performance, 428–55
Sri Lanka, 44, 206, 214, 217, 232, 246,
    252, 289, 481
stabilisation clauses, 180, 379–80,
    407–10
standards of treatment
    bilateral treaties, 233–7
    causes of action, 315–17
    customary law, 318–19
    fair and equitable treatment, 235–6,
        332–9
    full protection and security, 237,
        247, 342
    MAI, 295
    minimum. *See* minimum
        international standards
    most-favoured-nation treatment,
        236–7, 301, 308
    national treatment. *See* national
        treatment
    regional treaties, 320–1
    UNCTC draft code, 283
    WTO issue, 306–8
state agencies
    generally, 69–71
    in mixed economies, 26
    joint ventures, 65–6, 70, 103, 120–2
    monopolies, 70